Fundamentals of Social Statistics

Fundamentals of Social Statistics

THIRD EDITION

Kirk W. Elifson
Georgia State University

Richard P. Runyon and Audrey Haber

McGraw-Hill

Boston Burr Ridge, IL Dubuque, IA Madison, WI New York San Francisco St. Louis
Bangkok Bogotá Caracas Lisbon London Madrid
Mexico City Milan New Delhi Seoul Singapore Sydney Taipei Toronto

McGraw-Hill

*A Division of The **McGraw-Hill** Companies*

FUNDAMENTALS OF SOCIAL STATISTICS

This book is printed on acid-free paper.

1 2 3 4 5 6 7 8 9 0 DOC/DOC 9 0 9 8 7

ISBN 0-07-021579-0

Publisher: *Jane Vaicunas*
Sponsoring editor: *Jill Gordon*
Editorial coordinator: *Amy Smeltzley*
Marketing manager: *Sally Constable*
Project manager: *Christina Thornton-Villagomez*
Senior production supervisor: *Karen Thigpen*
Design manager: *Kiera Cunningham*
Compositor: *Interactive Composition Corporation*
Typeface: *10.5/12 Times Roman*
Printer: *R. R. Donnelley & Sons Company*

Library of Congress Cataloging-in-Publication Data

Elifson, Kirk W.
Fundamentals of social statistics / Kirk W. Elifson. —3rd ed.
p. cm.
Includes index.
ISBN 0-07-021579-0
1. Social sciences—Statistical methods. 2. Statistics.
I. Runyon, Richard P. II. Haber, Audrey. III. Title.
HA29.E482 1998
519.5—dc21 97-25763

http://www.mhhe.com

PREFACE

This book represents the collective wisdom of nearly a thousand statistics students whom I have taught. Much like myself when I was an undergraduate, students appreciate engaging, relevant, and concrete examples of statistics that are placed into a meaningful context. Their ability to learn is frequently hampered by computational steps that are omitted, the lack of clear definitions of new concepts, and the failure to include relevant presentations or the logic behind the techniques they are learning. My first encounter with statistics left me confused and floundering. I was unable to express the "faults" I found in the assigned text. This led me to write a text that students could more easily understand.

Students *can* learn statistics and have a satisfying experience at the same time, provided the material is presented appropriately. My students and I have worked hard to see that you will engage in some real problem solving, and not be asked to manipulate numbers within a meaningless context. A primary reason for writing this book was to create a text that is not a burden for students to use, one that could be appreciated even by those students who initially feared statistics. I believe that you will find this text to be very clear and useful.

Student and faculty response to the first and second editions of this textbook has been very satisfying. *Fundamentals of Social Statistics,* is widely used in social and behavioral science departments in the United States and in several English-speaking countries throughout the world. The publication of the third edition of a textbook is a great source of satisfaction to an author. In 1982, I was asked to rewrite Richard P. Runyon and Audrey Haber's best-selling behavioral science textbook, *Fundamentals of Behavioral Statistics;* I never dreamed that 15 years later I would be completing a third edition. I have sought to develop a text that meets the specific needs of those in sociology and in the related fields of criminology, family and urban studies, political science, and social welfare.

The current edition features a broader emphasis on the interpretation of data than the previous editions. The book now incorporates computer analysis from the Statistical Package for the Social Sciences (SPSS) along with a complete explanation of the interpretation and application of data. Case Examples are prominently displayed throughout the text. These examples are excerpted from a rich and varied selection of contemporary research in the social sciences and cover topics such as HIV/AIDS, health, gender, race, welfare, and crime. Statistics are presented as part of the real world, not as figures in a vacuum. The examples and raw data are presented and analyzed using the statistical techniques featured in that particular chapter. The Case Examples bring cohesion to statistical topics that often are perceived as separate and discrete.

Statistics in Action presents recently published material or research, including design, research goals, and raw data. The boxed examples first demonstrate statistical analysis at a level appropriate to student understanding at that point in the book, then offer additional data for analysis followed by solutions. The same studies are often repeated later in the text with more advance analyses, so students can observe the continuity and connectedness of statistical analysis.

The chapters on contingency tables, probability, and regression have undergone considerable revision; regression now includes a discussion on regression to the mean. The treatment of analysis of variance includes a more complete discussion of the F-test, and new sections dealing with hypothesis testing have been added to Chapters 13 and 14. Throughout the book, the examples have been updated and most exercises address current social issues, which provide students with meaningful, real-life knowledge. You also will find that the presentation of complex concepts has been clarified and simplified.

Features of the Book

A number of important features are included in this text. Key terms appear in boldface while terms that require emphasis are in italics. Visual devices—charts, figures, and graphs—help ensure maximum understanding by the student. New equations are discussed fully rather than applied mechanically, and ample examples of equations are provided initially to ensure comprehension.

Each chapter begins with an outline of the contents to provide the student with an overview of the material; each chapter ends with a glossary of key terms and summary. A completely updated student workbook has been designed by Philip Luck to provide a review and feedback for the student. The workbook incorporates study objectives for each chapter; a programmed review of terms, symbols, and concepts; selected computational exercises for application purposes; and sample test questions.

The Appendixes include a review of basic mathematics, a glossary of symbols keyed to the first page on which the symbols appear, a complete set of tables accompanied by explicit directions for their use, a master glossary of key terms and references. Other features of the book are a simplified chronological listing of equations most frequently used (inside the front and back covers), and a comprehensive index.

Acknowledgments

I owe a debt of gratitude to the many students who have participated in the revision of this edition and to the many colleagues who have contributed in ways that will always be appreciated.

Several persons at McGraw-Hill were particularly helpful in supporting me throughout this revision. Philip Butcher and Jill Gordon both encouraged and supported me as sponsoring editors at different phases of the project. Along with Amy Smeltzley, they kept me forging ahead while offering guidance when it was needed. Christina Thornton-Villagomez served as project manager who together with Charles Olson masterfully copyedited the third edition.

Charles Janet of Georgia State University provided a comprehensive review of earlier drafts. His assistance was invaluable and his keen eye and insight are much appreciated. Several other reviewers read all or part of the manuscript and offered important suggestions: Glenn Deane, State University of New York, Albany; Robin Franck, Southwestern College; Duane R. Monette, Northern Michigan University; and J. D. Robson, University of Arkansas at Little Rock. Thanks also must go to Dawn Baunach of Georgia State University and Edward Bell of Brescia College for their welcome suggestions.

Finally, my daughters Kristin and Shelley have been influential from the first edition to the present. My greatest supporters were undoubtedly Mam, Pap, and Andy Sheldon. Most important, Claire Sterk got me started, kept me going, and was with me as a pal and scholar from beginning to end.

Kirk W. Elifson
Atlanta, Georgia

CONTENTS

PART I Introduction

PART II Descriptive Statistics

PART V Appendixes

PART VI Answers to Selected Exercises

Fundamentals of Social Statistics

PART I

Introduction

CHAPTER 1

The Definition of Statistical Analysis

1.1 WHAT IS STATISTICS?

Think for a moment of the thousands of incredibly complex things you do during the course of a day. You are absolutely unique. No one else possesses your physical features, your intellectual makeup, your personality characteristics, and your value system. Yet, like billions of others of your species, you are among the most finely tuned and enormously sophisticated statistical instruments ever devised by natural forces. Every moment of your life provides testimony to your ability to receive and process a variety of information and then to use this information instantly to determine possible courses of action.

To illustrate, imagine you are driving in heavy traffic. You are continuously observing the road conditions, noting the speed of cars in front of you compared to your own speed, the position and rate of approach of vehicles to your rear, and the presence of automobiles in the oncoming lane. If you are an alert driver, you are constantly summarizing this information—usually without words or even awareness.

Imagine next that, without warning, the driver of the car in front of you suddenly jams on the brakes. In an instant you must act upon this prior information. You must brake the car, turn left, turn right, or pray. Your brain instantly considers alternative courses of action: If you jam on the brakes, what is the possibility that you will stop in time? Is the car behind you far enough away to avoid a rear-end collision? Can you avoid an accident by turning into the left lane or onto the right shoulder? Most of the time your decision is correct. Consequently, most of us live to a ripe old age.

In this situation, as in many others during the course of a lifetime, you have accurately assessed the possibilities and taken the right course of action. And you make such decisions thousands of times each and every day of your life. For this reason, you should regard yourself as a mechanism for making statistical decisions. In this sense you are already a statistician.

In daily living, our statistical functioning is usually informal and loosely structured. Consider the times you have contemplated the *likelihood* of someone you are attracted to, but do not know well, rejecting your invitation to have lunch. We *behave* statistically, although we may be totally unaware of the formal laws of probability, which will be presented in Chapter 12.

In this course, we will attempt to provide you with some of the procedures for collecting and analyzing data, and making decisions or inferences based on these analyses. Since we will frequently be building upon your prior experiences, you will often feel that you have made a similar analysis before: "Why, I have been calculating averages almost all my life—whenever I determine my test average in a course or the mileage my car gets," and "I compute range whenever I figure how much my time varies on my favorite two-mile jog." If you constantly draw upon your previous knowledge and relate course materials to what is familiar in daily life, statistics need not, and should not, be the bugaboo it is often painted to be.

What, then, is statistics all about? To many people, statistics is merely a collection of numerical facts that are expressed in terms of a summarizing statement such as: "Seven out of 10 doctors prescribe the pain reliever that is contained in Product X," or "During his current hitting streak, Ken Griffey, Jr., hit safely in 20 of his last 45 times at bat," or "During the Fourth of July weekend, 1986, more than 6 million New Yorkers and visitors participated in the centennial celebration of the unveiling of the Statue of Liberty."

However, this is not the way statistics is defined by scientists. Rather, **statistics** is a method for dealing with data and involves the organization and analysis of numerical facts or observations that are collected in accordance with a systematic plan. The plan for collecting data is called the **research design.** Broadly speaking, the design of a particular study is structured to provide answers to specific questions.

The material presented in Box 1.1 allows us to answer the following questions: Are smaller percentages of American children living in traditional families today than in the past? What percent of all children now live in traditional families? Is there a difference by race of the child? Ask yourself, are any trends apparent from reviewing the data? What might be some possible explanations for the trends and racial differences that are evident in Box 1.1?

A distinction may be made between the two functions of the statistical method: descriptive statistical techniques and inferential or inductive statistical techniques.

The major purpose of **descriptive statistics** is to present information in a convenient, usable, and understandable form. The statistical information presented in Figure 1.1 and the text of Box 1.1 are examples of statistics used for descriptive purposes. **Inferential or inductive statistics,** on the other hand, is concerned with making inferences about populations that are based on samples taken from those populations.

BOX 1.1

FAMILY COMPOSITION IN THE UNITED STATES, 1940–1990

A minority of Americans live in "traditional" families with a full-time working father and a homemaker mother. In 1940, only 43.1 percent of children lived in traditional families with a father who worked full time year-round and a mother who was not in the labor force. The proportion of children living in traditional families rose to 47.1 percent in 1950, but a majority of children continued to live in "nontraditional" families. After 1950, traditional family living declined rather dramatically, so that by 1980 only 26.3 percent of the families in the United States were of that type. Further decline occurred over the next 10 years; by 1990 fewer than one-fifth of all children lived in families with fathers as full-time providers and mothers as homemakers. Thus, for every child who lives in a traditional family, four children live in nontraditional families.

The percentage of white children living in traditional families peaked at 49.9 percent in 1950 and began a steep decline to 20.1 percent in 1990. Since 1940, fewer than 30 percent of African-American children lived with fathers who were full-time workers and mothers who were full-time homemakers, and this figure declined to 4.9 percent in 1990.

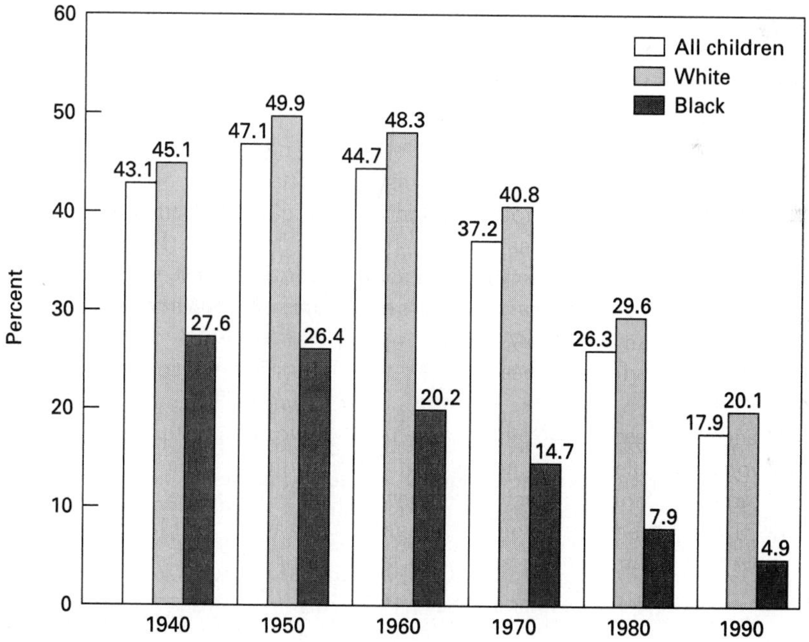

FIGURE 1.1
Children living with a father working full time and a mother not in the labor force, 1940–1990 (percent of children under 18 years old)

Source: U.S. Census of Population and Housing.

In describing the functions of statistics, we have already presented certain terms with which you may or may not be familiar. Before elaborating on the differences between descriptive and inductive statistics, we define certain terms you need to learn that will be employed repeatedly throughout the text.

1.2 DEFINITIONS OF TERMS COMMONLY USED IN STATISTICS

variable Any characteristic of a person, group, or environment that can vary *or* denote a difference. Thus, weight, occupational prestige, sex, political ideology, pollution count, group cohesion, and race are all variables because they can vary or denote a difference. A variable is contrasted with a constant, the value of which never changes (e.g., pi, which is equal to 3.14). Note that sex would be a constant in a study of only male delinquents and that a male–female comparison would not be possible.

data Numbers or measurements that are collected as a result of observations, interviews, and so on. They may be head counts such as the number or percentage of individuals stating a preference for a Republican presidential candidate; or they may be scores, as on a job satisfaction scale. Note that *data* is the plural form of *datum.* So you would say, "The data *are* available to anyone who wishes to see them or the data *show* that capital punishment is not a deterrent."

population A complete set of individuals, objects, or measurements having some common observable characteristic. We might focus, for example, on a population of Jews over 65 living in Los Angeles, handicapped students attending UCLA, or Korean entrepreneurs in "Koreatown."

When we think of populations, we think of very large groups such as all residents of the United States or all people who are schizophrenic. In many situations, however, the population may be considerably smaller. For example, all students enrolled in your statistics course may be thought of as representing a population. We could also say that all college students in the class of 2003 are a population.

Some statisticians prefer to distinguish between a population and a universe. Statisticians use the term *population* to refer only to numerical measurements or observations, and the term *universe* to refer to the origin of these observations. According to this distinction, voters in a national election are a universe and their votes are the population. We do not differentiate between populations and universes in this book. We prefer to focus on populations and do not distinguish between the behavior and the individual.

sample A subset or part of a population. For example, the newly elected members of the United States Senate constitute a sample of the population of all the current members of the Senate. All of the participants in a senior citizen center would constitute a sample of the senior citizens in the community. A sample could be drawn from the population of all female students in a college or from the population of all social work majors with a grade point average of at least 3.00.

In most cases populations are too large to measure. Therefore, we use a sample of individuals drawn from the population to represent the population. We assume that, if the sample is representative of the population, our descriptions of the sample can be applied to the population.

parameter Any characteristic of a population that is measurable. For example, the proportion of registered Democrats among Americans of voting age. In this text, we follow the practice of employing Greek letters (e.g., μ, σ) to represent population parameters. You will learn, for example, that if μ (pronounced "mu") equals 42, we are referring to an average for an entire population, and if σ (pronounced "sigma") equals 3.1, we are referring to a measure of variability for an entire population.

statistic A number that describes a characteristic of a sample. Commonly, we use a statistic that is calculated from a sample in order to estimate a population parameter; for example, a sample of Americans of voting age is used to estimate the proportion of Democrats in the entire population of voters. We will use italic letters (e.g., $\overline{X}$, s) to represent sample statistics. For example, if an author specifies that $\overline{X}$ (the mean of the X scores) equals 4.12, you know immediately that the referent is a sample and not a population. You should note that a statistic and a parameter are not the same thing. *Statistics are numbers based on direct observation and measurement: parameters are often inferred values based on sample statistics.*

Another difference between parameters and statistics involves the issue of variability. We assume that parameters are constants. Statistics, based on samples from the population, are variables. The reason for the variability of a statistic should be easy to understand. Let's use average height as an example. If we take a sample of women from the population, we can calculate the average height of these women. What would happen if we collected another sample and repeated our measurement? Would the average of the sample be exactly the same? No. Each sample will have different people. Each time we draw a sample the people we select will be of different height—sometimes shorter and sometimes taller. Although our sample statistics change, the parameter—average woman's height—does not change even though the statistics across samples vary.

random sampling* A method of selecting samples so that each sample of a given size in a population has an equal chance of being selected. This requires that all of the elements can be identified or listed. It would be possible, for example, to draw a random sample of prison inmates in the Pontiac State Penitentiary since a complete list of the inmates is available. The sample of senior citizens mentioned under the definition of "sample" would not be random. It would be possible, however, to draw a random sample from the senior citizen center participants if a complete list were available. Random sampling permits inferences about characteristics of the population from which the sample is selected.

It should be noted that random sampling is not an end in itself, merely a means to an end. The goal is that the sample accurately reflect all of the characteristics of the population from which it was drawn. Random sampling is only one way to achieve this goal.

> **EXAMPLE.** Imagine that you have been hired as a statistical consultant by a public health organization in a large metropolitan region. Your first assignment is to obtain statistical information on drug addiction among newborn infants. Treatment of these innocent victims of drug abuse requires some specialized equipment and round-the-clock medical supervision. Your immediate task is to estimate the extent and types of infant drug addiction so that the various clinics and hospitals in the city can make informed decisions about equipment and personnel needs for the coming year. Typically, your operating budget and the availability of trained assistants are limited. Therefore, there is no way you can hope to study the medical records of *all* the children born during the preceding year. At best, you can select only a small portion of the total records and subject these to

---

* Simple random sampling is more precisely defined in Section 12.2 as selecting samples in such a way that each sample of a given size has precisely the same probability of being selected.

intensive scrutiny. These selected records constitute the sample. If the sample is selected in such a way that each record has an equal probability of being chosen, we speak of the selection process as *random selection.* The variable of interest is the drug addiction status of each newborn baby. For our purposes, we shall assume that each record reveals either the presence or the absence of drug addiction. The data consist of the number of drug-addicted and non-drug-addicted infants in the sample. When computations are made on these data (such as calculating the proportion of drug-addicted babies), the resulting numerical values are called *statistics.*

The population to which we are interested in generalizing is all the infant births occurring in the metropolitan region during the preceding year. The "true" proportion of infant addicts in the population is the parameter (see Figure 1.2). Note that it is highly unlikely that the parameter will ever be known; to find it would require the examination of the medical records of every infant born in the region over one-year period. Since it is difficult, time consuming, and expensive to locate all members of a population, exhaustive studies of populations are not frequently undertaken. Consequently, parameters are rarely known, but as we shall see, they are commonly estimated from sample statistics.

A carefully selected sample can provide a very accurate description of the population from which it was drawn. Excellent samples are surprisingly small relative to

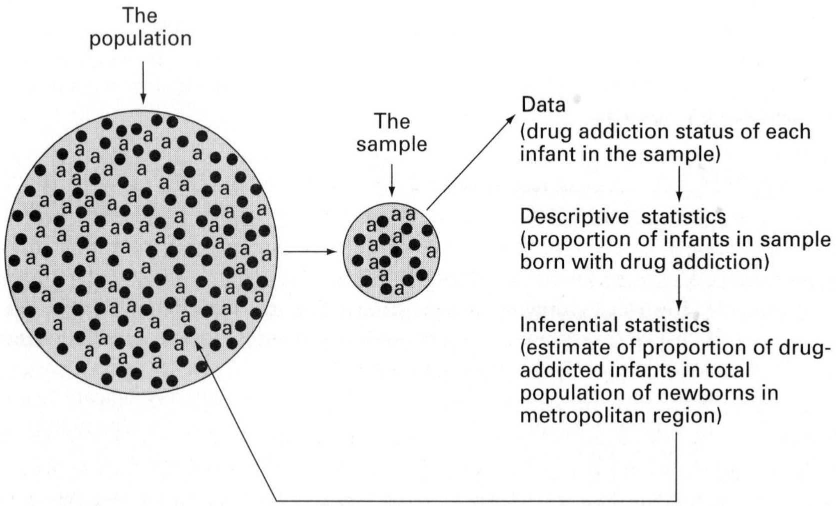

FIGURE 1.2

The proportion of drug-addicted infants among all newborns in a metropolitan region

The population consists of many thousands of babies born in a given metropolitan region over a specific time period. Some of these babies are addicted (a) and others are not (●). Because of cost or logistical reasons, the large size of the population rules out the possibility of a complete **census.** Thus, the parameter—that is, the true proportion of addicted infants in the population—is not knowable. A sample is selected from the population in such a way that it is likely to mirror the population. The *data* are collected, and various descriptive statistics are obtained. In inferential statistics, we attempt to estimate one or more population parameters, such as the proportion of drug-addicted infants among all newborn children in the metropolitan region.

the population. For example, a properly drawn national sample of 3,000 adults can provide extremely accurate information about the U.S. adult population. The logic will become clear once you have studied *sampling distributions* in Chapter 13.

It is of course possible to define a very small population by narrowing the definition of "common observable characteristic" to something like "all students attending their Sociology 201 class at Knox College today." In this event, calculating a parameter (e.g., the class average on the examination given today) would pose no difficulty. For such small populations, there is no reason to select samples and to calculate sample statistics.

From the point of view of the instructor, observations on the students in Sociology 201 at Knox College may be of supreme importance. However, such limited populations would be of little theoretical interest. In the real workaday world, the social scientist is usually interested in making statements having general validity over a wider set of people, and thus must *estimate* the (population) parameter. This estimate is based on the statistic that is calculated on the sample. Thus, we might use the observations on the students at Knox College as a basis for estimating parameters of the larger population.

Let us return to the two functions of statistical analysis for a closer look.

1.3 DESCRIPTIVE STATISTICS

When social scientists conduct a study, they usually collect a great deal of information or data about the problem at hand. The data may take a variety of forms: the number of medical schools in each state, the SAT scores of a group of college students, or responses to an attitude survey in a questionnaire. As collected in their original form, these data are usually a confusing hodgepodge of scores, frequency counts, and so forth. In performing the descriptive function, the statistician employs rules and procedures for presenting information about a variable or the relationship between variables in a more usable and meaningful form.

Rules are also followed when calculating various statistics from masses of raw data. Imagine that a team of social scientists administered a questionnaire concerning drug usage and attitudes to a group of high school students. What are some of the things they might do with the resulting information?

1. They might rearrange the scores and group them in various ways in order to see at a glance an overall picture of the data (Chapter 3, "Frequency Distributions and Graphing Techniques"). For example, how many of the students use drugs regularly? How many have never used drugs? Which drugs are used most frequently? What is the age distribution of the students? How do student attitudes toward drugs vary? What is the extent of multiple drug use?

2. They might construct tables, graphs, and figures to permit visualization of the results (Section 3.2, "Graphing Techniques," in Chapter 3). A pie chart might summarize the drugs most frequently used by the students, whereas a trend chart would provide a concise picture of the extent of drug use by year in school.

3. They might convert raw scores to other types of scores that are more useful for specific purposes. Thus, these scores could be used to rank the students, compare a student with the class average and so on. Other types of conversion will also be described in the text (Chapter 4, "Percentiles," and Chapter 7, "The Standard Deviation and the Standard Normal Distribution").

4. They might calculate averages to learn something about the typical attitudes of the students (Chapter 5, "Measures of Central Tendency"). What is the mean age when the students first used marijuana? What is the most frequently held attitude toward the legalization of marijuana?

5. Using the average as a reference point, they might describe the spread of scores about this central point. Statistics that measure this spread of scores are known as measures of variability or measures of dispersion (Chapter 6, "Measures of Dispersion"). Are the attitudes held by freshmen more or less homogeneous than those of seniors? Are males more likely to be multidrug users than females?

6. They may obtain a relationship between two different variables. Statistics are available for describing the relationship between two variables. The statistics for describing the extent of the relationship are referred to as *measures of association.*

Such statistics are extremely useful to the social scientist. For example, it might be important to determine the relationship between the number of books in the home and classroom grades or that between students' attitudes toward drugs and the extent to which they reported having committed delinquent acts. Once these relationships are known, the social scientist may use information from one variable to predict another (Chapter 8, "An Introduction to Contingency Tables," Chapter 9, "Correlation," and Chapter 10, "Regression and Prediction").

1.4 INFERENTIAL STATISTICS

As a social scientist, your task is not nearly over when you have completed the descriptive function. In fact, you are often nearer to the beginning than to the end of the task. The reason for this is clear when we consider that the purpose of the research is often to explore hypotheses of a general nature rather than simply to compare limited samples.

Imagine that you are a sociologist who is interested in determining the effectiveness of a videotape lecture approach compared with the usual approach of the professor delivering lectures in person. Consequently, you design a study involving two conditions: *experimental* and *control.* The question you wish to answer is which approach results in better student performance on a final sociology examination. The students in the experimental group view videotapes of the lectures attended by the control group. The students in the control group serve as a basis for comparison and are taught by means of the usual lecture approach. After all students have been tested, you might find that "on the average" the experimental group that viewed the videotapes did not perform as well on the final examination as the control group. In other words, the average of the experimental group on the final examination was lower than that of the control group. You then ask the question: Can I conclude that the teaching technique produced the difference between the two groups? To answer this question, it is not sufficient to rely solely upon *descriptive statistics.*

After all, you reason, even if both techniques worked, it is highly unlikely that the final examination averages of the two groups would have been *identical. Some* difference would have been observed. The operation of chance factors such as the time at which the classes are scheduled is certain to produce some differences in the final examination scores between the two groups. The critical question from the point of view of inferential statistics becomes: Is the difference between groups great enough to rule out chance factors in the experiment as a sufficient explanation? Stated another way: If you were to repeat the experiment, would you be able to predict with confidence that the same differences (i.e., the control group would consistently perform better than the experimental group) would systematically occur? Ultimately, we wish to infer to the population from which the study participants were drawn. Thus, we want to use the results of this experiment to reach conclusions about which technique would be better in similar sociology courses.

As you can see, *inference* is used in much the same way that logical reasoning is used when talking with friends. This notation of logical reasoning is sometimes employed to establish community standards in pornography litigation. Because the tolerance for pornography differs greatly from community to community, a survey of residents is often conducted to determine what sorts of sexually explicit activities should be available commercially. A well-drawn sample survey of 600 Milwaukee adults could be used by prosecution or defense lawyers in a pornography case to conclude that Milwaukee adults hold a particular attitude. If 78% of those interviewed believed that nude nightclubs should not be allowed, the prosecutors would seek to convince the jury members that the sample survey results allow for the inference that basically the same attitude is held by about three out of four adult residents in the entire population of Milwaukee.* In this instance, the sample was used to infer to the population from which it was drawn.

Most population parameters can never be known directly except in cases in which the population is small or if we have sufficient funds to study the population in its entirety. Counting election day ballots and taking the census are examples of measuring the population. We could also argue that the students in your statistics class are a population. Your instructor measures the population's knowledge of statistics each time he or she administers an exam. In most cases, however, we will almost certainly never know specific population parameters such as the percentage of people afflicted with acquired immune deficiency syndrome (AIDS). However, sampling from populations and subsequently applying inferential statistics permits us to build a bridge between the known and the unknown.

---

* Making inferences of this nature is specifically addressed in Section 14.7.2.

1.5 THE GOALS OF RESEARCH

Social scientists engage in a rich variety of different activities in diverse settings that involve the collection and analysis of numerical observations or data. These activities are generally subsumed under the label "research." The goals of these research activities may be classified into three broad categories: information gathering, describing relationships, and establishing causality. It should be noted that these goals are not mutually exclusive. All three are common components of many research efforts.

1.5.1 Information Gathering

The goal of statistical analysis can be to provide accurate information about some aspect of our professional activities that arouses our interest. For example, we may wish to know if the proportion of women entering the field of sociology is changing over the years, if the average starting salary of recent Ph.D.'s accepting positions at academic institutions has increased, or what percentage of criminal justice departments require statistics courses for their majors.

In answering these questions, we try to provide accurate descriptions of the situations studied. The information is considered valuable in its own right. Thus, there may not be any effort to relate the data to other events or situations. For example, we may make no attempt to answer the question, Why are the starting salaries of new Ph.D.'s in academia X dollars? Case Example 1.1 offers an additional example of descriptive statistics.

1.5.2 Describing Relationships between Variables

In the course of conducting research, we often obtain measurements on two or more variables from each respondent, and we wish to know whether or not the variables go together or covary. Does academic performance vary in relation to SAT scores? Is there a relationship between environment and aggressiveness as some researchers have claimed? Does our ability to recall childhood experiences relate to the pleasantness or unpleasantness associated with these experiences at the time they occurred?

Studies of this sort are referred to as correlational. They attempt to determine whether or not two variables are related (i.e., correlated—think of them as co-related) or vary together and, if so, to measure the direction and strength of the relationship. To illustrate, if we have measurements on two variables for each individual, we may raise questions such as the following: As the values of one variable increase (e.g., SAT scores), do the paired measures on the second variable also increase (e.g., academic performance)? Or are increases in one variable (e.g., age) associated with decreases in a second variable (e.g., income)? Or is there no detectable relationship between the two variables (e.g., health status and frequency of eating pizza).

It is important to note that correlations between naturally occurring variables such as income, gender, racial/ethnic backgrounds, or life satisfaction do not, as such,

CASE EXAMPLE 1.1

TABLE 1.1
Accidental deaths in 1992

Cause of death	**Number of deaths**
Passenger cars and taxis	21,257
Falls	12,646
Drowning	4,186
Fire and burns	3,958
Inhalation and ingestion of food	1,196
Falling objects	712
Agricultural machines	553
Drowning in bathtub	345
Side effects of therapeutic drug use	156
Caught in or between objects	119
Falls into holes and openings	99
Venomous plants and animals	68
Domestic wiring and appliances	66
Suffocation by falling earth	58
Lightning	53
Airplanes	**39**
Buses	23
Dog bites	13

Source: National Safety Council, 1992.

Table 1.1 presents descriptive statistics related to accidental causes of death in 1992. While many of us are greatly concerned when traveling by airplane, the probability of dying in an airplane crash is only three times as likely as dying from a dog bite and 1/100 as likely as dying from burns unrelated to an airplane crash. One statistician using Federal Aviation Administration data reported that you could board a plane at random every day for 21,000 years before dying in crash!

permit us to claim that changes in one variable *cause* changes in a second variable. They merely establish whether or not the two variables vary together. Many serious misinterpretations of data have occurred because people have ignored this fact. Thus, at various times in our history as a nation members of minority groups (e.g., African Americans, Hispanics, Asians, Italians, Poles, Jews) have labored under the label of inferiority because their low positions on the educational and socioeconomic ladders have been attributed to their racial and/or ethnic backgrounds. The point is that these groups differed from each other in many ways other than their ethnic/racial backgrounds—for example, command of the English language, educational and economic opportunities, and lifestyles. To focus on a single characteristic (e.g., ethnic background) that distinguished each of these groups from the majority and to attribute their social and economic position to this characteristic is to ignore the many other ways in which they differ.

1.5.3 Establishing Causality

One of the paramount goals of any science is to go beyond statements of relationships (e.g., If the value of *A* is high, then the value of *B* also is high) to those of causality (e.g., increases in the values of *A* *cause* the value of *B* also to increase). In spite of hundreds of years of speculating and writing about *causality,* it remains a somewhat elusive term. Not all scientists agree on the procedures for establishing cause-effect relationships. Indeed, some even doubt its feasibility while others question its necessity. However, the vast majority of scientists appear to agree that a statement such as "*A* causes *B*" is among the most powerful that a scientist can make and should be at the core of scientific inquiry.

Social scientists generally assume that three criteria must be met before causality can be established.

1. The two variables must covary. Let's consider an example involving personal income and health care. If we conduct a study and find that the more affluent respondents tend to receive better and more frequent health care than the poorer respondents, then we can conclude that there is some relationship between the two variables for our study participants.

2. The time-order in which the variables occur must show that the causal variable changes or comes into play before the effect/result occurs. In this particular example we suspect that health care is dependent on one's financial situation. If we find that in the vast majority of instances that changes in the respondents' incomes were followed by anticipated changes in their health care, we have established that the time-order of the variables is consistent with our assertion of causality.

3. Finally, and most difficult for social scientists, other possible explanations for the relationship we have observed must be eliminated. Perhaps the relationship is a result of a variable we did not consider. The poorer study participants may have been in excellent health and therefore did not need to seek health care. We will say much more on this third criteria for establishing causality later in Chapters 10 and 11.

1.6 A WORD TO THE STUDENT

The study of statistics need not and should not become a series of progressive exercises in calculated tedium. If it is approached with the proper frame of mind, statistics can be one of the most exciting fields of study; it has applications in virtually all areas of human endeavor and cuts across countless fields of study. H. G. Wells, the English novelist, prophesied, "Statistical thinking will one day be as necessary for efficient citizenship as the ability to read and write." Keep this thought constantly in mind. The course will be much more interesting and profitable to you if you develop the habit of "thinking statistically."

A common misconception held by laypersons is that statistics is merely a rather sophisticated method for fabricating lies or falsifying our descriptions of reality. We do not deny that some unscrupulous individuals employ statistics for these purposes. However, such uses of statistics are anathema to the social scientist dedicated to the establishment of truth. From time to time, we make references to various techniques that are used for lying with statistics. The purpose, though, is not to instruct you in these techniques but to make you aware of the various *misuses* of statistical analyses, so that you do not inadvertently "tell a lie" and that you are aware when others do.

When you see statistical information being exhibited, develop a healthy attitude of skepticism. Ask pertinent questions. When a national magazine sends a physically fit reporter to 10 different diet doctors and he or she receives an unneeded prescription from each, do not jump to the conclusion that all diet doctors are frauds. Do not say, "After all, 10 out of 10 is a rather high proportion" and dismiss further inquiry at this point. Ask how the reporter obtained the sample. Was it drawn at random, or is it possible that the doctors were selected purposely on the basis of prior information indicating they were rather careless in their professional practices? Question constantly, but reserve judgment until you have the answers.

Watch commercials on television; read newspaper advertisements. When the pitchman claims, "These food choppers are more effective," ask yourself, More effective than what? What is the evidence?

There also is something you can do to maximize the benefits derived from the course. You should set aside a separate section of your notebook to keep permanent records of your solutions to exercises. You will find that these solutions will provide an invaluable useful review of statistical procedures. For some of you, their use will long outlive the completion of this course. Of more immediate concern, however, is that it will be necessary to refer back to these solutions as you explore more advanced statistical techniques. Your notebook will reflect an important fact of statistical life: Researchers do not simply collect data, conduct a single statistical analysis of the data, and then share their results with others in the form of a published paper. Rather, they typically subject the same set of data to many levels of statistical analysis. It is hoped that this course will reflect the continuity among the various phases of ongoing research: Research design, descriptive and inferential data processing, and the ensuing conclusions are part of an organic whole. Something fundamental is lost if they are treated like discrete, independent elements of a jigsaw puzzle. To impart a flavor of real-world research, we will follow a number of research studies through all phases of their development, from their conception to a statement of conclusions that appear to be supported by the statistical facts.

SUMMARY

In this chapter, we saw that many people regard statistics merely as a collection of numerical facts. Scientists, however, stress the use of statistics as a method or tool concerned with the collection, organization, and analysis of numerical facts.

A distinction is made between two functions of the statistical methods, descriptive and inferential statistical analyses. The former is concerned with the organization and presentation of data in a convenient, usable, and communicable form. The latter is addressed to the problem of making broader generalizations or inferences from sample data to populations.

We also looked at the goals of research, which included gathering information, describing relationships, and establishing causality. We noted the important role of a systematic plan (the design of the study) in accomplishing these goals.

It was pointed out that statistics is frequently employed for the purpose of "telling lies." Such practices are inimical to the goal of establishing a factual basis for our conclusions and statistically based decisions. However, you should be aware of the techniques for telling statistical lies, so that you do not inadvertently tell one yourself or fail to recognize one when someone else does.

Finally, a number of terms commonly employed in statistical analysis were defined. In this and succeeding chapters, the new terms or concepts that have been introduced will be listed at the end of each chapter. Some of these terms will be more precisely defined in other chapters and consequently may appear again.

TERMS TO REMEMBER

data Numbers or measurements that are collected as a result of observations, interviews, and so forth.

descriptive statistics Procedures used to organize and present data in a convenient, usable summary form.

inferential or inductive statistics Procedures used to arrive at broader generalizations or inferences from sample data to populations.

parameter Any characteristic of a population that is measurable.

population A complete set of individuals, objects, or measurements having some common observable characteristic.

random sampling A method of selecting samples so that each sample of a given size in a population has an equal chance of being selected.

research design The plan for collecting data.

sample A subset or part of a population.

statistic A number that describes a characteristic of a sample.

statistics A collection of numerical facts expressed in summarizing statements; method of dealing with data: a tool for collecting, organizing, and analyzing numerical facts or observations that are collected in accordance with a systematic plan.

variable Any characteristic of a person, group, or environment that can vary or denotes a difference.

EXERCISES

1. Indicate whether each of the following represents a variable or a constant.
 (*a*) Number of days in the month of August.
 (*b*) The number of labor strikes per year in the United States since 1975.
 (*c*) The murder rate in Peoria last year.
 (*d*) Scores obtained on a 100-item multiple-choice examination.
 (*e*) Maximum score possible on a 100-item multiple-choice examination.
 (*f*) Age of freshmen entering college.

(*g*) Percentage of people in the United States who tried marijuana in 1997.
(*h*) Amount of money spent per year by students.
(*i*) Number of countries in Texas.

2. In your own words, describe what you understand the study of statistics to be. Compare your definition to the one provided in the book.

3. In the example cited in Section 1.2, imagine that 5% of the infants were addicted to an illicit drug.
(*a*) Can we assume that if the study were again conducted one year later the percentage of drug-addicted infants would remain the same?
(*b*) What factors might have caused the percent of drug-addicted infants to change?

4. What is the difference between a sample and a population? Is it possible to have a population consisting of only 20 respondents?

5. Football commentators frequently talk about the number of first downs in a game, passes attempted, passes completed, and so on. It is not uncommon for them to say, "Here are the half-time statistics. They really tell the story of this game!" Are these numbers they report statistics? If not, what are they?

Exercises 6 through 11 are based on the following: Imagine a researcher who decides to study risk-taking behavior in a randomly selected sample of male undergraduates at a large state university. The researcher administers a standardized test designed to assess this type of behavior. Based on this study, the researcher would like to make inferences about other male undergraduates at the college.

6. The students selected for study constitute the:
(*a*) Population (*b*) Statistic (*c*) Parameter (*d*) Sample

7. In this study, risk-taking behavior measured by the test constitutes a:
(*a*) Statistic (*b*) Variable (*c*) Parameter (*d*) Sample

8. The scores obtained by the individuals in this study constitute the:
(*a*) Data (*b*) Sample (*c*) Statistic (*d*) Population

9. The average test score of undergraduates in this sample constitutes a:
(*a*) Parameter (*b*) Statistic (*c*) Variable (*d*) Data

10. When we generalize our results, we make inferences to:
(*a*) Data (*b*) Variables (*c*) Statistics (*d*) Populations

11. The average score obtained by *all* undergraduates at the school constitutes a:
(*a*) Parameter (*b*) Variable (*c*) Data (*d*) Population

12. We wish to generalize from a sample to the:
(*a*) Data (*b*) Population (*c*) Statistic (*d*) Variable

13. You have interviewed 42 students attending a nearby university. Carefully consider how you might define the population from which the sample was drawn. (*Hint:* For example, were graduate students and part-time students sampled?)

14. Under what conditions might you poll the entire student body referred to in exercise 13?

15. In some urban areas, nearly 50% of all residential telephone numbers are unlisted.
(*a*) What types of persons would you expect to be underrepresented in a telephone survey in which the sample was drawn using the current telephone directory?
(*b*) Can you think of a procedure that might result in a more representative sample of all residential telephone numbers?

16. List five social science variables and briefly discuss how they might be measured.

17. Would it be possible to list all adults residing in Detroit on January 1, 1996? Why or why not?

18. Differentiate between the following pairs of words:
(*a*) Sample—population
(*b*) Statistic—parameter
(*c*) Inferential statistics—descriptive statistics
(*d*) Experimental group—control group

19. Indicate whether each of the following constitutes a statistic, data, or an inference from a statistic.
(*a*) A sample of 250 wage earners earn an average of $19,565.
(*b*) Based on a sample of 500 wage earners in Gotham City, it is believed that the average income of all wage earners in this city is $19,792.
(*c*) Slugs from a .22 rifle traveled 0.8, 0.96, and 1.1 miles.
(*d*) My tuition payment this year was $14,580; Sally's was $15,285.
(*e*) Based on a telephone survey, it is believed that the number of people viewing Monday night's television special was 33,520,000.

CHAPTER 2

Basic Mathematical Concepts

2.1 INTRODUCTION

"I'm not much good at math. How can I possibly pass a statistics course?" We have heard these words from the lips of countless undergraduate students. For many, this is probably a concern stemming from prior discouraging experiences with mathematics. A brief glance through the pages of this text may only serve to increase this anxiety because many of the equations appear complicated and may seem impossible to master. Therefore, it is most important to set the record straight right at the beginning of the course.

You do not have to be a mathematical genius to master the statistical principles in this text. The degree of mathematical sophistication necessary for a firm grasp of the fundamentals of statistics is often exaggerated. What statistics does require is a good deal of arithmetic computation, sound logic, and a willingness to stay with a point until it is mastered. To paraphrase Thomas Carlyle, success in statistics requires an infinite capacity for taking pains. Beyond this modest requirement, little is needed but the mastery of several algebraic and arithmetic procedures that most students learned early in their high school careers. In this chapter, we review the grammar of mathematical notations, discuss several types of numerical scales, and adopt certain conventions for rounding numbers.

If you wish to brush up on basic mathematics, Appendix A contains a review of all the math necessary to master this text.

2.2 SUMMATION RULES

Throughout the textbook you will be learning new mathematical symbols. For the most part, we will define these symbols when they first appear. However, four notations will appear so frequently that their separate treatment at this time is justified. These notations are X, Y, N, and the uppercase Greek letter Σ (pronounced "sigma").

While defining these symbols and demonstrating their use, we will also review the grammar of mathematical notation. It is not surprising that many students become so involved in the numerous mathematical formulas and symbols that they fail to realize that mathematics has its nouns, adjectives, verbs, and adverbs.

2.2.1 Mathematical Nouns

In grammar, we use nouns to represent persons, places, things, and ideas. In mathematics, our nouns are commonly quantities. The notation we use most frequently in statistics to represent quantity (or a score) is X, although we occasionally employ Y. More specifically, the letter X or Y represents a set of observations or data collected in a study. For example, if weight and height were two variables in a study, X would represent weight and Y would identify height. Another frequently used "noun" is the symbol N, which stands for the number of scores or quantities with which we are dealing. Thus, if we have 10 respondents participating in a study, $N = 10$; if there are 532 respondents interviewed in an opinion poll, $N = 532$.

2.2.2 Mathematical Adjectives

In grammar, we use adjectives to describe or modify nouns. When we want to modify a mathematical noun or identify it more specifically, we commonly employ subscripts. Thus, if we have a series of scores or quantities, we can represent them as X_1, X_2, X_3, X_4, and so on. The symbol X represents the measurement, and the subscript identifies the respondent, subject, or participant. We shall also frequently encounter X_i. The subscript i is a variable that may take on any value that we desire. In a study, we may have 10 respondents. The subscript represents the measurement for each respondent. Therefore, X_5 and Y_5 represent the X and Y measurements for the fifth respondent.

2.2.3 Mathematical Verbs

In grammar, we use verbs to denote actions related to nouns. In mathematics, notations that direct the reader to perform some action on the nouns have the same characteristics as verbs in a spoken language. One of the most important "verbs" is the symbol Σ. This notation directs us to sum all quantities or scores following the symbol. Thus, let X equal the data set with five numbers:

$$\begin{aligned} X_1 &= 5 \\ X_2 &= 3 \\ X_3 &= 6 \\ X_4 &= 7 \\ X_5 &= 2 \\ \Sigma X &= X_1 + X_2 + X_3 + X_4 + X_5 \\ \Sigma X &= 5 + 3 + 6 + 7 + 2 \\ \Sigma X &= 23 \end{aligned}$$

Therefore, ΣX indicates that we should add together all the quantities from X_1 to X_5. Other verbs we encounter frequently are $\sqrt{\ }$, which directs us to find the square root, and exponents (X^a), which tell us to raise a quantity to the indicated power. Mathematical verbs are commonly referred to as *operators*.

2.2.4 Mathematical Adverbs

In grammar, we use adverbs to describe or modify verbs. Likewise, in mathematics, adverbial notations are used to modify verbs. We frequently find adverbial notation modifying the summation sign (Σ). Let's imagine that we want to indicate that the following quantities are to be added together.

$$X_1 + X_2 + X_3 + X_4 + X_5 + \cdots + X_N$$

That is, we add all of these quantities in the set X from the first value (X_1) to the last or Nth value (X_N) starting with $i = 1$. Thus, if $X_1 = 7$, $X_2 = 5$, $X_3 = 9$, $X_4 = 8$ $X_5 = 11$, and $X_6 = 4$ and we wanted to find the sum of all the values, we would represent these operations as follows:

$$\sum_{i=1}^{N} X_i = 7 + 5 + 9 + 8 + 11 + 4 = 44$$

The notations above and below the summation sign indicate that i takes on successive values of 1, 2, 3, 4, 5, up to N. Stated verbally, the notation reads: We should sum all quantities from $i = 1$ (X_1) through $i = N$, that is, X_N. If we wanted to add all the quantities starting with the third value, we would place $i = 3$ under the summation sign instead of $i = 1$.

Sometimes this form of notation may direct us to add only selected quantities. Thus, if $X_1 = 7$, $X_2 = 5$, $X_3 = 9$, $X_4 = 8$, $X_5 = 11$, and $X_6 = 4$:

$$\sum_{i=2}^{6} X_i = 5 + 9 + 8 + 11 + 4 = 37$$

2.2.5 Rules of Priority

Many statistical equations have numerous steps expressed in a single equation. It is vital that you remember the rules of priority for interpreting a mathematical equation. Table 2.1 shows the general rules that apply to all mathematical operations.

TABLE 2.1
Rules of priority for mathematical operations*

Operator	Equation format	Example
1. Exponentiation and square root		
Exponentiation	X^2	$5^2 = 25$
Square root	$\sqrt{X}$	$\sqrt{25} = 5$
2. Negation	$-X$	$-(15) = -15$
3. Multiplication and division		
Multiplication	$X(Y)$	$3(4) = 12$
	$X \times Y$	$3 \times 4 = 12$
Division	X/Y	$12/4 = 3$
4. Addition and subtraction		
Addition	$X + Y$	$3 + 4 = 7$
Subtraction	$X - Y$	$12 - 4 = 8$

*The table is constructed from highest (first) priority to lowest (fourth) priority.

1. Work from the left to the right of the equation.
2. Perform all the operations *inside* the parentheses before performing those *outside* the parentheses.
3. Some mathematical operations are performed before others (see Table 2.1).

Here are some examples of multistep problems. When you come to problems like these, make sure that you show each step. Our experience is that most students make mistakes because they try to skip steps and make an error in the process.

EXAMPLE 1.

$$X = 49 - (28)(5) + 23$$

$$X = 49 - 140 + 23$$

$$X = -68$$

EXAMPLE 2.

$$X = 7^2 - (-7 + 4) + 8 - (-15)$$

$$X = 49 - (-3) + 8 + 15$$

$$X = 49 + 3 + 8 + 15$$

$$X = 75$$

Now we can apply these rules to several equations that are common to statistical analysis. For our purposes, we assume that data sets X and Y each consist of the following six values:

$X_1 = 7$	$Y_1 = 2$
$X_2 = 5$	$Y_2 = 7$
$X_3 = 9$	$Y_3 = 13$
$X_4 = 8$	$Y_4 = 2$
$X_5 = 11$	$Y_5 = 7$
$X_6 = 4$	$Y_6 = 8$

EXAMPLE: Sum of Observations in a Set

$$\Sigma X = X_1 + X_2 + X_3 + X_4 + X_5 + X_6$$
$$\Sigma X = 7 + 5 + 9 + 8 + 11 + 4$$
$$\Sigma X = 44$$

$$\Sigma Y = Y_1 + Y_2 + Y_3 + Y_4 + Y_5 + Y_6$$
$$\Sigma Y = 2 + 7 + 13 + 2 + 7 + 8$$
$$\Sigma Y = 39$$

EXAMPLE: Sum of Squared Observations in a Set

$$\Sigma X^2 = X_1^2 + X_2^2 + X_3^2 + X_4^2 + X_5^2 + X_6^2$$
$$\Sigma X^2 = 7^2 + 5^2 + 9^2 + 8^2 + 11^2 + 4^2$$
$$\Sigma X^2 = 49 + 25 + 81 + 64 + 121 + 16$$
$$\Sigma X^2 = 356$$

$$\Sigma Y^2 = Y_1^2 + Y_2^2 + Y_3^2 + Y_4^2 + Y_5^2 + Y_6^2$$
$$\Sigma Y^2 = 2^2 + 7^2 + 13^2 + 2^2 + 7^2 + 8^2$$
$$\Sigma Y^2 = 4 + 49 + 169 + 4 + 49 + 64$$
$$\Sigma Y^2 = 339$$

EXAMPLE: Sum of Observations in a Set, Quantity Squared

$$(\Sigma X)^2 = (7 + 5 + 9 + 8 + 11 + 4)^2$$
$$(\Sigma X)^2 = 44^2$$
$$(\Sigma X)^2 = 1936$$

$$(\Sigma Y)^2 = (2 + 7 + 13 + 2 + 7 + 8)^2$$
$$(\Sigma Y)^2 = 39^2$$
$$(\Sigma Y)^2 = 1521$$

EXAMPLE: Sum of Cross Products

$$\Sigma XY = X_1 Y_1 + X_2 Y_2 + X_3 Y_3 + X_4 Y_4 + X_5 Y_5 + X_6 Y_6$$
$$\Sigma XY = 7(2) + 5(7) + 9(13) + 8(2) + 11(7) + 4(8)$$
$$\Sigma XY = 14 + 35 + 117 + 16 + 77 + 32$$
$$\Sigma XY = 291$$

EXAMPLE: Product of Two Sums

$$(\Sigma X)(\Sigma Y) = (44)(39)$$
$$(\Sigma X)(\Sigma Y) = 1716$$

2.3 TYPES OF NUMBERS AND SCALES

In our numerically oriented society, we use numbers in many different ways long before we are expected to do complicated calculations. But if you were asked to define a number or to describe the ways in which numbers are used, you might be confused briefly and then realize that you have never thought about it before. You might further reply that numbers are symbols denoting amounts that can be added, subtracted, multiplied, and divided. That is partly correct, but some members are not used for these basic arithmetic operations. Is the symbol 7 on a baseball player's uniform such a number? What about your home address? Channel 2 on your television set? Do these numbers indicate amounts of things? Can they reasonably be added, subtracted, multiplied, or divided? Can you multiply the number on any football player's back by any other number and obtain a meaningful value? A careful analysis of our use of numbers in everyday life reveals an interesting fact: Most of the numbers we use do not have the mathematical properties we usually give to them; that is, they cannot be meaningfully added, subtracted, multiplied, and divided. A few examples are the serial number of a home appliance, a zip code number, a telephone number, a home address, an automobile registration number, and the catalog numbers on a book in the library.

The important point is that numbers are used in a variety of ways to achieve many different ends. Most of the time these ends do not include the representation of an amount or a quantity. Numbers are used in two different ways:

1. As **nominal numbers,** or numbers used to name.
2. As **ordinal numbers,** to represent position in a series.

Measurement is the assignment of numbers to objects or events according to sets of predetermined (or arbitrary) rules. The different levels of measurement that we will discuss represent different levels of numerical information contained in a set of observations (data), such as a series of house numbers, the order of finish in a horse race, a set of I.Q. scores, or the price per share of various stocks. The type of numerical scale obtained depends on the kinds of mathematical operations that can be legitimately performed on the numbers. In the social sciences, we encounter measurements at every level.

It should be noted that there are other schemata for classifying numbers and the ways they are used. We use the nominal-ordinal classification because it best handles the types of data we obtain in the social sciences. As you will see, we count, we place in relative position, and we obtain numerical scores. It should also be noted that the assignment to categories is not always clearcut or unambiguous. There are times when even experts cannot agree. To illustrate: Is the number in your street address nominal or ordinal? The answer depends on your need. For certain purposes it can be considered nominal, such as when used as a *name* of a dwelling. At the other times it can be considered ordinal, since the numbers place your house in a position relative to other houses on the block. Thus, 08 may be to the left of 12 and to the right of 04.

The fundamental requirements of observation and measurement are acknowledged by all the physical and social sciences as well as by any modern-day corporation interested in improving its competitive position. The things that we observe are often referred to as variables. Any particular observation is called the value of the variable. Let us look at two examples.

If we are studying the number of days of hospitalization among different kinds of patients, our variable is the number of days in the hospital. Thus, if a patient spends $8\frac{1}{2}$ days in the hospital, the value of the variable is 8.50.

If we are interested in determining whether an employer discriminates on the basis of racial background, the racial classification of the employees is our variable. This variable may have several values, such as black, black Hispanic, white, and white Hispanic.

2.3.1 Nominal Scales

Four basic levels of measurement scales are utilized by social and physical scientists. These include the nominal scale, the ordinal scale, the interval scale, and the ratio scale. Each type of scale has unique characteristics and, as we will see later, implications for the type of statistical procedures that can be used with it.

Nominal scales do not involve highly complex measurement. Instead, they involve rules for placing individuals or objects into categories. The categories must (1) be homogeneous, (2) be mutually exclusive, (3) be exhaustive, and (4) make no assumption about ordered relationships between categories. We refer to categories as **mutually exclusive** because it is impossible for a person's score to belong to more than one category. **Exhaustive** means that all scores can be placed within the established categories.

Consider a study of anti-Semitism. Let's classify the respondents into one of two categories: Jewish identified and non-Jewish. Such a dichotomy would satisfy each of the four classification rules for a nominal scale. All of the respondents in the Jewish category are *homogeneous* (similar) in terms of the variable religious identification in that only Jewish respondents are included. The respondents in the non-Jewish category are also homogeneous. The categories we have chosen are *mutually exclusive* because no respondent can be placed into both categories; that is, a person is either Jewish or non-Jewish. The categories are also *exhaustive* because all the respondents can be classified as Jewish identified or non-Jewish. Finally, we can make no assumptions about the ordered relationships between categories, only that the individuals in the Jewish category differ from those in the non-Jewish category in terms of their religious identification. Our data would consist of the number of individuals in each of these two categories. Note that we do not think of the variable religious affiliation as representing an ordered series of values, such as height, prestige, or speed. A person that is female does not have more of the variable sex than one that is male.

Observations of unordered variables are referred to as nominal scales of measurement. They constitute the lowest level of measurement because they are the least mathematically versatile of the four levels of measurement scales. We may assign numerical values to represent the various classes in a nominal scale, but these numbers function only as category labels. If we wish to compare female and male responses to a question concerning parenting and are using a computer to analyze our results, we might assign a number to each sex category. Thus, male might be assigned a 0 and female a 1.

If we wish to classify persons in terms of their present marital status, we might number the categories for convenience, but the numbers would serve only to identify each marital status category; for example, (1) married, (2) divorced, (3) separated, (4) single, and (5) widowed. Here we have assigned numbers only to label each category and it would be meaningless to add or subtract them. Other examples of nominal level variables include sex, religious affiliation, race, blood type, and astrological sign.

The data used with nominal scales consist of frequency counts or tabulations of the number of occurrences in each class of the variable under study. In the aforementioned anti-Semitism study, our frequency counts of Jewish and non-Jewish respondents would comprise our data. Such data are often referred to interchangeably as *frequency data, nominal data,* or *categorical data.*

2.3.2 Ordinal Scales

When we move into the next higher level of measurement, we encounter variables in which the categories *do* represent a rank-ordered series of relationships. Thus, the categories in **ordinal scales** are not only homogeneous, mutually exclusive, and exhaustive, but they stand in some kind of *relation* to one another. More specifically, the relationships are expressed in terms of the algebra of inequalities: a is less than b ($a < b$) or a is greater than b ($a > b$). In Figure 2.1 we see that B and C are higher than A, but we cannot say how much higher because we do not know the distance between A, B, and C since the values are measured on an ordinal scale.

Types of relationships encountered in an ordinal scale are greater, poorer, healthier, more prejudiced, more feminine, more prestigious, and so on. The numerals employed in ordinal scales indicate only position in an ordered series and not how much of a difference exists between successive positions on the scale (see Case Example 2.1). We can rank order the following educational degrees from higher to lower—for example, (1) doctorate, (2) master's degree, (3) bachelor's degree—but we cannot say that the doctor's degree is twice as high as the bachelor's degree or that a particular difference exists between categories.

Examples of ordinal scaling include rank ordering: the leading causes of death among the elderly, academic departments in a college according to their prestige, baseball teams according to their league standing, officer candidates in terms of their leadership qualities, and potential candidates for political office according to their name recognition with the people. Note that the ranks are assigned according to the ordering of individuals within the class. Thus, the most popular candidate may receive the rank of 1, the next most popular may receive the rank of 2, and so on down to the

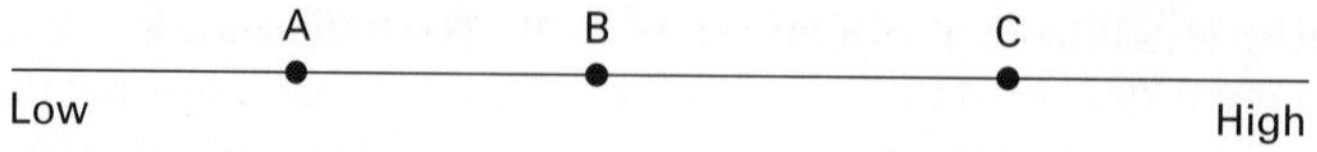

FIGURE 2.1
Relationship of three points on an ordinal scale

least popular candidate. It does not make any difference whether we give the best-known candidate the highest numerical rank or the lowest, *so long as we are consistent in placing the individuals accurately with respect to their relative position in the ordered series.*

CASE EXAMPLE 2.1

HELP IS WHERE YOU FIND IT

Offering advice is not the exclusive province of people specifically trained to give such help. Members of some occupational categories are necessarily involved in interpersonal relationships with their clients, often involving intimate revelations by the clients and attempts to render verbal assistance by the help-giver. One aspect of this study dealt with the response strategies of four different occupational groups (hairdressers, lawyers, supervisors, and bartenders) when clients sought help and advice concerning personal problems. The various strategies employed by members of each of these groups were rank ordered in an ordinal scale from most frequent to least frequent. Table 2.2 shows ordinal ranking of 11 different strategies among hairdressers and bartenders.

Table 2.2 reveals some interesting differences as well as similarities in the help-giving strategies of these two professions. Both rate offering support, trying to be lighthearted, and just listening high on their hierarchy of response strategies. The most notable disagreement involves telling the clients to count their blessings. Hairdressers are more inclined than bartenders to adopt this strategy.

TABLE 2.2
Ordinal position of response strategies of hairdressers and bartenders when clients seek advice and counsel

Strategy	Hairdressers	Bartenders
Offer support and sympathy	1	3
Try to be lighthearted	2	2
Just listen	3	1
Present alternatives	4	4
Tell person to count blessings	5	10
Share personal experiences	6	5
Try not to get involved	7	6
Give advice	8	7
Ask questions	9	9
Try to get person to talk to someone else	10	11
Try to change topic	11	8

Note: A rank of 1 corresponds to the most frequently used strategy and 11 to the least frequently used strategy.

Source: Based on Emory L. Cowen, "Help Is Where You Find It," *American Psychologist* 37 (1982), pp. 385–95.

We will be looking at these data again in Chapter 9 when we obtain the correlation between the rankings of response strategies of these two occupational groups.

It is important to realize that many social scientists believe all of the attitude scales employed in the social sciences are ordinal level scales. When you are asked, for example, to respond to a question with Likert-type response categories [e.g., (1) strongly disagree, (2) disagree, (3) agree, and (4) strongly agree], the responses are ordinal in nature. Consider course evaluations and the following statement: "My professor is well prepared for class." If a friend in the class responds "(1) strongly disagree" and you respond "(3) agree," we can only conclude that you ranked the professor more favorably on this question than your friend did. We cannot claim that your rating of "3" or "agree" indicates that you rated the professor three times as high as your friend did simply because the friend rated the professor "1" or "strongly disagree." Again, the numbers associated with the categories only indicate their ordered relationship, not how much of a difference exists between the categories. It should be noted, however, that consensus in this area is not complete.

2.3.3 Interval and Ratio Scales

Finally, the highest level of measurement in science is achieved with scales employing numbers that can be used in meaningful mathematical operations such as adding, subtracting, multiplying, and dividing (interval and ratio scales). In interval and ratio scales, equal differences between points on any part of the scale are equal. The only difference between the two scales is that the **interval scale** employs an arbitrary zero point, whereas the **ratio scale** employs a true zero point. Consequently, only the ratio scale permits us to make statements concerning the ratios of numbers in the scale; for example, 4 feet are to 2 feet are to 1 foot. A good example of the difference between an interval and a ratio scale is a person's height as measured from a table top (interval) versus height as measured from the floor.

With both interval and ratio scales, we can state exact differences between categories. This property or characteristic is particularly valuable because many statistical procedures can only be used with interval or ratio measures. Most statisticians consider the frequently used variables of age, education, and income as ratio variables because each has a true zero point. Age and education have a true zero point of zero years. We can say that if a wife has completed 14 years of formal education and her husband 7 years, she has had twice as much formal education as he has. We cannot of course assume that she has twice as much knowledge because knowledge cannot be measured in standard units. Additionally, four concepts you will study later in this chapter—proportions, percentages, rates, and ratios—are all ratio measures. I.Q., however, which has true zero point (it is impossible to say someone has no intelligence) is an interval measure.

Some statisticians enjoy pointing out that common social science variables such as income and education can be conceived of as only ordinal level measures in some instances. For example, they might ask, "Does a $1,000 raise mean the same thing to an individual whose annual income exceeds $100,000 as it does to someone whose annual income is $15,000?" Or, "Is the one-unit difference between 11 and 12 years of formal education really equivalent to the one-unit difference between 18 and 19 years of formal education?" The argument being made is that the *meaning* of the $1,000 or 1 additional year of formal education differs in these examples. While the implications of these examples are interesting to consider, we will treat variables like these as ratio measures. Also, apart from the difference in the nature of the zero point, interval and ratio scales have the same mathematical properties and will be treated alike throughout the text.

It should be clear that one of the most sought after goals of the social scientist is to achieve measurements that are at least interval in nature. Indeed, interval scaling is assumed for most of the statistical tests reported in this book. Although it is debatable that many of our scales achieve interval measurement, most social scientists are willing to make the assumption that they do.

One of the characteristics of higher-order scales is that they can readily be transformed into lower-order scales. Thus, the outcome of a one-mile foot race may be expressed as time scores measured in minutes and seconds (ratio scale); for example, 3 : 56, 3 : 58, and 4 : 02. The time scores may then be transformed into an ordinal scale; for example, first-, second-, and third-place finishers. However, the reverse transformation is not possible. If we know only the order of finishing a race, we cannot express the outcome in terms of a ratio scale (time scores). Although it is permissible to transform scores from higher-level to lower-level scales, it is not usually recommended since information is lost in the transformation. For example, risk-taking behavior might be scored from 0 to 10 depending on the number of 10 "risky" activities (e.g., driving over 100 miles per hour, skydiving, unprotected intercourse with a person having active genital herpes) in which a person has engaged. We could convert this interval-level measure into an ordinal-level measure by reclassifying everyone into three categories—(1) nonrisk taker, (2) moderate risk taker, (3) high risk taker—but we would lose information about the respondents.

The characteristics of nominal, ordinal, interval, and ratio scales are summarized in Table 2.3.

TABLE 2.3
Measurement scales and their characteristics

Scale	Characteristic	Examples
Nominal	Categories homogeneous, mutually exclusive, exhaustive, and no assumption made about ordered relationships between categories	Sex of subject (male = 0, female = 1) Religion of person Political party
Ordinal	All of the above plus the categories can be rank-ordered	Rank in class (1st, 2nd, or 3rd) Rank on personality dimension (low versus high self-esteem) Aggressiveness scale scores (1 = low aggression, 10 = high aggression)
Interval	All of the above plus exact differences between categories may be specified and an arbitrary zero point is assumed	Temperature of 98.6°F SAT verbal score of 540* Score on an IQ test Raw score on a statistics test
Ratio	All of the above with the exception that a true zero point is assumed	Height, weight, age, running speed Number of words recalled in a memory experiment Grams of fat consumed Number of problems solved

*Test scores are treated as interval scale data.

2.4 CONTINUOUS AND DISCRETE VARIABLES

Imagine that you are given the problem of trying to determine the number of children for each American family. Your scale of measurement would start with zero (no children) and would proceed, by *increments of 1,* to perhaps 15 or 20. Note that in moving from one value on the scale to the next, we proceed by *whole numbers* rather than by fractional amounts. Thus, a family has either 0, 1, 2, or more children. In spite of the statistical abstraction that the American family averages $1\frac{3}{4}$ children, we do not know a single couple that has achieved this marvelous state of family planning.

Such variables are referred to as **discrete** or **discontinuous variables,** and they have equality of *counting units* as their basic characteristics. Thus, if we are studying the number of children in a family, each child is equal with respect to providing one counting unit. Mathematical operations such as adding, subtracting, multiplying, and dividing are permissible with discrete variables. We can say that a family with four children has twice as many children as one with two children. Observations of discrete variables are always exact so long as the counting procedures are accurate. Examples of discrete variables are group size, the number of males in a class, the number of work stoppages in Illinois, and the number of welfare recipients in a country.

You should not assume from this discussion that discrete variables necessarily involve *only* whole numbers. However, most of the discontinuous variables used by social scientists are expressed in terms of whole numbers. For example, a political scientist tabulates the number of people who voted for a particular candidate or a sociologist tabulates the number of kindergarten children from family units of different sizes. In each of these examples we are clearly dealing with values that proceed by whole numbers.

In contrast, a **continuous variable** is one that has an unlimited number of *possible* values between *any two adjacent values.* Thus, if the variable is height measured in inches, then 4 inches and 5 inches would be two adjacent values on the scale. However, there can be an infinite number of intermediate values, such as 4.5 inches or 4.7 inches. If the variable is height measured in 10ths of inches, then 4.5 inches and 4.6 inches are two adjacent values of the scale, but there can *still* be an infinite of intermediate values such as 4.53 inches or 4.59 inches.

A variable that may take on an unlimited (infinite) number of intermediate values is referred to as a continuous variable. It is important to note that although our measurement of discrete variables may be exact, our measure of continuous variables is always approximate. If we were measuring the attitudes of Philadelphians toward their police, for example, we would find a wide variety of attitudes ranging from "very positive" to "very negative" because no two people can have *exactly* the same attitude. Figure 2.2 depicts the difference between continuous and discrete variables. Other social science examples of continuous variables include measures of achievement motivation, political activism, religiosity, and income.

Let's consider one additional point. Continuous variables are often expressed as whole numbers and therefore appear to be discontinuous. Thus, you may say that you are 5 feet, 8 inches tall and weigh 150 pounds. However, the decision to express height to the nearest inch and weight to the nearest pound was yours. You could just as easily have expressed height to the nearest fraction of an inch and weight to the nearest ounce.

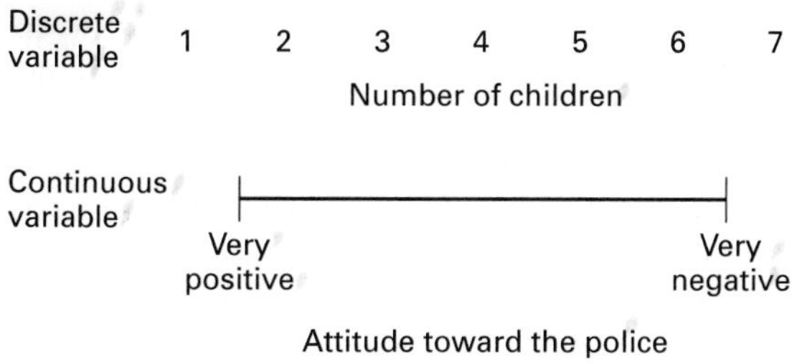

FIGURE 2.2
Discrete and continuous variables

You do not have such a choice when reporting such things as the number of children in a family. These must occur as whole numbers.

2.4.1 Continuous Variables and True Limits of Numbers

In our preceding discussion, we noted that continuously distributed variables can take on an unlimited number of intermediate values. Therefore, we can never specify the exact value for any particular measurement since it is possible that a more sensitive measurement can slightly increase the accuracy of our measurements. For this reason, we stated that numerical values of continuously distributed variables are always approximate. However, it is possible to specify the limits within which the true value falls; these limits are called **true limits** or, sometimes, **real limits.** For example, the true limits of the value of a continuous variable are equal to that number plus or minus one-half the unit of measurement. Let's look at a few examples. You have a bathroom scale that is calibrated in terms of pounds. When you step on the scale, the pointer is usually a little above or below a pound marker; however, you report your weight to the nearest pound. Thus, if the pointer were approximately three-quarters of the distance between 212 and 213 pounds, you would report your weight as 213 pounds. It would be understood that the true limit of your weight, assuming an accurate scale, falls between 212.5 pounds and 213.5 pounds. At times, you may be collecting data with precision to the first decimal place, for example, 6.1, 6.2, and 6.3. In this case, you would go to the 100ths column so that 6.2, for example, would represent all values between 6.15 and 6.25. Figure 2.2 illustrates this bracketing of the value of whole-number scores and scores reported to the nearest 10th.

Here are some examples of true limits. The true limits of:

11 are 10.5 and 11.5. Why?
11.5 are 11.45 and 11.55. Why?
112 are 111.5 and 112.5. Why?
112.2 are 112.15 and 112.25. Why?

2.5 ROUNDING NUMBERS

Imagine that you have some data that, in the course of conducting a statistical analysis, require you to divide one number into another. There will be innumerable occasions during this course and your later professional life when you will be required to perform this arithmetic operation. In some cases, the answer will be a value that extends to an endless number of decimal places. For example, if you were to express the fraction $\frac{1}{3}$ in decimal form, the result would be 0.33333. It is obvious that you cannot extend this series of numbers ad infinitum. You must stop at some point and assign a value to the last number in the series that best reflects the remainder. When you do this, the following three problems will arise.

1. To how many decimal places do we carry the final answer?
2. How do we decide on the last number in the series?
3. If the calculations involve a succession of multiplication and/or division steps in arriving at the final answer, do we round each intermediate step or round only after the final step has been completed?

The answer to the first question is frequently given in terms of the number of *significant digits.* The number of significant digits typically reflects the level of accuracy of the measurement. Suppose you have measured the time in seconds that it took subjects in an experiment to solve 10 anagrams. There were seven subjects, and the total of all the times was 93 seconds. When you calculate the average, it is $\frac{93}{7} = 13.285714286$. We recommend that the final report of measurements be rounded to the true limits of a measurement. In this example, you measured time to the nearest second. Therefore, the true limits of the time are ± 0.5 second. Consequently you should round to the first decimal place, converting the average to 13.3. What if you measured to the nearest $\frac{1}{100}$ second? The true limit would then be ± 0.0005 second. Therefore, we could round to 13.28571 seconds.

Not all researchers use the same conventions for reporting significant digits. In most examples in this text, we will report the final results to the second decimal place. This practice will allow you to check the accuracy of your own calculations. When you conduct your own research and statistical analyses, we encourage you to consider rounding to reflect the accuracy of measurement and report only the significant digits.

The second question asks when you should round up, down, or keep the last digit as it is. The rules of rounding are as follows.

1. If we are rounding to a specified number of decimal places (e.g., two) and the remainder that extends beyond that decimal place is less than 5 in decimal form, we drop the remainder. Thus, 53.56499 becomes 53.56.
2. If the remainder is greater than 5 in decimal form, we increase the last digit by 1. Thus, 53.56501 becomes 53.57.
3. If the remainder is exactly 5, we increase the last digit if it is an odd number and drop the remaining fraction if the last digit is even. Thus, 53.57500 is rounded to 53.58 since 7 is an odd number, and 53.58500 is rounded to 53.58 since 8 is an even number.

Finally, when calculating various statistical measures in this course, there will often be many intermediate steps when going from raw data to the final answer. It is important *not to do any rounding* until after you have computed the final statistic. Otherwise, the final answer will often have large rounding errors. The following two sets of calculations illustrate this point.

No intermediate rounding:	Much intermediate rounding:
$(1.7549)(3.6359)(0.8252) = 5.2653$	$(1.75)(3.64)(0.83) = 5.2871$
$= 5.27$	$= 5.29$

Note that there is a rounding error of 0.02 to the second decimal place. When many intermediate steps are involved in the calculation, the rounding error can be considerably larger.

Many of you will be using calculators to work through equations. You should be aware that minor differences may occur between your calculations, those of the book, or those of other students in the class. These minor differences may be attributed to the fact that different calculators carry the intermediate steps to a different number of decimal places. A calculator that carries the intermediate steps to 4 places will probably produce a slightly different final answer from one that carries all calculations to 14 places. Therefore, small differences that exist in the fourth or fifth decimal can be ignored (e.g., 5.56791 versus 5.56789). Larger differences suggest a problem (e.g., 5.5679 versus 5.1634).

2.6 RATIOS

One of the several ratios commonly used by social scientists is the *sex ratio* or the number of males per 100 females. We find that sex ratios vary between cities, rural-urban areas, and age groups. A city such as Washington, D.C., has a relatively low sex ratio (87.4) because of the large number of women employed in government positions, whereas Fairbanks, Alaska, which can be regarded as a frontier city, is characterized by a very high sex ratio (115.7) because of the high concentration of males in the workforce. A **ratio** is the number of cases in one category divided by the number of cases in another. In the sex ratio, the quantities are multiplied by 100 to eliminate the decimal.

Let's compute the sex ratio for the United States in 1994 when there were approximately 127.1 million males and 133.2 million females:*

$$\text{sex ratio} = \frac{\text{Number of males}}{\text{Number of females}} \times 100$$

$$\text{sex ratio} = \frac{127.1 \text{ million males}}{133.2 \text{ million females}} \times 100$$

$$= 95.42$$

We interpret our computed sex ratio as 95.4 males per 100 females. If we had calculated the sex ratio by age group (commonly referred as an age-specific sex ratio), we would observe the trend evident in Case Example 2.2 (Table 2.4). Can you explain why there are so few males per 100 females among the 65+ age group? A total of 13,475,000

* U.S. Bureau of the Census. The values have been rounded.

CASE EXAMPLE 2.2

TABLE 2.4
Sex ratio of males to females, by age group, 1950 to 1994, and projections, 2000 and 2025

							Projections	
Age	**1950**	**1960**	**1970**	**1980**	**1990**	**1994**	**2000**	**2025**
All ages	**98.6**	**97.1**	**94.8**	**94.5**	**95.1**	**95.4**	**95.7**	**96.3**
Under 14 years	103.7	103.4	103.9	104.6	104.9	104.9	105.2	105.4
14 to 24 years	98.2	98.7	98.7	101.9	104.6	104.4	104.4	104.7
25 to 44 years	96.4	95.7	95.5	97.4	98.9	99.1	99.1	98.6
45 to 64 years	100.1	95.7	91.6	90.7	92.5	93.4	94.1	94.2
65 years and over. . . .	89.6	82.8	72.1	67.6	67.2	68.5	70.5	82.0

Sources: U.S. Bureau of the Census, U.S. Census of Population, 1950, 1960, 1970; Current Population Reports; unpublished data.

males and 19,683,000 females were 65 years or older in 1994. Verify the age-specific sex ratio of 68.5 for the 65 years and older age group.

Another ratio used by social scientists is the *dependency ratio,* which indicates the number of individuals per 100 who are younger than 15 or older than 64 relative to those between the ages of 15 and 64. High dependency ratios characterize developing nations. Why? In Vietnam, the population totaled 76.6 million persons in 1996, of which 30.6 million or 40% were less than 15 and 3.8 million or 5% were over 64 years old. The dependency ratio in Vietnam is approximately 81.5, whereas in the United States it is 53.8:*

$$\text{dependency ratio} = \frac{\text{Persons younger than 15 or older than 64}}{\text{persons 15 to 64}} \times 100$$

$$\text{dependency ratio for Vietnam} = \frac{30.6 \text{ million} + 3.8 \text{ million}}{42.2 \text{ million}} \times 100$$

$$= 81.52$$

A more common use of ratios involves comparing one quantity to another. Nonwhites in the United States constituted approximately 45.1 million persons in 1995 and whites 218.3 million, for a total of approximately 263.4 million persons. We can express the ratio of nonwhites to whites as 45.1 to 218.3 (45.1 : 218.3) or 1 : 4.8. We

*Adapted from the 1996 World Population Data Sheet of the Population Reference Bureau, Inc. In industrial nations, the numerator is frequently adjusted to persons younger than 21 because few enter the workforce at age 15, as is common in developing nations. The ratio for the United States is based on the same equation as the Vietnam figure for comparative purposes.

will see that ratios provide the basis for proportions, percentages, and rates in that all are based on the relationship between two categories or quantities.

The ratio of cats to rats = 3:2

The proportion of cats = $\frac{3}{5}$ = .60

The percentage of cats = .60(100) = 60%

2.7 PROPORTIONS, PERCENTAGES, AND RATES

A **proportion** is a value calculated by dividing the quantity in one category by the total of all the categories. In 1992, the most frequent cause of death among persons ages 25 to 44 was unintentional injuries. During that year, 25,808 persons died following an unintentional injury (e.g., automobile, household), and a total of 112,727 persons in this age group died from the six leading causes of death (see Table 2.5). Given this information, we can calculate that the proportion of unintentional injuries out of the total number of deaths in 1992 attributable to the six leading causes of death for the 25 to 44 age group equaled 0.229 by dividing 25,808 by 112,727 using equation (2.1).

$$\text{proportion } (p) = \frac{f}{N} \tag{2.1}$$

$$p = \frac{25{,}808}{112{,}727} = 0.229$$

where f = frequency, the number of cases in any category
N = the number of cases in all categories

Proportions can range in value from 0 (if there are no cases in a category) to 1.000 (if a category contains all the cases). Note also in Table 2.5 that the proportions

TABLE 2.5
Six leading causes of death in 1992 among persons 25–44 years of age (both sexes)

	Number	Proportion	Percentage
Unintentional injuries	25,808	0.229	22.9%
HIV infection	24,629	0.218	21.8
Malignancies	22,185	0.197	19.7
Heart diseases	16,121	0.143	14.3
Suicide	12,181	0.108	10.8
Homicide	11,803	0.105	10.5
Total	112,727	1.000	100.0

Sources: Centers for Disease Control and Prevention; U.S. Center for Health Statistics, *Vital Statistics of the United States,* vol. II, *Mortality,* Part A, for data years 1980 and 1992, Public Health Service, Washington, D.C.: U.S. Government Printing Office, 1993.

associated with the six categories total 1.000 because they are mutually exclusive and exhaustive; hence, the categories constitute a nominal level of measurement.

A proportion can be converted to a **percentage** when it is multiplied by 100 as shown in equation (2.2):

$$\text{percentage } (\%) = \left(\frac{f}{N}\right) \times 100 \tag{2.2}$$

Box 2.1 provides an additional example of percentages based on national interviews.

Consider Table 2.5 again. We can convert the proportion of deaths associated with suicide to a percentage by multiplying the proportion 0.108 by 100. The other proportions associated with unintentional injuries also can be converted to a percentage when multiplied by 100. Hence, 10.8% died from suicide, and 22.9% from unintentional injuries, or a total of 33.7% of the deaths reported in Table 2.5 resulted from these two causes. If we added the 21.8% who were victims of HIV infection, the 19.7% who died of malignancies, the 14.3% who died of heart diseases, and the 10.5% who were victims of homicide, we could account for 100% of the 112,727 deaths.

We are frequently concerned with *percentage change*. While you probably have been calculating percentage change for many years, a brief review is worthwhile. Two points in time are involved when calculating percentage change. Consider how we might calculate the percentage of population increase in a small village in Wisconsin from the 1980 to 1990 census. If the population totaled 1,000 in 1980 and increased to 1,710 in 1990, how do we determine the percentage increase? Our first time period is 1980 and the second, 1990. Using the information and the following procedure, we can now calculate the percentage change:

$$\text{percentage change} = \frac{(\text{quantity at time 2}) - (\text{quantity at time 1})}{(\text{quantity at time 1})} \times 100 \tag{2.3}$$

$$\text{percentage change} = \frac{(1{,}710 - 1{,}000)}{1{,}000} \times 100$$

$$= \frac{710}{1{,}000} \times 100$$

$$= 0.71 \times 100 = 71\%$$

The procedure works equally well if the percentage change is negative. If the population of our fictitious village declined from 1,000 in 1980 to 900 in 1990, we would anticipate negative growth:

$$\text{percentage change} = \frac{(900 - 1{,}000)}{1{,}000} \times 100$$

$$= \frac{-100}{1{,}000} \times 100 = -10\%$$

The population decline is 10%. See also Case Example 2.2.

BOX 2.1

VICTIMIZATION BY VIOLENT CRIME: INCOME AND RACE

	Race	
Income level	White (%)	African American (%)
Under $3,000	6.26%	5.57%
$3,000–7,499	4.12	5.18
$7,500–9,999	3.67	4.06
$10,000–14,999	3.53	4.12
$15,000–24,999	2.87	3.04
$25,000 and above	2.50	2.74

Much of the data collected in the behavioral and social sciences consist of head counts—the number of people falling in one category as opposed to another category. We commonly use percentages or proportions to summarize such data. Various agencies of the criminal justice system rely heavily on the "head count" technique to summarize data on crimes and victims of crimes.

The accompanying table shows the percentage of victimization by violent crime (e.g., rape, robbery, or assault) during 1982, broken down in terms of race and income level. The data are based on interviews of about 60,000 households and represent 128,000 occupants age 12 and over. With the exception of the lowest income category, a greater percentage of African Americans are victims of crime within each income level. Note also that there appears to be an inverse relationship between income level and victimization rate: the higher the income level, the lower the rate of victimization. This relationship appears to hold for both African Americans and whites.

Source: P. A. Langan and C. A. Innes, "The Risk of Violent Crime," Bureau of Justice Statistics Special Report, NCI-97119, 1985.

Note that it is very important that you not disregard the minus sign in the numerator. The denominator will always constitute your base and is the quantity at time 1. Another way of looking at the concept of percentage change is to remember that we are interested in changes from our base (in this case the population in 1980). If the quantity at time 2 is less than the base (time 1), we know that the percentage change is negative. Consider another example. Suppose you earned $15,000 in 1996 and the next year received a major promotion that included an annual salary of $30,000. Your salary has doubled and the percentage increase is 100%. Demonstrate this to yourself.

We have seen the value of proportions and percentages; however, there is one more related value, the **rate,** which is a ratio of the occurrences in a group category to the total number of elements in the group with which we are concerned. The rate allows us to examine our data in another way. For example, the rate allows us to determine the number of deaths by each cause for a given number of persons. We know that 22.9% of the deaths attributable to the six leading causes in the 25–44 age group were caused by unintentional injuries (see Table 2.5). We do not know how many deaths per 100,000 persons in the 25–44 age group were caused by accidents. Or, put another way, if you are between 25 and 44 years of age, is it very likely that you will die in an accident? A total of approximately 82,313,000 persons were between the ages of 25 and 44 in 1992. We know that 25,808 died in accidents; therefore, we can calculate the proportion and percentage in this age group that died of accidental causes. You should find that the proportion of deaths attributable to accidents is approximately 0.0003135 (by dividing 25,808 by 82,313,000), the percentage is 0.03135 (by multiplying the proportion by 100), and the rate per 100,000 is 31.35 (by multiplying the proportion by 100,000). Case Example 2.3 shows the rate per 100,000 persons in 1992 for the most serious crimes tracked by the Federal Bureau of Investigation.

Rates are always reported for a specific number of cases, normally per 100, per 1,000, or per 100,000. Birthrates can be calculated in a variety of ways, including rate of live births per 1,000 population (demographers call it the "crude birth rate") and the rate per 1,000 women of childbearing age (normally 15 to 44), known as the "fertility rate." Therefore, be sure you know how a rate is calculated. The age-specific birthrate is the rate of live births per 1,000 women in specific age categories.

In 1992, the age-specific birthrate for U.S. women 15 to 19 years of age was 38.0, for women 20 to 24 it was 103.4, for women 25 to 29 it was 109.0, for women 30 to 34 it dropped to 76.1, and for women 35 to 39 it was only 38.0. The last figure of 38.0 contrasts with an age-specific birthrate of 22.1 in 1983 for women 35 to 39 and suggests that women have more recently delayed having children.* The importance of the age-specific birthrate is that we can determine which age groups are having disproportionate numbers of children.

Expressed as an equation:

$$\text{rate} = \frac{\text{number of occurrences in a group category}}{\text{total number of elements in the group}}$$

This ratio is then multiplied by a given number (normally 100, 1,000, or 100,000) to determine the rate per a given number of persons or events.

SUMMARY

In this chapter, we pointed out that advanced knowledge of mathematics is not a prerequisite for success in this course. A sound background in high school mathematics plus steady application to assignments should be sufficient to permit mastery of the fundamental concepts explained in this text.

To aid the student who may not have had recent contact with mathematics, we have attempted to review some of the basic concepts of mathematics. Included in this review are (1) the grammar of mathematical notations, (2) types of numbers, (3) types of numerical scales, (4) continuous and discrete scales, (5) rounding, and (6) ratios, proportions, percentages, and rates. Students requiring a more thorough review of mathematics may refer to Appendix A.

**Source:* U.S. Center for Health Statistics, *Vital Statistics of the United States,* annual.

CASE EXAMPLE 2.3

CRIME RATES AND PERCENTAGE CHANGE

Table 2.6 provides a summary of violent and property crime in the United States in 1992. The general trend from 1991 to 1992 indicates that crime has decreased in several areas during this one-year period; however, overall there has been a marked increase in crime from 1983 to 1992, with the exception of burglaries which declined 12.7%. The standardized rate per 100,000 persons ensures that the figures are independent of population growth. The rate per 100,000 for the total crime index in 1991 was 5,897.8 (not shown) and the 1992 rate as shown in Table 2.6 is 5,660.2. Verify the −4.0% change since 1991 by using equation (2.3). Recall that time 1 is 1991 and time 2 is 1992, so you will need to subtract 5897.8 from 5660.2 and divide by 5897.8 (which is your time 1 value). You should find that the crime index total rate per 100,000 persons declined approximately 4%.

TABLE 2.6
Crime in the United States, 1992

	Number of crimes reported	Rate per 100,000	Percent change since 1991	Percent change since 1983	Percent cleared by arrest
Crime index total	14,438,200	5,660.2	−4.0	+9.4	21.4
Violent crime	1,932,270	757.5	−0.1	+40.9	44.6
Property crime	12,505,900	4,702.7	−4.6	+5.7	17.7
Murder	23,760	9.3	−5.1	+12.0	64.6
Forcible rape	109.060	42.8	+1.2	+27.0	51.5
Robbery	672,480	263.6	−3.3	+21.8	24.0
Aggravated assault	1,126,970	441.8	+2.0	+58.2	56.2
Burglary	2,979,900	1,168.2	−6.7	−12.7	13.4
Larceny-theft	7,915,200	3,103.0	−3.9	+8.2	20.2
Motor vehicle theft	1,610,800	631.5	−4.2	+46.6	13.8
Arson	NA	NA	NA	NA	14.8

Source: Federal Bureau of Investigation, Uniform Crime Reports, 1983–1992.

If you were told that the burglary rate per 100,000 population in the San Diego Metropolitan Statistical Area (MSA) was 1,135 in 1994, you would know immediately that the rate was calculated by forming a ratio of the number of burglaries in the San Diego MSA (30,048) to the total population in the MSA (2,646,179) and multiplying by 100,000 (to obtain the rate per 100,000).* This is shown below:

$$\frac{30{,}048}{2{,}646{,}179} = 0.0113552 \times 100{,}000 = 1135.52$$

Source: Uniform Crime Reports, 1994.

TERMS TO REMEMBER

continuous variable A variable that can assume an unlimited number of intermediate values.
discrete variables (discontinuous variables) Variables that have equality of counting units.
exhaustive A grouped frequency distribution is said to be exhaustive when all possible scores can be placed within the established categories.
interval scale A scale in which exact distances can be known between categories. The zero point in this scale is arbitrary, and arithmetic operations are permitted.
measurement The assignment of numbers to objects or events according to sets of predetermined (or arbitrary) rules.
mutually exclusive Categories are said to be mutually exclusive because it is impossible for a person's score to belong to more than one category.
nominal numbers Numbers used to name.
nominal scale A scale in which the categories are homogeneous, mutually exclusive, exhaustive, and unordered.
ordinal numbers Numbers used to represent position or order in a series.
ordinal scale A scale in which the classes can be rank-ordered, that is, expressed in terms of the algebra of inequalities (e.g., $a < b$ or $a > b$).
percentage A proportion that has been multiplied by 100.
proportion A value calculated by dividing the quantity in one category by the total of all the categories.
rate A ratio of the occurrences in a group category to the total number of elements in the group with which we are concerned.
ratio The number of cases in one category divided by the number of cases in another category.
ratio scale The same as interval scale, except that there is a true zero point.
real limits See true limits.
true limits The true limits of a value of a continuous variable are equal to that number plus or minus one-half of the unit of measurement.

EXERCISES

The following exercises are based on this chapter and Appendix A.

1. Apply the rules of priority to the following.
(*a*) $(6 + 4)^2 + (3 + 4)^2 =$
(*b*) $(-3 + 7)^2 =$
(*c*) $3(5^2 + 2^2) =$
(*d*) $-8(5 + 2)^2 =$

2. Apply the rules of priority to the following.
(*a*) $(4 + 7)^2 + (-6)^2 =$
(*b*) $2(-3 + 7)^2 =$
(*c*) $-2(5^2 + 2^2) =$
(*d*) $4 - (5 + 2)^2 =$

3. Find Y when $N = 4$ and $20 + N = Y + 2$.

4. Find ΣX when $N = 20$ and $\overline{X} = 60$
where $\overline{X} = \dfrac{\Sigma X}{N}$.

5. Find N when $\bar{X} = 90$ and $\Sigma X = 360$
where $\bar{X} = \dfrac{\Sigma X}{N}$.

6. Find N when
$\Sigma(X - \bar{X})^2 = 640$, and $s^2 = 16$
where $s^2 = \dfrac{\Sigma(X - \bar{X})^2}{N}$

7. Find s^2 when
$\Sigma(X - \bar{X})^2 = 240$, and $N = 12$
where $s^2 = \dfrac{\Sigma(X - \bar{X})^2}{N}$

8. Determine the value of the following expressions in which $X_1 = 4$, $X_2 = 5$, $X_3 = 7$, $X_4 = 9$, $X_5 = 10$, $X_6 = 11$, $X_7 = 14$.

(*a*) $\sum_{i=1}^{4} X_i =$ (*b*) $\sum_{i=1}^{7} X_i =$ (*c*) $\sum_{i=3}^{6} X_i =$ (*d*) $\sum_{i=2}^{5} X_i =$ (*e*) $\sum_{i=1}^{N} X_i =$ (*f*) $\sum_{i=4}^{N} X_i =$

9. Using the values of X_i given in exercise 8, show that:

$$\sum_{i=1}^{N} X_i^2 \neq \left(\sum_{i=1}^{N} X_i\right)^2$$

10. Express the following in summation notation:
(*a*) $X_1 + X_2 + X_3$
(*b*) $X_1 + X_2 + \cdots + X_N$
(*c*) $X_3^2 + X_4^2 + X_5^2 + X_6^2$
(*d*) $X_4^2 + X_5^2 + \cdots + X_N^2$

11. Indicate the level of measurement for the following studies:
(*a*) The name recognition of several political candidates was coded into the following categories:
(1) Recognize the name
(2) Do not recognize the name
(*b*) Respondents in a community standards survey were asked to classify sexually explicit material as:
(1) Very obscene
(2) Obscene
(3) Not at all obscene
(*c*) The respondents in exercise 11(b) were also asked if the government should:
(1) Ban the material
(2) Protect the material
(*d*) A sample of middle-aged men was asked to rank-order their three biggest fears of growing older.
(*e*) The percentage of population loss or gain over the past 10 years was calculated by state.

12. The following questions were included in a recent series of student surveys. Indicate the level of measure for each question.

(*a*) How satisfied are you with your life?
  (1) Very satisfied
  (2) Satisfied
  (3) Neither satisfied nor unsatisfied
  (4) Unsatisfied
  (5) Very unsatisfied

(*b*) What type of job do you expect to obtain when you graduate? ________

(*c*) Of your five closest friends, how many are men? ________

(*d*) Estimate what percent of your study time is spent effectively. ________

(*e*) What is your current grade point average? ________

(*f*) Have you ever belonged to a:
  (1) Labor union ________ yes ________ no
  (2) Church or synagogue ________ yes ________ no
  (3) Social club ________ yes ________ no

(*g*) What is your race or ethnic background?
  (1) Hispanic
  (2) White, other than Hispanic
  (3) African American
  (4) Asian American
  (5) Native American
  (6) Other (specify ________)

13. Indicate which of the following italicized variables represent discrete or continuous scales.

(*a*) *The time it takes* you to complete these problems.
(*b*) *The number of newspapers* sold in a given city on December 19, 1996.
(*c*) *The amount of change in weight* for five women over a period of four weeks.
(*d*) *The number of home runs* hit by each of 10 randomly selected batters during the 1997 baseball season.
(*e*) *The number of stocks* on the New York Stock Exchange that increased in selling price on January 3, 1997.

14. State the true limits of the following numbers?

(*a*) 0 (*b*) 0.5 (*c*) 1.0 (*d*) 0.49 (*e*) −5 (*f*) −4.5

15. Round the following numbers to the second decimal place:

(*a*) 99.99500 (*e*) 16.46500
(*b*) 46.40501 (*f*) 1.05499
(*c*) 2.96500 (*g*) 86.2139
(*d*) 0.00501 (*h*) 10.0050

16. There are 18 males and 21 females in your social welfare class. What is the ratio of males to females?

17. (*a*) Calculate the ratio of male to female homicide rates for the following years.
(*b*) Also, calculate the male-female ratio for whites and African Americans for each year.

Homicide victims

	White		African American		
Year	**Male**	**Female**	**Male**	**Female**	**Total**
1982	9,620	2,179	7,730	1,743	21,272
1992	9,456	3,012	10,131	2,187	24,786

Source: U.S. Center for Health Statistics, *Vital Statistics of the United States,* annual.

18. New York State had a total of approximately 8,625,000 males and 9,365,000 females in 1990. What was the sex ratio?

19. In 1996, Japan had a total population of 125.8 million persons of whom 16% were younger than 15 and 15% were over 64. What was the dependency ratio and how would you interpret your answer?

20. Determine the proportion and percentage of the population in the Baltimore Metropolitan Statistical Area that is contained in each of the following areas (population estimated as of 1992):

Anne Arundel County	441,464
Baltimore County	705,138
Carroll County	130,466
Harford County	195,493
Howard County	199,930
Queen Anne's County	35,158
Baltimore City	726,096

Source: City and County Data Book, 1994, U.S. Department of Commerce, Bureau of the Census.

21. Examine the accompanying table.
(*a*) Calculate the women's earnings as a percentage of men's earnings by year.
(*b*) Determine the percentage change of men's earnings from 1960 to 1975.
(*c*) Determine the percentage change of women's earnings from 1960 to 1975.

Median annual earnings of year-round full-time workers 14 years and over by sex, 1960 to 1975

Year	**Annual earnings (dollars)**	
	Women	**Men**
1960	$3,293	$ 5,417
1965	3,823	6,375
1970	5,323	8,966
1975	7,504	12,758

Source: U.S. Department of Labor, Bureau of Labor Statistics, *U.S. Working Women: A Data Book,* 1977.

22. It has often been speculated that Californians cope with earthquake hazards by avoidance—simply not thinking about them. Professor Ralph H. Turner, a sociologist and the director of UCLA's Institute for Social Science Research, has collected data that bear on this common belief. Here are the data collected on a number of survey questions concerned with media coverage of earthquake-related information.

Find the proportion and percentage of individuals responding in each category to each of the questions raised in the survey.

Do the responses appear to support the common view that Californians avoid thinking about earthquakes?

(*a*) Do the media provide too little, too much, or sufficient coverage about what to do if an earthquake strikes?

	Number responding
Too little	386
About right	103
Too much	8
No opinion	3

(*b*) What about the news media's coverage on preparation for an earthquake?

	Number responding
Too little	357
About right	121
Too much	14
No opinion	8

(*c*) Do the media provide sufficient information about what the government is doing to prepare for an earthquake

	Number responding
Too little	413
About right	67
Too much	10
No opinion	10

(*d*) How about the attention the media pay to nonscientific earthquake predictions?

	Number responding
Too little	126
About right	142
Too much	215
No opinion	17

23. The local chapter of the John Birch Society lost 25 members from the previous year, and membership now totals 38. What is the percentage change?

24. An interviewer completed 150 interviews this month. How many interviews must be completed next month for a 25% increase?

25. In 1983, a total of 2,123,000 persons were on active military duty compared with 1,705,000 in 1993.

Assuming these estimated numbers are exact:

(*a*) Calculate the percentage change from 1983 to 1993.

(*b*) The number of military personnel in 1993 is what percentage of the number in 1983?

26. Following is a list showing the number of births in the United States (expressed in thousands) between 1950 and 1980. Calculate the percentage of males and females for each year.

Year	Males	Females
1950	1824	1731
1955	2074	1974
1960	2180	2078
1965	1927	1833
1970	1915	1816
1975	1613	1531
1980	1853	1760

Source: U.S. Center for Health Statistics, *Vital Statistics of the United States,* annual.

27. Using the figures shown in the accompanying table, answer the following questions:
(*a*) What percentage of the students majoring in each academic area is female?
(*b*) Considering only the males, what percentages are found in each academic area?
(*c*) Considering only the females, what percentages are found in each academic area?
(*d*) What percentage of students majoring in the five areas is male? What percentage is female?

	Males	Females
Business administration	400	100
Education	50	150
Humanities	150	200
Science	250	100
Social science	200	200

28. If there were 380 homicides in the Atlanta, Georgia, Metropolitan Statistical Area (MSA) in 1994, and the MSA population totaled 3,273,558, what is the homicide rate per 100,000 persons?

29. The total number of lawyers practicing in 1980 for selected states are shown below along with the 1980 population. Calculate the population per lawyer and the rate per 1,000 persons.

State	Population in 1980	Total lawyers in 1980
Alaska	402,000	1,355
Arkansas	2,286,000	3,188
California	23,668,000	64,840
District of Columbia	638,000	25,465
Georgia	5,463,000	11,087
Illinois	11,427,000	32,421
New York	17,558,000	62,745

Source: American Bar Foundation, Chicago, IL, *The Lawyer Statistical Report: A Statistical Profile of the U.S. Legal Profession in the 1980s,* 1985.

PART II

Descriptive Statistics

CHAPTER 3

Frequency Distributions and Graphing Techniques

3.1 GROUPING OF DATA

Imagine that you conducted a survey for the State Recreation Division assessing visitor use of a state park. Your job was to distribute questionnaires to the drivers of cars entering the park during a two-week period and to collect the completed questionnaires as the cars exited the park gate. Prior to a complete analysis of the 25 questions that were included on the questionnaires, your boss wants to get a sense of the visitors' ages. Because you collected forms from over 2,000 cars, it is obvious that you cannot examine all of them in a short period of time. You conduct random sampling, which is a method of selecting samples so that each sample of a given size in a population has an equal chance of being selected, of 75 completed questionnaires.

Altogether, the questionnaires returned by the drivers of the 75 cars indicate that the cars contained a total of 110 occupants. You write down the ages of the 110 occupants with the results listed in Table 3.1.

As you glance over the data in Table 3.1, it becomes clear that your boss will not be able to make heads or tails out of them unless you organize them in some systematic fashion.

TABLE 3.1
Ages of 110 park visitors selected at random

40	8	15	29	58	42	49	24	56	5
48	35	33	52	17	35	38	41	42	47
11	22	66	40	34	65	23	49	30	34
16	57	52	53	15	25	31	45	49	51
52	74	47	39	57	48	53	36	48	40
64	13	37	44	44	33	30	26	37	53
21	25	0	60	69	40	52	40	62	44
33	47	24	19	46	52	40	33	73	47
39	27	43	21	23	26	44	39	26	35
69	38	61	37	50	12	25	43	71	42
45	43	35	63	29	65	3	50	45	53

You decide to use one of the many statistical software programs that have become user-friendly and accessible. A computer program called the Statistical Package for the Social Sciences (SPSS) has a Windows version available in undergraduate and graduate student versions for the personal computer. If you enter the ages of the 110 park visitors that are shown in Table 3.1 and request a "frequency distribution," you could print the results shown in Table 3.2. The values correspond to the ages and the frequency indicates the number of persons of a particular age. For example, there were six persons who were 40 years old. You also see that there are no persons who were age 2, 4, 6, 7, 10, and so forth. The computer only prints those values for which there are valid scores. By doing this, you have constructed an **ungrouped frequency distribution** of scores. Note that in the park visitor example the ages are widely spread out and indicate no visually clear pattern. Under these circumstances, it is customary for most researchers to *group* the scores into what are referred to as class intervals and then obtain a frequency distribution of grouped scores (see Table 3.3).

The percent column indicates the percent of the total sample that is a given age. To verify the computation of the percent associated with the infant who is less than age one, divide 1 (the number of persons who are under one as displayed under the frequency column) by 110 (the total number of persons in the sample). Thus,

TABLE 3.2
Ungrouped frequency distribution of ages of 110 park visitors

VARIABLE1 Ages of Park Visitors

Value label	Value	Frequency	Percent	Valid percent	Cumulative percentage
Zero	0.00	1	.9	.9	.9
Three	3.00	1	.9	.9	1.8
Five	5.00	1	.9	.9	2.7
Eight	8.00	1	.9	.9	3.6
Eleven	11.00	1	.9	.9	4.5
Twelve	12.00	1	.9	.9	5.5
Thirteen	13.00	1	.9	.9	6.4
Fifteen	15.00	2	1.8	1.8	8.2
Sixteen	16.00	1	.9	.9	9.1

TABLE 3.2
(concluded)

VARIABLE1 Ages of Park Visitors

Value label	Value	Frequency	Percent	Valid percent	Cumulative percentage
Seventeen	17.00	1	.9	.9	10.0
Nineteen	19.00	1	.9	.9	10.9
Twenty-one	21.00	2	1.8	1.8	12.7
Twenty-two	22.00	1	.9	.9	13.6
Twenty-three	23.00	2	1.8	1.8	15.5
Twenty-four	24.00	2	1.8	1.8	17.3
Twenty-five	25.00	3	2.7	2.7	20.0
Twenty-six	26.00	3	2.7	2.7	22.7
Twenty-seven	27.00	1	.9	.9	23.6
Twenty-nine	29.00	2	1.8	1.8	25.5
Thirty	30.00	2	1.8	1.8	27.3
Thirty-one	31.00	1	.9	.9	28.2
Thirty-three	33.00	4	3.6	3.6	31.8
Thirty-four	34.00	2	1.8	1.8	33.6
Thirty-five	35.00	4	3.6	3.6	37.3
Thirty-six	36.00	1	.9	.9	38.2
Thirty-seven	37.00	3	2.7	2.7	40.9
Thirty-eight	38.00	2	1.8	1.8	42.7
Thirty-nine	39.00	3	2.7	2.7	45.5
Forty	40.00	6	5.5	5.5	50.9
Forty-one	41.00	1	.9	.9	51.8
Forty-two	42.00	3	2.7	2.7	54.5
Forty-three	43.00	3	2.7	2.7	57.3
Forty-four	44.00	4	3.6	3.6	60.9
Forty-five	45.00	3	2.7	2.7	63.6
Forty-six	46.00	1	.9	.9	64.5
Forty-seven	47.00	4	3.6	3.6	68.2
Forty-eight	48.00	3	2.7	2.7	70.9
Forty-nine	49.00	3	2.7	2.7	73.6
Fifty	50.00	2	1.8	1.8	75.5
Fifty-one	51.00	1	.9	.9	76.4
Fifty-two	52.00	5	4.5	4.5	80.9
Fifty-three	53.00	4	3.6	3.6	84.5
Fifty-six	56.00	1	.9	.9	85.5
Fifty-seven	57.00	2	1.8	1.8	87.3
Fifty-eight	58.00	1	.9	.9	88.2
Sixty	60.00	1	.9	.9	89.1
Sixty-one	61.00	1	.9	.9	90.0
Sixty-two	62.00	1	.9	.9	90.9
Sixty-three	63.00	1	.9	.9	91.8
Sixty-four	64.00	1	.9	.9	92.7
Sixty-five	65.00	2	1.8	1.8	94.5
Sixty-six	66.00	1	.9	.9	95.5
Sixty-nine	69.00	2	1.8	1.8	97.3
Seventy-one	71.00	1	.9	.9	98.2
Seventy-three	73.00	1	.9	.9	99.1
Seventy-four	74.00	1	.9	.9	100.0
		---	-----	-----	
	Total	110	100.0	100.0	

TABLE 3.3
Grouped frequency distribution of ages based on data appearing in Table 3.2

VARIABLE1 Ages of Park Visitors

Value label	Value	Frequency	Percent	Valid percent	Cumulative percentage
0-4	1.00	2	1.8	1.8	1.8
5-9	2.00	2	1.8	1.8	3.6
10-14	3.00	3	2.7	2.7	6.4
15-19	4.00	5	4.5	4.5	10.9
20-24	5.00	7	6.4	6.4	17.3
25-29	6.00	9	8.2	8.2	25.5
30-34	7.00	9	8.2	8.2	33.6
35-39	8.00	13	11.8	11.8	45.5
40-44	9.00	17	15.5	15.5	60.9
45-49	10.00	14	12.7	12.7	73.6
50-54	11.00	12	10.9	10.9	84.5
55-59	12.00	4	3.6	3.6	88.2
60-64	13.00	5	4.5	4.5	92.7
65-69	14.00	5	4.5	4.5	97.3
70-74	15.00	3	2.7	2.7	100.0
	Total	110	100.0	100.0	

$\frac{1}{110} = 0.009$; multiplying by 100 converts the proportion 0.009 to 0.9% as shown in the percent column to the right of zero years of age. The valid percent column is identical to the percent column in Table 3.2 because there are no missing data. Had respondents refused to provide their age or had an entry been illegible, for example, a valid score would not have been available for one or more persons and the two columns would have differed. The valid percent column is based on those persons for whom complete information is available. **Cumulative percentage** is the percentage of cases or frequencies at and below a given point. The column labeled cumulative percentage displays the **cumulative percentage distribution** of cases below the upper true limit of the corresponding class interval. The value of 2.7 in the cumulative percentage column, for example, indicates that 2.7% of the cases are five years or younger. The entries in the cumulative percentage column are obtained by the simple process of successive addition of the entries in the valid percent column. The value of 2.7 in the cumulative percentage column corresponding to age five was obtained by adding $0.9 + 0.9 + 0.9 = 2.7\%$. Now examine the cumulative percent value associated with age 40 which indicates that 50.9% of the visitors were age 40 or less. Also note that the last entry in the cumulative percent column is 100.0, which indicates that all of the 110 ages have been included.

3.1.1 Grouping into Class Intervals

Grouping into class intervals involves "collapsing the scale" and assigning scores to *mutually exclusive* and *exhaustive* (see Chapter 2, Section 2.3.1) classes where the classes are defined in terms of the grouping intervals used. The reasons for grouping are (1) that it is uneconomical and unwieldy to deal with a large number of cases spread out over many scores unless computers are available, (2) some of the scores have such low frequency counts associated with them that we are not justified in maintaining these scores as separate and distinct entities, and (3) categories provide a concise and meaningful summary of the data.

On the negative side is the loss of information that inevitably results from grouping. For example, individual scores lose their identity when we group into class intervals, and some small errors in statistics based on grouped scores are unavoidable.

The question now becomes, "On what basis do we decide upon the grouping intervals we will use?" Obviously, the interval selected must not be so large that we lose the information provided by our original measurement. For example, if we were to divide the previously collected ages into just two classes, those below 36 and those 36 and above, nearly all the information about the original ages would be lost. On the other hand, the class intervals should not be so small that they defeat the purposes of grouping. In answer to our question, there is, unfortunately, no general solution that can be applied to all data. Much of the time the choice of the number of class intervals must represent a judgment based on a consideration of how the data will be utilized. Some variables such as age and educational attainment lend themselves quite well to categorization. For example, high school and college graduation provide meaningful "cutting points."

Often the desired interval size determines the number of class intervals that will be used. Let's assume we will present the data from Table 3.2 in five-year age intervals; an examination of the raw scores reveals that 15 class categories will include all of the respondents who range in age from less than 1 to 74, as shown in Table 3.3.

Once we have decided on an appropriate number of class intervals for a set of data, the procedures for assigning scores to class intervals are fairly straightforward. Although several different techniques may be used, we will use only one for the sake of consistency. The procedures are as follows:

Procedure for establishing class intervals

Step 1. Find the difference between the highest and the lowest score values contained in the original data. Add 1 to obtain the total number of scores or potential scores. In the present example, this result is $(74 - 0) + 1 = 75$.

Step 2. Divide this figure by the number of class intervals that will provide the best summary of the data to obtain the number of scores or potential scores in each class interval. In most instances, 10 to 15 intervals will be adequate. If the resulting value is not a whole number (and it usually is not), we prefer to round to the nearest odd number so that a whole number will be at the middle of the class interval. However, this practice is far from universal and you would not be wrong if you rounded to the *nearest number*. In the present example, we use 15 intervals; therefore, the number of scores for each class interval is $75 \div 15$ or 5. We designate the width of the class interval by the symbol i. In the example, $i = 5$.

Step 3. Take the lowest score in the original data (0 in the present example) as the minimum value in the lowest class interval. Add to this $i - 1$ to obtain the maximum score of the lowest class interval. Thus, the lowest class interval of the data is $0 - 4$, because $(0 + i - 1 = 0 + 5 - 1 = 4)$.

Step 4. The next higher class interval begins at the integer following the maximum score of the lower class interval. In the present example, the next integer is 5. Follow the same procedures as in step 3 to obtain the maximum score of the second class interval. Follow these procedures for each successive higher class interval until all of the scores are included in their appropriate class intervals. Every score must fall in one, and only one, interval.

Step 5. Assign each obtained score to the class interval within which it is included. The frequency that the values of the variable are grouped into class intervals is called the **grouped frequency distribution.** The grouped frequency distribution obtained by using these procedures appears in Table 3.3.

You will note in Table 3.3 that by grouping you have obtained an immediate picture of the distribution of ages of park visitors. For example, you know that the ages of visitors ranged from an infant under 1 year old to someone 74 years of age. Also, the majority of park visitors in your sample are adults, with a clustering in the age class intervals between mid-30s and mid-50s. It also is apparent that the number of scores in the extremes tends to taper off. Thus, we have achieved one of our objectives in grouping: to provide a way of presenting our data that is concise and easy to understand.

The value labels used in the grouped frequency distribution appearing in Table 3.3 were obtained using these procedures. The value column is associated with the value labels. Value 1.00 is assigned to the value label 0–4, which is equivalent to the class interval 0–4. Indeed, an examination of the cumulative percentage column shows that only 10.9% of the 110 visitors sampled were less than age 20. If the survey had been conducted when school was in session, this might account for the few children and adolescents that are included in the sample. Both the Frequency and Percent columns indicate that the 40–44 class interval included the largest number and percentage of visitors.

Psychologists, educators, and other behavioral scientists typically use cumulative frequency and cumulative percentage tables in which the class intervals are presented from high to low. Sociologists and other social scientists normally present class intervals from low to high as shown in Table 3.3. Both approaches are equally valid.

If we chose to use 10 categories, we would divide 75 (see step 1) by 10 and find the width of i to be 7.5. Rounding to the nearest odd number (step 2) would give us an i equal to 7. To obtain the maximum score of the lowest class interval (step 3), we would add $(0 + i - 1 = 0 + 7 - 1 = 6)$. Step 4 would lead us to establish the following intervals:

0–6	42–48
7–13	49–55
14–20	56–62
21–27	63–69
28–34	70–76
35–41	

Note that rounding to the nearest odd number in step 2 resulted in 11 rather than 10 categories.

One word of caution: Most scores with which the social scientist deals are expressed as whole numbers rather than as decimals. This is why our examples involve whole numbers. However, scores are occasionally expressed in decimal form. The simplest procedure is to treat the scores as if the decimals did not exist; in other words, treat each score as a whole number. The decimals can then be reinserted at the final step. If in the preceding example the highest score had been 7.4 and the lowest 0.0, the calculations would have been exactly the same. At the last step, however, the highest interval would have been changed to 7.0 and 7.4 and the lowest to 0.0 and 0.4, with corresponding changes in between. The width of the class interval would have been 0.5.

3.1.2 The True Limits of a Class Interval

In our prior discussion of the true limits or real limits of a number (Section 2.4.1), we pointed out that the true value of a number is equal to its apparent value plus or minus one-half of the unit of measurement. The unit of measurement in Table 3.3 is 1; therefore, we will add and subtract $\frac{1}{2} = 0.5$ from the lower and upper real limit of each category. Thus, although we write the limits of the highest class interval as 70 to 74, the true limits of the interval are 69.5 ($70 - 0.5$) to 74.5 ($74 + 0.5$); that is, the lower real limit of 70 and the upper real limit of 74, respectively. Later, when calculating certain statistics for grouped data, we will make use of the *true limits* of the class interval.

3.2 GRAPHING TECHNIQUES

We have just examined some of the procedures involved in making sense out of a mass of unorganized data. As we pointed out, your work is usually just beginning when you have constructed frequency distributions of data. Commonly, the next step is to present the data in pictorial form so that the reader may easily determine the essential features of a frequency distribution and compare one with another if desired. Such pictures, called graphs, should not be thought of as substitutes for statistical treatment of data, but as *visual aids* for thinking about and discussing statistical problems.

3.3 MISUSE OF GRAPHING TECHNIQUES

As you may be aware, graphs that present data incorrectly can mislead the reader. For example, in Figure 3.1 the vertical (**ordinate,** or ***Y*-axis**) and horizontal (**abscissa,** or ***X*-axis**) have been lengthened to produce two distinctly different impressions.

It will be noted that Part A of Figure 3.1 tends to exaggerate the difference in frequency counts among the three classes, whereas Part B of Figure 3.1 tends to minimize these differences. The problem involves selection or scale units to represent

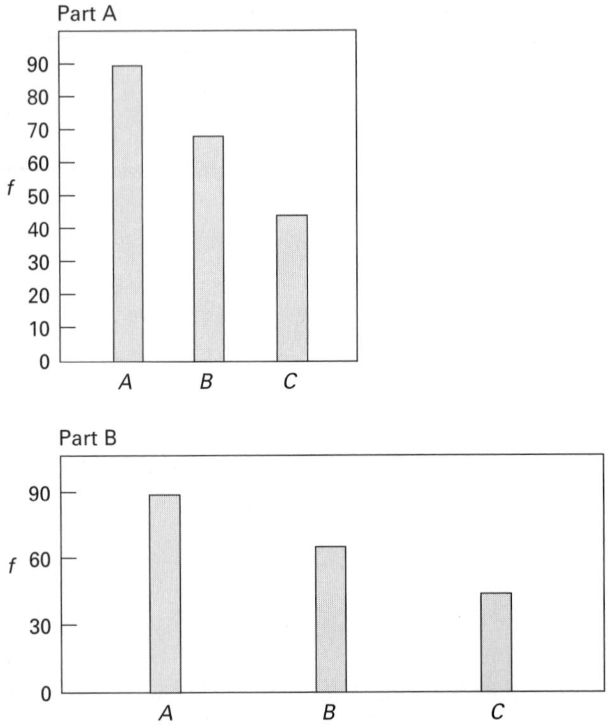

FIGURE 3.1
Bar graphs representing the same data but producing different impressions by varying the relative lengths of the Y-axis and the X-axis

the horizontal (X) and vertical (Y) axes. Clearly, the choice of these units is arbitrary, and the decision to make the Y-axis twice the length of the X-axis is just as correct as the opposite representation. It is clear that to avoid problems we need to present the data in a straightforward manner.

3.4 NOMINALLY SCALED VARIABLES

The **bar graph,** illustrated in Figure 3.2, is a device used to represent data that are either nominally or ordinally scaled. A vertical bar is drawn for each category, in which the *height* of the bar represents the number of members of that class. If we arbitrarily set the width of each bar at one unit, the *area* of each bar may be used to represent the frequency for that category. Thus, the total area of all of the bars is equal to N or 100%.

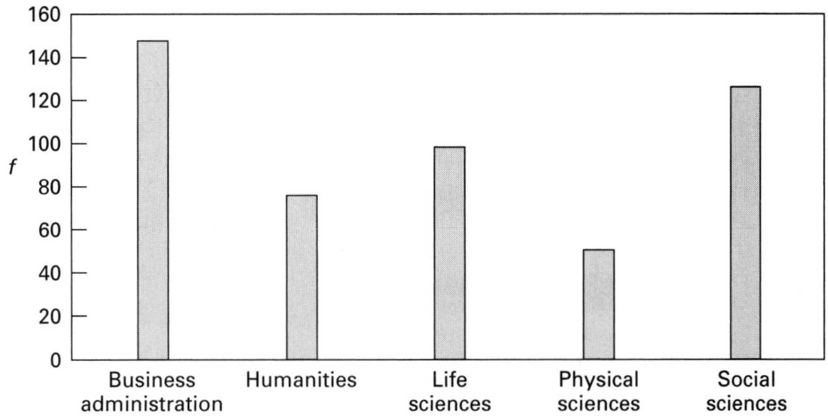

FIGURE 3.2
Vertical bar graph showing number of students enrolled in introductory sociology courses who are majoring in the various academic fields (hypothetical data)

Figure 3.3 shows a horizontal bar graph which contrasts women's share of employment in nontraditional and traditional occupations for 1972 and 1990. Bar graphs are sometimes drawn horizontally where the number of categories is large and the list may occupy a full page in length. Nevertheless, the vertical bar graph (see Figure 3.2) is more often used—and more easily understood at sight—because of its adaptability to a histogram or a frequency curve (see Figures 3.5 and 3.7).

In preparing frequency distributions of nominally scaled variables, you must keep two things in mind:

1. No order is assumed to underlie nominally scaled variables. Thus, the various categories can be represented along the horizontal axis (X-axis) in any order you choose. We prefer to arrange the categories alphabetically to eliminate any possibility of personal factors entering into the decision.

2. The bars should be separated rather than contiguous, so that any implication of continuity among the categories is avoided.

3.5 ORDINALLY SCALED VARIABLES

You will recall that the scale values of ordinal scales carry the implication of an ordering that is expressible in terms of the algebra of inequalities (i.e., greater than, less than). In terms of our preceding discussion, ordinally scaled variables should be treated in the same way as nominally scaled variables, except that the categories should be placed in their naturally occurring order along the horizontal (X) axis. Figure 3.4 illustrates the use of the bar graph with an ordinally scaled variable.

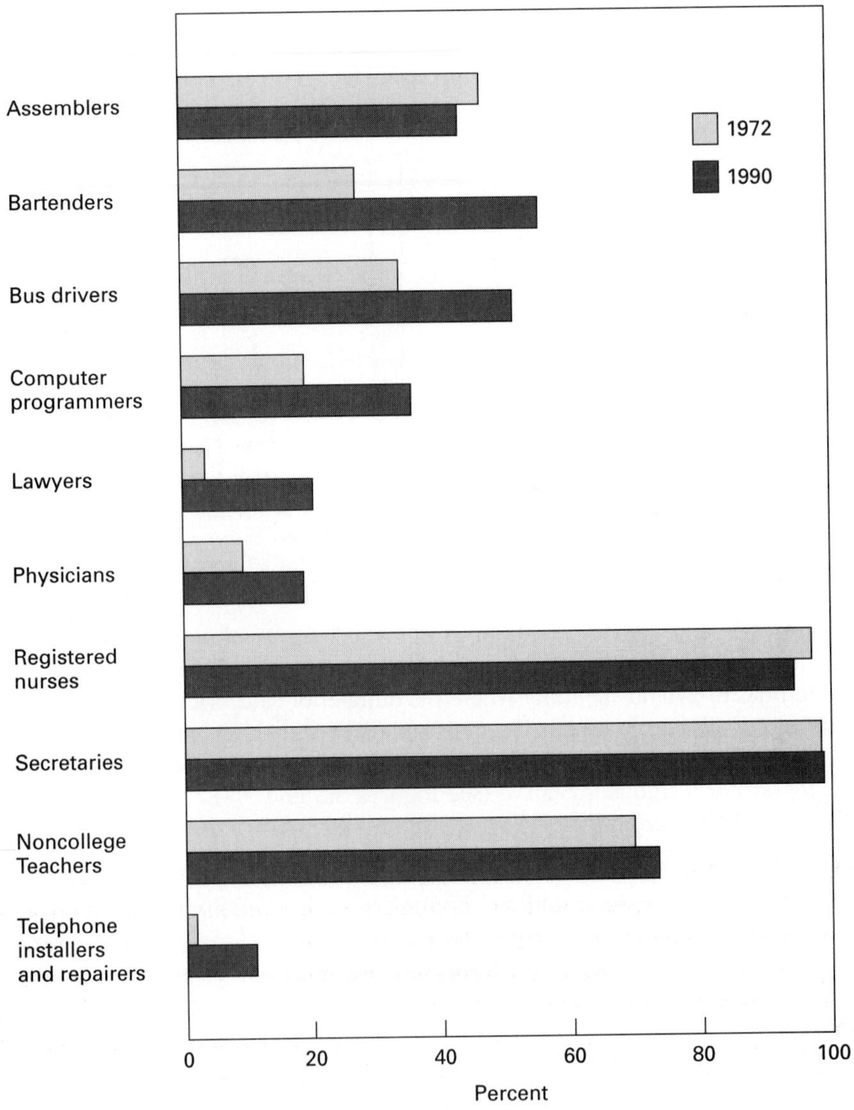

FIGURE 3.3
Women as a proportion of total employed persons in selected occupations, 1972 and 1990, annual averages
Source: Working Women: A Chartbook, U.S. Department of Labor, Bulletin 2385, Aug. 1991.

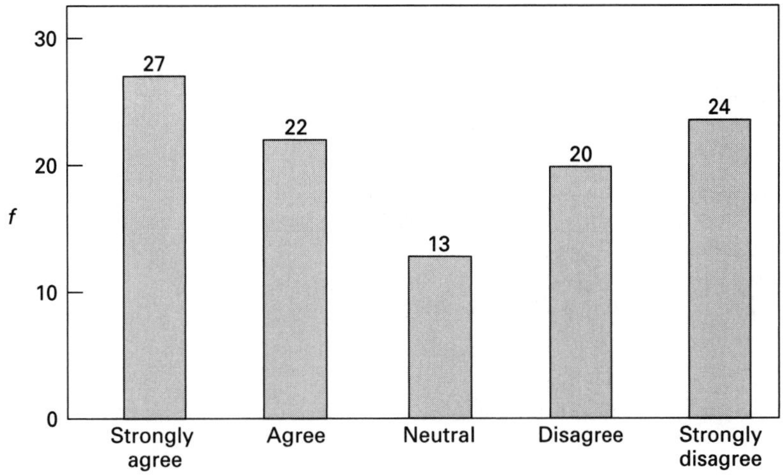

FIGURE 3.4
Bar graph showing distribution of 106 physicians' responses to the question, "Should venereal disease treatment be made available to minors without the knowledge of their parents?" (hypothetical data)

3.6 INTERVAL- AND RATIO-SCALED VARIABLES

3.6.1 Histogram

As discussed earlier, interval- and ratio-scaled variables differ from ordinally scaled variables in one important way; that is, equal differences in scale values are equal. This means that we permit the vertical bars to touch one another in graphic representations of interval- and ratio-scaled frequency distributions. Such a graph is referred to as a **histogram,** and it replaces the bar graph used with nominal and ordinal variables. Figure 3.5 illustrates the use of the histogram with a ratio-scaled variable.

We noted in Section 3.4 that frequency may be represented by either the area of a bar or its height. However, there are many graphic applications in which the height of the bar, or the ordinate, may give misleading information concerning frequency. Consider Figure 3.6, which shows the data grouped into *unequal* class intervals and the resulting histogram. The widths of the bars in Figure 3.6 have been drawn proportional to the size of the class intervals, and the heights of the bars indicate the relative frequency within each age category. Thus, the 30- to 34-year-old category is represented by a bar $2\frac{1}{2}$ times wider than the 14- to 15-year-old category. In this instance, the area under each bar does not reflect the frequency of cases, and confusion is sure to result. In general, it is advisable to construct histograms using equal intervals whenever you are dealing with variables in which an underlying continuity may be assumed.

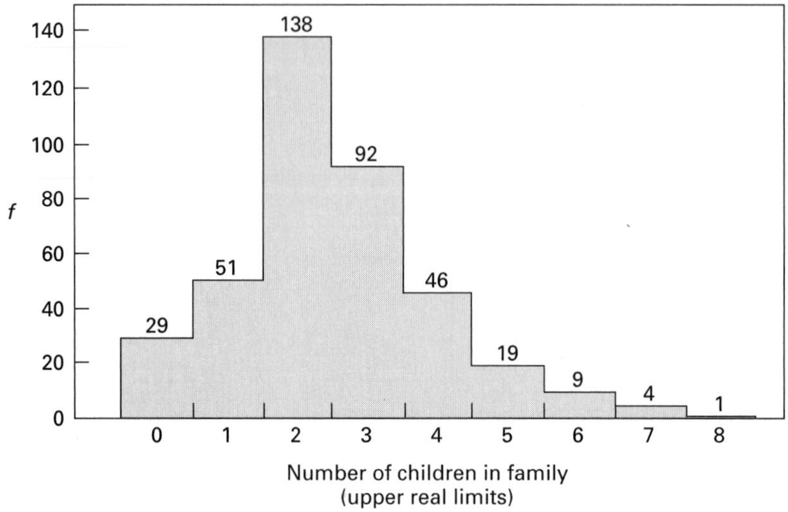

FIGURE 3.5
Frequency distribution of the number of children per family among 389 families surveyed in a small suburban community (hypothetical data)

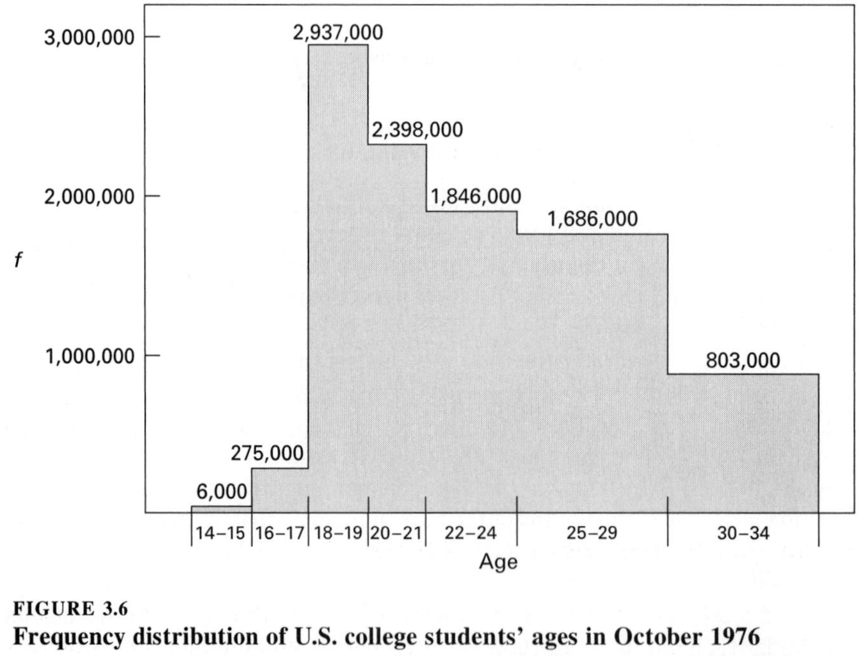

FIGURE 3.6
Frequency distribution of U.S. college students' ages in October 1976
Source: Digest of Educational Statistics, National Center for Education Statistics, 1977–1978, p. 92.

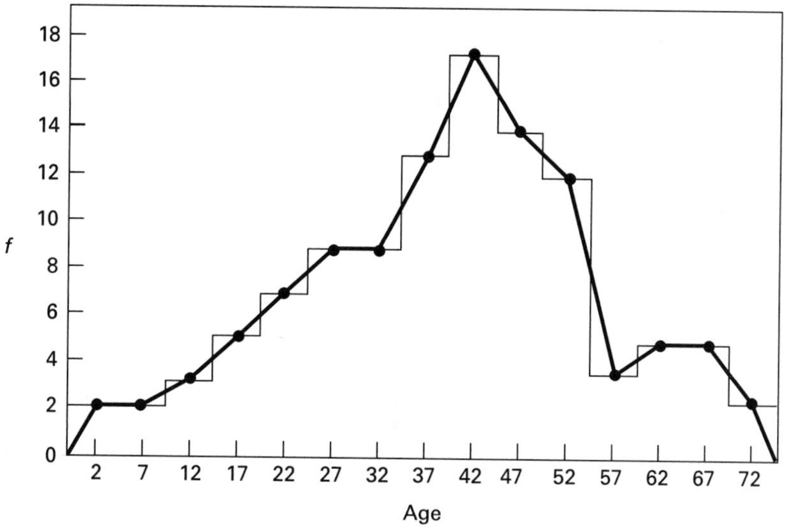

FIGURE 3.7
Frequency curve (frequency polygon) and histogram based on the grouped frequency distribution appearing in Table 3.3
Note: The values on the horizontal axis represent the midpoints of the class intervals in Table 3.3.

3.6.2 Frequency Curve (Frequency Polygon)

We can readily convert the histogram into another commonly used form of graphic representation, the **frequency curve,** or **frequency polygon,** by joining the midpoints of the bars with straight lines. However, it is not necessary to construct a histogram prior to the construction of a frequency curve. All you need to do is place a dot where the tops of the bars would have been, and join these dots. Some people prefer to use the histogram only for discrete distributions and the frequency curve for distributions in which the underlying continuity is explicit or may be assumed. Figure 3.7 shows a frequency curve superimposed on a histogram that is based on the grouped frequency distribution appearing in Table 3.3. In practice, we prefer to use the histogram for discrete distributions and the frequency curve for distributions in which the underlying continuity is explicit or may be assumed. The heights of the bars are determined by the frequencies in Table 3.3.

3.6.3 Cumulative Frequency Curve (Ogive)

In Section 3.1, we demonstrated the procedures for constructing cumulative percentage distributions. The corresponding graphic representations are the **cumulative frequency curve,** or **ogive,** and the cumulative percentage curve. These are both combined in Figure 3.8, with the left-hand *Y*-axis showing the **cumulative frequency,** or the number of cases (frequencies) at or below a given point, and the right-hand *Y*-axis showing cumulative percentages.

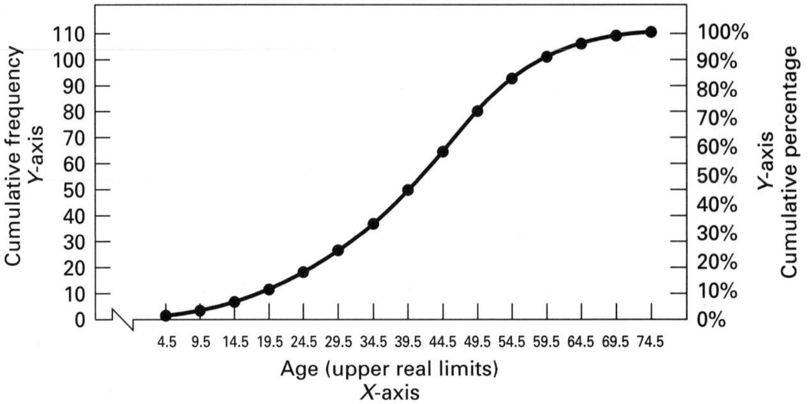

FIGURE 3.8
Cumulative frequency and cumulative percentage curve based on cumulative frequency and cumulative percentage distributions appearing in Table 3.4

There are two important points to remember: (1) the cumulative frequencies are plotted against the *upper true limit* of each interval and (2) the maximum value on the *Y*-axis in the cumulative frequency curve is *N*, and in the cumulative percentage curve it is 100%.

3.7 FORMS OF FREQUENCY CURVES

Frequency curves may take on an unlimited number of different shapes. However, many of the statistical procedures discussed in the text assume a particular form of distribution: namely, the bell-shaped **normal curve.**

In Figure 3.9 several forms of bell-shaped distributions are shown. Curve (a), which is characterized by a piling up of scores in the center of the distribution, is referred to as a **leptokurtic distribution.** Curve (c), in which the opposite condition prevails, is referred to as a **platykurtic distribution.** And finally, curve (b) takes on the form of a bell-shaped normal curve and is referred to as a **mesokurtic distribution.** Note that the height of frequency curves reflects the frequency at that point.

The normal curve is referred to as a symmetrical distribution because the two sides will coincide when it is folded in half.* Not all symmetrical curves are bell shaped, however. Three different nonnormal symmetrical curves are shown in Figure 3.10.

Certain distributions have been given names, for example, that in Figure 3.10(a) is called a *rectangular* distribution and that in Figure 3.10(b) a U-distribution. The

*A theoretical bell-shaped curve called a standard normal distribution will be discussed in Chapter 7.

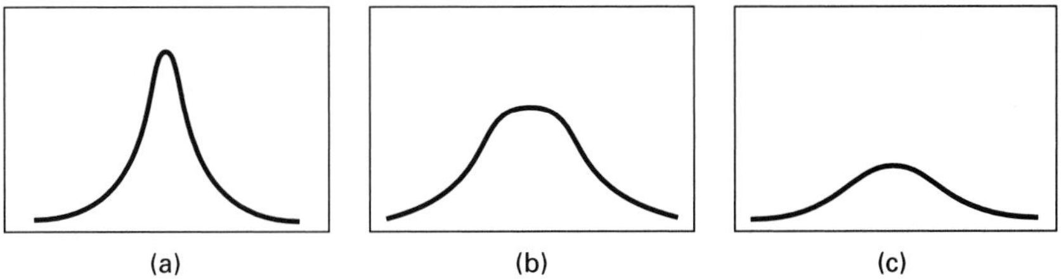

FIGURE 3.9
Three forms of bell-shaped distributions: (a) leptokurtic, (b) mesokurtic, and (c) platykurtic

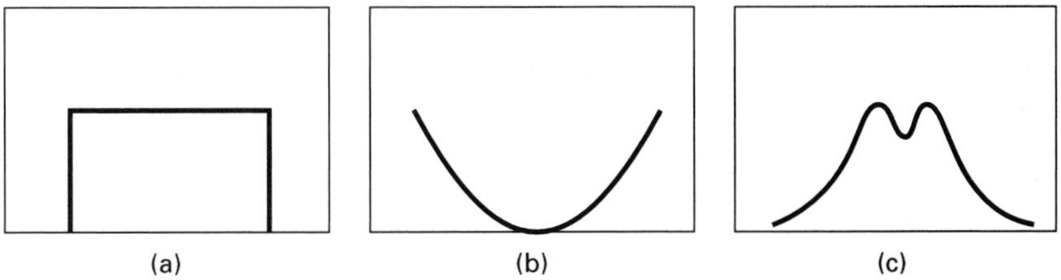

FIGURE 3.10
Three nonnormal symmetrical frequency curves: (a) rectangular, (b) U-distribution, and (c) bimodal distribution

distribution appearing in Figure 3.10(c) is found when a variable has a high concentration of frequencies around two separate values or if the frequency distributions of two different populations are represented in a single graph. This is sometimes called a bimodal distribution. For example, a frequency distribution of average adult male and female earnings might yield a curve similar to Figure 3.10(c) because the average annual income of males is considerably higher than that of females. Hence, the two peaks would reflect the income differential between males and females.

A distribution that is not symmetrical and "tails" off at one end is called **a skewed distribution.** A **positively skewed distribution,** or one that is skewed to the right, has relatively fewer frequencies at the high end of the horizontal axis. On the other hand, a **negatively skewed distribution,** or one that is skewed to the left, has relatively fewer frequencies at the low end of the horizontal axis. Figure 3.11(a) is positively skewed, and Figure 3.11(b) is negatively skewed.

It is not always possible to determine by inspection whether a distribution is skewed. Consider the frequency curve and histogram we plotted in Figure 3.7 for the sample of park visitors. Would you say that the curve is skewed to the left or right? In this instance, it is rather difficult to be certain. There is a precise mathematical method for determining both direction and magnitude of skew, but a detailed discussion of this topic is beyond the scope of this book.

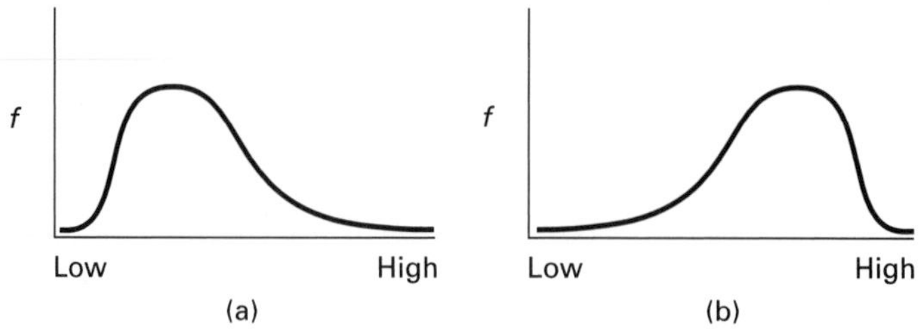

FIGURE 3.11
Illustrations of skewed frequency curves (scores increase from left to right)

3.8 OTHER GRAPHIC REPRESENTATIONS

Throughout this chapter, we have been discussing graphic representations of frequency distributions. However, other types of data are frequently collected by social scientists. We will briefly discuss a few graphic representations of such data. A frequently used graphic representation is the *pictograph,* which presents statistical data in pictorial shapes. Figure 3.12 depicts the declining numbers of elevator operators needed in the United States. The projection was that only 25,000 persons would be employed as elevator operators in 1985 because of the increased number of automatic elevators and a decline in the manual models.

The *pie chart* (see Figure 3.13) involved dividing the "pie" or circle into its component parts to represent the distribution of a nominal level variable. A protractor

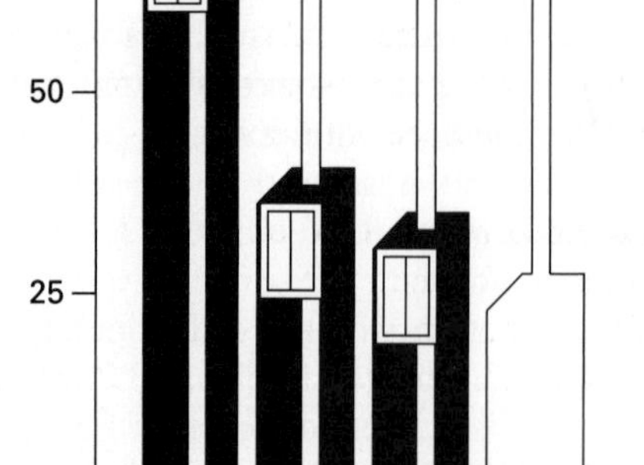

FIGURE 3.12
Pictograph of number of elevator operators, actual and projected for given years

Sources: 1960–1970 Decennial Census, Bureau of the Census; 1970–1985, Bureau of Labor Statistics. Data for 1970 and 1985 are unpublished; data for 1975 are in *Employment and Earnings,* Jan. 1976, p. 11, as cited in *Bureau of Labor Statistics Bulletin,* 1979.

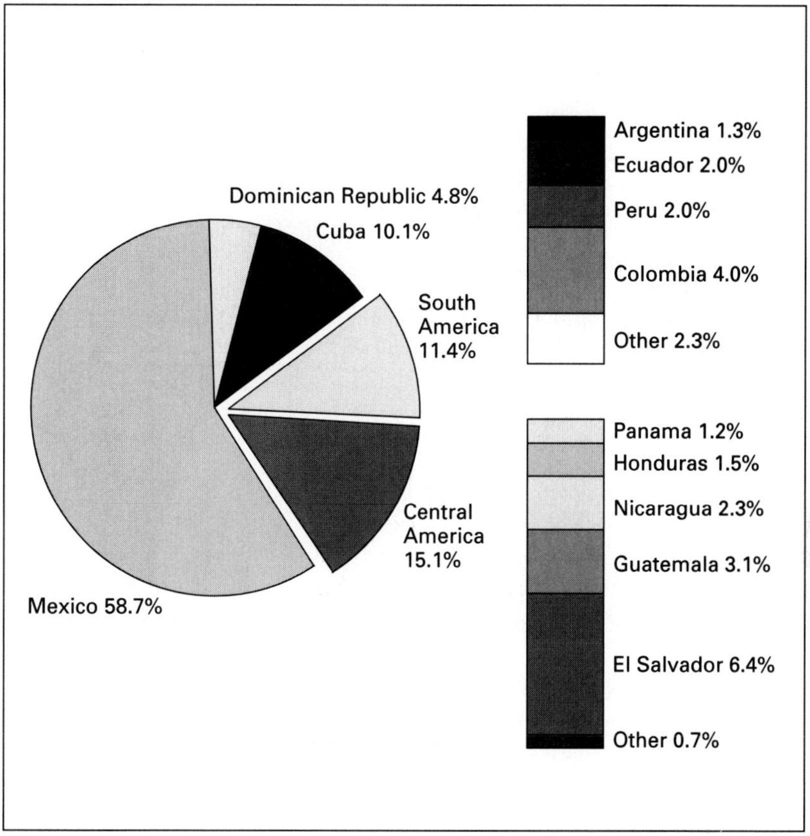

FIGURE 3.13

Pie chart of foreign-born persons in the United States from Spanish-speaking Latin America, 1990 (percent distribution)

Source: U.S. Bureau of the Census, Current Population Reports, Series P-23, no. 183, *Hispanic Americans Today,* Washington, D.C.: U.S. Government Printing Office, 1993.

is used to divide the 360 degrees in a circle into percentages to reflect the actual distribution of the variable. For example, we see in Figure 3.13 that about 58.7% of all foreign-born, Spanish-speaking persons from Latin America came from Mexico. The corresponding segment of the pie must be 211.3 degrees ($360 \times 0.587 = 211.3$).

Finally, an example of a *trend chart* is provided by the U.S. population projections in Figure 3.14. The four series have been determined by altering the three components of population change: births, deaths, and net immigration. Series II, II-X, and III are considered the most realistic projections, with Series I assuming an extremely high birthrate in the future.

Statistics in Action 3.1 provides an overview of frequency distributions, proportion, rates, and graphic representations.

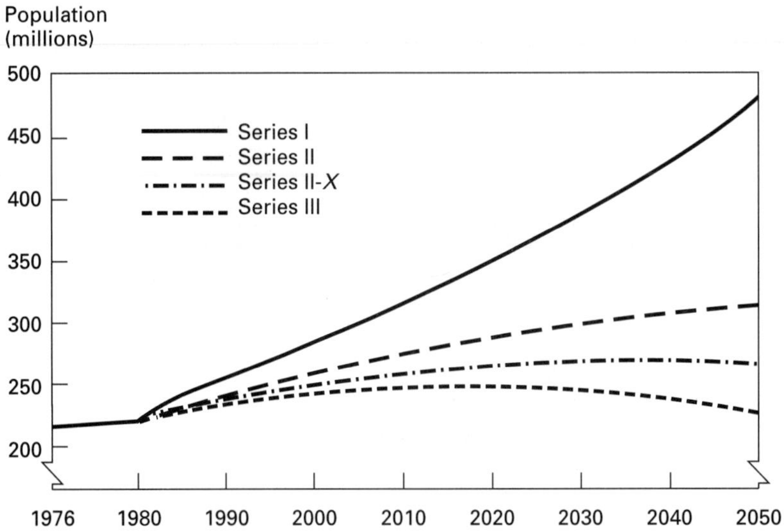

FIGURE 3.14

Trend chart of U.S. population—projections to 2050

Source: U.S. Bureau of the Census, Current Population Reports, Series P-25.

STATISTICS IN ACTION 3.1
Prison Crowding: Calculating Proportions and Rates

Overcrowding of prisons is at the core of one of the great social, political, and financial controversies of the 1990s. Should society mete out harsher mandatory sentences to criminal offenders, particularly those pushing drugs, and make plea bargaining and parole more difficult to negotiate? If this tack is taken, more prisons will have to be built, at great cost to society. If the cost of building and maintaining prisons is unacceptably high, prison overcrowding may increase to the breaking point. As an alternative to increased rates of incarceration, should society's emphasis be on social and rehabilitation services in which such programs as work furloughs and halfway houses are encouraged? Informed answers to these questions should depend, at least in part, on the results of coherent research.

One avenue of exploration has focused on the mortality rates of prisoners in various age groups. Table 3.4 shows two frequency distributions, grouped by age, of white and African-American male prison inmates. Also shown are the approximate number of deaths due to illness in each age group for both white and African-American inmates.

By dividing the estimated number of inmates within each age group by its column total, we obtain the proportion within each class. However, death rates per age groups are obtained by dividing the number of deaths within each age group by the number of inmates within that group. For example, for the death rate of whites in age group 15–24, you obtain $12/49{,}312 = 0.00024$. Because the rates of mortality statistics are typically low, they are often expressed in terms of deaths per thousand or deaths per hundred thousand. To express these proportions as rates of death per thousand, multiply the proportion of deaths in each age group by 1,000; for rates of death per hundred thousand, multiply each proportion by 100,000. Thus, for whites in age group 15–24, the deaths per $100{,}000 = 0.00024 \times 100{,}000 = 24$ (rounded). Table 3.5 shows the proportion of inmates within each age group, by race, and the rates of death per hundred thousand, also by race.

TABLE 3.4

Estimated numbers of white and African-American prison inmates in various age groupings and number of deaths due to illness within each racial grouping and age group

Age	Estimated number of white inmates	Number of deaths due to illness	Estimated number of African-American inmates	Number of deaths due to illness
15–24	49,312	12	46,375	18
25–34	77,669	38	80,686	106
35–44	37,326	56	30,540	126
45–54	12,065	62	6,032	71
55–64	4,147	65	2,639	68
65–74	1,131	42	754	34
Totals	181,650	275	167,026	423

Source: Based on R. B. Ruback and C. A. Innes, "The Relevance and Irrelevance of Psychological Research: The Example of Prison Crowding," *American Psychologist* 43, no. 9 (1988), pp. 683–702.

TABLE 3.5

Estimated proportions of white and African-American prison inmates in various age classes and mortality rates (deaths per 100,000) due to illness within each racial grouping and age class

Age	Proportion of white inmates	Rates of death per 100,000 due to illness	Proportion of African-American inmates	Rates of death per 100,000 due to illness
15–24	0.2715	24	0.2777	39
25–34	0.4276	49	0.4831	131
35–44	0.2055	150	0.1828	413
45–54	0.0664	514	0.0361	1177
55–64	0.0228	1567	0.0158	2577
65–74	0.0062	3714	0.0045	4509

Source: Based on R. B. Ruback and C. A. Innes, "The Relevance and Irrelevance of Psychological Research: The Example of Prison Crowding," *American Psychologist* 43, no. 9 (1988), pp. 683–702.

The relative frequency distributions of proportions of whites and African Americans in each age class are shown in Figure 3.15. It is clear that the greatest proportions of white and African-American inmates are 25 to 34 years old, and that the graphs are similar for whites and African Americans.

As would be expected, the death rates due to illness increased with increasing age among both whites and African Americans (see Figure 3.16). However, it is apparent that the rates of death per 100,000 are higher among African Americans in all age classes. Findings of this sort beg for follow-up studies to account for the differential death rates.

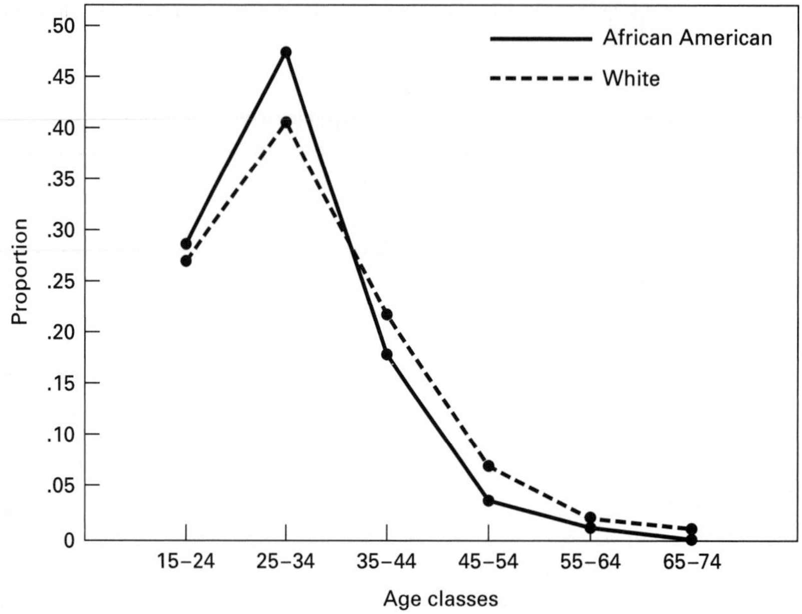

FIGURE 3.15
Relative frequency curve of white and African-American male prison inmates within different age classes

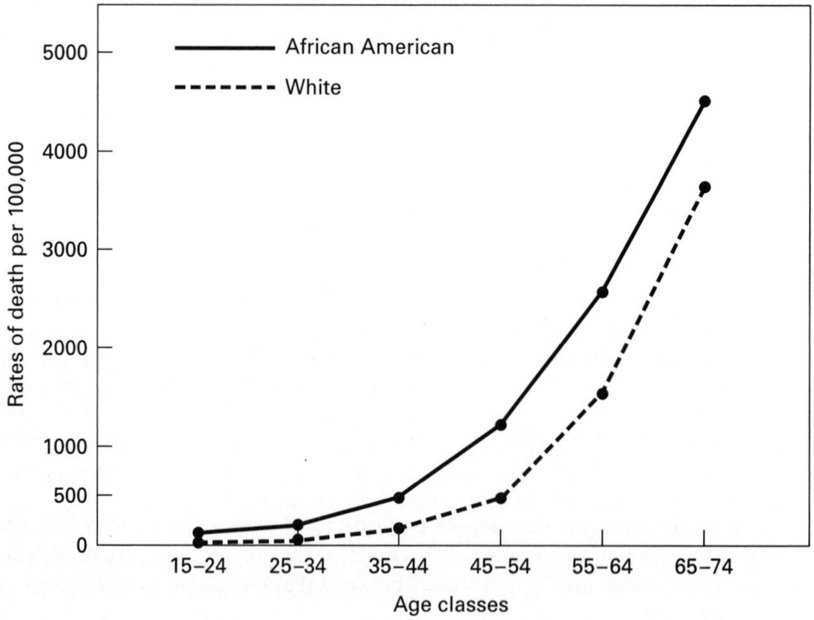

FIGURE 3.16
Rates of death from illness per 100,000 prison inmates for white and African-American male prisoners in various age classes

SUMMARY

This chapter was concerned with the techniques used in making sense out of a mass of data. We demonstrated the construction of frequency distributions of scores and presented various graphing techniques. When the scores are widely spread out, many have a frequency of zero. It is customary to group scores into class intervals. The resulting distribution is referred to as a grouped frequency distribution.

The basis for arriving at a decision concerning which grouping units to use and which procedures to follow to construct a grouped frequency distribution were discussed and demonstrated. We saw that the true limits of a class interval are obtained in the same way as the true limits of a score. The procedures for converting a frequency distribution into a cumulative frequency distribution, a cumulative proportion distribution, and a cumulative percentage distribution were demonstrated.

We also reviewed the various graphing techniques used in the social sciences. The basic purpose of graphic representation is to provide visual aids for considering and discussing statistical problems. The primary objective is to present data in a clear, unambiguous fashion so that the reader may determine at a glance the relationships that we want to portray.

We discussed devices that might mislead the unsophisticated reader. The use of the bar graph with nominally and ordinally scaled variables, and the use of the histogram and the frequency curve with continuous and discontinuous ratio- or interval-scaled variables were covered. Various forms of normally distributed data, nonbell-shaped symmetrical distributions, and asymmetrical or skewed distributions were presented. Finally, we discussed and demonstrated several graphic representations of data, other than frequency distributions, commonly used in the social sciences.

TERMS TO REMEMBER

abscissa (*X*-axis) Horizontal axis of a graph.

bar graph A form of graph that uses bars to indicate the frequency of occurrence of observations within each nominal or ordinal category.

cumulative frequency The number of cases (frequencies) at and below a given point.

cumulative frequency curve A curve that shows the number of cases below the upper true limit of an interval.

cumulative percentage The percentage of cases or (frequencies) at and below a given point.

cumulative percentage distribution A distribution that shows the cumulative percentage below the upper true limit of the corresponding class interval.

frequency curve (frequency polygon) A form of graph, representing a frequency distribution, in which a continuous line is used to indicate the frequency of the corresponding scores.

grouped frequency distribution A frequency distribution in which the values of the variable have been grouped into class intervals.

histogram A form of bar graph used with an interval- or ratio-scaled frequency distribution.

leptokurtic distribution A bell-shaped distribution characterized by a piling up of scores in the center of the distribution.

mesokurtic distribution Bell-shaped distribution; "ideal" form of normal curve.

negatively skewed distribution A distribution that has relatively fewer frequencies at the low end of the horizontal axis.
normal curve A frequency curve with a characteristic bell-shaped form.
ogive See *cumulative frequency curve.*
ordinate (*Y*-axis) The vertical axis of a graph.
platykurtic distribution A frequency distribution characterized by a flattening in the central position.
positively skewed distribution A distribution that has relatively fewer frequencies at the high end of the horizontal axis.
skewed distribution A distribution that departs from symmetry and tails off at one end.
ungrouped frequency distribution An ungrouped frequency distribution shows the number of times each score occurs when the values of a variable are arranged in order according to their magnitudes.

EXERCISES

1. Give the true limits, the width of interval, and the midpoints for each of the following class intervals:
(*a*) 8–12 (*b*) 6–7 (*c*) 0–2
(*d*) 5–14 (*e*) (−8)–(−2) (*f*) 2.5–3.5
(*g*) 1.50–1.75 (*h*) (−3)–(+3)

2. For each of the following sets of measurements, state (assume number of intervals = 15):
(*a*) The best width of class interval (*i*).
(*b*) The apparent limits of the lowest interval.
(*c*) The true limits of that interval.
(*d*) The midpoint of that interval.
(*i*) 0 to 106 (*iv*) −30 to +30
(*ii*) 29 to 41 (*v*) 0.30 to 0.47
(*iii*) 18 to 48 (*vi*) 0.206 to 0.293

3. Given the following list of scores in a statistics examination, use $i = 5$ for the class intervals and:
(*a*) Set up a frequency distribution.
(*b*) List the true limits and midpoint of each interval.
(*c*) Prepare a cumulative frequency distribution.
(*d*) Prepare a cumulative percentage distribution.

Scores on a statistics examination

63	88	79	92	86	87	83	78	40	67
68	76	46	81	92	77	84	76	70	66
77	75	98	81	82	81	87	78	70	60
94	79	52	82	77	81	77	70	74	61

4. Using the data in exercise 3, set up frequency distributions with the following, and discuss the advantages and the disadvantages of employing these widths.
(*a*) $i = 1$ (ungrouped frequency distribution)
(*b*) $i = 3$
(*c*) $i = 10$
(*d*) $i = 20$

5. The caseloads for social workers vary greatly. The accompanying table lists the number of clients to whom 40 social workers have been assigned (assume $i = 5$):
(*a*) Construct a grouped frequency distribution.
(*b*) List the true limits of each interval.
(*c*) Describe the distribution in words.

68	57	68	79	92	86	87	83	78	67
84	92	63	46	81	92	77	84	86	52
51	46	77	98	81	82	81	87	42	85
90	37	94	52	82	77	81	77	94	49

6. Several entries in a frequency distribution of children's ages are 1 to 5, 6 to 10, 11 to 15.
(*a*) What is the width of the interval?
(*b*) What are the lower and upper true limits of each of these three intervals?
(*c*) What are the midpoints of each interval?

7. Discuss the value of constructing a grouped frequency distribution from a set of ungrouped scores. Can you think of a situation when you would not want to group a set of data? Why?

8. Construct a grouped frequency distribution, using 5 to 9 as the lowest class interval, for the following scores on a job satisfaction scale. List the width and true limits of the highest class interval. If high scores indicate high satisfaction and it is possible to score as low as 0 or as high as 75, how would you characterize this distribution of scores?

67	63	64	57	56	55	53	53	54	54
45	45	46	47	37	23	34	44	27	44
45	34	34	15	23	43	16	44	36	36
35	37	24	24	14	43	37	27	36	26
25	36	26	5	44	13	33	33	17	33

9. Do exercise 8 again, using 3 to 7 as the lowest class interval. Compare the resulting frequency distribution with those of exercises 8, 10, and 11.

10. Repeat exercise 8, using 0 to 9 as the lowest class. Compare the results with those of exercises 8, 9, and 11.

11. Repeat exercise 8, using 4 to 5 as the lowest class. Compare the results with those of exercises 8, 9, and 10.

12. Give an example of a variable that would have a distribution that would be characterized as:
(*a*) Normal (*b*) Negatively skewed (*c*) Positively skewed

13. Given the following frequency distribution of the number of previous arrests for 50 inmates at a state prison (a) draw a histogram, (b) a frequency curve, and (c) a cumulative frequency curve. (Hint: you must first determine the cum *f* and cum % for the class intervals.)

Class interval	*f*	Class interval	*f*
0–2	0	15–17	3
3–5	17	18–20	1
6–8	15	21–23	1
9–11	8	24–26	0
12–14	4	27–29	1

14. Given the accompanying table, draw three histograms and compare the results for the three columns of data. Which columns do you believe most accurately portray the real picture?

Estimated number of illegitimate live births and illegitimacy rates and ratios: Selected years, 1940–1990

Year	Number	Rate per 1,000 unmarried women aged 14 to 44 years	Ratio per 1,000 total live births
1990	1,165,000	43.8	280.2
1980	665,700	29.4	184.3
1970	398,700	26.4	106.9
1960	224,300	21.6	52.7
1950	141,600	14.1	39.8
1940	89,500	7.1	37.9

Source: U.S. National Center for Health Statistics, *Vital Statistics of the United States,* annual.

15. Describe the types of distributions you would expect if you were to graph each of the following:
(*a*) Annual incomes of U.S. families.
(*b*) The heights of adult U.S. males.
(*c*) The heights of adult U.S. females.
(*d*) The heights of U.S. males and females combined in one graph.

16. Construct a bar graph to present the data in the accompanying table. (*Hint:* Consider superimposing the African-American population figures on the total figures.) Also, construct a trend chart that summarizes the relationship between the African-American and total population since 1790.

Total resident population in the United States for selected years, 1790–1990

	Millions of persons	
Year	**Total**	**African American**
1790	3.9	0.8
1860	31.4	4.4
1870	39.8	5.4

(concluded)

	Millions of persons	
Year	**Total**	**African American**
1890	62.9	7.5
1900	76.2	8.8
1910	92.2	9.8
1920	106.0	10.5
1930	123.2	11.9
1940	132.2	12.9
1950	151.3	15.0
1960	179.3	18.9
1970	203.2	22.6
1980	226.5	26.7
1990	249.4	30.6

Source: Bureau of the Census, Current Population Reports, Series P-23, no. 80, *The Social and Economic Status of the African-American Population in the United States: An Historical View, 1790–1978.*

17. Within recent years, a disabling type of physical disorder has surfaced that appears to be work-related—that is, related to the physical activities required by the hands and arms in performing a particular job. Referred to as repetitive strain disorder (RSI), it is placing the worker's compensation system in Australia in jeopardy because of the large number of employees in computer keyboard types of jobs that are afflicted. The following table shows the number of operators and number of cases reported in 14 occupational categories in Western Australia.

Cases of RSI reported among government employees through January 1985

Employment category	Number of operators	Reported cases
Secretary stenographers	397	70
Typists	1163	137
Clerk typists	838	60
Word processing operators	340	99
Data processing operators	379	84
Telephonists	172	6
Accounting machinists	72	7
Computer programmers	749	9
Clerks	1190	40
Clerical assistants	193	9
Telex operators	49	0
Journalists	12	0
Hansard/court reporters	32	7
Other keyboard operators	938	32

Source: Cited in S. Kiesler and T. Finholt, "The Mystery of RSI," *American Psychologist* 43, no. 12 (1988), pp. 1004–15.

Prepare a bar graph of the percentage of reported cases of RSI in the 14 employment categories. Because of the large number of categories, it is recommended that a *horizontal* graph be constructed.

18. Using the following data, construct a pie chart for 1984 and 1992. Contrast the differences in words.

Attendance figures for selected spectator sports, 1984 and 1992

	Attendance (in thousands)	
Sports	**1984**	**1992**
Major league baseball	45,262	70,257
Professional basketball	11,110	19,120
Professional football	14,053	14,774
Horse racing	74,076	49,275
Greyhound racing	22,076	28,003

Source: U.S. Department of Commerce, *Social Indicators*, 1985, 1993.

19. Construct a trend chart for the number of work stoppages and for the number of workers involved, 1950–1990. What trends are apparent to you?

Year	**Number of work stoppages**	**Workers involved (000s)**
1950	424	1,698
1955	363	2,055
1960	222	896
1965	268	999
1970	381	2,468
1975	235	965
1980	187	795
1985	54	324
1990	44	185

Source: U.S. Bureau of Labor Statistics, *Current Wage Developments*, monthly.

20. Using the following data, construct two pie charts to show the age composition of the U.S. Senate and House of Representatives in 1995.

	Age in years				
U.S. Congress	**Under 40**	**40–49**	**50–59**	**60–69**	**70 and over**
Senate	1	14	41	27	17
House of Representatives	53	155	135	79	13

Source: Congressional Directory, biennial.

21. The table below shows the estimated numbers of white and African-American prison inmates who died in prison as a result of suicide and homicide.

(*a*) Find the proportion of deaths in each age class due to suicide among white and African-American prisoners.

(*b*) Find the proportion of deaths in each age class due to homicide among white and African-American prisoners.

(*c*) Prepare a graph of the proportion of deaths due to suicide and homicide for each class of white and of African-American prisoners.

Age	Number of white suicides	Number of white homicides	Number of African-American suicides	Number of African-American homicides
15–24	10	6	5	33
25–34	20	13	16	100
35–44	9	5	5	20
45–54	3	1	1	4
55–64	1	0	0	1
65–74	1	0	0	0
Totals	44	25	27	158

Source: R. B. Ruback, and C. A. Innes, "The Relevance and Irrelevance of Psychological Research: The Example of Prison Crowding," *American Psychologist* 43, no. 9 (1988), pp. 683–702.

CHAPTER 4

Percentiles

4.1 INTRODUCTION

A declining birthrate and an increasing life span have resulted in major changes in the age composition of the U.S. population during the past century. Suppose someone told you that in 1994 approximately 32.0 million people in the United States were 65 years of age or older. What would be your reaction? Would you decide that the elderly are not nearly so numerous as you thought? Or that the United States is fast becoming a nation of elderly? You should conclude that you do not have enough information to offer a knowledgeable comment.

It should be clear that by itself a figure such as 32.0 million is not really meaningful. It takes on much more meaning when it can be compared to the total U.S. population of 259.6 million people and to the population of other age categories. If you were told that about 88% of the U.S. population was 65 or less years old, you would have a frame of reference for interpreting the information. You would know the **percentile rank** of the 65-year-old persons. The percentile rank of a score, then, represents the percent of cases in a distribution that had scores (in this case, ages) at or *lower* (younger) *than the one cited*. Thus, to say that an age of 65 has a percentile rank of 88 indicates that 88% of the population is 65 or less.

Consider one more example before we continue. Suppose you took the Advanced Graduate Record Examination in Political Science and received a score of 540. By itself, the score would not mean much, but assume that a score of 540 put you at the 79th percentile. Now you know that 79% of the persons who took the examination on the same day received an equal or lower score than you and 21% received a higher score. Knowing the percentile rank of a score allows you to compare it with other scores.

4.2
CUMULATIVE PERCENTILES AND PERCENTILE RANK

4.2.1 Obtaining the Percentile Rank of Scores from a Cumulative Percentage Graph

In Chapter 3, we learned how to construct cumulative frequency and cumulative percentage distributions. If we were to graph a cumulative percentage distribution, we could read the percentile ranks directly from the graph. Note that the reverse is also true; that is, given a percentile rank, we could read the corresponding scores. Figure 4.1 displays a graphic form of the cumulative percentage distribution presented in Table 4.1. Box 4.1 provides an additional example of a cumulative percentage graph.

To illustrate, imagine that we wanted to determine the percentile rank of people 60 years old. We locate 60 along the horizontal axis and construct a perpendicular at that point so that it intercepts the curve. From that point on the curve, we read directly across on the scale to the left and see that the percentile rank is approximately 85. On the other hand, if we wanted to know the score at a given **percentile,** we could reverse the procedure. For example, what is the score at the 75th percentile? We locate the 75th percentile on the vertical axis and read directly to the right until we meet the curve; at this point we construct a line perpendicular to the horizontal axis and read the value on the scale of scores. In the present example, it can be seen that the age at the 75th percentile is approximately 49.

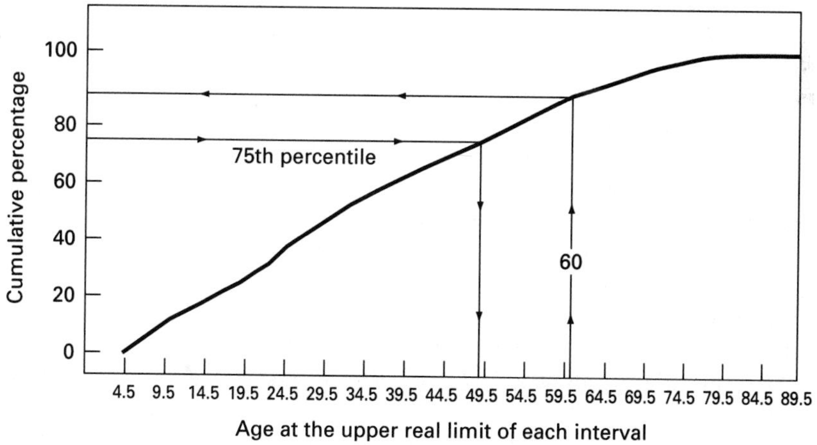

FIGURE 4.1
Graphic representation of a cumulative percentage distribution (age composition of the U.S. population in 1994, excluding persons over age 90)
Note: The cumulative percentage corresponding to a given score is the same as the percentile rank of that score.
Source: U.S. Bureau of the Census.

BOX 4.1

THE STRESS OF THE BEGINNING

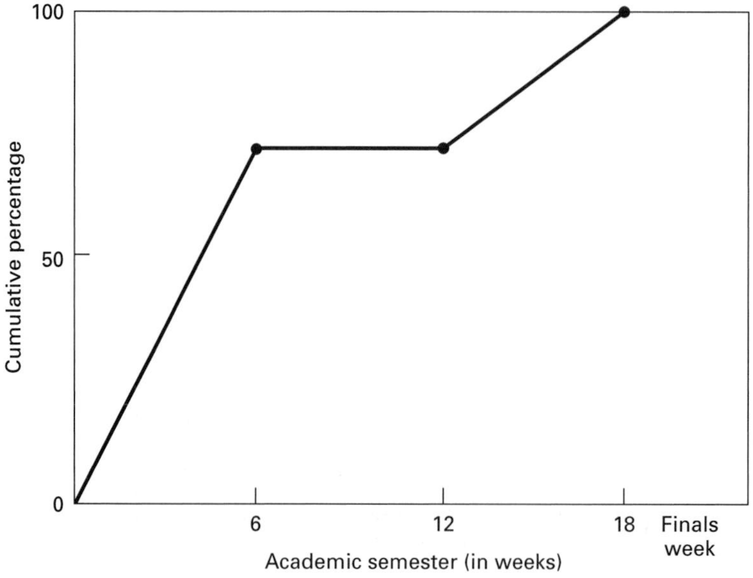

It has frequently been maintained that suicides among college students result from the stresses of final examinations. A long-term study at the University of California, Berkeley, investigated various factors related to student suicides. The figure above shows that the percentage of suicides was greatest in the opening weeks of the semester, leveled off at mid-semester, and showed a moderate increase during the last third of the semester. Thus, contrary to popular opinion, the period of greatest danger appears to be the beginning rather than the end of the semester.

Source: R. H. Seiden, "Campus Tragedy: A Story of Student Suicide," *Journal of Abnormal Psychology* 71 (1966), pp. 389–99.

4.2.2 Obtaining the Percentile Rank of Scores Directly

We are often called upon to determine the percentile rank of scores without the assistance of a cumulative percentage curve, or with greater precision than is possible with a graphical representation.

Using the grouped frequency distribution found in Table 4.1, let's determine directly the percentile rank of an age of 60, which we previously approximated by the use of the cumulative percentage curve. The first thing we should note is that an age of 60 falls within the interval 60 to 64. The total cumulative frequency *below* that

TABLE 4.1
Grouped frequency distribution and cumulative frequency distribution of the age composition of the United States, 1994

Age interval	Population (in millions)	Percent of population	Cumulative f (in millions)	Cumulative percent
0–4	19.7	7.6%	19.7	7.6%
5–9	18.9	7.3	38.6	14.9
10–14	18.8	7.2	57.4	22.1
15–19	17.6	6.8	75.0	28.9
20–24	18.3	7.0	93.3	35.9
25–29	19.2	7.4	112.5	43.3
30–34	22.2	8.6	134.7	51.9
35–39	22.0	8.5	156.7	60.4
40–44	20.0	7.7	176.7	68.1
45–49	16.7	6.4	193.4	74.5
50–54	13.2	5.1	206.6	79.6
55–59	10.9	4.2	217.5	83.8
60–64	10.1	3.9	227.6	87.7
65–69	10.0	3.9	237.6	91.6
70–74	8.7	3.3	246.3	94.9
75–79	6.6	2.5	252.9	97.4
80–84	4.4	1.7	257.3	99.1
85–89	2.3	0.9	259.6	100.0

Note: Excludes the 1,247,000 persons over 90 years of age because the over-90 age categories reported by the U.S. Bureau of the Census are not comparable with those in the table.

interval is 217.5 million. Since a percentile rank of a score is defined symbolically as:

$$\text{percentile rank} = \frac{\text{cum}f}{N} \times 100 \tag{4.1}$$

it is necessary to find the precise cumulative frequency corresponding to an age of 60. It is clear from Table 4.1 that the cumulative frequency corresponding to an age of 60 lies somewhere between 217.5 million and 227.6 million, the cumulative frequencies at both extremes of the interval. We must now establish the exact cumulative frequency of an age of 60 within the interval 60 to 64. In doing this, we are actually trying to determine the proportion of distance that we must move into the interval in order to find the number of cases included up to an age of 60.

An age of 60 is 0.5 years above the lower true limit of the interval (i.e., $60 - 59.5 = 0.5$). Since there are five ages within the interval (60, 61, 62, 63, and 64), 60 years of age is 0.5/5 of the distance through the interval. We now make a very important simplifying assumption that in reality is not exactly true: *the cases or frequencies within a particular interval are evenly distributed throughout that interval.* Since there are 10.1 million cases within the interval 60–64, we may now calculate that an age of 60 is $(0.5/5) \times 10.1$, or the 1.01-millionth case within the interval. In other words, the frequency 1.01 million corresponds to 60 years of age. We already know from Table 4.1 that in 1994, 217.5 million persons were younger than 60 years of age or will be less than the lower true limit of the interval 60 to 64. Adding the two together $(217.5 + 1.01)$, we find that an age of 60 has a cumulative frequency of 218.51 million. Substituting 218.51 into equation (4.1), we obtain:

$$\text{percentile rank of 60 years of age} = \frac{218.51}{259.6} \times 100 = 84.17$$

You will note that our answer agrees very closely with the approximation obtained by the use of the graphical representation of a cumulative percentage distribution (see Figure 4.1).

Equation (4.2) presents a generalized equation for calculating the percentile rank of a given score.

$$\text{percentile rank} = \frac{\text{cum } f_{ll} + \left(\dfrac{X - X_{ll}}{i}\right)(f_i)}{N} \times 100 \qquad (4.2)$$

where cum f_{ll} = cumulative frequency at the lower true limit of the interval containing X
X = given score
X_{ll} = score at lower true limit of interval containing X
i = width of interval
f_i = number of cases within the interval containing X

Let's calculate the percentile rank of 60 years of age using equation (4.2),

where cum $f_{ll} = 217.5$
$X = 60$
$X_{ll} = 59.5$
$i = 5$
$f_i = 10.1$
$N = 259.6$

Now the percentile rank can be calculated in the following manner:

$$\text{percentile rank} = \frac{217.5 + \left(\dfrac{60 - 59.5}{5}\right)(10.1)}{259.6} \times 100$$

$$= \frac{217.5 + 0.1(10.1)}{259.6} \times 100$$

$$= \frac{218.51}{259.6} \times 100$$

$$= 84.17$$

4.2.3 Finding the Score Corresponding to a Given Percentile Rank

What if you want to know the age above and below the 50 percentile in 1994?

To obtain the answer, we must work in the reverse direction, from the cumulative frequency scale to the scale of ages. We first must determine the cumulative frequency corresponding to the 50th percentile (which we will later refer to as the median of a distribution). Once we know the cumulative frequency, we will locate the interval that contains the cumulative frequency and then establish the age in question. Here is how we calculate the answer. It follows algebraically from equation (4.1) that :

$$\text{cum} f = \frac{\text{percentile rank}}{100} \times N \tag{4.3}$$

Since we are interested in an age at the 50th percentile and N is 259.6 million, the cumulative frequency of a score at the 50th percentile is:

$$\text{cum} f = \frac{50 \times 259.6}{100} = 129.8 \text{ million}$$

Referring to Table 4.1, we see that the frequency 129.8 million is in the 30–34 age interval which has true limits of 29.5 to 34.5. It is 17.3 million frequencies into the interval since the cum f at the lower true limit of the interval is 112.5 million, which is 17.3 million less than 129.8. There are 22.2 million persons in the age interval 30–34. Thus, the frequency 129.8 million is 17.3/22.2 of the way through an interval with a lower true limit of 29.5 and an upper true limit of 34.5. In other words, it is 17.3/22.2 of the way through the five ages in the interval. Expressed in age units $(17.3/22.2) \times 5$ or $0.779 \times 5 = 3.9$. By adding 3.9 to 29.5, we obtain the age at the 50th percentile, which is 33.4.

For students desiring a generalized method for determining scores (ages) corresponding to a given percentile, equation (4.4) should be helpful:

$$\text{Score at a given percentile} = X_{ll} + \frac{i(\text{cum} f - \text{cum} f_{ll})}{f_i} \tag{4.4}$$

where X_{ll} = score at lower true limit of the interval containing cum f
i = width of the interval
cum f = cumulative frequency of the score
cum f_{ll} = cumulative frequency at the lower true limit of the interval containing cum f
f_i = number of cases within the interval containing cum f

To illustrate the use of the equation, consider an example with which we are already familiar. What age is at the 84.17th percentile? First, by using equation (4.3), we obtain:

$$\text{cum} f = \frac{84.17 \times 259.6}{100} = 218.5 \text{ million}$$

If you refer to Table 4.1, you will see that our calculated cum f of 218.5 million is reasonable, given the 84.17th percentile. Try to get in the habit of ensuring that your answers are correct.

The age at the lower true limit of the interval containing the frequency 218.5 million is 59.5; i is 5; cum f to the lower true limit of the interval is 217.5; and the number of cases within the interval is 10.1 million. Substituting these values into equation (4.4), we obtain:

$$\text{age at 84.17th percentile} = 59.5 + \frac{5(218.5 - 217.5)}{10.1}$$

$$= 59.5 + 0.5 = 60 \text{ years of age}$$

Note that this is the age from which we previously obtained the percentile rank 84.17 and that this equation illustrates a good procedure for checking the accuracy of your calculations. In other words, whenever you find the percentile rank of a score (e.g., age), you may take that answer and determine the score corresponding to that percentile value. You should obtain the original score. Similarly, whenever you obtain a score corresponding to a given percentile rank, you may take that answer and determine the percentile rank of that score. You should always come back to the original percentile rank. Failure to do so indicates that you have made an error. Statistics in Action 4.1 provides a further illustration of calculating percentile rank.

STATISTICS IN ACTION 4.1
Male Prisoners: Calculating Percentile Rank

In Statistics in Action 3.1, we looked at data concerning the numbers of African-American and white male prison inmates and the causes of death during incarceration. Table 4.2 shows the combined African American and white frequency and cumulative-frequency distributions for the numbers of prisoners in six age classes.

Suppose that we want to know the age at and below which 60% of all prisoners fall. This age would correspond to the 60th percentile. Here are the steps in finding the age corresponding to a given percentile rank (the 60th percentile):

1. Sum the f column to obtain N. $N = 347{,}976$.
2. Cumulate frequencies by successive addition of frequencies from the lowest to the highest class. The last cumulative frequency *must* equal N.

TABLE 4.2
Estimated combined numbers of white and African-American male prison inmates in various age groupings

Class (age)	Estimated number of inmates (f)	Cum f
15–24	95,687	95,687
25–34	158,355	254,042
35–44	67,866	321,908
45–54	18,097	340,005
55–64	6,786	346,791
65–74	1,185	347,976
N	347,976	

Source: Based on R. B. Ruback and C. A. Jones, "The Relevance and Irrelevance of Psychological Research: The Example of Prison Crowding," *American Psychologist*, 43, no. 9 (1988), pp. 683–702.

3. Multiply the percentile rank in which we are interested (60) by N and divide by 100. Thus:

$$\frac{60 \times 347{,}976}{100} = 208{,}785.6$$

4. Find the age interval containing the 208,785.6th cumulative frequency. This is the class interval of 25 to 34 with the true limits of 24.5 to 34.5.
5. Subtract from the value obtained in step 3 the cumulative frequency at the upper true limit of the adjacent lower class; that is:
   208,785.6 − 95,687 = 113,098.6.
6. Divide the value found in step 5 by the frequency within the class (158,355) and multiply by the width of the class ($i = 10$). Thus, the number of years within the class corresponding to the 60th percentile is $(113{,}098.6/158{,}355) \times 10 = 7.14$.
7. Add the value found in step 6 to the score (age) at the lower true limit of the class containing the 208,785.6th cumulative frequency. Thus, 24.5 + 7.14 = 31.64. We may conclude that 60% of all male prisoners were 31.64 years of age or less.

Now, if we were to find the percentile rank of age 31.64, we should obtain our original percentile rank of 60. The following are the steps in obtaining the percentile rank of a score:

1. Sum the f column to obtain N. $N = 347{,}976$.
2. Cumulate frequencies by successive addition of frequencies from the lowest to the highest class. The last cumulative frequency *must* equal N.
3. Identify the class containing the score (age): 31.64.
4. Subtract the age at the lower true limit of that class from 31.64:
   31.64 − 24.5 = 7.14.
5. Note the frequency within the class: 158,355.
6. Divide the value found in step 4 by the width of the class and multiply by the frequency noted in step 5. Thus, $(7.14/10) \times 158{,}355 = 113{,}065.5$.* This value represents the frequency within the class 24.5 to 34.5 corresponding to an age of 31.64.
7. Note the cumulative frequency appearing in the adjacent lower class: cum $f = 95{,}687$.
8. Add the value found in step 6 to the value found in step 7. Thus, 113,075.5 + 95,687 = 208,762.5.
9. Divide the value found in step 8 by N and multiply by 100. Thus, $(208{,}762.5/347{,}976) \times 100 = 60$.

4.3 PERCENTILE RANK AND REFERENCE GROUP

Just as a score is meaningless in the abstract, so is a percentile rank. A percentile rank must always be expressed in relation to some reference group. Thus, if a friend claims that he obtained a percentile rank of 93 in a test of mathematical aptitude, you might not be terribly impressed if the reference group were made up of individuals who completed only the eighth grade. On the other hand, if the reference group consisted of individuals holding doctorate degrees in mathematics, your reaction would unquestionably be different.

---

* The slight discrepancy from step 5 in the previous illustration is due to rounding error.

Separate norms are frequently published for many standardized tests. Table 4.3 shows the raw score equivalents for selected percentile points on several advanced tests of the Graduate Record Examination. Note that a person scoring 500 would obtain a percentile rank of 73 on the Advanced Test in Sociology, but only have a percentile rank of 46 on the Advanced Test in History.

4.4 CENTILES, DECILES, AND QUARTILES

Occasionally you will encounter the terms centile, decile, and quartile. All refer to a specific division of the scale of percentile ranks. A scale of percentile ranks is comprised of 100 units. A **centile** is equivalent to a percentile and is a percentage rank that divides a distribution into 100 equal parts. The 13th centile is specified as C_{13} and is equivalent to the 13th percentile. A **decile** is a percentage rank that divides a distribution into 10 equal parts. The 9th decile (specified as D_9) is equivalent to the 90th centile (percentile). The 1st decile is the 10th centile, and so on. You should convince yourself that there are 9 deciles in any scale of percentile ranks. Why not 10?

A **quartile** is a percentile rank that divides a distribution into four equal parts. There are three quartiles in any scale of percentile ranks and they include the 1st quartile (Q_1), which is equivalent to the 25th centile, and 2nd quartile (Q_2), which is equivalent to the 50th centile or 5th decile, and the 3rd quartile (Q_3), which is equivalent to the 75th centile. Figure 4.2 shows the relationship among centiles, deciles, and quartiles.

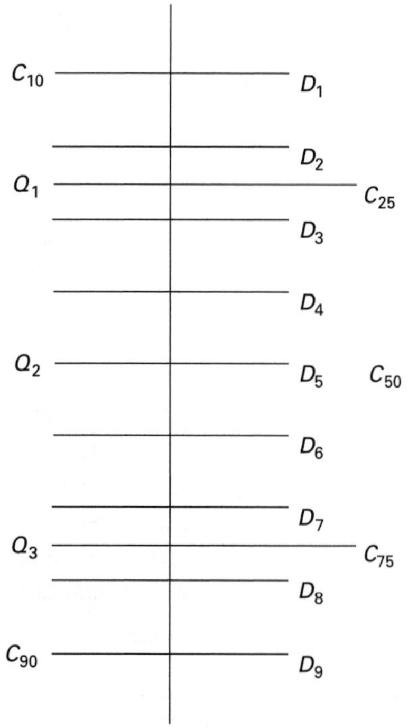

FIGURE 4.2
Comparison of centiles, deciles and quartiles

TABLE 4.3

Selected Graduate Record Examination Advanced Test Scores: percentile ranks used on score reports (percent of examinees scoring lower than selected scaled scores)

Scaled score	Edu-cation	French	History	Political science	Psychology	Sociology	Scaled score
800							800
780							780
760					99		760
740					99		740
720		99	99		97	99	720
700		99	99		95	99	700
680		96	98		92	99	680
660	99	94	96	99	88	98	660
640	98	90	94	98	83	96	640
620	96	86	90	97	77	95	620
600	93	82	86	94	71	92	600
580	90	76	80	90	63	89	580
560	85	69	73	85	56	87	560
540	79	61	65	79	48	83	540
520	73	52	55	72	40	78	520
500	65	44	46	64	33	73	500
480	57	35	35	56	26	66	480
460	49	27	26	46	20	60	460
440	40	20	17	38	15	53	440
420	32	14	11	30	11	46	420
400	25	9	6	23	7	38	400
380	18	6	2	17	5	30	380
360	13	3	1	12	3	24	360
340	9	2		8	2	18	340
320	6	1		5	1	14	320
300	4			3		9	300
280	2			1		6	280
260	1					3	260
240						1	240
Number of examinees	14,238	1,567	7,131	6,415	43,939	4,152	Number of examinees
Percent women*	72	74	34	31	64	50	Percent women
Percent men*	28	26	66	68	36	50	Percent men
Mean	458	512	509	462	539	434	Mean
Standard deviation	90	88	77	85	96	106	Standard deviation

* In some cases, percent women plus percent men is less than 100 percent because some examinees do not indicate their gender.

Source: Copyright by the Educational Testing Service, Princeton, N.J. Reproduced by permission. All rights reserved.

SUMMARY

In this chapter, we saw that a score by itself is meaningless unless it is compared to a standard base or scale. Scores are often converted into units of the percentile rank scale to provide a readily understandable basis for their interpretation and comparison.

We saw that percentile ranks of scores and scores corresponding to a given percentile may be approximated from a cumulative percentage graph. Direct computational methods were demonstrated to permit a more precise location of the percentile rank of a score and the score corresponding to a given percentile. A percentile rank was shown to be meaningless in the abstract. It must always be expressed in relation to some reference group. A distribution can be divided into centiles, deciles, and quartiles.

TERMS TO REMEMBER

centile A percentage rank that divides a distribution in 100 equal parts. Same as a percentile.
decile A percentage rank that divides a distribution into 10 equal parts.
percentile rank A number that represents the percentage of cases in a distribution that had scores at or lower than the one cited.
percentiles Numbers that divide a distribution into 100 equal parts. Same as a centile.
quartile A percentage rank that divides a distribution into 4 equal parts.

EXERCISES

1. Describe a percentile rank in your own words.

2. Estimate the percentile rank of the following ages, using Figure 4.1.
(*a*) 1 (*b*) 12 (*c*) 34

3. Calculate the percentile rank of the ages in exercise 2, using Table 4.1.

4. Estimate the ages corresponding to the following percentiles, using Figure 4.1.
(*a*) 25 (*b*) 50

5. Calculate the ages corresponding to the percentiles in exercise 4, using Table 4.1.

6. Your parents tell you that they have read in the newspaper that overall the public high school students in your county are at the 42nd percentile in a standard reading test. How might you clearly explain the meaning of the test results to them?

7. Refer to exercise 13 in Chapter 3.

(*a*) What is the percentile rank of an inmate who has been arrested six times?

(*b*) How many times would an inmate have to have been arrested to be in the 1st quartile? The 3rd quartile? The 2nd quartile?

8. The following questions are based on Table 4.2.

(*a*) John H. proudly proclaims that he obtained a "higher" percentile ranking than his friend Howard. Investigation reveals that John's score on the test was actually lower. Was John H. lying, or is some other explanation possible?

(*b*) Jean obtained a percentile rank of 56 on the political science test. What was her score? What score would she have had to obtain to achieve the same percentile rank on the psychology test?

(*c*) The Department of Sociology at Anomie University uses the Advanced Graduate Record Examination in Sociology as an element of the admissions procedure. No applicant obtaining a percentile rank below 73 is admitted regardless of other qualifications. Thus, the 73rd percentile might be called a cutoff point. What score constitutes the cutoff point for this distribution?

(*d*) The Department of Political Science uses the 72nd percentile as a cutoff point. Lee obtained a raw score of 500. What are his chances of being admitted?

9. A researcher administered a religious knowledge test to 36 persons whose scores are presented here.

(*a*) Which specific scores would be above the 3rd quartile?

(*b*) What score is at the 50th percentile?

(*c*) The 50th centile?

(*d*) The 9th decile?

Use $i = 3$ and assume that the lowest class interval is 0–2.

9	6	8	10
2	2	5	0
7	1	4	2
5	8	0	1
6	7	10	1
2	4	9	7
3	3	9	6
4	6	4	4
0	2	1	4

10. You are interested in comparing the scores of 25 students on a statistics test. Assigning one person to each letter, you record the following scores:

A. 55	F. 40	K. 50	P. 40	U. 40
B. 50	G. 60	L. 45	Q. 35	V. 30
C. 35	H. 45	M. 25	R. 25	W. 45
D. 45	I. 50	N. 35	S. 20	X. 35
E. 40	J. 30	O. 55	T. 30	Y. 40

Calculate the percentile rank for each person, employing $i = 5$ and assuming that the lowest class is 20 to 24.

11. In addition, you wish to study the number of statistical problems the students solve per day. You find the following number of problems completed per day for the same 25 students (the students are designated by the same letters as in exercise 10):

A. 45	F. 30	K. 40	P. 30	U. 30
B. 40	G. 50	L. 35	Q. 25	V. 20
C. 25	H. 35	M. 15	R. 15	W. 35
D. 35	I. 40	N. 25	S. 10	X. 25
E. 30	J. 20	O. 45	T. 20	Y. 30

Calculate the percentile rank for each person and compare it to the ranks in exercise 10. Employ $i = 5$ and a lowest class of 10 to 14.

12. Given the frequency distribution you constructed for the social worker's case load in exercise 5, Chapter 3, how many clients would a caseworker need to be placed in the: (*a*) 1st quartile? (*b*) 3rd quartile?

13. Using the accompanying table, calculate the percentile rank for the following size families: (*a*) 3 (*b*) 5 (*c*) 7

How does this table violate the standard procedure outlined in Chapter 3 for constructing frequency distributions?

Size of U.S. families of Spanish origin in 1977

Size	Number (000s)
2	662
3	636
4	625
5	408
6	218
7 or more persons	216

Source: U.S. Bureau of the Census, Current Population Reports, Series P-20, no. 339, *Persons of Spanish Origin in the United States,* March 1978 (Washington, D.C.: U.S. Government Printing Office, 1979).

14. Given exercise 13, what size family lies at the 5th decile? The 2nd quartile? The 3rd quartile?

15. Imagine that you have a population consisting of seven scores: 0, 1, 2, 3, 4, 5 and 6. You write each of these numbers on a paper tab and place them in a hat. Then you draw a number, record it, place it back in the hat, and draw a second number. You add the second number to the first to obtain a sum. You continue to draw pairs of scores and to obtain their sums until you have obtained all possible combinations of these seven scores, taken two at a time.

The following table shows all possible results from drawing samples of $N = 2$ from this population of seven scores. The values within each cell show the sum of the two scores.

		First draw						
		0	1	2	3	4	5	6
Second draw	0	0 + 0 = 0	1 + 0 = 1	2 + 0 = 2	3 + 0 = 3	4 + 0 = 4	5 + 0 = 5	6 + 0 = 6
	1	0 + 1 = 1	1 + 1 = 2	2 + 1 = 3	3 + 1 = 4	4 + 1 = 5	5 + 1 = 6	6 + 1 = 7
	2	0 + 2 = 2	1 + 2 = 3	2 + 2 = 4	3 + 2 = 5	4 + 2 = 6	5 + 2 = 7	6 + 2 = 8
	3	0 + 3 = 3	1 + 3 = 4	2 + 3 = 5	3 + 3 = 6	4 + 3 = 7	5 + 3 = 8	6 + 3 = 9
	4	0 + 4 = 4	1 + 4 = 5	2 + 4 = 6	3 + 4 = 7	4 + 4 = 8	5 + 4 = 9	6 + 4 = 10
	5	0 + 5 = 5	1 + 5 = 6	2 + 5 = 7	3 + 5 = 8	4 + 5 = 9	5 + 5 = 10	6 + 5 = 11
	6	0 + 6 = 6	1 + 6 = 7	2 + 6 = 8	3 + 6 = 9	4 + 6 = 10	5 + 6 = 11	6 + 6 = 12

(*a*) Obtain an ungrouped frequency distribution of the 49 sums.

(*b*) Construct a histogram from the frequency distribution. Note that the original distribution of scores was rectangular because each score occurred with the same frequency.

(*c*) Compare the form of the original distribution with the form of the frequency distribution of sums.

16. Calculate the percentage, cumulative frequency, and cumulative percentage for these ungrouped frequency data. What is the percentile rank of the 8th graders? The 11th graders?

Grade	Public elementary and secondary enrollment in 1990 Number (000s)
Kindergarten	3,612
1	3,499
2	3,328
3	3,299
4	3,249
5	3,197
6	3,112
7	3,067
8	2,981
9	3,169
10	2,897
11	2,612
12	2,380
Total	40,402

Source: U.S. National Center for Education Statistics, *120 Years of American Education: A Statistical Portrait* (Washington, D.C.: U.S. Government Printing Office, 1993).

CHAPTER 5

Measures of Central Tendency

5.1 INTRODUCTION

The ambiguity in the use of the term *average* can be confusing to the general public and perhaps leads to suspicion that statistics is more of a deceptive art than a tool of objective science (see Box 5.1). Unions and management speak of average salaries and frequently cite numerical values that are in sharp disagreement with each other; television programs and commercials are said to be prepared with the "average viewer" in mind; politicians are deeply concerned about the views of the average U.S. voter; the average family size is frequently given as a fractional value, a statistical abstraction that is ridiculous; the term *average* is commonly used as a synonym for the term *normal;* the TV weather reporter tells us we had an average day or that rainfall for the month is above or below average. Indeed, the term *average* has so many popular meanings that many statisticians prefer to drop it from the technical vocabulary and refer, instead, to **measures of central tendency**, which we define as an index of central location used in the description of frequency distributions. Since the center of a distribution may be defined in different ways, there are a number of different measures of central tendency. In this chapter, we concern ourselves with three of the most frequently used measures of central tendency: the mean, the median, and the mode.

5.1.1 Describing Frequency Distributions

Throughout the first four chapters, we dealt with organizing data into a meaningful and useful form. We want to go beyond that to describe our data, so that meaningful

BOX 5.1

THE AMBIGUITY OF "AVERAGE"

Annual salaries of XYZ Company (in dollars)	
60,000	
54,000	
44,000	
40,000	← Mean
39,000	
39,000	
39,000	
37,000	← Median
36,000	
36,000	
36,000	
35,000	← Mode
35,000	← Mode
35,000	← Mode
35,000	← Mode

The term *average* is frequently used by mass media, labor unions, corporations, hucksters, politicians, and students to describe scores or numerical values in the central part of a distribution. Unfortunately, there are three different measures of central tendency which, for a given distribution, may deviate substantially from one another. This disparity often gives rise to heated disagreements among individuals who focus their attention upon one or another measure of central tendency. Many people are confused by all this bickering and the endless citation of conflicting statistics. In dismay, they may conclude, "Statistics are meaningless. You can do anything you want with them."

In the accompanying table, we show an array of annual salaries of a hypothetical small business with a $600,000 payroll that employs 15 individuals, including the president and the vice president. The company has recently gone on strike. The leader of the strike cites the poor wages—pointing to the most frequently occurring wage (the mode). "The average salary is $35,000," shouts the leader, in a controlled rage. Management, looking at the arithmetic average (mean) of all the salaries, replies with righteous indignation. "Nonsense! The average salary is $40,000." A mediator, looking at exactly the same data but concentrating on the middle salary (the median), exclaims, "Nonsense! Both of you are wrong. The average salary is $37,000."

statements can be made about them. A frequency distribution represents an organization of data, but it does not in itself permit us to make statements describing the distribution or comparing two or more distributions.

Frequency distributions can be characterized by three different features:

1. Frequency data have a characteristic *form* or shape, as you learned in Section 3.7 where we discussed the forms of frequency data, including symmetrical and skewed distributions.
2. Frequency data cluster around a *central value* that lies between the two extreme values of the variable under study. This feature is the topic of this chapter.
3. Frequency data can be characterized by their degree of *dispersion,* spread, or variability about the central value. This last topic is discussed in Chapter 6.

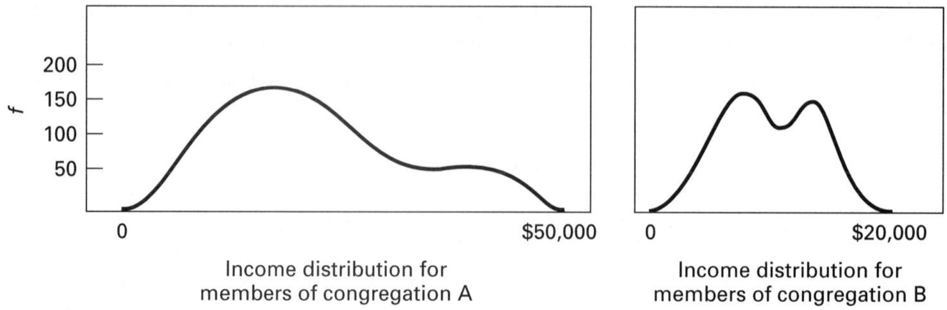

FIGURE 5.1
Hypothetical income distributions of two church congregations

Given these three features about a particular distribution, the social scientist can clearly convey to others the characteristics of a particular distribution. For example, the income distributions of the members of two church congregations might be summarized graphically as shown in Figure 5.1. The two distributions in Figure 5.1 differ with respect to form, a central value, and variability. In this and the following chapter, you will learn how to reduce considerable data to a few summary values. Being able to locate a single point of central tendency, particularly when combined with a summary description of the dispersion of scores about that point, can be very useful. While there is much to be gained by these summary values, the danger of course is that you lose considerable information that was available when the data were in their original form.

5.2 THE ARITHMETIC MEAN ($\overline{X}$)

5.2.1 Methods of Calculation

You are already familiar with the arithmetic **mean,** for whenever you obtain an "average" of grades by summing the grades and dividing by the number of grades, you are calculating the arithmetic mean. In short, the mean is the sum of the scores or values of a variable divided by the number of scores. Stated in algebraic form:

$$\overline{X} = \frac{X_1 + X_2 + \cdots + X_N}{N} = \frac{\Sigma X}{N} = \frac{\text{sum of scores}}{\text{number of scores}} \qquad (5.1)$$

where X = a raw score in a set of scores
$\overline{X}$ = the mean and is referred to as X bar*
N = the number of scores
Σ = sigma and directs us to sum all of the scores

---

* In Section 1.2, we indicated that italic letters would be used to represent sample statistics and Greek letters to represent population parameters. The Greek letter μ will be used to represent the population mean.

Note that we are using the shorthand version of $\overline{X}$ here. It is not necessary to include the subscript i because we are summing all of the X values.

The following equations show the procedure for computing the arithmetic mean of the scores 7, 28, 11, 25, and 10.

$$X_1 = 7, X_2 = 28, X_3 = 11, X_4 = 25, \text{ and } X_5 = 10$$

$$\overline{X} = \frac{7 + 28 + 11 + 25 + 10}{5} = \frac{81}{5} = 16.2$$

The mean serves as a summary value for the distribution of the five scores. Note that interval-level data are required before you can calculate the mean because both addition and division of the scores are required. However, social scientists often compute the mean on ordinal-level data. Statistics in Action 5.1 provides further examples of calculating and using the mean.

STATISTICS IN ACTION 5.1
Defining Sexual Harassment: Calculating the Mean

The U.S. Merit Systems Board conducted its first national sexual harassment survey of federal employees over 15 years ago. The initial survey in 1980 and the second and third surveys in 1987 and 1994 found widespread sexual harassment. Sexual harassment continues to be a serious problem in factories, small and large businesses, colleges and universities, and in medical facilities.

The accompanying survey results (see Table 5.1) show that the definition of sexual harassment has broadened over the three time periods. In 1994, some 83 percent of women found uninvited sexual teasing, jokes, and remarks from a supervisor to be a form of sexual harassment compared with 62 percent in 1980. The percentage of women who consider co-workers' sexual teasing, jokes, and remarks to be harassment rose from 54 to 77 percent during this same period.

Well over 90 percent of the men surveyed in 1994 believed that pressure for sexual favors from either a supervisor or co-worker constituted sexual harassment. Men also broadened what constituted sexual harassment over the past 15 years. The percentage who would include pressure for sexual favors from co-workers has jumped from 65 to 93 percent over the three survey periods.

Each of the arithmetic means shown in the far right column of Table 5.1 were computed using equation (5.1).* The first, 96.3, resulted from summing 91, 99, and 99 and dividing the total by 3. Thus, $289/3 = 96.3$. The six types of sexual harassment have consistently been presented under each of the four panels to facilitate comparison of women with men with respect to harassment from a supervisor versus harassment from a co-worker.

1. Recalculate the mean for several of the types of sexual harassment.
2. Do the women and men surveyed differ in their responses? Are their responses influenced by who is the source of the harassment? Summarize the pattern or patterns you observe in a paragraph or two.
3. How do the means assist you in understanding the survey results?

* We are assuming that the three samples are of equal size.

TABLE 5.1
Changing views on sexual harassment*

Type of uninvited behavior by a supervisor	Percentage of women who consider it harassment			
	1980	1987	1994	$\bar{X}$
Pressure for sexual favors	91	99	99	96.3
Deliberate touching, cornering	91	95	98	94.7
Suggestive letters, calls, materials	93	90	94	92.3
Pressure for dates	77	87	91	85.0
Suggestive looks, gestures	72	81	91	81.3
Sexual teasing, jokes, remarks	62	72	83	72.3
	Percentage of men who consider it harassment			
	1980	1987	1994	$\bar{X}$
Pressure for sexual favors	84	95	97	92.0
Deliberate touching, cornering	83	89	93	88.3
Suggestive letters, calls, materials	87	76	87	83.3
Pressure for dates	76	81	86	81.0
Suggestive looks, gestures	59	68	76	67.7
Sexual teasing, jokes, remarks	53	58	73	61.3
Type of uninvited behavior by a co-worker	**Percentage of women who consider it harassment**			
	1980	1987	1994	$\bar{X}$
Pressure for sexual favors	81	98	98	92.3
Deliberate touching, cornering	84	92	96	90.7
Letters, calls, other materials	87	84	92	87.7
Pressure for dates	65	76	85	75.3
Suggestive looks, gestures	64	76	88	76.0
Sexual teasing, jokes, remarks	54	64	77	65.0
	Percentage of men who consider it harassment			
	1980	1987	1994	$\bar{X}$
Pressure for sexual favors	65	90	93	82.7
Deliberate touching, cornering	69	82	89	80.0
Letters, calls, other materials	76	67	81	74.7
Pressure for dates	59	66	76	67.0
Suggestive looks, gestures	47	60	70	59.0
Sexual teasing, jokes, remarks	42	47	64	51.0

*Based on the percentage of respondents who indicated that they "definitely" or "probably" would consider the identified behavior sexual harassment.

Source: Sexual Harassment in the Federal Workplace: Trends, Progress, Continuing Challenges, U.S. Merit Systems Protection Board, 1995. Portions of the text originally appeared on pp. 12–13 of the report.

Obtaining the mean from an ungrouped frequency distribution. You will recall that we constructed a frequency distribution as a means of eliminating the constant repetition of scores that occur with varying frequency in order to permit a single entry in the frequency column to represent the number of times a given score occurs. Thus,

TABLE 5.2
Computational procedures for calculating the mean with ungrouped frequency distributions

X	f	fX
4	2	8
5	2	10
6	3	18
7	4	28
8	6	48
9	4	36
10	5	50
11	2	22
12	1	12
	$N = 29$	$\Sigma fX = 232$

$$\bar{X} = \frac{\Sigma fX}{N}$$

$$\bar{X} = \frac{232}{29}$$

$$\bar{X} = 8.00$$

in Table 5.2 we know from column f that the score of 8 occurred six times. In calculating the mean, then, it is unnecessary to add 8 six times since we may multiply the score by its frequency and obtain the same value of 48. Since each score is multiplied by its corresponding frequency prior to summing, we may represent the mean for frequency distributions as follows:

$$\bar{X} = \frac{\Sigma fX}{N} \tag{5.2}$$

Obtaining the mean from a grouped frequency distribution, raw score method. The calculation of the mean from a grouped frequency distribution involves essentially the same procedures that are used with ungrouped frequency distributions. To start, the midpoint of each interval is used to represent *all scores within that interval*. Thus, the assumption is made that the scores in an interval are evenly distributed. The midpoint of each interval (X_m) is multiplied by its corresponding frequency, and the product is summed and divided by N. If you encountered a distribution such as in exercise 13, Chapter 4, where an interval was not closed, it would be impossible to determine the midpoint and hence you could not calculate the mean. The procedures used to calculate the mean from a grouped frequency distribution are demonstrated in Table 5.3 using equation (5.3).

$$\bar{X} = \frac{\Sigma fX_m}{N} \tag{5.3}$$

5.2.2 Properties of the Arithmetic Mean

One of the most important properties of the mean requires that you understand the concept of deviation. A **deviation** is the distance and direction of a score from a reference point that is normally the mean. A deviation is positive when the score is larger than the mean and negative when the score is less than the mean.

TABLE 5.3
Computational procedures for calculating the mean from a grouped frequency distribution

1 Class interval	2 Frequency f	3 Midpoint X_m	4 Frequency multiplied by the midpoint fX_m	
75–79	3	77	231	
80–84	4	82	328	
85–89	8	87	696	
90–94	10	92	920	
95–99	15	97	1455	
100–104	20	102	2040	$\bar{X} = \frac{\Sigma fX_m}{N}$
105–109	15	107	1605	
110–114	10	112	1120	
115–119	8	117	936	$= \frac{10{,}195}{100}$
120–124	5	122	610	
125–129	2	127	254	$= 101.95$
	$N = 100$		$\Sigma fX_m = 10{,}195$	

1. The first important property of the mean is that it is the point in a distribution of measurements or scores about which the sum of the deviations are equal to zero. In other words, if we were to subtract the mean from each score and add the resulting deviations from the mean, this sum would equal zero. Symbolically:

$$\sum_{i=1}^{N} (X_i - \bar{X}) = 0$$

Therefore, the mean is the value that balances all of the scores on either side of it. You may wish to think of it as a center of gravity. In this sense, the mean is analogous to the fulcrum of a seesaw. In playing on seesaws, you may have noticed that it is possible for a small individual to balance a heavy individual if the latter moves closer to the fulcrum. Thus, if you wanted to balance a younger brother or sister (presumably lighter than you) on a seesaw, you would move yourself toward the center of the board. The arithmetic mean of the values $X_1 = 2$, $X_2 = 3$, $X_3 = 4$, $X_4 = 5$, $X_5 = 6$ is 4. Substituting these values into the symbolic equation above, we find that the sum of the deviations of these five values from their mean of 4 equals 0 as follows:

$$(2 - 4) + (3 - 4) + (4 - 4) + (5 - 4) + (6 - 4) =$$
$$(-2) + (-1) + (0) + (+1) + (+2) = 0$$

2. A second important property of the mean is that *the mean is very sensitive to extreme values when these are not dispersed evenly on both sides of it.* Observe the two arrays of scores in Table 5.4. An **array** is an arrangement of data according to their magnitude from the smallest to the largest value. Note that all of the scores in both distributions are the same except for the very large score of 33 in group 2. This one extreme score is sufficient to double the size of the mean. Thus, when a distribution is markedly skewed, the mean provides a misleading estimate of central tendency,

TABLE 5.4
Comparison of the means of two arrays of scores, one of which contains an extreme value

Group 1 Score, X	Group 2 Score, Y
2	2
3	3
5	5
7	7
8	33
$\Sigma X_i = 25$	$\Sigma Y_i = 50$
$\bar{X} = 5.00$	$\bar{Y} = 10.00$

whereas the median (see Section 5.3) better reflects the central region of that distribution. Annual income is a commonly studied variable in which the median is preferred over the mean, since the distribution is distinctly skewed in the direction of high incomes. The incomes of multimillionaires exert a much stronger upward pull on the mean than the incomes of paupers exert on a downward pull. Income does not go below zero, but there is no similar restraint on the upper end of the scale.

The sensitivity of the mean to extreme scores is a characteristic that has important implications governing our use of it. These implications will be discussed in Section 5.5, in which we compare the three measures of central tendency.

3. A third important property of the mean is that the **sum of squares** *of deviations from the arithmetic mean is less than the sum of squares of deviations about any other score or potential score.* To illustrate this property of the mean, Table 5.5 shows the squares and the sum of squares when deviations are taken from the mean and various other scores in a distribution. It can be seen that the sum of squares is smallest in column 4, when deviations are taken from the mean. This property of the mean provides us with another definition: *The mean is that measure of central tendency that makes the sum of squared deviations around it minimal.* The method of locating the mean by finding the minimum sum of squares is referred to as the **least-squares property of the mean.** The least-squares property of the mean is of considerable value in statistics, particularly when it is applied to curve fitting.

4. A fourth important property of the mean is that it is the most stable or reliable measure of central tendency. Let's say that we draw 25 separate random samples of 500 persons who are registered voters in New York State (it is possible that a few persons will be selected in more than one of the samples). If we computed the mean, the median, and the modal age for each of the 25 samples, we would find that in most instances the mean would show less fluctuation than either the median or mode. That is, the frequency distribution for the 25 mean ages would be more compact (show less variability) than either the frequency distribution of the 25 median ages or the 25 modal ages. The reason that stability or reliability is particularly important stems from our effort to infer from a sample to the population. We learned in Chapter 1 that

TABLE 5.5
The squares and sum of squares of deviations taken from various scores in a distribution

1 X	2 $(X - 2)^2$	3 $(X - 3)^2$	4 $(X - \bar{X})^2$	5 $(X - 5)^2$	6 $(X - 6)^2$
2	0	1	4	9	16
3	1	0	1	4	9
4	4	1	0	1	4
5	9	4	1	0	1
6	16	9	4	1	0
Totals	30	15	10	15	30
$N = 5$					
$\bar{X} = 4$					

the population parameter is frequently unknown, but that we can calculate sample statistics. Thus, the sample is a convenient way to estimate population characteristics or parameters. Normally, it is not possible to draw more than one sample so, because of its stability, we tend to use the sample mean as the best single estimate of its corresponding population parameter.

Each of these four properties of the arithmetic mean will be considered further in future chapters.

5.2.3 The Weighted Mean

Let's imagine that four classes in introductory sociology obtained the following mean scores on the final examination: 75, 78, 72, and 80. Could you sum these four means together and divide by 4 to obtain an overall mean for all four classes? This could be done only if the N in each class is identical. What if the mean of 75 is based on an N of 30, the second mean is based on 40 observations, the third on $N = 25$, and the fourth on $N = 50$?

To obtain the weighted mean, we need only apply the procedures we previously used to calculate the mean from an ungrouped frequency distribution. To do this, we regard each sample mean as if it is a score and the N for each mean as its frequency. We then make up a frequency distribution of means and follow the procedures that are already familiar. This frequency distribution of means is shown in Table 5.6* using equation (5.4) which is shown below:

$$\bar{X}_w = \frac{\Sigma f\bar{X}}{N_t} \tag{5.4}$$

As you see, the **weighted mean** is 77.03. Had we merely summed the sample means and divided by 4, we would have obtained an incorrect value of $305/4 = 76.25$. Weighted means are frequently used when we want to obtain the "average"

* It is not necessary to arrange these means in ascending or descending order unless you wish to calculate the median of the sample means. This is not often done.

TABLE 5.6
Obtaining the weighted mean by regarding each sample mean as a score and its associated N as a frequency and using procedures for calculating the mean from a frequency distribution*

$\overline{X}$	f	$f\overline{X}$	Computation
75	30	2,250	
78	40	3,120	$\overline{X}_w = \frac{\Sigma f\overline{X}}{N_t}$
72	25	1,800	$= \frac{11{,}170}{145}$
80	50	4,000	$= 77.03$
$N_t = 145$		$\Sigma f\overline{X} = 11{,}170$	

*$\overline{X}_w$ is the weighted mean, and N_t is the sum of the frequencies of means.

amount we paid per share on several different purchases of a given stock, when we calculate the lifetime batting average of a baseball player throughout his career, or when we wish to ascertain the overall mean we paid per pound for some product we purchased in different amounts over different times, to name but a few.

Your grade point average is also calculated by using the weighted mean. Exercise 17 at the end of the chapter is such an example. Statistics in Action 5.2 employs the weighted mean to highlight a statistical paradox.

5.3 THE MEDIAN (Md_n)

The **median** is defined as that score or potential score in a distribution of scores, above and below which one-half of the frequencies fall. If this definition sounds vaguely familiar to you, it is not by accident. The median is merely a special case of a percentile rank. Indeed, the median is the score at the 50th percentile.

5.3.1 Calculating the Median from an Array of Scores

Here are the results of standardized test scores for 11 children.

128 104 132 117 123 96 141 124 142 165 115

We can use these data to examine how to calculate the median.

Step 1. Arrange the numbers from lowest to highest.

96 104 115 117 123 124 128 132 141 142 165

Step 2. To find the location of the median, add 1 to N and divide the total by 2. In this example, the number of observations is 11. Therefore,

$$\text{Median location} = \frac{N+1}{2} = \frac{11+1}{2} = \frac{12}{2} = 6$$

Step 3. Starting with the lowest score, count up to the median. In this example, count to the sixth score.

96 104 115 117 123 **124** 128 132 141 142 165

We find that the sixth score, the median, is 124. Note that five scores are below 124 and five are above. The median divides the array of scores exactly in half.

If there is an even number of scores, the median is halfway between the two middle scores. Consider another set of test scores: that have been arranged from lowest to highest: 123 126 133 137 142 160

$$\frac{N+1}{2} = \frac{6+1}{2} = \frac{7}{2} = 3.5$$

The median is halfway between the third and fourth scores, 133 and 137. Thus, it is $(133 + 137)/2 = 135$.

5.3.2 Obtaining the Median of a Frequency Distribution

Table 5.7 shows the frequency and cumulative frequency distribution of 30 scores and Case Example 5.1 provides an example of the median used in a grouped frequency distribution. Calculating the median from a cumulative frequency distribution requires just two steps.

Step 1. Divide $N + 1$ by 2 to find the *location* of the middle frequency. In the present example, $N + 1 = 31$. Thus, the middle frequency is $31/2 = 15.5$—between the fourteen and fifteenth scores.

Step 2. This value falls between the lower and upper true limits of a score of 11.5 and 12.5. You can select the midpoint of that class—a score of 12—and identify it as the median. For most purposes, this is a satisfactory estimate of the median. If greater precision is needed or desired, calculate the 50th percentile using the techniques presented in Chapter 3.

TABLE 5.7
Cumulative frequency distribution of 30 scores

	X	f	Cum f	
	5	1	1	
	6	1	2	
	7	1	3	
	8	2	5	
The lower	9	1	6	
true limit	10	2	8	
of 12 is	11	5	13	
11.5 →				
	12	3	16	The 15.5th frequency is between 11.5 and 12.5.
12.5 →				
The upper	13	2	18	
true limit	14	2	20	
of 12	15	4	24	
	16	1	25	
	17	2	27	
	18	1	28	
	19	1	29	
	20	1	30	← total number of scores

USE OF THE MEDIAN

Women's earnings have traditionally have lagged behind men's for several reasons, including differences in occupational employment, years of work experience, number of hours worked, and discrimination in labor market practices. The median rather than the mean is frequently presented with census data because of its insensitivity to extreme values (see Section 5.3.3). Table 5.8 presents the median weekly earnings of men and women by age and race for two time periods. The top row of the table shows that women working full time in wage and salary jobs had median weekly earnings that were 62.5 percent of men's earnings in 1979 and 71.8 percent in 1990.

Increases in the women's to men's median earning ratio have occurred across all age groups, but they have been greatest for African American and white women 16 to 24 years of age. The ratio of women's to men's median earnings among African-American women of this age group was 86.2 percent in 1979, but it had risen to 94.0 percent in 1990. Their corresponding median weekly earnings increased from \$144 in 1979 to \$234 in 1990.

TABLE 5.8

Median weekly earnings for full time wage and salary workers by age, race, and sex, 1979 and 1990

Age and race	1979 Women	1979 Men	1979 Ratio of women's to men's earnings	1990 Women	1990 Men	1990 Ratio of women's to men's earnings
Total						
16 years and over	\$182	\$291	62.5	\$348	\$485	71.8
16 to 24 years	154	196	78.6	254	283	89.8
25 years and over	194	314	61.8	370	514	72.0
25 to 54 years	196	315	62.2	374	512	73.0
25 to 34 years	199	295	67.5	357	452	79.0
35 to 44 years	195	335	58.2	391	563	69.4
45 to 54 years	192	337	57.0	377	592	63.7
55 years and over	187	305	61.3	342	526	65.0
55 to 64 years	188	312	60.3	348	545	63.9
65 years and over . . .	170	219	77.6	300	402	74.6
White						
16 years and over	184	298	61.7	355	497	71.4
16 to 24 years	155	199	77.9	257	287	89.5
25 years and over	197	321	61.4	378	529	71.5
25 to 54 years	198	322	61.5	382	525	72.8
55 years and over . . .	190	313	60.7	348	554	62.8
Black						
16 years and over	169	227	74.4	308	360	85.6
16 to 24 years	144	167	86.2	234	249	94.0
25 years and over	177	245	72.2	320	386	82.9
25 to 54 years	179	249	71.9	321	387	82.9
55 years and over . . .	159	216	73.6	303	381	79.5

Source: Working Women: A Chartbook, U.S. Department of Labor, Bureau of Labor Statistics, 1991. Portions of the text originally appeared on pp. 22–23 of the report.

5.3.3 A Characteristic of the Median

An important characteristic of the median is its *insensitivity* to extreme scores. Consider the following set of scores: 2, 5, 8, 11, and 48. The median is 8. This is true in spite of the fact that the set contains one extreme score of 48. Had the 48 been a score of 97, the median would remain the same. This characteristic of the median makes it valuable for describing central tendency in certain types of distributions in which the *mean* is an unacceptable measure of central tendency due to its sensitivity to extreme scores. This point will be further elaborated in Section 5.5 where the uses of the three measures of central tendency are discussed.

5.4 THE MODE (M_o)

Of all measures of central tendency, the **mode** is the most easily determined because it is obtained by inspection rather than by computation. The mode is the score that occurs with greatest frequency. For grouped data, the mode is designated as the midpoint of the interval containing the highest frequency count. In Table 5.3, the mode is a score of 102 since it is the midpoint of the interval (100–104) containing the greatest frequency.

If the data in Table 5.3 were represented as a frequency curve (polygon) or as a histogram, the mode also would be 102. The mode of a frequency curve is the highest value on the curve. In a histogram, the mode is represented by the midpoint of the tallest column.

The mode can be determined for nominal-, ordinal-, or interval-level data, and therefore is the most versatile of the three measures of central tendency. Consider a study in which the respondents were classified by their religious affiliation in the following manner: Protestant, 47%; Catholic, 42%; and Jewish, 11%. The modal category would be Protestant. Note that the mode is located in the category with the plurality of cases. A majority of cases, that is, over 50%, is not required.

From a statistical perspective, the mode is also the most probable value. If the names of all of the respondents classified by religious affiliation were placed in a large container, the name drawn first would most probably be that of a Protestant simply because Protestants are most numerous in this particular study.

In some distributions, such as those shown in Figure 3.10(c) in Chapter 3, there are two high points that produce the appearance of two humps, as on a camel's back. Such distributions are referred to as *bimodal*. A distribution with more than two humps is referred to as *multimodal*.

5.5 COMPARISON OF MEAN, MEDIAN, AND MODE

We have seen that the mean is a measure of central tendency in which the *sum* of the deviations on one side equals the sum of the deviations on the other. The median divides a frequency distribution into two equal parts so that the *number* of scores below the median equals the *number* of scores above the median. The mode is the score that occurs with the greatest frequency.

In general, the arithmetic mean is the preferred statistic for representing central tendency because it has several desirable properties. To begin with, the mean is a member of a mathematical system, which permits its use in more advanced statistical analyses because it is based on interval-level data. It is the preferred measure of central tendency if the distribution of scores is not skewed. We have used deviations from the mean to demonstrate two of its most important characteristics; that is, the sum of deviations is zero and the sum of squares is minimal. Deviations of scores from the mean provide valuable information about any distribution. We will be making frequent use of deviation scores throughout the remainder of the text. In contrast, deviation scores from the median and the corresponding squared deviations have only limited applications to more advanced statistical considerations.

As previously noted, one important function of inferential statistics is to provide estimates of parameters. If we take a number of different samples from a population and wish to estimate the population mean from them, the mean would be a better estimator than the median. The size of the error of any given estimate using the mean of the sample is likely to be less than an estimate using the sample median because of the stability of the mean (see Section 5.2).

On the other hand, there are certain situations in which the median is preferred as the measure of central tendency. When the distribution is symmetrical, the mean, the median, and the mode are identical. Under these circumstances, the mean should be used. However, as we have seen, when the distribution is markedly skewed, the mean, which is analogous to a center of gravity, will provide a misleading estimate of central tendency because under these circumstances it is not a central score. The mean for group 2 in Table 5.4 is 10, even though four of the five scores are less than this value. Annual family income is a commonly studied variable in which the median is preferred over the mean since the distribution of this variable is distinctly skewed in the direction of high salaries, with the result that the mean overestimates the income obtained by most families. You will find upon examination of most census information that the median is used more frequently than the mean or mode because the median is less sensitive to the extreme values that are encountered with age, educational attainment, and income distributions. Computation of the median requires that the data be measured at the ordinal level or higher.

The mode is used far less than the mean and median in the social sciences. It is particularly appropriate whenever a quick, rough estimate of central tendency is desired. The mode, however, is very versatile in that it can be used with all levels of measurement.

5.5.1 Indeterminant Values

There are a number of different occasions when values of the variable are indeterminate. The highest class (and sometimes the lowest) in many summaries of health and age-related statistics do not include either an upper or lower boundary. If age is the variable of interest, the highest class may be 80 and above; if income is the variable, the lowest class may be under \$2,500 and the highest class may be \$50,000 and over. Since we are unable to specify the limits of these classes, we cannot ascertain the midpoint. Consequently, a mean cannot be calculated.

The inability, on occasion, to specify a value of a variable can also have important implications for the study of the environment. Many electronic and chemical tests for toxic substances in the environment (e.g., groundwater and air) are unable to detect quantities below certain values. It is not that these substances do not exist at these lower values, but that the test procedures are simply unable to find them. To illustrate, if a given substance is measured in parts per million per cubic meter and the available technology cannot measure amounts less than 50 parts per million, then samples containing 49, 48, 47, and fewer parts per million would not be detected. If there are many of these undetected values and they are all recorded as zero, the mean would be an inappropriate statistic since all of the recorded zeros would draw the mean toward them. The resulting sample mean could seriously underestimate the actual amount of the toxic substance in the environment studied. Under these circumstances, the median might provide a better estimate of central tendency since it would be unaffected by the spurious zeros—unless of course the majority of the readings are in the undetectable range.

5.6 THE MEAN, MEDIAN, MODE, AND SKEWNESS

In Chapter 3, we demonstrated several forms of skewed distributions. We pointed out, however, that skew cannot always be determined by inspection. If you understand the differences between the mean and the median, you should be able to suggest a method for determining whether a distribution is skewed and, if so, the direction of the skew. The basic fact to keep in mind is that the mean is pulled in the direction of the skew, whereas the median and mode, unaffected by extreme scores, are not. When the mean is higher than the median, the distribution may be said to be positively skewed; when the mean is lower than the median, the distribution is negatively skewed. Figure 5.2 demonstrates the relationship between the mean, the median, and the mode in positively skewed, negatively skewed, and symmetrical distributions.

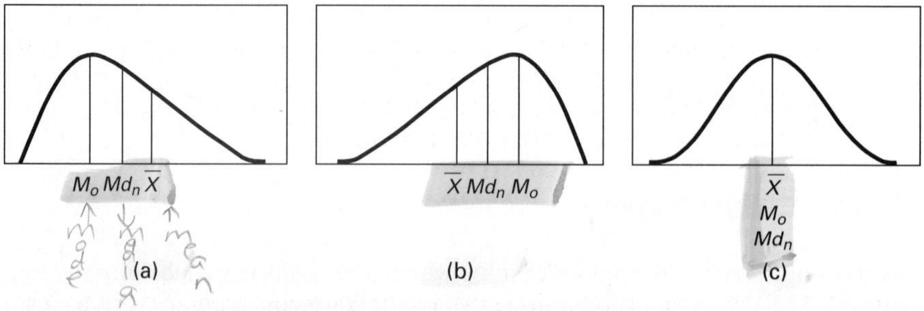

The relationship among the mean, median, and mode in (a) positively skewed, (b) negatively skewed, and (c) symmetrical distributions

STATISTICS IN ACTION 5.2
The Will Rogers Paradox: Patients Appear to Improve without Any Actual Change

Will Rogers was a colorful, often sardonic, social commentator of the 1920s and 1930s who brought smiles to an audience whose spirit was otherwise weighted down by the financial and emotional burdens of the Great Depression. Noting the mass migration of Oklahomans to California in search of employment (as described in John Steinbeck's *The Grapes of Wrath*), Rogers was reported to have said, "When the Okies left Oklahoma and moved to California, they raised the average intelligence of both states."

This observation derives its humor largely from the fact that it appears to be totally absurd. How could the average intelligence quotient (IQ) of both states increase as the result of a one-way migration from one state to another? Surprisingly, it is possible. Take a few moments and see if you can construct a scenario that would permit this to happen.

Here it is. Suppose that the mean IQ of Okies migrating to California is below the mean IQ of Oklahomans but above the mean IQ of Californians. This reverse "brain drain" would raise the mean IQ of Oklahoma. In addition, because the mean IQ of the migrating hordes is higher than the mean IQ of Californians, the migration would also raise the mean IQ of that state. Such a situation can occur under only one set of circumstances: if the mean IQ of Oklahomans is higher than the mean IQ of Californians.

No doubt Will Rogers said this with his typical sense of humor. But the biggest surprise of all is the recent resurrection of the *Will Rogers paradox* by a team of medical researchers who believe it provides a clue to an important source of misleading survival statistics.* Let's see how this works.

Physicians rank their patients' condition based on the status of the disease. Thus, a patient in the early stages of a disease is assigned to stage 1, a "good status" category. An advanced case is assigned to one of the two progressively deteriorating categories, stage 2 or stage 3. As might be expected, if the disorder is usually terminal, the patients in earlier stages will typically survive longer than those in the later stages *regardless of the treatment interventions that are undertaken.* As you can see in Table 5.9, patients diagnosed in stage 1 can expect to live, on average, for seven years, whereas patients diagnosed at stage 3 can expect to live for one and one-half years on average.

What would happen if there were a major improvement in the diagnosis of the disease, allowing physicians to better discriminate among the patients? One possible consequence is that patients who were once borderline would be placed into a different category. One example is cancer that originates in the lungs. Advances in diagnostic techniques allow physicians to detect patients with "silent" or early phases of the disease. These patients were previously placed in stage 1, but now are routinely placed in one of the advanced stages. Such a change is represented in Table 5.10.

The advances in diagnosis cause some patients originally placed in stage 1 to be placed in stage 2, and patients in stage 2 to be placed in stage 3. These reclassified patients are described as "migrating patients." Remember that the only thing that has changed is an improvement in diagnostic techniques; the treatment procedures are the same.

---

* Feinstein A. R., D. M. Sosin, and C. K. Wells (1985), "The Will Rogers Phenomenon: Stage Migration and New Diagnostic Techniques as a Source of Misleading Statistics for Survival in Cancer," *New England Journal of Medicine* 312 (25), pp. 1604–08.

TABLE 5.9
Mean survival times in three stages of lung cancer prior to the development of advanced diagnostic techniques*

Stage	N*	Expected survival years	Mean years
1	10	8	
	10	6	7.0
2	10	4	
	10	3	3.5
3	10	2	
	10	1	1.5

Expected mean survival years for the total sample: $\frac{(7 + 3.5 + 1.5)}{3} = 4.0$

*Equal *N*s do not require weighting.

TABLE 5.10
Weighted mean survival times in three stages of lung cancer subsequent to the development of advanced diagnostic techniques*

Stage	N*	Expected survival years	Weighted mean years
1	10	8	8
2	10	6 (migrating patients)	$\frac{(60 + 40)}{20} = 5$
	10	4	
3	10	3 (migrating patients)	$\frac{(30 + 20 + 10)}{30} = 2$
	10	2	
	10	1	

Expected mean survival years for the total sample: $\frac{(80 + 100 + 60)}{60} = 4.00$

*Unequal *N*s require weighting the means comprising each stage.

As you can see in Table 5.10, the average life expectancy for each stage has increased. Are people really living longer? No. If we look at the weighted mean, the average life expectancy remains four years. The only thing that has changed is that the criteria for being in any one of the stages have changed, thus changing the corresponding life expectancy for that stage.

Let's summarize this startling application of the Will Rogers paradox: Because of improved diagnostic techniques, many patients without overt symptoms migrate from lower to higher stages, thereby increasing the average survival time of those in both the promising and the dangerous stages of lung cancer without in any way affecting the overall survival times. Under these circumstances, it would be easy to attribute the apparent prolongation of life to the medical treatment used, even if it is completely ineffective.

Tables 5.9 and 5.10 present hypothetical data relating to the Will Rogers paradox as it may apply to survival statistics for lung cancer. Note that the survival times following the introduction of advanced diagnostic techniques are *greater within each stage:* Stage 1 has increased from seven years to eight years, stage 2 from three and one-half to five years, and stage 3 from one and one-half to two years. When looking at these statistics, it is easy to conclude that the use of new diagnostic techniques has improved the effectiveness of treatment at all stages of illness. Surprisingly, however, the total survival times remain precisely the same—four years—prior to and subsequent to the introduction of advanced diagnostic procedures.

SUMMARY

In this chapter we discussed, demonstrated the calculation of, and compared three indices of central tendency that are frequently used to describe frequency distributions: the mean, the median, and the mode.

We saw that the mean may be defined variously as the sum of scores divided by the number of scores, the point in a distribution that makes the summed deviations equal to zero, or the point in the distribution that makes the sum of the squared deviations minimal. The median divides the distribution in half, so that the number of scores below the median equals the number of scores above it. Finally, the mode is defined as the most frequently occurring score. We demonstrated the method for obtaining the weighted mean of a set of means when each of the individual means is based on a different N.

Because of special properties it possesses, the mean is the most frequently used measure of central tendency. However, because of the mean's sensitivity to extreme scores that are not balanced on both sides of the distribution, the median is usually the measure of choice when distributions are markedly skewed. The mode is rarely used in the social sciences.

Finally, we demonstrated the relationship among the mean, the median, and the mode in positively skewed, negatively skewed, and symmetrical distributions.

TERMS TO REMEMBER

array Arrangement of data according to their magnitude from the smallest to the largest value.

deviation The distance and direction of a score from a reference point.

least squares property of the mean The mean is that measure of central tendency that makes the sum of the squared deviations around it minimal.

mean The sum of the scores or values of a variable divided by their number.

measure of central tendency Index of central location used in the description of frequency distributions.

median Score in a distribution of scores, above and below which one-half of the frequencies fall.

mode Score that occurs with the greatest frequency.

sum of squares Deviations from the mean, squared and summed.

weighted mean Sum of the mean of each group multiplied by its respective weight (the N in each group), divided by the sum of the weights (total N).

EXERCISES

1. Find the mean, the median, and the mode for each of the following sets of measurements. Show that $\Sigma(X - \overline{X}) = 0$.
(*a*) 10, 8, 6, 0, 8, 3, 2, 5, 8, 0
(*b*) 1, 3, 3, 5, 5, 5, 7, 7, 9
(*c*) 119, 5, 4, 4, 4, 3, 1, 0

2. In which of the sets of data in exercise 1 is the mean a poor measure of central tendency? Why?

3. You have calculated measures of central tendency on family income and expressed your data in dollars. You decide to recompute after you have multiplied all the dollars by 100 to convert them to cents. How will this affect the measures of central tendency?

4. Give examples of data in which the preferred measure of central tendency would be the
(*a*) mean (*b*) median (*c*) mode

5. Calculate the measures of central tendency for the data in Table 3.3 in Chapter 3.

6. In exercise 1(c), if the score of 119 were changed to a score of 19, how would the various measures of central tendency be affected?

7. On the basis of the following measures of central tendency, indicate whether or not there is evidence of skew and, if so, its direction:
(*a*) $\overline{X} = 56$, median $= 62$, mode $= 68$
(*b*) $\overline{X} = 68$, median $= 62$, mode $= 56$
(*c*) $\overline{X} = 62$, median $= 62$, mode $= 62$
(*d*) $\overline{X} = 62$, median $= 62$, mode $= 30$, mode $= 94$

8. What is the nature of the distributions in exercises 7(c) and (d)?

9. Calculate the mean of the following array of scores: 3, 4, 5, 5, 6, and 7:
(*a*) Add a constant of, say, 2 to each score. Recalculate the mean.
Generalize: What is the effect on the mean of adding a constant to all scores?
(*b*) Subtract the same constant from each score. Recalculate the mean.
Generalize: What is the effect on the mean of subtracting a constant from all scores?
(*c*) Square all the scores. Recalculate the mean.
Generalize: What is the effect on the mean of squaring all the scores?
(*d*) Multiply each score by a constant of, say, 2. Recalculate the mean.
Generalize: What is the effect on the mean of multiplying each score by a constant?
(*e*) Divide each score by two. Recalculate the mean.
Generalize: What is the effect on the mean of dividing each score by a constant?

10. What is the mean, median, and mode for Figure 3.5 in Chapter 3? How is each affected by the skew of the distribution?

11. If we know that the mean and median of a set of scores are equal, what can we say about the form of the distribution?

12. Given the information in the following table, calculate the appropriate measures of central tendency.

Immigration to the United States, 1821–1990

Period	Number (in thousands)
1821–1830	152
1831–1840	599
1841–1850	1,713
1851–1860	2,598
1861–1870	2,315
1871–1880	2,812
1881–1890	5,247
1891–1900	3,688
1901–1910	8,795
1911–1920	5,736
1921–1930	4,107
1931–1940	528
1941–1950	1,035
1951–1960	2,515
1961–1970	3,322
1971–1980	4,493
1981–1990	7,338
	Total 56,993

Source: U.S. Immigration and Naturalization Service, annual report. Immigrants are nonresident aliens (i.e., non-U.S. citizens) admitted to the United States for permanent residence.

13. In a departmental final exam the following mean grades were obtained for classes of 25, 40, 30, 45, 50, and 20 students: 72.5, 68.4, 75.0, 71.3, 70.6, and 78.1.

(*a*) What is the total mean for all students in all sections who took this exam?

(*b*) Draw a line graph showing the size of the class along the *X*-axis and the corresponding means along the *Y*-axis. Does there appear to be a relationship between class size and mean grades on the final exam?

14. What can we say about the relationship between the mean and the median in a negatively skewed distribution? In a positively skewed distribution?

15. On the basis of examination performance an instructor identifies the following groups of students:

(*a*) Those with a percentile rank of 90 or higher.

(*b*) Those with a percentile rank of 10 or less.

(*c*) Those with percentile ranks between 40 and 49.

(*d*) Those with percentile ranks between 51 and 60.

Which group would the instructor work with if he or she wished to raise the *median* performance of the total group? Which group if he or she wished to raise the *mean* performance of the total group?

16. Given the information in the following table, calculate the mean, median, and mode for marriages and divorces:

Marriages and divorces in the United States

Year	Marriages (000s)	Divorces (000s)
1978	2,243	1,122
1979	2,331	1,181
1980	2,390	1,189
1981	2,422	1,213
1982	2,456	1,170
1983	2,446	1,158
1984	2,477	1,169
1985	2,413	1,190
1986	2,407	1,178
1987	2,403	1,166
1988	2,396	1,167

Source: U.S. Bureau of the Census, *Statistical Abstract of the United States 1995,* 115th ed., p. 102, Table 14.2 (Washington, D.C., 1995).

17. A student compiled the following academic record in college. What is her overall grade point average if $A = 4$, $B = 3$, $C = 2$, $D = 1$, and $F = 0$?

Credit hours	Grade
40	*A*
55	*B*
15	*C*
10	*D*
0	*F*

18. While backpacking on the Appalachian Trail, you encounter 20 hikers and note the number of days they have been out. Given the following data, demonstrate that the sum of deviations about the mean equals zero:

5	1	15	9
4	42	19	9
39	6	22	8
14	18	14	1
12	14	8	19

19. Surveys are typically pretested to identify procedural, sampling, and wording problems. A telephone interview was pretested using 10 respondents in a recent statewide survey of attitudes toward pornography.

Calculate the appropriate measures of central tendency for the following three variables. (*Hint:* Note the level of measurement for each of the variables.)

Respondent	**Age**	**Sex**	**Attitude toward pornography***
1	32	M	19
2	43	F	24
3	21	F	11
4	19	F	30
5	76	F	50
6	50	F	42
7	40	M	17
8	26	F	33
9	21	F	24
10	63	F	47

*Scores may range from 10 to 50 with a high score indicating opposition to pornography.

20. Calculate the median for the data in Table 5.3. (*Hint:* Construct a cumulative frequency or a cumulative percentage column to locate the class interval containing the median.)

21. Calculate the mean number of workers involved per work stoppage for each year represented in exercise 19 in Chapter 3. Describe the trend that you observe.

22. Which of the measures of central tendency is most affected by the degree of skew in the distribution? Explain.

23. In Section 5.5, we stated that the mean is usually *more reliable* than the median; that is, it is less subject to fluctuations. Suppose we conduct an experiment consisting of 30 tosses of three dice, obtaining the following results:

6, 6, 2	5, 4, 3	4, 3, 2	2, 1, 1	6, 5, 3	6, 5, 4
4, 1, 1	4, 4, 3	6, 4, 1	5, 4, 3	5, 1, 1	6, 2, 1
6, 5, 5	6, 6, 4	6, 4, 2	5, 4, 4	6, 5, 2	5, 4, 3
6, 4, 3	5, 3, 2	5, 1, 1	4, 3, 1	6, 3, 3	5, 4, 1
4, 2, 1	6, 3, 3	6, 5, 4	4, 2, 2	6, 6, 5	6, 3, 1

(*a*) Calculate the 30 means and 30 medians.
(*b*) Starting with the true limits of the lower interval 0.5–1.5, group the means and medians into separate frequency distributions.
(*c*) Draw histograms for the two distributions. Do they support the contention that the mean is a more stable estimator of central tendency? Explain.
(*d*) Assume that we place the means and medians into two separate hats and draw one at random from each. What is the likelihood that:
(i) A statistic greater than 5.5 would be obtained?
(ii) A statistic less than 1.5 would be obtained?
(iii) A statistic greater than 5.5 or less than 1.5 would be obtained?

CHAPTER 6

Measures of Dispersion

6.1 INTRODUCTION

In the introduction to Chapter 4, we saw that a score by itself is meaningless. A score takes on meaning only when it is compared with other scores or other statistics. If we know the mean of the distribution of a given variable, we can determine whether a particular score is higher or lower than the mean. But how much higher or lower? It is clear at this point that a measure of central tendency such as the mean provides only a limited amount of information. To describe a distribution more fully, or to interpret a score more fully, additional information is required concerning the **dispersion** of scores about our measure of central tendency.

Consider Figure 6.1. In both examples of frequency curves, the mean of the distribution is exactly the same. However, note the difference in the interpretations of a score of 128. In Figure 6.1(a), a score of 128 may be considered only moderately high because the scores are widely dispersed about the mean. Quite a few individuals in the distribution scored above 128, as indicated by the shaded area to the right of 128. In Figure 6.1(b), on the other hand, the scores are compactly distributed about the same mean. This is a more *homogeneous* distribution. Consequently, the score of 128 is now virtually at the top of the distribution and it may therefore be considered a very high score.

In interpreting individual scores, we must find a companion to the mean or the median. This companion must in some way express the degree of dispersion of scores about the measure of central tendency. We will discuss five such measures of dispersion or variability:

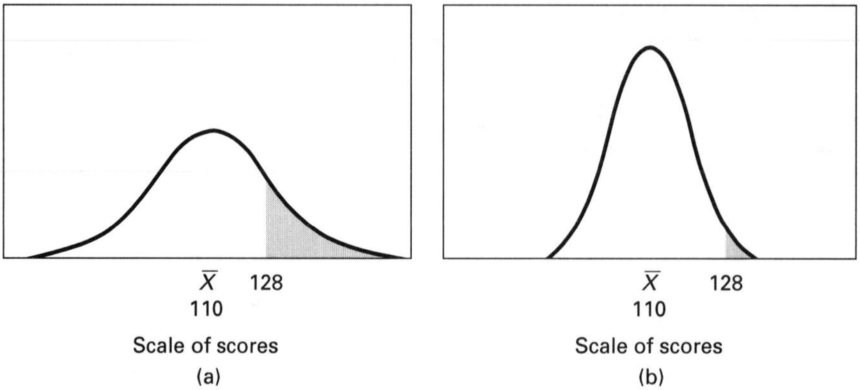

FIGURE 6.1
Two frequency curves with identical means but differing in dispersion or variability

1. Range
2. Interquartile range
3. Mean deviation
4. Variance
5. Standard deviation

Of the five, we will find the standard deviation to be our most useful measure of dispersion in both descriptive and inferential statistics. In advanced inferential statistics, as in analysis of variance (see Chapter 15), the variance will become a most useful measure of variability.

6.2 THE RANGE

When we calculated the various measures of central tendency, we located a *single point* along the scale of scores and identified it as the mean, the median, or the mode. When our interest shifts to measures of dispersion, however, we must look for an index of variability that indicates the *distance* along the scale of scores.

One of the first measures of distance that comes to mind is the range. The range is by far the simplest and the most straightforward measure of dispersion. It is the scale distance between the largest and smallest score.* In a recent study conducted by one of the authors, the youngest respondent was 28 years old and the oldest was 90. Thus, the range was 90 − 28 or 62.

Although the range is meaningful, it is of little use because of its marked instability, particularly when the range is based on a small sample. Note that if there is one

* Sometimes the range is computed by subtracting the lowest score from the highest score and adding 1.

extreme score in a distribution, the dispersion of scores will appear to be large when in fact the removal of that score may reveal an otherwise compact distribution. Several years ago, a resident of an institution for retarded persons was found to have an I.Q. score in the 140s. Imagine the erroneous impression that would result if the scores for the residents varied from 20 to 140 and the range was reported to be 120! Stated another way, the range reflects only the two most extreme scores in a distribution, and the remaining scores are ignored.

6.3 THE INTERQUARTILE RANGE

To overcome the instability of the range as a measure of dispersion, we sometimes calculate the interquartile range. The **interquartile range** is calculated by subtracting the score at the 25th percentile (referred to as the first quartile or Q_1) from the score at the 75th percentile (the third quartile or Q_3).

$$\text{interquartile range} = Q_3 - Q_1 \tag{6.1}$$

This measure of score variation is more meaningful than the range because it is not based on two extreme scores. Rather, it reflects the middle 50% of the scores. It does, however, have two shortcomings: (1) Like the range, it does not by itself permit the precise interpretation of a score within a distribution, and (2) like the median, it does not enter into any of the higher mathematical relationships that are basic to inferential statistics. Figure 6.2 provides a comparison of the range and interquartile range. Statistics in Action 6.1 includes an example of the interquartile range.

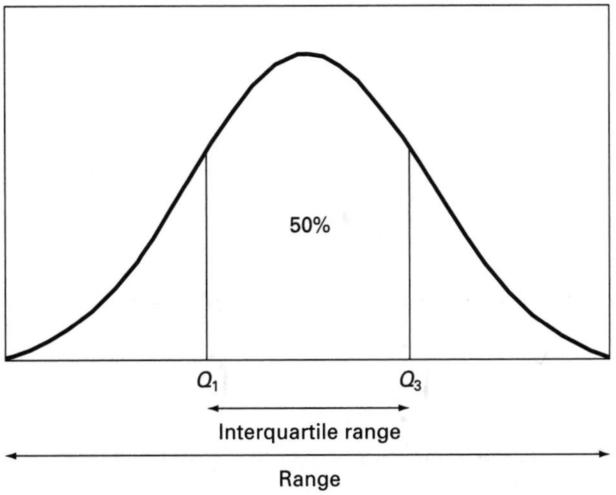

FIGURE 6.2
Comparison of range and interquartile range for a hypothetical distribution

STATISTICS IN ACTION 6.1
Reduction in Inequalities

Sociologists have long observed that great inequality in educational attainment can contribute to social tensions in much the same way that excessive income inequality does by fostering elitism, class differences, and political instability. Indeed, at one time a college education was a mark of rank and social standing as well as of acquired knowledge and skill. The situation in 1940 was not nearly this extreme because some able children from poor families had been attending colleges for some time. Still, the lack of even a high school diploma by many was striking and the relative number going to college was small. The growth in attainment that was to take place would change this situation, bringing with it a decrease in the amount of inequality in educational attainment.

Table 6.1 shows the distribution of the population 25 years old and over by years of schooling completed for 1940 and 1990, along with measures of the amount of variance or inequality in the distribution. Because there is a practical upper limit on the amount of formal education an individual can obtain, we expect that as more people attain higher levels, the closer together they would become. However, it is important to measure the degree to which this is happening, so that judgments can be made about how important the reductions are and comparisons can be made in different places and times.

Measures of absolute inequality (standard deviation, interquartile range) are essentially based on the absolute difference in years of attainment between individuals. As Table 6.1 shows, both measures declined significantly. The interquartile range shows that the range of attainment across the middle 50 percent of the population was 5.7 years of schooling in 1940 but only 3.3 years in 1990. The standard deviation declined over the same period from 3.8 to 3.4 years.

TABLE 6.1

Years of school completed by persons 25 years old and over and measures of dispersion, 1940 and 1990

1940	Less than 5 years	5 to 7 years	8 years	9 to 11 years	12 years	13 to 15 years	16 years and over
Percentage distribution	13.7	29.2	17.5	15.2	14.3	5.5	4.6
Median (years)					8.4		
Standard deviation (years)					3.8		
Interquartile range (years)					5.7		

1990	Less than 5 years	5 to 7 years	8 years	9 to 11 years	12 years	13 to 15 years	16 years and over
Percentage distribution	2.0	3.7	4.9	10.5	39.7	18.1	21.1
Median (years)					12.7		
Standard deviation (years)					3.4		
Interquartile range (years)					3.3		

Sources: U.S. Bureau of the Census, Special Demographic Analysis, CDS-85-1, *Education in the United States: 1940–1983* (Washington, D.C.: U.S. Government Printing Office, 1985). Portions of the text originally appeared on pp. 4–5 of the report. National Center for Education Statistics, *120 Years of American Education: A Statistical Portrait,* 1993.

6.4 THE MEAN DEVIATION

In Chapter 5, we pointed out that when we are dealing with data that are characterized by a bell-shaped distribution, the mean is our most useful measure of central tendency. We calculated the mean by adding together all of the scores and dividing them by N. If we carried these procedures one step further, we could subtract the mean from each score, sum the differences (deviations from the mean), and obtain an estimate of the amount of deviation from the mean. By dividing by N, we would have a measure that would be analogous to the arithmetic mean except that it would represent the average dispersion of scores from the arithmetic mean.

If you think for a moment about the characteristics of the mean, which we discussed in the preceding chapter, you will encounter one serious difficulty. The sum of the deviations of all scores from the mean must add up to zero. If we defined the **mean deviation** (also referred to as the **average deviation**) as this sum divided by N, the mean deviation would always have to be zero. You will recall in Chapter 5 that we used the fact that $\Sigma(X - \overline{X}) = 0$ to arrive at one of several definitions of the mean.

Now if we were to add all of the deviations *without regard to sign* and divide by N, we would still have a measure reflecting the mean deviation from the arithmetic mean. The resulting statistic would be based on the absolute value of the deviations. The **absolute value of a number** is the value of a number without regard to sign. The absolute value of a positive number or of zero is the number itself. The absolute value of a negative number can be found by changing the sign to a positive one. Thus, the absolute value of $+3$ *or* -3 is 3. The symbol for an absolute value is $|\ |$. Thus, $|-3| = 3$ and $|+3| = 3$.

The calculation of the mean deviation (MD) is shown in Table 6.2. The data in Tables 6.2 through 6.5 were compiled by the Joint Center for Political Studies in Washington, D.C. and include the number of African-American officials in 12 southern states holding elected state positions in 1993.*

As a basis for comparison of the dispersion of several distributions, the mean deviation has some value. For example, the greater the mean deviation is, the greater the dispersion of scores. However, for interpreting scores within a distribution, the mean deviation is less useful because there is no precise mathematical relationship between the mean deviation, as such, and the location of scores within a distribution.

You may wonder why we have bothered to demonstrate the mean deviation when it is of so little use in statistical analysis. As you will see, the standard deviation and the variance, which have great value in statistical analysis, are very closely related to the mean deviation.

---

* These figures do not include African-American officials holding congressional, regional, city, country, or other elected positions.

TABLE 6.2
Computational procedures for calculating the mean deviation from an array of scores

State	Number of African-American elected officials holding state positions X	$(\lvert X - \overline{X} \rvert)$	Computation
West Virginia	1	$\lvert -21.08 \rvert$	
Kentucky	4	$\lvert -18.08 \rvert$	
Arkansas	13	$\lvert -9.08 \rvert$	
Virginia	14	$\lvert -8.08 \rvert$	
Tennessee	16	$\lvert -6.08 \rvert$	$\text{MD} = \dfrac{\Sigma(\lvert X - \overline{X} \rvert)^{\dagger}}{N}$ (6.2)
Florida	22	$\lvert -0.08 \rvert$	
Alabama	23	$\lvert +0.92 \rvert$	$\text{MD} = \dfrac{125}{12} = 10.42$
South Carolina	26	$\lvert +3.92 \rvert$	
North Carolina	28	$\lvert +5.92 \rvert$	
Louisiana	33	$\lvert +10.92 \rvert$	
Mississippi	42	$\lvert +19.92 \rvert$	
Georgia	43	$\lvert +20.92 \rvert$	
	$\Sigma X = 265$	$\Sigma(\lvert X - \overline{X} \rvert) = 125.00$	
	$N = 12$		
	$\overline{X} = \dfrac{\Sigma X}{N} = \dfrac{265}{12} = 22.08$		

†For scores arranged in the form of a frequency distribution, the following equation for the mean deviation should be used:

$$\text{MD} = \Sigma f(\lvert X - \overline{X} \rvert)/N$$

Sources: U.S. Bureau of the Census, Current Population Reports, Series P-23, no. 80, Table 132; *The Social and Economic Status of the African-American Population in the United States: An Historical View, 1790–1978; African-American Elected Officials: A National Roster,* annual. Copyright by Joint Center for Political Studies, Washington, D.C. All rights reserved.

6.5 THE VARIANCE (s^2) AND STANDARD DEVIATION (s)†

After looking at Table 6.2, you might ask this question: "We had to treat the values in column $(X - \overline{X})$ as absolute numbers because their sum was equal to zero. Why couldn't we square each $(X - \overline{X})$ and then add the squared deviations? In this way we

† Italic letters will be used to represent sample statistics, and Greek letters to represent population parameters; for example, σ^2 represents the population variance and σ represents the population standard deviation. The problem of estimating population parameters from sample values will be discussed in Chapter 14.

would legitimately rid ourselves of the minus signs while still preserving the information that is inherent in these deviation scores."

The answer: We could, if by so doing, we arrived at a statistic of greater value in judging dispersion than those we have already discussed. It is fortunate that the standard deviation, based on the squaring of these deviation scores, is of considerable value in three different respects. (1) The standard deviation reflects dispersion of scores, so that the dispersion of different distributions may be compared by using the standard deviation (s). (2) The standard deviation permits the precise interpretation of scores within a distribution. (3) The standard deviation, like the mean, is a member of a *mathematical system,* which permits its use in more advanced statistical considerations. We will use measures based on s when we advance into inferential statistics, and will have more to say about the interpretive aspects of s after we have shown how it is calculated.

6.5.1 Calculation of Variance and Standard Deviation, Mean Deviation Method, with Ungrouped Scores

The **variance** is defined verbally as the sum of the squared deviations from the mean divided by N. Symbolically, it is represented as:

$$s^2 = \frac{\Sigma(X - \overline{X})^2}{N} \qquad (6.3)*$$

The **standard deviation** is the *square root* of the variance and is defined as:

$$s = \sqrt{\frac{\Sigma(X - \overline{X})^2}{N}} \qquad (6.4)$$

The computational procedures for calculating the standard deviation, utilizing the mean deviation method, are shown in Table 6.3.

You will recall from Section 5.2.2 that the sum of the $(X - \overline{X})^2$ column—that is, $\Sigma(X - \overline{X})^2$—is known as the **sum of squares** and that this sum is minimal when deviations are taken about the mean. From this point on in the text, we will encounter the sum of squares with regularity. It will take on a number of different forms, depending on the procedures that we elect for calculating it. However, it is important to remember that, whatever the form, the sum of squares represents the *sum of the squared deviations from the mean.*

The mean deviation method was shown to help you understand conceptually that the standard deviation is based on the deviation of scores from the mean. The mean deviation method [eq. (6.4)] for calculating the standard deviation is extremely unwieldy for use in calculation, particularly when the mean is a fractional value, which is usually the case.

---

* The important distinction between biased $\Sigma(X - \overline{X})^2/N$ and unbiased $\Sigma(X - \overline{X})^2/(N - 1)$ estimates of the population variance will be discussed in Chapter 14. Occasionally a calculator or computer software programmed to calculate various statistics (usually designated as *statistical* calculator or software) may use $N - 1$ in the denominator when calculating s^2 and s. If you have one of these calculators, simply multiply the variance given by your calculator by $(N - 1)/N$.

TABLE 6.3
Computational procedure for calculating *s*, mean deviation method, from an array of scores

State	Number of African-American elected officials holding state positions	$(X - \bar{X})$	$(X - \bar{X})^2$
West Virginia	1	−21.08	444.37†
Kentucky	4	−18.08	326.89
Arkansas	13	−9.08	82.45
Virginia	14	−8.08	65.29
Tennessee	16	−6.08	36.97
Florida	22	−0.08	00.01
Alabama	23	+0.92	00.85
South Carolina	26	+3.92	15.37
North Carolina	28	+5.92	35.05
Louisiana	33	+10.92	119.25
Mississippi	42	+19.92	396.81
Georgia	43	+20.92	437.65
	$\Sigma X = 265$	$\Sigma(X - \bar{X}) = 0.00$	$\Sigma(X - \bar{X})^2 = 1960.96$ $N = 12$ $\bar{X} = 22.08$

Steps

1. Count the number of scores to obtain N.
   $N = 12$
2. Sum the scores in the X column to obtain ΣX.
   $\Sigma X = 265$
3. Find the mean.
   $$\frac{\Sigma X}{N} = \frac{265}{12} = 22.08$$
4. Compute the deviation of each X value from the mean and place it in the $(X - \bar{X})$ column.
5. Square each value in the $(X - \bar{X})$ column and place it in the $(X - \bar{X})^2$ column.
6. Sum the squared deviations.
   $\Sigma(X - \bar{X})^2 = 1960.96$
7. Substitute the values found in steps 1 and 6 in the equation for s and solve.

$$s = \sqrt{\frac{\Sigma(X - \bar{X})^2}{N}} = \sqrt{\frac{1960.96}{12}} = \sqrt{163.41} = 12.78$$

†A comparison of the values in the $(X - \bar{X})$ column with those in the $(X - \bar{X})^2$ column demonstrates that the standard deviation weights extreme departures from the mean more heavily than the mean deviation does.

Sources: U.S. Bureau of the Census, Current Population Reports, Series P-23, no. 80, Table 132; *The Social and Economic Status of the African-American Population in the United States: An Historical View, 1790–1978; African-American Elected Officials: A National Roster,* annual.

6.5.2 Calculation of Standard Deviation, Raw Score Method with Ungrouped Scores

Equation (6.5) is the computational or raw score equation we use for s. It is mathematically equivalent to the mean deviation method equation (6.4) used to compute s.

$$s = \sqrt{\frac{\Sigma X^2}{N} - (\bar{X})^2} \tag{6.5}$$

TABLE 6.4
Computational procedures for calculating the standard deviation and variance, raw score method, from an array of scores

State	Number of African-American elected officials holding state positions X	X^2
West Virginia	1	1
Kentucky	4	16
Arkansas	13	169
Virginia	14	196
Tennessee	16	256
Florida	22	484
Alabama	23	529
South Carolina	26	676
North Carolina	28	784
Louisiana	33	1089
Mississippi	42	1764
Georgia	43	1849
$N = 12$ $\bar{X} = 22.08$	$\Sigma X = 265$	$\Sigma X^2 = 7813$

Steps

1. Count the number of scores to obtain N. $N = 12$.
2. Sum the scores in the X column to obtain ΣX. $\Sigma X = 265$.
3. Find the mean. $\Sigma X/N = 265/12 = 22.08$.
4. Square each score and place it in the adjacent X^2 column.
5. Sum the X^2 column to obtain $\Sigma X^2 = 7813$.
6. Substitute the values found in Steps 3 and 5 in the equation for s and solve:

$$s = \sqrt{\frac{\Sigma X^2}{N} - (\bar{X})^2}$$
$$= \sqrt{\frac{7813}{12} - (22.08)^2}$$
$$= \sqrt{651.08 - 487.53}$$
$$= \sqrt{163.55}$$
$$= 12.79$$

→ standard deviation

Also

$$s^2 = \frac{\Sigma X^2}{N} - (\bar{X})^2$$

→ variance

$$= \frac{7813}{12} - (22.08)^2$$
$$= 651.08 - 487.53$$
$$= 163.55$$

Sources: U.S. Bureau of the Census, Current Population Reports, Series P-23, no. 80, Table 132; *The Social and Economic Status of the African-American Population in the United States: An Historical View, 1790–1978; African-American Elected Officials: A National Roster,* annual.

You will note that the result using equation (6.5) agrees almost exactly with the answer we obtained by the mean deviation method equation (6.4) in Table 6.3. Table 6.4 summarizes the computational procedure that is used to calculate s with equation (6.5).

6.5.3 Calculation of Standard Deviation, Raw Score Method, from an Ungrouped Frequency Distribution

The data below are arranged into an ungrouped frequency distribution.

X	f
1	1
2	1
3	2
4	2
6	1
10	1
11	1
13	1
15	1

To calculate s, square each score and multiply by its corresponding frequency. Sum these products to obtain ΣfX^2. Place this value in equation (6.6):

$$s = \sqrt{\frac{\Sigma fX^2}{N} - (\bar{X})^2} \tag{6.6}$$

Table 6.5 summarizes the procedure for obtaining the standard deviation from an ungrouped frequency distribution using equation (6.6). Recall that

$$\bar{X} = \frac{\Sigma fX}{N}$$

TABLE 6.5
Procedures for calculating the standard deviation of scores from an ungrouped frequency distribution

X*	f	X^2	fX^2	Computation
1	1	1	1	
2	1	4	4	$s = \sqrt{\frac{\Sigma fX^2}{N} - (\bar{X})^2}$
3	2	9	18	
4	2	16	32	
6	1	36	36	$= \sqrt{\frac{706}{11} - 6.55^2}$
10	1	100	100	
11	1	121	121	$= \sqrt{64.18 - 42.90}$
13	1	169	169	
15	1	225	225	$= \sqrt{21.28} = 4.61$
	$N = 11$		$\Sigma fX^2 = 706$	$\bar{X} = 6.55$

Statistics in Action 6.2 demonstrates the calculation of the standard deviation and variance.

6.5.4 Errors to Watch For

In calculating the standard deviation using the raw score method, students commonly confuse the similar-appearing terms ΣX^2 (or ΣfX^2) and $(\Sigma X)^2$ [or $(\Sigma fX)^2$]. It is important to remember that the former represents the sum of the squares of each of the individual scores, whereas the latter represents the square of the sum of the scores. For example:

$$\text{Given: } X_1 = 2, X_2 = 3, X_3 = 4, X_4 = 5, X_5 = 6$$
$$\Sigma X^2 = 2^2 + 3^2 + 4^2 + 5^2 + 6^2 = 90$$
$$(\Sigma X)^2 = (2 + 3 + 4 + 5 + 6)^2 = 20^2 = 400$$
$$\Sigma X^2 \neq (\Sigma X)^2*$$

By definition, it is impossible to obtain a negative sum of squares or a negative standard deviation. In the event that you obtain a negative value under the square root sign, you have probably confused ΣX^2 and $(\Sigma X)^2$.

A rule of thumb for estimating the standard deviation is that the ratio of the range to the standard deviation is rarely smaller than 2 or greater than 6. Generally, you will find that the more scores (the larger the sample) you are dealing with, the larger the ratio is. In Table 6.5, the ratio was 14:4.61 = 3.04. Had our sample been considerably larger, the ratio would have been closer to 6. This will become clearer after learning about the normal distribution in Chapter 7. If you obtain a standard deviation that yields a ratio greater than 6 or smaller than 2 relative to the range, you have almost certainly made an error.

6.6 INTERPRETATION OF THE STANDARD DEVIATION

You may have noticed that the size of the standard deviation is related to the variability in the scores. The more homogeneous the scores are, the smaller the standard deviation. Conversely, the more heterogeneous the scores are, the larger the standard deviation. The means are equal in arrays A and B in the accompanying table, yet there is considerable difference in the variability of the scores and therefore in the size of the standard deviations. You also should note that extreme scores have a disproportionate effect on the standard deviation since we square the raw deviations from the mean. Examine the impact of the raw score 9 in array B, for example, on the $(X - \bar{X})^2$ column. These points are best illustrated by the mean deviation method of computation.

---

* Does not equal ($\neq$).

Array A

X	$X - \bar{X}$	$(X - \bar{X})^2$
4	0	0
4	0	0
4	0	0
4	0	0
4	0	0
$\Sigma X = 20$	$\Sigma(X - \bar{X}) = 0$	$\Sigma(X - \bar{X})^2 = 0$
$\bar{X} = 4$		
$N = 5$		
	$s = \sqrt{0/5} = 0$	

Array B

X	$X - \bar{X}$	$(X - \bar{X})^2$
2	−2	4
2	−2	4
3	−1	1
4	0	0
9	+5	25
$\Sigma X = 20$	$\Sigma(X - \bar{X}) = 0$	$\Sigma(X - \bar{X})^2 = 34$
$\bar{X} = 4$		
$N = 5$		
	$s = \sqrt{34/5} = 2.6$	

A complete understanding of the meaning of the standard deviation requires a knowledge of the relationship between the standard deviation and the normal distribution. To be able to interpret the standard deviations that are calculated in this chapter, we need to explore the relationship between the raw scores, the standard deviation, and the normal distribution. This material is presented in the following chapter.

SUMMARY

We have seen that to describe a distribution of scores fully, we require more than a measure of central tendency. We must be able to describe how these scores are dispersed about central tendency. In this connection, we discussed five measures of dispersion: the range, the interquartile range, the mean deviation, the standard deviation, and the variance. The summary procedure for calculating the variance and standard deviation from a grouped frequency distribution is presented in Table 6.7.

TABLE 6.7
Summary procedures: Calculating the variance and standard deviation from a grouped frequency distribution

1 Class interval	2 f	3 Midpoint of interval X_m	4 fX_m	5 fX_m^2
0–2	1	1	1	1
3–5	4	4	16	64
6–8	9	7	63	441
9–11	10	10	100	1,000
12–14	16	13	208	2,704
15–17	11	16	176	2,816
18–20	8	19	152	2,888
21–23	3	22	66	1,452
24–26	1	25	25	625
	$N = 63$		$\Sigma fX_m = 807$	$\Sigma fX_m^2 = 11,991$

(continued)

TABLE 6.7 *(continued)*

Steps

1. Sum the f column to obtain $N = 63$.
2. Prepare column 3, showing the mid point of each interval.
3. Multiply the f in each interval by the score at the midpoint of its corresponding interval. Values in column 2 are multiplied by corresponding values in col- umn 3. Place in column 4.
4. Sum column 4 to obtain $\Sigma\ fX_m$.
5. Divide $\Sigma\ fX_m$ by N to obtain $\overline{X}$. Thus $\overline{X} = 807/63 = 12.81$.
6. Multiply values in column 4 by corresponding values in column 3 to obtain fX_m^2. Sum this column to obtain $\Sigma\ fX_m^2 = 11{,}991$.
7. Substitute the values in steps 1, 5 and 6 in the equation for s^2:

$$s^2 = \frac{\Sigma\ fX_m^2}{N} - (\overline{X})^2$$

$$s^2 = \frac{11{,}991}{63} - (12.81)^2$$

$$= 190.33 - 164.10$$

$$= 26.23.$$

Then

$$s = \sqrt{26.23} = 5.12.$$

TERMS TO REMEMBER

absolute value of a number The value of a number without regard to sign.
average deviation See *mean deviation.*
dispersion The spread or variability of scores about the measure of central tendency.
interquartile range A measure of variability obtained by subtracting the score at the 1st quartile from the score at the 3rd quartile.
mean deviation Sum of the deviation of each score from the mean, without regard to sign, divided by the number of scores.
standard deviation Measure of dispersion defined as the square root of the sum of the squared deviations from the mean, divided by N. Also can be defined as the square root of the variance.
variance Sum of the squared deviations from the mean, divided by N.

EXERCISES

1. Calculate s^2 and s for the following array of scores: 3, 4, 5, 5, 6, and 7.
   (*a*) Add a constant, say, 2 to each score. Recalculate s^2 and s. Would the results be any different if you had added a larger constant, say, 200?
   Generalize: What is the effect on s and s^2 of adding a constant to an array of scores? Does the variability increase as we increase the magnitude of the scores?
   (*b*) Multiply each score by a constant, say, 2. Recalculate s and s^2.
   Generalize: What is the effect on s and s^2 of multiplying each score by a constant?

2. Why is it necessary to supplement measures of central tendency with measures of dispersion to describe a distribution completely?

3. Calculate the standard deviations for the following sets of measurements:
(*a*) 10, 8, 6, 0, 8, 3, 2, 2, 8, 0 (*c*) 20, 1, 2, 5, 4, 4, 4, 0
(*b*) 1, 3, 3, 5, 5, 5, 7, 7, 9 (*d*) 5, 5, 5, 5, 5, 5, 5, 5, 5, 5

4. Why is the standard deviation in exercise 3(c) so large? Describe the effect of extreme scores on s.

5. Determine the range for the sets of measurements in exercise 3. For which of these is the range a misleading index of variability and why?

6. What is the nature of a distribution if $s = 0$?

7. The list that follows presents the greatest distance (in miles) 15 children have ever traveled from their homes. Calculate the mean, standard deviation, and the variance. What are the advantages of each?

1,000	100	400
600	3,000	700
250	600	1,100
400	1,000	1,300
500	50	200

8. For the following grouped frequency distribution, find (*a*) the standard deviation and (*b*) the variance (hypothetical data).

Number of self-reported delinquent acts

Delinquent acts	f
0–2	13
3–5	6
6–8	3
9–11	2
12–14	4
15–17	2
	$N = 30$

9. Find (*a*) the standard deviation and (*b*) the variance for the following distribution. Which measure do you believe best reflects the distribution and why?

In how many political campaigns have you worked 10 or more hours? (hypothetical data)

Number of campaigns	f
1	22
2	15
3	11
4	9
5	4
6	2
7	1
8	1
	$N = 65$

10. Find the (*a*) mean, (*b*) standard deviation, and (*c*) range for each major in the following table. Which discipline has been most stable? Least stable? (*Hint:* Use the mean deviation method to ensure your calculator can accommodate the values.)

Earned bachelor's degrees in the United States

	Political science	History	Sociology
1969–1970	26,000	43,000	30,000
1970–1971	27,000	45,000	33,000
1971–1972	28,000	44,000	35,000
1972–1973	30,000	41,000	35,000
1973–1974	31,000	37,000	35,000
1974–1975	29,000	31,000	32,000
1975–1976	28,000	28,000	28,000

11. Three classes of math students took a test and received the following scores:

Class I	Class II	Class III
$\bar{X} = 72$	$\bar{X} = 74$	$\bar{X} = 70$
$s = 2.1$	$s = 5.6$	$s = 4.0$

Which class had the most variability on its test score? Which class had the least?

12. Compute the interquartile range and the mean deviation for the following scores:

18, 2, 4, 6, 10, 7, 9, 11, 14, 8, 3, 16, 20, 22, 24, 25

13. Recall from Chapter 1 the comparison of in-person lecture and videotape lecture approaches. The control and experimental group final examination scores are presented below:

Control group	Experimental group
$\bar{X} = 79$	$\bar{X} = 68$
$s = 2.6$	$s = 4.6$
$N = 27$	$N = 25$

Which teaching technique appears to be most successful? Is it possible that some individual students fared better with the videotape (experimental) approach?

14. Calculate the range, mean, standard deviation, and variance for the Appalachian Trail data in Chapter 5, exercise 18.

15. The outside appearances of homes in four neighborhoods were rated by a team of real estate appraisers. The ratings, which ranged from 0 (low) to 100 (high), reflected the expected resale value of the homes.

A random sample of 10 ratings from each of the neighborhoods is presented below. Which of the neighborhoods is most homogeneous? Most heterogeneous? Which neighborhood is most affluent? Least affluent?

A	B	C	D
37	96	24	22
42	78	36	16
40	84	17	9
32	69	49	14
35	88	56	20
36	84	17	6
39	92	59	8
29	90	32	20
31	80	66	19
42	71	19	14

16. Calculate the mean, standard deviation, and variance for the social worker data in Chapter 3, exercise 5. Assume $i = 5$ with a grouped frequency distribution.

17. Calculate the standard deviation and variance for the data in Table 5.3.

18. The annual accumulation of snow and ice pellets for selected cities is shown below. Calculate the standard deviation for the 10 cities. Recompute the standard deviation excluding Juneau, Alaska, and describe the change in your answer. Finally, exclude Atlanta and recompute for the other nine cities. Describe how extreme scores affect the standard deviation.

Annual snow and ice pellet accumulation (in inches)			
Juneau	102.8	St. Louis	19.8
Omaha	31.0	Atlanta	1.9
Wilmington	20.9	Chicago	40.3
Washington	17.0	Louisville	17.5
Denver	50.0	New York	28.7
Wilmington	120.9	New York	40.3

Source: U.S. National Oceanic and Atmospheric Administration, *Comparative Climatic Data,* annual, as cited in the *Statistical Abstract of the United States.*

CHAPTER 7

The Standard Deviation and the Standard Normal Distribution

7.1 INTRODUCTION

We have emphasized previously that scores are generally meaningless by themselves. To take on meaning, they must be compared to the distribution of scores from some reference group. Indeed, the scores derived from any index or scale become more meaningful when they are compared to some reference group of objects or persons. If we learned there were 491 violent crimes in San Antonio and 1,475 violent crimes in Cleveland during a comparable time period, we would not be able to determine which city had the highest rate of violence until we knew the population of each city during the same time period. Simply noting that there is approximately a 1 to 3 ratio in actual numbers of violent acts between the two cities would prove misleading. We would need to calculate rates for a comparable number of persons—for example, a rate per 100,000 population for each city—before we could make a valid comparison.

7.2 THE CONCEPT OF STANDARD SCORES

In interpreting a single score, we want to place it in some position with respect to a collection of scores from a reference group. In Chapter 4, you learned to place a score by determining its percentile rank. Recall that the percentile rank of a score tells the percentage of scores that are of lower-scale value. Another approach for interpretation of a single score might be to view it with reference to some central point, such as the mean. Thus, a score of 20 in a distribution with a mean of 23 might be reported as -3 because it is 3 units less than the mean, as can be seen in Figure 7.1. We can also express this deviation score as a **standard score (z)** in terms of standard deviation units. If the standard deviation of a set of scores is 1.5 (i.e., one standard deviation is 1.5), a score of 20 would be two standard deviations below the mean of 23 because the absolute difference between 20 and 23 is -3. Dividing -3 by our standard deviation of 1.5 yields -2, which is the number of standard deviations that the raw score of 20 is below the mean.

This process of dividing the deviation of a score from the mean by the standard deviation is known as the transformation of a raw score to a z score. Symbolically, z is defined as:

$$z = \frac{X - \bar{X}}{s} \quad \text{or} \quad z = \frac{X - \mu}{\sigma} \tag{7.1}$$

where X = the raw score
$\bar{X}$ = the sample mean
s = the sample standard deviation
μ = the population mean
σ = the population standard deviation

Thus, in the preceding example, where $\bar{X} = 23$, $s = 1.5$, and $X = 20$, we can confirm the z score equivalent of $X = 20$ using equation (7.1).

$$z = \frac{X - \bar{X}}{s}$$

$$z = \frac{20 - 23}{1.5}$$

$$z = -2.0$$

It is sometimes desirable to transform a z score to a raw score. Problem 6 in Section 7.6 demonstrates the use of equation (7.2) for this purpose:

$$X = zs + \bar{X}, \quad \text{or} \quad X = z\sigma + \mu \tag{7.2}$$

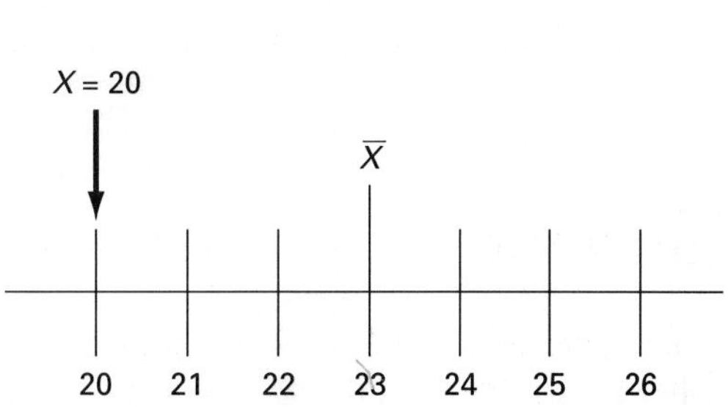

FIGURE 7.1
Example showing the relationship of the raw score to the mean

A z score represents the *deviation of a specific score from the mean expressed in standard deviation units.* For example, if the z score value of a raw score is +2.1, we know that the raw score lies 2.1 standard deviations to the right of the mean. A positive z score indicates the raw score is greater than the mean, a negative z score indicates the raw score is less than the mean, and a z score of zero indicates the raw score equals the mean.

To fully appreciate the value of transforming z scores, let's summarize three of their most important properties.*

1. The sum of the z scores is zero.
2. The mean of the z scores is zero.
3. The standard deviation and the variance of z scores are one.

---

*A complete mathematical explanation of several z score properties is provided here for those interested:

1. The sum of the z scores is zero. Symbolically stated:

$$\Sigma\, z = 0$$

2. The mean of z scores is zero. Thus:

$$\bar{z} = \frac{\Sigma\, z}{N} = 0$$

3. The sum of the squared z scores equals N. Thus:

$$\Sigma\, z^2 = N$$

This characteristic may be demonstrated mathematically:

$$\Sigma\, z^2 = \frac{\Sigma(X - \bar{X})^2}{s^2} = \frac{1}{s^2} \cdot \Sigma(X - \bar{X})^2$$

$$= \frac{N}{\Sigma(X - \bar{X})^2} \cdot \Sigma(X - \bar{X})^2$$

$$= N$$

4. The standard deviation and the variance of z scores are one. Thus:

$$S_z = S_z^2 = 1$$

To demonstrate, we have:

$$S_z^2 = \frac{\Sigma(z - \bar{z})^2}{N}$$

Since $\bar{z} = 0$, then:

$$S_z^2 = \frac{\Sigma\, z^2}{N}$$

Since $\Sigma\, z^2 = N$, then:

$$S_z^2 = \frac{N}{N} = 1$$

and

$$S_z = \sqrt{S_z^2} = \sqrt{1} = 1$$

STATISTICS IN ACTION 6.2
Male Prisoners: Calculating the Standard Deviation and Variance

In Statistics in Action 4.1, we used the prisoner data to illustrate the calculation of the score (age) corresponding to a given percentile rank and the percentile rank of a given score (age). In this chapter, we'll use the same data to demonstrate the procedures used to calculate the variance and standard deviation of a grouped frequency distribution.

TABLE 6.6
Estimated combined numbers of white and African-American male prison inmates in various age groupings*

Class (age)	Midpoint of class (X)	Estimated number of inmates (f)	fX	X^2	fX^2
15–24	19.5	95,687	1,865,896.5	380.25	36,384,981.75
25–34	29.5	158,355	4,671,472.5	870.25	137,808,438.75
35–44	39.5	67,866	2,680,707.0	1,560.25	105,887,926.50
45–54	49.5	18,097	895,801.5	2,450.25	44,342,174.25
55–64	59.5	6,786	403,767.0	3,540.25	24,024,136.50
65–74	69.5	1,185	82,357.5	4,830.25	5,723,846.25
		$N = 347{,}976$	$\Sigma\ fX = 10{,}600{,}002$		$\Sigma\ fX^2 = 354{,}171{,}504$

*Tabular entries necessary to calculate the variance and the standard deviation of a grouped frequency distribution

Step 1. Sum the values in the frequency column of Table 6.6 to obtain N. $N = 347{,}976$.

Step 2. Square each midpoint of class (X) and place the result in the column headed X^2.

Step 3. Multiply the midpoint of each class (X) by its corresponding frequency to obtain fX.

Step 4. Sum the values in the fX column to obtain ΣfX. $\Sigma fX = 10{,}600{,}002$. The mean equals $10{,}600{,}002/347{,}976 = 30.46$.

Step 5. Multiply each frequency (f) by its corresponding X^2 and place the result in the column headed fX^2.

Step 6. Sum the values in the column headed fX^2 to obtain ΣfX^2. In the present example, $\Sigma fX^2 = 354{,}171{,}504$.

Step 7. Using the values obtained in steps 2, 4, and 6, substitute in the following equation for the variance:

$$s^2 = \frac{\Sigma fX^2}{N} - \overline{X}^2$$

$$= 354{,}171{,}504/347{,}976 - (30.46)^2$$

$$= 1023.69 - 927.81 = 95.88$$

Step 8. To obtain the standard deviation, find the square root of s^2 (step 7). $s = \sqrt{95.88} = 9.79$.

Thus, if we compute the z scores for all the raw scores in a bell-shaped frequency distribution using equation (7.1), we find that the z scores sum to zero, their mean is zero, and their standard deviation and variance are one. See Box 7.1.

BOX 7.1

SO YOU WANT TO INTERPRET A TEST SCORE?

As we previously noted, a score in and of itself is meaningless. In this chapter, we see that the z-score transformation provides a precise means of interpreting any value of a variable when the scores are normally distributed. The following excerpt from *Winning with Statistics* illustrates the use of the z-score transformation in the interpretation of test scores on normally distributed standard psychological and educational tests.

The step-by-step procedures for taking all of the mystery out of the interpretation of test scores on standard tests are found on the next page.

1. Determine the mean and the standard deviation of the test. Sometimes different means and standard deviations are given for different age groups. Be sure to find these two measures for the age group in which you are interested.
2. Transform the score you are interested in interpreting to a z-score using the following equation:

$$z = \frac{\text{Score} - \text{Mean}}{\text{Standard deviation}}$$

If you are interested in interpreting a score of 40 and you know that the mean and standard deviation are 30 and 9, respectively you would have:

$$z = \frac{40 - 30}{9} = \frac{10}{9} = 1.1$$

3. Look up a positive value of 1.1 under column A of the accompanying table. Here we find an entry of 86. This means that 86 percent of the group with which this score is being compared obtained scores lower than 86. Only 14 percent (column C) scored higher.

There it is. It's as easy as that.

Percent of scores above and below a given z-score

A z	B Percent of cases below	C Percent of cases above
−2.2	1	99
−2.1	2	98
−2.0	2	98
−1.9	3	97
−1.8	4	96
−1.7	4	96
−1.6	5	95
−1.5	7	93
−1.4	8	92
−1.3	9	91
−1.2	12	88
−1.1	14	86

A z	B Percent of cases below	C Percent of cases above
−1.0	16	84
−0.9	18	82
−0.8	21	79
−0.7	24	76
−0.6	27	73
−0.5	31	69
−0.4	34	66
−0.3	38	62
−0.2	42	58
−0.1	46	54
0.00	50	50

(continued)

(continued)

A z	B Percent of cases below	C Percent of cases above	A z	B Percent of cases below	C Percent of cases above
0.1	54	46	1.2	88	12
0.2	58	42	1.3	91	9
0.3	62	38	1.4	92	8
0.4	66	34	1.5	93	7
0.5	69	31	1.6	95	5
0.6	73	27	1.7	96	4
0.7	76	24	1.8	96	4
0.8	79	21	1.9	97	3
0.9	82	18	2.0	98	2
1.0	84	16	2.1	98	2
1.1	86	14	2.2	99	1

Source: Excerpted from R. P. Runyon, *Winning with Statistics* (Reading, MA: Addison-Wesley, 1977).

What is the value of transforming a raw score to a z score? The conversion to z scores always yields a mean of 0 and a standard deviation of 1, but it does not "normalize" a nonnormal distribution. However, if the *population of scores* on a given variable is normal, we may express any score as a percentile rank by locating our z in the standard normal distribution. In addition, since z scores represent abstract numbers, as opposed to the concrete values of the original scores (e.g., inches, years of education, income), we may compare an individual's position on one variable with his or her position on a second. To understand these two important characteristics of z scores, we must make reference to the standard normal distribution.

7.3 THE STANDARD NORMAL DISTRIBUTION

The **standard normal distribution** is a theoretical model based on the mathematical equation in the footnote.* There is a family of curves that may be called normal. A normal curve's exact shape is determined by its population mean (μ) and its

---

* Recall that the Greek letters μ and σ represent the population mean and the standard deviation, respectively. The equation of the normal curve is:

$$Y = \frac{Ni}{\sigma\sqrt{2\pi}} e^{\frac{-(X-\mu)^2}{2\sigma^2}}$$

where Y = the frequency at a given value of X
σ = the standard deviation of the distribution
π = a constant equaling approximately 3.1416
e = approximately 2.7183
N = total frequency of the distribution
μ = the mean of the distribution
i = the width of the interval
X = any score in the distribution

It should be clear that there is a family of curves that may be called normal. By setting $Ni = 1$, a distribution is generated in which $\mu = 0$ and total area under the curve equals 1.

population standard deviation (σ). Each unique combination of a normally distributed population's μ and σ yields a unique normally distributed curve. Students sometimes have the mistaken impression that the shape of all normal curves is as regular as the coat hangers one particular dry cleaner might use. This is not the case. While all coat hangers share some basic characteristics, we all know that there are several variations of their characteristic shape. Normal curves also vary; for example, some are flatter than others and some are more peaked. All normal curves, however, share the characteristics summarized in Section 7.4.

7.4 CHARACTERISTICS OF THE STANDARD NORMAL DISTRIBUTION

Many variables are distributed in such a way that most observations are concentrated near the center of the distribution. As the distance between the values of the variable and the center of the distribution increases, the frequency of actual observations decreases, both above and below the central concentration of frequencies. This yields a bell-shaped distribution that is commonly referred to as the normal distribution. All standard normal distributions have a μ of 0, a σ of 1, and a total area equal to 1.00. They are also symmetrical. If you folded Figure 7.2 along a line that would connect the point where the horizontal axis equals 0 and the highest point on the curve, two mirror images would result. A normal curve is sometimes referred to as a bell-shaped curve in that the mean, median, and modal values are equal and both sides of the curve slope gently away from its highest point.

The normal distribution is a mathematical abstraction that is not found in the real world. It consists of a family of distributions in which the curves approach but never touch the horizontal axis. This is another way of saying that no matter how distant a given value of the variable is from the central concentration, there are other values, both negative and positive, that are more distant. In contrast, empirical distributions have upper and lower limits beyond which no real measurements are found. If we are measuring height, weight, and age of humans, for example, we will find no real-world negative values for these variables (such as −50 pounds, −4 years of age), nor will there be any real observations beyond some upper limit (e.g., according to the *Guinness Book of Records,* the heaviest person on record weighs 1,400 pounds, give or take a few).

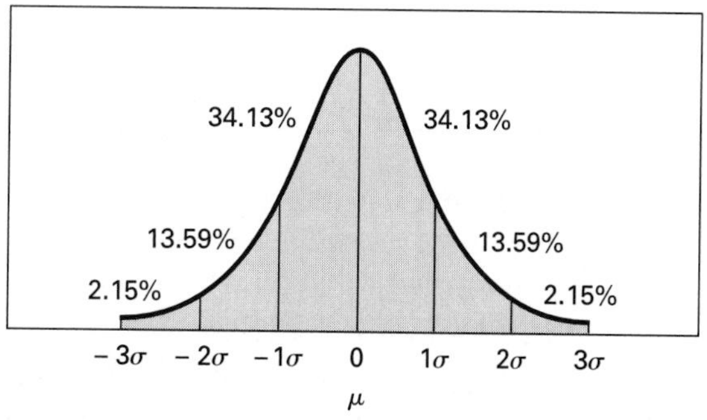

FIGURE 7.2
Areas between selected points under the normal curve

There also is a fixed proportion of cases between a vertical line, or ordinate, erected at any one point on the horizontal axis and an ordinate erected at any other point. Taking a few reference points along the normal curve, we can make the following statements.

1. Between the mean and 1 standard deviation above the mean is found 34.13% of all the cases. Similarly, 34.13% of all the cases fall between the mean and 1 standard deviation below the mean. Stated in another way, 34.13% of the *area* under the curve is found between the mean and 1 standard deviation above the mean, and 34.13% of the *area* falls between the mean and 1 standard deviation below the mean.

2. Between the mean and 2 standard deviations above the mean is found 47.72% of all the cases. Since the normal curve is symmetrical, 47.72% of the area also falls between the mean and 2 standard deviations below the mean.

3. Finally, between the mean and 3 standard deviations above the mean is found 49.87% of all the cases. Similarly, 49.87% of the cases fall between the mean and 3 standard deviations below the mean. Thus, 99.74% (49.87% + 49.87%) of all the cases fall between ±3 standard deviations. These relationships are shown in Figure 7.2.

We see that a total of 6 standard deviation units (±3 standard deviations from the mean) account for nearly 100% of the cases, and hence nearly 100% of the range of values. The remaining 0.26% (100% − 99.74%) of the cases lie beyond ±3 standard deviations from the mean. This leads us to another characteristic of the standard normal distribution: It is comprised of an infinite number of cases since the curve never closes.

7.5 TRANSFORMING RAW SCORES TO z SCORES

Many variables in the real world, such as the weight of a large number of persons, their attitudes toward the military, or their scores on a standardized examination, approximate a normal distribution. As a result, we can use our theoretical distribution, the standard normal distribution, as a basis for comparison. To make such a comparison, we must first transform the scores of the normally distributed variable to z scores. We are, in effect, creating a new variable with $\mu = 0$ and $\sigma = 1$, which is expressed in units of the standard normal curve. These units are referred to as standard deviation units or z scores. Figure 7.3 clarifies the relationships among raw scores on a standardized examination, z scores, and percentile ranks of a normally distributed variable. It assumes that $\mu = 500$ and $\sigma = 100$.

The mean of the raw scores in Figure 7.3 is 500 and the corresponding mean of the standard normal distribution is 0. A raw score of 600 is one standard deviation to the right of the mean of 500 because one standard deviation equals 100. The z score of +1, which is equivalent to 600 in raw units, is also located one standard deviation

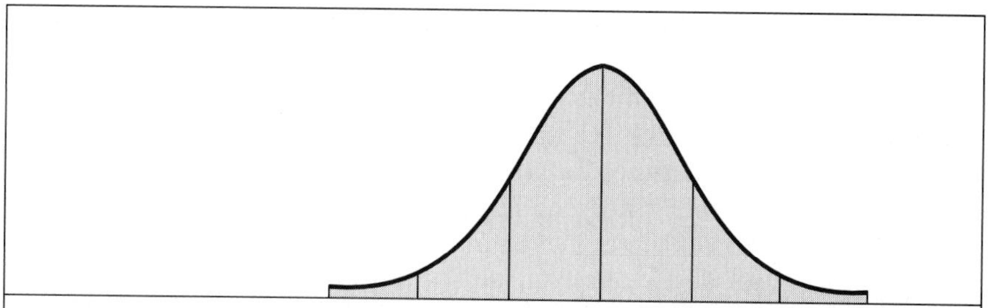

Raw score	200	300	400	500	600	700	800
z-score	−3	−2	−1	0	+1	+2	+3
Percentile rank	0.13	2.28	15.87	50.00	84.13	97.72	99.87

FIGURE 7.3
Relationships among raw scores, *z*-scores, and percentile ranks of a normally distributed variable in which the mean = 500 and the standard deviation = 100

to the right of its z score mean of 0. The following calculations provide further clarification. Applying equation (7.1), we have:

$$\text{if } X = 500,\ \mu = 500, \text{ and } \sigma = 100$$

$$\text{then } z = \frac{X - \mu}{\sigma} = \frac{500 - 500}{100} = 0$$

$$\text{if } X = 600,\ \mu = 500, \text{ and } \sigma = 100$$

$$\text{then } z = \frac{X - \mu}{\sigma} = \frac{600 - 500}{100} = +1$$

You should note carefully that these relationships apply *only to scores from normally distributed populations.* When scores are from a population that is skewed (e.g., the per capita income in the United States) rather than normally distributed, the standard normal distribution may not be used as a model for the data and z scores should not be computed. Transforming the raw scores to standard scores does not in any way alter the form of the original distribution nor does it, as we just saw, alter the relationship between the raw scores. The only change is to convert the mean to 0 and the standard deviation to 1. If the original distribution of scores is nonnormal, the *distribution* of z scores will be nonnormal. In other words, our transformation to z's will not convert a nonnormal distribution to a normal distribution.

By transforming the scores of a normally distributed variable to z-scores, we are, in effect, expressing these scores in units of the standard normal curve. For any given value of X with a certain proportion of area beyond it, there is a corresponding value of z with the same proportion of area beyond it. Thus, if we have a population in which $\mu = 30$ and $\sigma = 10$, the z of a score at the mean ($X = 30$) will equal zero, and the z of scores 1 standard deviation above and below the mean ($X = 40$ and $X = 20$) will be $+1.00$ and -1.00, respectively.

7.5.1 Finding the Area between Given Scores

Up to this point, we have confined our discussion of the area under the standard normal curve to selected points. As a matter of fact, however, it is possible to determine the percent of areas between *any* two points by making use of the tabled values of the area under the normal curve (see Table A in Appendix C). You have learned to convert a raw distribution of scores into a standard normal distribution so that you can use Table A, which was developed by a statistician who computed the area between the mean and every possible z score from 0 to 4.00. The left-hand column in Table A headed by z represents the deviation from the mean expressed in standard deviation units. *By referring to the body of the table, we can determine the proportion of total area between a given score and the mean (column B) and the area beyond a given score (column C).*

Thus, if a woman had a score of 24.65 on a normally distributed variable with $\mu = 16$ and $\sigma = 5$, her z score would be $+1.73$ using equation (7.1).

$$z = \frac{X - \mu}{\sigma} = \frac{24.65 - 16}{5} = +1.73$$

Referring to column B in Table A, we find that 0.4582 or 45.82%* of the area lies between her score and the mean. Since 50% of the area also falls below the mean in a symmetrical distribution, we may conclude that 50% + 45.82%, or 95.82%, of all the area falls below a score of 24.65. Note that we can now translate this score into a percentile rank of 95.82. Referring to column C in Table A, we find that 0.0418 or 4.18% of the area lies beyond a z score of $+1.73$.

Suppose another individual obtained a score of 7.35 on the same normally distributed variable. His z score would be -1.73, as opposed to her z score of $+1.73$, because the raw scores (24.65 and 7.35) are both 8.65 units from the mean of 16. Using equation (7.1), we obtain:

$$z = \frac{7.35 - 16}{5} = -1.73$$

Since the normal curve is symmetrical, only the areas corresponding to the positive z values are given in Table A. The proportion of cases between a negative z value and the mean will equal the proportion of cases between a positive z value of equal value and the mean. Thus, the area between the mean and a z of -1.73 is also equal to 0.4582 or 45.82% of the total area. The percentile rank of a score below the mean may be obtained by subtracting 45.82% either from 50% or directly from column C. In either case the percentile rank of a score of 7.35 is 4.18 because 4.18% of the scores were equal to or less than 7.35.

Before we consider some further uses of the normal curve, recall that one of its characteristics is that it contains an infinite number of cases. If you look at the value in column C associated with $z = 4.00$, you will find that the proportion of cases

---

* The areas under the normal curve are expressed as proportions of area. To convert to percentage of area, multiply by 100 or move the decimal two places to the right.

beyond $z = 4.00$ is 0.00003. The area beyond $z = 5.00$ is 0.0000003 (not shown in Table A) and, indeed, there will always be cases regardless of how far we move to the left or right of the mean in this theoretical curve. Most social science texts do not show the area beyond 4 or 5 standard deviations; however, the precision of physics, for example, requires measurement up to ± 10 to 15 standard deviations from the mean!

7.6 ILLUSTRATIVE EXAMPLES

Let's examine several examples in which we assume that $\mu = 100.0$ and $\sigma = 16.0$ on a state bar exam. The exam has been constructed so as to yield a normal distribution.

EXAMPLE 1. Frank obtained a score of 125.0 on a state bar exam. What percentage of cases fall between his score and the mean? What is his percentile rank in the general population? Let's start by drawing a diagram of the problem (see Figure 7.4). We can begin by assuming that the data are normally distributed. Therefore, we can draw a normal distribution. Next, we know that a score of 125.0 is above the mean. Therefore, the z-score is positive. To find the value of z corresponding to $X = 125.0$, we subtract the population mean from 125.0 and divide by 16. Thus:

$$z = \frac{(125.0 - 100.0)}{16.0}$$

$$z = \frac{25.0}{16.0} = 1.56$$

Looking up 1.56 in column B, Table A in the Appendix, we find that 44.06% of the area falls between the mean and 1.56 standard deviations above the mean. Therefore, Frank's percentile rank is 50 + 44.06 = 94.06. His score exceeds 94% of that of those taking the bar exam.

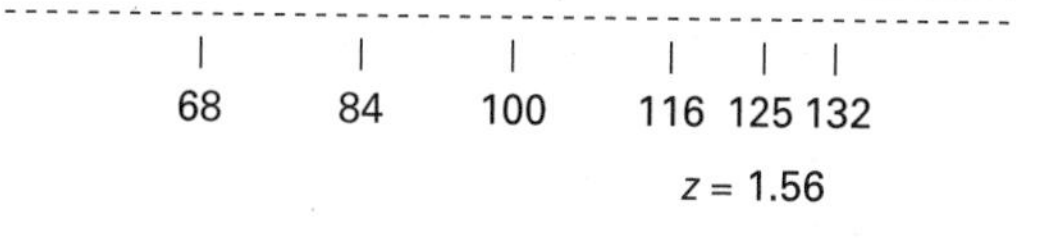

FIGURE 7.4
An illustration of example 1
The mean of the distribution is 100 and the standard deviation is 16. The observed score is 125. Using the calculations described in the text, a score of 125 is equal to a z-score of 1.56, which corresponds to the 94th percentile.

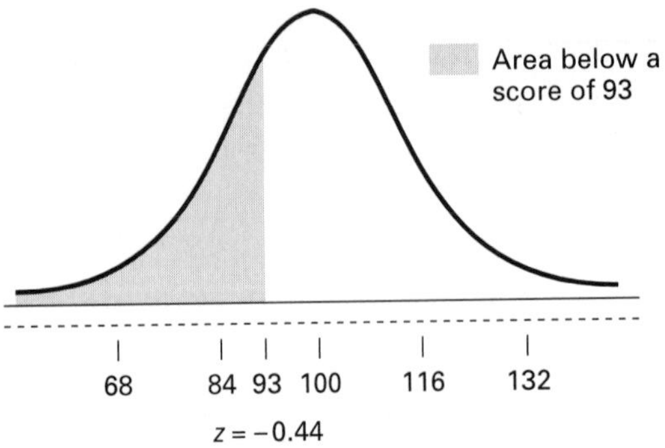

FIGURE 7.5
An illustration of example 2
The mean of the distribution is 100.0 and the standard deviation is 16.0. The observed score is 93.0. Using the calculations described in the text, a score of 93.0 is equal to a z-score of −0.44, which corresponds to the 33rd percentile.

EXAMPLE 2. Corinne scores 93.0 on the exam. What is her percentile rank in the general population (see Figure 7.5)? Her score is below the mean, and so we would expect to calculate a negative z-score and the percentile rank to be less than 50.0.

$$z = \frac{(93.0 - 100.0)}{16.0}$$

$$= \frac{-7.0}{16.0} = -0.44$$

The minus sign indicates that the score is below the mean. Looking up a z-score of 0.44 in Table A in the Appendix, we find in column C that 33.00% of the scores fall below her score. Thus, her percentile rank is 33. Note that we could also have taken the value in column B and subtracted it from 50.00.

EXAMPLE 3. What percentage of cases fall between a score of 120.0 and a score of 88.0 (see Figure 7.6)?

Note that to answer this question we do not subtract 88.0 from 120.0 and divide by s. The areas under the normal curve are designated in relation to the mean as a fixed point of reference. We must therefore calculate separately the area between the mean and a score of 120.0 and the area between the mean and a score of 88.0. We then add the two areas together. The procedure is as follows:

Step 1. To find the z corresponding to $X = 120.0$:

$$z = \frac{(120.0 - 100.0)}{16.0} = 1.25$$

Step 2. To find the z corresponding to $X = 88.0$:

$$z = \frac{(88.0 - 100.0)}{16.0} = -0.75$$

Step 3. Find the required areas by referring to column B, Table A. The area between the mean and $z = 1.25$ is 39.44%, and the area between the mean and $z = -0.75$ is 27.34%.

Step 4. Add the two areas together. Thus, the percentage of area between the scores 125.0 and 88.0 is 39.44% + 27.34% = 66.78%.

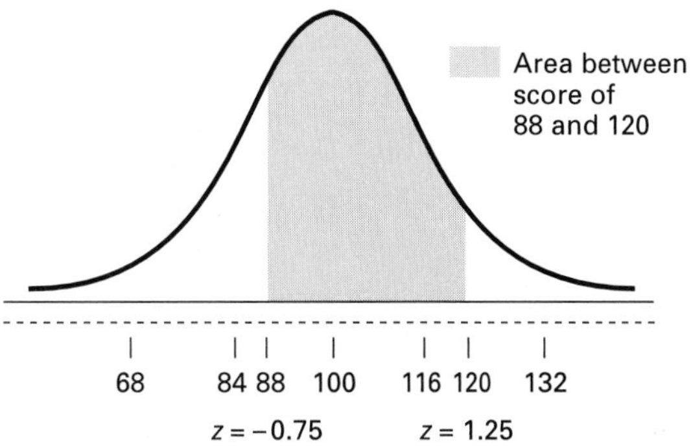

FIGURE 7.6

An illustration of example 3

The mean of the distribution is 100.0 and the standard deviation is 16.0. The observed scores are 88.0 and 120.0. Using the calculations described in the text, a score of 88.0 is equal to a z-score of -0.75. The area of the normal curve between 100.0 and 88.0 represents 27.34% of the distribution. A score of 120.0 is equal to a z-score of 1.25. The area of the normal curve between 100.0 and 120.0 represents 39.44% of the distribution. Therefore, 66.78% (27.34 + 39.44 = 66.78) of the normal curve is between 88.0 and 120.0.

EXAMPLE 4. What is the percentage of area between a score of 123.0 and a score of 135.0 (see Figure 7.7)? Here again, we cannot obtain the answer directly. We must find the area between the mean and a score of 123.0 and subtract this from the area between the mean and a score of 135.0. The procedure is as follows:

Step 1. Find the z corresponding to 135.0:

$$z = \frac{(135.0 - 100.0)}{16.0} = 2.19$$

Step 2. Find the z corresponding to 123:

$$z = \frac{(123.0 - 100.0)}{16.0} = 1.44$$

Step 3. Find the required areas by referring to column B, Table A. The area between the mean and $z = 2.19$ is 48.57%, and the area between the mean and $z = 1.44$ is 42.51%.

Step 4. Subtract to obtain the area between 123.0 and 135.0:

$$48.57\% - 42.51\% = 6.06\%$$

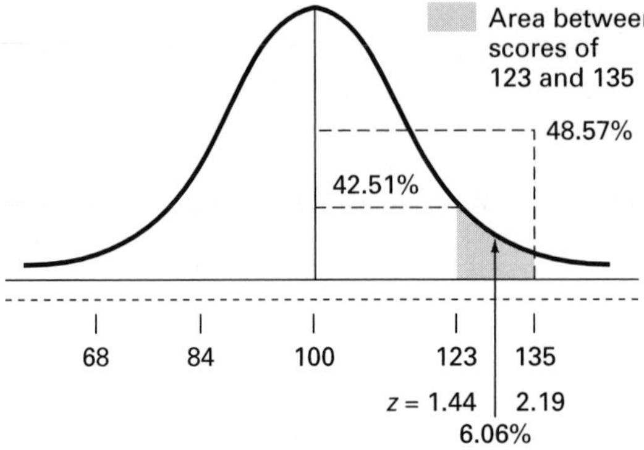

FIGURE 7.7

An illustration of example 4

The mean of the distribution is 100 and the standard deviation is 16.0. The observed scores are 135.0 and 123.0. Using the calculations described in the text, a score of 135.0 is equal to a z-score of 2.19. The area of the normal curve between 100.0 and 135.0 represents 48.57% of the distribution. A score of 123.0 is equal to a z-score of 1.44. The area of the normal curve between 100.0 and 123.0 represents 42.51% of the distribution. Therefore, 6.06% (48.57 − 42.51 = 6.06) of the normal curve is between 123.0 and 135.0.

EXAMPLE 5. We stated earlier that a transformation to z-scores permits us to compare an individual's position on one variable with her or his position on another. Let's look at this important use of z-scores.

On a standard aptitude test, Andrea obtained a score of 245.0 on the verbal scale and a score of 175.0 on the mathematics scale. The means and standard deviations of each of these normally distributed variables are:

Verbal test, $\mu = 220.0$, $s = 50.0$
Math test, $\mu = 150.0$, $\sigma = 25.0$

On which test did Andrea perform better?

All we need do is compare Andrea's z-score on each variable. Thus:

$$\text{Verbal } z = \frac{(245.0 - 220.0)}{50.0} = 0.50$$

$$\text{Math } z = \frac{(175.0 - 150.0)}{25.0} = 1.00$$

We conclude that, even though her raw score was lower on the math scale, she performed higher on the math scale than on the verbal scale. Her percentile rank is 84.13 on the math scale and 69.15 on the verbal scale.

EXAMPLE 6. In each of the preceding examples, we knew the mean, the standard deviation, and the value of the variable for which we wished to find the corresponding percentage of area. There are occasions when the percentage of area is known and we wish to find the value of the variable that yielded this percentage. To illustrate, imagine that you wish to join a highly selective intellectual society that requires that its members be in the upper 2% of the population in intelligence. The IQ test used for selection has a mean of 100.0 and a standard deviation of 16.0.

The first step is to find the value of z that cuts off the upper 2% (i.e., 0.0200) of the area under the standard normal curve. Referring to column C, Table A, we find that the area beyond a z of 2.05 excludes 2.02% of the area under the normal curve. This is sufficiently close for us to use this value in our calculations. Using equation (7.2), $X = z\sigma + \mu$ when the parameters are known or $X = zs + \overline{X}$ for normally distributed variables in which the sample standard deviation and mean are known, we find $X = 2.05(16.0) + 100.0 = 132.8$. Thus, a minimum IQ of 133.0 is needed to qualify for membership in this society. See Box 7.2 for an additional example.

BOX 7.2

DESIGNING SEAT SIZE IN COMMERCIAL CARRIERS: FOR COMFORT OR PROFIT?

Are you one of those rather wide-of-beam travelers who must gird your spirits for the next commercial airline flight (or take a trip on an intracity or intercity bus) because the seat width always seems to be about 2 inches shy of your comfort zone? Although measuring "beam widths" may not seem to be the most significant human enterprise, airlines may win or lose a fortune by a seemingly minor shift in the width of the passenger seats. To illustrate, if a given aircraft has 50 rows, 4 across, it can accommodate a maximum load of 200 passengers. However, if it can trim a few inches from each seat and a few more from the aisle, one more seat per row can be added, bringing the passenger capacity up to 250. That is a 25% increase $[(250 - 200)/200 \times 100 = 25\%]$ in seating capacity!

Let's assume that the "beam width" of airline passengers (including elbows) is normally distributed with a mean of 20 inches and a standard deviation of 2. Cheapflight Airlines finds that by reducing its old 20-inch seats by 3 inches and the aisle by 5 inches, it can accommodate five seats to a row. By doing so, it can reduce ticket fares considerably and increase the number of flights running at or near capacity.

Taking the opposite tack, Broadbeam Airlines decides to emphasize passenger comfort in its advertising campaign. By trimming 8 inches off the aisle, it can increase the seat width to 22 inches. However, its passenger capacity remains 200. Broadbeam justifies its higher fares in terms of its luxurious seating.

What percentage of the passengers in each airline will find the seat width comfortable?

Broadbeam Airlines:

$$z = (22 - 20)/2 = 1.00.$$

Presumably, all passengers with a $z \leq 1.00$ will luxuriate in posterior comfort. This comes to a generous 84.13% (50% + 34.13%).

Cheapflight Airlines:

$$z = (17 - 20)/2 = -1.5.$$

Only passengers with a $z \leq -1.50$ will find the seating capacity adequate. Referring to Table A, we find that the area beyond z is 0.0668. Thus, only about 7% of Cheapflight's passengers will emerge from the flight without severely pinched posteriors. About 93% will be at their wits' end.

Now, suppose another airline wanted to join the battle of the beams and base its advertising pitch on the claim that 97.5% of its passengers could sit in total comfort. How wide would the seats have to be to justify this claim?

(continued)

Notice that the problem here is the same as in example 6. We are given the desired percentage of area and would like to know the value of the variable that yields this percentage. The first step is to find the value of z that excludes 0.0250 (2.5%) of the area. Referring to column C in Table A, we find that the area beyond a z of 1.96 equals 0.0250. Using the equation $X = z\sigma + \mu$, we find $X = 1.96 \times 2 + 20 = 23.92$. In other words, the seats would have to be about 24 inches wide.

7.7 THE STANDARD DEVIATION AS AN ESTIMATE OF ERROR AND PRECISION

In the absence of any specific information, what is our best single basis for predicting a score that is obtained by any given individual? If the data are drawn from a normally distributed population, we find that the mean (or *any* measure of central tendency) is our best single predictor. The more compactly our scores are distributed about the mean, the smaller our errors will be in prediction, on the average. Conversely, the greater the spread or dispersion of scores about the mean, the greater will be our errors in prediction, on the average, when we use the mean to estimate or predict scores. Since the standard deviation reflects the dispersion of scores, it becomes, in a sense, an estimate of error. For the same reasons, the standard deviation is also a measure of precision. If two distributions have the same mean but different degrees of dispersion, the one with the smaller standard deviation provides more precise measures (i.e., measures closer to the mean), on the average.

To illustrate, imagine we are comparing two artillery units, Battery A and Battery B. A zero score means the shell was on target; a positive score means the shell went beyond the target, and a negative score indicates that it fell short of the target. Table 7.1 summarizes the results.

TABLE 7.1
Hypothetical scores made by two artillery batteries when firing at designated target

Distance from target (in meters)	Frequency: Battery A	Frequency: Battery B
200	2	0
150	4	1
100	5	5
50	7	10
0	9	13
−50	7	10
−100	5	5
−150	4	1
−200	2	0
	$N = 45$	$N = 45$
	$\overline{X} = 0$	$\overline{X} = 0$
	$s = 102.74$	$s = 65.83$*

*Although the mean accuracy of both batteries was identical, the shelling of Battery B showed less dispersion or scattering.

Although both batteries achieved the same mean, it is clear that more of the shells of Battery B landed close to the target than the shells of Battery A. In other words, the firing of Battery B was more precise. This greater precision is reflected in the lower standard deviation of Battery B.

7.8 INTERPRETING THE STANDARD DEVIATION

In Chapter 6, we noted that an interpretation of the standard deviation is dependent on an understanding of the normal distribution. Imagine two random samples, *A* and *B*, from a normally distributed population with a mean age of 40. A total of 100 persons are included in sample *A* and 100 persons in sample *B*. We find that the ages of the persons in the two samples are distributed as shown in Figure 7.8.

While both curves have a mean of 40, it is apparent that sample *A* exhibits more variability than sample *B*, as shown by their frequency curves and respective standard deviations of 14.0 and 11.7. But we can say much more about the two distributions in Figure 7.8. For instance, we know from Table A that 68.26 (2×34.13) percent of the persons in sample *A* are between the ages of 26 and 54 since these values are -1 and $+1$ standard deviation units from the mean ($40 + 14 = 54$; $40 - 14 = 26$ since $s_A = 14.0$). Recall that when we state that $s_A = 14.0$, we are saying that *one* standard deviation in sample *A* equals 14.0. By adding and subtracting one standard deviation (in this case it is 14.0 for sample A) to and from the mean of 40, we immediately know the ages equivalent to $z = +1$ and $z = -1$ since z scores are measured in standard deviation units. If you are interested in knowing the raw scores that are ± 2 standard deviations from the mean, move 28 (2×14.0) units to the right and left of the mean. Hence, the ages 12 and 68 are 2 standard deviations from the mean in sample *A*. Their z score equivalents are -2 and $+2$. Looking at Table A, you will find that 95.44 (2×47.72) percent of the persons in sample *A* are between the ages of 12 and 68.

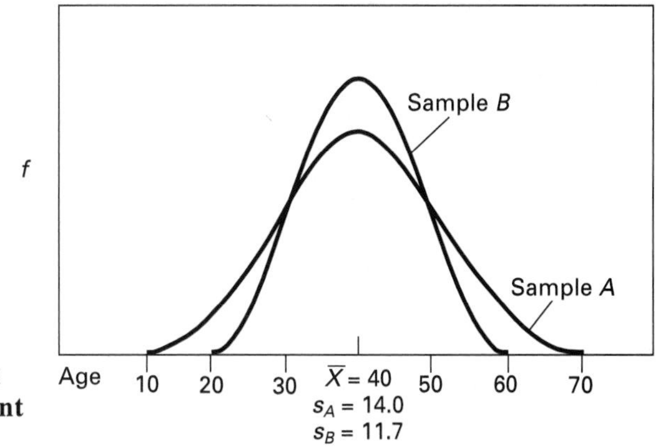

FIGURE 7.8
Two frequency curves with identical means but different standard deviations

For comparative purposes, consider sample *B* with its standard deviation of 11.7. The ages equivalent to $z = \pm 1$ can be calculated by adding 11.7 to the mean of 40 and subtracting 11.7 from the mean.

$$40 + 11.7 = 51.7$$
$$40 - 11.7 = 28.3$$

Whereas in sample *A* we found that the ages corresponding to $z = \pm 1$ were 26 and 54, we find that for sample *B* the ages are 28.3 and 51.7. This finding supports our earlier contention that sample *B* is more homogeneous (shows less variability) than sample *A*. Box 7.3 provides a summary discussion of interpreting aptitude tests using *z*-scores.

BOX 7.3

INTERPRETING STANDARDIZED APTITUDE TESTS

Table 7.2 shows the scores of Mary Cardinale on six scales of a standardized aptitude test. Also shown are the mean and the standard deviation of each scale. The conversion of each of Mary's scores into *z*-scores and percentile ranks is shown in Table 7.3.

Take note that Mary's raw score on logical reasoning is the second lowest of all her scores. Nevertheless, her percentile rank on this scale is her highest, exceeding 96% of the group against which the test was standardized. Conversely, her highest raw score, 105, was on the numerical reasoning scale, but her percentile rank was considerably lower than her percentile rank on the logical reasoning scale. How is it possible that a "high" raw score can be low and a "low" raw score can be high?

This example illustrates that performance is not necessarily judged on the basis of raw scores. What must be taken into account is the mean and the standard deviation of the comparison group on each scale of the aptitude test. Converting each score to a common scale of values (the *z*-scale) and a common reference standard (the standard normal curve) enables us to compare an individual's relative performance (percentile rank) on a diverse spectrum of abilities. Figure 7.9 shows a graph of Mary's raw scores and her relative performance (percentile rank) on several different measures of ability. Note again how misleading estimates of her abilities would be if you based your conclusions exclusively on her raw scores.

TABLE 7.2
The mean and standard deviation on six scales of a standardized test and the scores made by a single individual

	Clerical ability	Logical reasoning	Mechanical ability	Numerical reasoning	Spatial relations	Verbal fluency
Score	41	47	100	105	90	70
Mean	50	40	120	100	70	60
s	15	4	25	10	20	6

TABLE 7.3
Conversion of six scores on a standardized test to percentile ranks

Scale	*z*-score	Percentile rank
Clerical ability	(41 − 50)/15 = −0.60	27
Logical reasoning	(47 − 40)/4 = 1.75	96
Mechanical ability	(100 − 120)/25 = −0.80	21
Numerical reasoning	(105 − 100)/10 = 0.50	69
Spatial relations	(90 − 70)/20 = 1.00	84
Verbal fluency	(70 − 60)/6 = 1.67	95

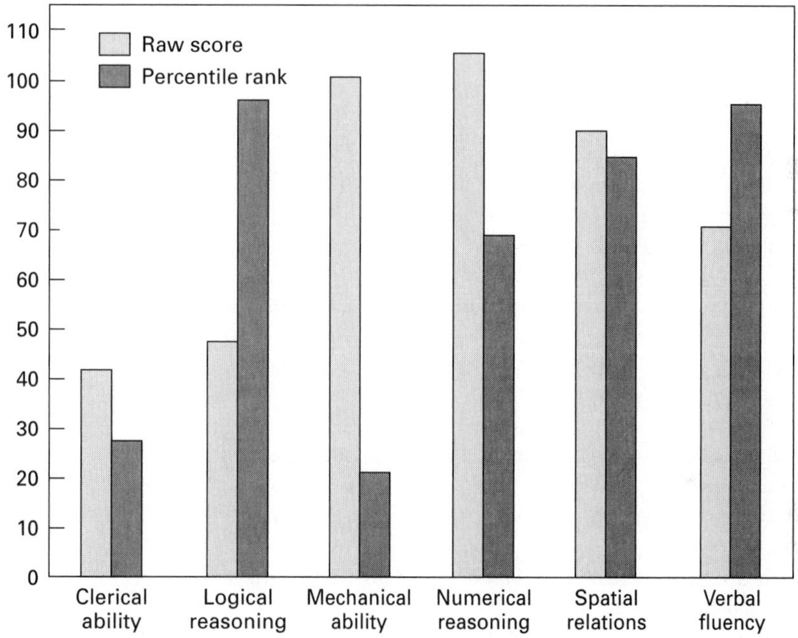

FIGURE 7.9
Bar graph of Mary Cardinale's relative performance on six scales of an aptitude test
The hatched bars show her raw scores, whereas the solid bars represent a measure based on relative performance (percentile rank).

SUMMARY

In this chapter, we demonstrated the value of the standard deviation for comparison of the dispersion of scores in different distributions of a variable, the interpretation of a score with respect to a single distribution, and the comparison of scores on two or more variables. We showed how to convert raw scores into units of the standard normal curve (transformation to *z* scores). Various characteristics of the standard normal curve were explained. A series of problems demonstrated the various applications of the conversion of normally distributed variables to z scores and z scores to raw scores.

We considered the standard deviation as an estimate of error and as an estimate of precision. Finally, we discussed the standard deviation as an interpretive tool.

TERMS TO REMEMBER

standard normal distribution A frequency distribution that has a mean of 0, a standard deviation of 1, and a total area equal to 1.00.

standard score (z) A score that represents the deviation of a specific score from the mean, expressed in standard deviation units.

EXERCISES

1. Given a normal distribution with a mean of 45.2 and a standard deviation of 10.4, find the standard score equivalents for the following scores:

(*a*) 55 (*c*) 45.2 (*e*) 68.4
(*b*) 41 (*d*) 31.5 (*f*) 18.9

2. Find the proportion of area under the normal curve between the mean and the following z scores:

(*a*) −2.05 (*c*) −0.25 (*e*) +1.65
(*b*) −1.90 (*d*) +0.40 (*f*) +1.96

3. Find the proportion of area under the normal curve beyond z:

(*a*) −2.05 (*c*) −0.25 (*e*) +1.65
(*b*) −1.90 (*d*) +0.40 (*f*) +1.96

4. Given a normal distribution based on 1,000 cases with a mean of 50 and a standard deviation of 10, find:

(*a*) The proportion of area and the number of cases *between* the mean and the following scores:
60 70 45 25

(*b*) The proportion of area and the number of cases *above* the following scores:
60 70 45 25 50

(*c*) The proportion of area and the number of cases *between* the following scores:
60–70 25–60 45–70 25–45

5. Below are a student's (Spiegel) scores, the mean, and the standard deviation on each of three normally distributed tests.

Test	μ	σ	Spiegel's score
Arithmetic	47.2	4.8	53
Verbal comprehension	64.6	8.3	71
Geography	75.4	11.7	72

(*a*) Convert each of Spiegel's test scores to standard scores.
(*b*) On which test did Spiegel do the best? The worst?
(*c*) Spiegel's score in arithmetic was surpassed by what proportion of students? His score in verbal comprehension? In geography?
(*d*) What assumption must be made to answer the preceding questions?
(*e*) Spiegel's friend Sue had a z score of -1.1 on the geography test. What was her raw score?

6. On a normally distributed mathematics aptitude test, for females:

$$\mu = 60, \qquad \sigma = 10$$

and for males:

$$\mu = 64, \qquad \sigma = 8.$$

(*a*) Arthur obtained a score of 62. What is his percentile rank relative to the male and female scores?
(*b*) Helen's percentile rank is 73 relative to the female scores. What is her percentile rank relative to the male scores?
(*c*) In comparison with other students of their own sex, who did better, Arthur or Helen?

7. If frequency curves were constructed for each of the following, which do you feel would approximate a normal curve?

(*a*) Heights of a large representative sample of adult American males.
(*b*) Means of a large number of samples with a fixed N (say, $N = 100$) drawn from a normally distributed population of scores.
(*c*) Weights in ounces of ears of corn selected randomly from a cornfield.
(*d*) Annual income in dollars of the breadwinner of a large number of American families selected at random.
(*e*) Weight in ounces of all fish caught in a popular fishing resort in a season.

8. In a normal distribution with $\mu = 72$ and $\sigma = 12$:

(*a*) What is the score at the 25th percentile?
(*b*) What is the score at the 75th percentile?
(*c*) What is the score at the 9th decile?
(*d*) Find the percent of cases scoring above 80.
(*e*) Find the percent of cases scoring below 66.
(*f*) Between what scores do the middle 50% of all cases lie?

9. Answer exercise 8(a) through (f), for:

(*a*) $\mu = 72$ and $\sigma = 8$
(*b*) $\mu = 72$ and $\sigma = 4$
(*c*) $\mu = 72$ and $\sigma = 2$

10. Given the following information, determine whether Larry did better on Test I or Test II. On which test did Mindy do better?

	Test I	**Test II**
μ	500	24
σ	40	1.4
Larry's scores	550	26
Mindy's scores	600	25

11. Are all sets of z scores normally distributed? Why or why not?

12. You have just completed interviewing 75 ministers. Initial calculations indicate that the number of years of formal education they have completed is normally distributed with a mean of 13.4 and a standard deviation of 3.0.

(*a*) How many years of education must a minister have completed to be in the top decile? (*Hint:* Find z at the 90th percentile.)
(*b*) How many years of education must a minister have completed to be one standard deviation above the mean?
(*c*) Approximately how many ministers will be within ± 2 z scores of the mean?
(*d*) Interpret the standard deviation for this problem. What does it tell you?

13. Your roommate has just received the results of her Graduate Record Examination in the mail. The mean of the verbal section was 510, the standard deviation 102, and the scores were normally distributed. Her reported score was 640, but the computer did not print her percentile rank. She has never had a statistics course and needs your assistance to calculate her percentile rank and help her understand the meaning of her score. State your explanation briefly. Feel free to use visual examples to supplement your answer.

14. Several of your friends also took the Graduate Record Examination discussed in exercise 13. Compute the z score and the percentile rank for each of the following scores.

Recall that:

$$\overline{X} = 510 \quad \text{and} \quad s = 102$$

X	z score	Percentile rank
270		
780		
500		
410		
565		

15. (*a*) Which of the scores in exercise 14 would place your friends in the top 10% of those who took the test?
(*b*) The upper quartile?
(*c*) Above the median?
(*d*) In the lowest quartile?
(*e*) What percent of the area under the curve lies between the lowest and highest score?
(*f*) Compute the two scores that lie equidistant from the mean and include 95% of the area under the curve.

16. Calculate the z score for each of the following:

(*a*) A score of 36 on a police sergeant's promotion examination, given a mean of 25 and a standard deviation of 3.1.
(*b*) An IQ of 110, given a mean of 100 and a standard deviation of 15.
(*c*) A height of 6 feet 5 inches in the National Basketball Association, given a mean of 6 feet 6 inches and a standard deviation of 5 inches. (*Hint:* Convert to inches.)
(*d*) A job satisfaction score of 59, given a mean of 75 and a standard deviation of 10.

17. Common colds normally require 7 to 10 days for complete remission. A friend who is a health-food advocate read that sucking on a zinc gluconate tablet three times a day is supposed to reduce the recovery time. She knows you are taking a statistics course and needs your help analyzing the following data she has collected from friends who used zinc tablets to recover quickly from a cold. They reported the following number of days to recover completely:

6	7	6
4	4	3
7	5	5
5	5	7
8	6	9
3	8	4
2	5	5
6	4	6

Assume the data approximate a normal curve.
(*a*) Compute the mean and standard deviation.
(*b*) Do the zinc tablets appear to work?
(*c*) How many recovery days place the patient at the 25th percentile?
(*d*) Again, assuming a normal curve, what proportion required four days or less? What proportion required seven or more days?

18. Is there more than one normal distribution?

19. Refer to Box 7.2. The values of μ and σ were given for the populations and included both males and females. Suppose the mean beam is 18 for females, 22 for males, and $\sigma = 2$ for both populations.

(*a*) What percentage of males and females flying Cheapflight will be comfortable?
(*b*) What percentage of males and females flying Broadbeam will be comfortable?

20. How wide would the seats have to be to achieve the comfort zone for 90.32% of the (*a*) females? (*b*) males?

21. Following are the means and standard deviations of five different normally distributed tests:

Test	μ	σ
A	50	10
B	50	20
C	100	15
D	100	10
E	120	30

(*a*) Relative to which test is a score of 70 the highest?
(*b*) Relative to which test is a score of 85 the lowest?

22. Refer to exercise 21. Monica obtained the following scores on each of the tests $A = 60$, $B = 80$, $C = 115$, $D = 112$, $E = 145$.

(*a*) Find her percentile rank on each test.
(*b*) On which test did she score the highest?
(*c*) On which test did she score the lowest?

23. In what sense can the standard deviation be regarded as a measure of precision?

CHAPTER 8

An Introduction to Contingency Tables

8.1 INTRODUCTION

In Chapters 3 to 7, we have considered one variable at a time, focusing on the frequency distribution, percentiles, measures of central tendency, and measures of dispersion. We now turn to examining the statistical relationship between two variables.

Social scientists are very interested in discovering how strongly two or more variables are related to each other in order to understand and predict behavior. Consider the following examples: In what manner is the variable years of educational attainment related to annual income? Are additional years of education a wise investment in terms of a person's potential earning power? Is a person's choice of leisure activities determined by his or her social class? To what extent is group cohesiveness a function of work group size? Is interest in politics related to a woman's parents' political involvement? To what extent is the "welfare experience" shared by two or more generations within a family?

8.2
DEPENDENT AND INDEPENDENT VARIABLES

All of the questions can be answered by analyzing two variables simultaneously. A *bivariate* or two-variable analysis normally involves specifying a dependent and an independent variable. The **dependent variable** (symbolized by Y) is the variable that is being predicted or explained. It is dependent on the **independent variable** (symbolized by X) which is the predictor variable. In an experimental context, the dependent variable is referred to as the criterion variable and the independent variable as the experimental or treatment variable. In the videotape instructional example outlined in Chapter 1, the instruction technique (lecture versus videotape of the lecture) would be the independent or experimental variable (X) and the students' test scores would be the dependent or criterion variable (Y).

Consider the relationship between marital status and employment status of U.S. women. It used to be fairly easy to predict the likelihood of a woman holding a job if we knew her marital status, because married women seldom worked outside the home. Such a relationship can be diagrammed as shown in Figure 8.1.

Marital status is the independent or predictor variable and employment status is the dependent variable or the variable we wish to predict. The arrow indicates that marital status hypothetically exerts an influence on employment status. Whether a variable is designated the independent variable or the dependent variable is determined by its usage. Marital status could be a dependent variable if we wished to predict it from one's age. Or employment status could be used to predict an adult's self-esteem, in which case it would be the independent variable and self-esteem the dependent variable. The point is that a variable must be placed into a framework or research situation before it can be designated as either independent or dependent.

8.3
THE BIVARIATE CONTINGENCY TABLE

You learned about frequency distributions in Chapter 3. We will now return to that topic as we begin to consider the relationship between two variables. The U.S. Department of Labor conducts national studies of employment patterns among U.S. women. Using data from these studies, let us consider the relationship between employment status and marital status, which was diagrammed in Figure 8.1. The tabulations and frequency distribution for these variables are presented in Table 8.1. The arrows in Table 8.1 indicate that the information from the tabulations of marital status and employment status allow us to construct the frequency distributions which are shown below the tabulations.

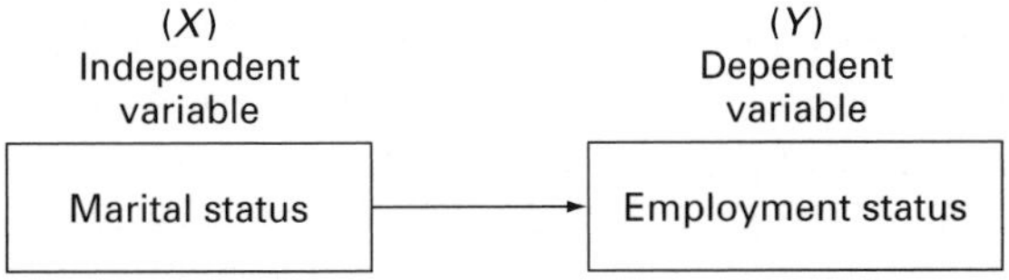

FIGURE 8.1
Relationship between marital status and employment status

TABLE 8.1
Tabulations and frequency distributions for marital status and employment status

Respondent	Marital status	Employment status
1	Divorced	Employed
2	Never married	Not employed
3	Married	Not employed
⋮	⋮	⋮
200	Married	Employed

Marital status	Frequency	%
Never married	(35)	17.5
Married	(125)	62.5
Divorced	(15)	7.5
Widowed	(25)	12.5
Total	(200)	100.0

Employment status	Frequency	%
Employed	(98)	49.0
Not employed	(102)	51.0
Total	(200)	100.0

The percentage of cases within each category reflects the responses from the actual national samples. However, to simplify the presentation, the distributions presented are based on only 200 responses. The frequency distribution is based on personal interviews with each of the 200 women included in this presentation. Among the 200 women presented, 98 (49%) were employed and 102 (51%) were not. Table 8.1 also shows that 35 respondents were never married, 125 were married, 15 were divorced, and 25 were widowed. Table 8.1 does not conveniently tell us the marital status of the 98 employed women nor of the 102 women not employed. We wish to know if a woman's marital status (the independent variable) might serve as a useful predictor of her employment status (the dependent variable).

Several other variables could have been considered as predictors of employment status, including the woman's financial needs, educational attainment, the number of children in her home, and so forth; however, here we seek a partial understanding of why some women work and others do not by examining only the relationship between employment status and marital status. The simultaneous use of two or more predictor variables is discussed in Chapter 11.

Table 8.2 presents a bivariate distribution or cross-tabulation of the two variables. The 21 women in the upper left-hand cell of Table 8.2 have never been married *and* are presently employed. We also can say that the 21 of the 35 never married respondents are employed and 14 are not employed. Had the tabulations of the individual respondents in Table 8.1 been shown in their entirety, we would be able to identify the 21 women whose pattern of responses was "never married-employed." We now have available the **conditional distribution** or **cross-tabulation** of the two variables, and we can examine the distribution of the categories of one variable under the differing conditions or categories of another.

A **contingency table** shows the cross-tabulation or the joint distribution of two variables. Table 8.2 has been presented in the manner generally used by social

TABLE 8.2
Contingency table summarizing the relationship between employment status and marital status

(*Y*) Employment status	(*X*) Marital status: Never married	Married	Divorced	Widowed	Total
Employed	21	60	11	6	98
Not employed	14	65	4	19	102
Total	35	125	15	25	$N = 200$

scientists. Normally, the independent variable (X) is the column variable and is placed at the top of the table; the dependent variable (Y) is the row variable and is placed to the left of the table. However, this convention is not followed by all social scientists, and it is important that you carefully examine tables to avoid misinterpretation. (Box 8.1, for example, includes a complex table that is not presented in a conventional manner—see Table 8.3.) The boxes or cells contain the cell frequencies (e.g., 21, 60, 11, 6, etc.) and/or the cell percentages. The column and row totals of the contingency table are referred to as **marginals.** There are as many column marginals as there are categories of the variable placed at the top of the table, and their values are the column totals (35, 125, 15, and 25). The row marginals are the row totals (98 and 102). Marginals provide a convenient summary of the distribution of cases for each of the variables. Indeed, you probably have noticed that the marginals in Table 8.2 are equivalent to the frequency distributions in Table 8.1.

Table 8.2 is a 2×4 table (read "2 by 4 table") because there are two rows and four columns. Tables can have any number of rows and columns, depending on the number of categories of the variables.

8.4 PERCENTAGING CONTINGENCY TABLES

Contingency tables can be percentaged in three ways, depending on the base (denominator) that is used.* Table 8.5 illustrates the three ways of percentaging a table. (See also Box 8.2 for an additional example.)

The most common way of percentaging a table (assuming that the independent variable is the column variable) is that of *percentaging down* as in Table 8.4(a) where you see that the percentages in each of the marital status columns total 100%. For example, 60% and 40% in the never married column total 100%. We typically percentage down because we are normally interested in assessing the effect of the independent variable on the dependent variable. When we percentage down, the

* In Chapter 2, you learned that a proportion is calculated by dividing a quantity in one category by the total of all the categories, and that a proportion can be converted to a percentage when multiplied by 100.

column marginals (35, 125, 15, and 25) become the base (the denominator) with which the percentages are calculated. Focusing again on the upper left-hand cell, we can calculate the 60.0% of the never married respondents are employed by dividing

BOX 8.1

THE PRESENTATION OF A COMPLEX TABLE

It was noted in Section 8.3 that the independent variable is normally presented as the column variable and the dependent variable as the row variable. This convention is not followed in this instance where we see that the placement of age, the independent variable, and type of college enrollment, the dependent variable, is reversed. Focusing first on the top panel, it is apparent that the table has been percentaged down (on the dependent variable). The row marginal percentages are presented in the far left-hand column under "all." Thus, 21.1% of the 13,898,000 college students enrolled in the fall of 1993 were 18 or 19 years of age. We can examine the status of the 18- and 19-year-old students by looking from left to right within the row marked 18 and 19. We see, for example, that 36.5% of the 18- and 19-year-old students were enrolled full-time in two-year undergraduate programs and 31.5% were full-time students in four year colleges.

The middle panel includes the 6,324,000 men and the bottom panel includes the 7,574,000 women who were combined with the men in the top panel. These two panels allow us to contrast men and women with respect to age and type of college enrollment. Do you feel there are enough differences in the table to warrant analyzing men and women separately? Why or why not?

TABLE 8.3
College enrollment by age of students, fall 1993

		Undergraduate					
		2-year		4-year		Graduate	
	All	Full-time	Part-time	Full-time	Part-time	Full-time	Part-time
All students							
15 to 17	0.9%	0.9%	0.8%	1.4%	0.4%	0.0%	0.0%
18 and 19.....	21.1	36.5	11.0	31.5	5.1	0.3	0.0
20 and 21.....	19.7	21.2	11.1	33.2	8.1	1.0	0.2
22 to 24	18.2	14.3	15.0	19.3	19.0	34.9	11.4
25 to 29	13.4	9.1	17.8	6.9	19.6	31.8	20.9
30 to 34	8.8	6.7	13.6	3.0	15.3	14.0	18.4
35 to 39	7.0	6.1	12.6	2.3	11.3	9.3	13.9
40 to 44	5.0	2.0	8.1	1.2	10.6	4.2	15.2
45 to 49	3.3	2.3	4.8	0.6	6.0	2.0	11.6
50 to 54	1.6	0.7	2.4	0.3	3.1	1.2	5.5
55 to 59	0.5	0.1	0.8	0.2	0.6	0.7	1.5
60 to 64	0.2	0.0	0.5	0.0	0.3	0.6	0.5
65 and older...	0.4	0.0	1.4	0.1	0.6	0.0	1.0
Number of students ..	13,898,000	2,274,000	1,922,000	5,720,000	1,591,000	1,025,000	1,366,000

(continued)

(concluded)

		Undergraduate					
		2-year		4-year		Graduate	
	All	**Full-time**	**Part-time**	**Full-time**	**Part-time**	**Full-time**	**Part-time**
Men							
15 to 17	0.8%	0.7%	1.1%	1.2%	0.3%	0.0%	0.0%
18 and 19.....	21.1	38.4	12.1	29.4	5.6	0.0	0.0
20 and 21.....	20.7	21.6	15.0	32.6	9.8	0.3	0.4
22 to 24	21.3	18.1	18.1	22.6	20.3	34.4	12.0
25 to 29	13.8	8.3	15.1	8.5	23.0	30.7	20.5
30 to 34	8.4	4.8	13.4	2.3	17.5	15.7	21.6
35 to 39	6.0	3.4	11.9	1.7	11.3	10.5	13.4
40 to 44	3.7	1.5	5.3	1.0	6.7	4.0	15.4
45 to 49	2.3	2.7	3.9	0.3	2.0	2.4	10.0
50 to 54	1.0	0.4	1.8	0.1	2.5	0.7	4.5
55 to 59	0.3	0.0	0.7	0.2	0.2	0.7	0.9
60 to 64	0.2	0.0	0.3	0.1	0.2	0.5	0.5
65 and older...	0.3	0.0	1.3	0.0	0.6	0.0	0.7
Number of students ..	6,324,000	1,006,000	742,000	2,806,000	640,000	579,000	551,000
Women							
15 to 17	0.9%	1.2%	0.7%	1.5%	0.4%	0.0%	0.0%
18 and 19.....	21.0	34.8	10.3	33.6	4.7	0.7	0.0
20 and 21.....	18.8	21.0	8.6	33.7	6.9	1.8	0.0
22 to 24	15.7	11.3	13.1	16.1	18.1	35.9	10.9
25 to 29	13.1	9.8	19.6	5.3	17.5	33.2	21.1
30 to 34	9.1	8.2	13.7	3.7	14.0	11.9	16.2
35 to 39	7.9	8.2	13.1	2.8	11.4	7.6	14.1
40 to 44	6.0	2.4	9.8	1.4	13.1	4.7	15.0
45 to 49	4.1	2.0	5.4	0.9	8.7	1.6	12.8
50 to 54	2.0	0.9	2.8	0.6	3.5	1.8	6.1
55 to 59	0.6	0.2	0.9	0.3	0.9	0.7	2.1
60 to 64	0.2	0.0	0.6	0.0	0.5	0.7	0.5
65 and older...	0.4	0.0	1.4	0.1	0.4	0.0	1.2
Number of students ..	7,574,000	1,268,000	1,179,000	2,914,000	951,000	446,000	815,000

Note: The figures are based on a Census Bureau survey of 60,000 households conducted in October 1993. The statistics may differ from enrollment data compiled by the U.S. Department of Education because of differences in survey methodology. Because of rounding, figures may not add to 100%.
Source: Census Bureau.

21 by 35, which is the column marginal for the never married respondents. *Percentaging down* is also referred to as *percentaging on the independent variable* when the independent variable is the column variable. Percentaging down allows us to determine the effect of the independent variable by comparing across the percentages within a row, that is, by comparing people in different categories of the independent variable. In Table 8.4(a) we see, by comparing across the employed row, that 60.0% of the never married respondents are employed, 48.0% of the married respondents are employed, as are 73.0% of the divorced respondents and 24.0% of the widowed respondents. Thus, we see that the overall relationship between the two variables is consistent with what we might assume logically.

BOX 8.2

A COMPUTER GENERATED CONTINGENCY TABLE

The Statistical Package for the Social Sciences (SPSS) was used to create the accompanying contingency table which is based on a national sample (The General Social Survey) of 1,500 persons in 1993. It shows the relationship between political party identification (the dependent variable) and the respondent's highest degree (the independent variable). The row marginals and percentages allow to see at a glance that 34.2% (511/1,496) of the respondents are Democrats, 34.4% (514/1,496) are Independents and 31.5% (471/1,496) are Republicans. The column marginals summarize the categories of the independent variable, highest degree. We see, for example, that those who did not complete high school total 18.6% (279/1,496) and persons with a high school degree comprise over one-half (52.1%) of the sample. Missing observations total 4; thus, information on the party identification and/or degree of four respondents was unavailable.

Notice the terms, "count," "row %," "col. %," "total %," in the upper left-hand corner of the table. They are your guide to the position and meaning of the numbers in each cell of the table. Count indicates the number of cases in each cell. Let's examine the upper right-hand cell in which 37 respondents have a graduate degree and are Democrats. Just below the count in the same cell we see the row percentage, 7.2%, which indicates that 7.2% (37/511) of the Democrats hold graduate degrees. Next, the column percentage indicates that 32.7% (37/113) of those persons with graduate degrees are Democrats. The final entry in the cell, the total percentage, indicates that 2.5% (37/1,496) have graduate degrees *and* are Democrats.

Does highest degree, our independent variable, have an effect on political party identification? Let's focus on the column percentages, which appear in boldface type to facilitate reviewing the effect of the independent variable on the dependent variable. Look across the Democrat, Independent, and Republican rows from left to right and note any differences in trends (see Table 8.4). Notice that among people with high school education or less, the least popular party choice is Republican, but among people with bachelors or graduate degrees, Republican is the most popular party choice. Based on these data, it appears that the more formal education people have, the more likely they are to identify with the Republican Party, and the less schooling they've had, the more likely they are to identify with the Democratic Party or as an independent.

TABLE 8.4
Political party identification by highest degree

Party ID	Count Row % Col. % Total %	Degree Less than high school 1	 High school 2	 Junior college 3	 Bachelor 4	 Graduate 5	Row Total
Democrat	1	107 20.9 **38.4** 7.2	274 53.6 **35.1** 18.3	29 5.7 **32.2** 1.9	64 12.5 **27.4** 4.3	37 7.2 **32.7** 2.5	511 34.2
Independent	2	98 19.1 **35.1** 6.6	282 54.9 **36.2** 18.9	32 6.2 **35.6** 2.1	67 13.0 **28.6** 4.5	35 6.8 **31.0** 2.3	514 34.4
Republican	3	74 15.7 **26.5** 4.9	224 47.6 **28.7** 15.0	29 6.2 **32.2** 1.9	103 21.9 **44.0** 6.9	41 8.7 **36.3** 2.7	471 31.5
	Column Total	279 18.6	780 52.1	90 6.0	234 15.6	113 7.6	1,496 100.0

Number of missing observations: 4

TABLE 8.5
Three ways of percentaging a contingency table

Original table

(*Y*) Employment status	(*X*) Marital status: Never married	Married	Divorced	Widowed	Total
Employed	21	60	11	6	98
Not employed	14	65	4	19	102
Total	35	125	15	25	$N = 200$

(a) Percentaging down using column marginals as the base

(*Y*) Employment status	(*X*) Marital status: Never married	Married	Divorced	Widowed
Employed	60.0%	48.0%	73.3%	24.0%
Not employed	40.0%	52.0%	26.7%	76.0%
Total	100.0%	100.0%	100.0%	100.0%

(b) Percentaging across using the row marginals as the base

(*Y*) Employment status	(*X*) Marital status: Never married	Married	Divorced	Widowed	Total
Employed	21.4%	61.2%	11.2%	6.1%	99.9%*
Not employed	13.7%	63.7%	3.9%	18.6%	99.9%*

* Does not add to 100.0% due to rounding error.

(c) Percentaging on the total using the total number of cases as the base

(*Y*) Employment status	(*X*) Marital status: Never married	Married	Divorced	Widowed	Total
Employed	10.5%	30.0%	5.5%	3.0%	
Not employed	7.0%	32.5%	2.0%	9.5%	
Total					100.0%

Percentaging across, as illustrated in Table 8.4(b), means the row marginals are used as the base and that the percentages in both of the employment status rows total 100%. We see that 21.4% of the employed respondents have never married, whereas 13.7% of those respondents who are not employed have never married. Rather than percentaging down and comparing across as we did in Table 8.4(a), we now are percentaging across and comparing up and down. One value of percentaging across in Table 8.4(b) is that a profile of the employed versus the not employed respondents can be established in terms of their marital status. Such a usage does *not* provide us with any indication of the extent to which the independent variable affects the dependent variable.

A third method of percentaging uses the total number of cases as the base; therefore, the sum of all the cell percentages is 100%. Percentaging on the total (200) as in Table 8.4(c) offers yet another interpretation of the data. The 10.5% figure in the upper left-hand cell indicates that 10.5% or 21 of the 200 respondents have never married *and* are employed. The joint percentage distribution that results from percentaging on the total, like the second method, also does *not* allow for determining the influence of the independent variable on the dependent variable and is rarely presented; however, it is an appropriate method of percentaging in certain instances. (See Statistics in Action 8.1, p. 163.)

8.5 EXISTENCE, DIRECTION, AND STRENGTH OF A RELATIONSHIP

We are now ready to consider whether two variables are statistically related and, if so, in what manner. Table 8.6 illustrates five unique relationships between family income and marital satisfaction. Family income is the independent variable because it is used to predict marital satisfaction, the dependent variable.

Labeling the categories of ordinal or interval scale variables normally follows a standard convention.* The lowest category of the independent variable (the column variable) is placed at the left, and the highest category of the independent variable is placed at the right. When labeling the dependent variable (the row variable), the highest category is placed at the top and the lowest category at the bottom.† You are cautioned that this convention is not followed by all social scientists; therefore, you should examine all tables carefully before interpreting the data.

Comparison of the conditional distribution of the two variables determines whether a relationship exists between the variables. In Table 8.6(a), for instance, all the conditional relationships are identical in that 60% of the low-income marriages are characterized as highly satisfying, as are 60% of the high-income marriages. There is also no difference when we compare percentages across the low marital satisfaction row; therefore, knowing a couple's income does not help us predict their

---

* The placement of the categories of a nominal-level variable in a contingency table is determined by the user's personal preference because the categories are not ordered.

† The placement of the variables and variable categories corresponds to other statistical graphs including the scatter diagrams presented in Chapters 9 and 10.

TABLE 8.6
Illustration of five types of relationships in contingency tables

(a) No relationship

(Y) Marital satisfaction	(X) Family income: Low	High
High	60%	60%
Low	40%	40%
Total	100%	100%

(b) Positive relationship

(Y) Marital satisfaction	(X) Family income: Low	High
High	40%	60%
Low	60%	40%
Total	100%	100%

(c) Negative relationship

(Y) Marital satisfaction	(X) Family income: Low	High
High	60%	40%
Low	40%	60%
Total	100%	100%

(d) Perfect positive relationship

(Y) Marital satisfaction	(X) Family income: Low	High
High	0%	100%
Low	100%	0%
Total	100%	100%

(e) Perfect negative relationship

(Y) Marital satisfaction	(X) Family income: Low	High
High	100%	0%
Low	0%	100%
Total	100%	100%

marital satisfaction. Stated another way, income and marital satisfaction are unrelated in Table 8.6(a). The difference in these percentages (0% in both instances), which was calculated by comparing the percentages within the categories of the dependent variable between the two extreme categories of the independent variable, is referred to as the **percentage difference** or **epsilon (ϵ)**. A relationship is said to exist between two variables when one or more of the epsilons are not equal to 0.

Table 8.6(b) has also been percentaged down due to the placement of the independent variable. Comparing the percentages across the high category of marital satisfaction, we note a 20% percentage difference. Forty percent of the low-income marriages and 60% of the high-income marriages reportedly are highly satisfying; thus, epsilon equals 20. The reverse is true upon comparing the percentages across the low category of marital satisfaction where we see that a larger percentage (60%) of the low-income marriages are characterized by low marital satisfaction than high-income marriages (40%); therefore, epsilon equals 20. We can conclude that income has a moderate **positive relationship** with marital satisfaction. Higher-income couples are more likely to report higher marital satisfaction than lower-income couples.

Relationships between two variables can be either positive or negative. A positive relationship is one in which high scores on one variable tend to be associated with high scores on the other variable and, conversely, low scores on one variable tend to be associated with low scores on the other variable. Naturally, we cannot specify the direction of a relationship when one or both of the variables are nominal level, as in Table 8.2. If the variables are not measured at the ordinal level, we can only speak of the existence and strength of a relationship.

Table 8.6(c) provides an example of a **negative relationship.** Variables are said to be negatively related when high scores on one variable tend to be accompanied by low scores on the other. Conversely, low scores on one variable tend to be associated with high scores on the other. We see in Table 8.6(c) that high-income marriages tend to be less satisfying than low-income marriages. The variables have a moderate, negative relationship.

The strength of a relationship can range from nonexistent to perfect. A **nonexistent relationship** is one in which knowledge of the independent variable does not improve our prediction of the dependent variable or when the variables are unrelated, as in Table 8.6(a). A **perfect relationship** is one in which knowledge of the independent variable allows a perfect prediction of the dependent variable or vice versa. Table 8.6(d) presents a *perfect positive relationship* between family income and marital satisfaction and Table 8.6(e) shows a *perfect negative relationship.*

8.6 INTRODUCTION TO MEASURES OF ASSOCIATION FOR CONTINGENCY TABLES

Several measures of association appropriate for contingency tables are presented in the remainder of this chapter, none of which requires that we make assumptions about the population distribution. Those measures that have been developed specifically for nominal-level data provide a measure of the strength of the relationship. The measures for ordinal-level or interval-level data include both a measure of the strength and the direction of the relationship.

All of the measures are either symmetric or asymmetric. **Symmetric measures of association** make no distinction between the independent and dependent variable. Symmetric measures provide a single summary value of mutual or two-way association. If we wished to establish the relationship between two items in a job satisfaction scale, a symmetric measure of association would be appropriate. We would be interested only in determining the relationship between the two items, neither of which would be classified as independent or dependent.

STATISTICS IN ACTION 8.1
Curiosity Is Dangerous to More than Cats: Finding Column, Row, and Total Percentages

Take the problem of the seemingly insatiable curiosity of children. Their explorations of the worlds of sight, smell, sound, and touch often get them into serious difficulties. Look at Table 8.7, which summarizes a study conducted on 950 children who had ingested products containing hydrocarbons. From the results, we can learn what dangerous hydrocarbons are most commonly ingested by children and how often hospitalization is required. Armed with such knowledge, community agencies can often undertake educational and preventive programs that are targeted on both careless adults and offending substances.

TABLE 8.7
Frequency of children hospitalized and not hospitalized following ingestion of substances containing hydrocarbons

	Substance ingested							
Outcome	Cleaning fluids	Furniture polish	Gasoline	Kerosene	Lighter fluid	Paint thinner	Other	Total
Hospitalized	6	48	28	12	23	23	10	150
Nonhospitalized	24	312	128	72	112	88	64	800

$N = 950$

Source: Anas, N., V. Namasthoni, and M. Ginsburg, "Criteria for Hospitalizing Children Who Have Ingested Products Containing Hydrocarbons," *Journal of the American Medical Association* 246, no. 8 (1981).

By looking across the "hospitalized" row, we see that furniture polish is the most frequent offender, followed by gasoline, lighter fluid, and paint thinner. Reading across the "nonhospitalized" row, we see that most cases (800) do not require hospitalization.

Prepare tables showing:

1. The column percentages, or percentage on the independent variable. (*Hint:* First add the hospitalized and nonhospitalized to obtain the column marginals.)
2. The row percentages.
3. The total percentages.
4. Looking at the raw data, identify the substance that accounted for the largest number of hospitalization cases. Which accounted for the least number?
5. Looking at Table (a), identify the substance that is most likely to result in hospitalization. Which substance is least likely to result in hospitalization?
6. Looking at Table (b), which substance accounted for the greatest percentage of total hospitalizations? Which accounted for the least?
7. On the basis of the consideration of all ways of calculating percentages, which substances appear to be most important to keep out of reach of children?

ANSWERS

1. Table (a) Column percentages

Outcome	Cleaning fluids	Furniture polish	Gasoline	Kerosene	Lighter fluid	Paint thinner	Other
Hospitalized	20	13	18	14	17	21	14
Nonhospitalized	80	87	82	86	83	79	86
	100%	100%	100%	100%	100%	100%	100%

2. Table (b) Row percentages

Outcome	Cleaning fluids	Furniture polish	Gasoline	Kerosene	Lighter fluid	Paint thinner	Other	Total
Hospitalized	4	32	19	8	15	15	7	100%
Nonhospitalized	3	39	16	9	14	11	8	100%

3. Table (c) Total percentages

Outcome	Cleaning fluids	Furniture polish	Gasoline	Kerosene	Lighter fluid	Paint thinner	Other	Total
Hospitalized	1	5	3	1	2	2	1	
Nonhospitalized	3	33	13	8	12	9	7	
								100%

4. Furniture polish produces the greatest number of hospitalizations and cleaning fluids produce the least. Looking only at the raw data, we might be tempted to assert that furniture polish is the most dangerous substance and cleaning fluid is the least.

5. Paint thinner is most likely to result in hospitalization (21% of the time) and furniture polish is least likely (13% of the time).

6. When we compute the row percentages, we find that ingesting furniture polish leads to the greatest percentage of hospitalizations and cleaning fluids leads to the least.

7. From the point of view of accessibility, it is apparent that many children have easy access to furniture polishes. Table (c) reveals that 38% (5 + 33) of all cases involved furniture polishes. However, Table (a) shows that furniture polishes produced a relatively low rate of hospitalization among children ingesting these products (13%). Paint thinner is both fairly accessible [11% of all cases—see Table (c)] and leads to the highest rate of hospitalization [21%—see Table (a)]. Table (c) indicates that cleaning fluids are least accessible (4% of all ingestions), but lead to a 20% hospitalization rate [see Table (a)]. So, there is no simple answer except all those substances are potentially dangerous—some because of the sheer numbers of children who ingest them and others because of their inherent danger once ingested.

An **asymmetric measure of association** is a summary value of one-way association and requires that the independent and dependent variables be specified. Two summary values are available when an asymmetric statistic is calculated: One value results from designating the row variable as independent, and a second value results from designating the column variable as independent.* An ordinal-level asymmetric measure of association would be an appropriate measure to use if the column variable were income and the row variable were quality of health care. In this special instance, you might wish to examine the relationship between these variables, first assuming that income has a casual effect upon quality of health care, and second assuming that quality of health care has a casual effect upon income. A summary statistic could be computed for each of these two relationships.

8.7 NOMINAL MEASURES OF ASSOCIATION: LAMBDA

Computing percentage differences, or epsilon (ϵ), for data in contingency form is only one way of determining the existence of a relationship between two variables. In addition, social scientists are interested in the degree to which a variable is helpful in predicting an attitude or behavior as measured by a second variable. **Lambda (λ)** is a statistic used to evaluate the usefulness of one variable in predicting another. It helps answer the question: Do we merely need to know the marginal values of the dependent variable to predict, or does it help to partition the dependent variable into categories of the independent variable?

Lambda is a measure of association for nominal-level variables, based on the logic of **proportional reduction in error,** known as **PRE.**† It is useful for any size table. While computational procedures are available for asymmetrical and symmetrical lambda, only asymmetrical lambda will be presented.‡

Let's consider the logic of PRE measures in general and lambda specifically using the data first presented in Table 8.2, repeated here as Table 8.8. If you knew that 102 women in a sample of 200 women were not employed and you were asked to predict or guess the employment status of the 200 women in the sample without knowledge of their marital status, you should guess that none of them is employed, given the row marginals. Such a strategy would result in your correctly predicting 102 of the 200 women in the sample because 102 are not employed. You would have incorrectly predicted the employment status of 98 women. Therefore, your guess of "not employed" would result in a slightly reduced number of errors.

If, on the other hand, you were asked to predict employment status while knowing marital status, you could make more correct guesses. If you knew a woman had been divorced *or* had never married, you would no longer want to guess "not employed" because the majority of women in *both* marital status categories are employed.

---

* Unless noted otherwise, we will assume that *X* designates the independent variable and that it is the column variable.

† Lambda can be computed using ordinal- or interval-level data; however, lambda ignores ranks and intervals, and information would be lost. Lambda or another appropriate statistic such as phi, Cramer's V, or the contingency coefficient (see Chapter 16) must be computed whenever *any* of the variables are measured at the nominal level.

‡ Symmetrical lambda measures the mutual influence of two variables on each other.

TABLE 8.8
Employment status by marital status

(Y) Employment status	Never married	Married	Divorced	Widowed	Total
	(X) Marital status				
Employed	21	60	11	6	98
Not employed	14	65	4	19	102
Total	35	125	15	25	$N = 200$

To analyze the usefulness of the partitioning of the data, social scientists calculate lambda, which expresses the relationship between the errors produced with the first type of guess and the errors produced with the second type of guess. To formalize this logic, statisticians refer to the predictions from tables as being based on one of two rules. Both rules govern procedures aimed at reducing the error in predictions. Rule I for lambda assumes no knowledge about the independent variable.

Rule I: Predict the modal category of the dependent variable.*

In essence, we use only the row marginals of the dependent variable to make our prediction.

Given additional information about our sample of women, we should be able to improve our prediction of their employment status. The data in Table 8.8 indicate, for example, that the women's employment status is related to their marital status. Now let us predict employment status given information about the respondent's marital status, which is the independent variable. We now use Rule II for lambda, which assumes knowledge of the independent variable.

Rule II: Predict the within-category mode of the independent variable.

Now we would predict that all of the never married respondents are employed because the within-category mode of the never married group is the employed category of the dependent variable. Rule II requires that we predict all of the married respondents are not employed, all of the divorced respondents are employed, and all of the widowed respondents are not employed.

Let's see how many errors in prediction we would make if we used Rule II. We would have correctly predicted the employment status of 21 out of the 35 never married respondents (therefore, 14 errors in prediction), 65 of the 125 married respondents (60 errors), 11 of the 15 divorced respondents (4 errors), and 19 of the 25 widowed respondents (6 errors). We have made a total of 84 prediction errors ($14 + 60 + 4 + 6$) given the respondents' marital status (using Rule II), compared with 98 prediction errors *without* knowledge of the respondents' marital status (using Rule I). Thus, we have reduced our prediction errors by 14 ($98 - 84 = 14$) now that we have information on the independent variable. Lambda can be calculated using the

* The mode of a category was defined in Chapter 5 as the score that occurs with the greatest frequency.

following equation, which is based on shifting from Rule I to Rule II once knowledge of the independent variable is available:

$$\lambda = \frac{(\text{errors using Rule I}) - (\text{errors using Rule II})}{\text{errors using Rule I}} \qquad (8.1)^*$$

Substituting into equation (8.1), we find that lambda equals 0.14.

$$\lambda = \frac{98 - 84}{98} = \frac{14}{98} = 0.14$$

While lambda is easily calculated using equation (8.1) in a table with few rows and cells, this is not the case with a larger table, and a computational equation is available for these purposes:

$$\lambda = \frac{\Sigma \text{ maximum frequency } (X) - \text{maximum frequency } (Y)}{N - \text{maximum frequency } (Y)} \qquad (8.2)$$

where maximum frequency (X) = the within-category mode for each category of the independent variable
maximum frequency (Y) = the modal frequency of the dependent variable, and
N = sample size

In words, equation (8.2) can be read:

$$\text{lambda} = \frac{\begin{array}{c}\text{sum of the within-category}\\ \text{modes of the independent}\\ \text{variable}\end{array} - \begin{array}{c}\text{modal frequency of}\\ \text{the dependent variable}\end{array}}{\text{sample size} - \begin{array}{c}\text{modal frequency of}\\ \text{the dependent variable}\end{array}}$$

Applying equation (8.2) to the data in Table 8.8, we obtain:

$$\lambda = \frac{(21 + 65 + 11 + 19) - 102}{200 - 102}$$

$$= \frac{14}{98}$$

$$= 0.14$$

8.7.1 Interpretation of Lambda

The value of lambda is determined by the proportional reduction in error when predicting the dependent variable on shifting from prediction Rule I to prediction Rule II.

---

* Equation (8.1) assumes Y is the dependent variable. Under these circumstances, lambda is frequently written λ_{yx} with the first subscript designating the dependent variable. Subscript variables, for example, x and y, will appear in lowercase italics throughout this text. Lambda also can be computed using Y as the independent variable and as a symmetric measure of association.

Formally stated, the prediction rules for lambda are:

Rule I: Predict the modal category of the dependent variable.

Rule II: Predict the within-category mode of the independent variable.

Lambda measures the strength of the relationship and ranges from 0 when the variables are not related to 1 when they are perfectly related. If lambda equals 0, knowledge of the independent variable is of no value when predicting the dependent variable, and we cannot predict any better when shifting from Rule I to Rule II than we can by using only Rule I. When lambda equals 1, knowledge of the independent variable allows you to predict the dependent variable perfectly.

A lambda of 0.14 indicates a weak relationship between marital status and employment status. Multiplying by 100 allows us to state that we have reduced the number of prediction errors by 14% when moving from Rule I to Rule II. Rule I resulted in an error rate of 98/200 or 49%, and Rule II resulted in an error rate of 84/200 or 42%. Shifting from Rule I to Rule II reduced the rate 7% (49% − 42% = 7%), which is the *absolute* reduction in error. To calculate *proportional* reduction in error, we divide the 7% absolute reduction in error by the original error rate of 49%, yielding a lambda of 0.14.

8.7.2 Limitations of Lambda

In spite of lambda's strengths, which include use with nominal-level data, no assumptions concerning the distribution of the variables (a normal distribution is unnecessary), and use with any size table, lambda does have two limitations. The first is that lambda has no sign and hence gives us no indication of the direction of the relationship, a limitation that stems from its use with nominal-level data. The second limitation results from the prediction rules on which lambda is based. Lambda equals 0 whenever *all* the within-category modes of the independent variable occur in the row containing the modal category of the dependent variable. In Table 8.9 lambda equals 0, yet it is clear that the variables are related because there is a 23.2% (85.7% − 62.5% = 23.2%) percentage difference between males and females who desire to have children, an 8.9% percentage difference between males and females who have no desire for children, and a 14.3% percentage difference between the undecided males and females. For males and females, the within-category modes of the independent variable (60 and 50) are both located in the row containing the modal category of the dependent variable; therefore, shifting from Rule I to Rule II will result in no reduction in prediction error, and lambda equals 0.

While we have found that lambda equals 0, it is apparent that a relationship does exist between sex and the desire to have children. As was noted in Section 8.5, we can only conclude that there is no relationship between two variables if the percentage differences between categories of the independent variable are zero.

TABLE 8.9
Desire to have children by sex of respondent (hypothetical study of college students)

(*Y*) Desire to have children?	(*X*) Sex of respondent: Male	Female	Total
Yes	85.7 (60)	62.5 (50)*	110
No	8.6 (6)	17.5 (14)	20
Undecided	5.7 (4)	20.0 (16)	20
Total	100.0 (70)	100.0 (80)	$N = 150$

Using equation (8.2), we have:

$$\lambda = \frac{\Sigma \text{ maximum frequency } (X) - \text{maximum frequency } (Y)}{N - \text{maximum frequency } (Y)}$$

$$= \frac{(60 + 50) - 110}{150 - 110}$$

$$= 0$$

* While a variety of conventions are available, we prefer that when cell percentages *and* frequencies are presented in a contingency table, the frequencies should be placed in parentheses. Contingency tables will be routinely percentaged on the independent variable unless stated otherwise.

8.8 ORDINAL MEASURES OF ASSOCIATION*

Measures of association for contingency tables using ordinal-level (or interval-level) data are based on the logic of **pair-by-pair comparison.** We will present Goodman and Kruskal's gamma, Somer's *d*, and Kendall's tau-*b*, three of the measures most frequently used by social scientists as ordinal measures of association.

8.8.1 The Logic of Pair-by-Pair Comparison

Each case in a contingency table can theoretically be paired with every other case in the table. Table 8.10 contains four cases, *A*, *B*, *C*, and *D*, which can form six distinct pairs. Upon pairing cases *A* and *B* in Table 8.10, we see that case *A* is lower on age (*X*) than case *B* (*A*'s age is young and *B*'s is middle-aged), but *A* is higher on income (*Y*) than case *B*. Table 8.11 presents a summary of the relationships between all pairs of cases.

* Gamma, Somer's *d*, and Kendall's tau-*b* can be used with interval-level data.

TABLE 8.10
Income by age

(*Y*) Income	(*X*) Age: Young	Middle-aged	Old
High	*A*		*D*
Medium		*B*	
Low			*C*

TABLE 8.11
Pairs of cases in Table 8.10

Pair	Summary	Relationship
AB	*A* lower on *X* than is *B* *A* higher on *Y* than is *B*	Discordant
AC	*A* lower on *X* than is *C* *A* higher on *Y* than is *C*	Discordant
AD	*A* lower on *X* than is *D* *A* and *D* tied on *Y*	Tied on *Y*
BC	*B* lower on *X* than is *C* *B* higher on *Y* than is *C*	Discordant
BD	*B* lower on *X* than is *D* *B* lower on *Y* than is *D*	Concordant
CD	*C* and *D* tied on *X* *C* lower on *Y* than is *D*	Tied on *X*

A **discordant pair** is one in which the two cases are ranked in the opposite order on both variables. A **concordant pair** is one in which the two cases are ranked in the same order on both variables. A **tied pair** is one in which the two cases are ranked similarly on one or both of the variables. To the extent that a pattern emerges in which discordant pairs predominate, the relationship between the variables is negative as shown in Table 8.12(a). A situation in which concordant pairs predominate and which is characterized by a positive relationship is shown in Table 8.12(b).

The diagonals have been shaded to highlight the predominant pattern in the tables. In Table 8.12(a), you will note that low scores on *X tend* to be paired with high scores on *Y* and vice versa. Gamma, Somer's *d*, and Kendall's tau-*b* are sensitive to patterns such as these, and their values reflect the extent to which concordant or discordant pairs predominate. If gamma, Somer's *d*, or Kendall's tau-*b* were calculated for Table 8.12(b), we would anticipate a positive relationship since the majority of cases lie on the positive diagonal; that is, low scores on *X* tend to be paired with low scores on *Y*, and high scores on *X* tend to be paired with high scores on *Y*.

Note that the patterns shown in Table 8.12 would differ if the conventional variable placement (column variable independent) or the ordering of the variable categories (low to high) were modified. It also should be stated that ordinal-level statistics such as those presented in this chapter may only be used if *both* the

TABLE 8.12
Concordant and discordant patterns in contingency tables

(a)

(Y) Income	(X) Age Young	Middle-aged	Old
High	20	6	2
Moderate	5	30	2
Low	1	4	10

Discordant pairs predominate. Relationship is *negative.*

(b)

(Y) Income	(X) Age Young	Middle-aged	Old
High	1	6	10
Moderate	5	30	2
Low	20	4	2

Concordant pairs predominate. Relationship is *positive.*

independent and dependent variables are measured at the ordinal level or higher. A contingency table in which one variable is measured at the nominal level (e.g., religious affiliation) and the other is measured at the ordinal level (e.g., frequency of church or synagogue attendance) would require that a nominal-level statistic be used.

8.9 GOODMAN AND KRUSKAL'S GAMMA

Gamma (*G* or γ)* is a symmetric measure of association for ordinal-level or interval-level data. No specification of which variable is independent and which is dependent is therefore necessary, and only one value of gamma is possible. Gamma ranges from -1 to $+1$, has a proportional reduction in error (PRE) interpretation, and is based on the logic of pair-by-pair comparison. Furthermore, gamma can be calculated for any size table.†

The equation for computing gamma compares the number of concordant pairs (C) to the number of discordant pairs (D). Gamma ignores ties, a weakness we will address later. The computation of gamma for Table 8.10 is shown below equation (8.3). Note that the sign of gamma in this instance is negative because discordant pairs outnumber concordant pairs three to one.

$$G = \frac{C - D}{C + D} \tag{8.3}$$

where C = number of concordant pairs
D = number of discordant pairs

$$G = \frac{1 - 3}{1 + 3} = \frac{-2}{4} = \frac{-1}{2} = -0.5$$

* Most social scientists symbolize gamma by G, although some prefer the lowercase Greek letter (γ).

† Yule's Q is a special case of gamma that was developed specifically for 2×2 tables. The values of G and Q are equivalent for 2×2 tables and are subject to the same interpretation and limitations. Social scientists generally prefer gamma because it can be used with any size contingency table containing ordinal-level or interval-level data.

8.9.1 Calculating Concordant and Discordant Pairs in Contingency Tables

Determining the number of concordant and discordant pairs for contingency tables with many cases is more complicated than the previous example, which included only four cases. The data in Table 8.13 are hypothetical results of a study of the relationship between political liberalism and year in college for a sample of college students.

Concordant pairs. The cells in Table 8.13 have been labeled with letters to facilitate the discussion. The lowest category of the independent variable, year in college, is freshman, and the highest category is senior. The not liberal category of the dependent variable is scored low, and the very liberal category scored high. The scores in Table 8.13, with some exceptions, tend to follow the *positive diagonal* connecting cells *i* and *d*.* We anticipate a positive relationship between *X* and *Y* due to the patterning of cases that are concentrated in cells *i*, *f*, *g*, and *d*. The positive diagonal in any contingency table connects the low-low cells of the dependent and independent variable (not liberal and freshman, therefore, cell *i* in Table 8.13) with the high-high cells of the dependent and independent variable (very liberal and senior, therefore, cell *d* in Table 8.13). The negative diagonal always connects the low-high cells of the dependent and independent variable (not liberal and senior, therefore, cell *l* in Table 8.13) with the high-low cells of the dependent and independent variables (very liberal and freshman, therefore, cell *a* in Table 8.13).

The first step in identifying the concordant pairs in any contingency table is to locate the cell on the positive diagonal that represents a low score on *X* and *Y*. The procedure we will follow for computing gamma assumes that the table is laid out in the standard manner described in Section 8.5. In this example, we must therefore begin at cell *i*. The cases that are concordant with the cases in cell *i* lie in those cells to the right and above cell *i*.† Cells concordant with cell *i* are cells *b*, *c*, *d*, *f*, *g*, and *h* because the cases in these cells are higher on both variables than the cases in cell *i*. The cells contain 3, 7, 10, 12, 9, and 7 cases, respectively, for a total of 48 cases. We can calculate the number of concordant *pairs* we have identified so far by multiplying the number of cases in cell *i* by the total number of cases in those cells above and to the right of cell *i*; therefore, we have identified 10×48, or 480 concordant pairs. We continue this procedure until we have counted all concordant pairs.

Our focal cell now is cell *j* because we must systematically move across the row, then up to the next row and across, and so on, until we have identified all concordant pairs. We note that only cells *c*, *d*, *g*, and *h* are above and to the right of cell *j*. The cases in these four cells are concordant with the cases in cell *j* because all of the cases are higher on both variables than the cases in cell *j*. A total of 33 cases $(7 + 10 + 9 + 7)$ lie in these cells. Multiplying by the 5 cases in cell *j*, we now have identified 165

---

* In contrast, Table 8.12(a) is characterized by a negative diagonal.

† The initial focal cell for computing concordant pairs could have been cell *d*, which lies at the opposite end of the positive diagonal. If we began with cell *d*, we would locate cells to the left and below cell *d* because they are concordant with cell *d*. Hence, either cell *i* or *d* could have been chosen as the starting point.

TABLE 8.13
Political liberalism by year in college

(Y) Political liberalism	(X) Year in college: Freshman	Sophomore	Junior	Senior	Total
Very liberal	*a* 2	*b* 3	*c* 7	*d* 10	22
Moderately liberal	*e* 8	*f* 12	*g* 9	*h* 7	36
Not liberal	*i* 10	*j* 5	*k* 4	*l* 3	22
Total	20	20	20	20	$N = 80$

TABLE 8.14
Calculation of concordant pairs

Focal cell	Paired cells	Calculation of concordant pairs	
i	*b, c, d, f, g, h*	$10(3 + 7 + 10 + 12 + 9 + 7) =$	480
j	*c, d, g, h*	$5(7 + 10 + 9 + 7) =$	165
k	*d, h*	$4(10 + 7) =$	68
e	*b, c, d*	$8(3 + 7 + 10) =$	160
f	*c, d*	$12(7 + 10) =$	204
g	*d*	$9(10) =$	90
		Total concordant pairs =	1,167

(5 × 33) additional concordant pairs. Continuing, we see that the 4 cases in cell *k* form concordant pairs with the cases in cells *d* and *h* for 68 (4 × 17) concordant pairs. The 8 cases in cell *e* are concordant with those in cells *b*, *c*, and *d*, and the 12 cases in cell *f* are concordant with the cases in cells *c* and *d*. Finally, the 9 cases in cell *g* are concordant with the 10 cases in cell *d*. The calculations to determine the number of concordant pairs are summarized in Table 8.14.

Discordant pairs. Identifying the discordant pairs of cases involves a procedure similar to identifying the concordant pairs. Our focal cell lies on the *negative diagonal* that runs from cell *a* to cell *l* in Table 8.13. We begin with cell *a* and work down the diagonal, locating those cells that contain cases whose value is less than the cases in cell *a* on the dependent variable, and greater on the independent variable. Therefore, cells *f*, *g*, *h*, *j*, *k*, and *l*, all of which lie below and to the right of cell *a*, contain cases discordant with those in cell *a*.* We then move systematically across and down to identify the remaining focal cells, which include cells *b*, *c*, *e*, *f*, and *g*. The calculations necessary to determine the discordant pairs are presented in Table 8.15.

* The discordant pairs could also be calculated by beginning with cell *l*, which is located at the opposite end of the negative diagonal, and locating cells above and to the left. The choice of either starting point is a matter of personal preference.

TABLE 8.15
Calculation of discordant pairs

Focal cell	Paired cells	Calculation of discordant pairs	
a	*f*, *g*, *h*, *j*, *k*, *l*	2(12 + 9 + 7 + 5 + 4 + 3) =	80
b	*g*, *h*, *k*, *l*	3(9 + 7 + 4 + 3) =	69
c	*h*, *l*	7(7 + 3) =	70
e	*j*, *k*, *l*	8(5 + 4 + 3) =	96
f	*k*, *l*	12(4 + 3) =	84
g	*l*	9(3) =	27
		Total discordant pairs =	426

We have found that concordant pairs predominate and can now calculate gamma, making use of equation (8.3).

$$G = \frac{C - D}{C + D} = \frac{1167 - 426}{1167 + 426} = +0.465$$

8.9.2 Interpreting Gamma

Gamma ranges from −1.00, when there is a perfect negative relationship between the variables (all untied pairs are discordant), to +1.00 where there is a perfect positive relationship (all untied pairs are concordant).* When the variables are unrelated, gamma equals 0 because there are an equal number of concordant and discordant pairs.

The gamma of +0.465 indicates a moderate, positive relationship between year in school and political liberalism. In other words, the seniors at the college we surveyed are more politically liberal than the freshmen. Our data of course do not allow us to know if the observed relationship is due to the liberalizing effect of a college education or if natural aging by four years would have the same liberalizing effect. Because gamma has a PRE interpretation, we also can say that using knowledge of the independent variable (year in college) to predict the order of the cases on the dependent variable (political liberalism), we have reduced our errors by 46.5%. However, because gamma is a symmetric measure of association, we also can say that, given knowledge of the dependent variable, we can reduce our errors by 46.5% when predicting the independent variable.

The procedure for determining the statistical significance of gamma is presented in Section 14.9.

8.9.3 Limitations of Gamma

Gamma ignores tied pairs; hence, a gamma value may reflect far less than all the possible pairs. There are $N(N - 1)/2$ or 3,160 possible pairs of cases in Table 8.13. Of these pairs, 1,593 (426 + 1,167) are discordant *or* concordant. Tied pairs total 1,567 (3,160 − 1,593), and therefore nearly 50% of all the possible pairs have been

* Recall that a tied pair is one in which two cases are ranked similarly on one or both of the variables.

ignored in the calculation of gamma. As a result, gamma tends to overstate the actual relationship. Indeed, it is possible for gamma to equal -1 or $+1$ when all but one pair of cases is tied! Somer's *d* and Kendall's tau-*b* overcome the problem, and are discussed in the following sections.

Gamma, along with all other ordinal-level statistics, can only detect a straight-line relationship between the variables. If a horseshoe-shaped curve best described the relationship between the variables, for example, the value of gamma would be very low. Naturally, you must learn to identify situations such as this in which a nonlinear* relationship exists, and not compute gamma.

In spite of these drawbacks, gamma is the most frequently used measure of association for ordinal-level and interval-level data in contingency form.

8.10 SOMER'S *d*

Somer's *d* is an asymmetrical measure of association for ordinal-level data that incorporates tied ranks. It is similar to gamma in that it is based on pair-by-pair comparison. Two values of *d* (d_{yx} where Y is the dependent variable and d_{xy} in which X is treated as the dependent variable) are possible; however, here we will assume Y is dependent. The computational equation requires that we determine the number of concordant pairs (C), the number of discordant pairs (D), and T_y, which is the number of pairs with different X values, but with the same Y value. Thus, the cases in cell *a* are tied with those in cells *b*, *c*, and *d* because all are ranked very liberal on Y, yet are in differing years in college. The computational procedure for Somer's *d* (with Y dependent) is presented in equation (8.4):

$$d_{yx} = \frac{C - D}{C + D + T_y} \tag{8.4}$$

where T_y = pairs with different X values but with the same Y values
C = number of concordant pairs
D = number of discordant pairs

The logic of including ties on the dependent variable when calculating a measure of association for contingency data is that a tie on the dependent variable given differing X values suggests that X exerts no influence on Y.† Instead of ignoring ties as gamma does, Somer's *d*, which is a more conservative measure, includes ties on the dependent variable to ensure a more accurate reflection of the true strength of association. Somer's *d* must always be less than or equal to gamma when calculated for the same contingency table due to the inclusion of the T_y term in the denominator. While Somer's *d* does not have a direct PRE interpretation, it has become very

---

* *Nonlinear* (or curvilinear) means not characterized by a straight line.

† Somer's d_{yx} ignores ties on the independent variable. If we wished to compute d_{xy} where X is dependent, the T_y term in equation (8.4) would be replaced by T_x, which includes pairs with different Y values but which share the same X value. For example, cell *a* is tied with cells *e* and *i* because all are freshmen, yet they are ranked differently on political liberalism. Ties on X will be discussed in Section 8.11.

TABLE 8.16
Computation of d_{yx} for the data in Table 8.13

(Y) Political liberalism	(X) Year in college: Freshman	Sophomore	Junior	Senior	Total
Very liberal	*a* 2	*b* 3	*c* 7	*d* 10	22
Moderately liberal	*e* 8	*f* 12	*g* 9	*h* 7	36
Not liberal	*i* 10	*j* 5	*k* 4	*l* 3	22
Total	20	20	20	20	$N = 80$

popular with social scientists in the past decade. Somer's d_{yx} has been calculated for the data in Table 8.13 (repeated here as Table 8.16).

$$d_{yx} = \frac{C - D}{C + D + T_y}$$

$$\left.\begin{aligned} C &= 1167 \\ D &= 426 \end{aligned}\right\}\text{(from Section 8.9.1)}$$

$$\begin{aligned} T_y &= 2(3 + 7 + 10) + 3(7 + 10) + 7(10) \\ &\quad + 8(12 + 9 + 7) + 12(9 + 7) + 9(7) \\ &\quad + 10(5 + 4 + 3) + 5(4 + 3) + 4(3) \\ &= 807 \end{aligned}$$

Using equation (8.4), we obtain:

$$d_{yx} = \frac{1167 - 426}{1167 + 426 + 807} = 0.309$$

You will note that this value is considerably less than the gamma of +0.465 that we computed for the same set of data. Somer's d ranges from -1 (perfect negative relationship) to $+1$ (perfect positive relationship) and assumes a linear or straight-line relationship between the variables. A Somer's d_{yx} of +0.309 indicates a weak to moderately positive relationship between year in school and political liberalism when year in college serves as the independent variable.

8.11 KENDALL'S TAU-*b*

Kendall's tau-*b* differs from Somer's d in that its computation involves pairs of cases that are tied on both X and Y. It is a symmetrical measure of association for ordinal-level data whose maximum value of ± 1 is possible in a square table (the number of rows equal the number of columns, i.e., $r = c$). Equation (8.5) for tau-*b* is:

$$\text{tau-}b = \frac{C - D}{\sqrt{(C + D + T_y)(C + D + T_x)}} \tag{8.5}$$

To compute tau-*b*, we must determine C, D, T_y, and T_x where T_x equals the number of pairs tied on X, but with different Y values. Using Table 8.16 as an illustration, we see that the cases in cell *a* are tied on X with cases in cells *e* and *i*, and the cases in cell *e* are tied on X with the cases in cell *i*. Likewise, the cases in cell *b* are tied on X with the cases in cells *f* and *j*, and the cases in cell *f* are tied with the cases in *j*. The procedure for determining ties on X, but not on Y is as follows:

$$\begin{aligned} T_x = {} & 2(8 + 10) + 8(10) \\ & + 3(12 + 5) + 12(5) \\ & + 7(9 + 4) + 9(4) \\ & + 10(7 + 3) + 7(3) = 475 \end{aligned}$$

Substituting the known values of C, D, and T_y from below Table 8.16 allows us to compute tau-*b*:

$$\begin{aligned} \text{tau-}b &= \frac{1167 - 426}{\sqrt{(1167 + 426 + 807)(1167 + 426 + 475)}} \\ &= \frac{741}{\sqrt{(2400)(2068)}} \\ &= \frac{741}{2227.8} \\ &= +0.333 \end{aligned}$$

A tau-*b* of +0.333 indicates a positive relationship between political liberalism and year in college. Tau-*b* is a symmetric statistic; therefore, we can say that our errors in prediction for either variable can be reduced by 33.3% given information about the order of pairs on the other variable. Table 8.16 is rectangular; therefore, the maximum value for tau-*b* is less than ±1. Its value may never be larger than gamma due to the incorporation of tied cases in the computation. In this particular instance, gamma would be a more appropriate ordinal-level statistic since $r \neq c$ in Table 8.16.

SUMMARY

In this chapter, we have learned about the presentation and interpretation of contingency tables. We also have discussed four distribution-free measures of association appropriate for nominal- or ordinal-level data.

Lambda is a measure of association for nominal data based on the logic of proportional reduction in error. Lambda can serve as either a symmetric or asymmetric measure. The value of lambda ranges from 0 to 1, and it can be used with tables of any dimension. Lambda equals 0 when the distribution of cases on the dependent variable is extremely skewed.

Gamma, Somer's *d*, and tau-*b* are measures of association for ordinal data based on the logic of pair-by-pair comparison. Gamma and tau-*b* are symmetric measures of association with a PRE interpretation, whereas Somer's *d* is an asymmetric measure and does not have a PRE interpretation. While gamma ignores ties, Somer's *d* and tau-*b* are more conservative measures that incorporate tied ranks on the dependent variable. Somer's d_{yx} incorporates ties on the dependent variable *Y*, and tau-*b*'s computation involves ties on *X* and *Y*. Gamma and Somer's *d* range from -1 to $+1$ can be used with tables of any dimension and assume the variables are linearly related. The maximum value for tau-*b* is less than ±1 when $r \neq c$.

TERMS TO REMEMBER

asymmetric measure of association A measure of the one-way effect of one variable upon another.

concordant pair Two cases are ranked similarly on two variables.

conditional distribution The distribution of the categories of one variable under the differing conditions or categories of another.

contingency table A table showing the cross-tabulation or joint distribution of two variables.

cross-tabulation See *conditional distribution.*

dependent variable The variable that is being predicted. Also referred to as the criterion variable.

discordant pair Two cases are ranked in the opposite order on two variables.

epsilon (ϵ) The percentage difference within a category of the dependent variable between the two extreme categories of the independent variable.

gamma (*G* or γ) A symmetric measure of association for ordinal-level data based on pair-by-pair comparison with a PRE interpretation.

independent variable The predictor variable. Referred to as the experimental variable in an experiment.

Kendall's tau-*b* A symmetric measure of association for ordinal-level data.

lambda (λ) An asymmetric or symmetric measure of association for nominal-level data.

marginals The column and row totals of a contingency table.

negative relationship High scores on one variable tend to be associated with low scores on the other; conversely, low scores on one variable tend to be associated with high scores on the other.

nonexistent relationship A relationship in which knowledge of the independent variable does not improve our prediction of the dependent variable or when the variables are unrelated.

pair-by-pair comparison An approach to prediction for ordinal-level data in contingency form.

percentage difference Differences in percentages normally measured between the two extreme categories of the independent variable within a category of the dependent variable. Also referred to as epsilon (ϵ).

perfect relationship A relationship in which knowledge of the independent variable allows a perfect prediction of the dependent variable or vice versa.

positive relationship High scores on one variable tend to be associated with high scores on the other; conversely, low scores on one variable tend to be associated with low scores on the other.

proportional reduction in error (PRE) A ratio of the prediction errors without information about the independent variable to the prediction errors having information about the independent variable.

Somer's *d* An asymmetrical measure of association for ordinal-level data that incorporates tied ranks.

symmetric measure of association A measure of the mutual association between two variables.

tied pair Two cases are ranked similarly on one or both of two variables.

EXERCISES

1. Percentage the following table down, across, and on the total. Interpret the data for each of the ways you have percentaged.

	High school grade point average		
Drug use	**Low**	**Moderate**	**High**
High	0	5	15
Moderate	15	10	10
Low	10	5	5

$N = 75$

2. Identify and defend your choice of independent and dependent variables for the table in exercise 1. Which direction would you percentage, given your selection?

3. Discuss the existence, direction, and strength of a relationship for the data in exercise 1 by examining the percentages and distribution of cases. Calculate an appropriate measure of association, defend your choice, and interpret the results.

4. Compute gamma, Somer's *d*, and tau-*b*. Compare and interpret your answers.

	(X) Social isolation		
(Y) **Perceived health**	**Low**	**Moderate**	**High**
Excellent	10	4	3
Average	5	6	7
Poor	2	4	9

$N = 50$

5. Compute lambda. Interpret your answer.

(*Y*) Educational attainment	(*X*) Religious affiliation: Protestant	Catholic	Jewish
College	10	15	15
High school	10	20	10

$N = 80$

6. Using a contingency table of your choice for illustrative purposes, discuss the logic underlying proportional reduction in error. Discuss the logic of pair-by-pair comparison using a different example.

7. Over 5 million adults in the United States reported that they wanted a job, yet were not seeking employment. Assuming that sex is the independent variable and that reason for not seeking work is the dependent variable, percentage the following table and compute an appropriate measure of association. Interpret the results.

(*Y*) Reason for not seeking work	(*X*) Sex: Male	Female	
In school	693	681	
Ill or disabled	326	394	
Keeping house	32	1,226	
Think cannot get a job	305	540	
Total	1,356	2,841	$N = 4{,}197$

(in thousands)

Source: U.S. Bureau of Labor Statistics, *Employment and Earnings,* monthly.

8. For the following research situations, construct a hypothetical table and select an appropriate measure of association:

(*a*) You have conducted a health survey and wish to examine the relationship between the number of close friends a person has and whether or not the respondent has seriously considered suicide.

(*b*) You wish to explore the relationship between the length of time U.S. senators have served in the Senate and the region of the country in which their home state is located.

(*c*) You wish to determine if lower-income persons are more likely than upper-income persons to be the victim of a street assault.

9. Interracially married couples in the United States totaled approximately 319,000 in 1970, 421,000 in 1977, and 762,000 in 1984. The following table indicates the racial composition of interracial marriages by year. Percentage the table, and discuss the relationship between year and racial composition of the marital pair.

Racial composition of marriage partners	Year 1970	1977	1984
Husband African American, wife white	41	95	111
Wife African American, husband white	24	30	64
Husband African American, wife other	8	20	17
Wife African American, husband other*	4	2	6
Husband white, wife other*	139	177	340
Wife white, husband other*	94	97	224
Total	310	421	762
	(in thousands)		

* "Other" indicates spouse is neither African American nor white, but is Asian or another unspecified category.

Source: U.S. Bureau of the Census.

10. Some studies have reported high rates of childhood abuse in adults with mental illness. One study examined the self-reports of 98 hospitalized women regarding childhood physical and sexual abuse.

History of physical abuse	History of sexual abuse No	Yes	Total
No	36	12	48
Yes	27	23	50
Total	63	35	98

Source: J. A. Chu and D. L. Dill, "Dissociative Symptoms in Relation to Childhood Physical and Sexual Abuse," *American Journal of Psychiatry* 147 (1990), pp. 887–92.

Based on these data, answer questions (*a*) through (*h*).

(*a*) Of the 98 women in the study, what percentage had a history of physical abuse?
(*b*) What percentage of the total had a history of sexual abuse?
(*c*) What percentage of the total had no history of either physical or sexual abuse?
(*d*) What percentage of the total had a history of both sexual *and* physical abuse?
(*e*) What percentage of the total had a history of sexual *or* physical abuse *or* both?
(*f*) Of the 35 women with a history of sexual abuse, what percentage reported also having been physically abused?
(*g*) Of the 50 women with a history of physical abuse, what percentage reported also having been sexually abused?
(*h*) Could you generalize these results to the general population? Could you generalize to all patients with a history of mental illness?

11. Discuss the strengths and weaknesses of lambda, tau-*b*, gamma, and Somer's *d*.

12. A study was conducted to examine the possible precipitating influences or causes of a person having a religious experience. Calculate lambda for the following table and interpret your results.

(Y) Religious experience?	(X) Possible precipitator: Death of a loved one	Breakup of a romantic relationship	Loss of a job	Severe physical pain
Yes	10	10	5	15
No	10	40	10	10
			$N = 110$	

13. Construct tables in which:
(*a*) Lambda = 1, lambda = 0.
(*b*) Tau-*b* =, tau-*b* = 0.
(*c*) Gamma = 1, gamma = 0.
(*d*) Somer's *d* = 1, Somer's *d* = 0.

14. (*a*) Compute lambda for this table.
(*b*) Interpret your answer
(*c*) Interpret the percentages.

(Y) Attitude toward labor unions	(X) Region of residence: Non-South	South	Total
Prounion	66.7 (40)	37.5 (15)	(55)
Antiunion	33.3 (20)	62.5 (25)	(45)
Total	100.0 (60)	100.0 (40)	$N = 100$

15. The following table summarizes the relationship between the use of cocaine and condoms among female prostitutes. Assuming use of cocaine is the independent variable, (*a*) percentage down, (*b*) compute gamma, Somer's *d*, and tau-*b*, and (*c*) discuss.

Use of condoms	Use of cocaine: Never	Sometimes	Frequently
Always	25	10	1
Sometimes	15	10	9
Never	4	6	20
			$N = 100$

16. Construct a table with ordinal-level variables in which there is a strong relationship between two variables, but because it is not linear—that is, it does not follow either the positive or negative diagonal—gamma, tau-*b*, and Somer's *d* will not accurately reflect the strong pattern that is evident. Calculate gamma, tau-*b*, or Somer's *d* and discuss. (*Hint:* Choose two variables that have several categories to allow for the demonstration of a nonlinear relationship.)

17. Many companies have reduced the size of work groups to promote group cohesion. Assuming work group size is the independent variable, (*a*) percentage down, (*b*) compute gamma, Somer's *d*, and tau-*b*, and (*c*) discuss the relationship shown in the following table.

	Size of work group		
Group cohesion	**3–6**	**7–10**	**11–14**
High	52	70	28
Moderate	22	75	12
Low	13	60	40

$N = 372$

18. For the accompanying table:
(*a*) Identify the independent and dependent variable.
(*b*) Given their level of measurement, identify an appropriate measure of association.
(*c*) Examine the cell percentages and discuss the relationship between the variables.
(*d*) Are the dependent variable categories presented in the conventional manner?

Educational attainment of the U.S. population by racial and ethnic group, 1990

Highest level reached	**All**	**Native American**	**Asian**	**African American**	**Hispanic**	**White**
8th grade or less	10.4%	14.0%	12.9%	13.8%	30.7%	8.9%
Some high school, no diploma	14.4	20.4	9.5	23.2	19.5	13.1
High school diploma	30.0	29.1	18.5	27.9	21.6	31.0
Some college, no degree	18.7	20.8	14.7	18.5	14.3	19.1
Associate degree	6.2	6.4	7.7	5.3	4.8	6.3
Bachelor's degree	13.1	6.1	22.7	7.5	5.9	13.9
Graduate or professional degree	7.2	3.2	13.9	3.8	3.3	7.7
Number of adults (in millions)	158.9	1.1	4.3	16.8	11.2	132.0

Note: The figures are based on the 1990 census and cover adults age 25 and older. The total includes those whose racial or ethnic group is not known. Hispanics may be of any race. The figures may not add to 100% because of rounding error.
Source: Census Bureau.

CHAPTER 9

Correlation

9.1 THE CONCEPT OF CORRELATION

We are frequently interested in determining the relationship between two interval- or ratio-scaled variables. For example, college admissions personnel are very concerned with the relationship between SAT scores and performance at college. Do students who score high on the SAT also perform well in college? Conversely, do high school students who score low on the SAT perform poorly in college? Is there a relationship between socioeconomic status and recidivism in crime? Is a spouse's power in a marriage related to his or her earnings? What is the relationship between the size of a law firm and beginning salaries for new members? To express the extent to which two variables are related, we need to compute a measure of association called a **correlation coefficient.** There are many types of measures of association, several of which were presented in Chapter 8.

Deciding which measure of association to use with a specific set of data depends on such factors as (1) the type of scale or measurement in which each variable is expressed (nominal, ordinal, interval, or ratio), (2) the nature of the underlying distribution (continuous or discrete), and (3) the characteristics of the distribution of scores (linear or nonlinear). Table 9.1 summarizes the measures of association that are included in this text. The level of measurement indicated is a minimal requirement. Lambda and the other nominal-level measures, for example, can be calculated if one of the variables is measured at the nominal level and the other is measured at the ordinal level.

TABLE 9.1
A summary of measures of association presented in this text

Scale	Symbol	Used with	Chapter
Nominal	λ (lambda)	Two nominal-level variables.	8
	ϕ (phi coefficient)	Two dichotomous variables.	16
	C (contingency coefficient)	Two nominal-level variables with equal rows and columns.	16
	V (Cramer's *V*)	Two nominal-level variables.	16
Ordinal	*G* (Goodman and Kruskal's gamma)	Two ordinal-level variables.	8
	d (Somer's *d*)	Two ordinal-level variables.	8
	tau-*b* (Kendall's tau-*b*)	Two ordinal-level variables.	8
	r_s (Spearman's rho)	Two ordinal-level variables. If one variable is ordinal level and one is interval level, both must be expressed as ranks prior to calculating r_s.	9
Interval/Ratio	*r* (Pearson's correlation coefficient)	Two interval-and/or ratio-level variables.	9
	R (multiple correlation coefficient)	Three or more interval- and/or ratio-level variables.	11

The Pearson correlation coefficient (*r*), also referred to as **Pearson's *r*, product-moment correlation coefficient,** and ***r*,** will be discussed in this chapter. Pearson's *r* is a measure of the linear or straight-line relationship between two interval-level variables. It is a symmetric statistic.

The form of the relationship between two interval- or ratio-level variables can be presented visually in a **scatter diagram** (also referred to as a *scattergram* or *scatter-plot*), which is a graphic device used to visually summarize the relationship between two variables. The *X*-axis is traditionally the horizontal axis and represents the independent variable. The vertical axis normally represents *Y*, the dependent variable.* The axes are drawn perpendicular to each other, approximately equal in length and marked to accommodate the full range of scores. Each coordinate represents two values: a score on the *X* variable and a score on the *Y* variable. Figure 9.1 displays the relationship between the desired number of children and the actual number of children reported by six hypothetical couples. Couple *A* preferred two children and have two children; therefore, their coordinate has been located at the point at which *X* and *Y* both equal 2. The scatter diagram allows for a visual inspection of the relationship between the two variables, and it is evident that three of the couples (*B*, *D*, and *E*) do not have the number of children that they desired. The Pearson correlation coefficient (*r*) for the data in Figure 9.1 equals +0.21. Let's consider the meaning of this value along with the correlation coefficients below the scatter diagrams in Figure 9.2.

*As with all statistical conventions, they are not always followed; therefore, always determine the independent and dependent variable before interpreting the data.

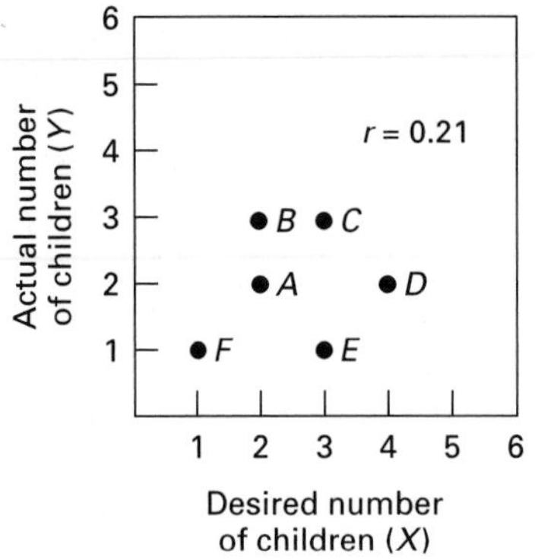

Couple	Desired number of children	Actual number of children
	(X)	(Y)
A	2	2
B	2	3
C	3	3
D	4	2
E	3	1
F	1	1

FIGURE 9.1
Scatter diagram showing the relationship between the desired and actual number of children for six couples (hypothetical data)

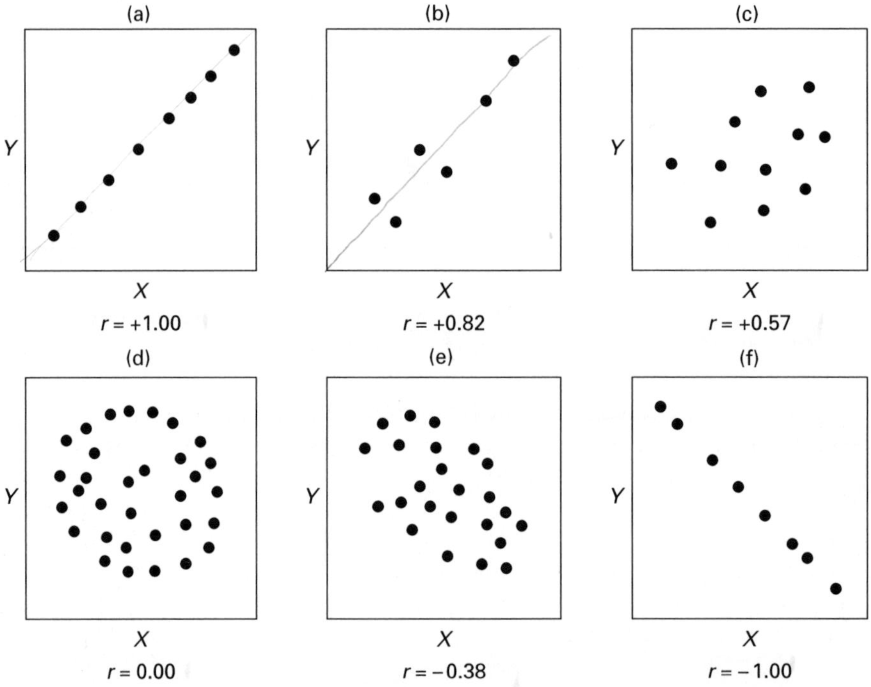

FIGURE 9.2
Scatter diagrams showing various degrees of relationship between two variables

The values of the Pearson correlation coefficient vary between +1.00 [see Figure 9.2(a)] and −1.00 [see Figure 9.2(f)]. Both extremes represent perfect linear relationships between variables, and 0.00 represents the absence of a relationship [see Figure 9.2(d)]. The *size* of the correlation coefficient indicates the strength of the relationship. The closer the points in the scatter diagram approach the form of a straight line, the stronger the relationship between X and Y. We ignore the sign of the coefficient when interpreting the strength of a relationship; hence the relationships in Figures 9.2(a) and (f) are equally strong in spite of their opposite signs.

The direction of a relationship is indicated by the *sign* of the correlation coefficient. A *positive relationship* (also referred to as a *positive correlation* or *direct relationship*) indicates that high scores on one variable tend to be associated with high scores on a second variable, and conversely, low scores on one variable tend to be associated with low scores on the second variable [see Figures 9.2(a), (b), and (c)]. A *negative relationship* (also referred to as a *negative correlation* or an *inverse or indirect relationship*) indicates that low scores on one variable tend to be associated with high scores on a second variable. Conversely, high scores on one variable tend to be associated with low scores on the second variable [see Figures 9.2(e) and 9.2(f)].

9.2 CALCULATION OF PEARSON'S *r*

9.2.1 Mean Deviation Method

The mean deviation method for calculating Pearson's r is not often used by social scientists because it involves more time and effort than other computational techniques. It is being presented here primarily because it sheds further light on the characteristics of Pearson's r. However, with small samples, it is as convenient a computational equation as any, unless a calculator or computer is available. The mean deviation computational equation for r is:

$$r = \frac{\Sigma(X - \bar{X})(Y - \bar{Y})}{\sqrt{[\Sigma(X - \bar{X})^2][\Sigma(Y - \bar{Y})^2]}} \tag{9.1}$$

Equation (9.1) provides a conceptual understanding of the Pearson correlation coefficient. The numerator of the equation is the **covariation** of X and Y or the extent to which X and Y vary together. It is the numerator that determines the *sign* of the correlation coefficient. A positive r results from high values of X tending to be paired with high values of Y, and conversely, low values of X tending to be paired with low values of Y. Substitute the values from Figure 9.1 into the numerator of equation (9.1) to ensure that you understand covariation and how it determines the sign of r. Also note that the covariation has an unrestricted upper range and that, by itself, it is not a good measure of association.

The denominator is always positive because the values are squared. It consists of the square root of the product of the standard deviation of X and Y since, in the more complex version of the equation on which equation (9.1) is based, both the numerator and denominator are divided by N. Thus, it is the denominator that restricts the range of r to ± 1 and results in r being independent of the measurement units of X and Y. The data in Table 9.2, which summarize educational attainment scores for seven female respondents and for their mothers, will be used to illustrate the mean deviation method for computing r.

TABLE 9.2
Computational procedures for *r* using the mean deviation method (hypothetical data)

Respondent	Mother's education X	$(X - \bar{X})$	$(X - \bar{X})^2$	Daughter's education Y	$(Y - \bar{Y})$	$(Y - \bar{Y})^2$	$(X - \bar{X})(Y - \bar{Y})$
A	1	−6	36	7	−6	36	36
B	3	−4	16	4	−9	81	36
C	5	−2	4	13	0	0	0
D	7	0	0	16	3	9	0
E	9	2	4	10	−3	9	−6
F	11	4	16	22	9	81	36
G	13	6	36	19	6	36	36
	$\bar{X} = 7$		$\Sigma(X - \bar{X})^2 = 112$	$\bar{Y} = 13$		$\Sigma(Y - \bar{Y})^2 = 252$	$\Sigma(X - \bar{X})(Y - \bar{Y}) = 138$

$$r = \frac{\Sigma(X - \bar{X})(Y - \bar{Y})}{\sqrt{[\Sigma(X - \bar{X})^2][\Sigma(Y - \bar{Y})^2]}}$$

$$= \frac{138}{\sqrt{(112)(252)}}$$

$$= \frac{138}{168.00} = 0.82$$

The computational procedures for the mean deviation method should be familiar to you. The symbols $\Sigma(X - \bar{X})^2$ and $\Sigma(Y - \bar{Y})^2$ were used to compute standard deviation in Chapter 6. In fact, in calculating r only one step has been added, that of obtaining the sum of cross-products $\Sigma(X - \bar{X})(Y - \bar{Y})$, which was identified earlier as the covariation of X and Y. This is obtained by multiplying the deviation of each individual's score from the mean of the X variable by its corresponding deviation on the Y variable and then summing all of the cross-products. Notice that if maximum deviations in X had lined up with maximum deviations in Y and so on down through the array, $\Sigma(X - \bar{X})(Y - \bar{Y})$ would have been equal to 168.00, which is the same as the value of the denominator, and would have produced a correlation of 1.00. In this instance we found the correlation between the mother's and daughter's education to be 0.82.

9.2.2 Raw Score Method

In calculating Pearson's r by the raw score method, we use equation (9.2):

$$r = \frac{N \Sigma XY - (\Sigma X)(\Sigma Y)}{\sqrt{[N \Sigma X^2 - (\Sigma X)^2][N \Sigma Y^2 - (\Sigma Y)^2]}} \qquad (9.2)$$

The procedure for calculating r by the raw score method is summarized in Table 9.3. Note that we calculate all of the quantities separately and substitute them into the equation. Here you find exactly the same coefficient ($r = 0.82$) as you did using the mean deviation method. As with that method, all of the procedures are familiar to you.

TABLE 9.3
Computational procedures for *r* using the raw score method (hypothetical data)

Respondent	Mother's education X	X^2	Daughter's education Y	Y^2	XY
A	1	1	7	49	7
B	3	9	4	16	12
C	5	25	13	169	65
D	7	49	16	256	112
E	9	81	10	100	90
F	11	121	22	484	242
G	13	169	19	361	247
$N = 7$	$\Sigma X = 49$ $\overline{X} = 7$	$\Sigma X^2 = 455$	$\Sigma Y = 91$ $\overline{Y} = 13$	$\Sigma Y^2 = 1435$	$\Sigma XY = 775$

$$r = \frac{N \Sigma XY - (\Sigma X)(\Sigma Y)}{\sqrt{[N \Sigma X^2 - (\Sigma X)^2][N \Sigma Y^2 - (\Sigma Y)^2]}}$$

$$= \frac{7(775) - (49)(91)}{\sqrt{[7(455) - (49)^2][7(1435) - (91)^2]}}$$

$$= \frac{5425 - 4459}{\sqrt{[3185 - 2401][10{,}045 - 8281]}}$$

$$= \frac{966}{\sqrt{[784][1764]}}$$

$$= \frac{966}{1176}$$

$$= 0.82$$

The quantity ΣXY is obtained by multiplying each X value by its corresponding Y and then summing these products. Also, be sure to make the distinction between ΣX^2 and $(\Sigma X)^2$ as well as between ΣY^2 and $(\Sigma Y)^2$.

9.3 PEARSON'S *r* AND *z* SCORES*

The Pearson correlation coefficient can also be computed using *z* scores and, furthermore, *z* scores provide an intutive interpretation that the raw score method is unable to offer. A high positive Pearson's *r* indicates that each individual obtains approximately the same *z* score on both variables. In a *perfect* positive correlation ($r = +1.00$), each individual obtains exactly the same *z* score on both variables.

With a high negative *r*, each individual obtains approximately the same *z* score on both variables, but the *z* scores are opposite in sign.

Remembering that the *z* score represents a measure of relative position in standard deviation units on a given variable (i.e., a high positive *z* represents a high score relative to the remainder of the distribution, and a high negative *z* represents a low

* *z* scores were initially discussed in Section 7.2.

score relative to the remainder of the distribution), we may now generalize the meaning of Pearson's r.

Pearson's r *represents the extent to which the same individuals, events, and so on occupy the same relative position on two variables.*

To explore the fundamental characteristics of the Pearson correlation coefficient, let's slightly modify the mother's and daughter's educational attainment scores example to demonstrate a perfect positive correlation. In Table 9.4, we find the educational attainment scores for the seven pairs of mothers and daughters on the two variables, X and Y, where X represents the educational attainment of the mother and Y represents the educational attainment of the daughter.

The scale values of X and Y do not need to be the same for the calculation of r. In this example, we see that X ranges from 1 through 13, whereas Y ranged from 4 through 22. This independence of r from specific scale values, which was initially noted in Section 9.2.1, permits us to investigate the relationships among an unlimited variety of variables. If we measure, for example, a person's yearly income in dollars *or* hundreds of dollars and separately correlate both measures of income with a second variable such as occupational status, the resulting correlation between income and status will be the same regardless of which income measure we use.

The z scores of each respondent on each variable are identical in the event of a perfect positive correlation. Had we reversed the order of either variable—that is, paired 1 with 22, paired 3 with 19, and so forth—the z scores would still be identical, but opposite in sign. In the latter case, the correlation would be a maximum *negative* ($r = -1.00$).

If we multiply the paired z scores and then sum the results, we will obtain maximum values only when the correlation is 1.00. Indeed, as the correlation approaches zero, the sum of the products of the paired z scores also approaches zero. Note that when the correlation is perfect, the sum of the products of the paired z scores

TABLE 9.4

Raw scores and corresponding z scores for seven pairs of mothers on two variables (hypothetical data)

Respondent	Mother's education X	$X - \overline{X}$	$(X - \overline{X})^2$	z_x	Daughter's education Y	$Y - \overline{Y}$	$(Y - \overline{Y})^2$	z_y	$z_x z_y$
A	1	−6	36	−1.5	4	−9	81	−1.5	2.25
B	3	−4	16	−1.0	7	−6	36	−1.0	1.00
C	5	−2	4	−0.5	10	−3	9	−0.5	0.25
D	7	0	0	0.0	13	0	0	0.0	0.00
E	9	2	4	0.5	16	3	9	0.5	0.25
F	11	4	16	1.0	19	6	36	1.0	1.00
G	13	6	36	1.5	22	9	81	1.5	2.25
	$\Sigma X = 49$	$\Sigma(X - \overline{X})^2 = 112$			$\Sigma Y = 91$	$\Sigma(Y - \overline{Y})^2 = 252$		$\Sigma z_x z_y = 7.00$	
	$\overline{X} = 7$	$s_x = \sqrt{\frac{112}{7}} = 4.00$			$\overline{Y} = 13$	$s_y = \sqrt{\frac{252}{7}} = 6.00$			

is equal to N, where N equals the number of pairs. These facts lead to an equation for r using z scores that is algebraically equivalent to equations (9.1) and (9.2).

$$r = \frac{\Sigma(z_x z_y)}{N} \tag{9.3}$$

Thus for Table 9.4:

$$r = \frac{7.00}{7} = 1.00$$

We suggest that you take the data in Table 9.1 and calculate r, using equation (9.3). You will arrive at a far more thorough understanding of r in this way.

Equation (9.3) is unwieldy because it requires calculation of separate z's for each score of each individual. Imagine the task of calculating r when N exceeds 50 cases, as it often does. For this reason computational equation (9.2) is normally used.

9.4 THE CORRELATION MATRIX

Researchers frequently present a **correlation matrix,** which is a summary of the statistical relationships between all possible pairs of variables. Table 9.5 presents the Pearson correlation coefficients for all of the possible relationships among five variables for 420 hypothetical respondents. Computation of the coefficients required that five measures, that is, one for each of the five variables in Table 9.5, be available for all of the respondents. The diagonal of a correlation matrix represents the correlation of a variable with itself; therefore, all of the values on the diagonal are 1.00. Each row in the matrix represents the correlation of a specific variable with other variables, as does each column.

The variable age, for example, is presented in row 1 and in column 1. If you wish to know the relationship between age and education, read down the age column until you come to the education row where you find $r = -0.23$. Notice that the scoring procedure for the attitude toward the federal funding for abortion variable has been stated explicitly to avoid misunderstanding. In this case, we see that a person who is opposed to federal funding for abortion would receive a low score and a person in

TABLE 9.5
Pearson correlation coefficients among five variables ($N = 420$) (hypothetical data)

	1	2	3	4	5
1. Age	1.00				
2. Occupational status	0.02	1.00			
3. Income	−0.19	0.33	1.00		
4. Education	−0.23	0.50	0.40	1.00	
5. Attitude toward federal funding of abortion (negative scored low)	−0.47	0.01	−0.19	0.14	1.00

favor of federal funding would receive a high score. Since it would be possible to score this item in the opposite manner (i.e., negative attitude scored high), it is always important to specify the scoring procedure in a potentially ambiguous situation such as this. If the scoring of the abortion item were reversed, all of the signs of the correlation coefficients associated with the abortion variable would also be reversed. The hypothetical example below shows the effect of scoring variable 5 in two ways.

	1. Age	5a. Attitude toward abortion (negative attitude scored low) (range = 0 to 10)	5b. Attitude toward abortion (negative attitude scored high) (range = 0 to 10)
Sue advocates the use of federal funds for abortion (very positive attitude)	30	10	0
Tom is neutral	42	5	5
Jim opposes the use of federal funds (very negative attitude)	50	0	10

Correlating age with variable 5a (equivalent to variable 5 in Table 9.5) would result in a negative correlation, whereas correlating age with variable 5b would result in a positive correlation. In either instance, the interpretation would be the same. The younger the respondent, the more likely he or she believes federal funds should be used to fund abortions.

Some social scientists prefer to display the correlation coefficients below the diagonal as shown in Table 9.5 and others prefer to display them above the diagonal. Table 9.6 in Statistics in Action 9.1 presents a correlation matrix in which the coefficients are displayed above the diagonal. Either approach is equally appropriate because the coefficients above and below the diagonal are a mirror image of each other. Pearson's r is a symmetrical measure of association; therefore, the correlation between two variables is exactly the same, regardless of which one, if either, serves as the independent or dependent variable—for example, $r_{13} = r_{31}$. You will occasionally see a *square matrix* with coefficients shown above and below the diagonal. For example, note the square matrix in exercise 29.

STATISTICS IN ACTION 9.1
Zero-Order Correlations with a Delinquency Scale

Scholars continue to search for explanations of why adolescents engage in delinquents acts. Table 9.6 summarizes the results of an Atlanta area study of self-reported deliquency among a sample of 600 adolescents.* A delinquency scale served as the dependent variable and was measured by combining 20 items that were weighted according to their seriousness (e.g., hurt

* Kirk W. Elifson, David M. Peterson, and C. Kirk Hadaway, "Religiosity and Delinquency: A Contextual Analysis," *Criminology* 21, November 1983, pp. 505–27.

TABLE 9.6
Zero-order correlations, means, and standard deviations (N = 498)

Variable	Mean	Standard deviation	1	2	3	4	5	6	7	8
1. Friends smoke marijuana ("all" = low)	3.69	1.09	1.00	−.28	.01	.25	−.17	.34	.25	−.31
2. Parent's attitudes toward friends (approve = low)	4.55	1.36		1.00	−.11	−.24	.30	−.27	−.27	.26
3. Sex (male = low)	1.49	0.51			1.00	.17	.00	.01	.10	−.15
4. High school grade average (A = 10)	6.89	2.09				1.00	−.06	.10	.16	−.22
5. Closeness to mother (close = low)	2.97	1.12					1.00	−.16	−.17	.19
6. Obey all parent's rules ("no" = low)	3.45	1.27						1.00	.28	−.21
7. Importance of religion (unimportant = low)	2.55	1.21							1.00	−.14
8. Weighted delinquency scale (not delinquent = low)	9.54	10.73								1.00

someone badly, steal something valued at more than $50, set fire to something, run away from home, hit a parent, intentionally damage school property, and take part in a gang fight). A computer was required to calculate the values in the tables.

The relationship of the independent (predictor) variables with each other and delinquency is shown in Table 9.6. We have also included the means and standard deviations for each of the variables. A guide for interpreting the correlations is included under each variable. Thus, the correlation between variable 1, "friends smoke marijuana," and variable 2, "parent's attitudes toward friends" ($r = -0.28$), tells us that those students who reported that their friends smoke marijuana also tend to have parents who do not approve of their friends. A dichotomous variable such as variable 3, "sex," can also be included in a correlation analysis. The correlation between sex and delinquency ($r = -0.15$) indicates that males are slightly more likely to have reported committing delinquent acts than females. Had you not known that males were scored "low" (0 in this analysis) and females were scored "high" (1 in this analysis), you would not have been able to interpret the correlation. Sex can be treated as an interval variable because the distance between being male (0) and female (1) is consistently 1.

9.5 INTERPRETING CORRELATION COEFFICIENTS

The correlation between age and attitude toward the federal funding of abortion in Table 9.5 is -0.47, which may also be written $r_{15} = -0.47$ where the subscripts 1 and 5 refer to the variables as numbered in Table 9.5. The negative coefficient indicates that there is a negative, inverse, or indirect relationship between the variables. Younger respondents tend to favor federal funding of abortion while, conversely, older respondents tend to be opposed to it. Although there is no established rule that specifies what constitutes a weak, moderate, or strong relationship, these general guidelines may be useful: a weak relationship, $r = \pm 0.01$ to ± 0.30; a moderate relationship, $r = \pm 0.31$ to ± 0.70; and a strong relationship, $r = \pm 0.71$ to ± 0.99. A perfect relationship is ± 1.00, and no relationship is indicated when $r = 0$.

Students frequently ask how large a coefficient must be before it is respectable. The magnitude and sign of a coefficient should be interpreted relative to previous inquiries whenever possible. The correlation between occupational status and educational attainment for a national sample of adult males normally falls between 0.50 and 0.60.* If an investigator found a marked departure from these values when studying similar variables, he or she would closely examine the computational procedures and data for errors.

Those social scientists who investigate the relationship between attitudes and behaviors, on the other hand, routinely expect the relationship to be weaker, generally between 0.20 and 0.40. Thus, previous studies can serve as guidelines in interpreting the relationship you choose to investigate.

When low correlations are found, one is strongly tempted to conclude that there is little or no relationship between the two variables under study. However, it must be remembered that r reflects only the *linear* relationship between two variables. The failure to find evidence of a relationship may be due to one of three possibilities: (1) The variables are unrelated, (2) the range of values on one or both of the variables is restricted, or (3) the variables are related but not linearly.† In the latter instance, Pearson's r would not be an appropriate measure of the degree of relationship between the variables because it assumes a linear relationship.

To illustrate, if we were plotting the relationship between age and church attendance, we might obtain a **scatter diagram** like that shown in Figure 9.3. It is usually possible to determine whether there is a substantial departure from a straight-line relationship by examining the scatter diagram. If the distribution of points in the scatter diagram is egg shaped or elliptical, without the decided bending that occurs in Figure 9.3, it may safely be assumed that the relationship is linear. Any small departures from linearity will not greatly influence the size of the correlation coefficient. On the other hand, where there is marked curvilinearity, as in Figure 9.3, a curvilinear coefficient of correlation would better reflect the relationship between the two variables under investigation. Although it is beyond the scope of this text to investigate

* The sign of a coefficient is frequently omitted when it is positive.

† A fourth possibility, that of a third variable suppressing the relationship, will not be discussed.

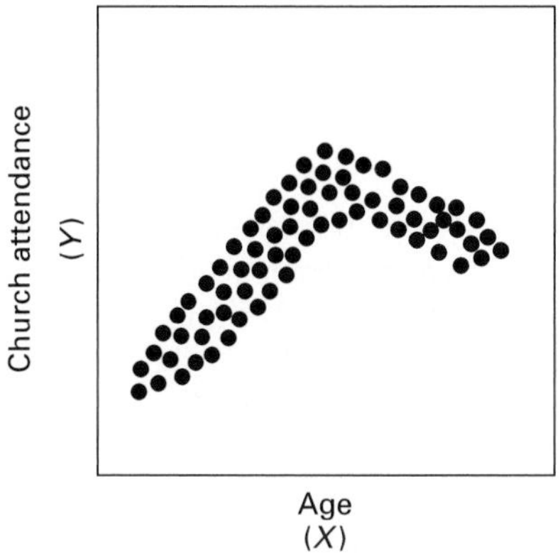

FIGURE 9.3
Scatter diagram of two variables that are related in a nonlinear fashion (hypothetical data)

nonlinear coefficients of correlation, you should be aware of this possibility and, as a matter of course, should construct a scatter diagram prior to calculating Pearson's r. Case Example 9.1 (Figure 9.4) provides additional examples of curvilinear relationships.

The assumption of linearity of relationship is the most important requirement to justify the use of Pearson's r as a measure of relationship between two variables. Pearson's r need not be calculated only with normally distributed variables, particularly when the sample size exceeds 50. So long as the distributions of the two variables are unimodal and relatively symmetrical, Pearson's r may legitimately be computed.

Another situation giving rise to artificially low correlation coefficients results from restricting the range of values of one or both of the variables. For example, if we were interested in the relationship between age and height for children from 3 to 16 years of age, we would undoubtedly obtain a rather high correlation coefficient between these two variables. However, suppose that we were to restrict the range of one of our variables? What effect would this have on the size of the coefficient? Consider that same relationship between age and height, but only for those children between the ages of 9 and 10. We would probably end up with a low coefficient.

You will note that the overall relationship illustrated in Figure 9.5 on p. 197 indicates a moderately strong negative relationship between age and life satisfaction ($r = -0.67$), but when we focus only on those respondents 40 years of age and less ($r = -0.51$) or those over 40 ($r = -0.38$), we see that the relationship is attenuated or weakened. A **restricted range** (sometimes referred to as **truncated range**) can normally be attributed to one of two causes: (1) a group of respondents might be inadvertently excluded from the study or (2) the respondents might be naturally homogeneous with respect to a particular variable. The exclusion of potential respondents can occur, for example, when home interviews are conducted only during daylight hours. Such a procedure results in interviewing very few respondents in the workforce and hence introduces the possibility of a restricted range in the respondents' ages. Note the reduced age variation to the left and right of the vertical line in Figure 9.5.

The second contributing factor, that of a naturally homogeneous group of respondents, is not uncommon in social science research because much of this research is

CASE EXAMPLE 9.1

CRANING AND GAWKING AT NOTHING

Bibb Latané proposed a theory of social impact that specifies the effect of other persons on an individual. Basing these conclusions on many different avenues of social research, the author states that "when other people are the source of impact and the individual is the target, impact should be a multiplicative function of the strength, immediacy, and number of other people." He presents considerable evidence that the relationship between impact and the number of people is not linear. In fact, the impact of each additional person added to the group is less than the impact of the preceding individual. This produces a curvilinear relationship between the number of people and social impact.

Have you ever been on a crowded city street and seen people craning and gawking at some nonexistent event? Figure 9.4(a) shows that as the size of the crowd increases, the percent of passersby who imitate craning and gawking behavior increases. Figure 9.4(b) shows that, similarly, in a study in which confederates gave incorrect answers to a length-of-line judging task, conformity increased with the size of the incorrect majority. In Figure 9.4(c) the size of the tip, in percent of total, decreases with the number of people seated at the table. Note that all describe curvilinear relationships between the independent variable (the number of people involved) and the dependent measure.

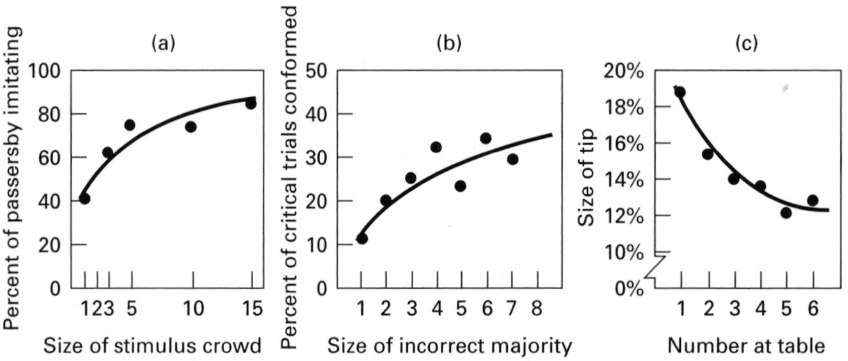

FIGURE 9.4

Several studies showing curvilinear relationships among variables

(*a*) Data from S. Milgram, L. Bickman, and L. Berkowitz, "Note on the Drawing Power of Crowds," *Journal of Personality and Social Psychology* 13 (1969), pp. 79–82; (*b*) data from H. B. Gerard, R. A. Wilhelmy, and E. S. Conolley, "Conformity and Group Size," *Journal of Personality and Social Psychology* 8 (1968), pp. 79–82; (*c*) data from S. Freeman, M. R. Walker, R. Borden, and B. Latané, "Diffusion of Responsibility and Restaurant Tipping. Cheaper by the Bunch," *Personality and Social Psychology Bulletin* 1 (1975), pp. 584–87.

Source: Based on Bibb Latané, "The Psychology of Social Impact," *American Psychologist* 36, no. 4 (1981), pp. 342–56.

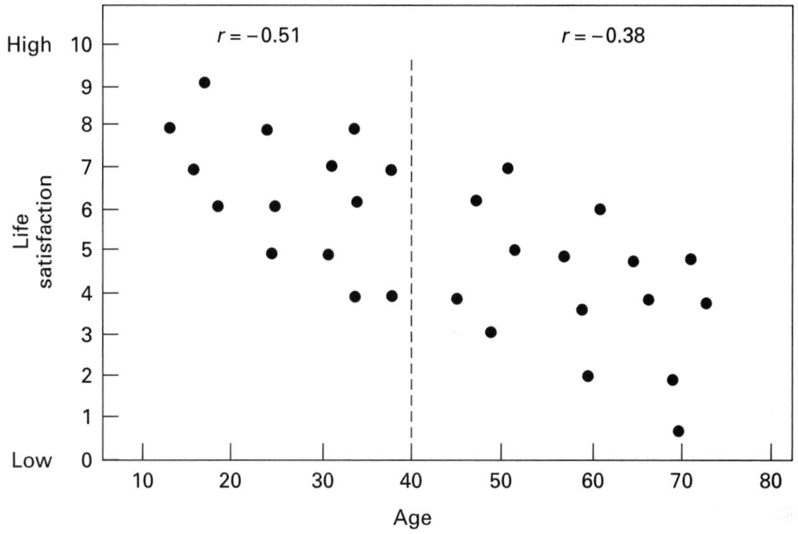

FIGURE 9.5
Scatter diagram illustrating high correlation over entire range of both variables ($r = -0.67$) but lower correlation when the range is restricted above or below 40 years of age (hypothetical data)

conducted in colleges and universities where respondents have been preselected for attitude and related variables. Thus, they represent a fairly homogeneous group with respect to these variables. Consequently, when an attempt is made to demonstrate the relationship between variables like SAT scores and college grades, the resulting coefficient may be low because of the restricted range. Furthermore, the correlations would be expected to be lower for colleges that select their students from within a narrow range of SAT scores.

Correlations can be artificially high when we are dealing with extremely small samples or when the data set contains extreme scores.* In the former instance, the correlation coefficient calculated using the sample data may not accurately reflect the actual correlation in the population from which the sample was drawn. This possibility will be considered further in Chapter 12. The significance test for r is presented in Section 14.8.

The impact of extreme scores on a correlation coefficient is shown in Figure 9.6 where the inclusion of the two extreme scores inflates the initial correlation of education and social participation from $r = 0.65$ to $r = 0.94$.

The influence of the extreme scores is exaggerated in this instance because of the small sample size. A few extreme scores in a sample with 500 cases, for example, would have little impact on the correlation coefficient.

---

*Also referred to as *deviant cases* or *outliers*.

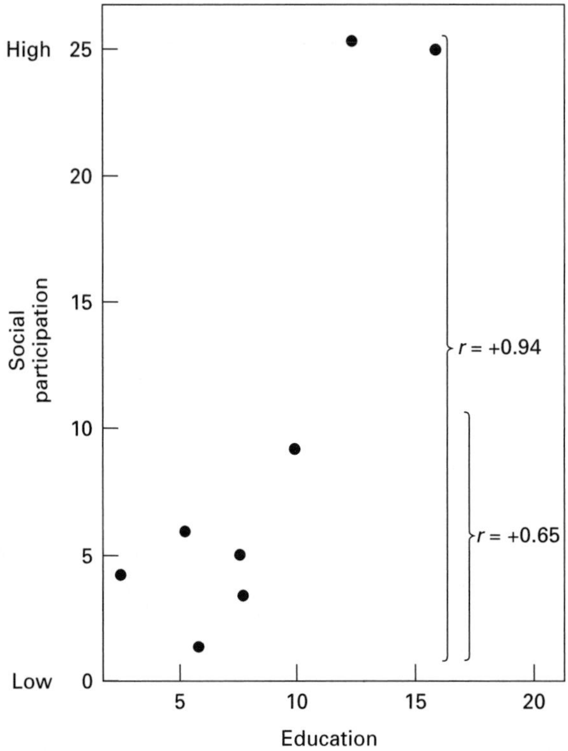

FIGURE 9.6
Scatter diagram illustrating the effect of extreme scores on the correlation coefficient (hypothetical data)

9.6 SPEARMAN'S RHO (r_s)

The second measure of correlation we discuss, r_s, is computed for ranked data on two variables. Imagine you are a sociologist. After long years of observation, you have developed a strong suspicion that the social class of husbands and wives *prior* to marriage is very similar. In an effort to test your hypothesis, you obtain a measure of the social class background for each of 15 men and women who are presently married. You are now able the use the premarriage social class measure to rank the wives from highest to lowest relative to the other wives, and you can rank the husbands in the some manner as shown in Table 9.7. For example, the wife who was ranked first would have had the highest social class score *prior* to her marriage of the 15 wives who were ranked. Her husband's social class score would have been the fourth highest among the men since he was ranked fourth.

Spearman's rho (r_s) requires that you obtain the differences in the ranks, square each difference, sum the squared differences, and substitute the resulting values into equation (9.4).

$$r_s = 1 - \frac{6 \Sigma D^2}{N(N^2 - 1)} \tag{9.4}$$

where D = rank X − rank Y, and
N = the number of ranked pairs

TABLE 9.7
Computational procedures for calculating r_s from ranked variables

Wife's rank (X)	Husband's rank (Y)	D	D^2
1	4	−3	9
2	2	0	0
3	9	−6	36
4	1	3	9
5	7	−2	4
6	10	−4	16
7	8	−1	1
8	13	−5	25
9	5	4	16
10	3	7	49
11	11	0	0
12	6	6	36
13	12	1	1
14	15	−1	1
15	14	1	1
		$\Sigma D = 0$	$\Sigma D^2 = 204$

$$r_s = 1 - \frac{6 \Sigma D^2}{N(N^2 - 1)}$$

$$= 1 - \frac{6(204)}{15(224)}$$

$$= 1 - \frac{1224}{3360}$$

$$= 1 - 0.36$$

$$= 0.64$$

As a matter of course, ΣD should be obtained even though it is not used in any of the calculations. It constitutes a useful check on the accuracy of your calculations up to this point since ΣD must equal zero. Case Example 9.2 provides a further discussion of r_s.

If you obtain any value other than zero, you should recheck your original ranks and the subsequent subtractions.

The value of r_s will equal $+1.00$ when the two sets of ranks are in perfect agreement, -1.00 when the two sets of ranks are in perfect disagreement, and 0 when there is no agreement, that is, the pairs are random; hence r_s is a measure of the extent to which the two sets of ranks are in agreement or disagreement. The computations in Table 9.7 in which r_s was found to equal 0.64 indicate that there is considerable similarity in the social class rankings prior to marriage of our sample of 15 wives and their husbands.

Occasionally, upon converting scores to ranks, you will find two or more tied scores. In this event, assign the mean of the tied ranks to each of the tied scores. The next score in the array receives the rank normally assigned to it. Thus, the ranks of the scores 128, 122, 115, 115, 115, 107, and 103 would be 1, 2, 4, 4, 4, 6, and 7, and the ranks of the scores 128, 122, 115, 115, 107, and 103 would be 1, 2, 3.5, 3.5, 5, and 6.

When there are tied ranks on either or both the X and the Y variables, the Spearman equation yields an inflated value, particularly when the number of tied ranks is high. The Pearson's r equation should be applied to the ranked data when there are numerous ties. The significance test for r_s is presented in Section 14.8.3.

CASE EXAMPLE 9.2

HELP IS WHERE YOU FIND IT!

We previously examined some of the data in Cowen's report when we discussed ordinal scales of measurement (Case Example 2.1). Table 9.8 presents the rankings of four different occupational groups in terms of how frequently they use various help-giving strategies when engaged with clients. We want to learn the extent to which they agree or disagree in their use of the 11 different strategies.

We must now find all possible intercorrelations among the four occupational groups. All told, six different correlations must be calculated: hairdressers versus bartenders, lawyers, and supervisors (three comparisons), bartenders versus lawyers and supervisors (two comparisons), and lawyers versus supervisors (one comparison). We'll show the calculation of r_s only for hairdressers versus bartenders (Table 9.9) and will summarize all their intercorrelations in Table 9.10.

The Spearman rank correlation for these data is

$$r_s = 1 - \frac{6(46)}{1320}$$

$$= 0.79$$

Table 9.10 shows the Spearman rank intercorrelations among all four occupational groups in terms of their help-giving strategies displayed in a correlation matrix. Examination of Table 9.10 reveals that hairdressers and bartenders correlate more highly than either does with lawyers and supervisors. The r_s of 0.79 is the highest of the six intercorrelations. Moreover, lawyers and supervisors intercorrelated higher with each other than they do with hairdressers and bartenders.

TABLE 9.8
Ordinal position of response strategies of four different occupations when clients seek advice and counsel

Strategy	Hairdressers	Bartenders	Lawyers	Supervisors
Offer support and sympathy	1	3	1	1.5
Try to be lighthearted	2	2	8	8
Just listen	3	1	5	1.5
Present alternatives	4	4	4	4
Tell person to count blessings	5	10	7	9
Share personal experiences	6	5	6	5
Try not to get involved	7	6	9.5	10
Give advice	8	7	3	7
Ask questions	9	9	2	3
Try to get person to talk to someone else	10	11	9.5	6
Try to change topic	11	8	11	11

Note: A rank of 1 corresponds to the most frequently used strategy and 11 to the least frequently used strategy.
Source: Based on Emory L. Cowen, "Help Is Where You Find It," *American Psychologist* 37, no. 4 (1982), pp. 285–395.

TABLE 9.9
Ordinal position of response strategies of two different occupations when clients seek advice and counsel

Strategy	Hairdressers	Bartenders	Difference	Difference squared
Offer support and sympathy	1	3	−2	4
Try to be lighthearted	2	2	0	0
Just listen	3	1	2	4
Present alternatives	4	4	0	0
Tell person to count blessings	5	10	−5	25
Share personal experiences	6	5	1	1
Try not to get involved	7	6	1	1
Give advice	8	7	1	1
Ask questions	9	9	0	0
Try to get person to talk to someone else	10	11	−1	1
Try to change topic	11	8	3	9
			$\Sigma D = 0$	$\Sigma D^2 = 46$

Note: A rank of 1 corresponds to the most frequently used strategy and 11 to the least frequently used strategy.

TABLE 9.10
Intercorrelations among four occupational groups on strategies for help-giving to clients

	Hairdressers	Bartenders	Lawyers	Supervisors
Hairdressers	1.00	0.79	0.43	0.46
Bartenders	—	1.00	0.30	0.43
Lawyers	—	—	1.00	0.78
Supervisors	—	—	—	1.00

SUMMARY

In this chapter, we discussed the concept of correlation and demonstrated the calculation of the Pearson correlation coefficient (r) using the mean deviation, raw score, and z score computational procedures. The scatter diagram was presented as an interpretive and summary device.

Correlation is concerned with determining the extent to which two variables are related or tend to vary together. The quantitative expression of the extent of the relationship is given in terms of the magnitude of the correlation coefficient. Correlation coefficients vary between values of -1.00 and $+1.00$; both extremes represent perfect relationships. A coefficient of zero indicates the absence of a relationship between two variables. The correlation matrix is used to summarize the correlations between all possible variable pairs.

Pearson's r is appropriate only for variables that are linearly related. Several situations that can contribute to artificially low or high correlations were discussed.

Spearman's rho (r_s) is a measure of association for ordinal data that provides a measure of the extent to which two sets of ranks are in agreement or disagreement. The value of r_s will equal $+1.00$ when the two sets of rankings are in perfect agreement and -1.00 when the two sets of rankings are in perfect disagreement.

TERMS TO REMEMBER

correlation coefficient A measure that expresses the extent to which two variables are related.

correlation matrix A summary of the statistical relationships among all possible pairs of variables.

covariation The extent to which two variables vary together.

Pearson's *r* (product-moment correlation coefficient; *r*) A correlation coefficient used with interval- or ratio-scaled variables.

restricted range A truncated range on one or both variables, resulting in a deceptively low correlation between these variables.

scatter diagram A graphic device used to summarize visually the relationship between two variables.

Spearman's rho (r_s) A measure of association for ordinal-level data that provides a measure of the extent to which two sets of ranks are in agreement or disagreement.

truncated range See *restricted range.*

EXERCISES

1. (*a*) Calculate the correlation between fear of crime (great fear scored high) and age.
(*b*) Reverse the scoring for fear of crime and recompute r. Assume fear of crime scores can theoretically vary between 1 and 15; therefore, 1 becomes 15, 2 becomes 14, and so on.

Age	Fear of crime
22	2
35	7
47	6
56	14
72	13

2. Explain in *your own words* the meaning of correlation.

3. In each of the following examples, identify a potential problem in the interpretation of the results of a correlational analysis.
(*a*) The relationship between age and frequency of drinking for an adolescent sample between the ages of 13 and 18.
(*b*) The correlation between aptitude and grades for honor students at a university.
(*c*) The relationship between vocabulary and reading speed among children in a "culturally deprived" community.

4. For a group of 50 individuals, $\Sigma z_x z_y$ is 41.3. What is the correlation between the two variables?

5. The following scores were made by five students on two tests. Calculate the Pearson r (using $r = \Sigma z_x z_y / N$). Convert to ranks and calculate r_s.

Student	Test X	Test Y
A	5	1
B	5	3
C	5	5
D	5	7
E	5	9

Generalize: What is the effect of tied ranks on r_s?

6. You have hypothesized that membership growth in large city churches is positively associated with distance from the central business district (CBD). Compute r for the following data set of 20 churches and determine if the data support your hypothesis.

Church	Percent growth in past year	Distance from CBD (in miles)	Church	Percent growth in past year	Distance from CBD (in miles)
1	14	6	11	3	0
2	8	3	12	1	6
3	9	21	13	14	12
4	2	0	14	6	3
5	4	3	15	2	1
6	0	4	16	4	7
7	15	9	17	7	4
8	22	9	18	8	2
9	7	4	19	11	9
10	9	3	20	6	7

7. Using distance from the CBD as the independent variable and percentage of growth in the past year as the dependent variable, construct a scatter diagram for the data in exercise 6. Does the relationship appear to be reasonably linear? Identify the two churches that can be characterized as having extreme scores (deviant cases or outliers).

8. Set up a data set demonstrating that gum disease is negatively related to the use of dental floss. Assume $N = 10$. Calculate r for your data.

9. Which correlation coefficient below indicates the strongest relationship? The weakest relationship? A negative relationship?
(*a*) -0.89 (*b*) $+0.32$ (*c*) $+0.58$

10. Calculate r for all pairs of the following variables and construct a correlation matrix.

Age	Education	Income	Family size
40	8	$ 7,000	6
32	17	46,000	4
21	16	33,000	3
36	14	30,000	3
51	12	31,000	5

11. A study focusing on political activism among African-American ministers reported that the Pearson *r* between age and an "attitude toward the police" scale (negative scored low) was −0.14. Interpret this finding. Church size and the minister's education were correlated +0.41. What does this finding tell you and how might it be interpreted? [*Source:* William M. Berenson, Kirk W. Elifson, and Tandy Tollerson III, "Preachers in Politics: Political Activism among the Black Ministry," *Journal of Black Studies* 6 (June 1976), pp. 373–92].

12. The following data show scores on advanced sections of the Graduate Record Examination and college grade point averages. What is the relationship between these two variables?

GRE scores	Grade point averages	GRE scores	Grade point averages
440	1.57	528	2.08
448	1.83	550	2.15
455	2.05	582	3.44
460	1.14	569	3.05
473	2.73	585	3.19
485	1.65	593	3.42
489	2.02	620	3.87
500	2.98	650	3.00
512	1.79	690	3.12
518	2.63		

13. Explain the difference between $r = -0.76$ and $r = +0.76$.

14. Construct a scatter diagram for each of the following four sets of data.

(*a*)		(*b*)		(*c*)		(*d*)	
X	*Y*	*X*	*Y*	*X*	*Y*	*X*	*Y*
1.5	0.5	0.5	5.0	0.5	0.5	0.5	1.0
1.0	0.5	0.5	4.5	1.0	1.0	0.5	2.5
1.0	2.0	1.0	3.5	1.0	1.5	0.5	4.5
1.5	1.5	1.5	4.0	1.5	2.5	1.0	3.5
1.5	2.0	1.5	2.5	1.5	3.5	1.5	1.0
2.0	2.0	2.0	3.0	2.0	2.5	1.5	2.5
2.5	2.5	2.5	2.0	2.0	3.5	1.5	4.0
2.5	3.2	2.5	3.5	2.5	4.5	2.0	1.0

(a)		(b)		(c)		(d)	
X	Y	X	Y	X	Y	X	Y
3.0	2.5	3.0	2.5	3.0	3.5	3.0	2.0
3.0	3.5	3.0	2.0	3.5	3.0	3.0	3.5
3.5	3.5	3.5	2.0	3.5	2.5	3.0	4.5
3.5	4.5	3.5	2.5	3.5	2.0	3.5	1.0
4.0	3.5	4.0	1.5	4.0	2.5	3.5	1.0
4.0	4.5	4.0	0.7	4.0	2.0	3.5	3.5
4.5	4.5	5.0	0.5	4.5	1.0	4.0	3.5
5.0	5.0			5.0	1.0	4.0	4.5
				5.0	0.5	4.5	2.5
						4.5	1.0

15. By inspecting the scatter diagrams for the data in exercise 14, determine which one represents:
(*a*) A curvilinear relation between *X* and *Y*.
(*b*) A positive correlation between *X* and *Y*.
(*c*) Little or no relation between *X* and *Y*.
(*d*) A negative correlation between *X* and *Y*.

16. Discuss the following correlation matrix, which is based on interviews with 275 lawyers (hypothetical data).

	1	2	3	4
1. Size of law firm	1.00			
2. Salary	0.40	1.00		
3. Age	−0.11	0.67	1.00	
4. Education	0.03	0.00	0.07	1.00

17. The following data show the scores obtained by a group of 20 students on a college entrance examination and a verbal comprehension test. (*a*) Calculate Pearson's *r* for these data and (*b*) prepare a scatter diagram.

Student	College entrance exam (X)	Verbal comprehension test (Y)	Student	College entrance exam (X)	Verbal comprehension test (Y)
A	52	49	K	64	53
B	49	49	L	28	17
C	26	17	M	49	40
D	28	34	N	43	41
E	63	52	O	30	15
F	44	41	P	65	50
G	70	45	Q	35	28
H	32	32	R	60	55
I	49	29	S	49	37
J	51	49	T	66	50

18. Outreach workers have identified seven neighborhoods that have the greatest predominance of intravenous drug users. The estimated number of drug users by neighborhood is shown below along with the area's median household income. Convert the data to ranks and compute r_s.

Neighborhood	Number of drug users	Median income
A	75	$ 9,000
B	20	20,000
C	0	27,000
D	110	6,200
E	40	14,000
F	200	7,500
G	60	12,000

19. The data in the following table represent scores obtained by 10 students on a statistics examination, and their final grade point average. Prepare a scatter diagram and calculate Pearson's r for these data.

Student	Score on statistics exam, X	Grade point average, Y	Student	Score on statistics exam, X	Grade point average, Y
A	90	2.50	*F*	70	1.00
B	85	2.00	*G*	70	1.00
C	80	2.50	*H*	60	0.50
D	75	2.00	*I*	60	0.50
E	70	1.50	*J*	50	0.50

20. Two consulting agencies have independently ranked 10 counties in terms of the quality of their public schools. Compute r_s to determine the extent to which the two sets of rankings correspond.

County	Rank of schools by agency *A*	Rank of schools by agency *B*
A	1	1
B	4	2
C	3	3
D	2	4
E	7	6
F	5	7
G	6	5
H	8	9
I	9	10
J	10	8

21. Twenty-five high school students were randomly selected from public high schools in the Boston area and asked to report anonymously the number of rock concerts they attended during the past year and the average number of days per week that they smoke marijuana. Given the accompanying data, compute *r* and interpret your answer. What does it tell you?

Number of rock concerts attended	Days per week marijuana smoked	Number of rock concerts attended	Days per week marijuana smoked
4	2	4	2
7	4	4	2
0	0	3	0
1	2	11	7
6	3	14	6
2	1	6	3
2	0	3	0
3	1	1	2
2	4	4	5
3	3	0	0
2	1	1	1
0	0	3	1
		0	1

22. A sociological study involved the rating of teachers. To determine the reliability of the ratings, the ranks given by two different observers were tabulated. Are the ratings reliable? Explain your answer.

Teacher	Rank by observer *A*	Rank by observer *B*	Teacher	Rank by observer *A*	Rank by observer *B*
A	12	15	*I*	6	5
B	2	1	*J*	9	9
C	3	7	*K*	7	6
D	1	4	*L*	10	12
E	4	2	*M*	15	13
F	5	3	*N*	8	8
G	14	11	*O*	13	14
H	11	10	*P*	16	16

23. What effect does departure from linearity have on Pearson's *r*?

24. How does the range of scores sampled affect the size of the correlation coefficient?

25. How well do you remember the names of the seven dwarfs from Disney's animated classic, *Snow White and the Seven Dwarfs?* The following table shows the order in which they were recalled, the percent of subjects recalling the names of each dwarf, and the percent who correctly identified them in a recognition task.

Dwarf	Order of recall	Recalled (%)	Recognized (%)
Sleepy	1	86	91
Dopey	2	81	95
Grumpy	3	75	86
Sneezy	4	78	93
Doc	5	58	80
Happy	6	62	70
Bashful	7	38	84

Source: G. E. Meyer and K. Hilterbrand, "Does It Pay to Be 'Bashful'?: The Seven Dwarfs and Long-Term Memory," *American Journal of Psychology* 97 (1984), pp. 47–55.

(*a*) What is the measure of relationship appropriate for these data?
(*b*) Prepare a correlation matrix showing the intercorrelations of these three variables.

26. What is the effect of reversing the scoring of a variable included in a correlation matrix?

27. Given the following two data sets:
(*a*) Compute r for each data set.
(*b*) Prepare the scatter diagrams.
(*c*) Discuss the influence of the extreme scores in data set 1 on the size of its correlation coefficient relative to the correlation coefficient for data set 2.

Data set 1		Data set 2	
X	Y	X	Y
1	4	1	4
5	6	5	6
6	2	6	2
8	3	8	3
8	5	8	5
10	9	10	9
13	25		
16	25		

28. Compute r for the following data set and prepare the scatter diagram. Can you explain why the correlation is so low?

X	Y
1	5
1	4
1	3
2	2
3	2
4	3
4	4
4	5

29. The square correlation matrix below was computer generated. What is the correlation between age and years of educational attainment, age and income, and income and educational attainment? (*Note:* The values in parentheses indicate the number of cases used to compute each coefficient.)

	Age	Education	Income
Age	1.0000 (1495)	−.2593 (1491)	−.0987 (1429)
Education	−.2593 (1491)	1.0000 (1496)	.4373 (1430)
Income	−.0987 (1429)	.4373 (1430)	1.0000 (1434)

Correlation coefficient/(Cases)

30. Discuss the scatter diagram below which shows the relationship between years of educational attainment and present salary for 474 bank employees ($r = +0.66$).

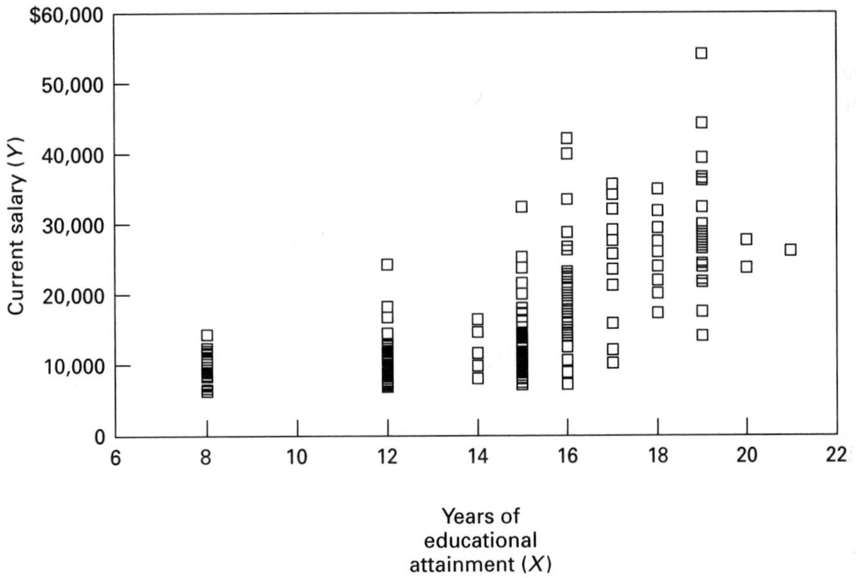

CHAPTER 10

Regression and Prediction

10.1 INTRODUCTION TO PREDICTION

Is length of courtship a good predictor of marital success? What role does sexual compatibility play in a successful marriage? Knowing a person's employment record, what can we say about the likelihood of him or her receiving a promotion? Knowing a student's mathematics aptitude score, can we estimate how well he or she will do in a statistics course?

Let's look at an example. Suppose we are trying to predict student Jones's score on the final exam. If the only information available was that the class mean on the final was 75 ($\overline{Y} = 75$), the best guess we could make is that he would obtain a score of 75 on the final.* However, far more information is usually available; for example, Jones obtained a score of 62 on the midterm examination. How can we use this information to make a better prediction about his performance on the final exam? If we know that the class mean on the midterm examination was 70 ($\overline{X} = 70$), we could reason that since he scored below the mean on the midterm, he would probably score below the mean on the final. At this point, we appear to be closing in on a more accurate prediction of his performance. How might we further improve the accuracy of our prediction? Simply knowing that he scored below the mean on the midterm does not give us a clear picture of his relative standing on this exam. If, however, we know the standard deviation of the whole class's scores on the midterm, we could express his

* See Section 5.2.2, in which we demonstrated that the sum of the deviations from the mean is zero and that the sum of squares of deviations from the arithmetic mean is less than the sum of squares of deviations about any other score or potential score.

score in terms of his relative position; that is, his z score. Let's imagine that the standard deviation on the midterm was 4 ($s_x = 4$). Since Jones scored a 62, which is 2 standard deviations below the mean ($z_x = -2.00$), would we be justified in guessing that he would score 2 standard deviations below the mean on the final ($z_y = -2.00$)? That is, if $s_y = 8$, would you predict a score of 59 ($75 - 16 = 59$) on the final? No! You will note that an important piece of information is missing: the correlation between the midterm and the final. You may recall from our discussion of correlation* that Pearson's r represents the extent to which the same individuals or events occupy the same relative position on two variables. Thus, we are justified in predicting a score of exactly 59 on the final only when the correlation between the midterm and the final exam is perfect (i.e., when $r = +1.00$). However, suppose that the correlation is equal to zero. Then it should certainly be obvious that we are not justified in predicting a score of 59; rather, we are once again back to our original prediction of 75, that is, $\overline{Y}$.

In summary, when $r = 0$, our best prediction is 75 ($\overline{Y}$); when $r = +1.00$, our best prediction is 59 ($z_y = z_x$). It should be clear that predictions from intermediate values of r will fall somewhere between 59 and 75.†

An important advantage of a correlational analysis, then, stems from its application to problems involving predictions from one variable to another. Sociologists, criminologists, political scientists, and economists are constantly called upon to make predictions. To provide an adequate explanation of r and to illustrate its specific applications, we need to proceed with a discussion of linear regression.

10.2 LINEAR REGRESSION

To simplify our discussion, let's start with an example of two variables that are usually perfectly or almost perfectly related: monthly salary and annual income. In Table 10.1, we have listed the monthly income of eight employees of a small welfare office. These data are shown graphically in Figure 10.1. As you recall, it is customary to refer to the horizontal axis as the X-axis and to the vertical axis as the Y-axis. If one variable occurs earlier in time (or before) the other, the earlier one (or the independent variable) is represented on the X-axis. It will be noted that all salaries are represented on a straight line extending diagonally from the lower left-hand corner to the upper right-hand corner.

10.2.1 Equation for Linear Relationships

The equation relating monthly salary to annual income may be represented as:

$$Y' = 12X$$

where the prime mark on Y indicates Y is being predicted.

---

* See Section 9.2.

† We are assuming that the correlation is positive. If the correlation were -1.00, our best prediction would be a score of 91, that is, $z_y = -z_x$.

TABLE 10.1
Monthly salaries and annual income of eight employees of a welfare office

Employee	Monthly salary	Annual income
A	1,800	21,600
B	1,900	22,800
C	1,925	23,100
D	1,950	23,400
E	2,000	24,000
F	2,050	24,600
G	2,100	25,200
H	2,175	26,100

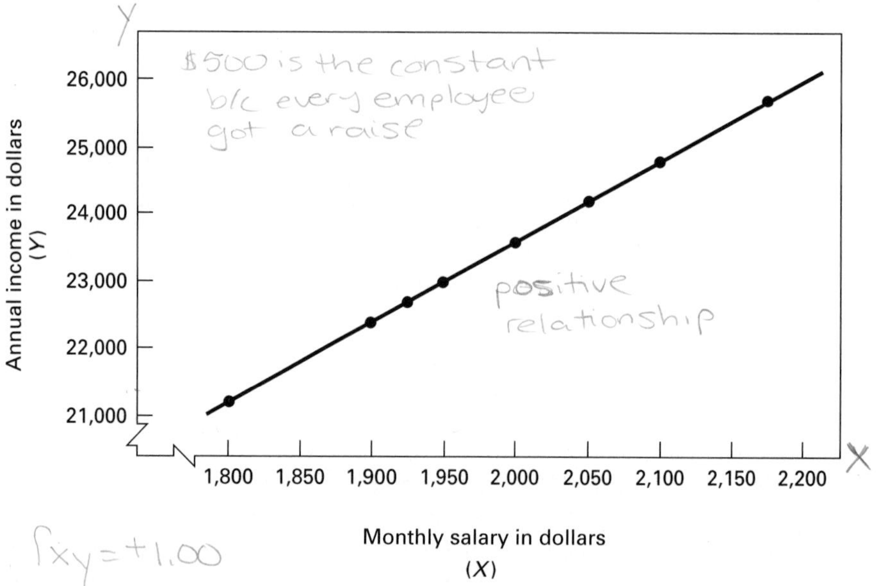

FIGURE 10.1
Monthly salaries and annual income of eight employees of a welfare office

You may substitute the value of X (the independent variable) into the equation and obtain the value of Y' (the predicted dependent variable) directly. For example, if another employee's monthly salary were \$2,200, her annual income would be:

$$Y' = 12(2{,}200) = 26{,}400$$

Let's add one more factor to this linear relationship. Suppose all of the employees received a \$500 raise. The equation would now read:

$$Y' = 500 + 12X$$

Thinking back to your algebra class, you will probably recognize this equation as a special case of the general equation for a straight line, that is:

$$Y' = a_y + b_y X \qquad (10.1)$$

in which Y and X represent variables that change from individual to individual, and a_y and b_y represent constants for a particular set of data. More specifically, b_y represents the *slope of a line* relating values of Y to values of X. Thus, Y is the dependent variable and X is the independent variable. This is referred to as the *regression of Y on X*. In the present example, the slope of the line is 12, which means that Y changes by a factor of 12 for each unit change in X. The letter a_y represents the value of Y when $X = 0$ and is referred to as the *Y-intercept* or the point at which the line crosses the Y-axis.

Equation (10.1) may be regarded as a method for predicting Y from known values of X. When the correlation is 1.00 (as in the present case), the predictions are perfect.

The line in Figure 10.1, if extended downward, would intersect the Y-axis at $Y = 0$; therefore, $a_y = 0$. The information presented in Figure 10.2 will help you understand the meaning of the intercept and the slope.

As you can see, five lines are shown in Figure 10.2. All five have an intercept of 50 because each crosses the Y-axis at 50. Each of the five lines, however, has a different

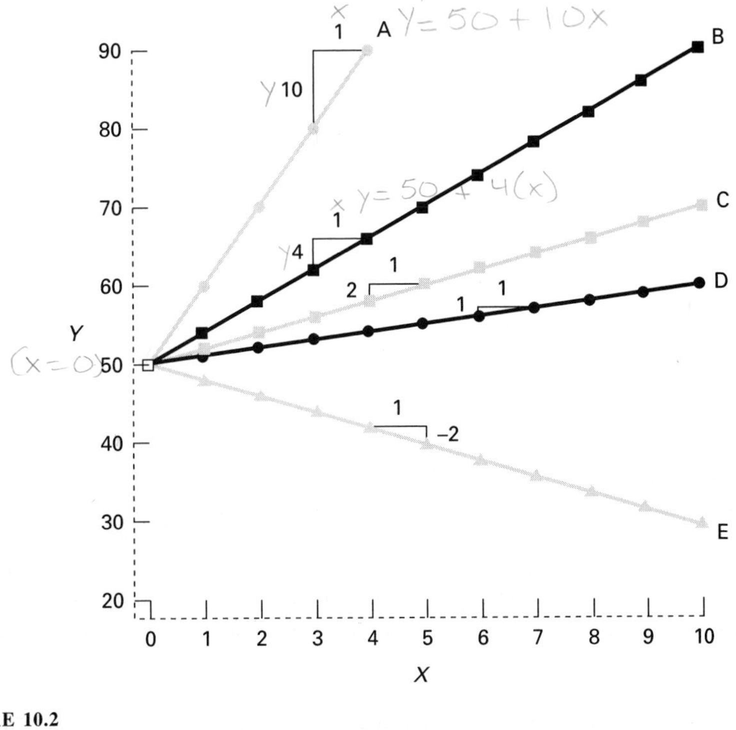

FIGURE 10.2
A graph representing five lines with different slopes
The slope refers to the change in Y relative to the change in X. A positive value indicates that the Y-variables increases as the X-variable increases. A negative slope indicates the Y-variable decreases as the X-variable increases. The size of the slope value determines if the line is more horizontal (small slope) or steep (large slope). The slopes for the lines in this figure are: line A, $b_y = 10$; line B, $b_y = 4$; line C, $b_y = 2$; line D, $b_y = 1$; line E, $b_y = -2$. For all lines the intercept is 50.

slope. The slope refers to the increase or decrease in Y that occurs as X increases. Consider the line that rises the fastest, line A. The line has a slope of 10; each 1-unit increase in X equals a 10-unit increase in Y. For this line, we say that the slope is 10 to 1 or, more simply, 10. Another way of expressing slope is with the equation:

$$b_y = \frac{\text{change in } Y}{\text{change in } X} \tag{10.2}$$

In words, the slope is the ratio of the change in Y to the change in X. When the change in Y is positive, the line increases from left to right, a positive relationship. When Y is negative, the line decreases from left to right, a negative relationship. As the slope becomes a smaller number, the line begins to level out. The line with a slope of 4, line B, is less steep than the line with a slope of 10. Likewise, with a slope of 2, line C represents a line that is less steep than the line with a slope of 4.

Line E represents a negative slope. Increases in X are associated with decreases in Y. You already saw diagrams like this when we examined negative correlations. For this line, the slope is -2, which means that each unit increase in X corresponds to a 2-unit decrease in Y.

Note that use of equation (10.1) may be regarded as a method for predicting Y from known values of X. In other words, we can use equation (10.1) to write an equation that describes each of the lines in Figure 10.2:

$$\begin{aligned}
\text{A:}\quad Y' &= 50 + 10(X) \\
\text{B:}\quad Y' &= 50 + 4(X) \\
\text{C:}\quad Y' &= 50 + 2(X) \\
\text{D:}\quad Y' &= 50 + 1(X) \\
\text{E:}\quad Y' &= 50 + -2(X)
\end{aligned}$$

Using any value of X, we can estimate the corresponding value of Y by multiplying the appropriate slope and adding the value of the intercept. When the correlation is 1.00 (as in the present case), the predictions are perfect.

10.2.2 Predicting *Y* from *X*

The correlations we obtain in social science research are almost never perfect and the data do not fall on a straight line. Therefore, we must find a straight line the *best fits* or describes our data and make predictions from that line. But what do we mean by "best fit"? When discussing the mean and the standard deviation, we defined the *mean* as that point in a distribution that makes the sum of squared deviations from it minimal; that is, less than the sum of squared deviations about any other score or potential score (see Section 5.2.2). When applying this principle to correlation and regression, we are defining the *best-fitting straight line* as a straight line that best represents the linear relationship between two variables, X and Y. This straight line is referred to as a **regression line.** Synonyms for the regression line include the **line of best fit,** least squares line, and the prediction line.

The term *predict,* which issued as a synonym for *estimate* in statistics, does not necessarily carry with it any implication about the future, simply refers to the fact that we are using information about one variable to obtain information about another. Thus, if we know a woman's occupational status, we may use this information to predict how much education she has completed (which we would assume preceded her having been hired for the job). On the other hand, regression is used in many situations where we want to estimate future events based on our knowledge of previous events. College admissions officers use students' high school GPA to predict whether they will be successful in college.

At this point, we will highlight a new symbol you recently encountered: Y'.* This may be read as "Y prime," "the predicted Y," or "estimated Y." We use this symbol with the regression line or the regression equation to estimate or predict a score on one variable from a known score on another.

Returning to the equation for a straight line ($y' = a_y + b_y X$), we are faced with the problem of determining b_y and a_y for a particular set of data so that Y' may be obtained. One equation for obtaining the slope of the line relating Y to X, which is known as the line of regression of Y on X, is the mean deviation equation:

$$b_y = \frac{\Sigma(X - \bar{X})(Y - \bar{Y})}{\Sigma(X - \bar{X})^2} \tag{10.3}$$

You may have noticed that the numerator for this equation and for the mean deviation computational equation (9.1) for r are identical. The numerator in equation (9.1) determined the sign of r, and the numerator of equation (10.3) also determines the sign of b_y. It follows that the sign of r will always be the same as the sign of b_y for a given data set. Equation (10.3) is mathematically equivalent to equation (10.4), which clearly shows the relationship between r and b_y; b_y is equal to r times the ratio of the standard deviation of Y and the standard deviation of X. Hence, r equals b_y only when the standard deviations of X and Y are equal:

$$b_y = r\left(\frac{s_y}{s_x}\right) \tag{10.4}$$

Equations (10.3) and (10.4) are mathematically equivalent to equation (10.5), which is the raw score computational equation preferred by many social scientists. You will note that it is similar to the raw score equation (9.2) used to compute r:

$$b_y = \frac{N(\Sigma XY) - (\Sigma X)(\Sigma Y)}{N(\Sigma X^2) - (\Sigma X)^2} \tag{10.5}$$

The intercept, a_y, is given by the equation:

$$a_y = \bar{Y} - b_y \bar{X} \tag{10.6}$$

When calculating Y', it is unwieldy to obtain each of these quantities separately and substitute them into the equation for a straight line. However, by algebraically combining equations (10.4) and (10.6) and relating the results to equation (10.1), we

* The symbol $\hat{Y}$ (read "Y hat or Y cap"), an alternative symbol that also designates the predicted Y, is preferred by some social and behavioral scientists.

can obtain a much more useful equation for Y':

$$Y' = \overline{Y} + r\left(\frac{s_y}{s_x}\right)(X - \overline{X}) \tag{10.7}*$$

Equation (10.7) produces the same results as equation (10.1). The main reason we use equation (10.7) is to help us to better explain the concept of regression analysis. Let us begin to examine the regression equation in greater detail.

Y'	=	$\overline{Y}$	+	r	$\left(\frac{s_y}{s_x}\right)$	$(X - \overline{X})$
Predicted value of Y	=	Mean of Y	+	Correlation between X and Y	$\frac{s \text{ of } y}{s \text{ of } x}$	Deviation score

One of the key elements of this equation is the slope of the regression line, $r\left(\frac{s_y}{s_x}\right)$. What are the factors that influence the slope of a line? Based on our definition, three factors affect the slope of the regression line: (1) the magnitude of the correlation coefficient, (2) the sign of the correlation coefficient, and (3) the ratio of the standard deviation of Y to the standard deviation of X. The data presented in Table 10.2 illustrate the relationship between these three factors.

The sign of the slope is always controlled by the sign of the correlation. Positive correlations produce positive slopes, negative correlations produce negative slopes, and correlations of 0 produce flat lines—lines with no slope.

The magnitude of the slope is influenced by the size of the correlation and the size of the ratio $\frac{s_y}{s_x}$. This ratio represents the proportional change in Y that occurs when X changes. As we have mentioned before, one of the advantages of correlation and regression statistics is that they allow us to use two scales that may have different means and standard deviations. The ratio $\frac{s_y}{s_x}$ allows us to estimate the proportional size of $(Y' - \overline{Y})$ given $(X - \overline{X})$. Stated another way, it allows us to adjust our predicted Y-score to accommodate any difference between the two measures in terms of their variability. If both X and Y have the same amount of variability ($s_x = s_y$), then the ratio will equal 1.0 and no adjustment will be needed. Two examples of $\frac{s_y}{s_x}$ are presented in Table 10.2. In example 1, the ratio is 2:1. As a consequence, small changes along the X-scale correspond to large changes along the Y-scale. In example 2, the ratio is 0.5:1. This smaller ratio means that changes along the X-scale correspond to relatively small changes along the Y-scale.

---

* Because $Y' = a_y + b_y X$, $a_y = \overline{Y} - b_y\overline{X}$, and $b_y = r\left(\frac{s_y}{s_x}\right)$, then $Y' = \overline{Y} - r\left(\frac{s_y}{s_x}\right)\overline{X} = \overline{Y} + r\left(\frac{s_y}{s_x}\right)(X - \overline{X})$.

TABLE 10.2
Two examples demonstrating the relation between the slope of a regression line and the magnitude of the correlation coefficient, its sign, and the magnitude of $\frac{s_y}{s_x}$

Example 1			Example 2		
$r = 1.0$	$\frac{s_y}{s_x} = \frac{2}{1}$	$b_y = 2.00$	$r = 1.0$	$\frac{s_y}{s_x} = \frac{1}{2}$	$b_y = 0.50$
$r = 0.5$	$\frac{s_y}{s_x} = \frac{2}{1}$	$b_y = 1.00$	$r = 0.5$	$\frac{s_y}{s_x} = \frac{1}{2}$	$b_y = 0.25$
$r = 0.0$	$\frac{s_y}{s_x} = \frac{2}{1}$	$b_y = 0.00$	$r = 0.0$	$\frac{s_y}{s_x} = \frac{1}{2}$	$b_y = 0.00$
$r = -0.5$	$\frac{s_y}{s_x} = \frac{2}{1}$	$b_y = -1.00$	$r = -0.5$	$\frac{s_y}{s_x} = \frac{1}{2}$	$b_y = -0.25$
$r = -1.0$	$\frac{s_y}{s_x} = \frac{2}{1}$	$b_y = -2.00$	$r = -1.0$	$\frac{s_y}{s_x} = \frac{1}{2}$	$b_y = -0.50$

Many researchers make the mistake of assuming that the larger the slope, the better. From an inspection of Table 10.2, however, you should be able to see that the size of the slope does not necessarily indicate the magnitude of the relationship between X and Y. It is true that when the correlation is zero, the slope will be zero. However, a larger slope doesn't always mean a stronger relationship. Consider the two examples presented in Table 10.2. In example 1 when $\frac{s_y}{s_x} = 2$ and $r = .5$, the slope of the line is 1.00. In contrast, example 2 indicates that when $\frac{s_y}{s_x} = .5$ and $r = 1$, the slope of the line is 0.5. Although it is smaller, a slope of 0.5, in this example, represents a greater degree of relatedness between the two variables. Of course, different values of r and $\frac{s_y}{s_x}$ produce different slopes. *Therefore, only the correlation coefficient can be used to describe the magnitude of the relation between two variables.*

Now look at the last part of the equation, $(X - \overline{X})$. This value tells us how much the observed score of X deviates from the mean of X. When we multiply this value by the slope, we determine how much the predicted score Y' will deviate from the mean of Y. In other words, multiplying the slope and the deviation of X gives the predicted deviation from the mean of Y resulting from the regression of Y on X. The amount of the deviation from the mean of Y is also affected by the magnitude of the correlation coefficient. The larger the r, the greater the deviation of Y' from $\overline{Y}$. Remember that it is the correlation coefficient that represents the relation between X and Y. The larger the correlation coefficient, the more closely matched the X and Y scores are in terms of their deviation from the group means.

When there is a perfect correlation, there is a perfect correspondence between the relative positions of the scores. When the correlation is 0, there is no correspondence between the relative position of the scores. Thus, when $r = 0$, $Y' = \overline{Y}$. This confirms what we noted earlier. When the correlation is 0 and no other information is available, the mean is the best estimate of individual performance.

Case Example 10.1 illustrates three regression problems.

CASE EXAMPLE 10.1

REGRESSION PROBLEMS

Here are three sample problems employing the data introduced in Section 10.1.

PROBLEM 1. Mr. Jones, you will recall, scored 62 on the midterm examination. What is our prediction concerning his score on the final examination? The relevant statistics are reproduced in the table below.

Midterm exam (X-variable)	Final exam (Y-variable)
$\overline{X} = 70$	$\overline{Y} = 75$
$s_x = 4$	$s_y = 8$

$r = 0.60$

Employing equation (10.7), we find:

$$Y' = 75 + 0.60\left(\frac{8}{4}\right)(62 - 70) = 75 - 9.60 = 65.40$$

PROBLEM 2. Alternatively, we could use equation (10.1) to predict Jones's score on the final examination in the following manner. Using equation (10.4), we can calculate b_y:

$$b_y = r\left(\frac{s_y}{s_x}\right) = 0.60\left(\frac{8}{4}\right) = 1.20$$

We see that $b_y = 1.20$ or that, as X increases one unit on the X-axis, Y increases 1.20 units on the Y-axis. Now we can calculate a_y, or our Y-intercept, using equation (10.6):

$$a_y = \overline{Y} - b_y\overline{X} = 75 - (1.20)70 = -9$$

We now know that $a_y = -9$ or that the regression line crosses the Y-axis at the value $Y = -9$. Using the values we have just calculated for b_y and a_y and his score of 62 on the midterm, we can now use equation (10.1) to predict Jones's score on the final exam:

$$Y' = a_y + b_yX = -9 + 1.20(62) = 65.40$$

Our prediction agrees with the less cumbersome calculation in problem 1, that Jones will receive a score of 65.40 on the final examination. This second example should begin to convey to you the interrelatedness of the various approaches to calculating a_y and b_y and predicting Y.

PROBLEM 3. On the same midterm test, Maureen scored 76. What is our prediction concerning her score on the final examination? Employing the tabular data of problem 1, we obtain the following results:

$$Y' = 75 + 0.60\left(\frac{8}{4}\right)(76 - 70) = 75 + 7.20 = 82.20$$

A reasonable question at this point is, "Since we know $\overline{Y}$ and s_y in the preceding problem, we presumably have all the observed data at hand. Therefore, why do we wish to predict Y from X?" It should be pointed out that the purpose of this example is to acquaint you with a prediction equation. In actual practice, however, regression techniques are often used to make predictions about future samples where Y is unknown.

For example, let's suppose that you are a demographer and over a period of years have accumulated a great deal of information concerning the relationship between the state of the economy and average family size. You find that it is now possible to use economic information (the independent variable, X) to predict average family size (the dependent variable, Y), and then use this information to establish population projections.

Since we discussed the relationship between Pearson's r and z scores in Chapter 9, it should be apparent that the prediction equation may be expressed in terms of z scores. Mathematically, it can be shown that:

$$z_{y'} = rz_x \qquad (10.8)$$

where $z_{y'} = Y'$ (the predicted final exam score) is expressed in terms of a z score.

Jones's score of 62 on the midterm can be expressed as $z_x = -2.00$, since it is two standard deviations to the left of the mean ($\overline{X} = 70$) and we know the correlation between the midterm and final exam scores is 0.60. Thus:

$$z_{y'} = 0.60(-2.00) = -1.20.$$

10.2.3 The Mean Deviation and Raw Score Computational Procedures for Linear Regression

Table 10.3 illustrates the mean deviation method of computation to provide you with a conceptual understanding of regression analysis. The computational procedures and the figures will be familiar to you as they were used to compute r in Table 9.2. We find b_y equals 1.232, which indicates that as X increases one unit, Y increases 1.232 units. The regression line intersects the Y-axis at 4.38 since $a_y = 4.38$. These two values, a_y and b_y, determine the regression line and also provide us with a general prediction equation for these data (see Figure 10.4). For example, using equation (10.1), we can predict respondent C's educational attainment knowing only her mother's educational attainment (five years of formal education) in the following manner. Because:

$$Y' = 4.38 + 1.232X$$

$$Y'_c = 4.38 + 1.232(5)$$

$$Y'_c = 10.54$$

TABLE 10.3
Computational procedures for linear regression using the mean deviation method (hypothetical data)

Respondent	Mother's education X	$(X - \bar{X})$	$(X - \bar{X})^2$	Daughter's education Y	$(Y - \bar{Y})$	$(X - \bar{X})(Y - \bar{Y})$
A	1	−6	36	7	−6	36
B	3	−4	16	4	−9	36
C	5	−2	4	13	0	0
D	7	0	0	16	3	0
E	9	2	4	10	−3	−6
F	11	4	16	22	9	36
G	13	6	36	19	6	36
$N = 7$	$\Sigma X = 49$ $\bar{X} = 7$	$\Sigma(X - \bar{X})^2 = 112$		$\Sigma Y = 91$ $\bar{Y} = 13$	$\Sigma(X - \bar{X})(Y - \bar{Y}) = 138$	

Dependent variable

↳ leave calculations to 3 decimal places

Using equation (10.3), we obtain:

$$b_y = \frac{\Sigma(X - \bar{X})(Y - \bar{Y})}{\Sigma(X - \bar{X})^2} = \frac{138}{112} = 1.232$$

Using equation (10.6), we have:

$$a_y = \bar{Y} - b_y(\bar{X}) = 13 - 1.232(7) = 4.38$$

Since:

$$Y' = a_y + b_y X$$
$$Y' = 4.38 + 1.232X$$

Also:

$$r = 0.82 \text{ (see Table 9.2)}$$

Our prediction is that respondent *C* has completed 10.54 years of education; however, we know she has actually completed 13 years, or 2.46 more years than we predicted (see Table 10.3 and Figure 10.3).

Table 10.4 illustrates raw score computational equation (10.5). The raw score procedure provides us with the same results as the mean deviation method presented in Table 10.3. Note that the correlation coefficient is positive ($r = +0.82$), as is the sign of the slope ($b_y = +1.232$).

10.2.4 Constructing a Regression Line

Let's return to the problem of constructing a regression line for predicting scores on the *Y* variables. As we have already pointed out, the regression line seldom passes through all the paired scores. It will, in fact, pass among the paired scores in a way that minimizes the squared deviations between the regression line (the predicted scores) and the obtained scores. Earlier, we pointed out that the mean is the point in a distribution that makes the sum of the squared deviations around it minimal. The regression line is analogous to the mean because, as we will demonstrate, the sum of deviations of scores around the regression line is zero and the sum of squares of these

TABLE 10.4
Raw score procedure for linear regression (hypothetical data)

Respondent	Mother's education X	X^2	Daughter's education Y	Y^2	XY
A	1	1	7	49	7
B	3	9	4	16	12
C	5	25	13	169	65
D	7	49	16	256	112
E	9	81	10	100	90
F	11	121	22	484	242
G	13	169	19	361	247
$N = 7$	$\Sigma X = 49$	$\Sigma X^2 = 455$	$\Sigma Y = 91$	$\Sigma Y^2 = 1435$	$\Sigma XY = 775$
	$\bar{X} = 7$		$\bar{Y} = 13$		

Using equation (10.5), we have:

use equation 10.9 instead $b_y = r\left(\frac{s_y}{s_x}\right)X$

$$b_y = \frac{N(\Sigma XY) - (\Sigma X)(\Sigma Y)}{N(\Sigma X^2) - (\Sigma X)^2}$$

$$= \frac{7(775) - (49)(91)}{7(455) - (49)^2}$$

$$= \frac{5425 - 4459}{3185 - 2401}$$

$$= \frac{966}{784}$$

$$b_y = 1.232$$

Also, using equation (10.6), we get:

$$a_y = \bar{Y} - b_y\bar{X}$$

$$a_y = 13 - 1.232(7)$$

$$a_y = 4.38$$

Using equation (10.1), we obtain:

$$Y' = a_y + b_yX$$

$$Y' = 4.38 + 1.232X$$

Also:

$$r = 0.82 \text{ (see Table 9.2)}$$

deviations is minimal. Some students find it helpful to think of the regression line as a "generalization" of the data.

The regression line always crosses the coordinate $(\bar{X}, \bar{Y})$; therefore, a convenient method of constructing our regression line involves locating the Y-intercept (a_y) on the Y-axis (in this instance, $a_y = 4.38$) and the coordinate determined by the means of X and Y. Connecting this coordinate with the Y-intercept determines the regression line that must pass through the coordinate determined by the means of X and Y $(\bar{X}, \bar{Y})$.

It is helpful to remember that the closer the data points (coordinates) are to the line, the larger the magnitude of r. When $r = 1.00$, all of the data points will lie on the line, and the predicted Y values will equal the actual Y values.

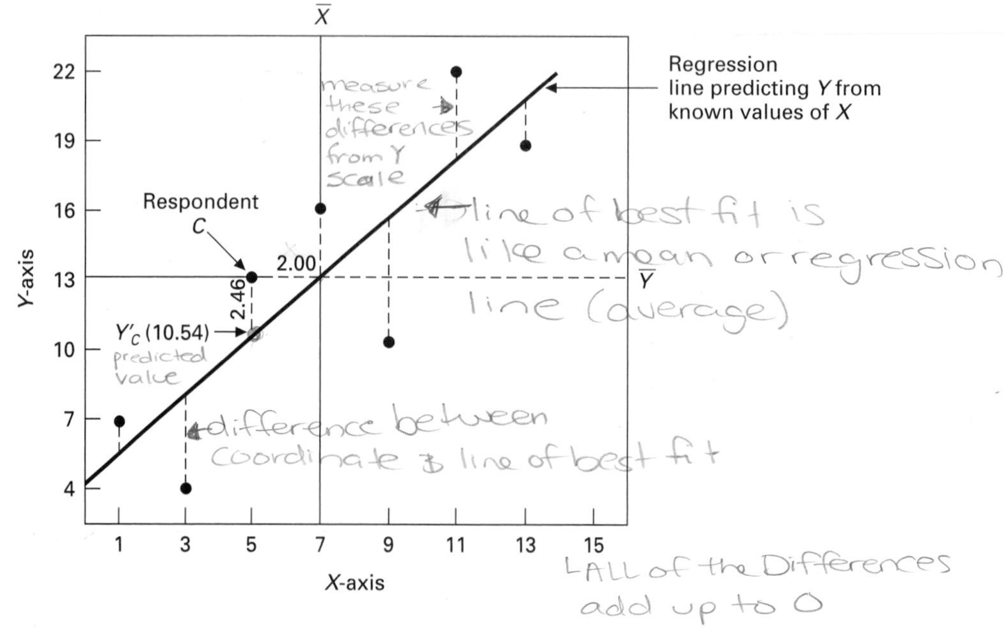

FIGURE 10.3
Scatter diagram representing paired scores on two variables and regression line for predicting *Y* from *X*
Note that the regression line minimizes the vertical or *Y*-axis deviations of the data points.

The coordinate for respondent *C* has been highlighted in Figure 10.3 to help you further understand prediction. Recall that in the previous section we predicted that respondent *C* would complete 10.54 years of education, given that her mother had completed the fifth grade. By examining Figure 10.3, you should see that the predicted *Y* value (Y') lies on the regression line predicting *Y* from known values of *X*.* Indeed, the regression line is also referred to as the *prediction line.* Projecting a *perpendicular* line from any point on the *X*-axis (assuming we are predicting *Y* from known values of *X*) to the prediction line allows us to determine the approximate predicted *Y* value for the corresponding *X* value from which the perpendicular line originated. As shown in Figure 10.3, the predicted *Y* value of 10.54 years (see Section 10.2.4), given that *X* equals 5 years, is 2.46 years lower than the actual *Y* value (13) for respondent *C*. That is, respondent *C* completed 2.46 more years of education than we predicted, given her mother's education.

The small triangle in Figure 10.3 confirms the slope that we calculated earlier for the data in Tables 10.3 and 10.4. You should see that as *X* increases 2.00 units, *Y* increases 2.46 units. Substituting into equation (10.2), we obtain:

$$b_y = \frac{\text{change in } Y}{\text{change in } X} = \frac{2.46}{2.00} = 1.23$$

* Predicting *X* from known values of *Y* is discussed in Section 10.2.6.

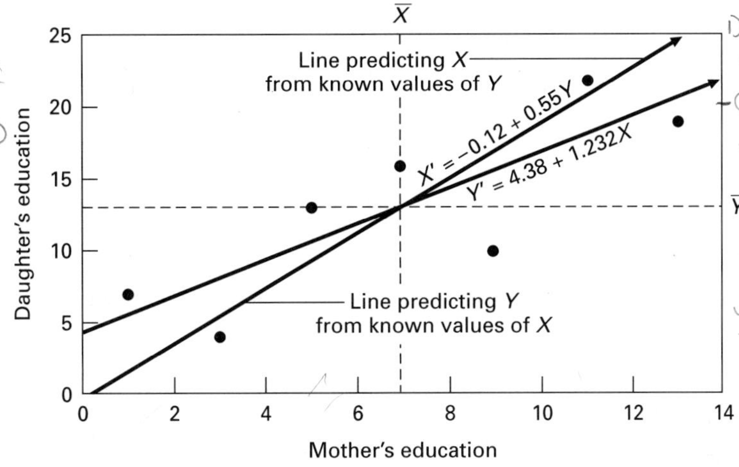

FIGURE 10.4
Scatter diagram representing paired scores for mother's and daughter's education (from Table 10.3) and predicting *X* from *Y* and *Y* from *X*

10.2.5 Constructing Lines of Regression

In Chapter 8, we differentiated between *symmetric* and *asymmetric* measures of association. Regression analysis is an asymmetric measure of association and the variables being analyzed must be designated as independent or dependent. Figure 10.4 shows the two resulting regression lines for the mother and daughter educational data in Table 10.3 when (1) the mother's education serves as the independent variable predicting her daughter's education and (2) the daughter's education serves as the independent variable predicting her mother's education. Normally, we would only be concerned with predicting the daughter's education from the mother's education; however, it is instructional to see that reversing the role of the two variables results in two entirely different regression lines.

Recall that all the values required to calculate predicted scores are readily found during the course of calculating r; that is, $\overline{X}$, $\overline{Y}$, s_x, and s_y. Now to construct our regression line for predicting *Y* from *X*, all we need to do is take two extreme values of *X*, predict *Y* from each of these values, and join these two points on the scatter diagram. The line joining these points represents the regression line for predicting *Y* from *X*, which is also referred to as the line of regression of *Y* on *X*. Similarly, to construct the regression line for predicting *X* from *Y*, we take two extreme values of *Y*, predict *X* for each of these values, and join these two points on the scatter diagram. This is precisely what was done in Figure 10.4 to construct the two regression lines from the data in Table 10.3.

Note that both regression lines intersect at the means of *X* and *Y*. In conceptualizing the relationship between the regression lines and the magnitude of r, we find it helpful to think of the regression lines as rotating around the joint means of *X* and *Y*.

When $r = 1.00$, both regression lines will have identical slopes and will be superimposed upon one another because they pass directly through all the paired scores. However, as r becomes smaller, the regression lines rotate away from each other, so that in the limiting case when $r = 0$, they are *perpendicular* to each other. At this point, the regression line for predicting X from known values of Y is $\overline{X}$, and the regression line for predicting Y from known values of X is $\overline{Y}$. As you examine Figure 10.4, note that the line predicting Y from X minimizes the vertical or Y-axis deviations of the coordinates (as shown in Figure 10.3). In contrast, the line predicting X from Y minimizes the horizontal or X-axis deviations. The discussion in Box 10.1 provides further information on why we use the term regression line.

10.3 RESIDUAL VARIANCE AND STANDARD ERROR OF ESTIMATE

Figure 10.5 shows a series of scatter diagrams (reproduced from Fig. 10.3) showing the regression of Y on X. The regression line represents our best basis for predicting Y scores from known values of X. As we can see, not all of the Y values fall on the regression line. However, if the correlation had been 1.00, all the Y scores (the years of education completed by the seven respondents) would have fallen exactly on the regression line. The deviations $(Y - Y')$ in Figure 10.5(c) and Table 10.5 represent our errors in prediction and reflect the vertical distance of each coordinate from the regression line.

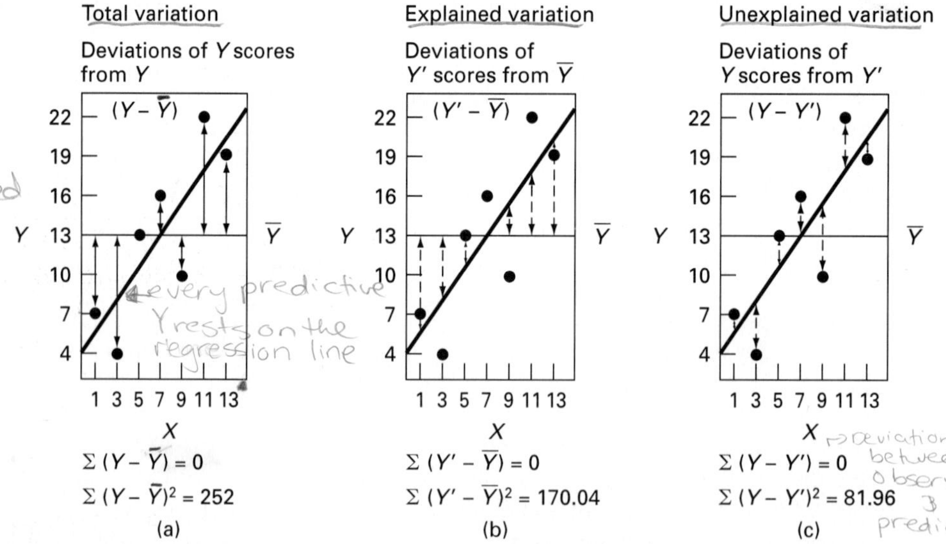

FIGURE 10.5
Scatter diagrams of paired scores on two variables, regression line for predicting Y values from known values of X, and the mean of the distribution of Y scores ($\overline{Y}$): $r = 0.82$ (from data in Table 10.4)

TABLE 10.5

Computational procedures for total, explained, and unexplained variation (data from Table 10.3)*

Respondent	X	Y	Y'	$(Y - \bar{Y})$	$(Y - \bar{Y})^2$	$(Y' - \bar{Y})$	$(Y' - \bar{Y})^2$	$(Y - Y')$	$(Y - Y')^2$
A	1	7	5.607	−6	36	−7.393	54.656	1.393	1.940
B	3	4	8.071	−9	81	−4.929	24.295	−4.071	16.573
C	5	13	10.536	0	0	−2.464	6.071	2.464	6.071
D	7	16	13.000	3	9	0	0	3.000	9.000
E	9	10	15.464	−3	9	2.464	6.071	−5.464	29.855
F	11	22	17.929	9	81	4.929	24.295	4.071	16.573
G	13	19	20.393	6	36	7.393	54.656	−1.393	1.940
	$\bar{X} = 7$	$\bar{Y} = 13$			$\Sigma(Y - \bar{Y})^2 = 252$		$\Sigma(Y' - \bar{Y})^2 = 170.04$*		$\Sigma(Y - Y')^2 = 81.96$*

*The values are computed to three significant decimals following a computer analysis.

The $(Y - Y')$ column in Table 10.5 shows the errors in prediction for each of the seven respondents. Earlier we calculated respondent *C*'s predicted *Y* score (Y') to be 10.54 (see Section 10.2.5). Substituting the more precise value 10.536 from Table 10.5 and the actual *Y* score for her, we can calculate the size *and* direction of the error in prediction.

$$Y_{\text{respondent } C} - Y'_{\text{respondent } C} = 13 - 10.536 = +2.464$$

The value +2.464 tells us that the coordinate for respondent *C* lies 2.464 years above the regression line. The size and direction of the error in prediction—referred to as a **residual**—for the remaining six respondents is shown in the $(Y - Y')$ column of Table 10.5. Note that there will be as many residuals as cases (e.g., respondents), although a residual will equal 0 if an obtained *Y* score lies on the prediction line, that is, $Y_i = Y'_i$.

Note the similarity of $Y - Y'$ (the deviation of the *Y* scores from the predicted scores, which always lie on the regression line) to $Y - \bar{Y}$ (the deviation of *Y* scores from $\bar{Y}$); the algebraic sum of the deviations around the regression line is equal to zero. Earlier, we saw that the algebraic sum of the deviations around the mean is also equal to zero.

You will recall that in calculating the variance (s^2), we squared the deviations from the mean, summed, and divided by *N*. The square root of the variance was the standard deviation. Now, if we were to square and sum the deviations of the scores from the regression line, $\Sigma(Y - Y')^2$, we would have a basis for calculating another variance and standard deviation. The variance around the regression line is known as the **residual variance** and is defined as

$$s^2_{\text{est } y} = \frac{\Sigma(Y - Y')^2}{N - 2} \qquad (10.9)*$$

The standard deviation around the regression line—referred to as the **standard error of estimate**—is the square root of the residual variance. The standard error of

* For now, don't be concerned about why the denominator is $(N - 2)$ rather than *N*. The explanation is concerned with making biased estimates of population parameters, which we will discuss shortly.

estimate provides a measure of how well the regression equation predicts Y, given information about X. Thus:

$$s_{\text{est } y} = \sqrt{\frac{\Sigma(Y - Y')^2}{N - 2}} \tag{10.10}$$

We learned in Table 10.4 that $\Sigma(Y - Y')^2 = 81.95$ and $N = 7$. Using this information, we can compute the standard error of estimate:

$$\begin{aligned} s_{\text{est } y} &= \sqrt{\frac{81.95}{7 - 2}} \\ &= \sqrt{16.368} \\ &= 4.048 \\ &= 4.05 \end{aligned}$$

As we have already indicated, the standard error of estimate has properties similar to those of the standard deviation. The smaller the standard error of estimate, the less dispersed are the scores around the regression line. You also should note that when $r = \pm 1.00$, $s_{\text{est } y} = 0$, which means that there are no deviations from the regression line and therefore no errors in prediction. On the other hand, when $r = 0$, the errors of prediction are maximal for that given distribution and will approach s_y; that is, $s_{\text{est } y} = s_y$.

10.4 EXPLAINED AND UNEXPLAINED VARIATION

If we look again at Figure 10.5, we can see that there are three separate sums of squares that can be calculated from the data. These are presented in three panels from left to right:

1. **The total sum of squares for *Y* (TSS).** This sum of squares is given by $\Sigma(Y - \bar{Y})^2$ [Figure 10.5(a)] and, as you know, is basic to finding the variance and standard deviation of the sample. The total sum of squares is a measure of the variation in the Y scores and is also referred to as the **total variation.**

2. **The sum of squares for explained variance in *Y*.** The variation of predicted scores about the mean of the distribution [Figure 10.5(b)]. This variation is given by $\Sigma(Y' - \bar{Y})^2$ and is referred to as the **regression sum of squares (RegSS)** and as **explained variation.** The reason for this terminology should be clear from our earlier discussion and our previous reference to predicted deviation (Section 10.3). Recall our observation that the greater the correlation, the greater the predicted deviation from the sample mean. It follows further that the greater the predicted deviation, the greater the explained variation. When the predicted deviations are maximum, the correlation is perfect and 100% of the variation is explained. When the predicted deviations are minimum, the correlation is 0 and there is no explained variation.

BOX 10.1

WHY THE LINE OF BEST FIT IS CALLED A REGRESSION LINE

Why do we call this statistical procedure "regression"? Why is the line of best fit called a "regression line"? The answer to these questions goes back to the originator of correlation and regression statistics, Sir Francis Galton (1822–1911). Galton was interested in how family traits are inherited. As you know, we inherit many of our personal characteristics from our parents. Height, hair and eye color, skin tone, and many other features are determined in part by our genetics. Galton spent much time studying how different physical and psychological traits are inherited by families. In his research, he noticed an extremely interesting phenomenon which he called **regression to the mean.** What was it that Galton saw? We can explain regression to the mean with an example.

Imagine that two extremely tall people are married and have children. We would expect their children to be tall; height is a physical trait that is influenced by genetics as well as environmental conditions such as diet. Will these children be as tall as their parents? Our prediction will be that the children will be closer to the average height of the other children in their generation. Remember that correlation and regression examine the relative deviations of scores from the mean. When we talk about regression to the mean we are saying the new scores will be, relatively speaking, closer to the mean.

What Galton discovered is an extremely important phenomenon in statistics and experimental design. Whenever we take a measurement of one variable, there is a tendency for the scores to cluster around the mean. If two variables are independent of one another, as is the case when $r = 0$, then an extreme score on one measure is as likely to be associated with a high score as with a low score on the other measure. More specifically, if we obtain an extreme score on one measure, the companion score is most likely to regress toward the mean for that measure. In this case, we say that there is a lot of regression toward the mean. By contrast, if two variables are highly interrelated, as is the case when $r = 1.00$, then extreme scores for one variable will be associated with extreme scores for the other variable and there will be no regression toward the mean.

Keep in mind that we are talking about predicted scores regressing toward the mean. Using the least squares method, which penalizes us when we are far off in our predictions—as a tennis player is penalized when his or her position is far from where it should be to make a satisfactory return—we find that we are safer standing in the center of the tennis court. But we all know that predictions are sometimes inaccurate and become increasingly inaccurate as the correlation between the two variables moves toward 0.

An application of regression to the mean is seen any time we administer a test to a student. What would happen if a student took a test and obtained an extremely low score and then took a similar test shortly thereafter? If there is a low correlation between the tests, then we would expect the student's performance to regress toward the mean and would predict that the score on the second test would be closer to the average. If there is a high correlation between the tests, the amount of regression toward the mean would be less. In this case, the student's second test score may not be as extreme, but it would still be lower than the average.

(continued)

Many people fail to recognize the regression to the mean effect when examining the results of a study. For example, suppose that a researcher claims that a new reading program is useful in helping students learn how to read. To justify her claim, she administers 100 students a reading test and then selects the 25 students with the lowest scores, the "poor readers." After a year in the reading program, all 25 students are reading at a higher grade level. Has the researcher demonstrated the effectiveness of the reading program? Probably not. We cannot use these data to determine why these students' scores increased. The apparent improvement observed in the 25 poor readers may have simply been a case of regression to the mean. On the day that they were first tested, they received low scores for reasons that cannot be identified. According to the regression to the mean phenomenon, we should not be surprised that they had higher scores the second time they were tested.

3. The sum of squares for unexplained variance in *Y*. The variation of scores around the regression line or line of predicted scores [Figure 10.5(c)]. This variation is given by $\Sigma(Y - Y')^2$ and is referred to as **residual sum of squares (RSS), unexplained variation,** and the **error sum of squares.** It is based on the sum of the differences between the obtained scores and the predicted scores. The reason for this terminology should be clear. If the correlation between two variables is ± 1.00, all the scores fall on the regression line. Consequently, we have explained all the variation in *Y* in terms of variations in *X* and, conversely, all the variation in *X* in terms of variations in *Y*. In other words, in the event of a perfect correlation, there is no unexplained variation. However, when the correlation is less than perfect, many of the scores do not fall right on the regression line. The deviations of these scores from the regression line represent variation that is not accounted for in terms of the correlation between the two variables. Hence the term *error sum of squares* or *unexplained variation* is used.

It can be shown mathematically that the total sum of squares consists of two components which may be added together. These two components represent explained variation and unexplained variation, respectively. Thus:

$$\Sigma(Y - \bar{Y}) = \Sigma(Y - Y')^2 + \Sigma(Y' - \bar{Y})^2 \qquad (10.11)$$

Total sum of squares	=	Unexplained variation or residual sum of squares	+	Explained variation or regression sum of squares

We can use the data in Table 10.5 to illustrate this point. As you can see, unexplained variation plus explained variation equals total variation.

$$\Sigma(Y - \bar{Y}) = \Sigma(Y - Y')^2 + \Sigma(Y' - \bar{Y})^2$$

$$252 = 81.96 + 170.04$$

Total variation = Unexplained variation + Explained variation

The ratio of the explained variation to the total variation is referred to as the **coefficient of determination (r^2)**. The equation for the coefficient of determination is:

$$r^2 = \frac{\text{explained variation}}{\text{total variation}} = \frac{\Sigma(Y' - \bar{Y})^2}{\Sigma(Y - \bar{Y})^2} \tag{10.12}$$

Referring to Figure 10.5, we see that the proportion of explained variation to total variation is:

$$r^2 = \frac{170.04}{252} = 0.67$$

The coefficient of determination indicates the proportion of total variation that is explained in terms of the magnitude of the correlation coefficient. When $r = 0$, the coefficient of determination, r^2, equals 0. When $r = 0.5$, the coefficient of determination is 0.25. In other words, 25% of the total variation is accounted for. Finally, when $r = 1.00$, then $r^2 = 1.00$ and all variation is accounted for or explained. In the preceding example, 67% of the variation in Y has been explained by X. Case Example 10.2 provides an additional example.

We have previously shown that the coefficient of determination r^2 is equal to 0.67 for the data summarized in Figure 10.5. Note that the square root of this number (i.e., $\sqrt{0.67}$) equals 0.82—which is r for these data.

Since r^2 represents the proportion of variation accounted for, $(1 - r^2)$ represents the proportion of variation that is *not* explained in terms of the correlation between X and Y.

As we have seen, $\Sigma(Y - Y')^2$ is the sum of squares for the differences between the predicted and actual values of Y. We consider this term the "error term" because it represents a deviation from our prediction and we have no way to explain this difference. Therefore, when we divide this term by the total sum of squares, we obtain the **coefficient of nondetermination ($1 - r^2$)**:

$$1 - r^2 = \frac{\text{unexplained variation}}{\text{total variation}} = \frac{\Sigma(Y - Y')^2}{\Sigma(Y - \bar{Y})^2} \tag{10.13}$$

For our current example:

$$1 - r^2 = \frac{\Sigma(Y - Y')^2}{\Sigma(Y - \bar{Y})^2} = \frac{81.96}{252} = 0.33$$

This finding confirms that $1 - r^2 = 1 - 0.82^2 = 0.33$. Thus, we can see that the coefficient of nondetermination is the proportion of the total variation that is unaccounted for by the regression of Y on X. Case Example 10.2 offers a further discussion of explaining variation.

10.5
CORRELATION AND CAUSATION

You have seen that when two variables are related, it is possible to predict one from your knowledge of the other. This relationship between correlation and prediction often leads to a serious error in reasoning; that is, the relationship between two

CASE EXAMPLE 10.2

EXPLAINING VARIATION

With many of our key resources in jeopardy and the acknowledged risk of the poisoning of our food and water supplies with toxic substances, the field of environmental psychology is receiving increased attention. Two researchers, Winkler and Winett, reviewed major efforts of behavioral interventions in resource conservation.* In part of their report, the authors looked at investigations of the effects of providing daily feedback on energy use. To ascertain the role of economic factors in energy conservation practices, they related the percentage of reduction in overall energy use to (1) gross annual household income, (2) cost per month of targeted energy source, and (3) budget share of gross monthly income expended for energy during the target month. The scatter diagrams for these data are shown in Figure 10.6 with accompanying correlation coefficients r and coefficients of determination r^2.

It can be seen in Figure 10.6(a) that there is a small relationship between reduction in energy use and annual household income. If $r = .15$ can be considered an estimate of the population correlation r, annual household income accounts for $r^2 = .15^2 = 0.0225$ or only about 2% of the variance in the reduction of energy use. However, when the energy cost is taken into account, the correlation becomes .50 and 25% of the variance in the reduction of energy use is taken into account. Finally, when proportion of the budget for energy is correlated with reduction in energy use illustrated in Figure 10.6(c), the correlation is .62 and approximately 38% of the variance is accounted for. These results suggest, but do not prove, the possibility that economic factors may be crucial in obtaining compliance with energy conservation practices. We may look forward to experimental studies (such as providing monetary incentives) to determine if economic factors cause people to conserve energy. One of the authors of this book, Richard Runyon, has demonstrated annual savings in excess of $1,000 by adopting coherent household energy conservation practices—a lot of money by any standard.

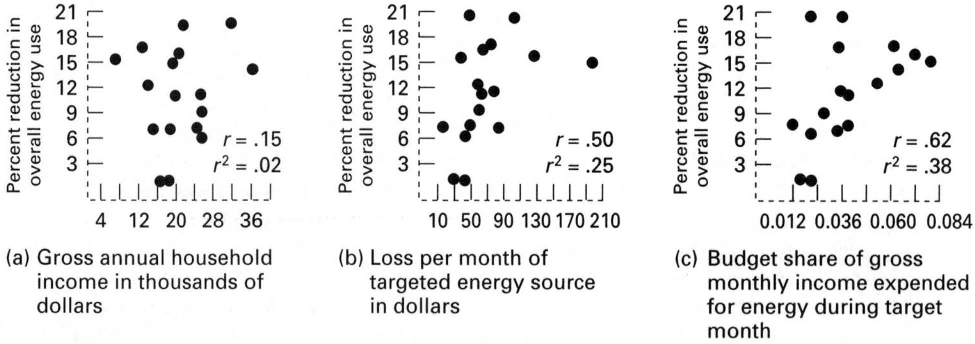

FIGURE 10.6
Percent change in overall targeted energy use in relation to factors (a), (b), and (c)

---

* Winkler, R. C. and Winett, R. A. "Behavioral Interventions in Resource Conservation: A Systems Approach Based on Behavioral Economics," *American Psychologist* 31 (1982), pp. 421–35.

variables frequently carries with it the implication that one has caused the other. This is especially true when there is a temporal relationship between the variables in question; that is, when one precedes the other in time. What is often overlooked is that the variables may not be causally connected in any way, but may vary together by virtue of a common link with a third variable. Thus, if you are a bird watcher, you may note that as the number of birds increases in the spring, the grass becomes progressively greener. However, recognizing that the extended number of hours and the increasing warmth of the sun is a third factor influencing both of these variables, you are not likely to conclude that the birds cause the grass to turn green. However, there are many occasions, particularly in the social sciences, when it is not so easy to identify the third factor.

Suppose that you have demonstrated that there is a high positive correlation between the number of hours students spend studying for an exam and their subsequent grades on that exam. You may be tempted to conclude that the number of hours of study causes grades to vary. This seems to be a perfectly reasonable conclusion, one that probably agrees closely with what your parents and instructors have been telling you for years. Let's look closer at the implications of a causal relationship. On the assumption that a greater number of hours of study causes grades to increase, we would be led to expect that *any* student who devotes more time to study is guaranteed a high grade and that one who spends less time on studying is going to receive a low grade. This is not necessarily the case. We have overlooked that the better student (by virtue of higher intelligence, stronger motivation, better study habits, and so on) who devotes more time to study might perform better simply because he or she has a greater capacity to do so.

Correlational studies simply do not permit inferences of causation. Correlation is a *necessary* but not a *sufficient* condition to establish a causal relationship between two variables.

Darrell Huff's book includes an excellent chapter devoted to the confusion of correlation with causation. He refers to faulty causal inferences from correlational data as the **post hoc fallacy.** The following excerpt illustrates a common example of the post hoc fallacy.

> Reams of pages of figures have been collected to show the value in dollars of a college education, and stacks of pamphlets have been published to bring these figures—and conclusions more or less based on them—to the attention of potential students. I am not quarreling with the intention. I am in favor of education myself, particularly if it includes a course in elementary statistics. Now these figures have pretty conclusively demonstrated that people who have gone to college make more money than people who have not. The exceptions are numerous, of course, but the tendency is strong and clear.
>
> The only thing wrong is that along with the figures and facts goes a totally unwarranted conclusion. This is the post hoc fallacy at its best. It says that these figures show that if *you* (your son, your daughter) attend college you will probably earn more money than if you decide to spend the next four years in some other manner. This unwarranted conclusion has for its basis the equally unwarranted assumption that since college-trained folks make more money, they make it because they went to college. Actually we don't know but that these are the people who would have made more money even if they had *not* gone to college. There are a couple of things that indicate rather strongly that this is so. Colleges get a disproportionate number of two groups of kids—the bright and the rich. The bright might show good earning power without college knowledge. And as for the rich

ones—well, money breeds money in several obvious ways. Few sons of rich men are found in low-income brackets whether they go to college or not.*

SUMMARY

Let's briefly review what we have learned in this chapter. We have seen that it is possible to "fit" a straight line to a bivariate distribution of scores for predicting Y scores from known X values.

We saw that when the correlation is perfect, all of the scores fall on the regression line. Thus, there is no error in prediction. The lower the degree of relationship, the greater the dispersion of scores around the regression line, and the greater the errors of prediction. Finally, when $r = 0$, the mean of the sample provides our best predictor for a given variable.

The regression line was shown to be analogous to the mean: The summed deviations around it are zero and the sum of squares are minimal. The standard error of estimate was shown to be analogous to the standard deviation.

We saw that three separate sums of squares, reflecting variability, may be calculated from correlational data. (1) Variation about the mean of the distribution for each variable: This variation is referred to as the *total variation* or *total sum of squares.* (2) Variation of each score about the regression line: This variation is known as *unexplained variation* or *residual sum of squares.* (3) Variation of each predicted score about the mean of the distribution for each variable: This variation is known as *explained variation* or *regression sum of squares.* We saw that the sum of the explained variation and the unexplained variation is equal to the total variation.

Finally, we saw that the ratio of the explained variation to the total variation provides us with the proportion of the total variation that is explained. The term applied to this proportion is *coefficient of determination.*

TERMS TO REMEMBER

coefficient of determination (r^2) The ratio of the explained variation to the total variation.

coefficient of nondetermination ($1 - r^2$) Proportion of variation not explained in terms of the correlation between the two variables.

error sum of squares See *unexplained variation.*

explained variation The variation of predicted scores about the mean of the distribution. Same as the regression sum of squares.

line of best fit See *regression line.*

post hoc fallacy Faulty causal inferences from correlational data.

regression line A straight line that best represents the linear relationship between two variables, X and Y.

regression sum of squares (RegSS) See *explained variation* and *total sum of squares for Y.*

---

* Huff (1954), pp. 93–94.

regression to the mean Individuals high or low on one testing or measure are found to be closer to (regress toward) the mean on subsequent testing or measures.
residual The size and direction of the error in prediction or the vertical distance from the observed data coordinate to the regression line.
residual sum of squares (RSS) See *unexplained variation* and *total sum of squares for Y*.
residual variance The variance around the regression line.
standard error of estimate The standard deviation of scores around the regression line.
total sum of squares for *Y* (TSS) The total sum of squares is a measure of the variation in the *Y* scores and is also referred to as the total variation.
total variation See the *total sum of squares for Y*.
unexplained variation The variation of scores around the regression line. Same as the residual sum of squares.

EXERCISES

1. Find the equation of the regression line for the following data.

X	1	2	3	4	5
Y	5	3	4	2	1

2. Using the data in exercise 1, construct a scattergram and draw the regression line. (*Hint:* The regression line always passes through the coordinate formed by $\overline{X}$ and $\overline{Y}$.)

3. Using the data in exercise 1, calculate the total sum of squares, the residual sum of squares, the regression sum of squares, r and r^2. Using equation (9.1) or (9.2), confirm your answer for r^2. Also compute the standard error of estimate.

4. Using the data in exercise 1, compute the residuals and the predicted Y values.

5. Assuming that TSS = 100, RSS = 75, and RegSS = 25, discuss the concepts of explained and unexplained variance. Compute the coefficients of determination and nondetermination and discuss.

6. In a study concerned with the relationship between two variables, X and Y, the following was obtained.

$$\overline{X} = 119 \qquad \overline{Y} = 1.30$$
$$s_x = 10 \qquad s_y = 0.55$$
$$r = 0.70$$
$$N = 100$$

(*a*) Sally B. obtained a score of 130 on the X variable. Predict her score on the Y variable.
(*b*) A score of 1.28 on the Y variable was predicted for Bill B. What was his score on the X variable?

7. You are investigating the relationship between family stability (X) and college grade point average (Y). A preliminary analysis of the following data yielded the accompanying results.

	Family stability	**College GPA**
1	22.00	2.20
2	35.00	2.90
3	46.00	3.00
4	48.00	3.40
5	49.00	3.35
6	52.00	3.00
7	57.00	3.10
8	60.00	2.85

$$\Sigma(Y - Y')^2 = 0.42186;\ \Sigma(Y' - \overline{Y})^2 = 0.53814;\ b_y = 0.01992;\ a_y = 2.05608$$

(*a*) Compute the total sum of squares, the standard error of estimate, and r^2.
(*b*) Write the regression equation for this data set.
(*c*) Plot the data and draw the regression line.
(*d*) Compute each of the eight predicted Y-values and the residuals.

8. Assume that $\overline{X} = 30$, $s_x = 5$; $\overline{Y} = 45$, $s_y = 8$. Draw a separate graph showing the regression line for the following values of r.
(*a*) $r = .00$ (*b*) $r = .20$ (*c*) $r = .40$ (*d*) $r = .60$ (*e*) $r = .80$
(*f*) $r = -.20$ (*g*) $r = -.45$ (*h*) $r = -.60$ (*i*) $r = -.80$ (*j*) $r = -.90$

9. What is the slope of the regression line for each of the following data sets?
(*a*) $r = .3$, $s_x = 3.5$, $s_y = 3.4$
(*b*) $r = -.6$, $s_x = 8.4$, $s_y = 9.1$
(*c*) $r = .25$, $s_x = 2.00$, $s_y = 6.00$
(*d*) $r = -.8$, $s_x = 12.00$, $s_y = 3.00$
(*e*) Write a short essay describing the relation between the slope of the regression line, r, s_x, and s_y.
(*f*) Using these data, explain why the size of the slope does not represent the strength of the relation between the two variables.

10. A researcher examines the correlations among three different tests and an outcome measure. The correlations are (1) $r = .45$, (2) $r = -.78$, and (3) $r = .62$. All else being equal, which of these correlations will produce the best overall prediction? Which correlations will have the greatest standard error of estimate?

11. For the following data (assume size of work group is the independent variable):
(*a*) What is your prediction of the measure of group cohesiveness for a work group numbering 15?
(*b*) What percent of the total variation in Y is explained by X?

Group	Size of work group	Measure of group cohesiveness (low value indicates a cohesive work group)
A	10	1
B	18	4
C	4	2
D	20	5
E	12	3
F	13	3
G	11	4

12. A psychologist wants to study the effectiveness of a new psychological treatment for depression. He administers a standard test of depression to a large number of subjects, selects those who are the most depressed, and provides them with the new treatment. The vast majority of the subjects experience some improvement in their mood. Can the psychologist assume that the treatment has brought about a relief from the depression? What concept have you learned in this chapter that can explain these results?

13. A sociologist is convinced that greater levels of education cause reduced levels of violent behavior. Based on the results of an extremely large data set, the sociologist finds that the correlation between years of education and number of criminal acts is −.25. Therefore, the sociologist argues that everyone should be required to complete a 12th-grade education. According to the results, a person who completes 12 years of school will commit, on average, 0.80 violent crimes. Do you think that the researcher's conclusions are justified? Defend your answer.

14. Review the magazine section of your Sunday newspaper, monthly magazines, television, and radio advertisements for examples of the post hoc fallacy.

15. A researcher finds that the slope of the regression equation is small ($b = 0.03$) and concludes that there is no meaningful relation between the two variables. Is this necessarily a correct conclusion?

16. Bob has just taken a job placement test. He is disappointed because he did very poorly. You discover that the correlation between the test scores of a person who takes the test on two occasions is .20. Would you encourage Bob to take the test again? Why? What if you discovered that the correlation between testings is .90?

17. On the basis of the obtained data (see table below), an experimenter asserts that the older a child is, the fewer irrelevant responses he or she makes in an experimental situation.
(*a*) Determine whether this conclusion is valid.
(*b*) Mindy, age 13, enters the experimental situation. What is the most probable number of irrelevant responses the experimenter would predict for Mindy?

Age	Number of irrelevant responses	Age	Number of irrelevant responses
2	11	7	12
3	12	9	8
4	10	9	7
4	13	10	3
5	11	11	6
5	9	11	5
6	10	12	5
7	7		

18. Hypothetical measures for X and Y.

X	3	4	5	6	7	8	9	10	11
Y	4	3	5	6	8	7	9	9	11

(*a*) Determine the correlation for the accompanying scores.
(*b*) Given this correlation and the computed mean for Y, predict the value of Y' for each X.
(*c*) Calculate $\Sigma(Y - \bar{Y})^2$.
(*d*) Calculate the unexplained variance.
(*e*) Calculate the explained variance.
(*f*) Calculate the coefficient of determination. Show that the square root of that value equals r.

19. A manager of a political campaign found a correlation of 0.70 between the number of people at a party and the loaves of bread consumed.

Number of people	**Number of loaves**
$\bar{X} = 50$	$\bar{Y} = 5$
$s_x = 15$	$s_y = 1.2$

(*a*) For a party of 60 people, calculate the predicted number of loaves needed.
(*b*) For a party of 35, calculate the predicted number of loaves needed.

CHAPTER 11

Multivariate Data Analysis

11.1 INTRODUCTION

In the previous chapters, we have examined univariate and bivariate statistical techniques. Often, however, the complexity of social science issues requires that several variables be analyzed simultaneously. When this is the case, we utilize **multivariate statistical techniques,** which allow us to determine the nature of the relationships between three or more variables.

When the relationship between marital status and employment status was considered in Chapter 8, "An Introduction to Contingency Tables," we concluded that a weak relationship existed between the two variables. That is, knowing a woman's marital status improved our ability to predict her employment status. In the process of establishing that a relationship existed, however, we ignored other variables that might have been useful in determining why some of the women in the sample chose to work and others did not. What if we had divided our sample into two groups: women who need to work for financial reasons and those who do not? It is very likely that introducing a third variable, in this instance the financial necessity of working, into the analysis would allow us to understand more fully the employment status of the women in our sample. Indeed, it is possible that a major reason for women working is the need for additional income. A fourth variable, the presence or absence of young children in the home, might also help clarify the complex reasons that determine whether or not a woman chooses to work outside the home.

In Chapter 9, "Correlation" you learned to assess the direction and strength of the relationship between two interval-level variables. Although it is valuable to know the correlation between two variables, you were later warned in Chapter 10 not to equate correlation with causation because a third variable might be responsible for the observed bivariate correlation.

You also may have concluded after studying Chapter 10, "Regression and Prediction" that using a single independent variable to predict a dependent variable was far too simplistic an approach given the complexity of human attitudes and behavior. Age by itself, for example, can be used as an independent variable to predict a person's life satisfaction. However, if several other independent variables, such as an individual's economic and health status, were used jointly with the individual's age, we would expect to improve our prediction of life satisfaction.

All of these examples require the use of multivariate data analysis. The multivariate techniques presented in this chapter are extensions of what you have learned in Chapters 8, 9 and 10. They include the topics of multivariate contingency table analysis, partial correlation analysis, and multiple regression and correlation analysis. You may wish to briefly review those chapters prior to reading this chapter.

11.2 THE MULTIVARIATE CONTINGENCY TABLE

Table 11.1(a) shows the relationship between high school seniors' plans to attend college and their parents' level of educational attainment. The table has been percentaged down, and comparisons made across the table reveal a positive relationship between parental educational attainment and seniors' plans to attend college (gamma = +0.443). Therefore, the more formal education the parent has completed, the more likely the student has plans to attend college following graduation from high school.

Before we can conclude that parental educational attainment is a key determinant of plans to attend college, we must consider the possibility that the relationship is due to a third variable. Perhaps the relationship between the initial two variables differs by sex. We can assess the effect of sex on college plans by analyzing the female and male respondents separately, as shown in Tables 11.1(b) and (c). Note that the distribution of cases shown in Table 11.1(a) would result if we combined Tables 11.1(b) and (c). For example, totaling the 347,000 cases in the upper right cell of Table 11.1(b) and the 362,000 cases in the upper right cell of Table 11.1(c) would result in the 709,000 cases in the upper right cell of Table 11.1(a).

The relationship between parental educational attainment and college plans of female seniors is presented in Table 11.1(b), and male seniors are included in Table 11.1(c). Tables 11.1(b) and (c) are referred to as **conditional tables** or **partial tables** because they summarize the relationship between two variables for subgroups, categories, or conditions of one or more other variables. The variable sex in this instance is referred to as a **control variable** or **test variable** and is designated by the letter Z. **Statistical elaboration** refers to the introduction of a control or test variable into an analysis to determine if a two-variable relationship remains the same or varies under the different categories or conditions of the control or test variable.

We are seeking to understand the bivariate relationship better by examining it under a variety of conditions. Although introducing a control variable cannot establish causation, if the bivariate relationship remains strong with the introduction of a

TABLE 11.1
College plans by educational attainment for head of family (in thousands)

(a) For females and males

(Y) College plans	(X) Educational attainment for head of family: Elementary	High school	College	Total
Plan to attend	31.6 (149)	42.4 (714)	71.4 (709)	(1572)
May attend	28.9 (136)	28.2 (475)	17.7 (176)	(787)
Will not attend	39.5 (186)	29.4 (495)	10.9 (108)	(789)
Total	100.0 (471)	100.0 (1684)	100.0 (993)	$N = 3148$

Gamma = +0.443

(b) For females

(Y) College plans	Females (Z) Educational attainment for head of family (X): Elementary	High school	College	Total
Plan to attend	34.7 (70)	45.7 (391)	75.6 (347)	(808)
May attend	26.7 (54)	24.8 (212)	15.7 (72)	(338)
Will not attend	38.6 (78)	29.5 (252)	8.7 (40)	(370)
Total	100.0 (202)	100.0 (855)	100.0 (459)	$N = 1516$

Gamma = +0.468

(c) For males

(Y) College plans	Males (Z) Educational attainment for head of family (X): Elementary	High school	College	Total
Plan to attend	29.4 (79)	39.0 (323)	67.8 (362)	(764)
May attend	30.5 (82)	31.7 (263)	19.5 (104)	(449)
Will not attend	40.1 (108)	29.3 (243)	12.7 (68)	(419)
Total	100.0 (269)	100.0 (829)	100.0 (534)	$N = 1632$

Gamma = +0.425

Source: Reported in U.S. Bureau of the Census, Current Population Reports, Series P-20, no. 299 *College Plans of High School Seniors,* (Washington, D.C.: U.S. Government Printing Office, 1994).

theoretically relevant control variable(s), we are more confident that the relationship is possibly causal.*

Tables 11.1(b) and (c) are also referred to as *first-order conditional tables.* The **order of a conditional table** is determined by the number of control or test variables that have been introduced. A *zero-order table* [like Table 11.1(a)] includes no control variables; a first-order conditional table [like Table 11.1(b) or (c)] includes one control variable; and a *second-order conditional table* contains two control variables employed simultaneously, and so forth.

The effect of sex, our control variable, has been physically removed in Table 11.1(b), which contains only females and in Table 11.1(c), which contains only males. Thus, both tables are homogeneous in terms of the test variable. Put another way, sex has been controlled or held constant. This was not the case in Table 11.1(a), which contained both females and males.

Controlling for the effect of sex has had a very minor influence on the bivariate relationship in Table 11.1(a). While the relationship between parental educational attainment and college plans is slightly stronger for females than males (gamma = 0.468 versus 0.425), the difference between the gammas is slight. Furthermore, a comparison of the percentages in Table 11.1(a) with those in Tables 11.1(b) and (c), as well as a comparison of the partial tables, supports the finding that controlling for the effect of sex had little impact.

We do see some differences as we compare the percentages in the three tables; however, the trends across rows are quite similar. For example, compare the percentages across the three rows labeled "Plan to attend" in Tables 11.1(a), 11.1(b), 11.1(c); then compare the three "May attend" rows; and finally, the three "Will not attend" rows.

Perhaps at this point you have asked yourself why sex was chosen as a control variable. Several other variables might have proven equally as important or more important than sex. The choice is based on logic and the theoretical context of the variables being investigated. Another potential test variable that could have an effect on the relationship between parental educational attainment and college plans of high school seniors is the student's academic aptitude. Studies have shown that students from a lower socioeconomic background with a high academic aptitude are more likely to attend college than students from a lower socioeconomic background with a low academic aptitude. Aptitude seems to have an influence independent of family economic and educational background. If we controlled for aptitude using an interval measure of a standardized test, it would be necessary to establish "cutting points." Dividing the scores into low, medium, and high categories would result in three, first-order partial tables, one for each category.

Controlling for an ordinal- or interval-level variable reduces but does not eliminate the influence of a test variable. For example, family income could be

* The following three criteria must be met to establish causality: (1) The two variables must be correlated or statistically related, (2) the independent variable must precede the dependent variable in time (i.e., must occur prior to the dependent variable), and (3) the bivariate relationship must not be due to the effect of a third variable (i.e., alternative explanations of the bivariate relationship must be eliminated by introducing control variables).

trichotomized into the following three categories: (1) less than \$20,000, (2) \$20,000–\$50,000, and (3) over \$50,000; yet within each of the categories, considerable variation remains. Family income cannot be held constant in the sense that all of the cases in a partial table are homogeneous with respect to the test variable, as was the case when we controlled for sex and analyzed males and females separately.

The variation within categories of an ordinally or intervally measured test variable can be *reduced* by increasing the number of categories. However, there may not be a sufficient number of cases for all the cells that would result, and too many cells can make the data very difficult to interpret. A 3×3 bivariate table and a test variable with three categories would result in three first-order partial tables, each containing 9 cells for a total of 27 cells ($3 \times 9 = 27$).

11.3 PARTIAL CORRELATION

11.3.1 Introduction

A study of African-American ministers in Nashville, Tennessee, was conducted, from which a model of their political involvement was developed.* Two demographic variables, the minister's age and years of formal education, were moderately correlated with civic participation (CP), a variable based on a combination of activities such as having worked in political campaigns, telephoned a state or local official about a community problem, contributed money to support a political campaign, and so forth. On the basis of the bivariate correlations (age with CP, $r = -0.30$ and education with CP, $r = 0.49$), the authors concluded that both age and education were important determinants of the minister's civic participation (the dependent variable).

Model A describes the expected relationships among the three variables. Education is shown as an **intervening variable** linking age and civic participation.

Model A   Age ⟶ Education ⟶ Civic participation

Two other models were considered. Model B assumes that age and civic participation are spuriously related because of their connection with education. A **spurious relationship** is said to exist when the zero-order relationship between two variables disappears or becomes significantly weaker with the introduction of a control or test variable. The variables are spuriously related because their relationship is due to the causal influence of the test variable on the variables. In model C, age serves as an intervening variable. Neither model B or C was considered plausible due to the unlikely causal ordering of education and age.

Model B   Education ⟶ Age; Education ⟶ Civic participation

Model C   Education ⟶ Age ⟶ Civic participation

* Berenson, Elifson, and Tollerson (1976), pp. 373–83.

To test model A, we calculated a partial correlation coefficient before proceeding with a test of the overall model. A **partial correlation coefficient** is a measure of the linear relationship between two interval-level variables, controlling for one or more other variables.* In this instance, the partial correlation coefficient between age and civic participation, controlling for educational attainment, was -0.04, suggesting that education was an intervening variable causally linking age and civic participation.

11.3.2 The Logic of the Partial Correlation Coefficient

Technically, the partial correlation of variables X and Y controlling for variable Z is the correlation of the residuals of the regressions of X on Z and Y on Z. In other words, you can think of the control variable Z serving as an independent variable to predict X and Y in two separate regression analyses. Two sets of residuals are computed in the process. The first set of residuals represents the variation in X not explained by Z, and the second set of residuals represents the variation in Y not explained by Z. The partial correlation coefficient between X and Y controlling for Z can be computed by correlating these two sets of residuals.

Partial correlation coefficients can be computed using the computational equation presented in the following section; however, a thorough understanding requires that one conceptual example be presented in which the logic of correlating two sets of residuals is developed. The partial correlation between age and civic participation, controlling for education, will serve as an illustration. Figure 11.1 is based on the scores presented in Table 11.2 of the five hypothetical male African-American ministers. Civic participation and age have been individually regressed on education, which serves as the control variable.

The *statistical control* procedure used in partial correlation analysis differs from the *physical control* procedure used with multivariate contingency tables in Section 11.2. Statistical control involves an adjustment process rather than placing the respondents into categories or subgroups as is the case when physical controls are used. Minister 2's 10 years of education has been highlighted using arrows in Figure 11.1(a) and (b). In Figure 11.1(a) the coordinate for minister 2 lies above the regression line, indicating that he scored higher on civic participation than was predicted given his 10 years of formal education. By the same token in Figure 11.1(b), the coordinate for minister 2 lies below the regression line, indicating that he is younger than was predicted given his 10 years of formal education.

The positive residual for minister 2 in Figure 11.1(a) indicates the extent to which his civic participation score is independent of (unexplained by) his education score. The negative residual shown in Figure 11.1(b) for minister 2 indicates the extent to

---

* Many social scientists routinely use ordinal-level variables that are evenly distributed and have five or more categories with interval statistical techniques. Violating the assumption of interval-level data given these restrictions does not have a marked impact on the outcome [Labovitz, (1970)]. As Blalock has noted, "if one becomes too much of a purist with respect to measurement criteria, there may be an equally dangerous tendency to throw away information that is not completely satisfactory" (1979, p. 444). Henkel (1975) offers an opposing argument.

TABLE 11.2
Raw scores, predicted scores, and residuals for five African-American ministers

African-American minister	Age (X)	Civic participation (Y)	Years of education (Z)	Y′ with Z independent	X′ with Z independent	Y − Y′	X − X′
1	28	4	15	3.56	36.44	+0.44	−8.44
2	42	3	10	2.29	45.57	+0.71	−3.57
3	50	2	12	2.79	41.92	−0.79	+8.08
4	34	2	15	3.56	36.44	−1.56	−2.44
5	41	5	16	3.81	34.62	+1.19	+6.38

which his age is independent of (unexplained by) his education score. The actual values of these two residuals (+0.71 and −3.57) are presented in Table 11.2.

Note in Figures 11.1(a) and (b) that both residuals for minister 2 are based on the same education score (10 years, in this instance); hence, education has been controlled or held constant. This is also true of the four other ministers, and therefore the residuals or deviations from the regression line shown in Figures 11.1(a) and (b) reflect the variation in civic participation and age that cannot be accounted for by education.

Table 11.2 includes the five ministers' ages, civic participation scores, and years of formal education, along with the predicted values for age (X') and civic participation (Y') when they were regressed independently on education (Z), the control variable. The actual values of the residuals shown in Figure 11.1 are also provided. These

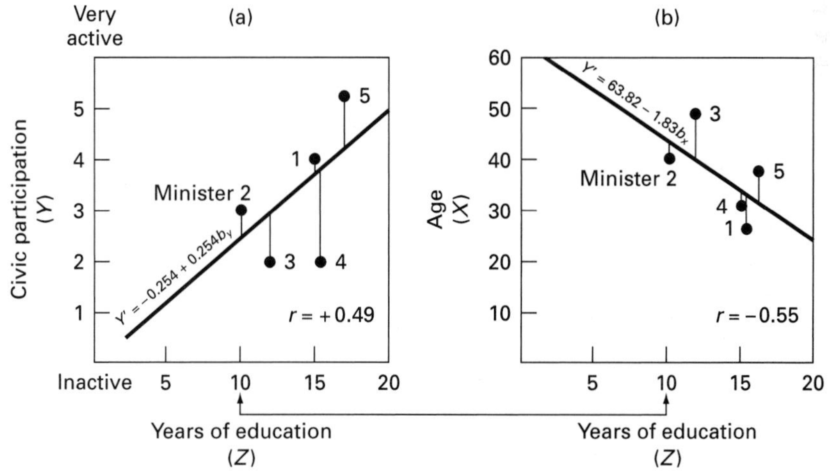

FIGURE 11.1
Regression of civic participation on years of education and regression of age on years of education

TABLE 11.3
Computational procedures for the partial correlation coefficient using residuals

African-American minister	Regression residual for civic participation with education independent $Y - Y'$	Regression residual for age with education independent $X - X'$	$(Y - Y')^2$	$(X - X')^2$	$(X - X')(Y - Y')$
1	+0.44	−8.44	0.19	71.23	−3.71
2	+0.71	−3.57	0.50	12.74	−2.53
3	−0.79	+8.08	0.62	65.29	−6.38
4	−1.56	−2.44	2.43	5.95	+3.81
5	+1.19	+6.38	1.42	40.70	+7.59
$N = 5$	$\Sigma = -0.01$*	$\Sigma = 0.01$*	$\Sigma = 5.16$	$\Sigma = 195.91$	$\Sigma = -1.22$

$$r = \frac{N\Sigma XY - (\Sigma X)(\Sigma Y)}{\sqrt{[N\Sigma X^2 - (\Sigma X)^2][N\Sigma Y^2 - (\Sigma Y)^2]}} \tag{9.2}$$

$$= \frac{5(-1.22) - (0.01)(-0.01)}{\sqrt{[5(195.91) - (0.01)^2][5(5.16) - (-0.01)^2]}}$$

$$= \frac{6.10}{\sqrt{25{,}272.39}}$$

$$= -0.04$$

Note: When substituting into equation (9.2), $X - X' = X$ and $Y - Y' = Y$.
* Does not sum to zero due to rounding error.

residual values are used with equation (9.2) in Table 11.3 to compute the partial correlation coefficient between age and civic participation controlling for education.

11.3.3 The Computational Equation

Now that you fully understand the logic of partial correlation coefficients, computational equation (11.1) is the preferable means of computing first-order partial correlation coefficients. The **order of a partial correlation coefficient** indicates the number of control or test variables.* Equation (11.1) requires that all of the relevant zero-order correlation coefficients be known, as shown in Table 11.4. It is not necessary to calculate the residuals to determine the partial correlation coefficient. Recall from Section 9.1 that the size of a correlation coefficient directly reflects the goodness of fit of the regression line to the coordinates, and therefore provides us with an explicit description of the residuals. [See equation (11.1)]

* Computational equations for higher-order partial correlation coefficients will not be discussed in this text. The interested reader should consult Blalock (1979).

TABLE 11.4
Zero-order correlation matrix

	X	*Y*	*Z*
(*X*) Age	1.00		
(*Y*) Civic participation	−0.30	1.00	
(*Z*) Education	−0.55	0.49	1.00

$$r_{XY.Z} = \frac{r_{XY} - r_{XZ}r_{YZ}}{\sqrt{(1 - r_{XZ}^2)(1 - r_{YZ}^2)}} \tag{11.1}$$

where X = the independent variable
Y = the independent variable
Z = the control variable

The partial correlation coefficient between X and Y controlling for Z is symbolized by $r_{XY \cdot Z}$ (read "r sub XY dot Z"). The numerator of equation (11.1) provides for a measure of the variation that variables X and Y share in common, less the product of the variation that X and Y share with Z, the control variable. The denominator involves taking the square root of the product of the variation in X and Y that is not explained by Z. Partial correlation coefficients can range from −1.00 to +1.00 and, when squared, are a measure of the proportion or percent of variation two variables have in common after controlling for the effects of a third (or third and fourth, and so on) variable. Squaring a partial correlation coefficient of −0.04 tells us that X and Y have less than 1% of their variance in common after Z has been controlled. Entering the correlation coefficients from Table 11.4 into equation (11.1) yields:

$$\begin{aligned} r_{XY.Z} &= \frac{-0.30 - (-0.55)(0.49)}{\sqrt{[1 - (-0.55)^2](1 - 0.49^2)}} \\ &= \frac{-0.03}{\sqrt{0.53}} \\ &= -0.04 \end{aligned}$$

This is the same value that was computed earlier. Comparison of the partial correlation coefficient (−0.04) with the zero-order correlation coefficient between age and civic participation ($r = -0.30$) suggests that education causally links age and civic participation.

Unfortunately, partial correlation coefficients cannot help us distinguish between a spurious relationship and one in which the control variable acts as an intervening variable as shown in the accompanying figure. Based on the logic developed in Section 11.3.1, the spurious interpretation appears to be far less plausible than an intervening variable interpretation.

Spurious Model Intervening Model

11.3.4 A Final Word

A partial correlation coefficient can also be defined as a weighted average of the zero-order correlation between two variables within categories of the control variable. To the extent that zero-order association between two variables is generally uniform across all categories of the control variable, a partial correlation coefficient can be a useful tool. However, when the association is not uniform within all categories of the control variable, the partial correlation coefficient is a misleading measure. A partial correlation coefficient of approximately zero could result, for instance, from two variables having a positive relationship below the median of the control variable and a negative relationship above the median. In the event that the relationship between X and Y is not uniform across all categories of the control variable, a multivariate contingency table should be used rather than partial correlation coefficients. (See Box 11.1.)

BOX 11.1

THE CONCEPT OF INTERACTION

Two variables are said to have **interaction** when their association is not uniform across all categories of a third variable. Consider the example in Section 11.3.2 in which we computed the partial correlation coefficient between age and civic participation controlling for education. Assume we had a large hypothetical sample (say, $N = 300$) and we divided the ministers into three categories based on their educational attainment (e.g., 0–7, 8–12, 13+ years). If we computed a zero-order correlation coefficient for each of the three subsamples we have created, we might get results such as shown in the table.

Age by civic participation controlling for education

Less than 8 years	8–12 years	13 or more years
$r = -0.26$	$r = +0.02$	$r = +0.32$

These results would indicate that interaction was present because the relationship between age and civic participation differs across the categories of educational attainment. If there was a consistent relationship across categories, or if there was consistently little or no relationship across categories, we would conclude there was no interaction. These results would indicate that a partial correlation coefficient would be inappropriate and misleading.

You should see that the same principles discussed here can be applied to multivariate contingency tables. If the measures of association for the partial or conditional tables are not consistent across the categories of a third variable, we can also say that we have interaction.*

* Interaction can be defined in several other ways including: (1) Two variables are said to interact when the effect of one variable on another is contingent upon the presence of a third variable, and (2) interaction is the joint effect of two or more independent variables on a dependent variable, independent of the separate effects of the independent variables.

11.4 MULTIPLE REGRESSION ANALYSIS

11.4.1 Introduction

Multiple regression analysis is a logical extension of simple regression (see Chapter 10). The basic concepts are very similar. Differences stem from multiple regression's use of two or more independent variables as predictors of a dependent variable; simple regression involves only one independent and one dependent variable. Several predictor variables used jointly can potentially account for considerably more variation in a dependent variable than can a single predictor variable.

A multiple regression equation with two independent variables is written in the following manner:

$$Y' = a_y + b_1 X_1 + b_2 X_2 \qquad (11.2)$$

where Y' = the predicted value of the dependent variable*
a_y = the Y-intercept
b_1 = the slope associated with the first independent variable (X_1), and
b_2 = the slope associated with the second independent variable (X_2)

The slopes are interpreted in the following manner: b_1 represents the units of change in Y given one unit increase in X_1, holding X_2 constant; and b_2 represents the units of change in Y given one unit increase in X_2, holding X_1 constant.

11.4.2 Visual Presentation of Multiple Regression Analysis

A visual presentation of multiple regression analysis with one dependent variable and two independent variables is shown in Figure 11.2.

Visualize, with the aid of three pencils, some tape, a flat piece of cardboard, and Figure 11.2, how the X_1-axis, X_2-axis, and Y-axis can be arranged to construct a three-dimensional model. Place two of the pencils on a flat surface so that the erasers touch and the pencils form an angle similar to that shown between the X_1-axis and X_2-axis. Extend the third pencil, which represents the Y-axis, vertically from the intersection of the first two pencils. The pencils can be taped together in this position. To locate a hypothetical coordinate such as $X_1 = 1$, $X_2 = 2$ and $Y = 4$, begin at the intersection of the three axes, move one unit (say, $\frac{1}{4}$ inch) out on the X_1-axis, and mark the distance. Move two units out on the X_2-axis, and mark the distance. Now extend vertical lines from the one-unit value on the X_1-axis and the two-unit value on the X_2-axis in the direction that allows them to intersect. Finally, move up four units relative to the Y-axis from this point of intersection, and the coordinate $X_1 = 1$, $X_2 = 2$, and $Y = 4$ has been established. Once all of the coordinates have been located, you will have created a three-dimensional figure with a "cloud" of points in space formed by the coordinates.

---

* Some texts use a "hat" symbol (e.g., $\hat{Y}$) to designate a predicted value.

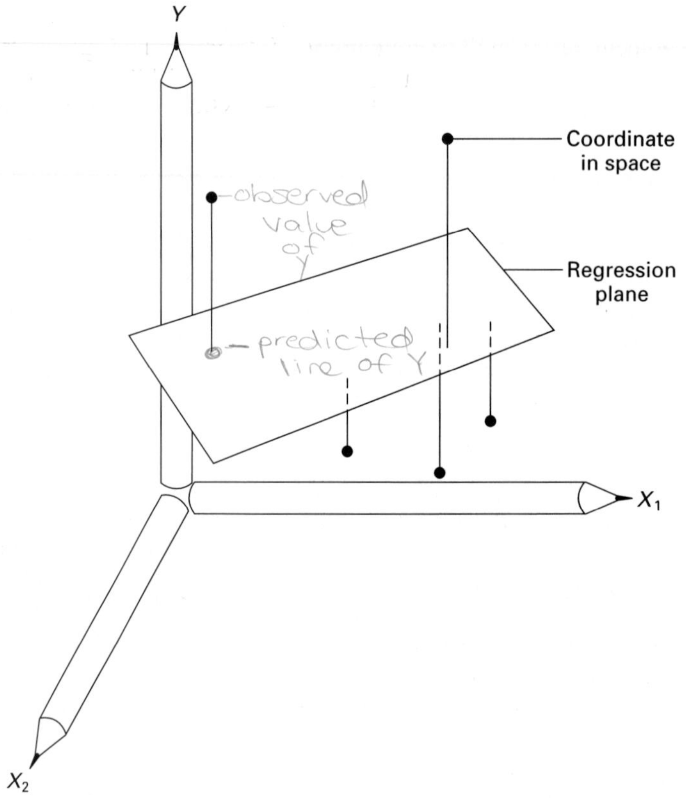

FIGURE 11.2
A three-dimensional portrayal of multiple regression analysis

A regression *line* of best fit relative to the coordinates in space would not be appropriate in this instance; however, a regression *plane* can be fitted to the points. A cardboard backing to a notepad can serve as the plane, as shown in Figure 11.2. Those coordinates that lie above the plane have positive residuals, and those that lie below the plane have negative residuals. Two slopes are required to know how to tilt the plane relative to the X_1-axis and X_2-axis, and a is the point at which the plane crosses the Y-axis.

11.4.3 Multiple Regression: An Example

In the preceding discussion of partial correlation coefficients civic participation among African-American ministers was the dependent variable, age the independent variable, and education the control variable. It was determined that education acted as an intervening variable linking age and civic participation.

Multiple regression analysis allows us to use two or more interval-level or ratio-level variables simultaneously as predictors of an interval-level dependent variable. Equation (11.3) is based on a multiple regression analysis of the data in Table 11.2.

Civic participation (Y) is the dependent variable, whereas age (X_1) and education (X_2) are the independent variables. The computation involved in multiple regression analysis is far too tedious and time-consuming for inclusion. While a computer was used to compute equation (11.3), the following example will allow you to understand the basic concepts of multiple regression:

$$Y' = 0.175 - 0.007X_1 + 0.242X_2 \tag{11.3}$$

Equation (11.3) can be rewritten in words as:

$$\begin{matrix}\text{a minister's} \\ \text{predicted} \\ \text{civic} \\ \text{participation} \\ \text{score}\end{matrix} = 0.175 - 0.007\begin{pmatrix}\text{the} \\ \text{minister's} \\ \text{age}\end{pmatrix} + 0.242\begin{pmatrix}\text{the} \\ \text{minister's} \\ \text{education}\end{pmatrix}$$

The value of a_y, which is 0.175, indicates that the regression plane intersects the Y-axis at 0.175. The **multiple regression coefficient*** associated with X_1 (age) indicates that Y' (civic participation) decreases 0.007 Y units with each one-year increase in X_1 (age), holding X_2 (education) constant. Similarly, the multiple regression coefficient associated with X_2 (education) indicates that Y' increases 0.242 Y units for each additional year of formal education, holding X_1 (age) constant. As was true of simple regression coefficients, the sign associated with a multiple regression coefficient must always be the same as the sign of the zero-order correlation of the independent variable with the dependent variable.† For example, age is correlated -0.30 with civic participation (see Table 11.4), and the sign of the coefficient for age in equation (11.3) is also negative.

Given equation (11.3), we can predict the civic participation scores of the five ministers. From Table 11.2, we see that the first minister is 28 years old and has completed 15 years of formal education. Substituting into equation (11.3), we obtain:

$$Y' = 0.175 - 0.007(28) + 0.242(15) = 3.61$$

Therefore, the predicted civic participation score for the first minister is 3.61, whereas his actual score was 4 (see Table 11.2). The difference between the actual (Y_1) and predicted score (Y'_1) yields the residual of +0.39 for the first minister ($Y_1 - Y'_1 = 4 - 3.61 = 0.39$), hence his coordinate lies 0.39 Y units above the regression plane. As was the case with simple regression, the five residuals (one for each minister) will sum to 0.

$$0.39 + 0.69 + (-0.74) + (-1.57) + 1.23 = 0$$

Equation (11.3) does not allow us to assess the *relative* importance of the independent variables in predicting civic participation, because the coefficients are based on different measurement units. Thus, an examination of *unstandardized regression*

* Multiple regression coefficients are also referred to as *partial regression coefficients, unstandardized partial regression coefficients,* and *unstandardized multiple regression coefficients.*

† If the zero-order correlation coefficients between two or more variables in a multiple regression equation are very close to 0.00, the signs may not be the same.

coefficients such as in equation (11.3) cannot reveal which predictor variables are of the greatest importance. Unlike r, which is independent of the measurement units of the variables involved (Section 9.2.1), b is not independent of measurement units in either a simple or multiple regression context.

Computer programs for multiple regression analysis routinely calculate unstandardized regression coefficients based on the raw data [equation (11.3)] and the *standardized regression coefficients* based on standard scores.* The following standardized regression equation for the five ministers is mathematically equivalent to the unstandardized equation (11.3), if one converts the raw X_1, X_2, and Y scores to z scores and substitutes these standardized scores into the equation:

$$Y' = -0.043X_1 + 0.465X_2$$

Note that there is no Y-intercept in a standardized regression equation. The means of all the variables are zero when they are standardized; therefore, because the regression plane must pass through the coordinate $(\bar{X}_1, \bar{X}_2, \bar{Y})$ or (0, 0, 0), the Y-intercept (a_y) always equals 0 in a standardized regression equation.

It is possible with standardized regression coefficients to assess the *relative* importance of the independent variables. The values (ignoring the signs) of the standardized regression coefficients are directly comparable, and because they are expressed in standardized units, it is evident that education (X_2) is the strongest predictor. The standardized coefficient associated with X_1 is interpreted in the following manner: Y' decreases 0.043 standard deviation units with each one standard deviation increase in X_1, holding X_2 constant. The standardized regression coefficient associated with X_2 indicates that Y' increases 0.465 standard deviation units with each one standard deviation increase in X_2, holding X_1 constant. Standardized regression coefficients are symbolized by the Greek letter β (beta).†

The relationship between the standardized and unstandardized coefficients is shown in equation (11.4):

$$\beta_{yx_1 \cdot x_2} = b_{yx_1 \cdot x_2}\left(\frac{s_{x_1}}{s_y}\right) \qquad (11.4)$$

The subscript $yx_1.x_2$ indicates that Y is the dependent variable, X_1 is the independent variable for which the standardized regression coefficient is being computed, and the second independent variable (X_2) has been statistically controlled.

In words:

$$\begin{matrix}\text{Standardized regression}\\ \text{coefficient for } X_1\\ \text{controlling}\\ \text{for } X_2\end{matrix} = \begin{matrix}\text{Unstandardized}\\ \text{coefficient for}\\ X_1 \text{ controlling}\\ \text{for } X_2\end{matrix}\left(\frac{\text{standard deviation of } X_1}{\text{standard deviation of } Y}\right)$$

The unstandardized coefficient associated with X_1 in equation (11.3) is -0.007, the standard deviation of X_1 is 8.37, and the standard deviation of Y is 1.30. Therefore,

---

* The concept of standard scores was discussed in Section 7.2.

† Standardized regression coefficients are also referred to as *beta weights* and *standardized path coefficients*. These coefficients are based on sample data.

substituting into equation (11.4), we have:

$$\beta_{yx_1 \cdot x_2} = -0.007\left(\frac{8.37}{1.30}\right)$$
$$= -0.045^*$$

Thus, it is possible to convert an unstandardized equation into the standardized form if the standard deviations of the independent and dependent variables are known. Both standardized and unstandardized coefficients are included in Statistics in Action 11.1.

STATISTICS IN ACTION 11.1
Zero-Order Correlation, Multiple Regression, and Multiple Correlation Analysis of a Delinquency Scale

The correlation matrix below Table 11.5 was first introduced in Statistics in Action 9.1. You will recall that the study was based on interviews with 600 adolescents. Table 11.6 provides the results of a multiple regression analysis of the weighted delinquency scale (the dependent

TABLE 11.5
Zero order correlations, means, and standard deviations (N = 498)

Variable	Mean	Standard deviation	1	2	3	4	5	6	7	8
1. Friends smoke marijuana ("all" = low)	3.69	1.09	1.00	−.28	.01	.25	−.17	.34	.25	−.31
2. Parents' attitudes toward friends (approve = low)	4.55	1.36		1.00	−.11	−.24	.30	−.27	−.27	.26
3. Sex (male = low)	1.49	0.51			1.00	.17	.00	.01	.10	−.15
4. High school grade average (A = 10)	6.89	2.09				1.00	−.06	.10	.16	−.22
5. Closeness to mother (close = low)	2.97	1.12					1.00	−.06	−.17	.19
6. Obey all parents' rules ("no" = low)	3.45	1.27						1.00	.28	−.21
7. Importance of religion (unimportant = low)	2.55	1.21							1.00	−.14
8. Weighted delinquency scale (not delinquent = low)	9.54	10.73								1.00

* Differs slightly from −0.043 computed earlier due to rounding error.

TABLE 11.6
Regression analysis of the weighted delinquency scale

Independent variable	Zero-order correlation	Unstandardized regression coefficient (b)	Standard error of b	Standardized regression coefficient (β)	F-ratio
Friends smoke marijuana	−0.31	−2.01	0.45	−0.20	19.8*
Parents' attitudes toward friends	+0.26	+0.93	0.37	+0.12	6.4*
Sex	−0.15	−2.46	0.88	−0.12	7.8*
High school grade point average	−0.22	−0.55	0.23	−0.11	6.0*
Closeness to mother	+0.19	+1.00	0.42	+0.10	5.8*
Obey all parents' rules	−0.21	−0.74	0.38	−0.09	3.7*
Importance of religion	−0.14	−0.11	0.39	+0.01	0.1
Y-intercept		2.11			
$R = 0.42$					
$R^2 = 0.17$					

*$p < .001$.

variable) which is based on 20 items that were weighted according to their seriousness (e.g., hurt someone badly, run away from home, steal something worth more than $50). The unstandardized and standardized regression coefficients are included.

Table 11.6 provides the results of the multiple regression analysis of the variables. The unstandardized and standardized regression coefficients are included along with the standard error of b (a measure of the extent to which the unstandardized regression coefficients would vary if a new sample were drawn and the data were reanalyzed) and the F-ratio (a measure which is discussed in conjunction with the analysis of variance that indicates the statistical significance of the regression coefficients, that is, the likelihood that the value of the coefficients in Table 11.6 reflect the relationships in the population from which the sample was drawn).* The asterisks in the table indicate that all of the variables with the exception of "importance of religion" are statistically significant predictors of "delinquency."

Looking at the standardized regression coefficients, that allow us to determine the relative importance of the predictors, we can see that whether or not one's "friends smoke marijuana" is the best predictor ($\beta = -0.20$). The predictor variables are presented in terms of their relative importance as can be seen by the size of the standardized regression coefficients. What parents think of their child's friends, closeness to one's mother, sex, and high school grade point average are important independent variables. Males are more likely to be delinquent than females and poorer students are more likely to be delinquent than good students. The importance of religion to the adolescent was clearly unimportant as a predictor.

The seven predictor variables accounted for 17% of the variance in the delinquency scale ($R = 0.42$ and $R^2 = 0.17$).

* t-values are sometimes used in place of the F-ratio. See Section 15.3.2 for a further discussion.

11.4.4 The Multiple Correlation Coefficient

The **multiple correlation coefficient (*R*)** is a measure of the linear relationship between a dependent variable and the combined effects of two or more independent variables. It is symbolized by a capital R to differentiate it from r, the zero-order correlation coefficient, which was discussed in Chapter 9. As was true of r, squaring R yields a far more interpretable measure. The **coefficient of multiple determination (R^2)** indicates the proportion of total variation in a dependent variable that is explained jointly by two or more independent variables. For the African-American minister example, $R = 0.49$ and $R^2 = 0.24$; thus, 24% of the variation in civic participation has been explained by age and education, and 76% ($100\% - 24\% = 76\%$) of the variation has not been explained.*

Figure 11.3 presents the concept of the coefficient of multiple determination diagrammatically. The shaded area designated by letters *a*, *c*, and *d* in Figure 11.3 represents the total variation in Y explained jointly by X_1 and X_2. Area *c* represents the independent contribution of X_2 to an explanation of the variation in Y and area *d* represents the independent contribution of X_1. Area *a* represents the joint contribution

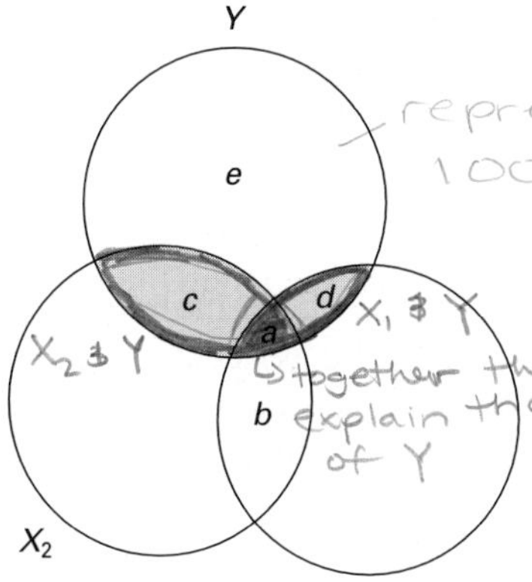

$a =$	Joint contribution of X_1 and X_2 to an explanation of the variation in Y.
$b =$	Variation shared by X_1 and X_2 independent of Y.
$c =$	Independent contribution of X_2 to an explanation of the variation in Y.
$d =$	Independent contribution of X_1 to an explanation of the variation in Y.
$e =$	Variation in Y not accounted for by X_1 and X_2 (equivalent to $1 - R^2$).
$a + b =$	Variation shared by X_1 and X_2.
$a + c + d =$	Total variation in Y accounted for by X_1 and X_2 (equivalent to R^2).

FIGURE 11.3
A diagrammatic presentation of the coefficient of multiple determination

* The unexplained variation is sometimes referred to as the *coefficient of nondetermination* and is symbolized by $1 - R^2$ for multiple regression or $1 - r^2$ for simple regression.

of X_1 and X_2. The total area represented by areas *a* and *b* indicates the variation shared by X_1 and X_2. Area *e* indicates the variation in *Y* that has not been accounted for by the two independent variables, X_1 and X_2.

Unfortunately, there is no way to partition the variation in *Y* that was explained by X_1 and the variation that was explained by X_2 unless X_1 and X_2 are unrelated. In this example, X_1 and X_2 are statistically associated as shown by their intersection (areas *a* and *b*), and it is impossible to know what proportion of the variation in *Y*, which is indicated by area *a*, is attributable to X_1 and what to X_2.

SUMMARY

In this chapter, we have learned about multivariate statistical techniques including multivariate contingency tables, partial correlation analysis, multiple regression analysis, and multiple correlation analysis. All of these techniques involve examining the relationship between three or more variables simultaneously.

Multivariate contingency tables allow us statistically to elaborate the relationship between two variables by introducing a control variable.

Partial correlation analysis provides us with a measure of the linear relationship between two interval-level variables having statistically controlled for one or more other interval-level variables. The concept and the computational procedure of statistical control was presented. The partial correlation coefficient should not be used when the zero-order association between two variables is not uniform across all categories of the control variable.

Multiple regression analysis allows us to use two or more interval-level variables simultaneously as predictors of an interval-level dependent variable. The interpretation and relationship of unstandardized and standardized multiple regression coefficients was presented, and the interpretation and use of multiple regression coefficients was discussed.

TERMS TO REMEMBER

coefficient of multiple determination (R^2) A measure of the proportion of total variation in a dependent variable that is explained jointly by two or more independent variables.

conditional table A contingency table that summarizes the relationship between two variables for categories or conditions of one or more other variables.

control variable A variable whose subgroups or categories are used in a conditional table to examine the relationship between two variables.

interaction Two variables are said to have interaction when their association is not uniform across all categories of a third variable.

intervening variable A variable that causally links two other variables.

multiple correlation coefficient (R) A measure of the linear relationship between a dependent variable and the combined effects of two or more independent variables.

multiple regression coefficient A measure of the influence of an independent variable on a dependent variable when the effects of all other independent variables in the multiple regression equation have been held constant. It can be standardized or unstandardized.

multivariate statistical technique A statistical technique used to determine the nature of the relationships among three or more variables.
order of a conditional table The order of a table is the number of control or test variables that are included.
order of a partial correlation coefficient The order of a partial correlation coefficient indicates the number of control or test variables.
partial correlation coefficient A measure of the linear relationship between two interval-level variables controlling for one or more other interval-level variables.
partial table See *conditional table.*
spurious relationship Exists when the zero-order relationship between an independent and dependent variable disappears or becomes significantly weaker with the introduction of a control variable.
statistical elaboration The process of introducing a control variable to determine whether a bivariate relationship remains the same or varies under the different categories or conditions of the control variable.
test variable See *control variable.*

EXERCISES

1. Discuss the advantages of using multivariate statistical procedures rather than bivariate statistical procedures.
2. Differentiate between physical control as used with multivariate contingency tables and statistical control as used with partial correlation analysis.
3. Given the following bivariate contingency table, introduce a control variable (e.g., education or another variable of your choice) and manipulate the data to show its influence on the relationship of age and attitude toward health maintenance organizations (HMOs).

	(*X*) Age		
(*Y*) Favor HMOs?	**Young**	**Old**	**Total**
Yes	34.7 (51)	63.6 (82)	(133)
No	65.3 (96)	36.4 (47)	(143)
Total	100.0 (147)	100.0 (129)	$N = 276$

4. The following table presents data obtained from a sample of college students. Based on the data, answer the following questions.
   (*a*) Identify the independent, dependent, and control variables that are included in this table.
   (*b*) Without doing any statistical operations beyond examining the percentages and numbers in the cells of the table, give an interpretation about the relationship between the variables in the table (what does this table tell us?) and describe the effect of the control variable.
   (*c*) Reconstruct or "collapse" this three-variable table into a two-variable table in a way that would allow you to examine the simple relationship between age and political

orientation, and indicate whether it appears that young or old students are more conservative (again, it is not necessary to do any statistical operation other than simple examination of percentages and numbers of cases).

	Under 25 years old		25 years and older		
	Level in school		Level in school		
Political orientation	Undergraduate	Graduate	Undergraduate	Graduate	
Liberal	75.0 (30)	25.0 (15)	60.0 (30)	50.0 (25)	
Conservative	25.0 (10)	75.0 (45)	40.0 (20)	50.0 (25)	
Total	100.0 (40)	100.0 (60)	100.0 (50)	100.0 (50)	$N = 200$

5. The data in Table A show the relationship between the length of prison sentence (in months) received by defendants charged with violations of the Federal Drug Abuse Prevention and Control Act during a two-year period. Table B shows the relationship between the length of sentence and year by the type of substance involved. Percentage the tables using the column totals as the base and discuss the influence of the control variable.

TABLE A

	Time period		
Sentence in months	Year 1	Year 2	Total
1–12	1404	885	2289
13–35	811	623	1434
36–59	1143	956	2099
60+	1310	1141	2451
Total	4668	3605	$N = 8273$

TABLE B

	Marijuana		Narcotics		Controlled substances (prescribed drugs)	
Sentence in months	Year 1	Year 2	Year 1	Year 2	Year 1	Year 2
1–12	466	241	757	412	181	232
13–35	281	158	410	328	120	137
36–59	274	245	749	518	120	193
60+	183	139	1022	739	105	263
Total	1204	783	2938	1997	526	825
	$N = 1987$		$N = 4935$		$N = 1351$	

Source: Administrative Office of the U.S. Courts.

6. The data in Tables A, B, and C are based on the General Social Survey which is conducted nationwide each year.

(*a*) Identify the independent, dependent, and control variable.

(*b*) Describe the relationship between health and family income in Table A.

(*c*) Discuss the influence of the control variable in Tables B and C.

(*d*) Propose alternative age categories to those used in Tables B and C, and defend your answer.

(*e*) Name other control variables that should be considered to understand the relationship between one's health and family income.

TABLE A
Respondent's health status by total family income

Count / Col. Pct. / Health (Row)	Income: Low	Moderate	High	Total
Excellent	181 24.9	188 32.0	193 43.4	562 32.0
Good	312 43.0	305 52.0	205 46.1	822 46.8
Fair or poor	233 32.1	94 16.0	47 10.6	374 21.3
Column Total	726 41.3	587 33.4	445 25.3	1758 100.0

Kendall's tau-*b*	+.200
Gamma	+.308
Somer's *d*: with health dependent	+.197

TABLE B
Respondent's health status by total family income controlling for . . .

Age value = 1.00 (40 years old or less)

Count
Col. Pct.

Health	Income: Low	Moderate	High	Row Total
Excellent	130 29.8	149 33.6	145 45.7	424 35.5
Good	202 46.3	232 52.4	142 44.8	576 48.2
Fair or poor	104 23.9	62 14.0	30 9.5	196 16.4
Column Total	436 36.5	443 37.0	317 26.5	1196 100.0

Kendall's tau-*b* +.150

Gamma +.235

Somer's *d*:
with health dependent +.145

TABLE C
Respondent's health status by total family income controlling for . . .

Age value = 2.00 (over 40 years old)

Count
Col. Pct.

Health	Income: Low	Moderate	High	Row Total
Excellent	50 17.4	39 27.3	48 37.5	137 24.5
Good	72 38.2	63 50.3	245 49.2	43.8
Fair or poor	128 44.4	32 22.4	17 13.3	177 31.7
Column Total	288 51.5	143 25.6	128 22.9	559 100.0

Kendall's tau-*b* +.264

Gamma +.408

Somer's *d*:
with health dependent +.270

Number of missing observations: 3

7. You are studying the relationship of church attendance, self-reported delinquent acts, and drug usage among a sample of high school students. Given the following correlation matrix, compute the first-order partial correlation coefficient between church attendance and self-reported delinquent acts controlling for drug usage, and interpret the results.

	1	2	3
1. Self-reported delinquent acts	1.00		
2. Church attendance	−0.32	1.00	
3. Drug usage	+0.41	−0.17	1.00

8. Explain why technically the partial correlation of variables X and Y controlling for variable Z is the correlation of the residuals of the regressions of X on Z and Y on Z.

9. Why should a partial correlation coefficient not be computed when the association between two variables is not uniform across all categories of the control variable?

10. If $r_{xy} = +0.80$, $r_{xz} = +0.61$, and $r_{yz} = +0.43$, compute $r_{xy \cdot z}$.

11. Income (X_1) and seniority (X_2) have been used as predictors of job satisfaction (Y) for a sample of municipal employees. Given the following regression equation, interpret the Y-intercept and the regression coefficients associated with income and seniority.

$$Y' = 0.93 + 0.28X_1 + 0.44X_2$$

12. Is the equation in exercise 11 in standardized or unstandardized form? How can you tell?

13. Given the scores for five of the employees included in the study summarized in exercise 11, compute the predicted Y scores and the residuals for each of the five employees.

	X_1	X_2	Y
Employee 1	10	2	6
2	15	3	5
3	9	6	7
4	21	9	9
5	46	15	21

14. Assume that the following table contains the results of regression analyses of data from a national sample survey of 11th grade African-American and white students. The purpose of the analysis is to see what factors account for students' performance levels on math achievement tests (the dependent variable). The independent variables are (1) the student's cumulative grade average, (2) the student's family socioeconomic status (SES), (3) the student's reading ability test score, (4) the percentage of the student's class that is white, and (5) a measure of the teaching ability of the student's math teacher. Using the standardized regression coefficients and other statistics in the table, answer the following questions.

Independent variables	White students	African-American students
1. Cumulative grade average	0.10	0.24
2. Family SES	0.42	0.49
3. Reading test score	0.39	0.05
4. % white in class	0.37	−0.19
5. Teacher's ability	0.17	0.34
Multiple correlation coefficient (R)	0.72	0.38
Coefficient of multiple determination (R^2)	0.52	0.14

(*a*) For which group, African Americans or whites, does the regression model using these five variables do a better job in predicting or explaining math achievement scores? How do you know that?

(*b*) Of the variables listed, which one seems to be the most important contributing factor to the math test achievement score? Which are the least important factors in this analysis?

(*c*) In multiple regression analysis, what is the meaning or interpretation of standardized regression coefficients such as those in the table? How would you interpret the fact that the standardized regression coefficient of teacher's ability is 0.17 for white students and 0.34 for African-American students? That is, what do these coefficients tell us?

15. The following questions refer to Statistics in Action 11.1.

(*a*) Write the unstandardized and standardized regression equations.

(*b*) Interpret the meaning of the unstandardized and standardized equations associated with grade point average.

(*c*) What does the *Y*-intercept tell us in this instance? Why is there no *Y*-intercept for the standardized equation?

(*d*) What is the dependent variable? How many independent variables are included in Table 11.6 and what are they?

(*e*) What proportion of the variation in the dependent variable has been explained by the independent variables? What percentage of the variation has been explained? What percentage of the variation in the dependent variable has not been explained?

(*f*) Which independent variable is the best predictor of delinquency? Which is the poorest?

16. The following questions refer to the summary of the SPSS multiple regression analysis below.

(*a*) Identify the dependent variable and the independent variables.

(*b*) How much of the variation in the dependent variable was explained jointly by the independent variables?

(*c*) Rank order the independent variables in order of their independent contribution to explaining variation in the dependent variable. *Hint:* Examine the beta coefficients (the standardized regression coefficients).

(*d*) Interpret the following coefficients: For education, B = −.045195 and Beta = −.162068; standard error of estimate = .70348 (*Hint:* This was discussed in Chapter 10.); and constant (Y-intercept or a_y) = 2.138544.

MULTIPLE REGRESSION

```
Equation Number 1    Dependent Variable..  HEALTH   CONDITION OF RESPONDENT'S HEALTH

Variable(s) entered on step number  1..   AGE      AGE OF RESPONDENT
                                    2..   EDUC     HIGHEST YEAR OF SCHOOL COMPLETED
                                    3..   SEX      RESPONDENTS SEX
                                    4..   SATJOB   SATISFACTION WITH JOB OR HOUSEWORK
                                    5..   INCOME   TOTAL FAMILY INCOME
Multiple R           .35320
R square             .12475
Standard error       .70348
  of estimate

------------------ Variables in the Equation ------------------
```

Variable	B	SE B	Beta	T	Sig T
INCOME	-.022305	.004172	-.142883	-5.346	.0000
SEX	-.007085	.037354	-.004685	-.190	.8496
SATJOB	.169152	.023583	.179041	7.173	.0000
EDUC	-.045195	.007330	-.162068	-6.166	.0000
AGE	.009472	.001485	.160856	6.380	.0000
(Constant)	2.138544	.146816		14.566	.0000

Note: The SE *B* (standard error of *B*) is a measure of the stability of *B* if a new sample were drawn and the regression analysis were repeated with these variables. All of the SE *B*s are stable with the exception of the coefficient associated with "sex," which is also the only independent variable that is not statistically significant.

Source: This analysis is based on the 1994 General Social Survey.

PART III

Inferential Statistics: Parametric Tests of Significance

CHAPTER 12

Probability

12.1 INTRODUCTION TO PROBABILITY

In the past few chapters, we have been concerned primarily with the presentation of techniques employed by statisticians and scientists to describe and present data. Statisticians and scientists study *some* people and/or events, but they want their conclusions to hold for other people and/or events that they have not specifically tested. In other words, they want to generalize their results to an entire population even though they specifically examined only a small sample.

Most national opinion polls are based on samples of less than 3,000 respondents and yet the results can be used to infer accurately how the adult population feels about the issues under consideration. Often you will read that a given percentage of those polled (e.g., 42%) favor a solution or hold a particular opinion and the results are accurate within ± 3 percentage points. As you will learn in Chapter 14, this means that if the entire population were interviewed, the actual percentage holding the opinion has a high probability of falling somewhere between 39% and 45%.

Probability theory is not so unfamiliar as many would think. Indeed, in everyday life you are constantly called upon to make probability judgements, although you may not recognize them as such (see Box 12.1). For example, suppose that, for various reasons, you are unprepared for class. You seriously consider not attending class. What are the factors that will influence your decision? Obviously, one consideration would be the likelihood that the instructor will discover you are not prepared. If the risk is high, you decide not to attend class; if low, then you will attend.

BOX 12.1

THE GAMBLER'S FALLACY

Probability theory is the foundation stone of inferential statistics. Without it, our interpretation of data would progress little beyond sheer guesswork. Considering its importance, it is surprising that mistaken notions about probability pervade the thinking of many people. One is the "Gambler's Fallacy," illustrated in this excerpt from *Winning with Statistics.*

I'm overdue for a run of luck

Famous last words! This one takes many forms and invades many fields. The gambler is tossing coins and loses four in a row. Reasoning that five losses in a row is exceedingly rare ($p = 0.031$, odds against $= 31.25:1$), he decides to increase the ante. "I'm due for a win," he proclaims confidently. Your favorite baseball player has gone 0 for 4. When he comes to bat for the fifth time, you exude confidence: "He's due for a hit." The opposing quarterback has just completed six consecutive passes against your team. You breathe a sigh of relief: "The next is bound to be incomplete or intercepted."

Although these examples are not exactly the same, they have one thing in common—the belief that events have memories. It is as if the gambler is reasoning, "The coin will remember that it came up heads four times in a row and will try to balance out the 'law of averages' by coming up tails on the next toss." This is sheer nonsense. So long as the coin is "honest," it is just as likely to come up heads as tails on the next toss or on any toss, for that matter. We speak of this condition as **independence**—the outcome of one trial has no effect on later trials. This is just another way of denying that coins or dice or cards or roulette wheels have memories.

It is somewhat different when dealing with activities involving behavior. Although a bat and ball have no memory, "turns at bat" are not always independent, particularly if they are against a pitcher of Greg Maddux's caliber. And your football team could have seven passes completed against it because of its porous defence. Nevertheless, it is incorrect to cite the "law of averages" as the reason for expecting something different on the next trial. The law of averages has no enforcement agency behind it, nor is there a Supreme Court to oversee the constitutionally of its "decisions." Indeed, the only thing it has in common with jurisprudence is its impartiality.

Source: Excerpted from Runyon, *Winning with Statistics* (1977).

Let's look at this example in slightly different terms. There are two alternative possibilities:

Event *A:* Your lack of preparation *will* be detected.
Event *B:* Your lack of preparation *will not* be detected.

There is uncertainty in this situation because more than one alternative is possible. Your decision whether or not to attend class will depend on the degree of assurance you associate with each of these alternatives. Thus, if you are fairly certain that the instructor will detect your lack of preparedness, you will decide not to attend class.

Suppose that your instructor frequently calls upon students to participate in class discussion. In fact, you have noted that most of the students are called upon in any given class session. This is an example of a situation in which event A is likely to occur. Stated another way, the probability of event A is higher than the probability of event B. Thus, you decide not to attend class. Although you have not used any formal probability laws in this example, you have actually made a judgment based on an *intuitive* use of probability.

Probability is a theory concerned with possible outcomes of studies. As social scientists, we concern ourselves with such questions as the probability that a prisoner will commit another crime after being released from prison, or the probability that a particular candidate will win an election.

You may have noted that many of the questions raised in the exercises earlier in the book began with, "What is the likelihood that . . . ?" These questions were in preparation for the formal discussion of probability occurring in this and subsequent chapters. However, before discussing the elements of probability, we should understand one of the most important concepts in inferential statistics, that of *randomness.*

12.2 THE CONCEPT OF RANDOMNESS

You will recall that when discussing the role of inferential statistics in Chapter 1, we pointed out that population parameters are rarely known or knowable. Thus, we are usually forced to draw samples from a given population and estimate the parameters from the sample statistics. We want to select these samples in such a way that they are representative of the populations from which they are drawn. One way to achieve representativeness is to employ simple random sampling: selecting samples in such a way that each sample of a given size has precisely the same probability of being selected, or, alternatively, selecting the events in the sample such that each event is equally likely to be selected in a sample of a given size.

Consider selecting samples of $N = 2$ from a population of five numbers: 0, 1, 2, 3, and 4. If, for any reason, any number is more likely to be drawn than any other number, each sample would not have an equal likelihood of being drawn. For example, if for any reason the number 3 were twice as likely to be drawn as any other number, there would be a preponderance of samples containing the value 3. Such sampling procedures are referred to as having **bias.** When we are interested in learning the characteristics of the general population for a given variable, we should not select our sample from automobile registration lists or "at random" on a street corner in New York City. The dangers of generalizing to a population from such biased samples should be clear. Unless the condition of randomness is met, we may never know to what population we should generalize our results. Furthermore, with nonrandom samples we find that many of the rules of probability do not apply.

Moreover, the statistical tests presented in this text require *independent* random sampling. Two events are said to be independent if the selection of one event has no effect on the probability of selecting the other. We can most readily grasp independence in terms of games of chance, assuming they are played honestly. Knowledge of the results of one toss of a coin, one throw of a die, one spin of the roulette wheel, or one selection of a card from a well-shuffled deck (assuming replacement of the card after each selection) will not aid us in our predictions of future outcomes.

When we are involved in conducting an experiment, we must concern ourselves with introducing randomness at two junctures of the study: *selecting* our subjects at random from the population of interest, and *assigning* these subjects at random to the experimental conditions.

It is beyond the scope of this text to go deeply into sampling procedures because that topic is a full course in itself. However, consider how we achieve randomness when drawing a sample from a population. Let's suppose we wish to select 25 persons randomly from a population totaling 300. One method to achieve randomness would be to place the names of each of the 300 persons in the population on a folded slip of paper. After shuffling the slips of paper and placing them in a container, we could reach into the container and draw 25 names.

An alternative method would be to use the table of random digits (Table M in Appendix C). Since the digits in this table have already been randomized by a computer, the effect of shuffling has been achieved. We assign each of our 300 persons comprising the population a number from 001 to 300. We may start with any row or column of digits in Table M. For example, if we start with the first row and choose consecutive sets of three digits, we obtain the following numbers: 100, 973, 253, 376, 520, 135, and so on. If any number over 300 or any repeated number appears, we disregard it and continue until we have chosen 25 "usable" numbers, which represent the 25 people who will constitute our sample.

Most present-day computers have a function that generates random digits. If you have access to a computer, you will save much time by letting the computer do the selecting for you. This randomization function is at the heart of the many games that computers play.

The reason for the great importance of random procedures will become clear in this chapter and the next. Fundamentally, it is based on a fascinating fact of inferential statistics: *Each event may not be predictable when taken alone, but collections of random events can take on predictable forms.* The binomial distribution, which we will discuss at greater length in Section 13.3, illustrates this fact. If we were to take, say, 20 unbiased coins and toss them into the air, we could not predict accurately the proportion that would land "heads." However, if we were to toss these 20 coins a great many times, record the number turning up heads on each trial, and construct a frequency distribution of outcomes in which the horizontal axis varies between no heads and all heads, the plot would take on a characteristic and predictable form known as the *binomial distribution* (see Figure 12.1). By employing the binomial model, we would be able to predict with considerable accuracy over a large number of trials the percentage of the time various outcomes will occur. What is perhaps more fascinating is that the distribution of outcomes of this two-category variable approximates the normal curve more and more closely as N (the number of tosses of a single coin or the number of coins tossed at one time) becomes larger. Indeed, with large Ns we may use the normal curve to describe the probability of various outcomes of a binomial variable.

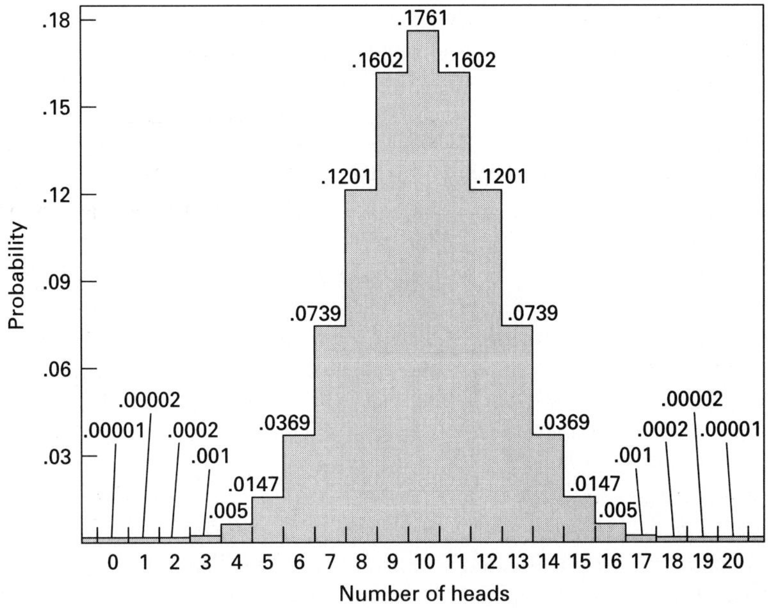

FIGURE 12.1
Probabilities of obtaining varying numbers of heads (from 0 to 20) on repeated tosses of an "honest" coin
Note how closely the histogram resembles the normal curve.

The same reasoning is true with respect to the normal-curve model. In the absence of any specific information, we might not be able to predict a person's status with respect to a given trait (e.g., intelligence, height, weight). However, as we already know, frequency distributions of scores on these traits commonly take the form of the normal curve. Thus, we may predict the proportion of individuals scoring between specified score limits.

What is perhaps more important from the point of view of inferential statistics is the fact that distributions of sample statistics ($\overline{X}$, s, median, etc.), based on random sampling from a population, also take on highly predictable forms. Chapter 13 deals with the concept of **sampling distributions,** which are theoretical probability distributions of a statistic that would result from drawing all possible samples of a given size from some population.

With this brief introduction to the concept of randomness, you are prepared to look at probability theory.

12.3 APPROACHES TO PROBABILITY

$0 \leq P(A) \leq 1.00$

As we mentioned earlier, *probability* is a theory that is concerned with the possible outcomes of a study. It must be possible to list every outcome that can occur, and we must be able to state the expected relative frequencies of these outcomes. It is the method of assigning relative frequencies to each of the possible outcomes that distinguishes the classical from the empirical approach to probability theory.

12.3.1 Classical Approach to Probability

The theory of probability has always been closely associated with games of chance. For example, suppose we want to know the probability that a single card selected from a 52-card deck will be an ace of spades. There are 52 possible outcomes. We assume an ideal situation in which we expect that each outcome is equally likely to occur. Thus, the probability of selecting an ace of spades is one out of 52 or $1/52$. This kind of reasoning has led to the following classical definition of probability:

$$p(A) = \frac{\text{number of outcomes in which event } A \text{ occurs}}{\text{total number of outcomes } (A \text{ occurs} + A \text{ does not occur})} \tag{12.1}$$

Note that probability is defined as a proportion (p). The most important point in the classical definition of probability is the assumption of an *ideal* situation in which the composition of the population is known; that is, the total number of possible outcomes (N) is known. The expected relative frequency of each of these outcomes is arrived at by deductive reasoning. Thus, the probability of an event is interpreted as a theoretical (or an idealized) relative frequency of the event. In the preceding example, the total number of possible outcomes was 52 (all cards in the deck), and each outcome was assumed to have an equal likelihood of occurrence. Thus, p (ace of spades) $= 1/52$; p (king of hearts) $= 1/52$, and so on.

12.3.2 Empirical Approach to Probability

Although it is usually easy to assign expected relative frequencies to the possible outcomes of games of chance, we cannot do this for most real-life situations in which expected relative frequencies are assigned on the basis of empirical findings. Thus, we may not know the exact proportion of students in a university who have worked in a political campaign, but we may conduct a simple random sample of students in the university and estimate the proportion who have worked in a campaign. Once we have arrived at an estimate, we can use classical probability theory to answer questions such as, "What is the probability that in a sample of 10 students, drawn at random from the student body, 3 or more will have worked in a political campaign?"

If, in a sample random sample of 100 students, we found that 30 had worked in a campaign, we could estimate that the proportion of experienced campaigners in the university was 0.30, using equation (12.1):

$$p(\text{campaigners}) = \frac{30}{100} = 0.30$$

TABLE 12.1
Proportion of male births, by race, in the United States, 1984–1993

Year	White	African American
1984	0.5131	0.5076
1985	0.5139	0.5074
1986	0.5143	0.5074
1987	0.5136	0.5069
1988	0.5141	0.5072
1989	0.5139	0.5081
1990	0.5138	0.5068
1991	0.5141	0.5076
1992	0.5140	0.5071
1993	0.5139	0.5070
Mean	0.5139	0.5073
Standard deviation	0.0003	0.0004

Thus, the probability is 0.30 that a student in the university will have campaigned previously.*

Although it is easy to assign expected relative frequencies to the possible outcomes of games of chance, we cannot do this for most real-life experiments. Take the gender of an about-to-be-born child. What is the probability that it will be a girl? On the surface, the answer would appear to be easy. Hypothetically, the birth of a boy or girl would appear to be equally likely, 0.50 in both cases. However, this is not the case. In the United States, the proportion of annual male births has been exceptionally stable for many years—0.5139 for white and 0.5073 for African American (see Table 12.1).

A gambler who made his livelihood on taking bets on the gender of children about to be born could do quite well, over the long run, by giving even odds that the child will be a boy. If he bet only on white babies, on every 10,000 bets, the gambler could expect to win, on the average, 5,139 times and lose 4,861 times.

The fundamental feature of empirical probabilities is that they are based on actual measurements rather than on theoretical proportions. There is usually little or no basis for assigning theoretical probabilities to most of the situations confronted by the student of behavior: for example, the probability that a person will require treatment for a disorder at some time in his or her life, the probability that a convicted felon will return to crime, or the probability that a child will be born with a congenital defect. Probabilities such as these must be obtained empirically and are always subject to revision in the light of additional data.

---

*This represents an *empirical* probability; that is, the expected relative frequency was assigned on the basis of empirical findings.

12.3.3 Subjective Approaches to Probability

There are many occasions when we lack the objective data for estimating probabilities. Nevertheless, we may have strong feelings that we term "a hunch," "common sense," or an intuition. Someone working on a suicide hot line may say, "I can't tell you precisely why I feel this way, but I believe that the caller is at high risk for suicide." We should not dismiss these subjective probabilities out of hand. Even though subjective probabilities cannot, by their very nature, be documented and substantiated, they may nevertheless arise from a lifetime of observation and assessment of subtle cues. Indeed, it is likely that any important decision we have made in life includes subjective probabilities as a basic ingredient. For this reason, we accept the notion of subjective probabilities. Once made, we expect them to follow the same rules as probabilities obtained by the classical or the empirical approach.

12.4 FORMAL PROPERTIES OF PROBABILITY

12.4.1 Probabilities Vary between 0 and 1.00

From the classical definition of probability, p is always between 0 and 1, inclusively. If an event is certain to occur, its probability is 1; if it is certain not to occur, its probability is 0. For example, the probability of drawing the ace of spades from an ordinary deck of 52 playing cards is 1/52. The probability of drawing a red ace of spades is zero because the ace of spades is never red. However, the probability of drawing a card with *some* marking on it is $p = 1.00$. Thus, for any given event, say, A, $0 \leq p(A) \leq 1.00$, in which the symbol $\leq$ means "less than or equal to" and the symbol $\geq$ means "greater than or equal to."

12.4.2 Expressing Probability

In addition to expressing probability as a proportion, several other ways are often used. It is sometimes convenient to express probability as a *percentage* or as the *number of chances* in 100.

To illustrate: If the probability of an event is 0.05, we expect this event to occur 5% of the time, or the chances that this event will occur are 5 in 100. This same probability may be expressed by saying that the odds are 95 to 5 against the event occurring, or 19 to 1 against it.

When expressing probability as the *odds against* the occurrence of an event, we use equation (12.2):

$$\text{odds against event } A = (\text{total no. of outcomes} - \text{no. of times event } A \text{ occurs}) \textit{ to } \text{no. of times event } A \text{ occurs} \qquad (12.2)$$

Thus, if $p(A) = 0.01$, the odds against the occurrence of event A are 99 to 1.

12.4.3 The Addition Rule

When we know the possible outcomes of an experiment, it is possible to identify any number of different events for purposes of probability analysis. To illustrate, we may raise questions such as:

1. What is the probability of obtaining one event or another; for example, drawing a queen *or* a club from a deck of playing cards?

2. What is the probability of obtaining two events simultaneously; for example, selecting a queen *and* a club from a deck of playing cards?

To answer the first question, we must make use of the **addition rule;** and for the second, we use the **multiplication rule.** We examine the addition rule in this section and the multiplication rule in Section 12.4.4.

When events are not mutually exclusive*

Suppose that in an effort to obtain data on current reasons for seeking professional help, a questionnaire was sent out to administrators at various mental health clinics throughout the country. One part of the questionnaire dealt with the abuse of drugs and alcohol among those receiving care at the clinics. The results of the questionnaires showed that out of 5,900 patients, 354 abused alcohol and 236 abused drugs; of these (the abusers of alcohol and drugs) 118 abused both. Let us define event A as the abuse of alcohol and event B as the abuse of drugs.

Based on the replies, we can estimate the probability of each event from the sample:

$$p(A) = \frac{354}{5{,}900} = 0.06$$

$$p(B) = \frac{236}{5{,}900} = 0.04$$

Now, if we wished to know the probability that a given patient was either an alcohol or drug abuser, we might be tempted to add together the number of patients abusing alcohol and the number abusing drugs, and divide by N to obtain $p(A \text{ or } B) = (354 + 236)/5{,}900 = 0.10$. However, this probability does not take into account the 118 people who are counted twice—once as alcohol abusers and once as drug abusers. In other words, the two categories are not mutually exclusive. The overlapping area in the Venn diagram in Figure 12.2 shows that alcohol and drug abuse are occurring at the same time (for the 118 people). Events A and B are said to be *mutually exclusive* if both cannot occur simultaneously. This is shown as the overlapping area in the Venn diagram in Figure 12.2.

To determine the probability of event A (alcohol abuse) or event B (drug abuse), we must subtract the 118 cases that overlap both categories. This leads to the general case of the addition rule. It is called the general case because it applies equally to

* Recall from Chapter 2 that two events would not be mutually exclusive if they *can* occur simultaneously.

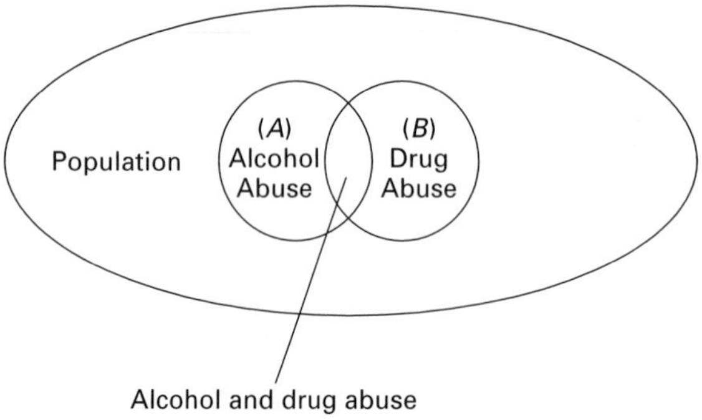

FIGURE 12.2
Venn diagram showing that two categories, alcohol abuse and drug abuse, are not mutually exclusive
To obtain $p(A \text{ or } B)$, we must subtract out the area of overlap

mutually exclusive and nonmutually exclusive categories:

$$p(A \text{ or } B) = p(A) + p(B) - p(A \text{ and } B) \tag{12.3}$$

where $p(A \text{ and } B)$ represents the probability associated with the overlapping events.

In the present example, $p(A \text{ or } B) = 354/5{,}900 + 236/5{,}900 - 118/5{,}900 = 0.08$. Thus, according to this survey, the probability is 0.08 that a given individual seeking help at a mental health clinic is either an alcohol or a drug abuser (or both).

Overlapping categories is also characteristic of many games of chance, for example, roulette or cards. To illustrate, if we want to know the probability of selecting either a heart (to fill a flush) or a jack (to fill a straight), we must take into account the fact that the jack of hearts overlaps both events. If we let event A equal the probability of a heart, $p(A) = 13/52$. The probability of event B (a jack) is $4/52$. However, the probability of both occurring (a jack of hearts) is $1/52$. Therefore, $p(A \text{ or } B) = 13/52 + 4/52 - 1/52 = 16/52 = 0.31$.

Mutually exclusive events

By definition, when events are mutually exclusive, there is no overlapping of the categories. Since both event A and event B cannot occur together, the probability of event A and event B is 0; that is, $p(A \text{ and } B) = 0$.

Therefore, if events A and B are mutually exclusive, the last term disappears (reduces to zero). Thus, the addition rule becomes:

$$p(A \text{ or } B) = p(A) + p(B) \tag{12.4}$$

where the events are mutually exclusive.

Furthermore, the addition rule for mutually exclusive events—equation (12.4)—can be rewritten to include more than two events. For example:

$$P(A \text{ or } B \text{ or } C) = p(A) + p(B) + p(C)$$

Consider a population comprised of 30% Catholics, 25% Methodists, 40% Baptists, and 5% Lutherans. What is the probability of getting a Catholic or a Methodist or a Baptist in a single draw?

$$\frac{30}{100} + \frac{25}{100} + \frac{40}{100} = \frac{95}{100} = 0.95$$

TABLE 12.2
Size of U.S. families of Hispanic origin

Size	Number (in thousands)	p
2	662	0.239
3	636	0.230
4	625	0.226
5	408	0.148
6	218	0.079
7 or more persons	216	0.078

Source: U.S. Bureau of Census, Current Population Reports, Series P-20, no. 339, U.S. Government Printing Office.

To illustrate further, in exercise 13 of Chapter 4, we presented census figures on the size of U.S. families of Hispanic origin. These figures are reproduced in Table 12.2.

What is the probability that a given family of Hispanic origin has either two or three members? Using equation (12.4), we find $p\,(2 \text{ or } 3) = p(2) + p(3) = 0.239 + 0.230 = 0.469$.

What is the probability that such a family will number 6 or more? $p(6 \text{ or } 7 \text{ or more}) = 0.079 + 0.078 = 0.157$.

Equation (12.4) can be extended to include any number of mutually exclusive events. Thus:

$$p(A \text{ or } B \text{ or } \ldots Z) = p(A) + p(B) + \cdots + p(Z)$$

In Chapters 13 and 16, we will be dealing with problems based on *dichotomous,* yes/no, or *two-category* variables, in which the events in question are not only mutually exclusive, but are also **exhaustive,** that is, all possible scores can be placed within established categories. For example, if women constitute 52% of the population in a given city and men constitute 48% of the population, what is the probability of drawing a woman and a man in one draw? Not only is it impossible to obtain both events simultaneously (i.e., they are mutually exclusive), but there is *no possible outcome other than a woman or a man.* In the case of mutually exclusive and exhaustive events, we arrive at the very useful formulation:

$$p(A) + p(B) = 1.00 \qquad (12.5)$$

In treating dichotomous populations, we commonly use the two symbols P and Q to represent, respectively, the probability of the occurrence of an event and the probability of the nonoccurrence of an event. Thus, if we are flipping a single coin, we can let P represent the probability of occurrence of a head and Q the probability of the nonoccurrence of a head (i.e., the occurrence of a tail). These considerations lead to three useful formulations:

$$P + Q = 1.00 \qquad (12.6)$$

$$P = 1.00 - Q \qquad (12.7)$$

$$Q = 1.00 - P \qquad (12.8)$$

when the events are *mutually exclusive and exhaustive.*

12.4.4 The Multiplication Rule

In the preceding section, we were concerned with determining the probability of obtaining one event or another based on a *single* draw (or trial) from a population. In statistical inference, we are often faced with the problem of ascertaining the probability of the **joint (or successive) occurrence** of two or more events when *more* than one draw or trial is involved. For example, what is the probability that we will draw a diamond and a heart on two successive draws from a deck of playing cards?

Much research has been done on the effects of physical attractiveness on various aspects of our behavior. In a field study by Benson, Karabenick, and Lerner* the objective was to ascertain whether favoritism for the physically attractive generalizes to behavioral helping responses. Graduate school applications, complete with mailing address, envelope, and stamps were "inadvertently" left in a number of telephone booths at a busy metropolitan airport. Pictures of the applicant were prominently displayed, some chosen to be physically attractive and others to be unattractive. Thus, physical attractiveness was the independent variable. The dependent response was whether or not the subject engaged in helping behavior, defined as "mailing the application or taking the envelope to one of the airport ticket counters."

Based on the results of the study, what is the probability that five out of five male subjects will engage in helping behavior (mailing the envelope containing the application or delivering it to an airport ticket counter)? Often our question will take on a somewhat modified form. If we assume an attractive female applicant, what is the probability that five out of five male subjects will engage in helping behavior? This last question is concerned with conditional probabilities. In this case, we are asking if the probability of obtaining helping behavior is conditional on the attractiveness of the applicant. In this section, we examine joint, marginal, and conditional probabilities as well as the multiplication rule for independent and nonindependent events.

Joint, marginal, and conditional probabilities

To illustrate joint, marginal, and conditional probabilities, let's study the data presented in Table 12.3.

If we divide each of the cell frequencies and the marginal (row and column) totals by *N*, we obtain a joint probability (see Table 12.4). Note that the table provides direct answers to such questions as "What is the probability that help was provided to an attractive applicant?"

TABLE 12.3
Number helping when applicant is attractive or unattractive female (whites and African Americans combined) and subject is male

	Characteristics of target		
Helping response	**Attractive**	**Unattractive**	**Row totals**
Helped	52	35	87
Did not help	62	71	133
Column totals	114	106	220

* Based on Benson, Karabenick, and Lerner (1976).

TABLE 12.4
Joint probability table of helping behavior when applicant is either attractive or unattractive*

Helping response	Attractive (A)	Unattractive ($\bar{A}$)	Marginal probability
Helped (B)	0.236 (52/220)	0.159 (35/220)	0.395 (87/220)
Did not help ($\bar{B}$)	0.282 (62/220)	0.323 (71/220)	0.605 (133/220)
Marginal probability	0.518 (114/220)	0.482 (106/220)	1.000 (220/220)

* Cell and marginal frequencies divided by total sample size are shown in parentheses.

Joint probabilities. **Joint probability** is the probability of two events occurring simultaneously. Each cell in Table 12.4 shows the joint probability associated with the column and row variables. For example, the joint probability that the applicant was both attractive (event A) and helped (event B) is:

$$p(A \text{ and } B) = \frac{52}{220} = 0.236$$

However, the joint probability of an applicant being unattractive (event $\bar{A}$) and helped (event B) is:

$$p(\bar{A} \text{ and } B) = \frac{35}{220} = 0.159$$

Also, the joint probability of an applicant being attractive (event A) and not helped (event $\bar{B}$) *is*:

$$p(A \text{ and } \bar{B}) = \frac{62}{220} = 0.282$$

Marginal probabilities. **Marginal probability** is a probability that reflects independent or unconditional events. Note that each marginal probability represents a simple probability of an event and is not conditional on other events. For this reason, marginal probabilities are also referred to as unconditional probabilities. Thus, in Table 12.4, the right-hand or row marginals show the simple probability of a person being helped or not helped without regard to her state of attractiveness. Thus, the unconditional probability of being helped is 0.395, whereas the unconditional probability of not being helped is 0.605.

Similarly, the column marginals show the probability that the applicant was attractive (0.518) or unattractive (0.482) whether or not she was helped.

Conditional probabilities. When the information we have about events is limited to the marginal probabilities, our best predictions concerning the probability of a given event is similarly restricted to these marginal probabilities. Thus, if we know only that a male entered the phone booth that contained a "lost" job application, our best estimate of the probability that he will help is 0.395 and that he will not help is

0.605. But what if we are given some additional information, such as "The applicant was attractive." Notice that we are now limited to attractive applicants rather than to all applicants, since we now have more information than we had before. Will this information permit us to "fine-tune" our assessment of the probability that the male entering the phone booth will engage in helping behavior? The answer is yes if helping behavior is conditional on the attractiveness of the applicant.

To illustrate, Table 12.4 provides three probabilities for each helping response—the marginal probability that help will be provided, the joint probability that the applicant is attractive and helped, and the joint probability that the applicant is attractive and not helped. Now suppose we know in advance that the applicant is attractive. Will this additional information provide a basis for a better assessment of the probability that she will be helped? Let's see.

Conditional probability is the probability of an event that is dependent on the presence of another event. To find the conditional probability that the applicant will receive help, we divide the joint probability that she is attractive and helped $P(A \text{ and } B)$ by the marginal probability that she is attractive $p(A)$. Thus, in the present example:

$$p(B \mid A) = \frac{p(A \text{ and } B)}{p(A)} = \frac{0.236}{0.518}$$
$$= 0.456$$

where $p(B \mid A)$ is the conditional probability of event B given that event A has occurred. Similarly:

$$p(A \mid B) = \frac{p(A \text{ and } B)}{p(B)}$$

where $p(A|B)$ is the conditional probability of event A given that event B has occurred.

Note that knowing only the marginal probability, we would have assessed the applicant's chance of being helped as 0.395. Knowing that she is attractive permitted us to raise our assessment of the probability to 0.456.

Let's look at one additional example. Knowing that an applicant is unattractive, what is our assessment of the probability of her not being helped, that is, of $p(\bar{B} \mid \bar{A})p$?

$$p(\bar{B} \mid \bar{A}) = \frac{p(\bar{A} \text{ and } \bar{B})}{p(\bar{A})} = \frac{0.323}{0.482}$$
$$= 0.670$$

Using only the marginal probabilities, we would have estimated the probability of any applicant not being helped as 0.605. Taking into account our knowledge of her unattractiveness, we were able to increase the probability assessment to 0.670.

Table 12.5 summarizes the conditional probabilities derived from Table 12.4. Note that the conditional probabilities shown in the two columns at the right relate to the probability of the applicant being attractive (A) and unattractive ($\bar{A}$) when the status of helping is known. Thus, we see that the probability of not being attractive when help has not been received $p(\bar{A} \mid \bar{B})$ is 0.534.

TABLE 12.5
Joint and conditional probability table of helping behavior when the applicant was either attractive or unattractive

Helping response	Attractive (A)	Unattractive $(\bar{A})$	Marginal probability	Conditional probability
Helped (B)	0.236	0.159	0.395	$p(A\|B)$ $p(\bar{A}\|B)$ 0.597 0.403
Did not help $(\bar{B})$	0.282	0.323	0.605	$p(A\|\bar{B})$ $p(\bar{A}\|\bar{B})$ 0.466 0.534
Marginal probability	0.518 $p(B\|A)$ 0.456 $p(\bar{B}\|A)$ 0.544	0.482 $p(B\|\bar{A})$ 0.330 $p(\bar{B}\|\bar{A})$ 0.670	1.000	

Note: The conditional probabilities are calculated by dividing the joint probabilities within each cell by its marginal probability.

Similarly, the two rows at the bottom of the table show the probabilities of the applicant receiving help (B) or not receiving help $(\bar{B})$ when the status of her attractiveness is known. Thus, the probability that an attractive person receives help $p(B \mid A)$ is 0.456.

The multiplication rule for independent events

Consider the following conceptual experiment. You toss a single coin into the air and a head appears. Assuming an ideal coin, the probability of a head is $1/2$ and the probability of a tail is $1/2$. Now toss the coin a second time. Does the outcome of the first toss in any way affect the outcome of the second toss? It it does not, the two outcomes are said to be independent. Since we have assumed an ideal coin (i.e., it is balanced, will not stand on end, is not motivated to change its behavior, and so on), we may assume that the two outcomes are independent, so that the probability of obtaining a head remains $1/2$ as does the probability of obtaining a tail. When outcomes or events are independent, the multiplication rule states:

> The probability of the simultaneous or successive occurrence of two events is the product of the separate probabilities of each event.

In symbolic form:

$$p(A \text{ and } B) = p(A)p(B) \tag{12.9}$$

Suppose we toss a single coin on three successive occasions. What is the probability of obtaining the events "all heads"? To obtain this event, all three outcomes must be a head. Thus:

$$\begin{aligned} p(H, H, \text{and } H) &= p(H)p(H)p(H) \\ &= \left(\frac{1}{2}\right)\left(\frac{1}{2}\right)\left(\frac{1}{2}\right) \\ &= \frac{1}{8} \quad \text{or} \quad 0.125 \end{aligned}$$

Sampling with replacement is an example of independent events. Suppose that we draw a single card from a deck of playing cards and obtain a king of hearts. The probability of this outcome is $1/52 = 0.019$. If we return the card to the deck, shuffle the cards well, and make a second selection, what is the probability of selecting the king of hearts again? It remains $1/52$. When sampling with replacement, what is the probability of selecting the king of hearts twice in succession? Using the multiplication rule for independent events, we obtain $p(KH \text{ and } KH) = (1/52)(1/52) = 1/2704$ or 0.00037.

The multiplication rule for nonindependent (dependent) events

Nonindependence or **dependence** is the condition that exists when the occurrence of a given event affects the probability of the occurrence of another event. The multiplication rule for nonindependent events can be grasped most readily by contrasting sampling with replacement with sampling without replacement. Imagine we were to make two successive draws from a deck of playing cards. What is the probability that we obtain two kings?

If we use sampling with replacement, the two events are independent. Since the probability of selecting a king is $4/52$, the probability of drawing two consecutive kings $p(K \text{ and } K)$ is $(4/52)(4/52) = 0.0059$.

However, if we use sampling without replacement, the events are not independent. If we select a king of the first draw, there will be only three kings left in a deck containing 51 cards. In other words, the results of the first draw influence the possible consequences of the second draw. In fact, the conditional probability of selecting a king on the second draw assuming that a king has been selected on the first draw $p(K \mid K)$ is $3/51 = 0.059$.

For nonindependent or dependent events, the multiplication rule becomes:

> Given two events A and B, the probability of obtaining both A and B jointly is the product of the probability of obtaining one of these events times the conditional probability of obtaining one event, given that the other event has occurred.

Stated symbolically:

$$p(A \text{ and } B) = p(A)p(B \mid A) = p(B)p(A \mid B) \qquad (12.10)$$

In the present example, the probability of selecting a king on the first draw $p(K)$ is equal to $4/52$. The probability of selecting a king on the second draw, given a king drawn on the first, is $3/51$. Thus, when using sampling without replacement, the probability of selecting two consecutive kings is:

$$\begin{aligned} p(K \text{ and } K) &= p(K)p(K \mid K) \\ &= \left(\frac{4}{52}\right)\left(\frac{3}{51}\right) \\ &= 0.0045 \end{aligned}$$

Figure 12.3 is a **tree diagram** of this statistical experiment that illustrates the calculation of the probability of all possible events. A tree diagram is a method for illustrating the sequence of several events. The outcome of each event has two or more alternatives.

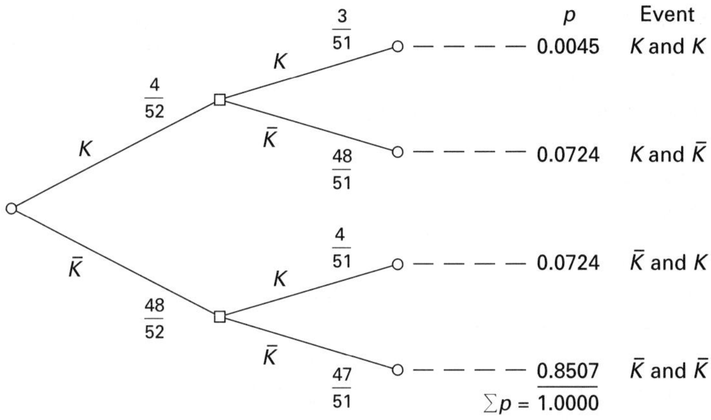

FIGURE 12.3
Tree diagram of the statistical experiment involving two draws, without replacement, from a deck of playing cards; the event of interest is the probability of selecting two consecutive kings

Note that we can calculate the probability of each event by successively multiplying the probability associated with each branch by the probability associated with connecting branches. Thus, the probability of selecting two kings is found by multiplying the probabilities of the two K branches (4/52) (3/51). Similarly, the two $\bar{K}$ branches provide the basis for calculating the selection of two nonkings on successive draws.

Figure 12.4 shows the tree diagram for calculating the conditional probabilities of the study concerned with physical attractiveness of the target and the helping behavior by the subjects: Case Example 12.1 will further your understanding of conditional probability.

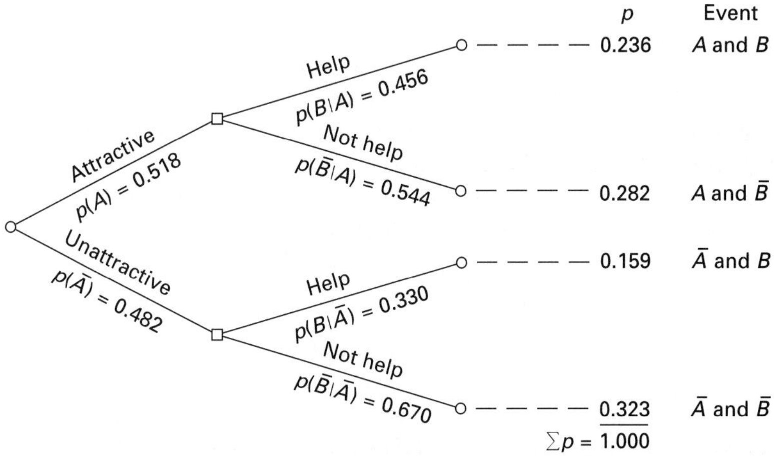

FIGURE 12.4
Tree diagram used to calculate the probability of various conditional events relating to physical attractiveness of the target and helping behavior by the subjects

A second example of the multiplication rule for nonindependent (dependent) events involves a contingency table. Given the following population in which the relationship between attitude toward busing for integration purposes and race is summarized, what is the probability of drawing a nonwhite person who favors busing?

	Race		
Attitude toward busing	**Nonwhite**	**White**	**Total**
Favor	200	300	500
Oppose	50	450	500
Total	250	750	1000

Event A is the probability of drawing a nonwhite person, and event B is the probability of drawing a person who favors busing. The probability of event A occurring is 0.25 because 250 of the 1,000 persons are nonwhite, and the probability of event B occurring is 0.5 because 500 of the 1,000 persons in the population favor busing. We also need to know the probability of B given A or A given B. The probability of A given B is 0.4 because 500 persons favor busing and 200 of these persons are nonwhite. The probability of B given A is 0.8 because 250 persons are nonwhite and, of these persons, 200 favor busing. Therefore, applying equation (12.10), we can solve the problem in one of two ways:

$$p(A \text{ and } B) = p(A)p(B \mid A) = (0.25)(0.8) = 0.2$$

But we also know that:

$$p(A \text{ and } B) = p(B)p(A \mid B)$$

Therefore:

$$p(A \text{ and } B) = (0.5)(0.4) = 0.2$$

Our answers agree and can be confirmed by locating the "favor-nonwhite" cell in the contingency table. Two hundred of the 1,000 persons in the population are nonwhite and favor busing; therefore, they constitute 20% or 0.2 of the population and we have confirmed our answer.

CASE EXAMPLE 12.1

THE CONDITIONAL PROBABILITY OF DOMESTIC VIOLENCE

Domestic violence is an all too common event in American society. In many marriages, it is common for either the husband, the wife, or both to use physical aggression in an argument. Daniel O'Leary and his associates (O'Leary et al., 1989) examined the use of physical aggression between spouses in a longitudinal study. Specifically, they wanted to determine if there are variables that predict the use of physical aggres-

TABLE 12.6
Frequency of reports of physical aggression against a partner

	Premarriage	18 Months	30 Months
Men = 272	Y = 84	Y = 43	Y = 25
			N = 18
		N = 41	Y = 12
			N = 29
	N = 188	Y = 28	Y = 15
			N = 13
		N = 160	Y = 16
			N = 144
Women = 272	Y = 120	Y = 71	Y = 51
			N = 20
		N = 49	Y = 8
			N = 41
	N = 152	Y = 24	Y = 14
			N = 10
		N = 128	Y = 14
			N = 114

sion in a marriage. The primary importance of these data is that they can help social scientists understand the use and patterns of physical aggression in marriages.

O'Leary and his colleagues asked 272 couples to complete a questionnaire that measured if physical aggression had been used in an argument during the previous year. Each couple completed the questionnaire 1 month before they were married, 18 months after their marriage, and 30 months after their marriage. These data are reported in Table 12.6. Let's examine the raw data. As you can see, 84 of the men and 120 of the women indicated that they used some form of physical aggression (e.g., throwing objects, pushing, slapping, hitting with a fist, or beating up) before the marriage. Of the men who indicated they used physical aggression before the marriage, 43 indicated that they had acted aggressively toward their wives after 18 months of marriage. Of these men, 25 continued to act aggressively after 30 months of marriage. As you can see, these data are something like the tree diagram for the coin toss. Each time the couple completed the questionnaire is similar to the tossing of a coin. The presence or absence of aggression is analogous to heads and tails. The real difference, and the one that we are most interested in, is that previous behavior may be used to predict future behavior—the use of aggression may not be an independent event.

Now that we have the frequencies, we can begin to use our knowledge of probability statistics to answer some very specific questions. Before we ask these questions, however, it may be useful to conduct a quick review of the principles discussed in this chapter to ensure that you understand the concepts as presented.

First, what type of variables are we using? Because we are concerned with the number of people who report using some form of physical aggression against their spouse, the data are best represented as a discrete variable.

The possible outcomes consist of the individual's responses to the three surveys. Are the responses *mutually exclusive?* Yes, the individuals' responses on the survey show whether they did or did not use violence against their spouse during the previous year. Are the responses *independent?* No, whether individuals report using physical aggression is dependent in part on their previous behavior as well as their willingness to disclose this information to a researcher. What will the data be used for? O'Leary and his associates are interested in the patterns of aggression in a marriage. Therefore, we can use the results of the study to make predictions about other couples in the population.

The first step is to convert the raw scores to joint probabilities by dividing each number in Table 12.6 by 272. Table 12.7 lists the joint probabilities for the presence or absence of reported aggression during each of the time periods. Using the basic rules of probability, we can answer some interesting questions.

To start, what percentage of men report that they use some form of aggression during the premarriage period and the first 30 months of marriage? This question asks whether there have been one or more incidents of aggression during the relationship. If we trace the numbers in Table 12.7, we find that 52.94% of the men reported never acting aggressively toward their wives. This means that there is a 47.06% (100 − 52.94) probability that a man will use aggression against his wife. Likewise, 41.91% of the women reported never acting aggressively toward their husbands. Therefore, we can estimate that there is a 58.09% (100 − 41.91) probability that a woman will use some form of aggression against her husband at least once in the relationship. What is the probability of a husband or a wife not acting aggressively during the premarriage period but acting aggressively during the marriage? In contrast, what is the probability that a husband or wife will act aggressively during the premarriage period and not act aggressively during the marriage? These are interesting questions that can be answered using the data provided and the addition rule.

We are now at the point where we can examine the conditional probabilities for these data. Remember, the importance of conditional probabilities is that they allow us to examine the probabilities of specific sequences. For this example, we are partic-

TABLE 12.7
Joint probabilities of reports of physical aggression against a partner

	Premarriage	18 Months	30 Months
Men	*Y* = .3088	*Y* = .1581	*Y* = .0919
			N = .0662
		N = .1507	*Y* = .0441
			N = .1066
	N = .6912	*Y* = .1029	*Y* = .0551
			N = .0478
		N = .5882	*Y* = .0588
			N = .5294
Women	*Y* = .4412	*Y* = .2610	*Y* = .1875
			N = .0735
		N = .1801	*Y* = .0294
			N = .1507
	N = .5588	*Y* = .0882	*Y* = .0515
			N = .0368
		N = .4706	*Y* = .0515
			N = .4191

ularly interested in looking at the use of aggression as the marriage progresses. We can ask, for example, about the probability that a spouse will act aggressively if he or she has used aggression on previous occasions. Using these data, we can trace the pattern of aggression in both men and women. The conditional probabilities are presented in Table 12.8.

The conditional probabilities were calculated using the same logic presented in the preceding section. We can use a specific example to trace the logic of the

TABLE 12.8
Conditional probabilities (boldface) of reports of physical aggression against a partner

	Premarriage	18 Months	30 Months
Men	*Y* = **.3088**	*Y* = .1581/.3088 = **.5120**	*Y* = .0919/.1581 = **.5813**
			N = .0662/.1581 = **.4187**
		N = .1507/.3088 = **.4880**	*Y* = .0441/.1507 = **.2926**
			N = .1066/.1507 = **.7074**
	N = **.6921**	*Y* = .1029/.6912 = **.1489**	*Y* = .0551/.1029 = **.5355**
			N = .0478/.1029 = **.4645**
		N = .5882/.6912 = **.8510**	*Y* = .0588/.5882 = **.1000**
			N = .5249/.5882 = **.9000**
Women	*Y* = **.4412**	*Y* = .2610/.4412 = **.5916**	*Y* = .1875/.2610 = **.7184**
			N = .0735/.2610 = **.2816**
		N = .1801/.4412 = **.4082**	*Y* = .0294/.1801 = **.1632**
			N = .1507/.1801 = **.3368**
	N = **.5588**	*Y* = .0882/.5588 = **.1578**	*Y* = .0515/.0882 = **.5839**
			N = .0368/.0882 = **.4172**
		N = .4706/.5588 = **.8422**	*Y* = .0515/.4706 = **.1094**
			N = .4191/.4706 = **.8906**

calculations. Consider the men who did or did not report using aggression prior to the marriage. Of all the men, 30.88% acted aggressively before marriage. Of the men who acted aggressively before marriage, 51.20% reported that they acted aggressively again within the next 18-month period. Finally, if a man reported that he had acted aggressively during the two preceding periods, there was a 58.13% chance that he would act aggressively again toward his wife. Using conditional probabilities, we see that although the minority of men in this study reported that they act aggressively toward their wives, previous bouts of aggression are an indicator that aggression will be used again. The same is true for women. Most women do not act aggressively toward their husbands. Those who do, however, are more likely to repeatedly use aggression as the marriage progresses. For both men and women, if aggression is used early in the marriage, there is an increased risk that it will be used throughout the marriage.

12.5 PROBABILITY AND CONTINUOUS VARIABLES

Up to this point, we have considered probability in terms of the expected relative frequency of an event. As you will recall, probability was defined in terms of frequency and expressed as the following proportion [equation (12.1)]:

$$p(A) = \frac{\text{number of outcomes in which event } A \text{ occurs}}{\text{total number of outcomes } (A \text{ occurs} + A \text{ does not occur})}$$

However, this definition presents a problem when we are dealing with continuous variables such as age or income. As we pointed out in Section 3.7, it is generally advisable to represent frequency in terms of areas under a curve when we are dealing with continuous variables. Thus, for continuous variables, we may express probability as the following proportion:

$$p = \frac{\text{area under portions of a curve}}{\text{total area under the curve}} \qquad (12.11)$$

Because the total area in a probability distribution is equal to 1.00, we define p as the proportion of total area under portions of a curve.

Chapters 13 through 15 use the standard normal curve as the probability model. Let's examine the probability-area relationship in terms of this model.

12.6 PROBABILITY AND THE NORMAL-CURVE MODEL

In Section 7.4, we stated that the standard normal distribution has a mean of 0, a standard deviation of 1, and a total area that is equal to 1.00. We saw that when scores on a normally distributed variable are transformed into z scores, we are, in effect, expressing these scores in units of the standard normal curve. This permits us to express the difference between any two scores as proportions of total area under the curve. Thus, we may establish probability values in terms of these proportions, as in equation (12.11). Let us look at several examples that illustrate the application of probability concepts to the normal-curve model.

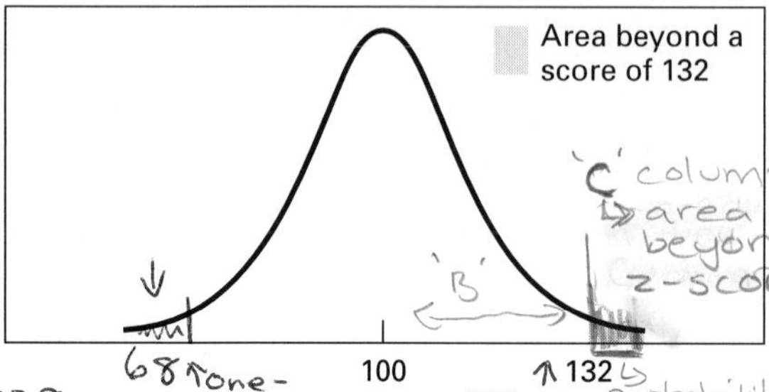

FIGURE 12.5
Proportion of area above a score of 132 in a normal distribution with $\mu = 100$ and $\sigma = 16$

12.6.1 Illustrative Problems*

For all problems, assume $\mu = 100$ and $\sigma = 16$.

PROBLEM 1. What is the probability of selecting at *random* from the general population a person with a test score of at least 132?

The answer to this question is given by the proportion of area under the curve above a score of 132 (see Figure 12.5).

First, we must find the z score corresponding to $X = 132$.

$$z = \frac{132 - 100}{16} = 2.00$$

In column C of Table A in Appendix C, we find that 0.0228 of the area lies at or beyond a z of 2.00. Therefore, the probability of selecting, at random, a person with a score of at least 132 is 0.0228.

PROBLEM 2. What is the probability of selecting, at random, an individual with a score of at least 92?

We are dealing with two mutually exclusive and exhaustive areas under the curve. The area under the curve above a score of 92 is P; the area below a score of 92 is Q. In solving our problem, we may therefore apply equation (12.7):

$$P = 1.00 - Q$$

By expressing a score of 92 in terms of its corresponding z, we may obtain the proportion of area below $X = 92$ (i.e., Q) directly from column C (Table A in Appendix C).

The z score corresponding to $X = 92$ is:

$$z = \frac{92 - 100}{16} = -0.50$$

The proportion of area below a z of -0.50 is 0.3085. Therefore, the probability of selecting, at random, an individual with a score of at least 92 becomes:

$$P = 1.00 - 0.3085 = 0.6915$$

* See Section 7.6.

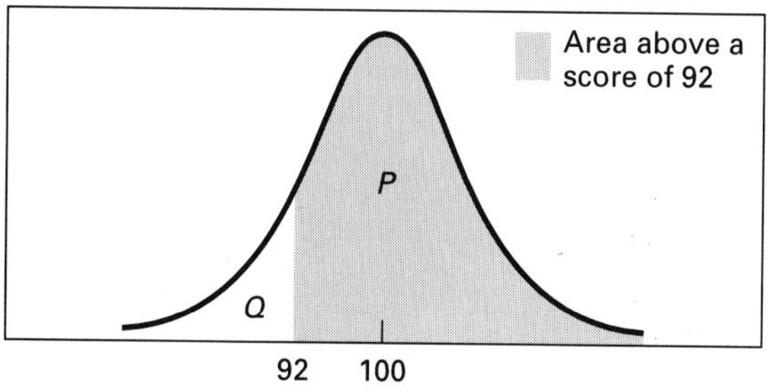

FIGURE 12.6
Proportion of area above (*P*) and below (*Q*) a score of 92 in a normal distribution with $\mu = 100$ and $\sigma = 16$

Figure 12.6 illustrates this relationship.

PROBLEM 3. Let's look at an example involving the multiplication law. Given that sampling with replacement is used, what is the probability of drawing, at random, three individuals with scores equaling or exceeding 124?

For this problem, we again assume that $\mu = 100$ and $\sigma = 16$.

The z score corresponding to $X = 124$ is:

$$z = \frac{124 - 100}{16} = 1.5$$

In column C (Table A of Appendix C), we find that 0.0668 of the area lies at or beyond $z = 1.50$. Therefore:

$$\begin{aligned} p(A, B, C) = p(A \text{ and } B \text{ and } C) &= p(A) \times p(B) \times p(C) \\ &= (0.0668)(0.0668)(0.0668) \\ &= 0.0003 \end{aligned}$$

12.7 ONE- AND TWO-TAILED *p* VALUES

In problem 1 we posed the question, "What is the probability of selecting a person with a score as high as 132?" We answered the question by examining only one tail of the distribution, namely, scores as high as or higher than 132. For this reason we refer to the probability value that we obtained as being a **one-tailed probability (*p*) value.**

In statistics and social science research, the following question is frequently asked: "What is the probability of obtaining a score (or statistic) this *deviant* from the mean? . . . or a score (or statistic) this *rare* . . . or a result this *unusual?*" Clearly, when the frequency distribution of scores is symmetrical, a score of 68 or lower is every bit as deviant from a mean of 100 as a score of 132. That is, both are two standard deviation units away from the mean (assuming $\sigma = 16$). We express the probability value that takes into account both tails of the distribution as a **two-tailed (*p*) value.** In symmetrical distributions two tailed p values may be obtained merely by doubling the one-tailed probability value. Thus, in the preceding problem the probability of selecting a person with a score as *rare* or *unusual* as 132 is $2 \times 0.0228 = 0.0456$.

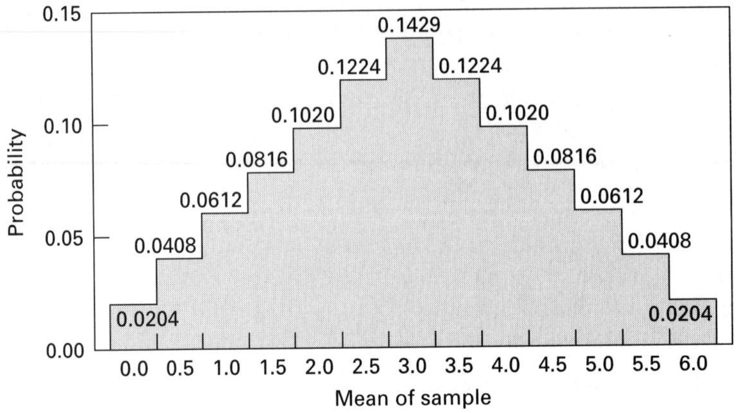

FIGURE 12.7
Probability histogram of means based on selecting, with replacement, samples of $N = 2$ from a population of seven numbers

TABLE 12.9
Frequency and probability distribution of means of samples of size $N = 2$ drawn with replacement from a population of seven scores (0, 1, 2, 3, 4, 5, 6)

$\overline{X}$	f	$p(\overline{X})$
6.0	1	0.0204
5.5	2	0.0408
5.0	3	0.0612
4.5	4	0.0816
4.0	5	0.1020
3.5	6	0.1224
3.0	7	0.1429
2.5	6	0.1224
2.0	5	0.1020
1.5	4	0.0816
1.0	3	0.0612
0.5	2	0.0408
0.0	1	0.0204
	$N_{\bar{x}} = 49$*	$\Sigma p = 0.9997$†

* We use $N_{\bar{x}}$ to refer to the total number of means obtained in our sampling experiment and to distinguish it from N, which is the number of scores on which each mean sampling is based. In this sampling experiment, $N_{\bar{x}} = 49$.

† $\Sigma p(\overline{X})$ should equal 1.000. The discrepancy of 0.0003 represents a rounding error.

We may illustrate the distinction between one- and two-tailed p values by referring to the sampling experiment we have used throughout the text. Figure 12.7 shows a probability histogram based on Table 12.9. Recall that this distribution was obtained by selecting, with replacement, all possible samples of $N = 2$ from a population of seven scores.

If we ask, "What is the probability of obtaining a mean equal to zero?" we need refer only to the left tail of the probability bar graph to find the answer of 0.0204. However, if we ask, "What is the probability of obtaining an outcome as deviant as a sample mean equal to zero?" we would have to look at both the left and the right tails. Since a mean of 6 is equally deviant from the mean of the distribution, we use the addition rule to obtain the two-tailed value:

$$p(\overline{X} = 0 \text{ or } \overline{X} = 6)$$
$$= p(\overline{X} = 0) \text{ and } p(\overline{X} = 6)$$
$$= 0.0204 + 0.0204 = 0.0408$$

Let's look at two additional examples.

EXAMPLE 1. What is the probability of obtaining a mean as low as 0.5 (i.e., a mean of 0.5 or lower)?

We find the probability of obtaining a mean of 0.5 and a mean of 0.0 (the only mean lower than 0.5), and add these probabilities together to obtain the one-tailed p value:

$$p(\overline{X} \leq 0.5) = p(\overline{X} = 0.5) + p(\overline{X} = 0.0)$$
$$= 0.0408 + 0.0204 = 0.0612$$

EXAMPLE 2. What is the probability of obtaining a mean as deviant from the distribution mean as a sample mean of 0.5?

The answer to this question calls for a two-tailed p value obtained by applying the addition rule to:

$$p(\overline{X} = 0.5) + p(\overline{X} = 0.0) + p(\overline{X} = 5.5) + p(\overline{X} = 6.0)$$

However, because the distribution is symmetrical and means of 5.5 and 6.0 are equally as deviant as 0.5 and 0.0, respectively, we need only double the p value obtained in example 1:

$$p(0.5 \geq \overline{X} \geq 5.5) = 2(0.0612)$$
$$= 0.1224$$

Incidentally, the left-hand member of this expression is read: *The probability of a mean equal to or less than 0.5 or equal to or greater than 5.5.*

The distinction between one- and two-tailed probability values takes on added significance as we progress into inferential statistics.

SUMMARY

In this chapter, we focused our discussion on five points:

1. *The importance of random sampling in inferential statistics.* Random sampling refers to selecting samples in such a way that each sample of a given size has

precisely the same probability of being selected. Independent random sampling refers to the fact that the selection of one event has no effect upon the probability of selecting another event. Although the individual events are unpredictable, collections of random events take on characteristic and predictable forms. The binomial distribution and the normal curve were cited in this regard.

2. *The theory of probability, which is concerned with the outcomes of experiments.* We learned to distinguish between probabilities established by assuming *idealized* relative frequencies and those established empirically by determining relative frequencies. Probability was defined as:

$$p = \frac{\text{number of outcomes favoring event}}{\text{total number of outcomes}}$$

3. *The formal properties of probability.*
   a. Probabilities vary between 0 and 1.00.
   b. The addition rule:

If A and B are two events, the probability of obtaining either of them is equal to the probability of A plus the probability of B minus the probability of their joint occurrence. Thus:

$$p(A \text{ or } B) = p(A) + p(B) - p(A \text{ and } B)$$

If events A and B are mutually exclusive, the addition rule becomes:

$$p(A \text{ or } B) = p(A) + p(B)$$

Allowing P to represent the probability of occurrence and Q to represent the probability of nonoccurrence, we find that three additional useful formulations for mutually exclusive and exhaustive events are:

$$P + Q = 1.00 \qquad P = 1.00 - Q \qquad Q = 1.00 - P$$

   c. The multiplication rule.

When events are independent. When sampling with replacement, the selection on one trial is independent of the selection on another trial. Given two events, A and B, the probability of obtaining both A and B in successive trials is the product of the probability of obtaining one of these events times the probability of obtaining the second of these events:

$$p(A \text{ and } B) = p(A)p(B)$$

When events are nonindependent. When sampling without replacement, the selection of one event affects the probability of selecting each remaining event. Thus, given two events, A and B, the probability of obtaining both A and B jointly or successively is the product of the probability of obtaining one of the events times the conditional probability of obtaining one event, given that the other event has occurred. Symbolically:

$$p(A \text{ and } B) = p(A)p(B \mid A) = p(B)p(A \mid B)$$

4. *The application of probability theory to continuously distributed variables.* Probability is expressed in terms of the proportion of area under a curve. Hence:

$$p = \frac{\text{area under portions of a curve}}{\text{total area under a curve}}$$

We saw how to employ z-scores and the standard normal curve to establish various probabilities for normally distributed variables.

5. *How to distinguish between one- and two-tailed probability values.*

TERMS TO REMEMBER

addition rule If A and B are mutually exclusive events, the probability of obtaining *either of them* is equal to the probability of A plus the probability of B. Symbolically:

$$p(A \text{ or } B) = p(A) + p(B)$$

bias In sampling, when selections favor certain events or certain collections of events.

conditional probability The probability of an event that is dependent on the presence of another event. Represented symbolically as $p(A \mid B)$, the probability of A given that B has occurred.

dependence See *nonindependence.*

exhaustive Two or more events are said to be exhaustive if they exhaust all posible outcomes. Symbolically:

$$p(A \text{ or } B \text{ or } \cdots) = 1.00$$

independence The condition that exists when the occurrence of a given event will not affect the probability of the occurrence of another event. Symbolically:

$$p(A \mid B) = p(A) \qquad \text{and} \qquad p(B \mid A) = p(B)$$

joint (or successive) occurrence The occurrence of two events simultaneously. Such events cannot be mutually exclusive.

joint probability The probability of two events occurring simultaneously. Symbolically:

$$p(A \text{ and } B)$$

marginal probability A probability that reflects independent or unconditional events.

multiplication rule Given two events, A and B, the probability of obtaining both A and B jointly is the product of the probability of obtaining one of these events times the conditional probability of obtaining one event, given that the other event has occurred. Symbolically:

$$p(A \text{ and } B) = p(A)p(B \mid A) = p(B)p(A \mid B)$$

nonindependence The condition that exists when the occurrence of a given event affects the probability of the occurrence of another event.

one-tailed probability (p) values Probability values obtained by examining only one tail of the distribution.

probability A theory concerned with possible outcomes of studies. Symbolically:

$$p(A) = \frac{\text{number of outcomes in which } A \text{ occurs}}{\text{total number of outcomes}}$$

sampling distribution A theoretical probability distribution of a statistic that would result from drawing all possible samples of a given size from some population.

tree diagram A method for illustrating the sequence of several events. The outcome of each event has two or more alternatives.

two-tailed probability (*p*) values Probability values that take into account both tails of the distribution.

unconditional probability See *marginal probability*.

EXERCISES

1. Mr. and Mrs. Smyth want a large family. So far they have five children, all boys. Mrs. Smyth is pregnant with another child. Mr. Smyth is sure that the next child will be a girl and says that the odds are in favor of a girl being born. Is Mr. Smyth correct to assume that the next child is more likely to be a girl? Defend your answer.

2. Dr. Jones gives unannounced quizzes. She tells the class that she uses a random number table to determine whether or not to give a quiz. For the past weeks Dr. Jones has given the quiz on Monday. It is late Sunday afternoon, and Mark is about ready to study. His roommate says that there is a great movie on television. Mark decides that there is very little chance that there will be a quiz tomorrow and decides to watch the movie. Is Mark's conclusion about the quiz correct? Defend your answer.

3. Denise is taking a general biology course. In class, her professor starts a lecture on environmental toxins. The professor states, "Of course, you all know that smoking is a serious health risk and leads to lung cancer." Mary objects to the professor's conclusion. She notes that her 85-year-old grandfather has been smoking two packs of cigarettes a day for the past 65 years and is still in relatively good health. Has Mary provided a good argument against her professor's claim?

4. The registrar of a large state university wants to conduct a survey of transcripts. For the study the registrar needs a representative sample of the student population. The university is divided into four colleges. According to current records, the enrollments in each of the colleges are:

College of Arts and Sciences	12,546
College of Business	8,534
College of Education	2,543
College of Engineering	10,343

Use this information to answer the following questions.

(*a*) What is the probability of selecting, at random, a student from each of the four colleges?

(*b*) Assume that the registrar decides to use simple random sampling. How would the students be selected? What are some advantages and disadvantages of this procedure?

5. List all the possible outcomes of a coin that is tossed three times. Calculate the probability of:

(*a*) Three heads (*b*) Three tails
(*c*) Two heads and one tail (*d*) At least two heads

6. A card is drawn at random from a deck of 52 playing cards. What is the probability that:
(*a*) It will be the ace of spades?
(*b*) It will be an ace?
(*c*) It will be an ace or a face card?
(*d*) It will be a spade or a face card?

7. In a single throw of two dice, what is the probability that:
(*a*) A seven will appear?
(*b*) A doublet (two of the same number) will appear?
(*c*) A doublet or an eight will appear?
(*d*) An even number will appear?

8. A bag contains six blue marbles, four red marbles, and two green marbles. If you select a single marble at random from the bag, what is the probability that it will be:
(*a*) Red? (*b*) Blue? (*c*) Green? (*d*) White?

9. Selecting *without* replacement from the bag described in exercise 8, what is the probability that:
(*a*) Three out of three will be blue?
(*b*) Two out of two will be green?
(*c*) None out of four will be red?

10. Selecting *with* replacement from the bag described in exercise 8, what is the probability that:
(*a*) Three out of three will be blue?
(*b*) Two out of two will be green?
(*c*) None out of four will be red?

11. Which of the following selection techniques will result in a true random sample? Explain your answers. If you believe that the sampling technique is not random, what would you do as an alternative?
(*a*) *Population:* Students attending a college. *Sampling technique:* Select every fifth person enrolled in Sociology 101.
(*b*) *Population:* Viewers of a talk show. *Sampling technique:* Select at random half of the studio audience for one evening chosen at random.
(*c*) *Population:* All children in a suburban high school. *Sampling technique:* Have each homeroom teacher select one student from the class.
(*d*) *Population:* Voters in a congressional district. *Sampling technique:* Calling a randomly selected group of voters on a Saturday.

12. The proportion of people who are Baptist in a particular city is 0.20. What is the probability that:
(*a*) A given individual, selected at random, will be a Baptist?
(*b*) Two out of two individuals will be Baptists?

(*c*) A given individual will not be a Baptist?
(*d*) Two out of two individuals will not be Baptists?

13. A researcher has developed a new test for colon cancer. The advantage of the procedure is that it is inexpensive and painless. The regular test, which is very accurate, requires expensive laboratory equipment and creates discomfort for the patient. To test the accuracy of the new test, the researcher selected 385 study participants who have a high risk of having colon cancer and administers the two tests: Here are the results.

Sample	New test	Regular test
385	154 positive	110 positive
		44 negative
	231 negative	30 positive
		201 negative

(*a*) Using these data, calculate the conditional probability that the new colon cancer test will correctly identify the presence of cancer.
(*b*) What is the conditional probability that the test will fail to detect a case of cancer?
(*c*) What is the probability that the new test will provide a correct result?

14. A well-known test of intelligence is constructed so as to have normally distributed scores with a mean of 100 and a standard deviation of 16.
(*a*) What is the probability that someone picked at random will have an IQ of 122 or higher?
(*b*) There are IQs so high that the probability is .05 that they will occur in a random sample of people. Such IQs are beyond what value?
(*c*) What is the probability that someone picked at random will have an IQ between 90 and 110?
(*d*) What is the probability of selecting two people at random:
i. With both having IQs of 122 or greater?
ii. With both having IQs between 90 and 110?
iii. With one having an IQs of 122 or greater and the other having an IQ between 90 and 110?
(*e*) An elementary school creates a special curriculum for talented and gifted students. Part of the entry requirement for the curriculum is to be in the 90th percentile for IQ. What IQ score will a child require to be considered for this curriculum?

15. A well-known college entrance test is constructed so as to have a normally distributed score with a mean of 500 and a standard deviation of 100.
(*a*) What proportion of all people who take the test will score 150 or higher?
(*b*) A large state university will admit any applicant who has a score of 550 or greater. What proportion of applications will the college reject because their scores are too low? (Assume that all people who take the test also apply to the university.)
(*c*) Another state university will admit any applicant who has a score at or above the 45th percentile. What score is required to be admitted to this university?

(*d*) Nancy scores 664 on the test. Convert her score to a percentile.
(*e*) Pat scores 305 on the test. Convert his score to a percentile.
(*f*) What scores on this test are associated with the 25th and 75th percentiles?

16. Given the following population, what is the probability that an upper-class person favors a tax cut? The probability that a lower-class person opposes a tax cut?

	Social class		
Attitude toward a tax cut	**Lower**	**Upper**	**Total**
Favor	75	25	100
Oppose	25	50	75
Total	100	75	$N = 175$

17. A political scientist is studying all 67 grassroots political organizations in a major U.S. city. The following table shows the political organizations by party allegiance and socioeconomic composition of their members.

	Socioeconomic status		
Party	**Low**	**Moderate**	**High**
Republican	5	11	19
Democrat	10	12	6
Socialist	2	1	1

If one of the political organizations were chosen at random from this city, what is the probability that its members will have the following characteristics:
(*a*) High income?
(*b*) Socialist?
(*c*) Socialist and high income?
(*d*) Not Republican?
(*e*) Not Democrat and low income?
(*f*) Not Republican and not Socialist?
(*g*) Not Republican and not moderate income?

18. Given the information in exercise 17, what is the conditional probability that if an organization is selected it will have the membership characteristics of:
(*a*) Moderate income, given that it is Republican?
(*b*) Democrat, given that it is low income?
(*c*) Not Socialist, given high income?

19. Refer back to Table 12.4. Construct a tree diagram of the conditional probabilities when the helping response of the subject is known.

20. In another facet of the study relating physical attractiveness to helping behavior, the target was either an attractive or unattractive male and the subjects were females. The results are shown in the following table.

Helping response	**Characteristics of target** Attractive	Unattractive	**Row totals**
Helped	19	13	32
Did not help	22	27	49
Column totals	41	40	81

(*a*) Prepare a joint probability table of the results.
(*b*) Calculate the conditional probabilities of events B and $\overline{B}$ when the attractiveness status of the subject is known.
(*c*) Construct a tree diagram of the conditional probabilities when the attractiveness status of the target person is known.
(*d*) Construct a tree diagram of the conditional probabilities when the helping status of the subject is known.

21. Imagine that we have a population of the following four scores: 0, 3, 6, and 9.
(*a*) Construct a probability distribution and histogram of all possible means when sampling with replacement, $N = 2$.
(*b*) Construct a probability histogram of all possible means when sampling with replacement, $N = 3$. (*Hint:* The table for finding the means appears below. The values in the cells represent the means of the three draws.)

1st draw		**0**				**3**				**6**				**9**			
2nd draw		**0**	**3**	**6**	**9**	**0**	**3**	**6**	**9**	**0**	**3**	**6**	**9**	**0**	**3**	**6**	**9**
3rd draw	0	0	1	2	3	1	2	3	4	2	3	4	5	3	4	5	6
	3	1	2	3	4	2	3	4	5	3	4	5	6	4	5	6	7
	6	2	3	4	5	3	4	5	6	4	5	6	7	5	6	7	8
	9	3	4	5	6	4	5	6	7	5	6	7	8	6	7	8	9

CHAPTER 13

Introduction to Statistical Inference

13.1 WHY SAMPLE?

You are the leader of a religious denomination, and for the purpose of planning recruitment you want to know what proportion of the adults in the United States claim church membership. How would you go about getting this information?

You are a sociologist, and you want to study the differences in child-rearing practices among parents of delinquent and nondelinquent children.

You are a market researcher, and you want to know what proportion of individuals prefer certain car colors and their various combinations.

You are a park attendant, and you want to determine whether the ice is sufficiently thick to permit safe skating.

You are a gambler, and you want to determine whether a set of dice is "biased."

What do each of these problems have in common? You are asking questions about the parameter of a population to which you want to generalize your answers, but you have no hope of ever studying the *entire* population. In Section 1.2, we defined a **population** as a *complete* or theoretical set of individuals, objects, or measurements having some common observable characterstic.* As has been noted, it is frequently

* It is recommended that you reread Section 1.2 to review several definitions of terms that will appear in this chapter.

impossible to study all of the members of a given population because the population as defined either has an infinite number of members or is so large that it defies exhaustive study. Moreover, when we refer to "the population" we are often dealing with a hypothetical entity. In some research situations, the actual population may not exist (e.g., the population of all babies regardless of whether or not they have been born) or certain elements may be difficult to locate (e.g., young black males are frequently undercounted in the census due to their high rate of geographical mobility).

Since populations can rarely be studied exhaustively, we must depend on **samples** as a basis for arriving at a hypothesis concerning various characteristics, or parameters, of the population. Our interest is not in descriptive statistics per se, but in making inferences from data. Thus, if we ask 100 people how they intend to vote in a forthcoming election, our primary interest is not in knowing how these 100 people will vote, but in estimating how the members of the entire voting population will cast their ballots.

Recall that in Chapter 1 we described polling a sample of registered voters in Wisconsin concerning their attitude toward the use of nuclear power as an energy source. The sample of respondents allowed us to estimate how *all* the registered voters in the state felt about the issue. A humorous example of a dog sampling its environment is included in Box 13.1.

Almost all research involves the observation and the measurement of a limited number of individuals or events. These measurements are presumed to tell us something about the population. To understand how we are able to make inferences about a population from a sample, we need to introduce the concept of sampling distributions.

A **sampling distribution** is a theoretical probability distribution of the possible values of some sample statistic that would occur if we were to draw all possible samples of a fixed size from a given population. We will discuss sampling distributions in Section 13.2.

13.1.1 Methods of Sampling

Simple random selection

By far, the simplest form of sampling is random sampling. For many years, researchers relied on random number tables to help them create sequences of random numbers. There is a well-known book that statisticians use that contains a million random numbers (Rand Corporation, 1955). An example of a random number table is printed in Table M of Appendix C. Today, many computer programs can generate a series of random numbers that meet your particular needs. Whichever technique you use, a printed table of numbers or a computer program, you should strive to ensure that your method for selecting subjects does not have some form of systematic bias.

Here is a quick example of how you could use a random number table in the selection of eligible voters. Assume that 250,000 people live in your county and that you decide you need 500 to have a fair and representative sample. You could use a computer program to generate random numbers between 1 and 250,000 or you could use a random number table. If you use a book of random digits, you should open the book to any page, place your finger or pencil somewhere on the page and select the closest three-digit number. That number will represent a page in the book. Turn to that page and again place your finger somewhere on the page. From that point on, select six-digit numbers that are less than or equal to 250,000.

Once you have the random digits, you can select the people to put into the sample. In this example, let's say the first person selected is listed as the 220,622nd voter on the voter registration roll.

For selection of a smaller sample, say 30, from the 100 sociology majors at your school, you could use the table of random numbers in this text (Appendix C, Table M). First assign a number to each student and choose two-digit numbers from the table. For very small samples, it is still possible to use the "names in the hat" technique and select names until you meet your required sample size, as long as you maintain your scientific objectivity and don't look at the names as you are selecting them.

Systematic selection

Another form of probability sampling is systematic sampling. In selecting voters for a sample, we may decide to choose the first registered voter at random and then select every 500th voter until we have the necessary sample. Although this technique is not truly a form of random sampling, it is easy to understand, does not require a random number table, and can produce a useful sample in most cases.

Stratified random selection

Sometimes there may be meaningful subgroups in a population. In our voting example, we may want to ensure that each voting district is equally and proportionally represented. Therefore, to select voters for this example, we need to divide the voter registration records into the separate voting districts and then conduct a random sample from each district. The stratified selection process can become more complicated if we know that there are differences in the voter turnout among the voting districts. For example, one district may consistently have 45% of its members casting votes, whereas another may average only a 30% turnout. Collecting a good stratified random sample may require a bit more work, but the reward will be a good and fair sample of the population.

There are many strategies for selecting a random sample. Likewise, there are many issues to be considered when creating a sampling strategy, including the number of items to be selected, the cost of sampling, and the accuracy of the sample. Readers interested in a more detailed account of sampling techniques should consult a textbook dedicated to the subject such as Henry's *Practical Sampling* (1990).

13.2
THE CONCEPT OF SAMPLING DISTRIBUTIONS

In actual practice, inferences about the parameters of a population are made from statistics that are calculated from a sample of N observations drawn at random from this population. If we continue to draw samples of size N from this population, we should not be surprised if we find some differences among the values of the sample statistics that are obtained. It would be extremely unlikely that we would draw exactly the same set of observations each time. On one occasion, we might, by chance, select a set of observations in which most of the scores are high. On another, we might select mostly low scores. On still another, there might be a good mix of high and low observations. Indeed, it is this observation that has led to the concept of a *sampling distribution.*

Imagine drawing simple random samples (with replacement) of $N = 50$ from the population of students at a medium-sized university. You calculate the mean age for the first sample and find that it is 20.2. Suppose you continue to draw an infinite number of samples of $N = 50$ and calculate the sample mean for each of the samples drawn. Each time you drew a sample you would record another mean, so that after you drew 1,000 samples you would end up with 1,000 means. Each of the means would be based on averaging the ages of 50 students who were drawn in a given sample. Although the actual ages of students at the university might vary, for example, between 16 and 64, you should see that each of the means will tend to cluster around the overall mean age of the entire university student body. By treating each of the sample means as a raw score, you could draw a frequency curve of the sample mean scores as shown in Figure 13.1. The original dispersion of ages for the population has been superimposed for comparative purposes. Note that the variation of the sampling distribution of means is far smaller than that of the actual population distribution of ages, a topic that is addressed in the following chapter.

Also realize that this exercise has been presented to demonstrate the logic behind constructing a sampling distribution. Normally, we draw only one sample from a population.

There is a sampling distribution for every statistic—mean, standard deviation, variance, proportion, median, and so on. It is one of the most important concepts in inferential statistics. You are already familiar with several sampling distributions, although we have not previously named them as such. Recall the various sampling problems we have introduced throughout the earlier chapters in the text. (See Box 13.1 for an example of the pervasiveness of sampling.)

In Chapter 12, Section 12.7 we started with a population of seven scores, and selected, with replacement, samples of $N = 2$. We obtained all possible combinations of these samples. We then constructed a frequency distribution and probability distribution of means drawn from that population with a fixed sample size of $N = 2$.

Recall also that in exercise 21 at the end of Chapter 12 we constructed sampling distributions based on drawing, with replacement, all possible samples of $N = 2$ and $N = 3$ from a population of four scores (0, 3, 6, 9). Table 13.1 shows these two

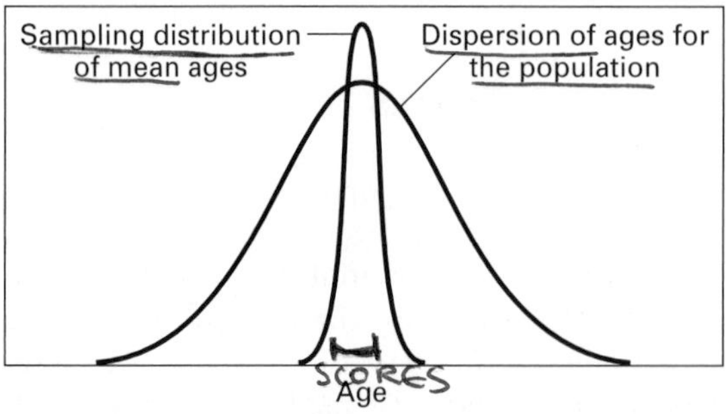

FIGURE 13.1
Hypothetical sampling distribution of mean ages and the original dispersion of ages for the population

TABLE 13.1
Sampling distributions of means drawn from a population of four scores (0, 3, 6, 9; $\mu = 4.5$, $\sigma = 3.35$) and sample sizes $N = 2$, $N = 3$, and $N = 4$. Sampling with replacement

$N = 2$		$N = 3$		$N = 4$	
$\overline{X}$	$p(\overline{X})$	$\overline{X}$	$p(\overline{X})$	$\overline{X}$	$p(\overline{X})$
9.0	0.0625	9.0	0.0156	9.0	0.0039
7.5	0.1250	8.0	0.0469	8.25	0.0156
6.0	0.1875	7.0	0.0938	7.50	0.0391
4.5	0.2500	6.0	0.1562	6.75	0.0781
3.0	0.1875	5.0	0.1875	6.00	0.1211
1.5	0.1250	4.0	0.1875	5.25	0.1562
0.0	0.0625	3.0	0.1562	4.50	0.1719
		2.0	0.0938	3.75	0.1562
		1.0	0.0469	3.00	0.1211
		0.0	0.0156	2.25	0.0781
				1.50	0.0391
				0.75	0.0156
				0.00	0.0039
$\overline{X} = 4.5$		$\overline{X} = 4.5$		$\overline{X} = 4.5$	
$s_{\overline{X}} = 2.37$		$s_{\overline{X}} = 1.94$		$s_{\overline{X}} = 1.68$	

sampling distributions in addition to the sampling distribution of the mean when $N = 4$.

Table 13.1 is not nearly so difficult as it may look. Concentrate on the situation in which $N = 2$. Here we see that if we sampled two scores, with replacement, from our population, only seven possible means could result (9.0, 7.5, 6.0, 4.5, 3.0, 1.5, and 0.0). A mean of 9.0, for example, could only occur if we drew two successive 9s, added them, and divided by 2. A mean of 7.5 would result if we drew a 6 and a 9 or a 9 and a 6. Note that the probability of drawing two 9s when $N = 2$ is 0.0625. You might be wondering how we arrived at this value. Since there are only four scores in the population (0, 3, 6, 9), the probability of drawing one 9 (or one 0 or 3 or 6) is one out of four or 0.25. Recall that the multiplication rule for independent events—equation (12.9)—states:

> The probability of the simultaneous or successive occurrence of two events is the product of the separate probabilities of each event.

Therefore, the probability of a 9 and a 9 can be calculated in the following manner:

$$\begin{aligned} p(9 \text{ and } 9) &= p(9)p(9) \\ &= (0.25)(0.25) \\ &= 0.0625 \end{aligned}$$

The probability of three successive 9s (see the middle column in which $N = 3$) is 0.0156 because the multiplication rule tells us to multiply 0.25 times 0.25 times 0.25, which yields 0.0156.

Finally, note that each of the three $p(\overline{X})$ columns sum to 1.0000, the means for the three sample sizes all equal 4.5, and the standard deviation of the sample means ($s_{\overline{X}}$)

BOX 13.1

SAMPLING: A MATTER OF SURVIVAL

We tend to think of sampling procedures as activities engaged in by only a handful of professionals—pollsters, laboratory scientists, and demographers, to name a few. As the following excerpt from *Winning with Statistics* makes clear, sampling followed by decision making are among the most pervasive activities of living organisms.

We have three dogs on our ranch on the outskirts of Tucson, Arizona. The baby of the three, Millie Muffin, is an eight-month-old black and white springer spaniel. Although "Mischief" should be her middle name, she is a sheer delight. She is constantly exploring the desert flora and fauna with the indefatigable curiosity of a three-year-old human child. When spying something that moves on its own (such as a giant spider, better known as a tarantula), she leaps about two feet off the ground—ears flapping—and retreats several feet away, all the while barking like a fierce Doberman. But I know better. In reality, she is the world's greatest coward. I'll tell you how I know.

While she is prancing mindlessly about the giant saguaro, the ocotillo, the cholla, and other assorted exotic plants of the desert, I will sneak downwind of her. Then I will raise myself on the balls of my toes, stretch my arms in front of me, and shuffle my feet as I advance toward her in my best Frankenstein-monster style. When she spies me, she lets out a startled "yip," springs into the air, and begins a barking retreat. But all the while, her nose is probing the air, sniffing constantly, desperately drawing in samples in an effort to make inferences about the nature of the intruder.

While observing Millie's antics, it occurred to me that the actions involved in taking samples and drawing inferences from these samples are among the most pervasive of mammalian activities. The pet dog, the family feline, the lion in the jungle, the gorilla in the rain forest, and the wife, husband, daughter, son, businessperson, doctor, lawyer, and Indian chief have this characteristic in common. They are continuously probing aspects of their environment, assessing the risks against the benefits, making probability judgments concerning alternative avenues of behavior, and pursuing those lines of activity that appear most likely to lead to desired goals. By this I do not mean to imply that all this sampling and probability assessment is conscious or deliberate. The truth of the matter is that nature has designed us all to be exquisite probability generating machines. Without the ability to sample and thereby judge peril, or the availability of food, or the receptivity of a sexual partner, all species presently inhabiting the earth would have come from a long line of unborn ancestors.

Source: Excerpted from Runyon, *Winning with Statistics* (1977).

becomes smaller as the sample sizes increase. This last point will become clear at the beginning of Chapter 14.

Why is the concept of a sampling distribution so important? The answer is simple. Once you are able to describe the sampling distribution of *any statistic,* be it mean, standard deviation, or proportion, you are in a position to entertain and test a wide variety of hypotheses. For example, suppose you draw four numbers from some population for which you know neither the mean nor the standard deviation. You obtain a sample mean of 6.00. You ask, "Is it reasonable that this sample was drawn from the population of four numbers upon which the sampling distribution in Table 13.1 was based?" The mean of the sampling distribution was 4.5, and your sample mean was 6.00. Is such a departure from the population mean an extraordinary or rare event, or will departures this large occur with regularity?

In the absence of a frame of reference, these questions would be meaningless. However, if we knew the sampling distribution of the mean for the population of interest, we would have the necessary frame of reference, and the answer would be quite straightforward. If we were to tell you that the appropriate sampling distribution is given in Table 13.1, you would have little trouble in answering the question. A sample mean of 6.00 would be drawn about 12% of the time ($p = 0.1211$), and a mean of 6.00 or greater would occur almost 26% of the time ($p = 0.1211 + 0.0781 + 0.0391 + 0.0156 + 0.0039 = 0.2578$). Roughly one chance in four is not terribly unusual. Thus, you would have no overriding reason to suspect that the sample was selected from a population different from the one represented in Table 13.1, $N = 4$.

But what if you had selected a sample mean equal to 9.0? Referring to the same sampling distribution of means in Table 13.1, we see that such an event would be quite rare—less than 1 in 100, or, to be more precise, 39 times in 10,000 ($p = 0.0039$). At this point, we might entertain serious doubts that the sample was drawn at random from the four scores shown in Table 13.1.

Or, to put this into everyday experiences, suppose you have a friend who often accompanies you to lunch. After the meal, when the tab is presented, your friend always produces a coin and cheerfully intones, "Heads you pay, tails I pay." After the toss, you friend's cheerfulness is undiminished: "Heads, bad luck, you pay." It has come up heads 10 times in a row. As with the sample mean equal to 9.00, might you not begin questioning the honesty of the coin in your friend's possession? Perhaps, with his coin, the probability of obtaining a heads and a tails are not equal. A weighted coin, or even a two-headed coin, perhaps? Rare or unusual outcomes must always alert us to the possibility that we must look elsewhere for explanations of things we observe.

Whenever we estimate a population parameter from a sample, we ask such questions as: "How good an estimate do I have? Can I conclude that the population parameter is identical with the sample statistic? Or is there likely to be some error? If so, how much?" To answer each of these questions, we compare our sample results with the "expected" results. The expected results are in turn given by the appropriate sampling distribution. But what does the sampling distribution of a particular statistic look like? How can we ever know the form of the distribution, and thus what the expected results are? Fortunately, there are known and predictable relationships between the form of the sampling distributions we shall be considering and the sample size of the statistics on which they are based. As we increase the sample size of the statistics that make up the sampling distribution, (1) the dispersion of the sample statistics becomes less—that is, the sample statistics tend to cluster closer to the parameter of interest—and (2) the form of the distribution becomes increasingly symmetrical and bell-shaped. These features are found even when the original population of scores is not distributed in a symmetrical and bell-shaped form. These points are shown in Figure 13.2.

- As sample size increases -> it becomes more bell shaped

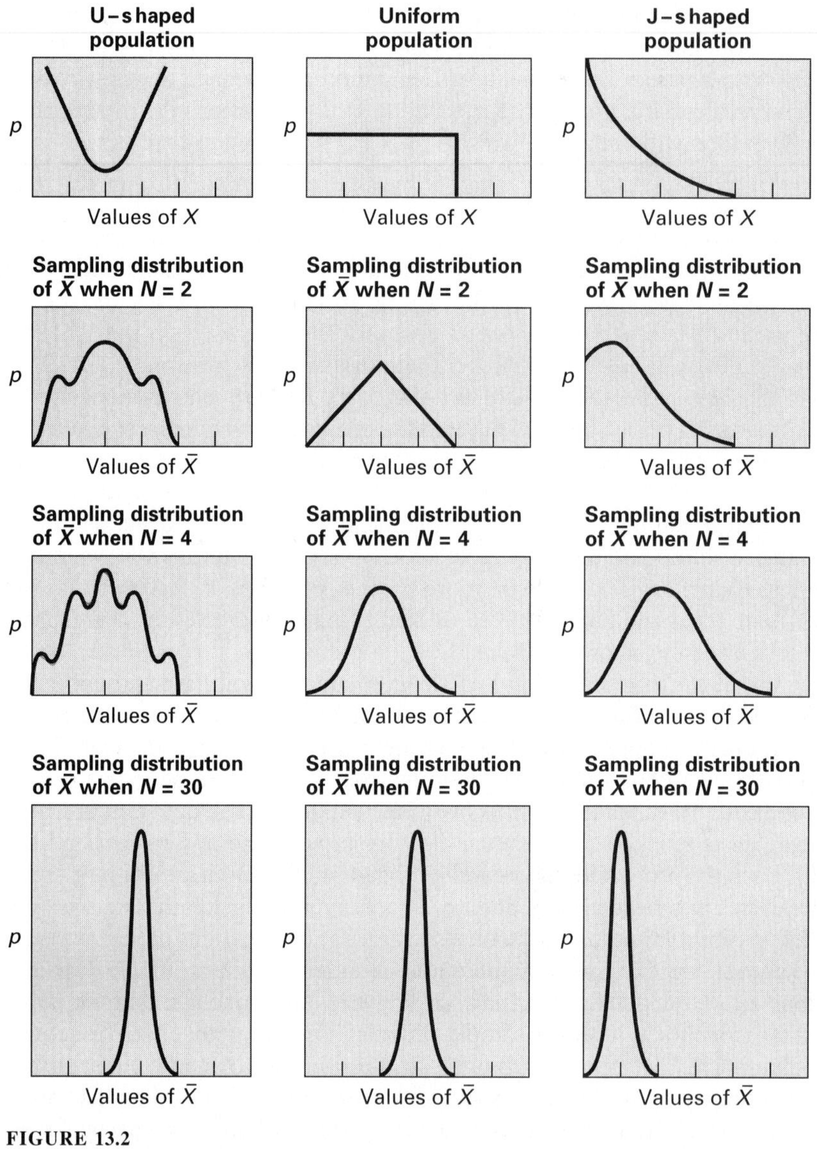

FIGURE 13.2

Sampling distributions of means of samples $N = 2$, $N = 4$, and $N = 30$ from three different types of populations

These figures illustrate the central limit-theorem by showing how, regardless of the form of the parent population, the sampling distribution of means approaches normality as N increases.

In many of the remaining chapters, the inferences we draw imply knowledge of the form of the sampling distribution. We will be looking at two idealized models whose mathematical properties are known: the normal curve and the **binomial distribution.** Both are frequently used as models to describe particular sampling distributions. Thus, for example, if we know that the sampling distribution of a particular statistic takes the form of a normal distribution, we may raise questions such as: "How likely is it that the value of the statistic we obtained was drawn from the sampling distribution under consideration?"

The following sections should serve to clarify these important points.

13.3
TESTING STATISTICAL HYPOTHESES: LEVEL OF SIGNIFICANCE

Let us say that you have a favorite coin that you use constantly in everyday life as a basis of "either–or" decision making. For example, you may ask, "Should I study tonight for the statistics quiz, or should I relax at one of the local movie houses? Heads I study, tails I don't." Over a period of time, you have sensed that the decision has gone against you more often than for you—in other words, you have to study more often than relax! You begin to question the accuracy and the adequacy of the coin. Does the coin come up heads more often than tails? How might you find out?

One thing is clear. The true proportion of heads and tails characteristic of this coin can never be known. You could start tossing the coin this very minute and continue for a million years (granting a long life and a remarkably durable coin) and you would not exhaust the population of possible outcomes. In this instance, the true proportion of heads and tails is unknowable because the universe, or population, is unlimited.

That the *true* value is unknowable does not prevent us from trying to estimate what it is. We have already pointed out that since populations can rarely be studied exhaustively, we must depend on sample statistics to estimate population parameters.

Returning to our problem with the coin, we clearly see that to determine whether or not the coin is biased, we shall have to obtain a sample of the "behavior" of that coin and arrive at some generalization concerning its possible bias. For example, if we toss our coin 10 times and obtain 5 heads and 5 tails, would we begin to suspect our coin of being biased? Of course not, since this outcome is exactly a 50–50 split, and is in agreement with the hypothesis that the coin is not biased. What if we obtained six heads and four tails? Again, this is not an unusual outcome. In fact, we can answer the question of how often, given a theoretically perfect coin, we may expect an outcome at least this much different from a 50–50 split. Looking at Figure 13.3, which represents the theoretical probability distribution of various numbers of heads when $N = 10$, we see that departures from a 50–50 split are quite common. Indeed, whenever we obtain either six or more heads, or four or fewer heads, we are departing from a 50–50 split. Such departures will occur fully 75.4% ($1 - 0.246 = 0.754 \times 100 = 75.4\%$) of the time when we toss a perfect coin in a series of trials with 10 tosses per trial.

What if we obtained nine heads and one tail? Clearly, we begin to suspect the honesty of the coin. Why? At what point do we change from attitudes accepting the "honesty" of the coin to attitudes rejecting its "honesty"? This question takes us to the crux of the problem of inferential statistics. We have seen that the more unusual or rare the event is, the more prone we are to look for nonchance explanations of the event. When we obtained 6 heads in 10 tosses of our coin, we felt no necessity to find

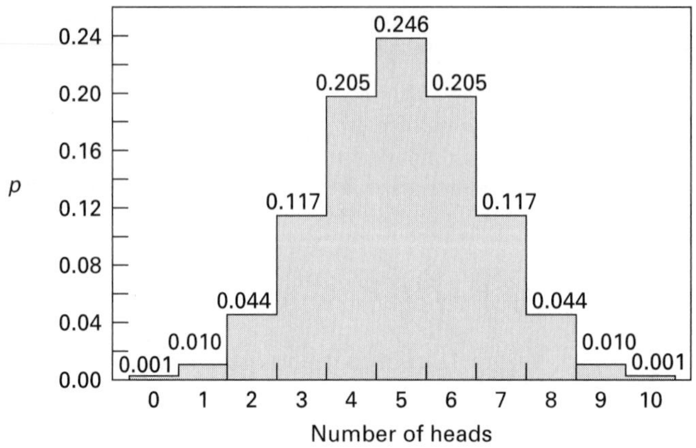

FIGURE 13.3
Histogram of binomial sampling distribution of various numbers of heads obtained by tossing an unbiased coin 10 times ($N = 10$), or by tossing 10 coins 1 time

an explanation for its departure from a 50–50 split, other than to state that such a departure would occur frequently "by chance." However, when we obtained heads nine times, we had an uncomfortable feeling concerning the "honesty" of the coin. Nine heads out of 10 tosses is such a rare occurrence that we begin to suspect that the explanation may be found in terms of the characteristics of the coin rather than in the so-called laws of chance. The critical question is, Where do we draw the line that determines what inferences we make about the coin?

The answer to this question reveals the basic nature of science: its probabilistic rather than its absolutistic orientation. In the social sciences, most researchers have adopted one of the following two cutoff points as the basis for *inferring the operation of nonchance factors*.

1. When the event or one more deviant would occur 5% of the time or less, *by chance,* some researchers are willing to assert that the results are due to nonchance factors. This cutoff point is known variously as the 0.05 **significance level,** or the 5.00% significance level.

2. When the event or one more deviant would occur 1% of the time or less, *by chance*, other researchers are willing to assert that the results are due to nonchance factors. This cutoff point is known as the 0.01 *significance level,* or the 1.00% significance level.

The level of significance set by the researchers for inferring the operation of nonchance factors is known as the **alpha (α) level.** Thus, when using the 0.05 level of significance, $\alpha = 0.05$; when using the 0.01 level of significance, $\alpha = 0.01$.

To determine whether the results were due to nonchance factors in the present coin experiment, we need to calculate the probability of obtaining an event as *rare* as nine heads out of 10 tosses. In determining the rarity of an event, we must consider that the rare event can occur in both directions (e.g., nine tails and one head) and that it includes more extreme events. In other words, the probability of an event as rare as nine or ten heads out of 10 tosses or as rare as one or zero heads out of 10 tosses as well is equal to:

$$p(9 \text{ heads}) + p(10 \text{ heads}) + p(1 \text{ head}) + p(0 \text{ heads})$$

Since this distribution is symmetrical:

$$p(9 \text{ heads}) = p(1 \text{ head})$$

and

$$p(10 \text{ heads}) = p(0 \text{ heads})$$

Thus:

$$p(9 \text{ heads}) + p\ (10 \text{ heads}) + p(1 \text{ head}) + p(0 \text{ heads})$$
$$= 2[p(9 \text{ heads}) + p(10 \text{ heads})]$$

These p values may be obtained from Figure 13.3 as follows.

$$p(9 \text{ heads}) = 0.010$$

and

$$p(10 \text{ heads}) = 0.001$$

Therefore, the two-tailed probability of an event as rare as nine or ten heads out of 10 tosses or as rare as one or zero heads out of 10 tosses is $2(0.010 + 0.001) = 0.022$ or 2.2%. A **two-tailed probability value** is a probability value that takes into account both tails of the distribution.

Applying the 0.05 significance level ($\alpha = 0.05$), we would conclude that the coin was biased (i.e., the results were due to nonchance factors). However, if we employed the 0.01 significance level ($\alpha = 0.01$), we would not be able to assert that these results were due to nonchance factors.

It should be noted and strongly emphasized that you do *not* conduct a study, analyze the results, arrive at a probability value, and then decide upon the α-level. The α-level must be specified *prior* to the study as part of the overall strategy of designing the study.

13.4 TESTING STATISTICAL HYPOTHESES: NULL HYPOTHESIS AND ALTERNATIVE HYPOTHESIS

At this point, many students become disillusioned by the arbitrary nature of decision making in science. Let's examine the logic of statistical inference a bit further and see if we can resolve some of the doubts. Prior to the beginning of any study, the researcher sets up two mutually exclusive and exhaustive hypotheses.

1. The **null hypothesis (H_0)**, which specifies hypothesized values for one or more of the *population parameters*. For example, we could state a null hypothesis in which

we expect there to be no difference between the incomes of male and female professors in the following manner:

$$H_0\text{: } \mu \text{ males} = \mu \text{ females}$$

2. The **alternative hypothesis (H_1),** which asserts that the *population parameter* is some value other than the one hypothesized. An alternative hypothesis to the null hypothesis just stated could be:

$$H_1\text{: } \mu \text{ males} \neq \mu \text{ females}$$

where $\neq$ means "does not equal."

The alternative hypothesis is sometimes referred to as the *research hypothesis.* It is the hypothesis that we wish to verify and is stated in a way that anticipates the expected outcome or relationship. The null hypothesis is sometimes referred to as the hypothesis to be nullified. The researcher anticipates that it will be rejected. Thus, the preceding null hypothesis anticipates that the incomes of male and female professors will differ and the alternative hypothesis is stated in a manner that is consistent with that expectation.

In the present coin experiment, these two hypotheses read as follows:

H_0: the coin is unbiased; that is:

$$P = Q = \tfrac{1}{2}$$

where P = probability of heads
Q = probability of tails

H_1: the coin is biased; that is

$$P \neq Q \neq \tfrac{1}{2}$$

The alternative hypothesis may be either a **directional hypothesis** or a **nondirectional hypothesis.** When H_1 asserts *only* that the population parameter is *different from* the one hypothesized, it is referred to as a nondirectional or two-tailed hypothesis, for example:

$$P \neq Q \neq \tfrac{1}{2}$$

Very frequently in the social sciences hypotheses are *directional* or *one-tailed.* In this instance, in addition to asserting that the population parameter is different from the one hypothesized, we assert the *direction* of that difference, for example:

$$P > Q \text{ or } P < Q$$

In evaluating the outcome of a study, we should use one-tailed probability values whenever our alternative hypothesis is directional. A **one-tailed probability value** is a probability value obtained by examining only one tail of the distribution. When the alternative hypothesis is directional, so is the null hypothesis. For example, referring back to the income of male versus female professors, if the alternative hypothesis is that μ males $>$ μ females, the corresponding null hypothesis is that μ males $\leq$ μ females. Conversely, if H_1 is μ males $<$ μ females, H_0 reads: μ males $\geq$ μ females.

13.4.1 The Indirect Proof of a Hypothesis

One of the basic rules of logic is that claims can often be proved false but never proved true. Consider the simple statement, "All crows are black." Can you *prove* this statement true? In fact, you cannot. The word "all" in the statement refers to crows that are currently living, crows that are dead, and crows yet to be hatched. Have you now and will you have the opportunity to observe all crows to confirm this statement to be true? The answer is no. You may be confident that the statement is true because all the crows you have seen are black and therefore make an induction that based on your experience the statement is true. Unfortunately, there may be a group of crows that you have never seen that are not black. Indeed, if you found one red crow, your initial statement, "All crows are black," would be proved wrong. Thus, with one disconfirming case you are able to falsify or prove wrong the statement, "All crows are black." How does this problem relate to a statistical hypothesis? The problem is that no statement can ever really be proved to be true, only false.

Statistical logic operates in exactly the same way. We cannot prove the null hypothesis, nor can we directly prove the alternative hypothesis. However, if we can *reject* the null hypothesis, we can assert its alternative, namely, that the population parameter is some value other than the one hypothesized.* Applied to the coin problem, if we can reject the null hypothesis that $P = Q = \frac{1}{2}$, we can assert the alternative, namely, that $P \neq Q \neq \frac{1}{2}$. Note that the support of the alternative hypothesis is always *indirect*. We have supported it by rejecting the null hypothesis. On the other hand, since the alternative hypothesis can neither be proved nor disproved directly, we can *never prove the null hypothesis* by rejecting the alternative hypothesis. The strongest statement we are entitled to make in this respect is that we *failed to reject the null hypothesis.*

What, then, are the conditions for rejecting the null hypothesis? Simply this: When using the 0.05 level of significance, you reject the null hypothesis when a given result occurs, by chance, 5% of the time or less. When using the 0.01 level of significance, you reject the null hypothesis when a given result occurs, by chance, 1% of the time or less. Under these circumstances, of course, you *affirm* the alternative hypothesis.

In other words, one rejects the null hypothesis when the results occur, by chance, 5% of the time or less (or 1% of the time or less), *assuming that the null hypothesis is the true distribution.* That is, one assumes that the null hypothesis is true, calculates the probability on the basis of this assumption, and if the probability is small, rejects the assumption.

For reasons stated previously, R. A. Fisher, the eminent British statistician, affirmed:

> In relation to any experiment we may speak of this hypothesis as the "null hypothesis," and it should be noted that the null hypothesis is never proved or established, but is possibly disproved, in the course of experimentation. *Every experiment may be said to exist only in order to give the facts a chance of disproving the null hypothesis.*†

---

* The null hypothesis can be thought of as the hypothesis to be nullified by a statistical test.

† R. A. Fisher, *The Design of Experiments* (Edinburgh: Oliver & Boyd, 1935), p. 16.

13.4.2 Comparing the Criterion Probability, α, and the Observed Probability, p

The researcher sets the α-level to determine when to reject H_0 and when to fail to reject H_0. Once α is set, the data can be collected and the probability of the outcome calculated. If $p \leq \alpha$, then we reject H_0 in favor of the alternative hypothesis. If $p > \alpha$, then we cannot reject H_0. For example, if the α-level is .05 and the probability of the sample statistic is $p = .02$, then $p < \alpha$ and we can reject the null hypothesis. If $p = .06$, then we cannot reject the null hypothesis because $p > \alpha$.

When H_0 is rejected, many researchers say that they have statistically significant results. What does the term *statistically significant* really mean? For us it means that the results are worthy of further consideration and discussion. "Statistically significant" is a short-hand phrase meaning, "These results are not likely to be due to chance or random events and are worthy of further analysis." Does "significant" mean "important"? Not necessarily. There are many times when the results can be statistically significant but not all that important. As we will see, many factors contribute to statistical significance, including the size of the sample. Using a large sample, it is possible to obtain results that are statistically significant, yet have little meaning in everyday life. For example, many studies have found that there is a statistically significant difference between men and women on standardized math tests. Although this difference is frequently significant, the difference between the average scores of men and women is very small relative to the variance within each group (Hyde, Fennema, & Lamon, 1990). There are other cases where statistical significance does translate into important differences. What you should learn is that rejecting H_0 is just one step in a long line of steps taken in any research project. Once you decide to reject H_0, you must still determine what specific inferences you are willing to make from the data.

You should be careful how you use this phrase and wary of how others use it. Many people are confused by statistical procedures and do not understand hypothesis testing. Consequently, when they read or hear, "Research has determined that there is a statistically significant relation between eating carrots and losing weight," they assume that eating carrots has an impressive effect on weight loss. What if you learned that the researcher had made this conclusion after using $\alpha = .4$? These results are not impressive. The probability of obtaining results like these by chance is 40%. What if $\alpha = .001$? These results are more impressive because the probability of getting results like these by chance alone are 1 in 1,000.* But we still have to ask a basic question: How much weight did the subjects lose? It is possible that a two-pound difference is statistically significant, but is it really all that important for someone who is 15–20 pounds overweight? Here are some examples to illustrate these points.

You decide you will accept your friend's claim that he is psychic if he can correctly guess eight or more tosses of a coin. In essence, $\alpha = .055$. Your friend correctly predicted only 6 of the 10 tosses. You decide not to reject the null hypothesis because

* The authors know of no research that links carrots to weight loss. Carrots are a good vegetable with many vitamins, but we cannot endorse the assertion that they *cause* weight loss.

$p = .3767$, which is greater than .055 (e.g., $p > \alpha$), and to conclude that your friend has not provided sufficient evidence that he is psychic.

You want to decide if the rate of cancer is greater than average in a specific county. You decide to set $\alpha = .10$. You then examine the cancer rate in the county and compare it to national averages. According to your calculations, the rate of cancer is above the mean and the probability of getting a rate that high by chance alone is $p = .043$. You may reject H_0 and infer that the rate of cancer in the county is greater than the national average. Although you have a statistically significant result, you cannot yet determine the cause of the higher-than-average cancer rate. The statistically significant result merely suggests that you should further examine the situation.

You decide that you will reject H_0 based on $\alpha = .01$. When you determine the probability, $p = .012$. You must fail to reject the null hypothesis because $p > \alpha$. Although the difference between the two is small, we must hold fast to our rule and base our hypothesis on consistently applied and logically derived rules of evidence.

13.5 TESTING STATISTICAL HYPOTHESES: THE TWO TYPES OF ERROR

You may now ask, "But aren't we taking a chance that we will be wrong in rejecting the null hypothesis? Is it not possible that we have, in fact, obtained a statistically rare occurrence by chance?"

The answer to this question must be a simple and humble yes. This is precisely what we mean when we say that science is probabilistic. If there is any absolute statement that scientists are entitled to make, it is that we can never assert with complete confidence that our findings or propositions are true. There are countless examples in science in which an apparently firmly established conclusion has had to be modified in the light of further evidence.

Even if all the tosses in the coin experiment had resulted in heads, it is possible that the coin was not, in fact, biased. By chance, once in every 1,024 experiments, "on the average," the coin will turn up heads 10 out of 10 times. When we use the 0.05 level of significance, approximately 5% of the time we will be wrong when we reject the null hypothesis and assert its alternative.

These are some of the basic facts of the reality of inductive reasoning to which the student must adjust. The student of behavior who insists on absolute certainty before speaking on an issue is a student who has been mute throughout life, and who will remain so (probably).

These same considerations have led statisticians to formulate two types of errors that may be made in statistical inference.

13.5.1 Type I Error (Type α Error)

Back pain has become one of the most common disabling disorders of this century. In a number of cases, trauma and aging have caused the disks (shock absorbers) between the vertebrae to lose elasticity and the gap between the vertebrae to narrow.

Speculating that by surgically fusing vertebrae together, the patient might be better able to absorb shock and thereby reduce pain, spinal fusion was introduced. The initial results of this surgical procedure were so positive that the null hypothesis (H_0: Spinal fusion does not relieve pain) was rejected. More recent evidence no longer supports the view that spinal fusion is effective in relieving back pain (i.e., there have been many failures to reject H_0). It is now a relatively rare surgical procedure. As a result of the false rejection of H_0, many people underwent expensive and temporary incapacitating surgery without achieving any pain relief.

In a **type I error (type α error),** we reject the null hypothesis when it is actually true. The probability of making a type I error is *alpha* (α). We have already pointed out that if we set our rejection point at the 0.05 level of significance, we will mistakenly reject H_0 approximately 5% of the time. It would seem, then, that to avoid this type of error, we should set the rejection level as low as possible. For example, if we were to set $\alpha = 0.001$, we would risk a type I error only about one time in every thousand. It should be noted that the 0.05 level is rather routinely used in the social and behavioral sciences unless there is a particular reason to be extremely conservative about making a type I error. For example, suppose we were comparing a totally new teaching method to the technique currently in use. Suppose also that the null hypothesis were really true, that is, there were *no* differences between the two methods. If a type I error were made and the null hypothesis falsely rejected, this could conceivably lead to an extremely costly and time-consuming changeover to a method that was no better than the one being used. Similarly, in medicine a type I error could lead to the implementation of a procedure that is costly, involves high levels of risk, and leads to severe discomfort for the patient.

In situations such as these we might want to set a more conservative level of significance; for example, $\alpha = 0.01$. To familiarize you with the use of both α-levels, we have arbitrarily employed the $\alpha = 0.01$ and $\alpha = 0.05$ levels in examples presented throughout the text. However, the lower we set α, the greater the likelihood that we will make a type II error.

13.5.2 Type II Error (Type β Error)

When DDT was first introduced into the household and on farms as an effective pesticide, there was no accumulated evidence that permitted the null hypothesis (H_0: DDT is not harmful) to be rejected. As a result of widespread use over a period of years, evidence was accumulated concerning its harmful effects on humans (cancer), domestic animals, and wildlife. Failure to reject H_0 had led to the false conclusion that DDT was not harmful (i.e., safe). Even though now banned, residual quantities still show up in water supplies, in soil samples, and in the food chain. The decision-making error exemplified by DDT and many later pesticides and solvents is known as a type II error. As you can see, the consequences of such an error can be devastating.

In a **type II error (type β error),** we fail to reject the null hypothesis when it is actually false. *Beta* (β) is the probability of making a type II error. This type of error is far more common than a type I error. For example, if we apply the 0.01 level of significance as the basis of rejecting the null hypothesis and then conduct a study in which the result we obtained would have occurred by chance only 2% of the time, we cannot reject the null hypothesis.

It is clear that the lower we set the rejection level, the less we face the likelihood of a type I error and the greater the likelihood of a type II error. Conversely, the higher we set the rejection level, the greater is the likelihood of a type I error and the smaller the likelihood of a type II error.

The fact that the rejection level is set as low as it is attests to the conservatism of scientists; that is, the greater willingness on the part of the scientist to make an error in the direction of *failing* to claim a result than to make an error in the direction of *claiming* a result when he or she is wrong.

Table 13.2 summarizes the type of error made as a function of the true status of the null hypothesis and the decision we have made. We should note that type I and type II errors are sampling errors and refer to samples drawn from hypothetical populations. (See also Statistics in Action 13.1.)

Let's look at a few examples in which we supply the following information about the underlying population:

H_0, α-level, obtained p, statistical decision made, and the true status of H_0.

Let's ascertain what type of error, if any, has been made.

1. H_0: $\mu_1 = \mu_2$, $\alpha = 0.05$, two-tailed test. Obtained $p = 0.03$, two-tailed value. Statistical decision: H_0 is false. Actual status of H_0: True.

Consequence. Type I—rejecting a true H_0.

2. H_0: $\mu_1 = \mu_2$, $\alpha = 0.05$, two-tailed test. Obtained $p = 0.04$, two-tailed value. Statistical decision: H_0 is false. Actual status of H_0: False.

Consequence. No error has been made. A correct conclusion was drawn since H_0 is false and the statistical decision was that H_0 is false.

3. H_0: $\mu_1 = \mu_2$, $\alpha = 0.01$, two-tailed test. Obtained $p = 0.10$, two-tailed value. Statistical decision: fail to reject H_0. Actual status of H_0: False.

Consequence. Type II—failing to reject a false H_0.

TABLE 13.2
Various statistical decisions and their outcomes when H_0 is true or false*

	True status of H_0	
Decision	**H_0 is true**	**H_0 is false**
Fail to reject H_0	Correct $p = 1 - \alpha$	Type II error $p = \beta$
Reject H_0	Type I error $p = \alpha$	Correct $p = 1 - \beta$

*Each cell represents the decision made and the probability, p, that the decision is correct or in error.

4. H_0: $\mu_1 = \mu_2$, $\alpha = 0.01$, two-tailed test. Obtained $p = 0.06$ two-tailed value. Statistical decision: fail to reject H_0. Actual status of H_0: True.

Consequence. No error has been made, since the statistical decision has been to accept H_0 when H_0 is actually true.

You may now ask, "In actual practice, how can we tell when we are making a type I or a type II error?" The answer is simple: We can't! If we examine once again the logic of statistical inference, we will see why. We have already stated that with rare exceptions we cannot or will not know the true parameters of a population. Without this knowledge, how can we know whether our sample statistics have approximated or have failed to approximate the true value? How can we know whether we have mistakenly rejected a null hypothesis? If we did know a population value, we could know whether we made an error. Under these circumstances, however, the need for sampling statistics is eliminated. We collect samples and draw inferences from samples only because our population values are unknowable for one reason or another. When they become known, the need for statistical inference is lost.

Is there no way to know which surveys or experiments reporting significant results are accurate and which are not? The answer is a conditional yes. If we were to repeat the survey and obtain similar results, we would have increased confidence that we were not making a type I error. For example, if we tossed our coin in a second series of 10 trials and obtained 9 heads, we would feel far more confident that our coin was biased. Parenthetically, replication of studies is one of the weaker areas in social science research. The general attitude is that a study is not much good unless it is "different" and is therefore making a novel contribution. Replicating studies, when they are performed, frequently go unpublished. In consequence, we may feel assured that in studies using the 0.05 significance level, approximately 1 out of every 20 that reject the null hypothesis is making a type I error.*

STATISTICS IN ACTION 13.1
Type I and Type II Errors Applied to Decision-Making Processes, Including Medical, Psychological, Sociological, Economic, and Other Areas

Table 13.2 (Section 13.5.2) may be modified to exemplify an extremely broad spectrum of situations in which we must make decisions concerning one of two alternative courses of action. We may formulate two hypotheses; H_0: A given procedure will not work and H_1: A given procedure will work. If it does not work, we have made a correct decision when we "accept" the null hypothesis. Thus, a physician who says "I will not use treatment A because it is ineffective" when the treatment is truly ineffective will have made a correct decision. Imagine that the treatment is really effective (i.e., H_0 is false), but the physician fails to reject

* The proportion is probably even higher, since our methods of accepting research reports for publication are heavily weighted in terms of the statistical significance of the results. Thus, if four identical studies were conducted independently, and only one obtained results that permitted rejection of the null hypothesis, *this* one would most likely be published. There is virtually no way for the general scientific public to know about the three studies that *failed* to reject the null hypothesis.

H_0. This is analogous to a type II error. Because of this error, the patient may be denied a treatment that will cure the disorder. Thus, you see, type II errors *can* have serious consequences in the everyday world of decision making.

Let's look at another example. When considering the use of asbestos wrapping as an insulating material for hot water lines, the null hypothesis might be: H_0: Asbestos is not harmful. For years we failed to reject this hypothesis and acted as if asbestos is harmless, when, in fact, the null hypothesis was false (type II error: We failed to reject a false null hypothesis). Because of this failure to reject a false null hypothesis (i.e., H_0: Asbestos is not harmful), untold thousands of workers and others exposed to asbestos fibers are now at high risk for the development of lung cancer and other disorders of the lung. The National Institute of Occupational Safety and Health (NIOSH) has established exposure limits for well over 100 substances, many previously thought not to be harmful (NIOSH Recommendations for Occupational Safety and Health Standards, *Morbidity and Mortality Weekly Report, Supplement* 34/(1S) 1985). An interesting historical note in this connection is that early in his career as a medical doctor, Sigmund Freud regarded cocaine as a miracle drug. His failure to reject a false null hypothesis (H_0: Cocaine is not addictive) led to the mistaken advocacy of cocaine as a harmless way to relieve a number of disorders, including morphine addiction (cited in Dusek and Girdano, 1980).

Table 13.3 summarizes the errors that can be made as a result of accepting a false H_0 concerning the safety of a substance or incorrectly failing to reject a false H_0.

(*a*) One of the logical problems in dealing with type I and type II errors is that the null hypothesis is usually expressed in the negative form. To illustrate, suppose that a pharmaceutical house is investigating the effectiveness of a new compound for the treatment of

TABLE 13.3

Type of errors and correct decisions that can be made as a function of true status of safety of substance*

	H_0: Product is not harmful	**True status of H_0** — **Product is not harmful (H_0: True)**	**True status of H_0** — **Product is harmful (H_0: False)**
Decision	Fail to reject H_0 (treat as harmless)	Correct failure to reject The product may be used without jeopardizing public health.	Incorrect failure to reject (type II error) Harmful substance is treated as if harmless (i.e., safe). Public health is jeopardized (e.g., DDT).
Decision	Reject H_0 (treat as harmful)	Incorrect rejection (type I error) Harmless product is treated as harmful. Public is denied a possible treatment.	Correct rejection Product is banned. Public health is not jeopardized.

*H_0: Suspected substance is not harmful. H_1: Suspected substance is harmful. If we fail to reject H_0, we treat the substance as if it is not harmful (i.e., safe). If we reject H_0, we regard the substance as harmful (i.e., unsafe).

AIDS. The most likely null hypothesis is: H_0: The compound is ineffective. Rejection of H_0 involves a double negative. We do *not* accept the hypothesis that the compound is *in*effective. Two negatives make a positive. Thus, rejecting H_0 leads to the assertion that the compound is effective. Assuming that H_0 is true, show the consequences of a false rejection. Assuming H_0 is false, show the consequences of a failure to reject.

(*b*) A parole board must decide whether or not to parole a previously dangerous prisoner. What is H_0? Show the consequences of the two types of decisions that can be made when H_0 is true and when H_0 is false.

(*c*) A mental health team must decide whether the client's symptoms and complaints are "psychological" or "organic" before initiating treatment. The null hypothesis is that the symptoms are not organic. Show the consequences of falsely rejecting H_0 and failing to reject a false H_0.

ANSWERS

(*a*) If H_0 is falsely rejected (the compound is found to be effective when it is not), the compound is likely to be used and discovered to be ineffective only after the continued deterioration and death of a number of patients. Its use may also preclude the adoption of other treatment regimes that may be effective. Many medical procedures, standard at one time, were dropped only after repeated failures, such as purging and blood letting. Also, the literature of medicine and psychology abounds with examples of charlatans who took advantage of the misfortunes of others to promote useless compounds and/or procedures as safe and effective treatments of serious disorders.

On the other hand, if the compound is truly effective, the failure to reject H_0 may lead to the false belief that the compound is ineffective. Thus, research on a promising compound may be abandoned and patients may be denied effective treatments for life-threatening disorders.

(*b*) H_0: The prisoner is not dangerous. If H_0 is true and the prisoner is released, a correct decision has been made. If H_0 is true and a prisoner remains incarcerated (i.e., H_0 is rejected), society loses a possible productive individual (type I error). If H_0 is false and the prisoner is released, a dangerous person has been let loose in society (type II error). If H_0 is false and the prisoner is not released, a correct decision has been made.

(*c*) If H_0 is falsely rejected (i.e., the symptoms are not organic) and the client is treated exclusively for an organic disorder, the client is unlikely to show improvement (except possibly due to a placebo effect). If H_0 is falsely accepted (i.e., the disorder really is organic), the root cause of the disorder is unlikely to be touched by psychotherapy while an effective course of therapy may be neglected.

13.6
A FINAL WORD OF CAUTION

There is a very fine line between a significant and a nonsignificant finding. For example, if you tested a hypothesis at the 0.05 significance level and found that the probability of the results occurring by chance was 0.06, you would not reject the null hypothesis. If a friend tested the same hypothesis at the 0.05 level, using another sample from the population for which you tested your hypothesis, and found the probability of the results occurring by chance to be less than 0.05 (sometimes written as $P < 0.05$), he or she would reject the null hypothesis.

Consider another example in which you hypothesize that the mean age of two groups of people does not differ. The mean age of group 1 is 36 and the mean age of group 2 is 37. You test the hypothesis at the 0.01 level of significance and conclude they differ significantly. What you have found is that a mean difference of one year is statistically significant but also possibly trivial. Significance must be interpreted within meaningful context. Had you found a mean difference of one year between two groups of preschoolers, we would be far less likely to call the difference trivial. In the latter instance, the difference probably would be considered both practically and statistically significant because of the difference one year can have on the maturational process of a preschooler.

Finally, as you study the material in the following chapters, be aware that large samples are more likely to result in a statistically significant finding than small samples because of the influence of the sample size when testing hypotheses.

SUMMARY

In this chapter, we explained that one of the basic problems of inferential statistics involves estimating population parameters from sample statistics.

In inferential statistics, we are frequently called upon to compare our *obtained* values with *expected* values. The expected values are given by the appropriate sampling distribution, which is a theoretical probability distribution of the possible values of a sample statistic. We discussed how to use sampling distributions to interpret sample statistics.

We also learned that there are two mutually exclusive and exhaustive statistical hypotheses in every study: the null hypothesis (H_0) and the alternative hypothesis (H_1). If the outcome of a study is *rare* (i.e., it has some arbitrary but accepted probability value), we reject the null hypothesis and assert its alternative. If the event is not rare (i.e., the probability value is greater than what we have agreed upon as being significant), we fail to reject the null hypothesis. However, in no event are we permitted to claim that we have *proved* H_0.

The researcher is faced with two types of errors in establishing a cutoff probability value that he or she will accept as significant:

Type I: rejecting the null hypothesis when it is true.
Type II: failing to reject ("accepting") the null hypothesis when it is false.

The basic conservatism of scientists causes them to establish a low level of significance, resulting in a greater incidence of type II errors than of type I errors. Without replication of studies, we have no basis for knowing when a type I error has been made, and even with replication we cannot claim knowledge of absolute truth.

Finally, and perhaps most important, we have seen that scientific knowledge is probabilistic and not absolute.

TERMS TO REMEMBER

alpha (α) level The level of significance set by the researcher for inferring the operation of nonchance factors.

alternative hypothesis (H_1) A statement specifying that the population parameter is some value other than the one specified under the null hypothesis.

binomial distribution A model with known mathematical properties used to describe the distribution of discrete random variables.

directional hypothesis An alternative hypothesis (H_1) that states the direction in which the population parameter differs from the one specified under H_0.

nondirectional hypothesis An alternative hypothesis that states only that the population parameter is *different* from the one specified under H_0.

null hypothesis (H_0) A statement that specifies hypothesized values for one or more of the population parameters. It commonly, although not necessarily, involves the hypothesis of "no difference" and can be thought of as the hypothesis to be nullified by a statistical test.

one-tailed probability value A probability value obtained by examining only one tail of the distribution.

population A complete set of individuals, objects, or measurements having some common observable characteristic.

research hypothesis See *alternative hypothesis.*

sample A subset of a population or universe.

sampling distribution A theoretical probability distribution of a statistic that would result from drawing all possible samples of a given size from some population.

significance level A probability value that is considered so rare in the sampling distribution specified under the null hypothesis that one is willing to assert the operation of nonchance factors. Common significance levels are 0.05, 0.01, and 0.001.

two-tailed probability value A probability value that takes into account both tails of the distribution.

type I error (type α error) The rejection of H_0 when it is actually true. The probability of a type I error is given by the α-level.

type II error (type β error) The probability of accepting H_0 when it is actually false. The probability of a type II error is given by β. Research hypothesis see alternative hypothesis.

EXERCISES

1. Explain, in your own words, the nature of drawing inferences in social science. Be sure to specify the types of risks that are taken and the ways in which the researcher attempts to keep these risks within specifiable limits.

2. Give examples of studies in which:
(*a*) A type I error would be considered more serious than a type II error.
(*b*) A type II error would be considered more serious than a type I error.

3. After completing a study, Nelson W. concluded, "I have proved that no difference exists between the two groups." Criticize his conclusion according to the logic of drawing inferences in science.

4. Explain what is meant by the following statement: "It can be said that the purpose of any study is to provide the occasion for rejecting the null hypothesis."

5. Identify H_0 and H_1 in the following:
   (*a*) The population mean age is 31.
   (*b*) The proportion of Democrats in Watanabe County is not equal to 0.50.
   (*c*) The population mean age is not equal to 31.
   (*d*) The proportion of Democrats in Watanabe County is equal to 0.50.

6. Suppose that you are a welfare eligibility employee responsible for approving clients for welfare. What type of error would you be making if:
   (*a*) The hypothesis that a client is qualified for welfare (H_0) is erroneously accepted?
   (*b*) The hypothesis that a client is qualified for welfare is erroneously rejected?
   (*c*) The hypothesis that a client is qualified for welfare is correctly accepted?
   (*d*) The hypothesis that a client is qualified for welfare is correctly rejected?

7. A public opinion analyst recommends a political campaign strategy for a candidate on the basis of hypotheses she has formulated about future trends in the candidate's popularity. What type of error is she making if she makes the following predictions under the given conditions?
   (*a*) H_0: The candidate's popularity will remain stable.
   Fact: It goes up precipitously.
   (*b*) H_0: The candidate's popularity will remain stable.
   Fact: It falls abruptly.
   (*c*) H_0: The candidate's popularity will remain stable.
   Fact: It shows only minor fluctuation about a central value.

8. An investigator sets $\alpha = 0.01$ for rejection of H_0. She conducts a study in which she obtains a p value of 0.02 and fails to reject H_0. Is it more likely that she is accepting a true or a false H_0? Discuss.

9. A student has collected a mass of data to test 100 different null hypotheses. On completion of the analysis, he finds that 5 of the 100 comparisons yield p values ≤ 0.05. He concludes: "Using $\alpha = 0.05$, I have found a true difference in five of the comparisons." Comment.

10. Does the null hypothesis in a one-tailed test differ from the null hypothesis in a two-tailed test? Give an example.

11. Does the alternative hypothesis in a one-tailed test differ from the alternative hypothesis in a two-tailed test? Give an example.

12. Describe what happens to the distribution of sample means when you:
    (*a*) Increase the size of each sample.
    (*b*) Increase the number of samples.

13. Suppose you want to test the hypothesis that there is not an equal number of male and female executives in a given large company. The appropriate null hypothesis would be:
    (*a*) There are more female than male executives.
    (*b*) The numbers of male and female executives are equal.
    (*c*) There are more male than female executives.

14. Suppose a small groups expert finds a significant difference between the time it takes a group to reach a decision with three members and the time it takes to reach a decision with

seven members. Although $\alpha = 0.05$ or $\alpha = 0.01$ is traditionally applied as the level of significance, this choice is arbitrary. For each of the following levels of significance, state how many times in 1,000 this difference would be expected to occur by chance.

(*a*) 0.001 (*c*) 0.005 (*e*) 0.05 (*g*) 0.004
(*b*) 0.01 (*d*) 0.06 (*f*) 0.095 (*h*) 0.10

15. With reference to exercise 14, the adoption of which level of significance would be most likely to result in the following statements?
(*a*) There is a significant difference between the decision-making times of the two groups.
(*b*) It cannot be concluded that there is a significant difference between the decision-making times of the two groups.

16. Refer again to exercise 14. The adoption of which level of significance would be most likely to result in the following errors? Identify the type of each error.
(*a*) There is a significant difference between the decision-making times of the two groups.
Fact: There is no difference.
(*b*) It cannot be concluded that there is a significant difference between the decision-making times of the two groups.
Fact: There is a difference.

17. Refer to Table 13.2. Suppose you are working with a clinician engaged in the diagnosis of individuals seeking help for emotional disorders. Assume that a person has or does not have a disorder. Construct a table that describes the types of error that a clinician might make.

18. In view of the table you constructed in exercise 17, what are some circumstances in which a type II error may have more serious consequences than a type I error?

In exercises 19 through 23, H_0, α, obtained p, and true status of H_0 are given. State whether or not an error in statistical decision has been made. If so, state the type of error.

19. H_0: $\mu_1 \geq \mu_2$, $\alpha = .01$, one-tailed test. Obtained $p = .008$, one-tailed value (in predicted direction). Actual status of H_0: true.

20. H_0: $\mu_1 = \mu_2$, $\alpha = .05$, two-tailed test. Obtained $p = .08$, two-tailed value. Actual status of H_0: True.

21. H_0: $\mu_1 = \mu_2$, $\alpha = .05$, two-tailed test. Obtained $p = .06$, two-tailed value. Actual status of H_0: False.

22. H_0: $\mu_1 = \mu_2$, $\alpha = .05$, two-tailed test. Obtained $p = .03$, two-tailed value. Actual status of H_0: False.

23. H_0: $\mu_1 = \mu_2$, $\alpha = .01$, two-tailed test. Obtained $p = .005$, two-tailed value. Actual status of H_0: False.

CHAPTER 14

Statistical Inference and Continuous Variables

14.1 INTRODUCTION

You were first introduced to the concepts of *sample, population,* and *statistical inference* in Chapter 1. In the process of studying these terms, you learned that a statistic is a number that describes a characteristic of a sample and that a parameter describes a characteristic of a population. Furthermore, you learned that in many instances (but not always) the parameter is unknown and must be estimated from information about a sample drawn from the population. Statistical inference involves a number of procedures that allow us to estimate parameters from sample statistics.

Recall the example in Chapter 1 in which a poll was conducted for a U.S. senator to estimate the percentage of a state's registered voters who approve of nuclear energy as an energy source. A simple random sample was drawn from the list of the state's registered voters, and the percentage favoring nuclear energy was computed. How confident are we that the statistic we computed from the sample of voters provides a good estimate of the population parameter? Or, how do we test the hypothesis that a sample of prisoners drawn from a prison is representative of the entire prison population from which the sample was drawn? If we find that the Pearson correlation coefficient between educational attainment and income is +0.65 for those persons attending a school's 10-year reunion, can we be sure that if we contacted the population of all former graduates of the school the correlation would be +0.65? The statistical inference procedures to answer these and other questions are the topic of this chapter.

In Chapter 13, we illustrated the use of a sampling distribution for a discrete two-category nominal variable (the binomial distribution) and for all possible means when drawing samples of a fixed N from a population of four scores. Table 13.1 showed the frequency and probability distributions of means when all possible samples of a given size were selected from the population of four scores. Figure 14.1, which is based on Table 13.1, shows probability histograms, with superimposed curves obtained by connecting the midpoints of each bar.

Before proceeding with the discussion of sampling distributions for interval or ratio-scaled variables, examine Table 13.1 and Figure 14.1 carefully. See if you can answer the following questions:

1. How does the mean of each sampling distribution of means compare with the mean of the population from which the samples were drawn?

2. How does the variability or dispersion of the sample means change as we increase the sample size on which each sampling distribution is based?

Now compare your answers with ours:

1. The mean of the population of four scores is 4.5. The mean of each sampling distribution of means is 4.5. Thus, the mean of a sampling distribution of means is the same as the population mean from which the sample means were drawn. This statement is true for all sizes of N. In other words, the mean of the sampling distribution does not vary with the sample size.

2. As you increase the sample size, the dispersion of sample means becomes less. A greater proportion of means are close to the population mean, and extreme deviations are rarer as N becomes larger. To verify these statements, note the probability of obtaining a mean as rare as 0 or 9 at different sample sizes. Note also that the proportion of means in the middle of the distribution becomes greater as sample size is increased. For example, the proportion of means between and including 3 and 6 is 0.6250 when $N = 2$, 0.6874 when $N = 3$, and 0.7265 when $N = 4$.

Finally, in Chapter 13 we introduced the standard deviation of the sample means—which we will call the **standard error of the mean ($s_{\bar{X}}$)** from this point forward—shows that the dispersion of sample means decreases as sample size is increased.* The relationship between the sample size and the standard error of the

---

**Standard error of the mean* is a theoretical standard deviation of sample means, of a given sample size, drawn from some specified population. When based on a known population standard deviation, $\sigma_{\bar{X}} = \sigma/\sqrt{N}$; when estimated from a single sample, $s_{\bar{X}} = s/\sqrt{N-1}$.

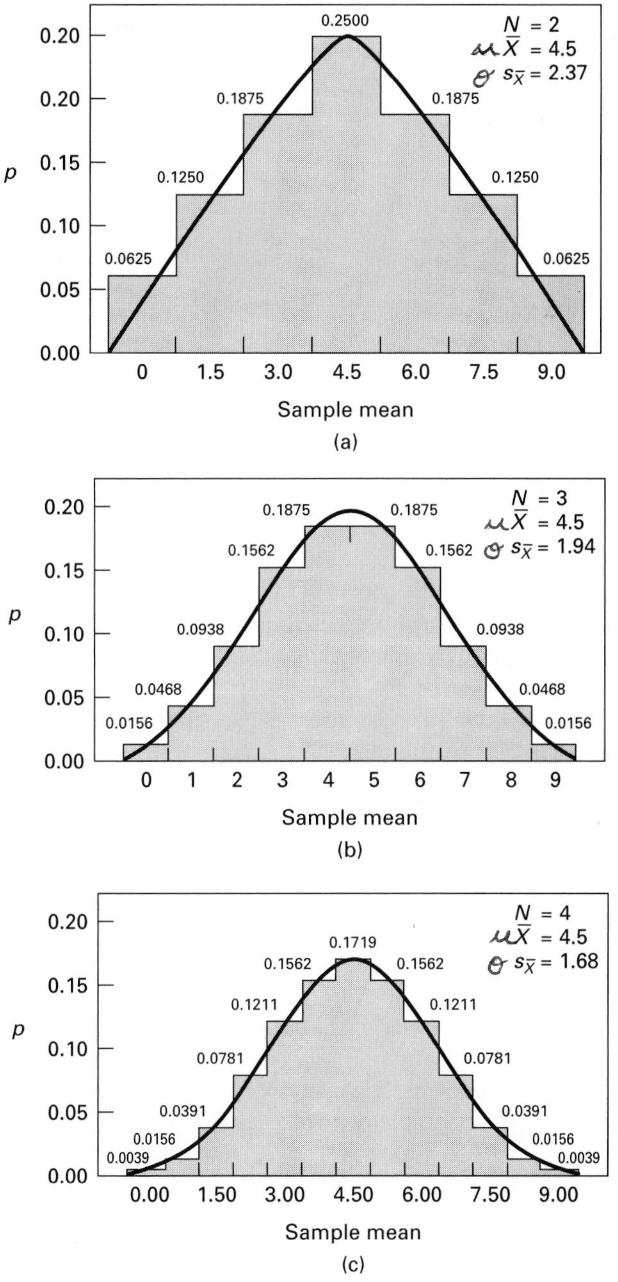

FIGURE 14.1

Probability histograms based on sampling distributions of means drawn, with replacement, from a population of four scores and sample sizes $N = 2$, $N = 3$, and $N = 4$

mean is specified by the **law of large numbers;** that is, as the sample size increases, the standard error of the mean decreases.

In forthcoming chapters, we will calculate many different standard errors in addition to the standard error of the mean. These standard errors represent bench-

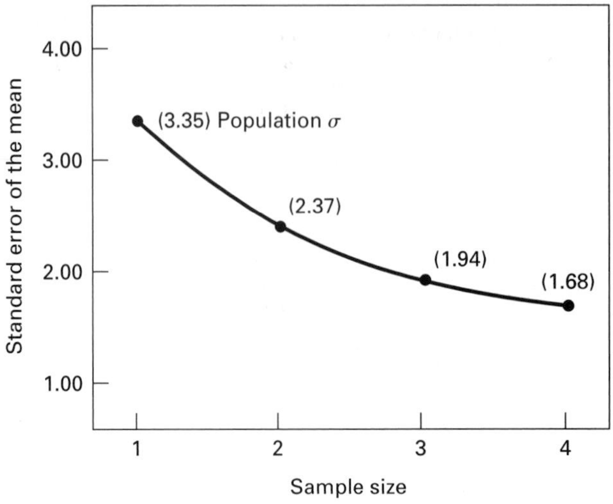

FIGURE 14.2
A line drawing showing the decreasing magnitude of $s_{\overline{X}}$ as the sample size increases
Shown are the population standard deviations of four scores and the standard error of the mean for the sampling distributions when $N = 2$, $N = 3$, and $N = 4$.

marks against which we evaluate differences in means, proportions, correlations, and so forth. The smaller the standard error is for a particular data set, the more precise our estimates will become. Thus, increasing sample size is one way of increasing the precision of our statistical decisions.

However, notice that the decrease in not linear. In going from $N = 1$ to $N = 2$ in Figure 14.2, the decrease in $s_{\overline{X}}$ equals $3.35 - 2.37 = 0.98$; from $N = 2$ to $N = 3$, the decrease is $2.37 - 1.94 = 0.43$; and from $N = 3$ to $N = 4$ the decrease is $1.94 - 1.68 = 0.26$. Thus, increasing the sample size is a curve of diminishing returns. A point will be reached when nonstatistical considerations (the difficulty of obtaining subjects, time, economics, and logistics) will outweigh the advantage of increasing *N*.

14.2 SAMPLING DISTRIBUTION OF THE MEAN

Let us imagine that we are conducting a sampling experiment in which we randomly draw (with replacement)* a sample of two scores from a population containing the values 2, 3, 4, 5, 6, 7, and 8 in which $\mu = 5.00$, and $\sigma = 0.99$ (see Table 14.1). For example, we might draw scores of 3 and 6. We calculate the sample mean and find $\overline{X} = 4.5$. Now suppose we continue to draw samples of $N = 2$ (e.g., we might draw scores of 2, 8; 3, 7; 4, 5; and 5, 6) until we obtain an infinitely large number of samples. If we calculate the sample mean for each sample drawn and treat each of these means as a raw score, we may set up a frequency distribution of these sample means.

* If the population is infinite or extremely large, the difference between sampling with or without replacement is negligible.

TABLE 14.1
An approximately normally distributed population with $\mu = 5.00$ and $\sigma = 0.99$

X	f	$p(X)$
2	4	0.004
3	54	0.054
4	242	0.242
5	400	0.400
6	242	0.242
7	54	0.054
8	4	0.004
	$N = 1{,}000$	$\Sigma\, p(X) = 1.000$

Let's repeat these procedures with increasingly larger sample sizes, for example, $N = 5$, $N = 15$. We now have three frequency distributions of sample means based on three different sample sizes.

Intuitively, what might we expect these distributions to look like? Since we are selecting at random from the population, we would expect the mean of the distribution of sample means to approximate the mean of the population.

How might the dispersion of these sample means compare with the variability in the original distribution of scores? In the original distribution, when $N = 1$ the probability of obtaining an extreme score such as 8 is $4/1{,}000$ or 0.004 (see Table 14.1). The probability of obtaining a sample *mean* equal to 8 when $N = 2$ (e.g., drawing scores of 8, 8) is equal to 0.004×0.004 or 0.000016. This is based on equation (12.9), which was stated earlier as:

> The probability of the simultaneous or successive occurrence of two events is the product of the separate probabilities of each event.

In other words, the probability of selecting a sample with an extreme *mean* is less than the probability of selecting a single score that is equally extreme. What if we increase our sample size to $N = 4$? The probability of obtaining results this extreme ($\overline{X} = 8$) is exceedingly small $(0.004)^4 = 0.0000000003$. Generalizing, the probability of drawing extreme values of the sample mean is less as N increases. Since the standard deviation is a direct function of the number of extreme scores (see Chapter 6), it follows that a distribution containing proportionately fewer extreme scores will have a lower standard deviation. Therefore, if we treat each of the sample means as a raw score and then calculate the standard deviation of the means around the population mean ($\sigma_{\overline{X}}$, referred to as the *standard error of the mean**), it is clear that,

* This notation represents the standard deviation of a sampling distribution of means. This is purely a theoretical notation since, with an infinite number of sample means, it is not possible to assign a specific value to the number of sample means involved.

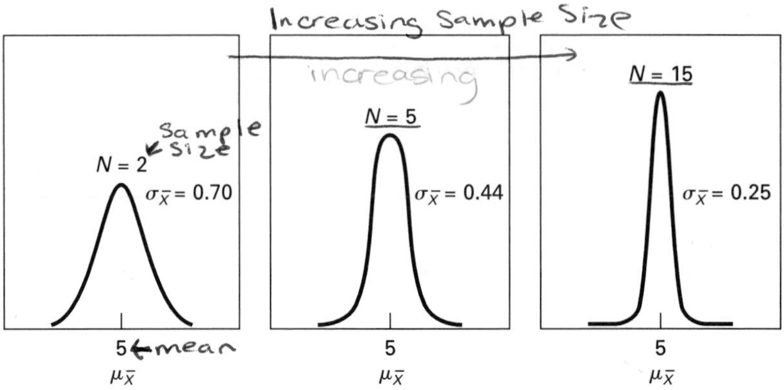

FIGURE 14.3
Frequency curves of sample means drawn from a population in which μ = 5.00 and σ = 0.99
mean variance

as the sample size increases, the variability of the sample means decreases. The standard error of the mean is interpreted in the same way that the standard deviation is interpreted with respect to the normal curve. Looking at the frequency curve in Figure 14.3 that is based on $N = 2$, we see that $\sigma_{\bar{X}} = 0.70$; therefore, we know that approximately 68% of the area under the curve lies within ± 0.70 units of the population mean ($\mu = 5$). Therefore, approximately 68% of the area lies between 4.30 $(5 - 0.70)$ and 5.70 $(5 + 0.70)$.

If the sampling experiment that was based on samples of $N = 2$, 5, and 15 was actually conducted, the frequency curves of sample means would be obtained as in Figure 14.3.

There are three important lessons that may be learned from a careful examination of Figure 14.3:

1. The distribution of sample means, drawn from a normally distributed population, is bell-shaped or "normal." Indeed, it can be shown that even if the underlying distribution is skewed, the distribution of sample means will tend to be normal.

2. The mean of the sample means ($\mu_{\bar{X}}$) is equal to the mean of the population (μ) from which these samples were drawn.

3. The distribution of sample means shows less and less dispersion as we increase the size of the sample. In Figure 14.3, for example, $\sigma_{\bar{X}} = 0.70$ for the curve based on $N = 2$, $\sigma_{\bar{X}} = 0.44$ for the curve based on $N = 5$, and $\sigma_{\bar{X}} = 0.25$ for the curve based on $N = 15$. This is an extremely important point in statistical inference, about which we soon will have a great deal more to say.

If we base our estimate of the population mean on a *single* sample drawn from the population, our approximation to the parameter is likely to be closer as we increase the size of the sample. In other words, if it is true that the dispersion of sample means decreases with increasing sample size, it also follows that the mean of any single sample is more likely to be closer to the mean of the population as the sample size increases (see Case Example 14.1 on page 330).

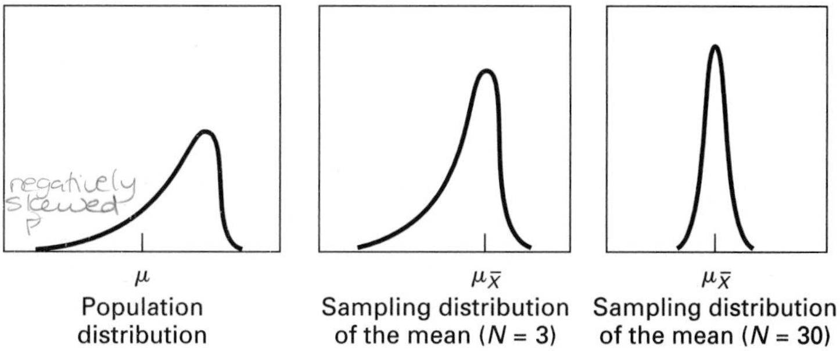

FIGURE 14.4
Effect of the central limit theorem

These three observations illustrate a rather startling theorem that is of fundamental importance in inferential statistics, that is, the **central limit theorem,** which states:

> If random samples of a fixed N are drawn from *any* population (regardless of the form of the population distribution), as N becomes larger, the distribution of sample means approaches normality, with the overall mean approaching μ, the variance of the sample means $\sigma_{\bar{X}}^2$ being equal to σ^2/N, and a standard error $\sigma_{\bar{X}}$ of $\sigma/\sqrt{N}$.

Stated symbolically:

$$\text{variance of sample means} = \sigma_{\bar{X}}^2 = \frac{\sigma^2}{N} \tag{14.1}$$

and

$$\text{standard error of the mean} = \sigma_{\bar{X}} = \frac{\sigma}{\sqrt{N}} \tag{14.2}$$

In essence, the central limit theorem allows us to understand that if the underlying population distribution is skewed, the distribution of sample means will approach the form of a normal curve as the sample size increases. The effect of the central limit theorem is shown in Figure 14.4.

14.3 TESTING STATISTICAL HYPOTHESES: POPULATION MEAN AND STANDARD DEVIATION KNOWN

14.3.1 Finding the Probability That a Sample Mean Will Fall within a Certain Range

Let's briefly examine some of the implications of the relationships we have just discussed. When μ and σ are *known* for a given population, it is possible to describe the form of the distribution of sample means that are drawn randomly from this population when N is large (regardless of the form of the original distribution). It will be a

A STATISTICAL SAMPLING EXPERIMENT

Most of us are aware of the information-processing revolution that was ushered in by the advent of the computer. Calculations that previously took hours, days, and even weeks to perform, are now completed within time frames that include microseconds and milliseconds. Moreover, as long as the data entry is accurate and the programming is flawless, the computer simply does not make errors. For this reason, the computer has become an indispensable element of human endeavor, be it in business, education, or the social sciences.

What is perhaps less appreciated by the general public is that the computer's capabilities are not limited to high-speed computation. For example, it may be used to conduct statistical experiments that illuminate some of the shadowy corners of statistical thinking.

In one statistical experiment, the author had a computer select samples from a population and calculate the mean, variance, and standard deviation of each sample. The samples were selected from a population that was distributed in a completely uniform fashion—numbers from 1 to 85. The mean and standard deviation of the population were 43 and 24.54, respectively. Two sets of 22 samples were selected from this population—one with $N = 5$ and the other with $N = 15$. The results are shown in Table 14.2.

TABLE 14.2
Sample means obtained by randomly selecting 22 samples of $N = 5$ and 22 samples of $N = 15$ from a uniform population of 85 integers from 1 through 85

$N = 5$		$N = 15$	
25.4	45.6	25.07	42.27
29.2	46.0	31.07	42.40
34.2	47.0	31.40	43.00
35.4	48.8	33.00	43.60
35.6	48.8	36.67	43.60
36.2	49.0	37.40	44.07
38.6	49.2	37.67	45.07
38.8	50.6	40.00	45.73
42.6	51.6	40.80	50.07
42.8	57.8	41.50	54.13
43.6	61.8	41.60	55.93
$\Sigma \bar{X} = 958.6$		$\Sigma \bar{X} = 906.05$	
$N_s = 22$		$N_s = 22$	
$\bar{X}_{\bar{X}} = 43.47$		$\bar{X}_{\bar{X}} = 41.18$	
$s_{\bar{X}} = 8.65$		$s_{\bar{X}} = 7.41$	

where N_s is the number of sample means, $\bar{X}_{\bar{X}}$ is the mean of the sample means, and $s_{\bar{X}}$ is the standard deviation of the sample means.

Before looking at the table, however, try answering the following questions: Do you expect that each sample mean will equal the population mean? What about the distribution of the means of each of the 22 samples based on N_s equal to 5 and 15, respectively? Do you expect the variability of the sample means to change in any systematic way as the sample size increases from $N = 1$ (the population distribution) to $N = 15$? What about the form of the distribution of the sample means? Does it mimic the population distribution of scores or does it tend to change with increasing sample size? Now look at Table 14.2 and Figure 14.5 and compare your answers with the results of the sampling experiment.

When examining Table 14.2 notice that:

1. Each sample mean is not equal to the population mean. However, the mean of the sample means is a pretty good approximation to the population mean. It can be shown that the means of randomly selected samples, averaged over all possible samples, will yield the population mean as the averaged value. The means are said to be unbiased estimators of the population mean. An **unbiased estimate of a parameter** is an estimate that equals, on the average, the value of the corresponding parameter.

2. The variability among the sample means decreases as the sample size increases. The range and standard deviation of the population were 84 and 24.54, respectively. When $N = 5$, the range and standard deviations of the sample means were 36.4 and 8.65, respectively. Finally, with $N = 15$, the range fell to 30.86, and the standard deviation declined to 7.41.

3. The form of the distribution of means also changed with increased sample size. Remember that the population distribution was absolutely flat, with all 85 values having an associated frequency of 1. Figure 14.5 presents grouped frequency histograms of the sample means. Note how nicely they illustrate the central limit theorem. With sample sizes as small as 15, the distribution of the sample means already begins to take on the classic bell-shaped form of the normal probability distribution.

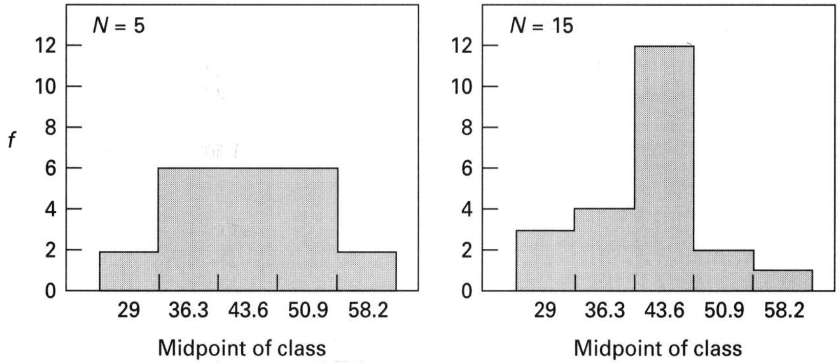

FIGURE 14.5

Grouped frequency histograms of sample means based on N_s equal to 5 and 15, respectively

The samples were randomly and independently selected from a population in which the measurements are uniformly distributed.

Source: Based on Runyon, "A Statistical Sampling Experiment" (1985).

normal distribution with a mean ($\mu_{\overline{X}}$) equal to μ and a standard error ($\sigma_{\overline{X}}$) equal to $\sigma/\sqrt{N}$. It now becomes possible to determine probability values in terms of areas under the normal curve. Thus, we may use the known relationships of the normal probability curve to determine the probabilities associated with any sample mean (of a given N) randomly drawn from this population.

We have already seen (Section 7.3) that any normally distributed variable may be transformed into the normally distributed z-scale. We have also seen (Section 12.6) that we may establish probability values in terms of the relationships between z-scores and areas under the normal curve. That is, for any given raw score value X with a certain proportion of area beyond it, there is a corresponding value of z with the same proportion of area beyond it. Similarly, for any given value of a sample mean $\overline{X}$ with a certain proportion of area beyond it, there is a corresponding value of z with the same proportion of area beyond it. Thus, assuming that the form of the distribution of sample means is normal, we may establish probability values in terms of the relationship between z-scores and areas under the normal curve.

To illustrate: Suppose we have a population of Baptist churches with a mean membership size of 250 ($\mu = 250$) and a standard deviation of 50 ($\sigma = 50$), from which we randomly draw 100 churches ($N = 100$). What is the probability that the sample mean ($\overline{X}$) will be equal to or greater than 255 members? Thus H_0: $\mu = \mu_0 = 250$. Figure 14.6 illustrates the area under the normal curve, which represents the probability that $\overline{X} \geq 255$.

The value of z corresponding to $\overline{X} = 255$ is obtained as follows:

$$z = \frac{\overline{X} - \mu_0}{\sigma_{\overline{X}}} \tag{14.3}$$

where μ_0 = value of the population mean under H_0:

$$\sigma_{\overline{X}} = \frac{\sigma}{\sqrt{N}} = \frac{50}{\sqrt{100}} = 5.00$$

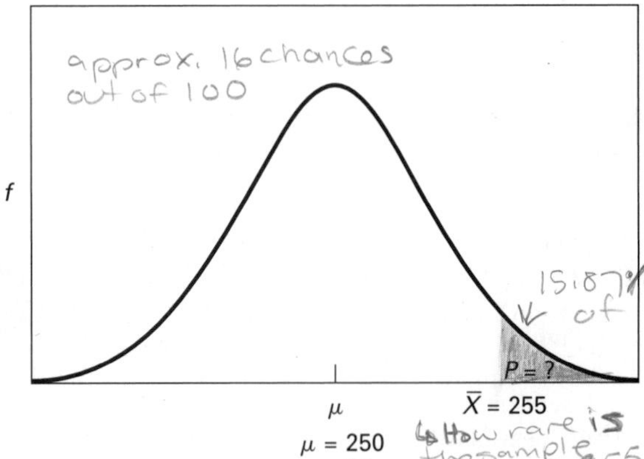

FIGURE 14.6
The probability of $\overline{X} \geq 255$ if $\mu = 250$ and $\sigma = 50$

and

$$z = \frac{255 - 250}{5.00} = 1.00$$

↑z-score

Looking up a z of 1.00 in column C (Table A of Appendix C), we find that 0.1587 (15.87%) of the sample means fall at or above $\overline{X} = 255$. Thus, there are approximately 16 chances in 100 of obtaining a sample mean equal to or greater than 255 from this population when $N = 100$. Note that $\sigma_{\overline{X}} = 5.00$ is considerably less than $\sigma = 50$. Why?

14.3.2 Testing Hypotheses about the Sample Mean

Now extend this logic to a situation in which we do not know from what population a sample is drawn. We suspect that it may have been selected from the preceding population of churches with $\mu = 250$ and $\sigma = 50$, but we are not certain. We wish to test the hypothesis that our sample mean was indeed selected from this population. Let's imagine that we had obtained $\overline{X} = 263$ for $N = 100$. Is it reasonable to assume that this sample was drawn from the preceding population of churches?

Setting up this problem in formal statistical terms involves the following six steps, which are common to all hypothesis-testing situations:

1. *Null hypothesis* (H_0). The mean membership size of the population (μ) from which the sample of churches was drawn equals 250; that is, $\mu = \mu_0 = 250$.

2. *Alternative hypothesis* (H_1). The mean of the population from which the sample was drawn does *not* equal 250; $\mu \neq \mu_0$. Note that H_1 is nondirectional; consequently, a two-tailed test of significance will be used.

3. *Statistical test.* The z statistic is used since σ is known.

4. *Significance level:* $\alpha = 0.01$. If the difference between the sample mean and the specified population mean is so extreme that its associated probability of occurrence under H_0 is equal to or less than 0.01, we reject H_0.

5. *Sampling distribution.* The normal probability curve.

α=0.01 6. *Critical region for rejection of* H_0: $|z| \geq 2.58$.* A **critical region** is the portion of the area under the curve that includes those values of a statistic that lead to rejection of the null hypothesis.

The critical region is chosen to correspond with the selected level of significance. Thus, for $\alpha = 0.01$, two-tailed test, the critical region is bounded by those values of $z_{0.01}$ that mark off a total of 1% of the area. Referring again to column C, Table A of Appendix C, we find that the area beyond a z of 2.58 is approximately 0.005. We

---

* Since $z_{0.01} = \pm 2.58$, $z \geq |z_{0.01}|$ is equivalent to stating $z \geq 2.58$ or $z \leq -2.58$. Recall that the symbol $|\;|$ indicates the absolute value of the number, that is, without regard to sign.

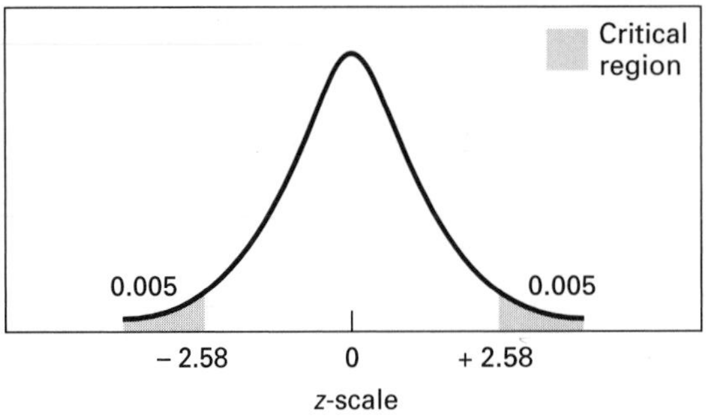

FIGURE 14.7
Critical region for rejection of H_0 when $\alpha = 0.01$, two-tailed test

double 0.005 to account for both tails of the distribution. Figure 14.7 depicts the critical region for rejection of H_0 when $\alpha = 0.01$, in a two-tailed test.

Therefore, to reject H_0 at the 0.01 level of significance, the absolute value of the obtained z must be equal to or greater than $|z_{0.01}|$ or 2.58. Similarly, if we are to be allowed to reject H_0 at the 0.5 level of significance, the absolute value of the obtained z must be equal to or greater than $|z_{0.05}|$ or 1.96.

In the present example using equation (14.3), the value of z corresponding to $\overline{X} = 263$ is:

$$z = \frac{\overline{X} - \mu_0}{\sigma_{\overline{X}}} = \frac{263 - 250}{5.00} = 2.60$$

Decision. Because the obtained z falls within the critical region—that is, $2.60 > z_{0.01}$—we may reject H_0 at the 0.01 level of significance. Thus, we conclude that the sample in question ($\overline{X} = 263$) was not drawn from the population in which $\mu = 250$ and $\sigma = 50$. Having established α at the 0.01 level of significance, we know that the probability of rejecting the null hypothesis when it is actually true (and therefore making a type I error) is 1 out of 100, a rare event that is very unlikely to occur by chance.

14.4 ESTIMATION OF PARAMETERS: POINT ESTIMATION

So far we have been concerned with testing hypotheses when the population parameters are known. However, we have taken some pains in this book to point out that population values are rarely known, particularly when the population is extremely large. Every 10 years, when the federal government undertakes that massive data collection effort called the census, we come close to knowing the parameters on the various questions. But knowledge of parameters is not the usual case. However, the fact that we do not know the population values does not prevent us from using the logic developed in Section 14.3.

Whenever we make inferences about population parameters from sample data, we compare our sample results with the expected results given by the appropriate sampling distribution. A hypothetical sampling distribution of sample means is associated with any sample mean. This distribution has a mean, $\mu_{\overline{X}}$, and a standard error,

$\sigma_{\overline{X}}$. So far, to obtain the values of $\mu_{\overline{X}}$ and $\sigma_{\overline{X}}$, we have required a knowledge of μ and σ. In the absence of knowledge concerning the exact values of the parameters, we are forced to estimate μ and σ from the statistics calculated from sample data. Since we rarely select more than one sample in actual practice, our estimates are generally based on the statistics calculated from a single sample. All such estimates of population parameters involving the use of single sample values (e.g., mean age of a sample) are known as **point estimation** which is defined as an estimate of a population parameter that involves a single sample value, selected by the criterion of "best estimate."

14.4.1 Estimating $\sigma_{\overline{X}}$ from Sample Data

You will recall that we previously defined the variance of a sample as:

$$s^2 = \frac{\Sigma(X - \overline{X})^2}{N}$$

in equation (6.3). We obtained the standard deviation s by finding the square root of this value. These definitions are perfectly appropriate as long as we are interested only in *describing* the variability of a sample. However, when our interest shifts to *estimating* the population variance from a sample value, we find that the preceding definition is inadequate since $\Sigma(X - \overline{X})^2/N$ tends, on the average, to *underestimate* the population variance. In other words, it provides a biased estimate of the population variance, whereas an unbiased estimate is required.

A **biased estimate of a parameter** is an estimate that does not equal, on the average, the value of the parameter.

We define an **unbiased estimate of a parameter** as an estimate that equals, on the average, the value of the parameter; that is, when we state that a statistic is an unbiased estimate of a parameter, the mean of the distribution of an extremely large number of sample statistics drawn from a given population tends to center on the corresponding value of the parameter. We demonstrate in Box 14.1 that an unbiased estimate of the population variance may be obtained by dividing the sum of squares by $N - 1$. We will use the symbol $\hat{s}^2$ to represent a sample variance providing an *unbiased estimate of the population variance,* and $\hat{s}$ to represent a sample standard deviation based on the unbiased variance estimate. Thus:

$$\text{unbiased estimate of } \sigma^2 = \hat{s}^2 = \frac{\Sigma(X - \overline{X})^2}{N - 1} \qquad (14.4)$$

and

$$\text{estimated } \sigma = \hat{s} = \sqrt{\hat{s}^2} \qquad (14.5)$$

We are now able to estimate $\sigma^2_{\overline{X}}$ and $\sigma_{\overline{X}}$ from sample data. We will use the symbols $s^2_{\overline{X}}$ and $s_{\overline{X}}$ to refer to the estimated variance and standard error of the mean, respectively. Since we do not know σ^2, we accept the unbiased variance estimate $\hat{s}^2$ as the best estimate we have of the population variance.

BOX 14.1

UNBIASED ESTIMATE OF THE POPULATION VARIANCE

Throughout this book, we have turned to a sampling experiment whenever we wanted to illustrate a concept of fundamental importance in statistical analysis. Let's take a look at the denominator of the variance equation, and show that $N - 1$ in the denominator provides an unbiased estimate of the population variance, whereas N in the denominator underestimates the population variance.

Let's imagine the following sampling experiment. You place the following population of four scores in a hat: 1, 2, 3, and 4. The mean of this population is 2.5 and the variance is 1.25. You select, with replacement, all possible samples of $N = 2$ and calculate the variance of each sample, using N and $N - 1$ in the denominator. Just as we previously placed the mean of each sample in the cell corresponding to both draws, we now place the *variance* of each sample in the appropriate cell.

First, let's do this using N in the denominator when calculating each sample variance. Use equation (6.3) and confirm that the variance for a sample draw of 1 and 1 is 0.00 and that the variance for a sample draw of 0 and 4 is 2.25.

Now let's construct a frequency distribution of these variances and calculate the mean variance.

The mean variance is found to be $10/16 = 0.625$. Recall that the variance of the population is 1.25. In this sampling experiment, using N in the denominator of the variance equation, the mean variance of all possible samples of $N = 2$ underestimates the population variance. Generalizing, sample variances that use N in the denominator provide a biased estimate of the population variance.

Variance of each sample when using N in the denominator ($N = 2$)

		First draw			
		1	**2**	**3**	**4**
Second draw	1	0.00	0.25	1.00	2.25
	2	0.25	0.00	0.25	1.00
	3	1.00	0.25	0.00	0.25
	4	2.25	1.00	0.25	0.00

s^2	f	fs^2
2.25	2	4.50
1.00	4	4.00
0.25	6	1.50
0.00	4	0.00
	$\Sigma f = 16$	$\Sigma fs^2 = 10.00$

Variance of each sample when using $N - 1$ in the denominator ($N = 2$)

		First draw			
		1	**2**	**3**	**4**
Second draw	1	0.00	0.50	2.00	4.50
	2	0.50	0.00	0.50	2.00
	3	2.00	0.50	0.00	0.50
	4	4.50	2.00	0.50	0.00

s^2	f	fs^2
4.50	2	9.00
2.00	4	8.00
0.50	6	3.00
0.00	4	0.00
	$\Sigma f = 16$	$\Sigma fs^2 = 20.00$

Now let's repeat the same procedures, using $N - 1$ to calculate the variance of each sample. The frequency distribution and mean of the sample variances are shown in the bottom table.

Now the mean variance is 20/16 = 1.25. Note that this is identical to the original variance of the population. Thus, using $N - 1$ in the denominator provides an unbiased estimate of the population variance since the variability of a sample tends not to be as that large as that of a population. Using $N - 1$ in the denominator serves as a correction factor.

Thus, the equation for determining the variance of the mean from sample data is:

$$\text{estimated } \sigma_{\bar{X}}^2 = s_{\bar{X}}^2 = \frac{\hat{s}^2}{N} \tag{14.6}$$

We estimate the standard error of the mean by finding the square root of this value:

$$\text{estimated } \sigma_{\bar{X}} = s_{\bar{X}} = \sqrt{\frac{\hat{s}^2}{N}} = \frac{\hat{s}}{\sqrt{N}} \tag{14.7}$$

If the sample variance (not the unbiased estimate) is used, we may estimate $\sigma_{\bar{X}}$ as:

$$\text{estimated } \sigma_{\bar{X}} = s_{\bar{X}} = \frac{s}{\sqrt{N-1}} = \sqrt{\frac{\Sigma(X-\bar{X})^2}{N(N-1)}} \tag{14.8}$$

Equation (14.8) is the one most frequently used in the social sciences to estimate the standard error of the mean. We will follow this practice.

Before proceeding further, let's review some of the symbols we have been discussing. Table 14.3 shows the various symbols for the means, variances, and standard deviations, depending on whether we are dealing with population parameters, unbiased population estimators, or sample statistics.

TABLE 14.3
Review of symbols

	Population parameters (theoretical)	Parameters of sampling distribution of mean (theoretical)	Unbiased population estimators for sampling distribution of mean (empirical)	Sample statistics (empirical)
Means	μ, μ_0	$\mu_{\bar{X}}$	$\bar{X}$	$\bar{X}$
Variances	σ^2	$\sigma_{\bar{X}}^2$	$\hat{s}^2$, $s_{\bar{X}}^2$	s^2
Standard deviations	σ	$\sigma_{\bar{X}}$	$\hat{s}$, $s_{\bar{X}}$	s

14.5 TESTING STATISTICAL HYPOTHESES WITH UNKNOWN PARAMETERS: STUDENT'S *t*

We previously pointed out that when the parameters of a population are known, it is possible to describe the form of the sampling distribution of sample means. It will be a normal distribution with $\sigma_{\overline{X}}$ equal to $\sigma/\sqrt{N}$. By employing the relationship between the z-scale and the normal distribution, we were able to test hypotheses using:

$$z = \frac{(\overline{X} - \mu_0)}{\sigma_{\overline{X}}}$$

as a test statistic. When σ is not known, we are forced to estimate its value from sample data. Consequently, estimated $\sigma_{\overline{X}}$ (i.e., $s_{\overline{X}}$) must be based on the estimated σ, that is, $\hat{s}$:

$$s_{\overline{X}} = \frac{\hat{s}}{\sqrt{N}}$$

Now, if substituting $\hat{s}$ for σ provided a reasonably good approximation to the sampling distribution of means, we could continue to use z as our test statistic and the normal curve as the model for our sampling distribution. However, this is not the case. At the turn of the century, William Gosset, a statistician who published under the pseudonym of Student, noted that the approximation of $\hat{s}$ to σ is poor, particularly for small samples. This failure of approximation is due to the fact that, with small samples, $\hat{s}$ will tend to underestimate σ more than one-half of the time. Compared to the normal distribution, the statistic:

$$\frac{\overline{X} - \mu_0}{\hat{s}/\sqrt{N}}$$

will tend to be flatter in the central region and spread out more in extreme regions (see Figure 14.8).

Gosset's major contribution to statistics consisted of his description of a distribution, or rather, a family of distributions, that permits the testing of hypotheses with samples drawn from normally distributed populations when σ is not known. These distributions are referred to variously as the *t-distributions* or *Student's t*. The ratio used in the testing of hypotheses is known as the *t-ratio:*

$$t = \frac{\overline{X} - \mu_0}{s_{\overline{X}}} \qquad (14.9)$$

where μ_0 is the value of the population mean under H_0.

We can now formally define ***t*-distributions** (or **Student's *t***) as theoretical symmetrical sampling distributions with a mean of zero and a standard deviation that becomes smaller as *degree of freedom* (*df*) increase. They are employed in relation to the ***t*-ratio,** which can be defined as a test statistic for determining the significance of a difference between means (two-sample case), or for testing the hypothesis that a given sample mean was drawn from a population with the mean specified under the null hypothesis (one-sample case). The t-ratio is employed when the population standard deviation (or standard deviations) is not known.

The t-statistic is similar in many respects to the z-statistic. Both statistics are expressed as the deviation of a sample mean from a population mean (known or hypothesized) in terms of the standard error of the mean. By reference to the appropriate sampling distribution, we may express this deviation in terms of probability. When the z-statistic is used, the standard normal curve is the appropriate sampling distribution. For the t-statistic there is a family of distributions that varies as a function of degrees of freedom.

The term **degrees of freedom (df)** refers to the number of values that are free to vary after we have placed certain restrictions on our data. To illustrate, let's imagine that we have four numbers: 18, 23, 27, and 32. The sum is 100 and the mean is $\overline{X} = 100/4 = 25$. Recall that if we subtract the mean from each score, we should obtain a set of four deviations that add up to zero. Thus:

$$(18 - 25) + (23 - 25) + (27 - 25) + (32 - 25)$$
$$= (-7) + (-2) + 2 + 7 = 0$$

Note also that the four deviations are not independent. Once we have imposed the restriction that the deviations are taken from the mean, the values of only three deviations are free to vary. As soon as three deviations are known, the fourth is completely determined. Stated another way, the values of only three deviations are free to vary. For example, if we know three deviations to be -7, -2, and $+2$, we may calculate the unknown deviation by use of the equality:

$$(X_1 - \overline{X}) + (X_2 - \overline{X}) + (X_3 - \overline{X}) + (X_4 - \overline{X}) = 0$$

Therefore:

$$(X_4 - \overline{X}) = 0 - [(X_1 - \overline{X}) + (X_2 - \overline{X}) + (X_3 - \overline{X})]$$

In the present example, we find the fourth value to be $+7$.

$$(X_4 - \overline{X}) = 0 - [(-7) + (-2) + (2)]$$
$$= 0 + 7 + 2 - 2 = +7$$

To generalize: For any given sample on which we have placed a single restriction, the number of degrees of freedom is $N - 1$. In the preceding example, $N = 4$; therefore, degrees of freedom are $4 - 1 = 3$.

Note that when $s/\sqrt{N - 1}$ [equation (14.8)] is used to obtain $s_{\overline{X}}$, the quantity under the square root sign $(N - 1)$ is the degrees of freedom.

We noted earlier that the use of Student's t-ratio depends on the assumption that the underlying population is normally distributed. This requirement stems from a unique property of normal distributions:

> Given that observations are independent and random, the sample means and sample variances are independent only when the population is normally distributed.

As we previously pointed out, two scores or statistics are independent only when the values of one do not depend on the values of the other and vice versa. Tests of significance of means, which are discussed in the following sections, demand that the means and variances be independent of one another. They cannot vary together in some systematic way—for example, with the variances becoming larger as the means become larger. If they do vary in a systematic way, the underlying population cannot be normal and tests of significance based on the assumption of normality may be invalid. It is for this reason that the assumption of normality underlies the use of the t-ratio, which is referred to as a **robust test,** meaning that statistical inferences are likely to be valid even when there are fairly large departures from normality in the population distribution. This robustness is another consequence of the central limit theorem. If we have serious doubts concerning the normality of the population distribution, it is wise to increase the N in each sample.

14.5.1 Characteristics of t-Distributions

Let's compare the characteristics of the t-distributions with the already familiar standard normal curve. First, both distributions are symmetrical about a mean of zero. Therefore, the proportion of area beyond a particular positive t-value is equal to the proportion of area below the corresponding negative t.

Second, the t-distributions are more spread out than the normal curve. Consequently, the proportion of area beyond a specific value of t is *greater* than the proportion of area beyond the corresponding value of z. However, as sample size increases—and therefore the greater are the degrees of freedom—the more the t-distributions resemble the standard normal curve. To see the contrast between the t-distributions and the normal curve, we have reproduced three curves in Figure 14.8: the sampling distributions of t when degrees of freedom $= 3$, degrees of freedom $= 10$, and the normal curve.

Figure 14.8 permits several interesting observations. We have already seen that with the standard normal curve, $|z| \geq 1.96$ defines the region of rejection at the 0.05 level of significance. However, when degrees of freedom equal 3, $|t| \geq 1.96$ includes approximately 15% of the total area. Consequently, if we were to use the normal curve for testing hypotheses when N is small (therefore, degrees of freedom are small) and σ is unknown, we would be in serious danger of making a type I error; that is, rejecting H_0 when it is true. A much larger value of t is required to mark the bounds of the critical region of rejection. Indeed, when degrees of freedom equal 3, the absolute value of the obtained t must be equal to or greater than 3.18 to reject H_0 at the 0.05 level of significance (two-tailed test). However, as degrees of freedom increase, the differences in the proportions of area under the normal curve and the t-distributions become negligible.

In contrast to our use of the normal curve, the tabled values for t (see Table C in Appendix C) are **critical values,** that is, those values that bound the critical rejection regions corresponding to varying levels of significance. Thus, in using the table for the distributions of t, we locate the appropriate number of degrees of freedom in the left-hand column and then find the column corresponding to the chosen α. The tabled

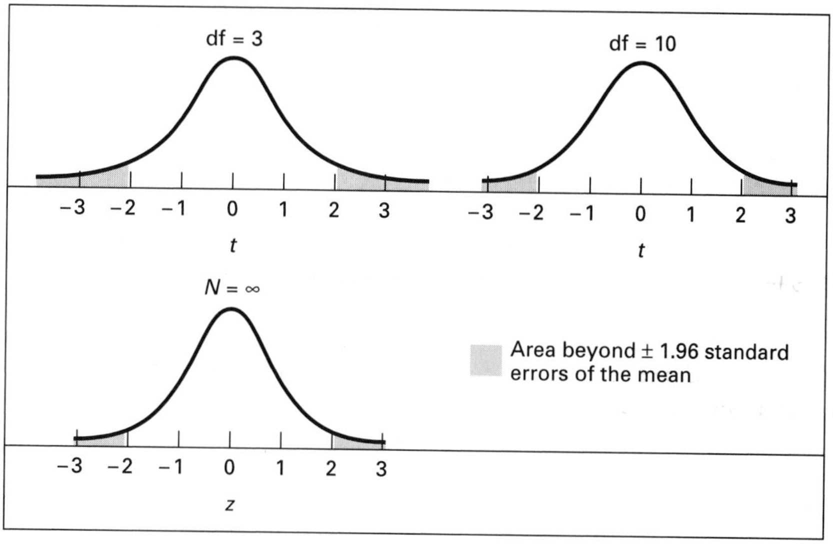

FIGURE 14.8
Sampling distributions of $t = (\overline{X} - \mu_0)/s_{\overline{X}}$ when df = 3, and 10, compared to the standard normal curve

values represent the t-ratio required for significance. If the absolute value of our obtained t-ratio equals or exceeds this tabled value, we may reject H_0.

14.5.2 Illustrative Problem: Student's *t*

Let's now examine an example involving a small sample. A group of 17 male prisoners in federal, maximum-security penitentiaries was randomly selected from the federal prison population to participate in a new rehabilitation program. The 17 prisoners had a mean score on a "dangerousness to society" index (low score = not dangerous, high score = extremely dangerous) of 84 and a standard deviation of 16. Therefore, we know that:

$$\overline{X} = 84, \qquad s = 16, \qquad N = 17$$

Can we assume that the 17 prisoners who were randomly chosen to participate in the rehabilitation program are representative of a prison population in which $\mu = 78$?

Let's set up this problem in more formal statistical terms:

1. *Null hypothesis* (H_0): The mean of the population from which the sample was drawn equals 78 ($\mu = \mu_0 = 78$).
2. *Alternative hypothesis* (H_1): The mean of the population from which the sample was drawn does not equal 78 ($\mu \neq \mu_0$).
3. *Statistical test:* The Student's t-ratio is chosen because we are dealing with a normally distributed variable in which σ is unknown.

4. *Significance level:* $\sigma = 0.05$.

5. *Sampling distribution:* The sampling distribution is the Student's t-distribution with df = 16. (*Note*: df = $N - 1$.)

6. *Critical region:* $|t_{0.05}| \geq 2.12$. Since H_1 is nondirectional, the critical region consists of all values of $t \geq 2.12$ and $t \leq -2.12$. In the present example, the value of t corresponding to $\overline{X} = 84$ is:

$$t = \frac{\overline{X} - \mu_0}{s_{\overline{X}}} = \frac{84 - 78}{16/\sqrt{16}} = 1.50$$

where equation (14.8) allows us to calculate $s_{\overline{X}}$, the estimated error:

$$s_{\overline{X}} = \frac{s}{\sqrt{N - 1}}$$

Decision. Since the obtained t does not fall within the critical region (i.e., $1.50 < t_{0.05}$), we fail to reject H_0 (see Figure 14.9). In other words, we have statistical justification to believe that the sample of 17 prisoners is (in terms of their dangerousness to society) representative of the federal prison population; therefore, the rehabilitation program can proceed with the sample of 17 prisoners. Had our decision been that the sample was unrepresentative, a new sample would have to be drawn and tested for representativeness before continuing with the program. Why? We wish to increase the likelihood that if the program is successful, it was not successful due to a unique sample. Once the program's success is established with a representative sample of prisoners, it should be effective for the prison population.

14.6 ESTIMATION OF PARAMETERS: INTERVAL ESTIMATION

We have repeatedly pointed out that one of the basic problems in inferential statistics is the estimation of the parameters of a population from statistics calculated from a sample. This problem, in turn, involves two subproblems: (1) point estimation and (2) interval estimation. Recall that we defined *point estimation* as an estimate of a

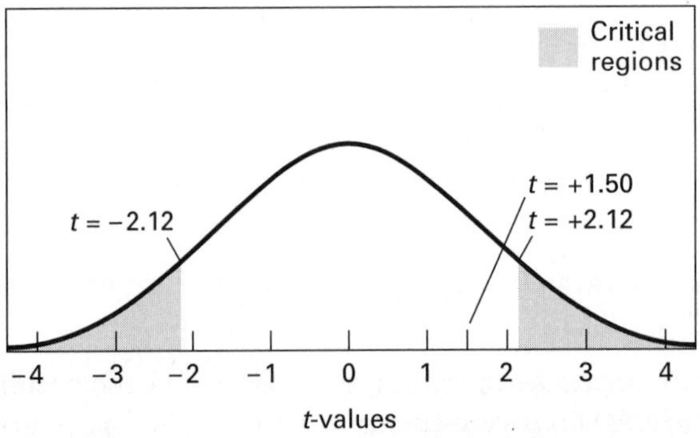

FIGURE 14.9
Sampling distribution of t and critical regions for a two-tailed test, $t_{0.05}$, df = 16

population parameter that involves a single value, selected by the criterion of "best estimate." **Interval estimation** is the determination of an interval within which the population parameter is presumed to fall.

In Section 14.4, you learned that when we estimate parameters using single sample values, these estimates are known as point estimates. A single sample value drawn from a population provides an estimate of the population parameter. But how good an estimate is it? If a population mean were known to be 100, would a sample mean of 60 constitute a good estimate? How about a sample mean of 130, 105, 98, or 99.4? Under what conditions do we consider an estimate good? Since we know that the population parameters are virtually never known and that we generally use samples to estimate these parameters, is there any way to determine the amount of error we are likely to make? The answer to this question is no. It is possible, however, not only to estimate the population parameter (*point estimation*), but also to state a range of values that we are confident includes or encompasses the population parameter (*interval estimation*). Moreover, we may express our confidence in terms of probabilities, and as a result social scientists generally prefer interval estimates over point estimates.

Have you ever seen a weight-guesser at a carnival who promises to guess your correct weight to within a specified number of pounds? Suppose you are that weight-guesser who is trying to estimate the weight of a man, basing the estimate on physical inspection.

Let's assume that you are unable to place him on a scale, and that you cannot ask him his weight. This problem is similar to many you have faced throughout this text. You cannot know the population value (the man's true weight), and hence you are forced to estimate it. Let's say that you have the impression that he weighs about 200 pounds. If you are asked, "How confident are you that he weighs *exactly* 200 pounds?" you would probably reply, "I doubt that he weighs exactly 200 pounds. If he does, you can credit me with a fantastically lucky guess. However, I feel reasonably confident that he weighs between 190 and 210 pounds." In doing this, you have stated the interval within which you feel confident that the true weight falls. After a moment's reflection, you might hedge slightly, "Well, he is almost certainly between 180 and 220 pounds. In any event, I feel perfectly confident that his weight is included in the interval between 170 and 230 pounds." Note that the greater the size of the interval, the greater is your feeling of certainty that the true value is encompassed between these limits. Note also that in stating these confidence limits, you are, in effect, making two statements: (1) You are stating the limits that include the man's weight and (2) you are rejecting the possibility that his weight is not included in these limits. Thus, if someone asks, "Is it conceivable that our subject weighs as much as 240 pounds or as little as 160 pounds?" your reply would be negative.

14.7 CONFIDENCE INTERVALS AND CONFIDENCE LIMITS

In the preceding example, we were in a sense concerning ourselves with the problem of estimating *confidence limits*. In effect, we were attempting to determine the interval within which any hypotheses concerning the weight of the man might be considered tenable and outside which any hypotheses would be considered untenable. The interval within which we consider hypotheses tenable is known as the **confidence interval,** and the limits defining the interval are referred to as **confidence limits.**

Let's look at a sample problem and apply our statistical concepts to the estimation of confidence levels. A local health systems agency is trying to decide on the feasibility of establishing a health care clinic in a particular neighborhood. In part, the decision will depend on estimates of the health care needs of the neighborhood. A limited budget does not allow assessing the needs of all the residents in the neighborhood. Consequently, we must be content with selecting a simple random sample from the neighborhood and basing our estimates on the sample. The medical team screens a simple random sample of 26 residents; each resident is assigned an overall health care needs score. We obtain the following results:

$$\overline{X} = 108, \qquad s = 15, \qquad N = 26$$

Our best estimate of the population mean (i.e., the mean health care needs score within the neighborhood) is 108. However, even though our sample statistics provide our best estimates of population values, we recognize that such estimates are subject to error. As with the weight problem, we would be very lucky if the mean of the neighborhood were actually 108. On the other hand, if we use truly random selection procedures, we have a right to believe that our sample value is fairly close to the population mean. The critical question becomes, "What confidence limits are likely to include the value of the population mean (μ) in the neighborhood?"

We have seen that the mean of the sampling distribution of sample means ($\mu_{\overline{X}}$) is equal to the mean of the population. We have also seen that since we can determine for any given N how far sample means are likely to deviate from any given or hypothesized value of μ, we may determine the likelihood that a particular $\overline{X}$ could have been drawn from a population with a mean of μ_0, where μ_0 represents the value of the population mean under H_0. Now, since we do not know the value of the population mean, we are free to hypothesize *any* value we desire.

It should be clear that we could consider an unlimited number of hypotheses concerning the population mean and subsequently reject them, or fail to reject them, on the basis of the size of the t-ratios. This problem requires that we use a t-ratio because of the small sample size and unknown population parameter. Use of t values to estimate confidence intervals will be presented in the following example.

In the present problem, let's select a number of hypothetical population means. We will use the 0.05 level of significance (two-tailed test) and test the hypothesis that $\mu_0 = 98$. The value of t corresponding to $\overline{X} = 108$ is 3.333:

$$t = \frac{\overline{X} - \mu_0}{s_{\overline{X}}} = \frac{108 - 98}{15/\sqrt{25}} = \frac{10}{3} = 3.333$$

In Table C (Appendix C), we find that $t_{0.05}$ for 25 df is 2.060. Since our obtained t is greater than this critical value, we reject the hypothesis that $\mu_0 = 98$. In other words, it is unlikely that $\overline{X} = 108$ was drawn from a population with a mean of 98.

Our next hypothesis is that $\mu_0 = 100$, which gives a t of:

$$t = \frac{108 - 100}{15/\sqrt{25}} = 2.667$$

Since $2.667 > t_{0.05}$ (or 2.060), we may reject the hypothesis that the population mean is 100.

If we hypothesize $\mu_0 = 102$, the resulting t-ratio of 2.000 is less than $t_{0.05}$. Consequently, we may consider the hypothesis that $\mu_0 = 102$ is tenable. Similarly, if we obtained the appropriate t-ratios, we would find that the hypothesis $\mu_0 = 114$ is tenable, whereas hypotheses of values greater than 114 are untenable. Thus, $\overline{X} = 108$ was probably drawn from a population whose mean falls in the interval 102–114 (note that these limits, 102 and 114, represent approximate limits, that is, the closest *integers*). The hypothesis that $\overline{X} = 108$ was drawn from a population with $\mu < 102$ or $\mu > 114$ may be rejected at the 0.05 level of significance. The interval within which the population mean probably lies is the confidence interval. We refer to the limits of this interval as the confidence limits. Since we have been using $\alpha = 0.05$, we call it the 95% confidence interval. Similarly, if we used $\alpha = 0.01$, we could obtain the 99% confidence interval.

Now that we have considered the hypothesis-testing approach to confidence intervals, we will calculate the exact limits of the 95% confidence interval directly. It is not necessary to perform all of these previous calculations to establish the confidence limits.

To determine the upper limit for the 95% confidence interval, we have:

$$\text{upper limit } \mu_0 = \overline{X} + (t_{0.05})(s_{\overline{X}}) \tag{14.10}$$

We know that $\overline{X} = 108$ and that $s_{\overline{X}} = 15/\sqrt{25} = 3$.* Table C (in Appendix C) shows that $t_{0.05}$ with 25 degrees of freedom equals 2.060. Multiplying the critical value of t times $s_{\overline{X}}$ (the estimated standard error) provides us with the number of units we must move to the right of the mean to encompass one-half of the 95% confidence interval. The resulting value is the upper limit of the 95% confidence interval.

Applying equation (14.10), we find that the upper 95% confidence limit in the preceding problem is:

$$\begin{aligned}\text{upper limit } \mu_0 &= 108 + (2.060)(3.0)\\ &= 108 + 6.18 = 114.18\end{aligned}$$

To compute the lower limit, we apply equation (14.11):

$$\text{lower limit } \mu_0 = \overline{X} - (t_{0.05})(s_{\overline{X}}) \tag{14.11}$$

Using equation (14.11), we find that the lower confidence limit is:

$$\begin{aligned}\text{lower limit } \mu_0 &= 108 - (2.060)(3.0)\\ &= 108 - 6.18 = 101.82\end{aligned}$$

*Applying equation (14.8).

Note that to compute the lower confidence limit, we *subtracted* the same value (6.18) from the sample mean of 108 that we *added* to the sample mean when determining the upper limit. Hence, the sample mean is equidistant from the upper and lower limits.

You should also note that equations (14.10) and (14.11) are derived algebraically from equation (14.9):

$$t_{0.05} = \frac{\overline{X} - \mu_0}{s_{\overline{X}}}$$

Therefore:

$$\mu_0 = \overline{X} + (t_{0.05})(s_{\overline{X}})$$

Having established the lower and the upper limits as 101.82 and 114.18, respectively, we may now conclude: On the basis of our obtained mean and standard deviation, which were computed from scores drawn from a population in which the true mean is unknown, we assert that the population mean probably falls within the interval that we have established.

If we wish to compute the 99% confidence interval, it is necessary to substitute $t_{0.01}$ in the preceding equation. To compute the upper limit of the 99% confidence interval, we obtain:

$$108 + (2.787)(3.0) = 108 + 8.36 = 116.36$$

To compute the lower limit, we have:

$$108 - (2.787)(3.0) = 108 - 8.36 = 99.64$$

Notice that the 99% confidence interval is wider than the 95% confidence interval by comparing the confidence limits in the two examples.

Some words of caution in interpreting the confidence interval: In establishing the interval within which we believe the population mean falls, we have not established any probability that our obtained mean is correct. In other words, we cannot claim that the chances are 95 in 100 (or 99 in 100) that the population mean is 108. Our statements are valid only with respect to the interval and not to any particular value of the sample mean. In addition, since the population mean is a fixed value and does not have a distribution, our probability statements never refer to μ. The probability we assert is about the interval; that is, the probability that the interval contains μ.

Finally, when we have established the 95% confidence interval of the mean, we are not stating that the probability is 0.95 that the particular interval we have calculated contains the population mean. It should be clear that if we were to select repeated samples from a population, both the sample means and the sample standard deviations would differ from sample to sample. Consequently, our estimates of the confidence interval also would vary from sample to sample. When we have established the 95% confidence interval of the population mean, we are stating that if repeated samples of a given size are drawn from the population, 95% of the interval estimates will include the population mean. Figure 14.10 provides an illustration.

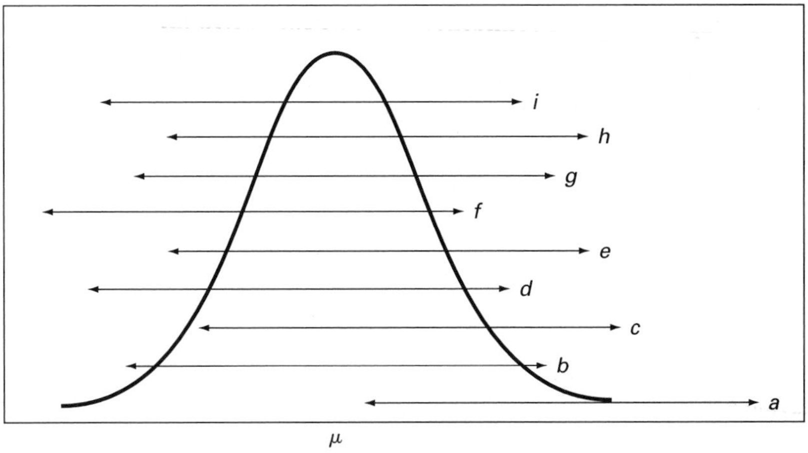

FIGURE 14.10
Confidence intervals based on repeated samples from a population. Interval a does not include μ

14.7.1 Confidence Intervals and Limits for Large Samples

In many instances, the sample size exceeds 50 and the z distribution may be used to compute confidence intervals for a population mean. Assume we have conducted a random sample of 600 Atlanta area adolescents whose family income averaged \$25,000 with a standard deviation of \$2,500. We wish to compute the 95% confidence interval for the mean family income:

$$\bar{X} = \$25{,}000, \qquad s = \$2{,}500, \qquad N = 600$$

We can compute $s_{\bar{X}}$ in the following manner using equation (14.8):

$$s_{\bar{X}} = \frac{s}{\sqrt{N-1}} = \frac{2500}{\sqrt{599}} = \frac{2500}{24.47} = 102.17$$

To compute the upper limit, we find that:

$$\text{upper limit } \mu_0 = \bar{X} + z(s_{\bar{X}}) \qquad (14.12)$$

To compute the lower limit, we obtain:

$$\text{lower limit } \mu_0 = \bar{X} - z(s_{\bar{X}}) \qquad (14.13)$$

In Table A (Appendix C), we find that the z value that includes 47.5% of the area ($95/2 = 47.5$) to the right (or left) of the mean is 1.96. Substituting this value into equations (14.12) and (14.13), we can now determine the upper and lower limits of the 95% confidence interval for μ, the unknown population parameter:

$$\text{upper limit} = 25{,}000 + 1.96(102.17) = \$25{,}200.25$$

$$\text{lower limit} = 25{,}000 - 1.96(102.17) = \$24{,}799.75$$

↳ 95%

14.7.2 Confidence Intervals and Limits for Percentages

Confidence intervals and limits also can be computed for percentages and proportions. Suppose we drew a random sample of 200 from the list of registered voters in Wisconsin that we discussed in Chapter 1 and in the introduction to this chapter in an effort to estimate the percent favoring nuclear power as an energy source. What if 56% favored nuclear energy? Hypothetically, it is possible that if we had drawn four more samples from the list of registered voters (with replacement), the following percentages of voters would favor nuclear power as an energy source: 52%, 55%, 58%, and 57%.

Our concern is that of establishing a confidence interval around the 56% value determined by the actual survey. While it *appears* that a majority of voters prefer nuclear energy, it is possible that this is not the case. To establish the confidence interval, we must first determine the **standard error of the proportion** [see equation (14.14)], which is an estimate of the standard deviation of the sampling distribution of proportions. Converting 56% to a proportion allows us to use equation (14.14) and determine the standard error of the proportion.

$$\sigma_P = \sqrt{\frac{P(1 - P)}{N}} \tag{14.14}$$

where P = the sample proportion
N = sample size

Therefore:

$$\sigma_P = \sqrt{\frac{0.56(0.44)}{200}} = \sqrt{\frac{0.2464}{200}} = 0.035$$

The 95% confidence interval may now be computed by determining the upper and lower confidence limits of the proportion.

1.96 – 95% CI

$$\begin{aligned} \text{upper limit} &= P + z(\sigma_P) \\ &= 0.56 + 1.96(0.035) \\ &= 0.56 + 1.96(0.035) \\ &= 0.56 + 0.07 \\ &= 0.63 \end{aligned} \tag{14.15}$$

$$\begin{aligned} \text{lower limit} &= P - z(\sigma_P) \\ &= 0.56 - 1.96(0.035) \\ &= 0.56 - 0.07 \\ &= 0.49 \end{aligned} \tag{14.16}$$

We now know the lower confidence limit to be 0.49 or 49% and the upper confidence limit to be 0.63 or 63%. The confidence interval therefore includes the percentages between 49 and 63%. We have not established that the percentage of all voters favoring nuclear energy is 56% or that the chances are 95 out of 100 that 56% favor nuclear energy. What we can say is that if we drew a large number of samples ($N = 200$) from the population, 95% of the interval estimates would include the actual population percentage. Had we increased the sample size, the standard error of the proportion would decrease and the 95% confidence interval would be narrower. Examine equation (14.14) and demonstrate this to yourself.

14.8
TEST OF SIGNIFICANCE FOR PEARSON'S r: ONE-SAMPLE CASE

In Chapter 9, we discussed the calculation of two statistics—r_s and Pearson's r—commonly used to describe the extent of the relationship between two variables. If you recall, the coefficient of correlation varies between ± 1.00, with $r = 0.00$ indicating the absence of a relationship. It is easy to overlook the fact that correlation coefficients based on sample data are only estimates of the corresponding population parameter and, as such, will distribute themselves about the population value. Thus, it is quite possible that a sample drawn from a population in which the true correlation is zero may yield a high positive or negative correlation by *chance*. The null hypothesis most often investigated in the one-sample case is that the *population correlation coefficient* (ρ, pronounced "rho") is zero.

It is clear that a test of significance is called for. However, the test is complicated by the fact that the sampling distribution of ρ is usually nonnormal, particularly as ρ approaches the limiting values of ± 1.00. Consider the case in which ρ equals $+0.80$. You may determine that sample correlation coefficients drawn from this population will distribute themselves around $+0.80$ and can take on any value from -1.00 to $+1.00$. It is equally clear, however, that there is a definite restriction in the range of values that sample statistics greater than $+0.80$ can assume, whereas the range of possible values less than $+0.80$ is greater: from $r < +0.80$ to $r = -1.00$ to be precise. The result is a negatively skewed sampling distribution. The departure from normality will usually be less as the number of paired scores in the sample increases. When the population correlation from which the sample is drawn is equal to zero, the sampling distribution is more likely to be normal.

14.8.1 Testing H_0: $\rho = 0$

When testing the null hypothesis that the population correlation coefficient is zero, the following t-test should be used:

$$t = \frac{r\sqrt{N-2}}{\sqrt{1-r^2}} \qquad (14.17)$$

The number of degrees of freedom for testing r is equal to $N - 2$.

Let's look at an illustrative example. A team of social psychologists has developed a scale that purports to measure social isolation. The scores made on the scale by 15 respondents are correlated with their scores on an index revealing the degree of prejudice felt toward minority groups. They obtain a Pearson's r of 0.60. May they conclude that the obtained correlation is not likely to have been drawn from a population in which the true correlation is $\rho = 0$?

Let's set up this problem in formal statistical terms.

1. *Null hypothesis* (H_0). The population correlation coefficient from which this sample was drawn equals 0.00 or is negative ($\rho \leq 0.00$).
2. *Alternative hypothesis* (H_1). The population correlation coefficient from which the sample was drawn is greater than 0.00 ($\rho > 0.00$).
3. *Statistical test.* The t-test, with $N - 2$ degrees of freedom.
4. *Significance level.* $\alpha = 0.05$, one-tailed test because the hypotheses are directional.
5. *Sampling distribution.* The Student's t-distributions with df $= 13$ ($15 - 2 = 13$).
6. *Critical region.* $|t_{0.05}| \geq 1.771$. Since H_1 is directional, the critical region consists of all values of $t \geq 1.771$.

In the present example:

$$t = \frac{0.60\sqrt{13}}{\sqrt{0.64}} = \frac{2.163}{0.8} = 2.70$$

Decision. Since the obtained $t > t_{0.05}$, it falls within the critical region for rejecting H_0. Thus, it may be concluded that the sample was drawn from a population in which $\rho > 0.00$.

This example was for a one-tailed test. If we had decided to use nondirectional hypotheses, our null hypothesis would have been $\rho = 0$ and the alternative hypothesis would have been $\rho \neq 0$. The alpha level would remain at .05 and the degrees of freedom would remain at 13, but the critical value would change to 2.160.

14.8.2 Testing Other Null Hypotheses Concerning ρ

The t-test should not be used for testing hypotheses other than $\rho = 0.00$ because, as we pointed out earlier, the sampling distribution is not normal for values of ρ that are different from zero.

Fisher has described a procedure for transforming sample r's to a statistic z_r, which yields a sampling distribution more closely approximating the normal curve, even for samples employing small N's.

The value of z_r can then be converted to a conventional z-score using the equation

$$z = \frac{z_r - Z_r}{\sqrt{1/(N - 3)}} \tag{14.18}$$

where z_r = the transformed value of the sample r (see Table E in Appendix C)

Z_r = the transformed value of the population correlation coefficient specified under H_0

Using the same example, let's test H_0 that the population ρ from which the sample was drawn is 0.25. Recall that $r = 0.60$ and $N = 15$.

Obtaining z_r is greatly simplified by Table E, Appendix C, which shows the value of z_r, corresponding to each value of r in steps of 0.01, between 0.00 and 0.99. Thus, referring again to Table E, we see that an r of 0.60, for example, has a corresponding z_r of 0.693.

Similarly, ρ of 0.25 has a corresponding Z_r of 0.256. Substituting these values in the equation of z, we find:

$$z = \frac{0.693 - 0.256}{\sqrt{1/(15 - 3)}} = \frac{0.437}{0.289} = 1.51$$

Decision. At the 0.05 level, two-tailed test, $|z_{0.05}| \geq 1.96$ is required for significance. Since $z = 1.51$ is less than the critical values, we cannot reject H_0. It is quite possible that the sample was drawn from a population in which the true correlation is 0.25.

14.8.3 Test of Significance of r_s: One-Sample Case

Table F in Appendix C presents the critical values of r_s, one- and two-tailed tests, for selected values of N from 5 to 30. In Chapter 9, we demonstrated the calculation of r_s from data consisting of the social-class backgrounds of 15 married couples. A correlation of 0.64 was computed. Since $N = 15$ is not listed in Table F, it is necessary to interpolate, using the critical values of $N = 14$ and 16. The critical value at the 0.05 level, two-tailed test, for $N = 14$ is 0.544; at $N = 16$ it is 0.506. By using linear interpolation, we may roughly approximate the critical value corresponding to $N = 15$.

With Table F, linear interpolation merely involves adding together the boundary values of r_s and dividing by 2. Thus:

$$r_{s(0.05)} = \frac{0.544 + 0.506}{2} = 0.525$$

Since our obtained r_s of 0.64 exceeds the critical value at the 0.05 level, we may conclude that the population value of the Spearman correlation coefficient from which the sample was drawn is greater than 0.00.

14.9 TEST OF SIGNIFICANCE FOR GOODMAN AND KRUSKAL'S GAMMA

Goodman and Kruskal's gamma was discussed in Chapter 8, using an example in which the relationship between political liberalism and year in college was explored. Gamma was found to equal +0.465. Overall, there were 1,167 concordant pairs and

426 discordant pairs. Let's test the hypothesis that in the population from which the sample was drawn, γ (the Greek letter symbolizing the parameter) is greater than 0. Therefore, our null hypothesis is H_0: $\gamma \leq 0$ and we will test it at the 0.01 level of significance with a one-tailed test using the following equation, which allows us to convert G to a z-score:

$$z = (G - \gamma)\sqrt{\frac{C + D}{N(1 - G^2)}}$$

where $G = 0.465$
$C = 1167$
$D = 426$
$N = 80$, and
$\gamma = 0$ because H_0: $\gamma \leq 0$

Therefore:

$$z = (0.465 - 0)\sqrt{\frac{1{,}167 + 426}{80(1 - 0.216)}}$$

$$= (0.465)\sqrt{\frac{1{,}593}{62.72}}$$

$$= (0.465)(5.03)$$

$$= +2.34$$

The computed z score of 2.34 falls into the critical region that begins at $z = 2.33$ (see Table A in Appendix C); therefore, we reject the null hypothesis that the association between political liberalism and year in college in the population from which the 80 students was drawn equals 0.

SUMMARY

We have seen that if we take a number of samples from a given population, then:

1. The distribution of sample means tends to be normal.
2. The mean of these sample means ($\mu_{\bar{X}}$) is equal to the mean of the population (μ).
3. The standard error of the mean ($\sigma_{\bar{X}}$) is equal to $\sigma/\sqrt{N}$. As N increases, the variability decreases.

We used these relationships in the testing of hypotheses (e.g., $\mu = \mu_0$) when the standard deviation of a population was known, using the z-statistic and the standard normal curve.

When σ is not known, we demonstrated the use of sample statistics to estimate these parameters. We used these estimates of the parameters to test hypotheses, using the Student's t-ratio and the corresponding sampling distributions. We compared these t-distributions, which vary as a function of degrees of freedom (df), with the standard normal curve.

We used the t-ratio and the normal distribution as a basis for establishing confidence intervals for means and proportions.

Finally, we demonstrated the test of significance for Pearson's r, Spearman's r_s, one-sample case, and for gamma.

TERMS TO REMEMBER

biased estimate of a parameter An estimate that does not equal, on the average, the value of the parameter.

central limit theorem If random samples of a fixed N are drawn from *any* population (regardless of the form of the population distribution), as N becomes larger the distribution of sample means approaches normality, with the overall mean approaching μ, the variance of the sample means $\sigma_{\bar{X}}^2$ being equal to σ^2/N, and a standard error $\sigma_{\bar{x}}$ of $\sigma/\sqrt{N}$.

confidence interval Specifies a range of values for a parameter bounded by two endpoints called confidence limits. Common confidence intervals are 95% and 99%.

confidence limits The two endpoints of a confidence interval.

critical region The portion of the area under a curve that includes those values of a statistic that lead to rejection of the null hypothesis.

critical values of t Those values that bound the critical rejection regions corresponding to varying levels of significance.

degrees of freedom (df) The number of values that are free to vary after we have placed certain restrictions upon our data.

interval estimation The determination of an interval within which the population parameter is presumed to fall. (Contrast *point estimation.*)

law of large numbers As the sample size increases, the standard error of the mean decreases.

point estimation An estimate of a population parameter that involves a single sample value selected by the criterion of "best estimate." (Contrast *interval estimation.*)

robust test A statistical test from which statistical inferences are likely to be valid even when there are fairly large departures from normality in the population distribution.

standard error of the mean ($s_{\bar{X}}$) A theoretical standard deviation of sample means, of a given sample size, drawn from some specified population. When based on a known population standard deviation, $\sigma_{\bar{X}} = \sigma/\sqrt{N}$; when estimated from a single sample, $s_{\bar{X}} = s/\sqrt{N-1}$.

standard error of the proportion An estimate of the standard deviation of the sampling distribution of proportions.

t-distributions (Student's t-distributions or Student's t) Theoretical symmetrical sampling distributions with a mean of zero and a standard deviation that becomes smaller as degrees of freedom (df) increase. Used in relation to Student's t-ratio.

t-ratio A test statistic for determining the significance of a difference between means (two-sample case) or for testing the hypothesis that a given sample mean was drawn from a population with the mean specified under the null hypothesis (one-sample case). Used when population standard deviation (or standard deviations) is unknown.

unbiased estimate of a parameter An estimate that equals, on the average, the value of the corresponding parameter.

EXERCISES

1. Describe what happens to the distribution of sample means when you:
(*a*) Increase the size of each sample.
(*b*) Increase the number of samples.

2. Explain why the standard deviation of a sample will usually underestimate the standard deviation of a population. Give an example.

3. Given that $\overline{X} = 24$ and $s = 4$ for $N = 15$, use the t-distribution to find:
(*a*) The 95% confidence limits for μ.
(*b*) The 99% confidence limits for μ.

4. Given that $\overline{X} = 24$ and $s = 4$ for $N = 121$, use the t-distribution to find:
(*a*) The 95% confidence limits for μ.
(*b*) The 99% confidence limits for μ.

Compare the results with exercise 3.

5. A professor gives the class an examination that, as he knows from years of experience, yields $u = 78$ and $\sigma = 7$. The present class of 22 obtains a mean of 82. Is the professor correct in assuming that this is a superior class? Use $\alpha = 0.01$, two-tailed test.

6. A professor gives the class an examination that, as he knows from years of experience, yields $u = 78$. The present class of 22 obtains $\overline{X} = 82$ and $s = 7$. Is the professor correct in assuming that this is a superior class? Use $\alpha = 0.01$, two-tailed test.

7. Explain the difference between exercises 5 and 6. What test statistic is used in each case, and why? Why is the decision different?
Generalize: What is the effect of knowing σ upon the likelihood of a type II error?

8. The superintendent of Zody school district claims that the children in her district are brighter, on average, than the general population of students. To determine the aptitude of school children in the district, a study was conducted. The results are as follows.

Test scores
105
109
115
112
124
115
103
110
125
99

The mean of the general population of school children is 106. Set this up in formal statistical terms (i.e., H_0, H_1) and draw the appropriate conclusions. Use a one-tailed test, $\alpha = 0.05$.

9. For a particular population with $\mu = 28.5$ and $\sigma = 5.5$, what is the probability that, in a sample of 100, $\bar{X}$ will be:
(*a*) Equal to or less than 30.0? (*c*) Equal to or more than 29.5?
(*b*) Equal to or less than 28.0? (*d*) Between 28.0 and 29.0?

10. Given that $\bar{X} = 40$ for $N = 24$ from a population in which $\sigma = 8$, find:
(*a*) The 95% confidence limits for μ.
(*b*) The 99% confidence limits for μ.

11. Overton University claims that its superior facilities and close faculty supervision allow its students to complete the Ph.D. program earlier than usual. The university bases its assertion on the fact that the national mean age for completion is 32.11, whereas the mean age of its 26 Ph.D.'s is 29.61 with $s = 6.00$. Test the validity of the school's assumption.

12. Using the data in the preceding exercise, find the interval within which you are confident that the true population mean (average age for Ph.D.'s at Overton University) probably falls, using the 95% confidence interval.

13. A sociologist asserts that the average length of courtship is longer before a second marriage than before a first marriage. He bases this assertion on the average for first marriages of 265 days, whereas the average for second marriages (of his 626 respondents) is 268.5 days, with $s = 50$. Test the validity of his assumption.

14. Using the data in the preceding exercise, find the interval within which you are confident that the true population mean (average courtship days for a second marriage) probably falls, using the 99% confidence interval.

15. Random samples of size 2 are selected from the following finite population of scores: 1, 3, 5, 7, 9, and 11.
(*a*) Calculate the mean and standard deviation of the population.
(*b*) Construct a histogram showing the sampling distribution of means when $N = 2$. Sample *without* replacement.
(*c*) Construct a histogram showing the means of all possible samples that can be drawn. Sample *with* replacement.

16. Given (*b*) in exercise 15, answer the following: Selecting a sample with $N = 2$, what is the probability that:
(*a*) A mean as high as 10 will be obtained?
(*b*) A mean as low as 2 will be obtained?
(*c*) A mean as deviant as 8 will be obtained?
(*d*) A mean as low as 1 will be obtained?

17. Given (*c*) in exercise 15, answer the following: Selecting a sample with $N = 2$, what is the probability that:
(*a*) A mean as high as 10 will be obtained?
(*b*) A mean as low as 2 will be obtained?
(*c*) A mean as deviant as 8 will be obtained?
(*d*) A mean as low as 1 will be obtained?

18. A census field supervisor ranked 25 of her workers on the length of their employment with the Census Bureau and their rate of interview completion. She correlated these ranks and obtained an $r_s = -0.397$. Assuming $\alpha = 0.05$, two-tailed test, what do you conclude?

19. Matthew ranked the 17 waiters he supervises in terms of their speed and efficiency on the job. He correlated these ranks with the total amount of tips each of these waiters received for a 1-week period and obtained $r_s = .438$. What do you conclude? Use $\alpha = .05$.

20. As a requirement for admission to Blue Chip University, a candidate must take a standardized entrance examination. The correlation between performance on this examination and college grades is 0.43.

(*a*) The director of admissions claims that a better way to predict college success is by using high school averages. To test her claim, she randomly selects 52 students and correlates their college grades with their high school averages. She obtains $r = 0.54$. What do you conclude? Use $\alpha = 0.05$.

(*b*) The director's assistant constructs a test that he claims is better for predicting college success than the one currently used. He randomly selects 67 students and correlates their grade point averages with performance on his test. The obtained $r = 0.61$. What do you conclude? Use $\alpha = 0.05$.

21. What are the statistics used to describe the distributions of a sample? The distribution of sample statistics?

22. Is s^2 an unbiased estimate of σ^2? Why?

23. Is $\hat{s}^2$ an unbiased estimate of σ^2? Why?

24. What is a confidence interval? A confidence limit? What is their relationship?

25. Give an example to show the effect of the α level on the precision of a confidence interval.

26. How do t-distributions differ from normal distributions? Are they ever the same?

27. In a study of marital success and failure, Bentler and Newcomb (1978) gave a personality questionnaire to 162 newly married couples. Four years later, 77 couples from the original sample were located; of these, 53 were still married while 24 had separated or divorced. Among the still-married group, the correlation between the husband's and wife's scores on an attractiveness scale was 0.59, and the correlation between their scores on a generosity scale was 0.23. Among the divorced group, the correlation between the ex-husband's and ex-wife's scores on the attractiveness scale was 0.07, and the correlation between their scores on the generosity scale was 0.13.

(*a*) Using $\alpha = 0.05$, set up and test the null hypothesis that the correlation between the married couples' scores on attractiveness is equal to zero. Also, set up and test the null hypothesis that the correlation between the divorced couples' scores on attractiveness is equal to zero.

(*b*) Using $\alpha = 0.05$, set up and test the null hypothesis that the correlation between the married couples' scores on generosity is equal to zero. Also, set up and test the null hypothesis that the correlation between the divorced couples' scores on generosity is equal to zero.

28. Assume that the mean number of religious conversions a year in the Methodist church is 50. A group of 16 Methodist ministers who attended a special seminar for increasing conversions show the following number of conversions in their churches during the year following the seminar:

Number of conversions	
55	85
50	60
45	50
75	65
80	60
75	50
80	80
80	50

Calculate the value of t. Can you conclude that the seminar produced ministers with superior abilities to attract converts?

29. A Los Angeles criminologist found an r_s of 0.15 between the number of times 20 male prostitutes had been arrested and the number of years they had worked as prostitutes. Can she conclude that this correlation is significant? Use $\alpha = 0.05$, two-tailed test.

30. Mr. Smith stated that his training program for selling life insurance enables a company to sell more life insurance than the "average" company. The mean amount of life insurance sold by all salespeople per month is \$100,000. A sample of 10 people who have been through the training program show monthly selling rates of:

Selling rates (in \$000s)	
\$100	90
120	130
130	135
120	140
125	110

If you were a supervisor of insurance salespeople, would you adopt Mr. Smith's training program? Calculate the value of t.

CHAPTER 15

An Introduction to the Analysis of Variance

15.1 MULTIGROUP COMPARISONS

We are often concerned with comparisons between only two groups. Yet the complexity of the phenomena that the social scientist investigates does not allow us to restrict our observations to two groups. Events in nature rarely order themselves conveniently into two groups. The questions we pose more commonly are: Which type of juvenile detention facility is more successful in terms of the recidivism rate? Do the median incomes of the residents in several neighborhoods differ significantly? Are Southern Baptists significantly more orthodox than Lutherans and Methodists? Are persons over 60 more socially isolated than the middle-aged and the young? Which of three teaching techniques is most effective?

The research design necessary to provide answers to these questions would require comparison of more than two groups. You may wonder why multigroup comparisons should provide any obstacles. Can we not simply compare the mean of each group with the mean of every group and obtain a Student's *t*-ratio for each comparison? For example, if we had four groups, *A*, *B*, *C*, and *D*, could we not calculate Student's *t*-ratios comparing *A* with *B*, *C*, and *D*; *B* with *C* and *D*; and *C* with *D*?

If you will think for a moment of the errors in inference, which we have so frequently discussed, you will recall that our greatest concern has been to avoid type I errors. When we establish the region of rejection at the 0.05 level, we are, in effect, acknowledging our willingness to take the risk of being wrong as often as 5% of the time in our rejection of the null hypothesis. Now, what happens when we have numerous comparisons to make? For an extreme example, let us imagine that we have conducted a study involving the calculation of 1,000 separate Student's t-ratios. Would we be terribly impressed if, say, 50 of the t's proved to be significant at the 0.05 level? Of course not. Indeed, we would probably murmur something to the effect that, "With 1,000 comparisons, we would be surprised if we don't obtain approximately 50 comparisons that are significant *by chance,* that is, due to predictable sampling error."

The **analysis of variance (ANOVA)** is a method, described by R. A. Fisher, partitioning the sum of squares for survey or experimental data into known components of variation. This technique of statistical analysis permits us to overcome the ambiguity involved in assessing significant differences when more than two group means are compared, by allowing for a single decision at a specified level of significance. It allows us to answer the question, Is there an overall indication that the independent variable is producing differences among the means of the various groups? Although ANOVA may be used in the two-sample case (in which event it yields precisely the same probability values as the Student's t-ratio), it is most commonly used when three or more categories or groups of the independent variable are involved. The focus of this chapter is **one-way analysis of variance,** which derives its name from the fact that various groups represent different categories or levels of a *single* independent variable (sometimes referred to as a *treatment variable*).

The procedures discussed may be generalized to any number of independent variables. We will now consider the two-group situation before examining the more complex three-group situation.

15.2
THE CONCEPT OF SUMS OF SQUARES

Imagine that we have conducted a study (see Table 15.1) with two groups of students concerning their attitude toward the legalization of marijuana. None of the students in group 1 has ever used marijuana, and all of the students in group 2 use it at least once a month. A high score indicates the student strongly favors legalization. We will test the hypothesis that the two groups of students have been drawn from the same population (or that there is no difference in the attitudes of users and nonusers toward legalization of marijuana).

The mean for group 1 is 4; the mean for group 2 is 8. The overall mean, $\overline{X}_{\text{tot}}$, is 48/8 or 6. If we were to subtract the overall mean from each score and square, we would obtain the total sum of squares (SS_{tot})

$$SS_{\text{tot}} = \Sigma(X - \overline{X}_{\text{tot}})^2 \qquad (15.1)$$

For the data in Table 15.1, the total sum of squares using equation (15.1) is:

$$SS_{\text{tot}} = (1-6)^2 + (2-6)^2 + (5-6)^2 + (8-6)^2 + (6-6)^2 + (7-6)^2 + (9-6)^2 + (10-6)^2 = 25 + 16 + 1 + 4 + 0 + 1 + 9 + 16 = 72$$

TABLE 15.1
Nonuser's and user's attitude toward the legalization of marijuana

(nonusers) Group 1 X_1	X_1^2	(users) Group 2 X_2	X_2^2
1	1	6	36
2	4	7	49
5	25	9	81
8	64	10	100
Σ 16	94	32	266
$N_1 = 4$,	$\bar{X}_1 = 4$	$N_2 = 4$,	$\bar{X}_2 = 8$
$\Sigma X_{tot} = 48$	$N = 8$	$\bar{X}_{tot} = 6$	

Thus, we see that the **total sum of squares (TSS)** is the sum of the squared deviations from the overall mean, and hence is a measure of the total variation in the data. We have already encountered the sum of squares in calculating the standard deviation, the variance, and the total variation of a dependent variable when studying regression analysis. The alternative raw score equation for the total sum of squares is:

$$SS_{tot} = \Sigma X_{tot}^2 - \frac{(\Sigma X_{tot})^2}{N} \tag{15.2}$$

For the data in Table 15.1, the total sum of squares is:

$$SS_{tot} = 94 + 266 - \frac{(48)^2}{8}$$

$$= 360 - 288 = 72$$

We will now partition the total variance (total sum of squares) into two smaller components: the within-group variance (within-group sum of squares) and the between-group variance (the between-group sum of squares).

The **within-group sum of squares (SS_w)** is the sum of the sum of squares obtained within each group and is a measure of the variability within the groups. Figure 15.1 shows, for example, that the scores of the students in group 1 (nonusers) and group 2 (users) vary widely about each of their respective group means of 4 and 8. The source of the within-group variation includes all of the variables influencing the dependent variable (attitude toward the legalization of marijuana) other than the independent variable. Could the variability we observed in Figure 15.1 in the attitude toward marijuana legalization scores within group 1 or within group 2 have stemmed from the independent variable (nonuse versus use)? No, since everyone in group 1 was a nonuser and everyone in group 2 was a user. Thus, all within-group variability must stem from variables other than the specified independent variable.

In this instance, the within-group sum of squares measures the sum of the squared deviations of the scores in group 1 around $\bar{X}_1$ *plus* the sum of the squared deviations of the scores in group 2 around $\bar{X}_2$:

$$SS_w = SS_1 + SS_2$$

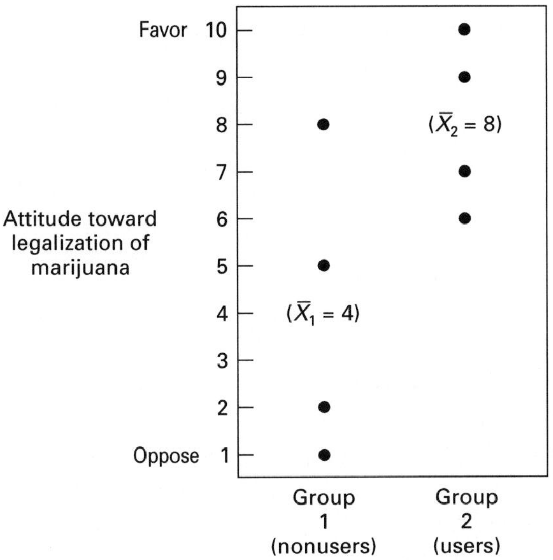

FIGURE 15.1
Scattergram of attitude toward legalization of marijuana scores for nonusers and users

where $SS_1 = \Sigma(X - \bar{X}_1)^2$
$SS_2 = \Sigma(X - \bar{X}_2)^2$

For the data in Table 15.1, the within-group sum of squares is:

$$\begin{aligned}
&\Sigma(X - \bar{X}_1)^2 + \Sigma(X - \bar{X}_2)^2 \\
&= (1 - 4)^2 + (2 - 4)^2 + (5 - 4)^2 + (8 - 4)^2 \\
&\quad + (6 - 8)^2 + (7 - 8)^2 + (9 - 8)^2 + (10 - 8)^2 \\
&= 9 + 4 + 1 + 16 + 4 + 1 + 1 + 4 = 40
\end{aligned}$$

Using the raw score equation (15.3) for the within-group sum of squares, we also find that $SS_w = 40$.

$$SS_w = SS_1 + SS_2$$

$$SS_1 = \Sigma X_1^2 - \frac{(\Sigma X_1)^2}{N_1}$$

$$= 94 - \frac{(16)^2}{4} = 94 - 64 = 30 \qquad (15.3)$$

$$SS_2 = \Sigma X_2^2 - \frac{(\Sigma X_2)^2}{N_2}$$

$$= 266 - \frac{(32)^2}{4} = 266 - 256 = 10$$

$$SS_w = 30 + 10 = 40$$

The **between-group sum of squares (SS_{bet})** is the sum of the sum of squares between each group and reflects the influence of the independent or treatment variable. It may be obtained by subtracting the overall mean from each group mean, squaring the result, multiplying by N in each group, and summing across all of the groups. Thus:

$$SS_{bet} = \Sigma N_i(\bar{X}_i - \bar{X}_{tot})^2 \tag{15.4}$$

where N_i is the number in the ith group, and $\bar{X}_i$ is the mean of the ith group.

$$SS_{bet} = 4(4 - 6)^2 + 4(8 - 6)^2 = 32$$

The raw score equation for calculating the between-group sum of squares is:

$$SS_{bet} = \Sigma \frac{(\Sigma X_i)^2}{N_i} - \frac{(\Sigma X_{tot})^2}{N} \tag{15.5}$$

and

$$\begin{aligned} SS_{bet} &= \frac{(16)^2}{4} + \frac{(32)^2}{4} - \frac{(48)^2}{8} \\ &= 64 + 256 - 288 \\ &= 320 - 288 = 32 \end{aligned}$$

It will be noted that the total sum of squares is equal to the sum of the between-group sum of squares and the within-group sum of squares. In other words:

$$SS_{tot} = SS_w + SS_{bet} \tag{15.6}$$

In this example, $SS_{tot} = 72$, $SS_w = 40$, and $SS_{bet} = 32$. Thus, $72 = 40 + 32$. Therefore, we have partitioned the *total sum of squares,* which is a measure of total variation in the dependent variable into two components: the within-group and between-group sum of squares. The *within-group sum of squares component* is a measure of the variability of the dependent variable scores *within* each of the categories or groups of the independent variable, and hence is the variation in the dependent variable that cannot be attributed to the independent variable. The *between-group sum of squares component* is a measure of the variation *between* the categories or groups of the independent variable, and hence is the variation in the dependent variable that is attributable to the independent or treatment variable.

15.3 OBTAINING VARIANCE ESTIMATES

The analysis of variance consists of obtaining two independent estimates of variance, one based on variability between groups, or **between-group variance,** and the other based on the variability within groups, or **within-group variance.** The within- and between-group variance estimates are known as **mean squares.** The significance of the difference between these mean squares is provided by Fisher's F-distributions. In analysis of variance, the ***F*-ratio** is the between-group **variance estimate** divided by the within-group variance estimate. If the between-group variance estimate is large (i.e., the difference between means is large) relative to the within-group variance estimate, the F-ratio is large. Conversely, if the between-group variance estimate is small relative to the within-group estimate, the F-ratio will be small.

A test of our null hypothesis that the two samples do not differ in their attitudes toward the legalization of marijuana (H_0: $\mu_1 = \mu_2$) requires that we create a ratio of the between- and within-group sum of squares. You may have observed, however, that both values will increase as the sample size increases. Therefore, as a "corrective" factor we control for sample size by dividing both values by their respective degrees of freedom.* This procedure allows us to arrive at variance estimates for the between- and within-group sum of squares. The *degrees of freedom of the between-group sum of squares* are the number of categories or groups (k) of the independent variable minus 1:

$$df_{bet} = k - 1 \tag{15.7}$$

With two groups, $k = 2$. Therefore, $df = 2 - 1 = 1$. Thus, our between-group variance estimate for the problem at hand is:

$$\hat{s}^2_{bet} = \frac{SS_{bet}}{df_{bet}} = \frac{32}{1} = 32, \qquad df = 1 \tag{15.8}$$

The number of *degrees of freedom of the within-groups sum of squares* is the total N minus the number of categories within the independent variable. Thus:

$$df_w = N - k \tag{15.9}$$

In the present problem, $df_w = 8 - 2 = 6$ and our within-group variance estimate becomes:

$$\hat{s}^2_w = \frac{SS_w}{df_w} = \frac{40}{6} = 6.67, \qquad df = 6 \tag{15.10}$$

Now all we have left to do is to calculate the F-ratio and determine whether our two variance estimates could have reasonably been drawn from the same population. If not, we will conclude that the significantly larger between-group variance is due to the operation of the group differences. In other words, we will conclude that the groups' differences in marijuana usage produced a significant difference in their mean attitudes toward the legalization of marijuana.

As we stated earlier, the F-ratio is the between-group variance estimate divided by the within-group variance estimate. The F-ratio uses the same logic as the z-score and the t-ratio. The F-ratio creates a standardized value that compares the size of the between-group variance relative to the size of the within-group variance.

$$F = \frac{\text{between-group variance estimate}}{\text{within-group variance estimate}}$$

---

* The rationale for the degrees of freedom concept was presented in Section 14.5. The same rationale applies here. Degrees of freedom represent the number of values that are free to vary once we have placed certain restrictions on our data.

Symbolically:

$$F = \frac{\hat{s}^2_{\text{bet}}}{\hat{s}^2_{\text{w}}} \tag{15.11}$$

For this problem, our F-ratio is:

$$F = \frac{32}{6.67} = 4.80, \qquad \text{df} = 1, 6$$

Looking up the F-ratio under 1 and 6 degrees of freedom in Table D, Appendix C, we find that an F-ratio of 5.99 or larger is required for significance at the 0.05 level. For the present problem, then, we cannot reject the null hypothesis that there is no difference in the two groups' attitudes toward legalizing marijuana. You should note that Table D provides two-tailed values. The analysis of variance test for significance is automatically two-tailed because *any* difference among the sample means will enlarge the entire value of F, not just the difference in which the researcher is interested.

In summary, we must conclude that the nonusers and users we have studied do not differ significantly in their attitudes toward the legalization of marijuana and that they were drawn from the same population.

The data entry to compute the one-way ANOVA we have just completed is shown below, using SPSS along with the analysis of variance summary. The independent or treatment variable is designated by "group" 1 or 2 on the data entry summary and "attitude" indicates the students' scores on the dependent variable, the attitude toward marijuana use. Thus, the first student is in group 1 and has a score of 1 (see also Table 15.1). The first four students are in group 1 and the second four students are in group 2.

	Group	**Attitude**
1	1.00	1.00
2	1.00	2.00
3	1.00	5.00
4	1.00	8.00
5	2.00	6.00
6	2.00	7.00
7	2.00	9.00
8	2.00	10.00

The one-way ANOVA summary in Table 15.2 provides the between groups, within groups, and total sum of squares along with their corresponding degrees of freedom (df). The degrees of freedom between groups equals 1 and the degrees of freedom within groups equals 6. The total degrees of freedom are found by:

$$df_{tot} = N - 1 \tag{15.12}$$

In the present example, the number of degrees of freedom for the total is:

$$df_{tot} = 8 - 1 = 7$$

You are familiar with the sum of squares, mean squares, and the F-ratio. The very specific F probability provided by the SPSS analysis is consistent with our decision not to reject the null hypothesis because it is greater than the 0.05 significance level we had designated earlier.

15.4 RELATION BETWEEN THE t-RATIO AND THE F-RATIO

When we use ANOVA to compare the means of two groups, we have a special case of the t-ratio. Specifically, statisticians have shown that $t^2 = F$ when $k = 2$. This means that if you want to compare two means, you could use ANOVA or a t-ratio with a *nondirectional hypothesis* and obtain the same statistical conclusion. This may raise a few questions such as: Why even study the t-ratio? and Why is ANOVA a test of a nondirectional hypothesis?

The answer to the first question is that the t-ratio is an essential statistic for comparing means when the researcher has a specific, logically derived directional hypothesis to test. In other words, the t-ratio, not the F-ratio, allows us to make directional comparisons between means.

The answer to the second question is related to how the sampling distribution for the F-ratio is constructed when $k = 2$. Figure 15.2 presents the sampling distribution for the t-ratio for 20 degrees of freedom and the sampling distribution for the F-ratio when the degrees of freedom are 1 and 20. For the t-ratio, the critical region for α is divided at both ends of the distribution. The sampling distribution for the F-ratio represents similar characteristics. The shapes of the distributions are different because the sampling distribution for t is based on the distribution of differences between means, whereas the sampling distribution for F is based on the distribution of variances. The differences between means can be negative, consequently the t-distribution is symmetrical. The ratio of variances can only be positive, thus the F-distribution always has a positive skew.

TABLE 15.2
One-way analysis of variance

Attitude toward legalization of marijuana (dependent variable) by group (1=nonusers; 2=users)

Source	df	Sum of squares	Mean squares	F-ratio	F-probability
Between groups	1	32.0000	32.0000	4.8000	.0710
Within groups	6	40.0000	6.6667		
Total	7	72.0000			

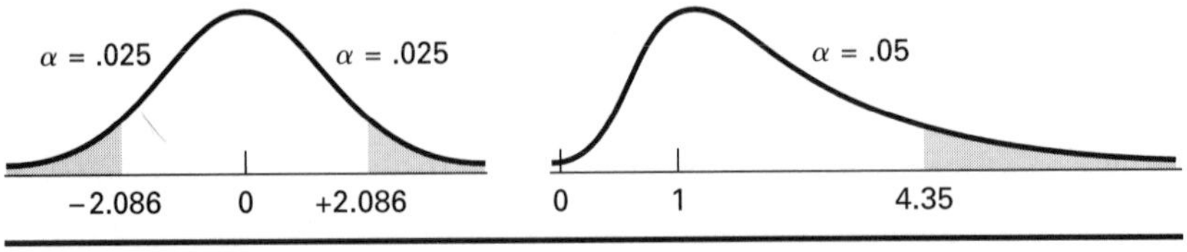

FIGURE 15.2
Sampling distributions for the *t*-ratio and *F*-ratio
The degrees of freedom for the *t*-ratio are 20. The degrees of freedom for the *F*-ratio are 1 and 20. The critical region ($\alpha = .05$) for both distributions are shaded.

15.5
FUNDAMENTAL CONCEPTS OF ANALYSIS OF VARIANCE

In these few pages, we have examined all of the basic concepts necessary to understand simple analysis of variance. Before proceeding with an example involving three groups, let's briefly review these fundamental concepts:

1. We have seen that in a study involving two or more groups, it is possible to identify two different bases for estimating the population variance: the between-group and the within-group.

   a. The between group variance estimate reflects any systematic differences in the ways the groups were treated and the influence of the independent or treatment variable on the dependent variable. The larger the difference is between the group means, the larger the between-group variance.

   b. The within group variance estimate reflects the dispersion of scores within each group due to individual differences and/or other uncontrolled factors. In well-conducted research, the impact of "other factors" is kept to a minimum.

2. The null hypothesis is that the samples were drawn from the same population, or that $\mu_1 = \mu_2 = \cdots = \mu_k$.

3. The alternative hypothesis is that the samples were not drawn from the same population; that is, $\mu_1 \neq \mu_2 \neq \cdots \neq \mu_k$.

4. The *F*-ratio consists of the between-group variance estimate divided by the within-group variance estimate. The within- and between-group variance estimates are known as *mean squares.* By consulting Table D (in Appendix C) of the distribution of *F*, we can determine whether the null hypothesis of equal population means can reasonably by entertained. In the event of a significant *F*-ratio, we may conclude that the group means are not all estimates of a common population mean.

5. In the two-sample case, the *F*-ratio yields probability values identical to those of the Student's *t*-ratio. Indeed, in the one-degree-of-freedom situation (i.e., $k = 2$), $t = \sqrt{F}$ or $t^2 = F$. You may check this statement by calculating the Student's *t*-ratio for the sample problem we have just completed.

15.6
ASSUMPTIONS UNDERLYING ANALYSIS OF VARIANCE

Like the *t*-test, ANOVA is a parametric statistic that makes several basic assumptions about the data that are collected. These assumptions involve the distribution of error. We assume that:

1. Sampling error is distributed normally around μ in each treatment population.
2. The distribution of error is the same for each population, $\sigma_1 = \sigma_2$. This assumption is known as **homogeneity of variance.**
3. The observations in each sample are independent of each other. That is, there is no systematic relation between pairs of scores for each group.

There is some controversy among statisticians about how robust ANOVA is against violations of the homogeneity of variance and normal distribution assumptions. For example, Milligan, Wong, and Thompson (1987) demonstrated that ANOVA is not robust when variances and sample sizes are radically different. Their study, however, examined extreme violations of homogeneity and used large differences in sample size. As a generality, ANOVA can be considered robust to violations of homogeneity of variance and the normal distribution if the sample sizes are equal and large. Therefore, when you collect data for research, you should attempt to place a premium on collecting as many respondents or subjects as possible and to ensure that there are the same number of respondents or subjects in each group.

15.7
AN EXAMPLE INVOLVING THREE GROUPS

Imagine we have just completed a study to assess attitudes toward welfare payments, and we have three samples of nine respondents each: Group 1 is a middle-class sample, group 2 is a sample of persons presently on welfare, and group 3 is a lower-middle-class sample. A high score indicates strong support of welfare payments. Our null hypothesis is that these samples were drawn from the same population or that the groups do not differ in their attitudes toward welfare. If we reject the null hypothesis, we would conclude that one or more of the group means is significantly different from one or both of the other group means. The results of this study are presented in Table 15.3.

The following steps are followed in a three-group analysis of variance:

Step 1. Using equation (15.2), we find that the total sum of squares is:

$$SS_{tot} = 1216 - \frac{(158)^2}{27} = 291.41$$

Step 2. Using equation (15.5) for three groups, we find that the between-group sum of squares is:

$$SS_{bet} = \frac{(46)^2}{9} + \frac{(78)^2}{9} + \frac{(34)^2}{9} - \frac{(158)^2}{27} = 114.96$$

Step 3. By employing equation (15.3) for three groups or by subtracting SS_{bet} from SS_{tot}, we obtain the within-group sum of squares:

$$SS_w = \left(292 - \frac{(46)^2}{9}\right) + \left(756 - \frac{(78)^2}{9}\right) + \left(168 - \frac{(34)^2}{9}\right) = 176.45$$

$$SS_w = SS_{tot} - SS_{bet} = 291.41 - 114.96 = 176.45$$

Step 4. The between-group mean square is:

$$df_{bet} = k - 1 = 2, \qquad \hat{s}^2_{bet} = \frac{114.96}{2} = 57.48$$

Step 5. The within-group mean square is:

$$df_w = N - k = 24, \qquad \hat{s}^2_w = \frac{176.45}{24} = 7.35$$

Step 6. Using equation (15.11), we find that the value of F is:

$$F = \frac{57.48}{7.35} = 7.82, \qquad df = 2, 24$$

To summarize these steps, we use the format shown in Table 15.4.

By following the format recommended in Table 15.4, you have a final check upon your calculation of sum of squares and your assignment of degrees of freedom. Thus, $SS_{bet} + SS_w$ must equal SS_{tot}.

TABLE 15.3
Attitude toward welfare scores of three groups of respondents

Group 1 (middle-class sample)		Group 2 (welfare sample)		Group 3 (lower-middle-class sample)	
X_1	X_1^2	X_2	X_2^2	X_3	X_3^2
4	16	12	144	1	1
5	25	8	64	3	9
4	16	10	100	4	16
3	9	5	25	6	36
6	36	7	49	8	64
10	100	9	81	5	25
1	1	14	196	3	9
8	64	9	81	2	4
5	25	4	16	2	4
Σ 46	292	78	756	34	168
$N_1 = 9$,	$\bar{X}_1 = 5.11$	$N_2 = 9$,	$\bar{X}_2 = 8.67$	$N_3 = 9$,	$\bar{X}_3 = 3.78$

$\Sigma X_{tot} = 46 + 78 + 34 = 158$

$\Sigma X^2_{tot} = 292 + 756 + 168 = 1{,}216$

$N = 27$

TABLE 15.4
SPSS summary table for representing the relevant statistics in analysis of variance problems
Attitude toward welfare (dependent variable) by group (1=middle; 2=welfare; 3=lower-middle)

Source	df	Sum of squares	Mean squares	F-ratio	F-probability
Between groups	2	114.9630	57.4815	7.8186	.0024
Within groups	24	176.4444	7.3519		
Total	26	291.4074			

15.7.1 Interpreting the *F*-ratio

When we look up the *F* required for significance with 2 and 24 degrees of freedom, we find that an *F* of 3.40 or larger is significant at the 0.05 level. Since our *F* of 7.82 exceeds this value, we may conclude that the three-group means are not all estimates of a common population mean or that the attitudes of the groups toward welfare differ. Now, do we stop at this point? After all, are we not interested in determining whether one of three samples is more in favor of welfare than the other two? The answer to the first question is no and the answer to the second is yes.

The truth of the matter is that our finding an overall significant *F*-ratio now permits us to investigate the following specific hypotheses, which will allow us to determine exactly which means are significantly different:

$$H_0: \mu_1 = \mu_2$$

$$H_0: \mu_1 = \mu_3$$

$$H_0: \mu_2 = \mu_3$$

In the absence of a significant *F*-ratio, any significant differences between specific comparisons would have to be regarded as representing a chance difference.

Over the past several years, statisticians have developed a large number of tests that permit the researcher to investigate specific hypotheses concerning population parameters. Two broad classes of such tests exist:

1. A priori or planned comparisons

When comparisons are planned in advance of the investigation, an a priori test is appropriate. The term *a priori* means "before the fact." For statisticians, a priori means that the hypotheses for the multiple comparisons were stated prior to the start of the data analysis. For a priori tests, it is not necessary that the overall *F*-ratio be significant.

2. A posteriori comparisons

When the comparisons are not planned in advance, an a posteriori test is appropriate. The term *a posteriori* means "after the fact." Applied to statistics, an a posteriori comparison is a statistical test that is created after the data have been collected and analyzed. The hallmark of an a posteriori comparison is that the null and alternative hypotheses are created after one has examined the data.

In the present example, we illustrate the use of an a posteriori test for making pairwise comparisons among means. Tukey (1953) has developed such a test, which he named the HSD (honestly significant difference) test. To use this test, the overall F-ratio must be significant. A difference between two means is significant at a given α-level if it equals or exceeds HSD, which is:

$$\text{HSD} = q_\alpha \sqrt{\frac{\hat{s}_\text{w}^2}{n}} \tag{15.13}$$

where HSD = critical difference required to consider the means statistically different

$\hat{s}_\text{w}^2$ = the within-group mean square

n = number of individuals in each group

q_α = tabled value for a given α-level found in Table K (in Appendix C) for df_w and k (number of means)

15.7.2 A Worked Example

Let's use the data from Section 15.6 to illustrate the application of the HSD test. We will assume $\alpha = 0.05$ for testing the significance of the difference between each pair of means.

Step 1. Prepare a matrix showing the mean of each group and the differences between pairs of means. This is shown in Table 15.5.

Step 2. We must now determine the value of q. Given that the within-group sum of squares degrees of freedom equals 24 ($N - k = 27 - 3 = 24$), $k = 3$, and $\alpha = 0.05$, we find by referring to Table K (Appendix C) that $q_{0.05} = 3.53$.

Step 3. Find HSD by multiplying $q_{0.05}$ by $\sqrt{\hat{s}_\text{w}^2/n}$. The quantity $\hat{s}_\text{w}^2$ is found in Table 15.4 under within-group mean square. The n per group is 9. Thus:

$$\text{HSD} = 3.53 \sqrt{\frac{7.35}{9}} = 3.53(0.90) = 3.18$$

Step 4. Referring to Table 15.5, we find that the differences between $\overline{X}_1$ versus X_2 and X_2 versus $\overline{X}_3$ both exceed HSD $= 3.18$. We may therefore conclude that these differences are statistically significant at $\alpha = 0.05$. Since the group 2 mean (welfare sample) is significantly higher than the mean of the other two samples, we may conclude that the respondents' experience with welfare has influenced their attitude toward welfare in such a manner as to result in a high score relative to the other two samples.

Our conclusion is confirmed by the SPSS output in Table 15.6, in which the stars (*) indicate that group 2 differs significantly from groups 1 and 3 when we employ the Tukey-HSD test with a significance of .050. The means for the three groups are also shown in Table 15.6.

TABLE 15.5
Differences among means

	$\bar{X}_1$ $\bar{X}_1 = 5.11$	$\bar{X}_2$ $\bar{X}_2 = 8.67$	$\bar{X}_3$ $\bar{X}_3 = 3.78$
$\bar{X}_1 = 5.11$	. . .	3.56	1.33
$\bar{X}_2 = 8.67$	. . .	. . .	4.89
$\bar{X}_3 = 3.78$	. . .	. . .	. . .

TABLE 15.6
Tukey-HSD test with significance level .050

```
(*) Indicates significant differences
                                 G G G
                                 r r r
                                 p p p

                                 3 1 2
-----------------------------------------
Mean          Group
-----------------------------------------
3.7778         Grp 3
5.1111         Grp 1
8.6667         Grp 2             * *
-----------------------------------------
```

SUMMARY

We began this chapter with the observation that the researcher is frequently interested in conducting studies that are more extensive than the classical two-group design. However, when more than two groups are involved in a study, we increase the risk of making a type I error if we accept as significant any comparison that falls within the rejection region. In multigroup studies, it is desirable to know whether there is an indication of an overall effect of the independent variable before we investigate specific hypotheses. The analysis of variance technique provides such a test.

In this chapter, we presented an introduction to the complexities of analysis of variance. We showed that total sums of squares can be partitioned into two component sums of squares: the within-group and the between-group. These two component sums of squares provide us in turn with independent estimates of the population variance. A between-group mean square that is large relative to the within-group mean square suggests that the independent variable or experimental treatments are responsible for the large differences among the group means. The significance of the difference in mean squares is obtained by reference to the F table (Table D, Appendix C).

When the overall *F*-ratio is found to be statistically significant, we are free to investigate specific hypotheses, employing a multiple-comparison test.

TERMS TO REMEMBER

analysis of variance (ANOVA) A method, described initially by R. A. Fisher, for partitioning the sum of squares for experimental or survey data into known components of variation.
a posteriori comparisons Comparisons not planned in advance to investigate specific hypotheses concerning population parameters. A posteriori means after the fact.
a priori or planned comparisons Comparisons planned in advance to investigate specific hypotheses concerning population parameters. A priori means before the fact.
between-group sum of squares (SS_{bet}) The sum of the sum of squares between each group.
between-group variance An estimate of variance based on variability between groups.
***F*-ratio** The between-group variance estimate divided by the within-group variance estimate.
homogeneity of variance The condition that exists when two or more sample variances have been drawn from populations with equal variances.
mean square The sum of the squared deviations from the mean divided by degrees of freedom.
one-way analysis of variance Statistical analysis of various categories, groups, or levels of one independent (experimental) variable.
total sum of squares (TSS) Sum of the squared deviations from the overall mean.
variance estimate See *mean square.*
within-group sum of squares (SS_w) The sum of the sum of squares within each group.
within-group variance An estimate of variability based on variance within groups.

EXERCISES

1. The accompanying table is a summary table for an analysis of variance. Some of the information has been left out. Fill in the missing material and then continue with the following questions.

Source	SS	df	MS	*F*
Between-groups	______	3	______	6.25
Within-groups	______	16	2.114	
Total	______	______		

(*a*) How many categories (levels) of the independent variable were there?
(*b*) Assuming equal sample sizes, how many individuals were in each treatment condition?
(*c*) What are the degrees of freedom for the *F*-ratio?
(*d*) Assuming that $\alpha = .05$, what is the critical value of *F* required to reject the null hypothesis?
(*e*) Given the data reported in the summary table, can the null hypothesis be rejected?

2. The accompanying table is a summary table for an analysis of variance. Some of the information has been left out. Fill in the missing material and then continue with the following questions.

Source	SS	df	MS	F
Between-groups	12.450	______	6.225	______
Within-groups	______	27	______	
Total	60.609	29		

(*a*) How many categories (levels) of the independent variable are there?
(*b*) Assuming equal sample sizes, how many individuals were in each treatment condition?
(*c*) What are the degrees of freedom for the F-ratio?
(*d*) Assuming that $\alpha = .05$, what is the critical value of F required to reject the null hypothesis?
(*e*) Given the data reported in the summary table, can the null hypothesis be rejected?

3. Professor Stevens negotiates contracts with 10 different independent research organizations to compare the effectiveness of his marital satisfaction assessment instrument with that designed by another sociologist 10 years earlier. A significant difference (0.05 level) in favor of Professor Stevens's instrument is found in 1 of 10 studies. He subsequently claims that independent research has demonstrated the superiority of his instrument over the instrument developed earlier. Criticize this conclusion.

4. A random sample of four interviewers associated with a large public opinion firm have completed four interviews each, and the time in minutes necessary to complete the interviews is indicated in the accompanying table. Test the null hypothesis that the interviewers require an equal amount of time to complete an interview.

Interviewer A	Interviewer B	Interviewer C	Interviewer D
28	34	29	22
19	23	24	31
30	20	33	18
25	16	21	24

5. A labor organization randomly selected three medium-sized businesses for a study of worker grievances. The number of official grievances during the past five calendar years was tabulated. Set up and test an appropriate null hypothesis that will assess the extent to which a particular business has significantly more grievances than the others. Conduct an HSD test comparing each business with every other business, using $\alpha = 0.05$.

Business A	Business B	Business C
42	52	38
36	48	44
47	43	33
43	49	35
38	51	32

6. If the *F*-ratio is equal to 1.00, what do we conclude? If it is greater than 1.00, what do we conclude?

7. Tracy wants to repeat an experiment that was reported in a research journal. The author of the article noted that the results were significant. Specifically, the researcher wrote, "The results of a one-way ANOVA were statistically significant, F (2, 19) = 3.75 $p < .05$." Use this information to answer the following questions.
(*a*) How many levels of the independent variable were there?
(*b*) In total, how many subjects did the experimenter use?
(*c*) Was the *F*-ratio significant?

8. Given the SPSS output below, discuss the results, paying special attention to the following:
(*a*) Is there a significant difference in the family stability scores between the four schools?
(*b*) Which school or schools significantly differ(s) from the others using $\alpha = .05$?
(*c*) Do your calculations confirm the computer output?

One-way analysis of variance

Source	df	Sum of squares	Mean squares	F-ratio	F-probability
Between groups	3	919.7917	306.5972	6.4265	.0032
Within groups	20	954.1667	47.7083		
Total	23	1873.9583			

Tukey-HSD test with significant level .050.
(*) Indicates significant differences

Mean	School	Grp A	Grp B	Grp C	Grp D
52.5000	Grp A				
61.6667	Grp B				
61.6667	Grp C				
70.0000	Grp D	*			

9. A nutritional expert divides a sample of bicyclists into three groups. Group B is given a vitamin supplement and group C is given a diet of health foods. Group A is instructed to eat as they normally do. The expert subsequently records the number of minutes it takes each person to ride six miles.

A	B	C
15	14	13
16	13	12
14	15	11
17	16	14
15	14	11

Set up the appropriate hypothesis and conduct an analysis of variance.

10. For exercise 9, determine which diet or diets are superior. Use $\alpha = 0.01$.

11. A set of data are presented in the accompanying table.

X_1	X_2	X_3	X_4
16	18	18	20
14	17	19	26
12	13	18	17
10	14	13	15
8	7	9	11

Use an analysis of variance to analyze these data. Compare the means, using Tukey's HSD test.

12. Determine whether there is a significant difference in the number of major work stoppages between the three geographical areas given (hypothetical data).

New England		Mid-Atlantic		Far West	
Maine	8	New York	7	Washington	9
New Hampshire	7	New Jersey	7	Oregon	7
Vermont	8	Pennsylvania	8	Nevada	6
Massachusetts	6.5	Delaware	7	California	7
Rhode Island	8	Maryland	7	Alaska	8
Connecticut	8	District of Columbia	7	Hawaii	5

13. Suppose a family stability measure were administered in four public high schools to a sample of 24 students who attend the schools. The following scores were obtained.

School A	School B	School C	School D
50	55	50	70
50	60	65	80
55	65	75	65
60	55	55	70
45	70	60	75
55	65	65	60

Note: Low score = family instability.

Is there a significant difference in the family stability scores between the four groups of students?

PART IV

Inferential Statistics: Nonparametric Tests of Significance

CHAPTER 16

Statistical Inference with Categorical Variables: Chi-Square and Related Measures

16.1 INTRODUCTION

In recent years, there has been a broadening in both scope and penetration of research in the social sciences. Much provocative and stimulating research has been initiated in such diverse areas as socialization, welfare rights, public opinion polling, groups processes, and social stratification. New variables have been added to the arsenal of the researcher, many of which do not lend themselves to traditional parametric statistical treatment, either because of the scales of measurement used or because of flagrant violations of the assumptions of these parametric tests. For these reasons, many new statistical techniques have been developed (see Box 16.1). In this chapter and the next, we present a few techniques from among over 40 nonparametric procedures,* none of which require that we make any assumptions about the shape of the population distribution. See Table 16.1 for nonparametric tests that appear in Chapters 16 and 17 as well as several parametric tests of significance that appeared earlier in the text. Tests in parentheses are not covered.

Parametric techniques are usually preferable because of their greater sensitivity; that is, they are more likely to lead to the rejection of H_0 when it is actually false. This

*A nonparametric test of significance is one that makes no assumptions concerning the shape of the parent distribution or population; accordingly, it is commonly referred to as a distribution-free test of significance.

BOX 16.1

DOGS: THE BEST FRIEND OF A CORONARY PATIENT?

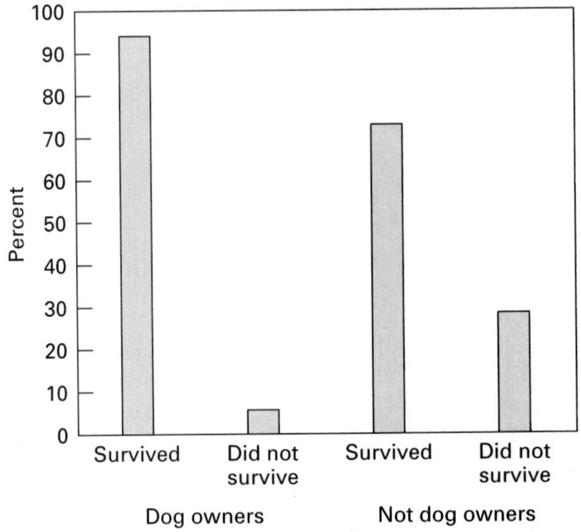

The cliché "Dog is man's best friend" is celebrated in both song and legend. Recent evidence suggests that the presence of a dog may also be therapeutic. A group of coronary patients were studied for one year following their release from the hospital. Fifty-three of these patients owned dogs and 39 did not. One year later, 11 of the patients who did not own dogs had died, whereas only three of the dog owners succumbed.

In this study, there are two nominal variables—status with respect to ownership of a pet dog and survival record after suffering a heart attack. There are two values of each variable: owning or not owning a dog, and surviving or not surviving a heart condition. At the descriptive level, we could determine the percent of pet owners versus the percent of nonowners who survived and failed to survive at least one year following hospitalization. These results are summarized in the bar graph above.

At the inferential level, the data can be cast in the form of a 2 × 2 contingency table. Reading downward, we see that 50 of 53 dog owners survived at least one year. In contrast, only 28 of 39 nondog owners enjoyed a similar survival record. The appropriate test of significance—the chi squre test—permits us to ascertain whether or not dog ownership and survival are related.

	Status of dog ownership		
Survival status	**Owners**	**Not owners**	**Total**
Survived one year	50	28	78
Did not survive	3	11	14
Totals	53	39	92

2 × 2 contingency table showing number of dog owners and number of nondog owners who survived at least one year following onset of a coronary disease.

Source: Friedman (1978), pp. 57–58.

TABLE 16.1
Summary of nonparametric and parametric tests

Scale of measurement	One-sample case	Two-sample case: Related samples	Two-sample case: Independent samples
Nominal	Pearson χ^2 test Section 16.2	(McNemar test for significance of change)	Pearson χ^2 test Sections 16.3–16.4
Ordinal	(Kolmogorov-Smirnov one-sample test	Sign test Section 17.4	
	(One sample runs test)	Wilcoxon matched-pairs signed-rank test Section 17.5	Mann-Whitney U Section 17.2
Interval/ratio	Student's t Section 14.5	(Student's t for correlated groups)	(Student's t for two samples) (z-statistic for two samples)

generalization is not true, however, when the underlying assumptions are seriously violated. Indeed, under certain circumstances (e.g., badly skewed distributions, particularly with small sample sizes), a nonparametric test may well be as powerful as its parametric counterpart. Consequently, the researcher is frequently faced with the difficult choice of a statistical test appropriate for his or her data.

At this point, let us interject a word of caution with respect to the choice of statistical tests of inference. For heuristic purposes, we take a few sample problems and subject them to statistical analyses employing several different tests of significance. This procedure will serve to clarify points of difference among the various tests. However, you may inadvertently draw an erroneous conclusion; namely, that researchers first collect their data, then "shop around" for a statistical test that will be the most sensitive to any differences that exist. Actually, nothing could be further from the truth. The null hypothesis, alternative hypothesis, statistical test, sampling distribution, and level of significance should all be specified in *advance* of the collection of data. If we "shop around," so to speak, after the collection of the data, we tend to maximize the effects of any chance differences that favor one test over another. As a result, the possibility of a type I error (rejecting the null hypothesis when it is true) is substantially increased.

Usually, we do not have the problem of choosing statistical tests in relation to categorical variables because nonparametric tests alone are suitable for enumerative data. Even here, however, parametric estimation tests are available when N is sufficiently large.

When our scales of measurement are either interval or ratio, the problem of choosing a statistical treatment usually arises when we employ small samples* or

* When large samples are employed, the parametric tests are almost always appropriate because of the *central limit theorem* (Section 14.2).

when there is doubt concerning the normality of the underlying population distribution. In Chapter 17, we demonstrate several nonparametric statistical tests employed when such doubts arise.

16.2
THE χ^2 ONE-VARIABLE CASE

Following a course in research methods, 86 nursing students completed a course-evaluation questionnaire that was administered to the entire class (Van Bree, 1981). One item in the questionnaire dealt with the importance of research to the nursing profession. The observed frequencies are presented in Table 16.2.

This is the type of problem for which the χ^2* **one-variable test** is ideally suited. In single-variable applications, the χ^2 test has been described as a **"goodness-of-fit" technique:** It permits us to determine whether a significant difference exists between the *observed* number of cases falling into each category and the *expected* number of cases, based on the null hypothesis. In other words, it permits us to answer the question, "How well does our observed distribution fit the theoretical distribution?"

If the responses from the 86 students were randomly distributed across all five possible response categories, we would theoretically *expect* that approximately 17 students would choose each category since $86/5 = 17.2$. The observed distribution of responses that was presented in Table 16.2 will be contrasted with the expected distribution (Table 16.3). What we require, then, is a null hypothesis that allows us to specify the expected frequencies in each category, and subsequently to test this null hypothesis. The null hypothesis may be tested by:

$$\chi^2 = \sum_{i=1}^{k} \frac{(f_0 - f_e)^2}{f_e} \qquad (16.1)$$

where f_0 = the observed number in a given category
f_e = the expected number in that category
$\sum_{i=1}^{k}$ = directs us to sum this ratio over all k categories

In our example, the null hypothesis would be that there is an equal preference for each response category; that is, $86/5 = 17.2$ is the expected frequency in each category (Table 16.3).

As is readily apparent from equation (16.1), if there is close agreement between the observed frequencies and expected frequencies, the resulting χ^2 will be small, leading to a failure to reject the null hypothesis. If the observed and expected values for all cells in the table are equal, χ^2 will reach its lower limit of 0.[†] As the

* We use the symbol χ^2 to represent the test of significance as well as the quantity obtained from the test for observed frequencies. The term *chi-square* refers to the theoretical sampling distribution known as the chi-square distribution.

[†] The upper limit of χ^2 is $N(k - 1)$ where N is the total number of cases and k the number of rows or columns in the table, whichever is smaller. For example, in a 3×3 table with 100 cases, the maximum value of χ^2 would be 200 because $100(3 - 1) = 200$.

TABLE 16.2
Contingency table showing observed frequencies

	Student response				
Item	**Strongly agree**	**Agree**	**Undecided**	**Disagree**	**Strongly disagree**
Research is important to nursing profession	34	41	7	3	1

Source: Van Bree (1981), pp. 39–41.

TABLE 16.3
Contingency table showing expected frequencies

	Student response				
Item	**Strongly agree**	**Agree**	**Undecided**	**Disagree**	**Strongly disagree**
Research is important to the nursing profession	17.2	17.2	17.2	17.2	17.2

Source: Van Bree (1981), pp. 39–41.

TABLE 16.4
Computation of chi-square

f_0	f_e	$f_0 - f_e$	$(f_0 - f_e)^2$	$(f_0 - f_e)^2/f_e$
34	17.2	−16.8	282.24	16.409
41	17.2	23.8	566.44	32.933
7	17.2	−10.2	104.04	6.049
3	17.2	−14.2	201.64	11.723
1	17.2	−16.2	262.44	15.258
86	86.0			$\chi^2 =$ 82.372

discrepancy ($f_0 - f_e$) increases, the value of χ^2 increases. The larger the χ^2, the more likely we are to reject the null hypothesis.

Substituting the observed and expected values into equation (16.1), we find χ^2 to be 82.372 as shown in Table 16.4 and in these calculations. Either technique works equally well. Figure 16.1 shows that we can reject the null hypothesis.

$$\chi^2 = \frac{(34 - 17.2)^2}{17.2} + \frac{(41 - 17.2)^2}{17.2} + \frac{(7 - 17.2)^2}{17.2} + \frac{(3 - 17.2)^2}{17.2} + \frac{(1 - 17.2)^2}{17.2}$$

$$= 16.409 + 32.933 + 6.049 + 11.723 + 15.258$$

$$= 82.372$$

In studying the Student's t-ratio (Section 14.5), we saw that the sampling distributions of t varied as a function of degrees of freedom. The same is true for χ^2. However, assignments of degrees of freedom with the Student's t-ratio are based on

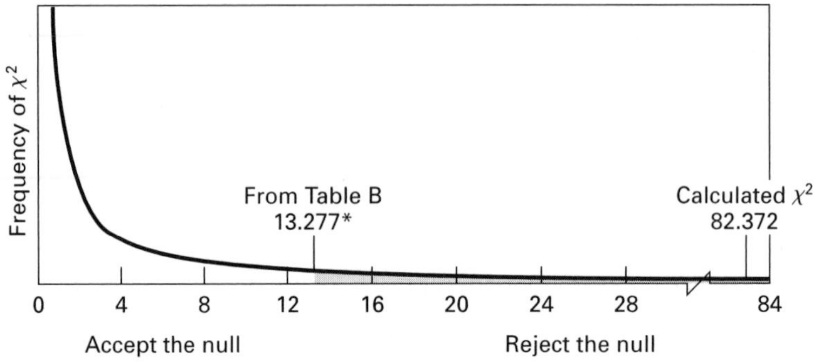

*Assumes α = 0.01

FIGURE 16.1
Sampling distribution: of χ^2 for four degrees of freedom

N, whereas the degrees of freedom for χ^2 are a function of the number of cells (k). In the one-variable case, df $= k - 1$ because the marginal total is fixed, and only $k - 1$ cells are free to vary. Given that the total is 86, as soon as four cells or categories are filled, the fifth is completely determined. Thus, there are four degrees of freedom.

In the one-variable case, df $= k - 1$. Table B, Appendix C, lists the critical values of χ^2 for various α-levels. If the obtained χ^2 value *exceeds* the critical value at a given probability level, the null hypothesis may be rejected at that level of significance. Hence, we are concerned only with the right-hand tail of the distribution as all χ^2 tests are one-tailed.

In this example, $k = 5$. Therefore, df $= 4$. Employing $\alpha = 0.01$, we find that Table B (Appendix C) indicates that a χ^2 value of 13.277 or greater is required for significance. Since our obtained value of 82.372 is greater than 13.277, we may reject the null hypothesis (see Figure 16.1) and assert instead that each response category was not equally preferred. Incidentally, we are free to investigate any form of hypothetical distribution suggested for prior research or theoretical considerations. If we had prior reason to suspect that the distribution might be 0.25, 0.25, 0.20, 0.20, or 0.10, we could investigate this H_0 by multiplying each hypothesized proportion by *N* to obtain the expected frequency in each cell.

Before proceeding, we should note that the shape of the theoretical χ^2 distribution is determined by the degrees of freedom. Figure 16.2 shows the distribution for 1, 2, and 10 degrees of freedom.

As is apparent in Figure 16.2, for all degrees of freedom the χ^2 distribution is skewed to the right, with those curves associated with large degrees of freedom reaching far to the right before approaching the horizontal axis, which designates the value of χ^2. For example, from Table B (Appendix C) we see that the critical region for a test, given $\alpha = 0.01$ and degrees of freedom equal to 1, begins at 6.635. By following the 0.01 column down, you will see that as we deal with greater degrees of freedom (i.e., more cells), the corresponding value of χ^2 from Table B that must be exceeded to reject the null hypothesis increases until it reaches 50.892 for 30 degrees of freedom.

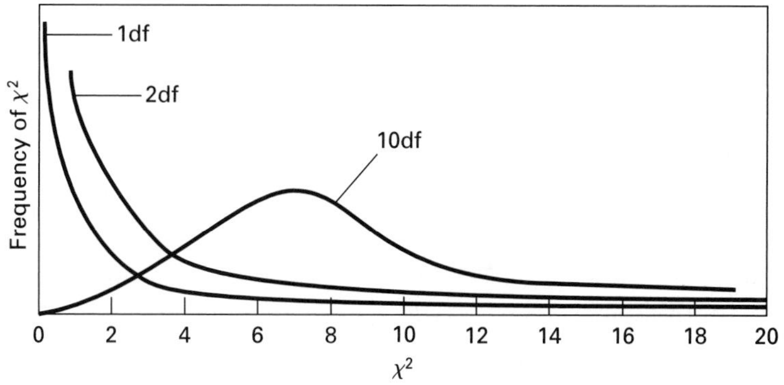

FIGURE 16.2
χ^2 distribution for 1, 2, and 10 degrees of freedom

16.3 THE χ^2 TEST OF THE INDEPENDENCE OF VARIABLES

So far we have been concerned with the one-variable case. In practice, we do not encounter the one-variable case very frequently when using categorical variables. More often we ask questions concerning the interrelationships between and among variables. For example, we may ask:

1. Is there a difference in the crime rate of children coming from different socioeconomic backgrounds? (In other words, is the crime rate independent of socioeconomic background, or does it depend in part on this background?)

2. If we are conducting an opinion poll, can we determine whether there is a difference between males and females in their opinions about a given issue? (Stated another way, does the opinion on a given issue depend to any extent on the gender of the respondent?)

These are only two examples of problems for which the χ^2 technique can be used. You could undoubtedly extend this list to include many campus activities, such as the attitudes of fraternity and sorority members versus nonfraternity and nonsorority students toward certain basic issues (e.g., cheating on exams), or differences in grading practices among professors in various academic departments. All of these problems have certain characteristics in common: (1) They deal with two or more variables in which (2) the data consist of a frequency count that is tabulated and placed in the appropriate cells.

These examples also share an additional and more important characteristic: (3) There is no immediately obvious way to assign expected frequency values to each category. However, as we will point out shortly, we must consequently base our expected frequencies on the observed frequencies themselves.

Let's look at another example. Political scientists, sociologists, and politicians have long been interested in the relationship between religious affiliation and political

TABLE 16.5
Two-by-two contingency table showing the relationship between religious and political affiliation

Political affiliation	Religious affiliation c_1 Catholic	c_2 Protestant	Total
Democrat r_1	*a* 125	*b* 225	350
Republican r_2	*c* 75	*d* 125	200
Total	200	350	550

party affiliation. Traditionally, Catholics have aligned themselves with the Democratic party, whereas Protestants were more likely to support Republican candidates. The following study of 550 registered voters in California will allow us to test the null hypothesis that Catholics are no more likely than Protestants to affiliate with either party (see Table 16.5).

We will now apply a test of significance. In formal statistical terms:

1. *Null hypothesis* (H_0). Political party affiliation and religious affiliation are independent (statistically unrelated).

2. *Alternative hypothesis* (H_1). Political party affiliation and religious affiliation are not independent.

3. *Statistical test.* Since we are assuming that religious and political affiliations are independent and the data are in terms of frequencies in discrete categories, the χ^2 test of independence is the appropriate statistical test.

4. *Significance level.* $\alpha = 0.05$.

5. *Sampling distribution.* The sampling distribution is the chi-square distribution with df $= (r - 1)(c - 1)$. Since marginal totals are fixed, the frequency of only one cell is free to vary; that is, once one cell value is known in a 2×2 table, the other three cell values are determined. Therefore, we have a 1-degree-of-freedom situation. The general rule for finding df in the two-variable case is $(r - 1)(c - 1)$, in which r = number of rows and c = number of columns. Thus, in the present example df $= (2 - 1)(2 - 1) = 1$.

6. *Critical region.* Table B in Appendix C shows that for df $= 1$, $\alpha = 0.05$, the critical region consists of all values of $\chi^2 \geq 3.841$. Thus, χ^2 is calculated from equation (16.1):

$$\chi^2 = \sum_{i=1}^{k} \frac{(f_0 - f_e)^2}{f_e}$$

The main problem now is to decide on a basis for determining the expected cell frequencies. Recall from Chapter 12, equation (12.9), that "the probability of the

TABLE 16.6
Relationship between religious and political affiliation (expected frequencies in parentheses)

Political affiliation	Religious affiliation: Catholic	Religious affiliation: Protestant	Total
Democrat	*a* 125 (127.3)	*b* 225 (222.7)	350
Republican	*c* 75 (72.7)	*d* 125 (127.3)	200
Total	200	350	550

simultaneous or successive occurrence of two events is the product of the separate probabilities of each event." In Table 16.5 the probability of a respondent in the total sample being Catholic is 200/550 or 0.364 and the probability of a respondent being a Democrat is 350/550 or 0.636; therefore, the joint probability of being a Catholic and a Democrat (see cell *a*) is (0.364)(0.636) or 0.2315. Multiplying 0.2315 by our total sample size of 550 results in an expected frequency in cell *a* of 127.3. You could proceed further in this manner and calculate the expected frequency for the remaining cells. However, there is a simple rule that may be followed in determining expected frequency of a given cell: Multiply the two marginal frequencies common to that cell and divide by *N*.

Let's again concentrate on cell *a*. The two marginal totals common to cell *a* are row 1 marginal and column 1 marginal. If the null hypothesis is correct and political affiliation is independent of religious affiliation, we would expect the same proportion of respondents who are Catholics to affiliate with the Democratic party as would those who are Protestants. Since 200 of the total sample of 550 are Catholic, we would expect that $(200 \times 350)/550$ would be found in cell *a*. This figure comes to 127.3, a value identical to the expected frequency we calculated utilizing the more cumbersome *joint-probability method*.

Table 16.6 presents the observed data, with the expected cell frequencies within parentheses. Incidentally, you may have noted that the four expected frequencies total 550 and that the expected frequencies for a given column or row sum to the respective observed column or row marginal.

Table 16.6 shows that 125 of the 200 Catholics claimed an affiliation with the Democratic party and that 225 of the 350 Protestants were also affiliated with the Democrats. Do these data indicate that political affiliation is independent of religious affiliation? Table 16.7 summarizes the necessary calculations.

Since the χ^2 value of 0.17 (see Table 16.7) is less than the value of 3.84 (1df, $\alpha = 0.05$) from Table B (in Appendix C) required for significance at the 0.05 level, we fail to reject H_0. In other words, we must conclude that political party affiliation and religious affiliation are independent; that is, there is no difference in political party affiliation between Catholics and Protestants.

TABLE 16.7
Computation of chi-square

Cell	f_0	f_e	$f_0 - f_e$	$(f_0 - f_e)^2$	$(f_0 - f_e)^2/f_e$
a	125	127.3	−2.3	5.29	0.04
b	225	222.7	2.3	5.29	0.02
c	75	72.7	2.3	5.29	0.07
d	125	127.3	− 2.3	5.29	0.04
	550	550.0			$\chi^2 =$ 0.17

In research, we often find that we have more than two subgroups within a nominal class. For example, we might have three categories in one scale and four in another, resulting in a 3×4 contingency table. The procedure for obtaining the expected frequencies is the same as the one for the 2×2 contingency table. Of course, the degrees of freedom will be greater than 1 (e.g., 3×4 contingency table, df $= 6$). See Case Example 16.1 on page 390 for an example of a 2×3 table, and Box 16.2 for an example of the SSPS output that accompanies a chi-square analysis.

16.4 LIMITATIONS IN THE USE OF χ^2

A fundamental assumption in the use of χ^2 is that each observation or frequency is independent of all other observations. Consequently, you may not make several observations on the same individual and treat each as though it were independent of all the other observations. Such an error produces what is referred to as an **inflated** N because you are counting or including some people more than once, that is, you are treating the data as though you had a greater number of independent observations than you actually have. This error is extremely serious and may easily lead to the rejection of the null hypothesis when it is in fact true.

Consider the following hypothetical example. Imagine that you are a student in a sociology course. As a class project, you decide to poll the student body to determine whether male and female students differ in their opinions on some issue of contemporary significance. Each of 15 members of the class is asked to obtain replies from 10 respondents, 5 male and 5 female. The results are listed in Table 16.8 in which the expected cell frequencies are included in parentheses.

Assuming $\alpha = 0.05$, we find that the critical region consists of all the values of $\chi^2 \geq 3.84$. Since the obtained χ^2 of $10.71 > 3.84$, you reject the null hypothesis of no difference in the opinions of male and female students on the issue in question. You conclude instead that approval of the issue is dependent on the sex of the respondent.

After completing the study, you discover that a number of students were inadvertently polled as many as two or three times by different members of the class. Consequently, the frequencies within the cells are not independent because some individuals had contributed as many as two or three responses. In a reanalysis of the data, in which only one frequency per respondent was permitted, we obtained the results shown in Table 16.9.

Note that now the obtained χ^2 of $2.72 < 3.84$; thus, you fail to reject H_0. The failure to achieve independence of responses resulted in a serious error in the original

TABLE 16.8
Response to question in class project

Response to question	Sex: Male	Sex: Female	Total
Approve	30 (40)	50 (40)	80
Disapprove	45 (35)	25 (35)	70
Total	75	75	150

$\chi^2 = 10.71$

TABLE 16.9
Reanalysis of response to question

Response to question	Sex: Male	Sex: Female	Total
Approve	28 (32.5)	32 (27.5)	60
Disapprove	37 (32.5)	23 (27.5)	60
Total	65	55	120

$\chi^2 = 2.72$

conclusion. Incidentally, you should note that the requirement of independence within a cell or condition is basic to *all* statistical tests. We have mentioned that specifically in connection with the χ^2 test because violations may be very subtle and not easily recognized.

An equally important limitation of χ^2 stems from the fact that its value is proportional to the sample size. For example, if the sample in Table 16.9 were doubled to 240 and the observed frequencies were increased proportionately (i.e., 56, 64, 74, and 46) χ^2 would equal 5.44 rather than 2.72. Consequently, despite the unchanged relationship, we would reject rather than fail to reject the H_0. For this reason, many social scientists prefer to avoid χ^2 when dealing with large samples because the results can be very misleading. Indeed, it is difficult not to reject the H_0 when the sample size is over 1,000 cases!

With small N's or when the expected proportion in any cell is small, the approximation of the sample statistics to the chi-square distribution may not be very close. A rule that has been generally adopted, in the one-degree-of-freedom situation, is that the *expected frequency* in all cells should be equal to or greater than 5. When df > 1, the expected frequency should be equal to or greater than 5 in at least 80% of the cells. When these requirements are not met, other statistical tests are available. [See Siegel and Castellan (1988).]

When a contingency table is larger than 2×2, it is possible to collapse rows or columns in such a manner as to increase the frequencies within the resulting cells.

CASE EXAMPLE 16.1

THE SUCCESSFUL WOMEN

With the relatively recent changes in the traditional roles of women in society, much attention has been directed to their possible impact on various aspects of the behavior and emotions of contemporary women. In this hypothetical study, 70 women completed Horner's multiple-item scale on the fear of success as well as other items aimed at assessing attitudes about traditional sex-roles and basic demographic questions about their age, income, and educational attainment.

In one portion of the study, the women were placed into two groups: those with a fear of success and those with no fear of success. This dependent variable was analyzed in a contingency analysis with the women's educational level serving as the independent variable. The results from a SPSS analysis are summarized in Table 16.10 along with the computations using equation (16.1).

The observed and expected frequencies are displayed in each cell. The row marginals indicate that 44 (62.9%) of the women were classified as having a fear of success and 26 (37.1%) did not have a fear of success. The column marginals display the distribution of the women's educational attainment.

Let's test the null hypothesis that fear of success is independent of educational attainment against the alternative hypothesis that they are not independent. The Pearson χ^2 (named after E. S. Pearson) value is shown as 9.21911, there are two degrees of freedom (df = 2), and the calculated significance is .00996. The minimum expected frequency is 6.69 (see Section 16.4) and there are no missing observations.

The critical value of χ^2 at $\alpha = 0.05$ with df = 2 is 5.991 (from Table B in Appendix C). Since the calculated χ^2 exceeds this value, we may reject H_0 and assert H_1. Examination of the significance value shown in the SPSS output (.00996) confirms our decision.

The data reveal a tendency for the women to have a greater fear of success as their educational attainment increases. Although we can conclude that there is a statistically significant increase in fear of success with higher educational attainment, we cannot assume causality. An alternative explanation is that well-educated women are employed in positions that place them in direct competition with men and these women may in turn demand more of themselves.

Source: Adapted from Caballero, Giles, and Shaver (1975), pp. 319–26.

Such a practice is used widely in the social sciences with the understanding that the categories that are combined logically fit together and that the procedure is not intended to increase or decrease the value of χ^2.

TABLE 16.10
Relationship between educational level and fear of success

	Educational level				
	Observed expected	No BA 1.00	BA 2.00	Grad school 3.00	Row total
Fear of Success	Yes 1.00	12 17.60	12 11.31	20 15.09	44 62.9%
	No 2.00	16 10.40	6 6.69	4 8.91	26 37.1%
	Column total	28 40.0%	18 25.7%	24 34.3%	70 100.0%

Chi-square	Value	df	Significance
Pearson	9.21911	2	.00996

Minimum expected frequency - 6.69
Number of missing observations: 0

$$\chi^2 = \frac{(12 - 17.60)^2}{17.60} + \frac{(12 - 11.31)^2}{11.31} + \cdots + \frac{(4 - 8.91)^2}{8.91}$$
$$= 1.78 + 0.04 + 1.60 + 3.02 + 0.07 + 2.71$$
$$= 9.22$$
$$\text{df} = (r - 1)(c - 1) = 2$$

16.5 NOMINAL MEASURES OF ASSOCIATION BASED ON χ^2

Although we are able to reject the null hypothesis regarding differences between groups using the χ^2-test, the results provide no information about the *strength* of the relationship between the independent and the dependent variables. In the next section, we will show you how to determine the degree to which the independent and dependent variables are related to each other.

We learned in Section 16.4 that the value of χ^2 is directly proportional to the sample size. This characteristic of χ^2 plus the observation that $\chi^2 = 0$ when two variables are statistically independent led to the development of the **phi coefficient,** which is used primarily with 2 × 2 tables.

$$\phi = \sqrt{\frac{\chi^2}{N}} \qquad (16.2)$$

or

$$\phi^2 = \frac{\chi^2}{N} \qquad (16.3)$$

For any table in which either the number of rows or columns equals two, phi ranges from 0 when the variables are independent to 1 when the variables are perfectly related.* Phi is sometimes referred to as a measure of the degree of diagonal

* The maximum value of phi exceeds 1 when a table contains more than two rows and two columns.

concentration; hence, when two diagonally opposite cells are both empty as in the following example, phi equals 1, as is demonstrated in Tables 16.11 and 16.12. As is the case with the other two measures of association to be discussed, phi only requires nominal-level data and provides us with a measure of the strength, but not the direction, of association since the sign of phi will always be positive. By examining the percentage distribution of cases in the cells, we can, of course, determine the pattern of the relationship (see Chapter 8).

TABLE 16.11
Special case in which phi equals 1, example 1

	Sex		
Vote	**Male**	**Female**	**Total**
Yes	50	0	50
No	0	50	50
Total	50	50	$N = 100$

$$\chi^2 = \frac{(50 - 25)^2}{25} + \frac{(0 - 25)^2}{25} + \frac{(0 - 25)^2}{25} + \frac{(50 - 25)^2}{25}$$

$$= 25 + 25 + 25 + 25$$

$$= 100$$

Using equations (16.2) and (16.3):

$$\phi = \sqrt{\frac{100}{100}} = 1 \quad \text{and} \quad \phi^2 = \frac{100}{100} = 1$$

TABLE 16.12
Special case in which phi equals 1, example 2

	Sex		
Vote	**Male**	**Female**	**Total**
Yes	0	50	50
No	50	0	50
Total	50	50	$N = 100$

$$\chi^2 = \frac{(0 - 25)^2}{25} + \frac{(50 - 25)^2}{25} + \frac{(50 - 25)^2}{25} + \frac{(0 - 25)^2}{25}$$

$$= 25 + 25 + 25 + 25$$

$$= 100$$

$$\phi = \sqrt{\frac{100}{100}} = 1 \quad \text{and} \quad \phi^2 = \frac{100}{100} = 1$$

The **contingency coefficient** was developed primarily for use with square tables having more than two rows and columns, for example, 3 × 3 or 4 × 4.

$$C = \sqrt{\frac{\chi^2}{\chi^2 + N}} \tag{16.4}$$

The contingency coefficient equals 0 when the variables are independent; however, its maximum value is always less than 1 and is determined by the number of rows and columns in the table.* C has been calculated for the data in Table 16.13.

In this instance $C = 0.55$, and we can conclude that there is a moderately strong relationship between educational attainment and political activism since the maximum value for C with a 3 × 3 table is 0.816. By examining Table 16.13, we can also see that the respondents who have completed higher levels of education tend to be more politically active than those who have had less education.

A disadvantage of the contingency coefficient, in addition to its interpretability when the variables are neither independent nor perfectly related, is the difficulty of comparing contingency coefficients for tables of unequal size (differing numbers of rows and columns). The fluctuation of its maximum value has led to the development of **Cramer's *V*,** a third measure of association for nominal-level data based on χ^2, which can be used with square and nonsquare tables of any size. Cramer's V ranges from 0 when the variables are independent to 1 when they are perfectly related.

$$V = \sqrt{\frac{\chi^2}{N \cdot \text{minimum}\ (r - 1 \text{ or } c - 1)}} \tag{16.5}$$

The denominator of Cramer's V is calculated by multiplying N times the smaller of the two quantities, $r - 1$ or $c - 1$. Calculating V for Table 16.13, we find it to equal 0.47 versus 0.55 for C. This example should help clarify the problems of interpreting ϕ, C, and V. They are not equivalent measures with one limited exception.†

$$V = \sqrt{\frac{66.0}{150(3 - 1)}} = \sqrt{0.220} = 0.47$$

Cramer's V is the most versatile of the three measures of association since its range is always 0 to 1 and it can be used with a table of any dimension. It does share limitations with the phi and contingency coefficients. Cramer's V does not allow for a proportional reduction in error (PRE) interpretation, nor does it provide an indication of the direction of relationship.

---

* The maximum value for a square table (e.g., 2 × 2, 3 × 3) is calculated using the equation $\sqrt{(k - 1)/k}$ when k equals the number of rows or columns, whichever is less. For a 2 × 2 table, the maximum value would be $\sqrt{(2 - 1)/2} = \sqrt{1/2} = 0.707$, and for a 3 × 3 table, the maximum value would be $\sqrt{(3 - 1)/3} = 0.816$.

† $V^2 = \phi^2$ in a 2 × k table.

TABLE 16.13
Educational attainment by political activism

	Educational attainment			
Political activism	**Low**	**Moderate**	**High**	**Total**
High	5	10	35	50
Moderate	15	30	5	50
Low	30	10	10	50
Total	50	50	50	$N = 150$

$$\chi^2 = \frac{(5 - 16.7)^2}{16.7} + \frac{(10 - 16.7)^2}{16.7} + \frac{(35 - 16.7)^2}{16.7} + \frac{(15 - 16.7)^2}{16.7}$$

$$+ \frac{(30 - 16.7)^2}{16.7} + \frac{(5 - 16.7)^2}{16.7} + \frac{(30 - 16.7)^2}{16.7} + \frac{(10 - 16.7)^2}{16.7}$$

$$+ \frac{(10 - 16.7)^2}{16.7}$$

$$= 8.2 + 2.7 + 20.1 + 0.2 + 10.6 + 8.2 + 10.6 + 2.7 + 2.7$$

$$= 66.0$$

$$C = \sqrt{\frac{\chi^2}{\chi^2 + N}} = \sqrt{\frac{66.0}{66.0 + 150}} = 0.55$$

BOX 16.2

DOG OWNERSHIP AND SURVIVAL

Research involving coronary patients and the relationship between their survival status and the ownership of a dog was introduced in Box 16.1. Table 16.14 is based on the data presented in that ex-example and shows the relationship between survival status, the dependent variable, and dog ownership, the independent variable. Using an SPSS analysis, we have tested the null hypothesis that survival of a heart attack is independent of dog ownership ($\alpha = 0.05$). Pearson's χ^2 value is 8.85109, df = 1, and the significance is shown as .00293. We can therefore reject the null hypothesis that survival of a heart attack and dog ownership are independent. You can confirm this by referring to Table B in Appendix C where you will see that the critical value of χ^2 at $\alpha = 0.05$ with df = 1 is 3.841. The SPSS-computed Pearson's χ^2 value shown below Table 16.4 exceeds 3.841 and falls in the critical region. Equation (16.1) has also been used to compute χ^2.

Phi, the contingency coefficient, and Cramer's *V*, the three nominal measures of association based upon chi-square, have been computed using SPSS and equations (16.2), (16.4), and (16.5). Only in the special instance in which a table's dimensions are 2×2 are all three measures of association appropriate for one table.

TABLE 16.14
Status of dog ownership and survival of a heart attack

Dog ownership

Survival status	Observed / expected	Owners	Nonowners	Row total
	Survived one year	50 44.93	28 33.06	78 84.8%
	Did not survive	3 8.07	11 5.93	14 15.2%
	Column total	53 57.6%	39 42.4%	92 100.0%

Chi-square	Value	DF	Significance
Pearson	8.85109	1	.00293
Minimum expected frequency	5.93		

Statistic	Value
Phi	.31017
Cramer's *V*	.31017
Contingency coefficient	.29625

Number of missing observations: 0

Calculations using equation 16.1 are shown below:

$$\chi^2 = \frac{(50 - 44.93)^2}{44.93} + \frac{(28 - 33.06)^2}{33.06} + \frac{(3 - 8.07)^2}{8.07} + \frac{(11 - 5.93)^2}{5.93}$$
$$= 0.57 + 0.77 + 3.18 + 4.33$$
$$= 8.85$$
$$\text{df} = (c - 1)(c - 1) = 1$$

$$\phi = \sqrt{\frac{8.85}{92}} = \sqrt{0.0962} = 0.310$$

$$C = \sqrt{\frac{8.85}{8.85 + 92}} = \sqrt{\frac{8.85}{100.85}} = 0.296$$

$$V = \sqrt{\frac{8.85}{92(1)}} = \sqrt{0.0962} = 0.310$$

SUMMARY

In this chapter, we have discussed two tests of significance used with categorical variables; that is, the χ^2 one-variable test and the χ^2 two-variable test.

The χ^2 one-variable test has been described as a "goodness-of-fit" technique, permitting us to determine whether a significant difference exists between the *observed* number of cases appearing in each category and the *expected* number of cases specified under the null hypothesis.

The χ^2 test of independence of variables may be used to determine whether two variables are related or independent. If the χ^2 value is significant, we may conclude that the variables are interdependent or related.

We discussed three limitations on the use of the χ^2 test. In the one-degree-of-freedom situation, the expected frequency should equal or exceed 5 to permit the use of the χ^2 test. When df > 1, the expected frequency in 80% of the cells should equal or exceed 5. A second, and most important, restriction is that the frequency counts must be independent of one another. Failure to meet this requirement results in an error known as the inflated *N* and may well lead to the rejection of the null hypothesis when it is true (type I error). A third limitation is that χ^2 is directly proportional to *N* and hence can be misleading.

Three nominal measures of association were discussed, including the phi coefficient, the contingency coefficient, and Cramer's *V*.

TERMS TO REMEMBER

contingency coefficient A nominal measure of association based on χ^2 and used primarily for square tables, makes it the most versatile of the 3 measures of association.

Cramer's *V* A nominal measure of association based on χ^2 suitable for tables of any dimension.

inflated *N* An error produced whenever several observations are made on the same individual and treated as though they were independent observations.

one-variable test ("goodness-of-fit" technique) A test of whether or not a significant difference exists between the *observed* number of cases falling into each category and the *expected* number of cases, based on the null hypothesis.

phi coefficient A nominal measure of association based on χ^2 used with 2×2 tables.

EXERCISES

1. Is birth order related to one's selection of a career? Bohmer and Sitton (1993) wanted to test the hypothesis that last born children may be more likely to accept nontraditional occupations. For their research, they compared the career choice of prominent women born between the years 1857 and 1943. According to their review, first-born women were equally likely to become scientists, social reformers, performing artists, or writers. Women who were born last in their families had a different pattern of career choice. The data are presented below:

Career choices of last-born women				
Scientist	**Social reformer**	**Performing artist**	**Writer**	**Total**
23	13	34	14	84

Source: P. Bohmer and S. Sitton, "The Influence of Birth Order and Family Size on Notable American Women's Selection of Careers," *The Psychological Record* 43 (1993), pp. 375–80.

Set up this study in formal statistical terms and draw appropriate conclusions.

2. Let's suppose that you are a demographer conducting research on the number of children preferred by American couples. Research in 1992 indicated that 16% of the couples polled preferred no children, 65% preferred one or two children, and 19% preferred three or four children (hypothetical data). Realizing that attitudes may have changed in five years, you conducted a national study of 600 couples selected by an accepted sampling technique. The distributions for 1992 and 1997 are presented here. Using χ^2, test the null hypothesis that the preferred number of children has not changed from 1992 to 1997. Assume that the 1992 distribution is expected, the 1997 distribution is observed, and $\alpha = 0.01$.

Expected frequencies (1992)

		Preferred number of children		
	0	**1 or 2**	**3 or 4**	**Marginal total**
Number of couples preferring	96	390	114	600

Observed frequencies (1997)

		Preferred number of children		
	0	**1 or 2**	**3 or 4**	**Marginal total**
Number of couples preferring	120	400	80	600

3. Given the following table in which $N = 80$ and only the marginal values are shown, enter the cell values that would yield a χ^2 of 0. Calculate χ^2 and confirm its value. Calculate ϕ.

	X		
Y			40
			40
	40	40	$N = 80$

4. For the following values of χ^2, determine if the obtained value is significant using $\alpha = .01$ and also $\alpha = .05$

(*a*) $\chi^2 = 4.12$, df $= 1$
(*b*) $\chi^2 = 3.94$, df $= 2$
(*c*) $\chi^2 = 7.99$, df $= 3$
(*d*) $\chi^2 = 7.99$, df $= 1$

5. Interviews are conducted with 70 homosexual and 110 heterosexual males concerning their fear of contracting AIDS. State an appropriate null hypothesis, assume $\alpha = 0.01$, and test the hypothesis using χ^2. Also, calculate Cramer's *V*, percentage down, and discuss.

	Sexual orientation		
Fear of AIDS	Homosexual males	Heterosexual males	
Great	40	15	55
Moderate	20	35	55
Low	10	60	70
	70	110	

6. The World Series may last from four to seven games. During the period 1922 to 1989, the distribution of the number of games played per series was as follows:

Number of games	4	5	6	7
Frequency of occurrence	11	15	13	29

For these data, test the hypothesis that each number of games is equally likely to occur. Use $\alpha = .05$.

7. Suppose that a recording company is interested in testing a cover to put on a CD. It sends the same CD with three different covers to a store. At the end of a month, it has found that the following number of CDs have been sold:

Type A cover	Type B cover	Type C cover
41	50	20

Compute χ^2 and draw appropriate conclusions.

8. Marital status and depression has long been a topic of interest for social scientists. Given the following data, calculate χ^2, an appropriate measure of association, and interpret the results if $\alpha = 0.05$.

	Marital status		
Depression	Married	Never married	Formerly married
High	20	15	15
Moderate	26	12	10
Low	18	9	8

9. Jackie conducted a study in which she compared the helping behavior of passersby under two conditions. What can you conclude from the results shown in the accompanying table?

	Condition A	**Condition B**
Helped	75	45
Did not help	40	80

Set up this study in formal statistical terms and draw appropriate conclusions.

10. Professor Stevens has the following data that do not meet the assumptions of χ^2 and must be altered. Combine categories in a defensible manner and calculate χ^2. Assume $\alpha = 0.05$ and interpret.

	Country of birth					
Educational attainment	**United States**	**Germany**	**England**	**Vietnam**	**Thailand**	**Korea**
Graduate school	6	4	3	3	1	1
College	8	4	3	2	2	2
High school	9	2	5	4	3	0
Grade school	4	3	2	1	3	4

11. A study was conducted to determine if there is a relationship between socioeconomic status and attitudes toward a new urban renewal program. The results are listed in the accompanying table.

	Socioeconomic status	
Attitude	**Lower**	**Middle**
Approve	90	60
Disapprove	200	100

Set up this study in formal statistical terms and draw the appropriate conclusion.

12. Why does $\chi^2 = 0$ when two variables are independent?

13. Discuss the ways in which ϕ, C, and V are unique with respect to each other and similar to each other.

14. In a study concerned with preferences of schools for their children, 100 people in an upper-income group and 200 people in a lower-income group were interviewed. The results of their choices follow.

Preference stated	Lower-income group	Upper-income group
Private, nonreligious	84	36
Private, religious	51	39
Public	44	16
No preference	21	9

Set up this study in formal statistical terms and draw appropriate conclusions. Use $\alpha = .05$.

15. Infections acquired while the patient is hospitalized are a continuing problem in hospitals. One study traced the mortality rates of patients with urinary-tract infections who had a catheter inserted by medical doctors, by registered nurses, and by others. The results are shown in the following table.

	Catheter inserted by		
Patient outcome	Medical doctor	Registered nurse	Other
Survived	510	542	345
Died	11	38	28
Total	521	580	373

Source: Platt, Polk, Murdock, and Rosner (1982), pp. 637–000.

(*a*) Percentage down. Which group of professionals was associated with the highest mortality rate?
(*b*) What is the appropriate test of significance?
(*c*) Using $\alpha = 0.01$, test H_0 that mortality is independent of the professional inserting the catheter.

16. Neil is conducting research on memory. He asks 50 participants to think about the earliest memory of their father and the earliest one of their mother. Then he asks them to evaluate each memory as positive or negative. He obtains the results listed in the accompanying table.

	Memory of mother	Memory of father
Positive	35	31
Negative	15	19

Neil plans to analyze his data using χ^2. Do you think such an analysis is appropriate? Explain.

17. The following table shows the number of females helping an attractive or an unattractive male.

Helping response	Characteristics of target		Total
	Attractive	Unattractive	
Helped	17	13	30
Did not help	24	27	51

(*a*) What is the appropriate test of significance?
(*b*) Conduct a test of significance using $\alpha = 0.05$.

CHAPTER 17

Statistical Inference: Ordinally Scaled Variables

17.1 INTRODUCTION

In the previous chapter, we pointed out that the researcher is frequently faced with a choice about which statistical test is appropriate for the data. You will recall that this was not really a problem in relation to categorical variables because nonparametric tests alone are suitable for nominally scaled data.

In this chapter, we discuss several statistical techniques that are frequently employed as alternatives to parametric tests. Before examining them in detail, let's look at a brief summary of the situations in which their use is appropriate.

Mann-Whitney U. Used in two-group situations in which the groups are independent; that is, the respondents are not matched in any way nor are before-after measures involved. The respondents are randomly assigned to the experimental conditions. The scale of the independent measures is either ordinal or interval/ratio. If interval/ratio, the Mann-Whitney U is used as a substitute for Student's t-ratio when the validity of the assumption of normality is questionable.

Sign test. Used in two-group correlated samples designs, before-after measures are employed or pairs of respondents are matched on some basis. Although the underlying scale of the dependent measures is ordinal, we are unwilling to assume that the scores have any precise quantitative properties. We ignore the amount of difference between scores and concentrate only on the direction of the differences (larger than or smaller than).

Wilcoxon matched-pairs signed-rank test. Used in matched-pairs two-group designs in which we assume the scores are quantitative and that the differences in scores achieve an ordinal level of measurement; that is, the differences in scores may legitimately be ranked from smallest to largest or vice versa.

17.2 MANN-WHITNEY *U*-TEST

The **Mann-Whitney *U*-test** is one of the most powerful nonparametric statistical tests because it utilizes most of the quantitative information that is inherent in the data. It is most commonly employed as an alternative to Student's *t*-ratio when the measurements fail to achieve interval scaling or when the researcher wishes to avoid the assumption of normality.

Imagine that we have drawn two independent samples of N_1 and N_2 observations. The null hypothesis is that both samples are drawn from populations with the same distributions. The two-tailed alternative hypothesis, against which we test the null hypothesis, is that the parent populations from which the samples were drawn are different. Imagine further that we combine the $N_1 + N_2$ observations and assign a rank of 1 to the smallest value, a rank of 2 to the next smallest value, and continue until we have assigned ranks to all the observations. Let's refer to our two groups as *E* and *C*, respectively. If we were to count the number of times each *C* precedes each *E* in the ranks, we would expect under the null hypothesis that it would equal the number of times each *E* precedes a *C*. In other words, if there is no difference between the two groups, the order of *E*'s preceding *C*'s, and vice versa, should be random. However, if the null hypothesis is not true, we would expect a bulk of the *E* scores or the *C* scores to precede their opposite number.

For example, suppose you have the hypothesis that leadership can be learned. You set up two groups, one to receive special training in leadership (*E*) and the other to receive no special instruction (*C*). Following the training, independent estimates of the leadership qualities of all the subjects are obtained. The results are:

E-scores	12	18	31	45	47
C-scores	2	8	15	19	38

When using the Mann-Whitney test, we are concerned with the sampling distribution of the statistic "*U*." To find *U*, we must first rank all of the scores from the lowest to the highest, retaining the identity of each score as *E* or *C* (see Table 17.1).

You will note that the number of *E*'s preceding *C*'s is less than the number of *C*'s preceding *E*'s. The next step is to count the number of times each *E* precedes a *C*. Note that the first *E* (score of 12) precedes three *C*'s (scores of 15, 19, and 38, respectively). The second *E* (score of 18) precedes two *C*'s (scores of 19 and 38). The third *E* (score of 31) precedes one *C* (score of 38). Finally, the last two *E*'s precede no *C*'s. *U* is the sum of the number of times each *E* precedes a *C*. Thus, in our hypothetical problem, $U = 3 + 2 + 1 + 0 + 0 = 6$. Had we concentrated on the number of times *C*'s precede *E*'s, we would have obtained a sum of $5 + 5 + 4 + 3 + 2 = 19$. We refer to this greater sum as U'. Under the null hypothesis, U and U' should be equal. The

TABLE 17.1
Data for hypothetical leadership study

Rank	**1**	**2**	**3**	**4**	**5**	**6**	**7**	**8**	**9**	**10**
Score	2	8	12	15	18	19	31	38	45	47
Condition	*C*	*C*	*E*	*C*	*E*	*C*	*E*	*C*	*E*	*E*

question is whether the magnitude of the observed difference is sufficient to warrant the rejection of the null hypothesis.

The sampling distribution of U under the null hypothesis is known. Tables N_1 through N_4 (in Appendix C) show the values of U and U', which are significant at various α levels. To be significant at a given α level, the obtained U must be equal to or *less* than the tabled value, or the obtained U' must be equal to or *greater* than its corresponding critical value. Employing $\alpha = 0.05$, two-tailed test, we find (Table N_3, Appendix C) that for $N_1 = 5$ and $N_2 = 5$, either $U \leq 2$ or $U' \geq 23$ is required to reject H_0. Since our obtained U of $6 > 2$, we may not reject the null hypothesis.

Equation (17.1) may be used as a check on the calculation of U and U':

$$U = N_1 N_2 - U' \tag{17.1}$$

The counting technique for arriving at U can become tedious, particularly with large N's, and frequently leads to error. An alternative procedure, which provides identical results, is to *assign ranks* to the combined groups as we did before, and then to employ either of the following equations to arrive at U and/or U':

$$U = N_1 N_2 + \frac{N_1(N_1 + 1)}{2} - R_1 \tag{17.2}$$

or

$$U' = N_1 N_2 + \frac{N_2(N_2 + 1)}{2} - R_2 \tag{17.3}$$

where R_1 = the sum of ranks assigned to the group with a sample size of N_1
R_2 = the sum of ranks assigned to the group with a sample size of N_2

Psychologists often conduct studies to determine the effects of a drug on the reaction time to a visual stimulus. Since reaction time and related measures (e.g. latency, time to traverse a maze) are commonly skewed to the right because of a restriction on the left of the distribution (i.e., no score can be less than zero) and no restrictions on the right (i.e., the score can take *any* value greater than zero), the Mann-Whitney U-test was selected in preference to Student's t-ratio. The results of the hypothetical study and the computational procedures are shown in Table 17.2.

To check the following calculations, we should first obtain the value of U', employing equation (17.3):

$$U' = N_1 N_2 + \frac{N_2(N_2 + 1)}{2} - 39 = 45$$

TABLE 17.2
Calculation of Mann-Whitney U using equation (17.2) (hypothetical data)

Experimental		Control		
Time (milliseconds)	**Rank**	**Time (milliseconds)**	**Rank**	**Computation**
140	4	130	1	$U = N_1N_2 + \frac{N_1(N_1+1)}{2} - 81$
147	6	135	2	
153	8	138	3	
160	10	144	5	$= 56 + \frac{8(9)}{2} - 81$
165	11	148	7	
170	13	155	9	
171	14	168	12	$= 56 + 36 - 81$
193	15			$= 11$
	$R_1 = 81$		$R_2 = 39$	
	$N_1 = 8$		$N_2 = 7$	

We use equation (17.1) as a check of our calculations:

$$U = N_1N_2 - U'$$
$$= 56 - 45 = 11$$

As a check on our calculations of the sums of the ranks, the total sum of the ranks (R_T) is given by:

$$R_T = \left(\frac{N_1 + N_2}{2}\right)(N_1 + N_2 + 1) \tag{17.4}$$

In the present example, $R_1 + R_2 = (15/2)(16) = 120$. In our calculations, we found $R_1 = 81$ and $R_2 = 39$. Note that $R_1 + R_2 = 81 + 39 = 120$. Using $\alpha = 0.01$, two-tailed test, for $N_1 = 8$ and $N_2 = 7$, we find (in Table N_1, Appendix C) that a $U \leq 6$ is required to reject H_0. Since the obtained U of 11 is greater than this value, we accept H_0. We do not have a valid statistical basis for asserting that the drug affected reaction time.

Tables N_1 through N_4 in Appendix C have been constructed so that it is unnecessary to calculate both U and U'. Indeed, it is not even necessary to identify which of these statistics has been calculated. For any given N_1 and N_2, at a specific α level, the tabled values represent the upper and the lower limits of the critical region. The obtained statistic, whether it is actually U or U', must fall *outside* these limits to be significant. Thus, you need not be concerned about labeling which of the statistics you have calculated.

17.2.1 Mann-Whitney U-Test with Tied Ranks

A problem that often arises with data is that several scores may be exactly the same. Although the underlying dimension on which we base our measures may be continuous, our measures are, for the most part, quite crude. Even though theoretically there should be no ties (if we had sufficiently sensitive measuring instruments), we do in fact obtain ties quite often. The procedures for converting tied scores to ranks are the same as we used with the Spearman r_s (Section 9.6). We assign the mean of the tied ranks to each of the tied scores, with the next rank in the array receiving the rank that is normally assigned to it. Although ties within a group do not constitute a problem (U is unaffected), we do face some difficulty when ties occur between two or more observations that involve both groups. There is an equation available that corrects for the effects of ties. Unfortunately, the use of this equation is involved and is thus beyond the scope of this introductory textbook.* However, the failure to correct for ties results in a test that is more "conservative," that is, decreases the probability of a type I error (rejecting the null hypothesis when it should not be rejected). Correcting for ties is recommended only when their proportion is high and when the uncorrected U approaches our previously set level of significance.

In the event that several ties occur, we recommend that you calculate the Mann-Whitney without correcting for ties. If the uncorrected U approaches but does not achieve the α-level we have set for rejecting the null hypothesis, consult the source shown in the footnote and recalculate the Mann-Whitney U, correcting for ties.

The data entry to compute the Mann-Whitney U-test for the example presented in Section 17.2 is shown below. Subjects 1–8 are included in the experimental group (group 1) and subjects 9–15 are in the control group (group 2). The variable "time" is measured in milliseconds and an entry is made for each of the 15 subjects.

subjects	group	time
1	1.00	140.00
2	1.00	147.00
3	1.00	153.00
4	1.00	160.00
5	1.00	165.00
6	1.00	170.00
7	1.00	171.00
8	1.00	193.00
9	2.00	130.00
10	2.00	135.00
11	2.00	138.00
12	2.00	144.00
13	2.00	148.00
14	2.00	155.00
15	2.00	168.00

*See Siegel and Castellan (1988) for corrections when a large number of ties occur.

The SPSS computer output below shows that when the Mann-Whitney U-test *ignores ties* the exact two-tailed P-value is 0.0541 whereas when the Mann-Whitney U-test with tied ranks is employed, the two-tailed P-value corrected for ties is 0.0491. Assuming $\alpha = 0.05$, the exact two-tailed P-value does not lead us to reject the null hypothesis (also see Section 17.2). However, when ties are taken into consideration, the P-value corrected for ties is less than 0.05 and we would reject the null hypothesis and conclude that the drug does affect reaction time. The output also includes the mean rank on time for the experimental and control groups. They are based on the ratio of R_1/N_1 and R_2/N_2 in Table 17.2; thus, $81/8 = 10.13$ and $39/7 = 5.57$. The output confirms that $U = 11$.

```
                              Mann-Whitney U-Test

Mean Rank      Cases

    10.13          8    Experimental group = 1.00
     5.57          7    Control group = 2.00
                  --
                  15    Total
                                 Exact                    Corrected for ties
       U                  2-tailed probability                 2-tailed probability
    11.0                         .0541                               .0491
```

17.2.2 Mann-Whitney U-Test When N_1 or N_2 Exceeds 20

Tables N_1 through N_4 (in Appendix C) provide critical values of U for sample sizes up to and including $N_1 = 20$ and $N_2 = 20$. What test of significance should be used when either N_1 or N_2 exceeds 20? As with many other statistics, the sampling distribution approaches the normal curve as the sample size becomes larger. As long as both N's are approximately equal in number and one exceeds 20, the normal curve and the z-statistic may be used to evaluate the significance of the difference between ranks. The z-statistic takes the following form:

$$z = \frac{U_1 - U_E}{s_U}$$

in which U_1 is the sum of ranks of group 1, U_E is the sum expected under H_0, and s_U is the standard error of the U-statistic.

In turn:

$$U_E = \frac{N_1(N_1 + N_2 + 1)}{2} \tag{17.5}$$

and

$$s_U = \sqrt{\frac{N_1 N_2(N_1 + N_2 + 1)}{12}} \tag{17.6}$$

Imagine that an investigator has completed a study in which $N_1 = 22$ and $N_2 = 22$. The sum of the ranks of group 1 was found to be 630.* At $\alpha = 0.05$, test the null hypothesis that both groups were drawn from populations with the same mean rank. The critical value of z is ± 1.96.

The standard error of the ranks using equation (17.6) is:

$$s_U = \sqrt{\frac{22[22(22 + 22 + 1)]}{12}}$$

$$s_U = \sqrt{\frac{21{,}780}{12}}$$

$$s_U = \sqrt{1{,}815}$$

$$s_U = 42.60$$

The expected rank under H_0 is:

$$U_E = \frac{22(22 + 22 + 1)}{2}$$

$$U_E = \frac{900}{2}$$

$$U_E = 495$$

The test statistic z becomes:

$$z = \frac{630 - 495}{42.60} = 3.17$$

Because the obtained z of 3.17 exceeds the critical value of 1.96, we may reject the null hypothesis and assert that the experimental treatment produced a significant difference between conditions. Statistics in Action 17.1 provides an additional example of computing Mann-Whitney U.

17.3 NONPARAMETRIC TESTS INVOLVING CORRELATED SAMPLES

A **correlated-samples design** (also known as a **matched-group design**) is one in which pairs of respondents are matched on a variable known to be correlated with the dependent variable. The result is a set of paired respondents in which each member of a given pair obtains approximately the same score on the matching variable. Then one member of each pair is randomly assigned to the experimental condition and the other is assigned to the control group. Thus, if we wanted to determine the effect of some

---

*Using equation (17.4), we find the sum of all the ranks equals $[(22 + 22)/2](22 + 22 + 1) = 44/2(45) = 990$. By subtraction, $R_2 = R_T - R_1 = 990 - 630 = 360$. Note that $U_1 - U_E$ equals $U_2 - U_E$. Thus, we could just as easily have used $z = (U_1 - U_E)/s_U$. However, *if the sample sizes differ,* U_E must be changed to equation (17.5) in order to use U_2 in the equation for z. Both yield identical probability values and both test H_0: $\mu_1 = \mu_2$.

drug on the ease of learning the solution to a mathematical problem, we might match individuals on the basis of IQ estimates, the amount of mathematical training, grades in statistics, or performance on other mathematics problems. Such a design has two advantages:

1. It ensures that the experimental groups are "equivalent" in initial ability.

2. It permits us to take advantage of the correlation based on initial ability and allows us in effect to remove one source of error from our measurements.

The same advantages accrue to nonparametric tests involving matched or correlated samples. In the following sections, we discuss two such tests for ordinally scaled variables—the *sign test* and the *Wilcoxon signed-rank test.*

17.4 THE SIGN TEST

Suppose that we are repeating the leadership experiment with which we introduced the chapter, employing larger samples. On the expectation that intelligence and leadership ability are correlated variables, we set up two groups, an experimental and a control, that are matched on the basis of intelligence. On completion of the leadership training course, independent observers are asked to rate the leadership qualities of each respondent on a 50-point scale. We will use the **sign test,** which is a nonparametric statistical test for ordinally scaled variables, used with matched or correlated samples. The sign test simply utilizes information concerning the *direction* of the differences between pairs of scores. The results are listed in Table 17.3.

TABLE 17.3
Ratings of two groups of matched subjects on qualities of leadership (hypothetical data)

	Leadership score		Sign of difference
Matched pair	**Experimental group**	**Control group**	**Experimental minus control**
A	47	40	+
B	43	38	+
C	36	42	−
D	38	25	+
E	30	29	+
F	22	26	−
G	25	16	+
H	21	18	+
I	14	8	+
J	12	4	+
K	5	7	−
L	9	3	+
M	5	5	(0)

STATISTICS IN ACTION 17.1
Polonium-210, Smoking, and Cancer in Directly Exposed Tissue: Calculating Mann-Whitney *U*

The recent discovery of a radioelement in cigarettes (polonium-210) suggests the possibility that directly exposed sites (e.g., buccal cavity, pharynx) in smokers may put them at greater risk for the development of cancer at these sites. Health data for various risk groups are frequently expressed as an o/e ratio (observed to expected). Because the ratios appear to be markedly positively skewed and raise doubts concerning the normality of the population distribution, the Mann-Whitney *U* is chosen over its parametric counterpart (Student's *t*-ratio for independent samples). However, the decision to use the Mann-Whitney *U* is not engraved in stone. Some researchers would use Student's *t*-ratio based on the robustness of the *t*-test.

The following table shows the o/e ratios for indirectly exposed and directly exposed tissues, the conversion to ranks, and the application of the Mann-Whitney *U*-test. An o/e ratio greater than 1 means a higher-than-average risk.

Based on the known carcinogenic properties of radioelements, we'll use a directional test of H_0 at $\alpha = 0.01$. Since a two-tailed $\alpha = 0.02$ yields a one-tailed $\alpha = 0.01$, we'll use Table N_2 (Appendix C) to evaluate the significance of the results.

Cancer of indirectly exposed tissue	O/E ratio	Rank	Cancer of directly exposed tissue	O/E ratio	Rank
Stomach	1.52	7	Buccal cavity	4.23	12
Intestines	1.11	3.5	Pharynx	13.14	16
Rectum	1.11	3.5	Larynx	11.75	15
Liver/biliary ducts	2.35	11	Lung and bronchus	11.29	14
Pancreas	1.79	9	Esophagus	6.5	13
Prostate	1.31	5			
Kidney	1.41	6			
Bladder	2.16	10			
Brain	1.05	1			
Malignant lymphomas	1.07	2			
Leukemias	1.61	8			
Sum of ranks		66			70

$$U = (11)(5) + \frac{11(12)}{2} - 66$$
$$= 55 + 66 - 66$$
$$= 55$$

Reference to Table N_2 (Appendix C) shows the one-tailed critical value of *U*, at $\alpha = 0.01$, to be 48. Because obtained *U* exceeds this value, we reject H_0 and assert that directly exposed tissues are at a greater risk for the development of cancer.

1. Can we conclude that polonium-210 caused the greater risk of cancer at directly exposed sites?
2. Analyze these data with Student's *t*-ratio for independent samples, using $\alpha = 0.01$, one-tailed test. Compare the conclusions drawn from the two different tests of significance.

Answers

1. Not necessarily. There may be other carcinogens in cigarette smoke that increase the risk of cancer in directly exposed tissue.

2. $\overline{X}_1 = 1.50, \overline{X}_2 = 9.38, t = -7.05$ with df $= 14$. Critical value $\alpha = -2.624$. Reject H_0 at $\alpha = 0.01$, one-tailed test.

Source: Based on Ravenholt (1982), p. 312.

The rating scales in Table 17.3 seem to be extremely crude and we are unwilling to affirm that the scores have any precise quantitative properties. The only assumption we feel justified in making is that any existing difference between two paired scores is a valid indicator of the direction and not the magnitude of the difference.

There are 13 pairs of observations in Table 17.3. Since pair M is tied and there is consequently no indication of a difference one way or another, we drop these paired observations. Of the remaining 12 pairs, we would expect, on the basis of the null hypothesis, half the changes to be in the positive direction and half the changes to be in the negative direction. In other words, under H_0 the probability of any difference being positive is equal to the probability that it will be negative. Since we are dealing with a two-category population (positive differences and negative differences), H_0 may be expressed in precisely the same fashion as in the binomial test when $P = Q = 1/2$. That is, in the present problem, H_0: $P = Q = 1/2$. Indeed, the sign test is merely a variation of the binomial test.

Of 12 comparisons showing a difference ($N = 12$) in the present example, 9 are positive and 3 are negative. Since $P = Q = 1/2$, we refer to Table I (in Appendix C) under $x = 9$, $N = 12$, and find that the critical value at $\alpha = 0.05$, two-tailed test, is 10. Because x is less than the critical value, we fail to reject H_0.

The assumptions underlying the use of the sign test are that the pairs of measurements must be independent of each other and that these measurements must represent, at least, ordinal scaling.

One of the disadvantages of the sign test is that it completely eliminates any quantitative information that may be inherent in the data (e.g., $-8 = -7 = -6$). The sign test treats all plus differences as if they were the same and all minus differences as if they were the same.

If this is the only assumption warranted by the scale of measurement employed, we have little choice but to employ the sign test. If, on the other hand, the data *do* permit us to make such quantitative statements as "a difference of $8 > 7 > 6 > \cdots$," we lose power when we employ the sign test.

17.5 WILCOXON MATCHED-PAIRS SIGNED-RANK TEST

We have seen that the sign simply utilizes information concerning the direction of the differences between pairs. If the *magnitude* as well as the *direction* of these differences may be considered, a more powerful test may be employed. The **Wilcoxon**

matched-pairs signed-rank test is a nonparametric test for ordinally scaled variables used with matched or correlated samples. It is more powerful than the sign test because it utilizes the quantitative information concerning the magnitude of the differences between the pairs.

For heuristic purposes, let's return to the data in Table 17.3 and make a different assumption about the scale of measurement employed. Suppose the rating scale is not so crude as we had imagined; that is, not only do the measurements achieve ordinal scaling, but also the differences between measures achieve ordinality. Table 17.4 reproduces these data, with an additional entry indicating the magnitude of the differences.

Note that the difference column represents differences in scores rather than in ranks. The following column represents the ranking of these differences from the smallest to largest without regard to the algebraic sign. We have placed the negative sign in parentheses so that we can keep track of the differences bearing positive and negative signs. Now, if the null hypothesis were correct, we would expect the sum of the positive and that of the negative ranks to balance each other more or less. The more the sums of the ranks are preponderantly positive or negative, the more likely we are to reject the null hypothesis.

The statistic T is the sum of the ranks with the smaller sum. In this problem T is equal to -13. Table O (Appendix C) presents the critical values of T for sample sizes up to 50 pairs. All entries are for the absolute value of T. In the present example, we

TABLE 17.4
Rating of two groups of matched respondents on qualities of leadership (hypothetical data)

	Leadership score				
Pair	**Experimental**	**Control**	**Difference $E - C$**	**Rank of the differences**	**Ranks with negative value**
A	47	40	+7	9	
B	43	38	+5	5	
C	36	42	−6	(−)7	(−)7
D	38	25	+13	12	
E	30	29	+1	1	
F	22	26	−4	(−)4	(−)4
G	25	16	+9	11	
H	21	18	+3	3	
I	14	8	+6	7	
J	12	4	+8	10	
K	5	7	−2	(−)2	(−)2
L	9	3	+6	7	
M	5	5	(0)		
					$T = -13$

find that a T of 13 or less is required for significance at the 0.05 level (two-tailed test) when $N = 12$. Note that we dropped the M-pair from our calculations because, as with the sign test, a zero difference in scores cannot be considered as either a negative or a positive change. Our obtained T was 13, so we may reject the null hypothesis. We may conclude that the leadership training produced higher ratings for the experimental respondents.

You will recall that the sign test applied to these same data did not lead to the rejection of the null hypothesis. The reason should be apparent; that is, we were not taking advantage of all the information inherent in our data when we employed the sign test.

The SPSS computer output below is based on Table 17.4 and confirms that the sign test does not lead to rejection of the null hypothesis (2-tailed P-value $= 0.1460$) while the Wilcoxon matched-pairs ranks test 2-tailed P-value $= 0.0414$ does, assuming $\alpha = 0.05$.

```
                         Sign Test

Cases

          3   - Diffs (EXPER  <  CONTROL)
          9   + Diffs (EXPER  >  CONTROL)
          1     Ties  (EXPER  =  CONTROL)
         --
         13     Total       2-tailed P = .1460


        Wilcoxon Matched-Pairs Signed-Ranks Test

Mean Rank     Cases
   4.33           3   - Ranks   (EXPER < CONTROL)
   7.22           9   + Ranks   (EXPER > CONTROL)
                  1     Ties    (EXPER = CONTROL)
                 --
                 13     Total

                                 2-tailed P = .0414
```

17.5.1 Assumptions Underlying Wilcoxon's Matched-Pairs Signed-Rank Test

An assumption used in the Wilcoxon signed-rank test is that the scale of measurement is at least ordinal in nature. In other words, the assumption is that the scores permit the ordering of the data into relationships of greater than and less than. However, the signed-rank test makes one additional assumption, which may rule it out of some potential applications; namely, it assumes that the differences in scores also constitute an ordinal scale. It is not always clear whether this assumption is valid for a given set of data. Take, for example, a personality scale purported to measure "manifest anxiety" in a testing situation. Can we validly claim that a difference between matched pairs of, say, five points on one part of the scale is greater than a difference of four points on another part of the scale? If we cannot validly make this assumption, we must employ another form of statistical analysis, even if it requires that we move to a less sensitive test of significance. Once again, our basic conservatism as scientists makes us more willing to risk a type II rather than a type I error.

SUMMARY

In this chapter, we have pointed out that the social scientist does not first collect data and then shop around for a statistical test to determine the significance of differences between experimental conditions. The researcher must specify in advance of the experiment the null hypothesis, alternative hypothesis, test of significance, and the probability value that is acceptable as the basis for rejecting the null hypothesis.

We demonstrated the use of the Mann-Whitney *U*-test as an alternative to Student's *t*-ratio when the measurements fail to achieve interval scaling or when the researcher wishes to avoid the assumptions of normality. It is one of the most powerful of the nonparametric tests because it utilizes most of the quantitative information that is inherent in the data.

We have seen that by taking into account correlations between respondents on a variable correlated with the dependent measure, we can increase the sensitivity of our statistical test. The sign test accomplishes this objective by using before-after measures on the same individuals. We have also seen that the sign test, although taking advantage of the direction of differences involved in ordinal measurement, fails to make use of information concerning magnitudes of difference.

The Wilcoxon matched-pairs signed-rank test takes advantage of both the direction and magnitude implicit in ordinal measurement with correlated samples. When the assumptions underlying the test are met, this Wilcoxon technique is an extremely sensitive basis for obtaining probability values.

Table 17.5 summarizes the conditions under which each of these tests might be used.

TABLE 17.5
Three ordinal tests used to replace statistical tests when the validity of the assumptions of the parametric tests are questionable

Test of significance	Experimental design	Number of conditions	Type of data	Test statistic	Test replaced
Mann-Whitney *U*-test	Independent samples	2	Ordinal, interval, ratio	U or U'	Student's *t*-ratio for independent samples
Sign test	Correlated samples	2	Ordinal, but only the direction of the difference (+ or −)	Binomial	Student's *t*-ratio and Wilcoxon matched-pairs signed-rank test
Wilcoxon matched-pairs signed-rank test	Correlated samples	2	Ranks of differences between scores or ranks	T	Student's *t*-ratio for correlated samples

TERMS TO REMEMBER

correlated-samples design See *matched-group design.*

Mann-Whitney U-test A powerful nonparametric statistical test commonly employed as an alternative to the Student t-ratio when the measurements fail to achieve interval scaling.

matched-group design A design which pairs of respondents are matched on a variable correlated with the dependent variable. Each member of a pair receives different experimental conditions.

sign test A nonparametric statistical test for ordinally scaled variables, used with matched or correlated samples. The sign test simply utilizes information concerning the *direction* of the differences between pairs of scores.

Wilcoxon matched-pairs signed-rank test A nonparametric statistical test for ordinally scaled variables used with matched or correlated samples; more powerful than the sign test since it utilizes information concerning the *magnitude* of the differences between pairs of scores.

EXERCISES

1. From the data presented in the accompanying table, determine whether there is a significant difference in the number of stolen bases obtained by two leagues, employing:
(*a*) The sign test.
(*b*) The Wilcoxon matched-pairs signed-rank test.
(*c*) The Mann-Whitney U-test.

Which is the best statistical test for these data? Why?

	Number of stolen bases	
Team standing	**League 1**	**League 2**
1	91	81
2	46	51
3	108	63
4	99	51
5	110	46
6	105	45
7	191	66
8	57	64
9	34	90
10	81	28

2. In a study to determine the effect of a drug on aggressiveness, group A received a drug and group B received a placebo. A test of aggressiveness was applied following the drug administration. The scores obtained are shown in the accompanying table (the higher the score, the greater the aggressiveness).

Group A	Group B
10	12
8	15
12	20
16	18
5	13
9	14
7	9
11	16
6	

(*a*) What do you believe the null and alternative hypotheses are for this study?
(*b*) Which nonparametric test do you believe is appropriate for analyzing these data?
(*c*) Apply the statistic you selected to these data.
(*d*) Is there sufficient evidence to reject the null hypothesis, assuming $\alpha = .05$? How should these data be interpreted?

3. The human resources director at a large insurance office claims that insurance agents trained in personal-social relations make a more favorable impression on prospective clients. To test this hypothesis, 22 individuals are randomly selected from among those recently hired and half are assigned to a personal-social relations course. The remaining 11 individuals received no training and constitute the control group. Following the training period, all 22 individuals are observed in a simulated interview with a client and rated on a 10-point scale (0 to 9) for their ease in establishing relationships. The higher the score, the better the rating. The data are listed in the accompanying table.

Personal-social training	Control group
8	5
7	6
9	2
4	6
7	0
9	2
3	6
7	5
8	1
9	0
3	5

(*a*) What do you believe the null and alternative hypotheses are for this study?
(*b*) Which nonparametric test do you believe is appropriate for analyzing these data?
(*c*) Apply the statistic you selected to these data.
(*d*) Is there sufficient evidence to reject the null hypothesis, assuming $\alpha = .05$? How should these data be interpreted? What would the interpretation of the data be if $\alpha = .01$?

4. Assume that the individuals in exercise 3 were matched on a variable known to be correlated with the criterion variable. Employ the appropriate test and repeat exercise 3(*c*) and (*d*).

5. Fifteen husbands and their wives were administered an opinion scale to assess their attitudes about the particular political issue. These results are shown in the accompanying table (the higher the score, the more favorable the attitude).

Husband	Wife
37	33
46	44
59	48
17	30
41	56
36	30
29	35
38	38
32	46
35	32
39	29
37	45
36	29
45	48
40	35

(*a*) What do you believe the null and alternative hypotheses are for this study?
(*b*) Which nonparametric test do you believe is appropriate for analyzing these data?
(*c*) Apply the statistic you selected to these data.
(*d*) Is there sufficient evidence to reject the null hypothesis, assuming $\alpha = .05$? How should these data be interpreted?

6. Suppose that during the last track season there was no difference in the mean running speeds of the runners from two schools. Assume that the same people are on the teams this year. Runners from school A train as usual; however, the coach from school B introduces bicycle work as a part of the training cycle. During a meet, the times were recorded (in seconds) for the runners from the two schools in the 50-yard dash and are listed in the accompanying table.

School A	School B
10.2	9.9
11.1	10.3
10.5	11.0
10.0	10.1
9.7	9.8
12.0	9.5
10.7	10.8
10.9	10.6
11.5	9.6
10.4	9.4

(*a*) What do you believe the null and alternative hypotheses are for this study?
(*b*) Which nonparametric test do you believe is appropriate for analyzing these data?
(*c*) Apply the statistic you selected to these data.
(*d*) Is there sufficient evidence to reject the null hypothesis, assuming $\alpha = .05$? How should these data be interpreted? What would be the interpretation of the data if $\alpha = .01$?

7. Suppose that in exercise 6 the people on each team had been previously matched on running speed for the 50-yard dash. The matches are as listed in exercise 6. Using the sign test and the Wilcoxon matched-pairs signed-rank test, set up and test the null hypothesis.

8. An investigator wanted to measure the effectiveness of an advertisement promoting his brand of toothpaste. He matched respondents (none of whom had ever bought this brand of toothpaste) according to the number of tubes of toothpaste they usually buy in six months. He then divided the sample into two groups and showed one group the advertisement. The accompanying table lists the number of tubes of this brand of toothpaste sold during the next six months.

Advertisement	**No advertisement**
4	1
4	2
3	0
1	2
2	0
0	1
1	0
0	1

(*a*) What do you believe the null and alternative hypotheses are for this study?
(*b*) Which nonparametric test do you believe is appropriate for analyzing these data?
(*c*) Apply the statistic you selected to these data.
(*d*) Is there sufficient evidence to reject the null hypothesis, assuming $\alpha = .05$? How should these data be interpreted? What would be the interpretation of the data if $\alpha = .01$?

PART V

Appendixes

APPENDIX A

Review of Basic Mathematics

Arithmetic Operations
Algebraic Operations
Reducing Fractions to Simplest Expressions

ARITHMETIC OPERATIONS

You already know that addition is indicated by the sign +; subtraction by the sign −; multiplication in one of three ways, 2×4, $2(4)$, or $2 \cdot 4$; and division by a slash, /, an overbar, —, or the symbol ÷. However, it is not unusual to forget the rules concerning addition, subtraction, multiplication, and division, particularly when these operations occur in a single problem.

Addition and Subtraction

When numbers are added together, the order of adding the numbers has no influence on the sum. Thus, we may add $2 + 5 + 3$ in any of the following ways:

$$2 + 5 + 3, \quad 5 + 2 + 3, \quad 2 + 3 + 5$$
$$5 + 3 + 2, \quad 3 + 2 + 5, \quad 3 + 5 + 2$$

When a series of numbers containing both positive and negative signs are added, the order of adding the numbers has no influence on the sum. It is often desirable, however, to group together the numbers preceded by positive signs, group together the numbers preceded by negative signs, add each group separately, and subtract the latter sum from the former. Thus:

$$-2 + 3 + 5 - 4 + 2 + 1 - 8$$

may best be added by grouping in the following ways:

$$\begin{array}{rr} +3 & \\ +5 & -2 \\ +2 & -4 \\ \underline{+1} & \underline{-8} \\ +11 & -14 = -3 \end{array}$$

Incidentally, to subtract a larger numerical value from a smaller numerical value, as in the above example $(11 - 14)$, we ignore the signs, subtract the smaller number from the larger, and affix the sign of the larger to the sum. Thus, $-14 + 11 = -3$.

Multiplication

The order in which numbers are multiplied has no effect on the product. In other words:

$$\begin{aligned} 2 \times 3 \times 4 &= 2 \times 4 \times 3 = 3 \times 2 \times 4 \\ &= 3 \times 4 \times 2 = 4 \times 2 \times 3 = 4 \times 3 \times 2 = 24 \end{aligned}$$

When addition, subtraction, and multiplication occur in the same expression, we must develop certain procedures governing *which* operations are to be performed first. In the expression:

$$2 \times 4 + 7 \times 3 - 5$$

multiplication is performed first. Thus, the above expression is equal to:

$$\begin{aligned} 2 \times 4 &= 8 \\ 7 \times 3 &= 21 \\ -5 &= -5 \end{aligned}$$

Thus:

$$8 + 21 - 5 = 24$$

We may *not* add first and then multiply. Thus, $2 \times 4 + 7$ is *not* equal to $2(4 + 7)$ or 22.

If a problem involves finding the product of one term multiplied by a second expression that includes two or more terms either added or subtracted, we may multiply first and then add, or add first and then multiply. Thus, the solution to the following problem becomes:

$$\begin{aligned} 8(6 - 4) &= 8 \times 6 - 8 \times 4 \\ &= 48 - 32 \\ &= 16 \end{aligned}$$

or

$$\begin{aligned} 8(6 - 4) &= 8(2) \\ &= 16 \end{aligned}$$

In most cases, however, it is more convenient to reduce the expression within the parentheses first. Thus, generally speaking, the second solution appearing above will be more frequently used.

Finally, if numbers having like signs are multiplied, the product is always positive; for example:

$$(+2) \times (+4) = +8$$

and

$$(-2) \times (-4) = +8$$

If numbers bearing unlike signs are multiplied, the product is always negative; for example:

$$(+2) \times (-4) = -8$$

and

$$(-2) \times (+4) = -8$$

The same rule applies also to division. When we obtain the quotient of two numbers of like signs, it is always positive; when the numbers differ in sign, the quotient is always negative.

Multiplication as successive addition

Many students tend to forget that multiplication is a special form of successive addition. Thus:

$$15 + 15 + 15 + 15 + 15 = 5(15)$$

and

$$(15 + 15 + 15 + 15 + 15) + (16 + 16 + 16 + 16) = 5(15) + 4(16)$$

This formulation is useful in understanding the advantages of "grouping" scores into what is called a frequency distribution. In obtaining the sum of an array of scores, some of which occur a number of times, we want to multiply each score by the frequency with which it occurs and then add the products. Thus, if we were to obtain the following distribution of scores:

12, 13, 13, 13, 14, 14, 14, 14, 15, 15, 15, 15,
15, 15, 15, 16, 16, 16, 17, 17, 17, 17, 18

and wanted the sum of these scores, it would be advantageous to form the following frequency distribution.

X	f	fX
12	1	12
13	3	39
14	4	56
15	7	105
16	3	48
17	4	68
18	1	18
	$N = 23$	$\Sigma fX = 346$

ALGEBRAIC OPERATIONS

Transposing

To transpose a term from one side of an equation to another, you merely have to *change the sign* of the transposed term. All the following are equivalent statements:

$$a + b = c$$

$$a = c - b$$

$$b = c - a$$

$$0 = c - a - b$$

$$0 = c - (a + b)$$

Solving Equations Involving Fractions

Much of the difficulty encountered in solving equations that involve fractions can be avoided by remembering one important mathematical principle:

Equals multiplied by equals are equal.

Let's look at a few sample problems.

1. Solve the following equation for x:

$$b = \frac{a}{x}$$

In solving for x, we want to express the value of x in terms of a and b. In other words, we want our final equation to read, $x =$ ______. Note that we may multiply both sides of the equation by x/b and obtain the following:

$$\not{b} \cdot \frac{x}{\not{b}} = \frac{a}{\not{x}} \cdot \frac{\not{x}}{b}$$

This reduces to:

$$x = \frac{a}{b}$$

2. Solve the same equation for a.

Similarly, if we wanted to solve the equation in terms of a, we could multiply both sides of the equation by x. Thus:

$$b \cdot x = \frac{a}{\not{x}} \cdot \not{x}$$

becomes $bx = a$, or $a = bx$.

In each of the preceding solutions, you will note that the net effect of multiplying by a constant has been to rearrange the terms in the numerator and the denominator of the equations. We may state two general rules that will permit us to solve the preceding problems without having to use multiplication by equals (although multiplication by equals is implicit in the arithmetic operations):

a. A term that is in the denominator on one side of the equation may be moved to the other side of the equation by multiplying it by the numerator side. Thus:

$$\frac{x}{a} = b \qquad \text{becomes} \qquad x = ab$$

b. A term in the numerator on one side of an equation may be moved to the other side of the equation by dividing the numerator on that side by it. Thus:

$$ab = x \qquad \text{may become} \qquad a = \frac{x}{b} \qquad \text{or} \qquad b = \frac{x}{a}$$

Thus, we have seen that all of the following are equivalent statements:

$$b = \frac{a}{x} \qquad a = bx \qquad x = \frac{a}{b}$$

Similarly:

$$\frac{\Sigma X}{N} = \overline{X} \qquad \Sigma X = N\overline{X} \qquad \frac{\Sigma X}{\overline{X}} = N$$

Dividing by a sum or a difference

It is true that

$$\frac{x+y}{z} = \frac{x}{z} + \frac{y}{z} \qquad \text{and} \qquad \frac{x-y}{z} = \frac{x}{z} - \frac{y}{z}$$

We cannot, however, simplify the following expressions as easily:

$$\frac{x}{y+z} \qquad \text{or} \qquad \frac{x}{y-z}$$

Thus:

$$\frac{x}{y+z} \neq \frac{x}{y} + \frac{x}{z}$$

in which $\neq$ means "not equal to."

REDUCING FRACTIONS TO SIMPLEST EXPRESSIONS

A corollary to the rule stating that equals multiplied by equals are equal is:

Unequals multiplied by equals remain proportional.

Thus, if we were to multiply 1/4 by 8/8, the product, 8/32, is in the same proportion as 1/4. This corollary is useful in reducing the complex fractions to their simplest expression. Let's look at an example.

EXAMPLE. Reduce:

$$\frac{a/b}{c/d} \quad \text{or} \quad \frac{a}{b} \div \frac{c}{d}$$

to its simplest expression.

Note that if we multiply both the numerator and the denominator by:

$$\frac{bd/1}{bd/1}$$

We obtain:

$$\frac{(a/b) \cdot (bd/1)}{(c/d) \cdot (bd/1)}$$

which becomes ad/bc.

However, we could obtain the same result if we were to *invert the divisor* and multiply. Thus:

$$\frac{a/b}{c/d} = \frac{a}{b} \cdot \frac{d}{c} = \frac{ad}{bc}$$

We may now formulate a general rule for dividing one fraction into another fraction. In dividing fractions, we *invert the divisor and multiply.* Thus:

$$\frac{x/y}{a^2/b} \quad \text{becomes} \quad \frac{x}{y} \cdot \frac{b}{a^2} \quad \text{which equals} \quad \frac{bx}{a^2y}$$

To illustrate: If $a = 5$, $b = 2$, $x = 3$, and $y = 4$, the preceding expressions become:

$$\frac{3/4}{5^2/2} = \frac{3}{4} \cdot \frac{2}{5^2} = \frac{2 \cdot 3}{4 \cdot 5^2} = \frac{6}{100}$$

A general practice to follow when substituting numerical values into fractional expressions is to reduce the expression to its simplest form *prior* to substitution.

Multiplication and Division of Terms Having Exponents

An exponent indicates how many times a number is to be multiplied by itself. For example, X^5 means that X is to be multiplied by itself five times, or:

$$X^5 = X \cdot X \cdot X \cdot X \cdot X$$

If $X = 3$

$$X^5 = 3 \cdot 3 \cdot 3 \cdot 3 \cdot 3 = 243$$

and

$$\left(\frac{1}{X}\right)^5 = \frac{1^5}{X^5} = \frac{1 \cdot 1 \cdot 1 \cdot 1 \cdot 1}{3 \cdot 3 \cdot 3 \cdot 3 \cdot 3} = \frac{1}{243}$$

To multiply X to the ath power (X^a) times X raised to the bth power, you simply *add the exponents,* thus raising X to the $(a + b)$th power. The reason for the addition of exponents may be seen from the following illustration.

If $a = 3$ and $b = 5$, then:

$$X^a \cdot X^b = X^3X^5 = (X \cdot X \cdot X)(X \cdot X \cdot X \cdot X \cdot X)$$

which equals X^8.

Now, if $X = 5$, $a = 3$, and $b = 5$, then:

$$X^a \cdot X^b = X^{a+b} = X^{3+5} = X^8 = 5^8 = 390{,}625$$

If $X = 1/6$, $a = 2$, and $b = 3$:

$$X^a \cdot X^b = X^{a+b} = \left(\frac{1}{6}\right)^{2+3} = \left(\frac{1}{6}\right)^5 = \frac{1^5}{6^5} = \frac{1}{7{,}776}$$

To divide X raised to the ath power by X raised to the bth power, you simply *subtract* the exponent in the denominator from the exponent in the numerator.* The reason for the subtraction is made clear in the following illustration. If $X = 3$, $a = 5$, and $b = 2$, then:

$$\frac{X^a}{X^b} = \frac{X^5}{X^2} = \frac{X \cdot X \cdot X \cdot X \cdot X}{X \cdot X} = X^3 = 3^3 = 27$$

If $X = 5/6$, $a = 4$, $b = 2$, then:

$$\frac{X^a}{X^b} = X^{a-b} = X^{4-2} = X^2$$

Substituting $5/6$ for X, we have:

$$X^2 = \left(\frac{5}{6}\right)^2 = \frac{5^2}{6^2} = \frac{25}{36}$$

---

* This leads to an interesting exception to the rule that an exponent indicates the number of times a number is multiplied by itself; that is:

$$\frac{X^N}{X^N} = X^{N-N} = X^0$$

However,

$$\frac{X^N}{X^N} = 1 \qquad \text{therefore} \qquad X^0 = 1$$

Any number raised to the zero power is equal to 1.

APPENDIX B

Glossary of Symbols

Mathematical Operators
Greek Letters
English Letters

Following are definitions of the symbols that appear in the text, followed by the page number showing the first reference to the symbol.

English letters and Greek letters are listed separately in their alphabetical order. Mathematical operators are also listed separately.

Symbol	Definition	Page
	Mathematical operators	
$\neq$	Not equal to	124
$a < b$	a is less than b	26
$a > b$	a is greater than b	26
$\leq$	Less than or equal to	272
$\geq$	Greater than or equal to	272
$\sqrt{\ }$	Square root	21
X^a	X raised to the ath power	21
$\|X\|$	Absolute value of X	117
Σ	Sum all quantities or scores that follow	21
$\sum_{i=1}^{N} X_i$	Sum all quantities X_1 through X_N: $X_1 + X_2 + \cdots + X_N$	21
%	Percentage	36
	Greek letters	
$1 - \alpha$	Probability of correct failure to reject H_0	315
$1 - \beta$	Probability of correctly rejecting H_0	315
α	Probability of a type I error, probability of rejecting H_0 when it is true	314
β	**1.** Probability of a type II error, probability of accepting H_0 when it is false	314
	2. Standardized multiple regression coefficient.	250

Mathematical Operators
(continued)

Symbol	Definition	Page
ϵ	Epsilon: percentage difference in a contingency table	165
γ	Goodman and Kruskal's gamma for ordinal-level contingency data	171
λ	Lambda: an asymmetric or symmetric measure of association for nominal-level contingency table data	165
μ	Mu; population mean	7
μ_0	Value of the population mean under H_0	332
$\mu_{\bar{X}}$	Mean of the distribution of sample means	328
σ	Sigma; population standard deviation	7
σ^2	Sigma squared; population variance	335
σ_P	Standard error of the proportion	348
$\sigma^2_{\bar{X}} = \frac{\sigma^2}{N}$	Variance of the sampling distribution of the mean	329
$\sigma_{\bar{X}} = \frac{\sigma}{\sqrt{N}}$	True standard error of the mean given random samples of a fixed N	329
τ_b	Kendall's tau-*b* for ordinal-level contingency data	176
ϕ	Phi coefficient	391
χ^2	Chi-square	382

English letters

Symbol	Definition	Page
a_y	Constant term in a regression equation (Y-intercept)	215
b_y	Unstandardized slope of a line relating values of Y to values of X	214
c	Number of columns in a contingency table	154
C	**1.** Centile: Equivalent to a percentile and is a percentage rank that divides a distribution into 100 equal parts	84
	2. Concordant pairs in a contingency table	172
	3. Contingency coefficient	393
cum f	Cumulative frequency	79
cum f_{ll}	Cumulative frequency at the lower true limit of the interval containing X	80
cum %	Cumulative percentage	52
D	**1.** Rank on X-variable − rank on Y-variable (r_s equation)	198
	2. Score on X-variable − score on Y-variable ($X - Y$)	198
	3. Decile: a percentage rank that divides a distribution into 10 equal parts	84
	4. Discordant pairs in a contingency table	174
d_{yx}	Somer's d for ordinal-level data that incorporates tied pairs	175
df	Degrees of freedom: number of values free to vary after certain restrictions have been placed on the data	339
F	A ratio of the between-group mean square to the within-group mean square	362
f	Frequency	35
f_i	Number of cases within the interval containing X	80
f_e	Expected number in a given category	382
f_O	Observed number in a given category	382
fX	A score multiplied by its corresponding frequency	95
Gamma	Goodman and Kruskal's symmetric measure of association for ordinal-level contingency table data, sometimes written γ	171

Mathematical Operators
(continued)

Symbol	Definition	Page
H_0	The null hypothesis; hypothesis actually tested	309
H_1	The alternative hypothesis; hypothesis entertained if H_0 is rejected	310
HSD	Tukey's honestly significant difference	370
i	Width of the class interval	53
k	Number of groups or categories or cells	382
Md_n	Median	99
M_0	Mode	102
MD	Mean deviation	117
N	**1.** Number of pairs	198
	2. Number in sample	35
	3. Total number of scores or quantities	20
N_s	Total number of means obtained in a sampling experiment	268
(p)	Proportion	35
PRE	Proportional reduction in error	165
p	Probability	270
$p(A)$	Probability of event A	270
$p(B \mid A)$	Probability of B given that A has occurred	278
P	**1.** Probability of the occurrence of an event	275
	2. Proportion of cases in one class in a two-category population	275
Q	**1.** Probability of the nonoccurrence of an event	275
	2. Yule's special case of gamma for 2×2 tables	171
Q_1	First quartile, 25th percentile	84
Q_3	Third quartile, 75th percentile	84
r	**1.** Pearson product-moment correlation coefficient (Pearson's r)	185
	2. Number of rows in a contingency table	154
r^2	Coefficient of determination	229
r_s	Spearman rank-order correlation coefficient (Spearman's rho)	198
$r_{XY \cdot Z}$	Partial correlation coefficient	244
R	Multiple correlation coefficient	253
R_1	Sum of ranks assigned to the group with a sample size of N_1 (Mann-Whitney U)	404
R_2	Sum of ranks assigned to the group with a sample size of N_2 (Mann-Whitney U)	404
R^2	Coefficient of multiple determination	253
$1 - r^2$	Coefficient of nondetermination	229
$s^2 = \dfrac{\Sigma(X - \overline{X})^2}{N}$	Variance of a sample	119
$s = \sqrt{\dfrac{\Sigma(X - \overline{X})^2}{N}}$	Standard deviation of a sample	119
$\hat{s}^2 = \dfrac{\Sigma(X - \overline{X})^2}{N - 1}$	Unbiased estimate of the population variance	335
estimated $\sigma^2_{\overline{X}} = s^2_{\overline{X}} = \dfrac{\hat{s}^2}{N}$	Estimated variance of the sampling distribution of the mean	337

Mathematical Operators
(concluded)

Symbol	Definition	Page
$s_{\bar{X}} = \frac{\hat{s}}{\sqrt{N}} = \frac{s}{\sqrt{N-1}}$	Estimated standard error of the mean	324
$\hat{s}^2_{\text{bet}}$	Between-group variance estimate	363
$\hat{s}^2_w$	Within-group variance estimate	363
$s_{\text{est}\,y}$	Standard error of estimate when predictions are made from X to Y	225
$\Sigma(X - \bar{X})^2$	Sum of squares, sum of the squared deviations from the mean	119
SS_{tot}	Total sum of squares, sum of the squared deviations of each score (X) from the overall mean ($\bar{X}_{\text{tot}}$)	359
SS_w	Within-group sum of squares, sum of the squared deviations of each score (X) from the mean of its own group ($\bar{X}_i$)	360
SS_{bet}	Between-group sum of squares, sum of the squared deviations of each group mean ($\bar{X}_i$) from the overall mean ($\bar{X}_{\text{tot}}$), multiplied by the N in each group	362
t	Statistic employed to test hypotheses when σ is unknown	339
T	Sum of the ranks with the least frequent sign. Used with the Wilcoxon matched-pairs signed-rank test.	411
T_y	Tied pairs with different X values but which share the same Y value. Used with Somer's *d*.	175
U, U'	Statistics in the Mann-Whitney test	403
V	Cramer's V	393
X, Y	Variables; quantities or scores of variables	20
X_i, Y_i	Specific quantities indicated by the subscript i	20
$\bar{X}$, $\bar{Y}$	Arithmetic means of a sample	7
$\bar{X}_i$	Mean of the ith group	362
$\bar{X}_w$	The weighted mean	98
$\bar{X}_{\text{tot}} = \frac{\Sigma X_{\text{tot}}}{N}$	Overall mean	359
$(X - \bar{X})$	Deviation of an x-score from its mean	118
ΣX^2	Sum of the squares of the raw scores	120
$(\Sigma X)^2$	Sum of the raw scores, the quantity squared	124
X_{ll}	Score at lower true limit of interval containing X	80
X_m	Midpoint of an interval	95
Y'	Scores predicted by regression equations (also $\hat{Y}$)	215
z	**1.** Deviation of a specific score from the mean, expressed in standard deviation units	131
	2. Statistic employed to test hypotheses when σ is known	329
$z_{0.01} = \pm 2.58$	Critical value of z, minimum z required to reject H_0 at the 0.01 level of significance, two-tailed test	333
$z_{0.05} = \pm 1.96$	Minimum value of z required to reject H_0 at the 0.05 level of significance, two-tailed test	334
z_y	Y' expressed in terms of a z-score	219
Z	Control variable in a multivariate context	243

APPENDIX C

Tables

A	**Proportions of area under the normal curve**
B	**Table of χ^2**
C	**Critical values of t**
D	**Critical values of F**
D_1	**Critical values of F that cut off the upper and lower 2.5% of the F-distribution**
E	**Transformation of r to z_r**
F	**Critical values of r_s**
G	**Functions of r**
H	**Binomial coefficients**
I	**Critical values of x or $N - x$ (whichever is larger) at 0.05 and 0.01 levels when $p = Q = 1/2$**
J	**Critical values of x for various stages of P and Q when $N \leq 49$**
K	**Percentage points of the Studentized range**
L	**Squares, square roots, and reciprocals of numbers from 1 to 1000**
M	**Random digits**
$N_1 - N_4$	**Critical values of U and U'**
O	**Critical values of T**

THE USE OF TABLE A

The use of Table A requires that the raw score be transformed into a z-score and that the variable be normally distributed.

The values in Table A represent the proportion of area in the standard normal curve, which has a mean of 0, a standard deviation of 1.00, and a total area also equal to 1.00.

Because the normal curve is symmetrical, it is sufficient to indicate only the areas corresponding to positive z values. Negative z values will have precisely the same proportions of area as their positive counterparts.

Column B represents the proportion of area between the mean and a given z.

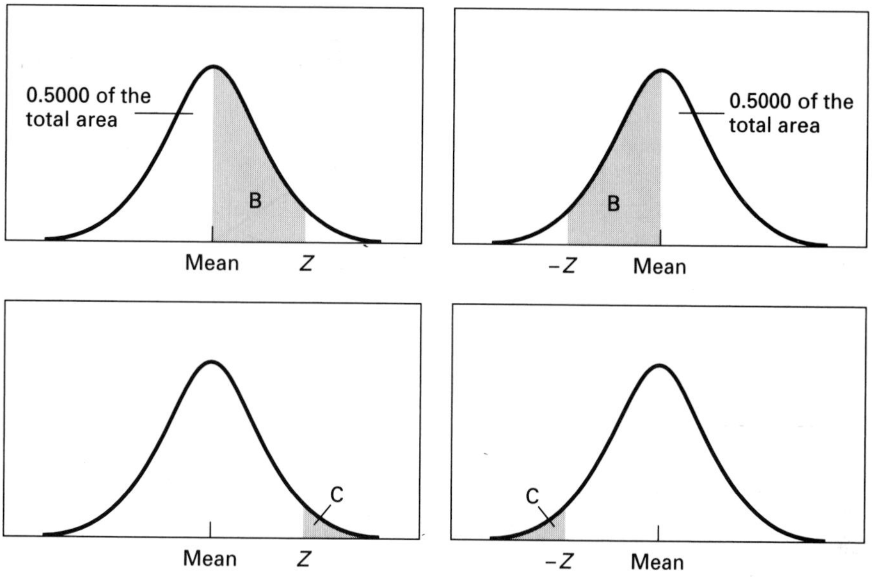

TABLE A

Proportions of area under the normal curve

(A) z	(B) Area between mean and z	(C) Area beyond z
0.00	0.0000	0.5000
0.01	0.0040	0.4960
0.02	0.0080	0.4920
0.03	0.0120	0.4880
0.04	0.0160	0.4840
0.05	0.0199	0.4801
0.06	0.0239	0.4761
0.07	0.0279	0.4721
0.08	0.0319	0.4681
0.09	0.0359	0.4641
0.10	0.0398	0.4602
0.11	0.0438	0.4562
0.12	0.0478	0.4522
0.13	0.0517	0.4483
0.14	0.0557	0.4443
0.15	0.0596	0.4404
0.16	0.0636	0.4364
0.17	0.0675	0.4325
0.18	0.0714	0.4286
0.19	0.0753	0.4247
0.20	0.0793	0.4207
0.21	0.0832	0.4168
0.22	0.0871	0.4129
0.23	0.0910	0.4090
0.24	0.0948	0.4052
0.25	0.0987	0.4013
0.26	0.1026	0.3974
0.27	0.1064	0.3936
0.28	0.1103	0.3897
0.29	0.1141	0.3859
0.30	0.1179	0.3821
0.31	0.1217	0.3783
0.32	0.1255	0.3745
0.33	0.1293	0.3707
0.34	0.1331	0.3669
0.35	0.1368	0.3632
0.36	0.1406	0.3594
0.37	0.1443	0.3557
0.38	0.1480	0.3520
0.39	0.1517	0.3483
0.40	0.1554	0.3446
0.41	0.1591	0.3409
0.42	0.1628	0.3372
0.43	0.1664	0.3336
0.44	0.1700	0.3300
0.45	0.1736	0.3264
0.46	0.1772	0.3228
0.47	0.1808	0.3192
0.48	0.1844	0.3156
0.49	0.1879	0.3121
0.50	0.1915	0.3085
0.51	0.1950	0.3050
0.52	0.1985	0.3015
0.53	0.2019	0.2981
0.54	0.2054	0.2946
0.55	0.2088	0.2912
0.56	0.2123	0.2877
0.57	0.2157	0.2843
0.58	0.2190	0.2810
0.59	0.2224	0.2776

TABLE A *(continued)*

(A) z	(B) Area between mean and z	(C) Area beyond z	(A) z	(B) Area between mean and z	(C) Area beyond z	(A) z	(B) Area between mean and z	(C) Area beyond z
0.60	0.2257	0.2743	1.00	0.3413	0.1587	1.40	0.4192	0.0808
0.61	0.2291	0.2709	1.01	0.3438	0.1562	1.41	0.4207	0.0793
0.62	0.2324	0.2676	1.02	0.3461	0.1539	1.42	0.4222	0.0778
0.63	0.2357	0.2643	1.03	0.3485	0.1515	1.43	0.4236	0.0764
0.64	0.2389	0.2611	1.04	0.3508	0.1492	1.44	0.4251	0.0749
0.65	0.2422	0.2578	1.05	0.3531	0.1469	1.45	0.4265	0.0735
0.66	0.2454	0.2546	1.06	0.3554	0.1446	1.46	0.4279	0.0721
0.67	0.2486	0.2514	1.07	0.3577	0.1423	1.47	0.4292	0.0708
0.68	0.2517	0.2483	1.08	0.3599	0.1401	1.48	0.4306	0.0694
0.69	0.2549	0.2451	1.09	0.3621	0.1379	1.49	0.4319	0.0681
0.70	0.2580	0.2420	1.10	0.3643	0.1357	1.50	0.4332	0.0668
0.71	0.2611	0.2389	1.11	0.3665	0.1335	1.51	0.4345	0.0655
0.72	0.2642	0.2358	1.12	0.3686	0.1314	1.52	0.4357	0.0643
0.73	0.2673	0.2327	1.13	0.3708	0.1292	1.53	0.4370	0.0630
0.74	0.2704	0.2296	1.14	0.3729	0.1271	1.54	0.4382	0.0618
0.75	0.2734	0.2266	1.15	0.3749	0.1251	1.55	0.4394	0.0606
0.76	0.2764	0.2236	1.16	0.3770	0.1230	1.56	0.4406	0.0594
0.77	0.2794	0.2206	1.17	0.3790	0.1210	1.57	0.4418	0.0582
0.78	0.2823	0.2177	1.18	0.3810	0.1190	1.58	0.4429	0.0571
0.79	0.2852	0.2148	1.19	0.3830	0.1170	1.59	0.4441	0.0559
0.80	0.2881	0.2119	1.20	0.3849	0.1151	1.60	0.4452	0.0548
0.81	0.2910	0.2090	1.21	0.3869	0.1131	1.61	0.4463	0.0537
0.82	0.2939	0.2061	1.22	0.3888	0.1112	1.62	0.4474	0.0526
0.83	0.2967	0.2033	1.23	0.3907	0.1093	1.63	0.4484	0.0516
0.84	0.2995	0.2005	1.24	0.3925	0.1075	1.64	0.4495	0.0505
0.85	0.3023	0.1977	1.25	0.3944	0.1056	1.65	0.4505	0.0495
0.86	0.3051	0.1949	1.26	0.3962	0.1038	1.66	0.4515	0.0485
0.87	0.3078	0.1922	1.27	0.3980	0.1020	1.67	0.4525	0.0475
0.88	0.3106	0.1894	1.28	0.3997	0.1003	1.68	0.4535	0.0465
0.89	0.3133	0.1867	1.29	0.4015	0.0985	1.69	0.4545	0.0455
0.90	0.3159	0.1841	1.30	0.4032	0.0968	1.70	0.4554	0.0446
0.91	0.3186	0.1814	1.31	0.4049	0.0951	1.71	0.4564	0.0436
0.92	0.3212	0.1788	1.32	0.4066	0.0934	1.72	0.4573	0.0427
0.93	0.3238	0.1762	1.33	0.4082	0.0918	1.73	0.4582	0.0418
0.94	0.3264	0.1736	1.34	0.4099	0.0901	1.74	0.4591	0.0409
0.95	0.3289	0.1711	1.35	0.4115	0.0885	1.75	0.4599	0.0401
0.96	0.3315	0.1685	1.36	0.4131	0.0869	1.76	0.4608	0.0392
0.97	0.3340	0.1660	1.37	0.4147	0.0853	1.77	0.4616	0.0384
0.98	0.3365	0.1635	1.38	0.4162	0.0838	1.78	0.4625	0.0375
0.99	0.3389	0.1611	1.39	0.4177	0.0823	1.79	0.4633	0.0367

TABLE A *(continued)*

(A) z	(B) Area between mean and z	(C) Area beyond z	(A) z	(B) Area between mean and z	(C) Area beyond z	(A) z	(B) Area between mean and z	(C) Area beyond z
1.80	0.4641	0.0359	2.20	0.4861	0.0139	2.60	0.4953	0.0047
1.81	0.4649	0.0351	2.21	0.4864	0.0136	2.61	0.4955	0.0045
1.82	0.4656	0.0344	2.22	0.4868	0.0132	2.62	0.4956	0.0044
1.83	0.4664	0.0336	2.23	0.4871	0.0129	2.63	0.4957	0.0043
1.84	0.4671	0.0329	2.24	0.4875	0.0125	2.64	0.4959	0.0041
1.85	0.4678	0.0322	2.25	0.4878	0.0122	2.65	0.4960	0.0040
1.86	0.4686	0.0314	2.26	0.4881	0.0119	2.66	0.4961	0.0039
1.87	0.4693	0.0307	2.27	0.4884	0.0116	2.67	0.4962	0.0038
1.88	0.4699	0.0301	2.28	0.4887	0.0113	2.68	0.4963	0.0037
1.89	0.4706	0.0294	2.29	0.4890	0.0110	2.69	0.4964	0.0036
1.90	0.4713	0.0287	2.30	0.4893	0.0107	2.70	0.4965	0.0035
1.91	0.4719	0.0281	2.31	0.4896	0.0104	2.71	0.4966	0.0034
1.92	0.4726	0.0274	2.32	0.4898	0.0102	2.72	0.4967	0.0033
1.93	0.4732	0.0268	2.33	0.4901	0.0099	2.73	0.4968	0.0032
1.94	0.4738	0.0262	2.34	0.4904	0.0096	2.74	0.4969	0.0031
1.95	0.4744	0.0256	2.35	0.4906	0.0094	2.75	0.4970	0.0030
1.96	0.4750	0.0250	2.36	0.4909	0.0091	2.76	0.4971	0.0029
1.97	0.4756	0.0244	2.37	0.4911	0.0089	2.77	0.4972	0.0028
1.98	0.4761	0.0239	2.38	0.4913	0.0087	2.78	0.4973	0.0027
1.99	0.4767	0.0233	2.39	0.4916	0.0084	2.79	0.4974	0.0026
2.00	0.4772	0.0228	2.40	0.4918	0.0082	2.80	0.4974	0.0026
2.01	0.4778	0.0222	2.41	0.4920	0.0080	2.81	0.4975	0.0025
2.02	0.4783	0.0217	2.42	0.4922	0.0078	2.82	0.4976	0.0024
2.03	0.4788	0.0212	2.43	0.4925	0.0075	2.83	0.4977	0.0023
2.04	0.4793	0.0207	2.44	0.4927	0.0073	2.84	0.4977	0.0023
2.05	0.4798	0.0202	2.45	0.4929	0.0071	2.85	0.4978	0.0022
2.06	0.4803	0.0197	2.46	0.4931	0.0069	2.86	0.4979	0.0021
2.07	0.4808	0.0192	2.47	0.4932	0.0068	2.87	0.4979	0.0021
2.08	0.4812	0.0188	2.48	0.4934	0.0066	2.88	0.4980	0.0020
2.09	0.4817	0.0183	2.49	0.4936	0.0064	2.89	0.4981	0.0019
2.10	0.4821	0.0179	2.50	0.4938	0.0062	2.90	0.4981	0.0019
2.11	0.4826	0.0174	2.51	0.4940	0.0060	2.91	0.4982	0.0018
2.12	0.4830	0.0170	2.52	0.4941	0.0059	2.92	0.4982	0.0018
2.13	0.4834	0.0166	2.53	0.4943	0.0057	2.93	0.4983	0.0017
2.14	0.4838	0.0162	2.54	0.4945	0.0055	2.94	0.4984	0.0016
2.15	0.4842	0.0158	2.55	0.4946	0.0054	2.95	0.4984	0.0016
2.16	0.4846	0.0154	2.56	0.4948	0.0052	2.96	0.4985	0.0015
2.17	0.4850	0.0150	2.57	0.4949	0.0051	2.97	0.4985	0.0015
2.18	0.4854	0.0146	2.58	0.4951	0.0049	2.98	0.4986	0.0014
2.19	0.4857	0.0143	2.59	0.4952	0.0048	2.99	0.4986	0.0014

TABLE A *(concluded)*

(A) z	(B) Area between mean and z	(C) Area beyond z	(A) z	(B) Area between mean and z	(C) Area beyond z	(A) z	(B) Area between mean and z	(C) Area beyond z
3.00	0.4987	0.0013	3.12	0.4991	0.0009	3.24	0.4994	0.0006
3.01	0.4987	0.0013	3.13	0.4991	0.0009	3.25	0.4994	0.0006
3.02	0.4987	0.0013	3.14	0.4992	0.0008	3.30	0.4995	0.0005
3.03	0.4988	0.0012	3.15	0.4992	0.0008	3.35	0.4996	0.0004
3.04	0.4988	0.0012	3.16	0.4992	0.0008	3.40	0.4997	0.0003
3.05	0.4989	0.0011	3.17	0.4992	0.0008	3.45	0.4997	0.0003
3.06	0.4989	0.0011	3.18	0.4993	0.0007	3.50	0.4998	0.0002
3.07	0.4989	0.0011	3.19	0.4993	0.0007	3.60	0.4998	0.0002
3.08	0.4990	0.0010	3.20	0.4993	0.0007	3.70	0.4999	0.0001
3.09	0.4990	0.0010	3.21	0.4993	0.0007	3.80	0.4999	0.0001
3.10	0.4990	0.0010	3.22	0.4994	0.0006	3.90	0.49995	0.00005
3.11	0.4991	0.0009	3.23	0.4994	0.0006	4.00	0.49997	0.00003

Tabled values are two-tailed.

TABLE B
Table of χ^2

Degrees of freedom df	0.10	0.05	0.02	0.01
1	2.706	3.841	5.412	6.635
2	4.605	5.991	7.824	9.210
3	6.251	7.815	9.837	11.341
4	7.779	9.488	11.668	13.277
5	9.236	11.070	13.388	15.086
6	10.645	12.592	15.033	16.812
7	12.017	14.067	16.622	18.475
8	13.362	15.507	18.168	20.090
9	14.684	16.919	19.679	21.666
10	15.987	18.307	21.161	23.209
11	17.275	19.675	22.618	24.725
12	18.549	21.026	24.054	26.217
13	19.812	22.362	25.472	27.688
14	21.064	23.685	26.873	29.141
15	22.307	24.996	28.259	30.578
16	23.542	26.296	29.633	32.000
17	24.769	27.587	30.995	33.409
18	25.989	28.869	32.346	34.805
19	27.204	30.144	33.687	36.191
20	28.412	31.410	35.020	37.566
21	29.615	32.671	36.343	38.932
22	30.813	33.924	37.659	40.289
23	32.007	35.172	38.968	41.638
24	33.196	36.415	40.270	42.980
25	34.382	37.652	41.566	44.314
26	35.563	38.885	42.856	45.642
27	36.741	40.113	44.140	46.963
28	37.916	41.337	45.419	48.278
29	39.087	42.557	46.693	49.588
30	40.256	43.773	47.962	50.892

THE USE OF TABLE C

For any given df, Table C shows the values of t corresponding to various levels of probability. Obtained t is significant at a given level if it is equal to or *greater than* the value shown in the table.

TABLE C
Critical values of t

	Level of significance for one-tailed test					
	0.10	**0.05**	**0.025**	**0.01**	**0.005**	**0.0005**
	Level of significance for two-tailed test					
df	**0.20**	**0.10**	**0.05**	**0.02**	**0.01**	**0.001**
1	3.078	6.314	12.706	31.821	63.657	636.619
2	1.886	2.920	4.303	6.965	9.925	31.598
3	1.638	2.353	3.182	4.541	5.841	12.941
4	1.533	2.132	2.776	3.747	4.604	8.610
5	1.476	2.015	2.571	3.365	4.032	6.859
6	1.440	1.943	2.447	3.143	3.707	5.959
7	1.415	1.895	2.365	2.998	3.499	5.405
8	1.397	1.860	2.306	2.896	3.355	5.041
9	1.383	1.833	2.262	2.821	3.250	4.781
10	1.372	1.812	2.228	2.764	3.169	4.587
11	1.363	1.796	2.201	2.718	3.106	4.437
12	1.356	1.782	2.179	2.681	3.055	4.318
13	1.350	1.771	2.160	2.650	3.012	4.221
14	1.345	1.761	2.145	2.624	2.977	4.140
15	1.341	1.753	2.131	2.602	2.947	4.073
16	1.337	1.746	2.120	2.583	2.921	4.015
17	1.333	1.740	2.110	2.567	2.898	3.965
18	1.330	1.734	2.101	2.552	2.878	3.922
19	1.328	1.729	2.093	2.539	2.861	3.883
20	1.325	1.725	2.086	2.528	2.845	3.850
21	1.323	1.721	2.080	2.518	2.831	3.819
22	1.321	1.717	2.074	2.508	2.819	3.792
23	1.319	1.714	2.069	2.500	2.807	3.767
24	1.318	1.711	2.064	2.492	2.797	3.745
25	1.316	1.708	2.060	2.485	2.787	3.725
26	1.315	1.706	2.056	2.479	2.779	3.707
27	1.314	1.703	2.052	2.473	2.771	3.690
28	1.313	1.701	2.048	2.467	2.763	3.674
29	1.311	1.699	2.045	2.462	2.756	3.659
30	1.310	1.697	2.042	2.457	2.750	3.646
40	1.303	1.684	2.021	2.423	2.704	3.551
60	1.296	1.671	2.000	2.390	2.660	3.460
120	1.289	1.658	1.980	2.358	2.617	3.373
∞	1.282	1.645	1.960	2.326	2.576	3.291

Table C is taken from Table III (page 46) of Fisher and Yates, *Statistical Tables for Biological, Agricultural, and Medical Research,* 6th ed., published by Longman Group Ltd., 1974. London (previously published by Oliver and Boyd, Edinburgh), and by permission of the authors and publishers.

HOW TO USE TABLE D

The obtained F is significant at a given level if it is equal to or *greater than* the value shown in Table D. 0.05 (lightface row) and 0.01 (boldface row) values for the distribution of F.

The values shown are the right tail of the distribution obtained by dividing the larger variance estimate by the smaller variance estimate. To find the complementary left or lower tail for a given df and α-level, reverse the degrees of freedom and find the reciprocal of that value in the F-table. For example, the value cutting off the top 5% of the area for df 7 and 12 is 2.85. To find the cutoff point of the bottom 5% of the area, find the tabled value at the $\alpha = 0.05$ level for 12 and 7 df. This is found to be 3.57. The reciprocal is $1/3.57 = 0.28$. Thus, 5% of the area falls *at or below an* $F = 0.28$.

TABLE D
Critical values of F

Degrees of freedom for denominator	Degrees of freedom for numerator																							
	1	2	3	4	5	6	7	8	9	10	11	12	14	16	20	24	30	40	50	75	100	200	500	∞
1	161	200	216	225	230	234	237	239	241	242	243	244	245	246	248	249	250	251	252	253	253	254	254	254
	4052	**4999**	**5403**	**5625**	**5764**	**5859**	**5928**	**5981**	**6022**	**6056**	**6082**	**6106**	**6142**	**6169**	**6208**	**6234**	**6258**	**6286**	**6302**	**6323**	**6334**	**6352**	**6361**	**6366**
2	18.51	19.00	19.16	19.25	19.30	19.33	19.36	19.37	19.38	19.39	19.40	19.41	19.42	19.43	19.44	19.45	19.46	19.47	19.47	19.48	19.49	19.49	19.50	19.50
	98.49	**99.01**	**99.17**	**99.25**	**99.30**	**99.33**	**99.34**	**99.36**	**99.38**	**99.40**	**99.41**	**99.42**	**99.43**	**99.44**	**99.45**	**99.46**	**99.47**	**99.48**	**99.48**	**99.49**	**99.49**	**99.49**	**99.50**	**99.50**
3	10.13	9.55	9.28	9.12	9.01	8.94	8.88	8.84	8.81	8.78	8.76	8.74	8.71	8.69	8.66	8.64	8.62	8.60	8.58	8.57	8.56	8.54	8.54	8.53
	34.12	**30.81**	**29.46**	**28.71**	**28.24**	**27.91**	**27.67**	**27.49**	**27.34**	**27.23**	**27.13**	**27.05**	**26.92**	**26.83**	**26.69**	**26.60**	**26.50**	**26.41**	**26.30**	**26.27**	**26.23**	**26.18**	**26.14**	**26.12**
4	7.71	6.94	6.59	6.39	6.26	6.16	6.09	6.04	6.00	5.96	5.93	5.91	5.87	5.84	5.80	5.77	5.74	5.71	5.70	5.68	5.66	5.65	5.64	5.63
	21.20	**18.00**	**16.69**	**15.98**	**15.52**	**15.21**	**14.98**	**14.80**	**14.66**	**14.54**	**14.45**	**14.37**	**14.24**	**14.15**	**14.02**	**13.93**	**13.83**	**13.74**	**13.69**	**13.61**	**13.57**	**13.52**	**13.48**	**13.46**
5	6.61	5.79	5.41	5.19	5.05	4.95	4.88	4.82	4.78	4.74	4.70	4.68	4.64	4.60	4.56	4.53	4.50	4.46	4.44	4.42	4.40	4.38	4.37	4.36
	16.26	**13.27**	**12.06**	**11.39**	**10.97**	**10.67**	**10.45**	**10.27**	**10.15**	**10.05**	**9.96**	**9.89**	**9.77**	**9.68**	**9.55**	**9.47**	**9.38**	**9.29**	**9.24**	**9.17**	**9.13**	**9.07**	**9.04**	**9.02**
6	5.99	5.14	4.76	4.53	4.39	4.28	4.21	4.15	4.10	4.06	4.03	4.00	3.96	3.92	3.87	3.84	3.81	3.77	3.75	3.72	3.71	3.69	3.68	3.67
	13.74	**10.92**	**9.78**	**9.15**	**8.75**	**8.47**	**8.26**	**8.10**	**7.98**	**7.87**	**7.79**	**7.72**	**7.60**	**7.52**	**7.39**	**7.31**	**7.23**	**7.14**	**7.09**	**7.02**	**6.99**	**6.94**	**6.90**	**6.88**
7	5.59	4.74	4.35	4.12	3.97	3.87	3.79	3.73	3.68	3.63	3.60	3.57	3.52	3.49	3.44	3.41	3.38	3.34	3.32	3.29	3.28	3.25	3.24	3.23
	12.25	**9.55**	**8.45**	**7.85**	**7.46**	**7.19**	**7.00**	**6.84**	**6.71**	**6.62**	**6.54**	**6.47**	**6.35**	**6.27**	**6.15**	**6.07**	**5.98**	**5.90**	**5.85**	**5.78**	**5.75**	**5.70**	**5.67**	**5.65**
8	5.32	4.46	4.07	3.84	3.69	3.58	3.50	3.44	3.39	3.34	3.31	3.28	3.23	3.20	3.15	3.12	3.08	3.05	3.03	3.00	2.98	2.96	2.94	2.93
	11.26	**8.65**	**7.59**	**7.01**	**6.63**	**6.37**	**6.19**	**6.03**	**5.91**	**5.82**	**5.74**	**5.67**	**5.56**	**5.48**	**5.36**	**5.28**	**5.20**	**5.11**	**5.06**	**5.00**	**4.96**	**4.91**	**4.88**	**4.86**
9	5.12	4.26	3.86	3.63	3.48	3.37	3.29	3.23	3.18	3.13	3.10	3.07	3.02	2.98	2.93	2.90	2.86	2.82	2.80	2.77	2.76	2.73	2.72	2.71
	10.56	**8.02**	**6.99**	**6.42**	**6.06**	**5.80**	**5.62**	**5.47**	**5.35**	**5.26**	**5.18**	**5.11**	**5.00**	**4.92**	**4.80**	**4.73**	**4.64**	**4.56**	**4.51**	**4.45**	**4.41**	**4.36**	**4.33**	**4.31**
10	4.96	4.10	3.71	3.48	3.33	3.22	3.14	3.07	3.05	2.97	2.94	2.91	2.86	2.82	2.77	2.74	2.70	2.67	2.64	2.61	2.59	2.56	2.55	2.54
	10.04	**7.56**	**6.55**	**5.99**	**5.64**	**5.39**	**5.21**	**5.06**	**4.95**	**4.85**	**4.78**	**4.71**	**4.60**	**4.52**	**4.41**	**4.33**	**4.25**	**4.17**	**4.12**	**4.05**	**4.01**	**3.96**	**3.93**	**3.91**
11	4.84	3.98	3.59	3.36	3.20	3.09	3.01	2.95	2.90	2.86	2.82	2.79	2.74	2.70	2.65	2.61	2.57	2.53	2.50	2.47	2.45	2.42	2.41	2.40
	9.65	**7.20**	**6.22**	**5.67**	**5.32**	**5.07**	**4.88**	**4.74**	**4.63**	**4.54**	**4.46**	**4.40**	**4.29**	**4.21**	**4.10**	**4.02**	**3.94**	**3.86**	**3.80**	**3.74**	**3.70**	**3.66**	**3.62**	**3.60**
12	4.75	3.88	3.49	3.26	3.11	3.00	2.92	2.85	2.80	2.76	2.72	2.69	2.64	2.60	2.54	2.50	2.46	2.42	2.40	2.36	2.35	2.32	2.31	2.30
	9.33	**6.93**	**5.95**	**5.41**	**5.06**	**4.82**	**4.65**	**4.50**	**4.39**	**4.30**	**4.22**	**4.16**	**4.05**	**3.98**	**3.86**	**3.78**	**3.70**	**3.61**	**3.56**	**3.49**	**3.46**	**3.41**	**3.38**	**3.36**
13	4.67	3.80	3.41	3.18	3.02	2.92	2.84	2.77	2.72	2.67	2.63	2.60	2.55	2.51	2.46	2.42	2.38	2.34	2.32	2.28	2.26	2.24	2.22	2.21
	9.07	**6.70**	**5.74**	**5.20**	**4.86**	**4.62**	**4.44**	**4.30**	**4.19**	**4.10**	**4.02**	**3.96**	**3.85**	**3.78**	**3.67**	**3.59**	**3.51**	**3.42**	**3.37**	**3.30**	**3.27**	**3.21**	**3.18**	**3.16**

TABLE D *(continued)*

Degrees of freedom for numerator (columns) / Degrees of freedom for denominator (rows)

Denom. df	1	2	3	4	5	6	7	8	9	10	11	12
14	4.60	3.74	3.34	3.11	2.96	2.85	2.77	2.70	2.65	2.60	2.56	2.53
	8.86	**6.51**	**5.56**	**5.03**	**4.69**	**4.46**	**4.28**	**4.14**	**4.03**	**3.94**	**3.86**	**3.80**
15	4.54	3.68	3.29	3.06	2.90	2.79	2.70	2.64	2.59	2.55	2.51	2.48
	8.68	**6.36**	**5.42**	**4.89**	**4.56**	**4.32**	**4.14**	**4.00**	**3.89**	**3.80**	**3.73**	**3.67**
16	4.49	3.63	3.24	3.01	2.85	2.74	2.66	2.59	2.54	2.49	2.45	2.42
	8.53	**6.23**	**5.29**	**4.77**	**4.44**	**4.20**	**4.03**	**3.89**	**3.78**	**3.69**	**3.61**	**3.55**
17	4.45	3.59	3.20	2.96	2.81	2.70	2.62	2.55	2.50	2.45	2.41	2.38
	8.40	**6.11**	**5.18**	**4.67**	**4.34**	**4.10**	**3.93**	**3.79**	**3.68**	**3.59**	**3.52**	**3.45**
18	4.41	3.55	3.16	2.93	2.77	2.66	2.58	2.51	2.46	2.41	2.37	2.34
	8.28	**6.01**	**5.09**	**4.58**	**4.25**	**4.01**	**3.85**	**3.71**	**3.60**	**3.51**	**3.44**	**3.37**
19	4.38	3.52	3.13	2.90	2.74	2.63	2.55	2.48	2.43	2.38	2.34	2.31
	8.18	**5.93**	**5.01**	**4.50**	**4.17**	**3.94**	**3.77**	**3.63**	**3.52**	**3.43**	**3.36**	**3.30**
20	4.35	3.49	3.10	2.87	2.71	2.60	2.52	2.45	2.40	2.35	2.31	2.28
	8.10	**5.85**	**4.94**	**4.43**	**4.10**	**3.87**	**3.71**	**3.56**	**3.45**	**3.37**	**3.30**	**3.23**
21	4.32	3.47	3.07	2.84	2.68	2.57	2.49	2.42	2.37	2.32	2.28	2.25
	8.02	**5.78**	**4.87**	**4.37**	**4.04**	**3.81**	**3.65**	**3.51**	**3.40**	**3.31**	**3.24**	**3.17**
22	4.30	3.44	3.05	2.82	2.66	2.55	2.47	2.40	2.35	2.30	2.26	2.23
	7.94	**5.72**	**4.82**	**4.31**	**3.99**	**3.76**	**3.59**	**3.45**	**3.35**	**3.26**	**3.18**	**3.12**
23	4.28	3.42	3.03	2.80	2.64	2.53	2.45	2.38	2.32	2.28	2.24	2.20
	7.88	**5.66**	**4.76**	**4.26**	**3.94**	**3.71**	**3.54**	**3.41**	**3.30**	**3.21**	**3.14**	**3.07**
24	4.26	3.40	3.01	2.78	2.62	2.51	2.43	2.36	2.30	2.26	2.22	2.18
	7.82	**5.61**	**4.72**	**4.22**	**3.90**	**3.67**	**3.50**	**3.36**	**3.25**	**3.17**	**3.09**	**3.03**
25	4.24	3.38	2.99	2.76	2.60	2.49	2.41	2.34	2.28	2.24	2.20	2.16
	7.77	**5.57**	**4.68**	**4.18**	**3.86**	**3.63**	**3.46**	**3.32**	**3.21**	**3.13**	**3.05**	**2.99**
26	4.22	3.37	2.89	2.74	2.59	2.47	2.39	2.32	2.27	2.22	2.18	2.15
	7.72	**5.53**	**4.64**	**4.14**	**3.82**	**3.59**	**3.42**	**3.29**	**3.17**	**3.09**	**3.02**	**2.96**

Denom. df	14	16	20	24	30	40	50	75	100	200	500	∞
14	2.48	2.44	2.39	2.35	2.31	2.27	2.24	2.21	2.19	2.16	2.14	2.13
	3.70	**3.62**	**3.51**	**3.43**	**3.34**	**3.26**	**3.21**	**3.14**	**3.11**	**3.06**	**3.02**	**3.00**
15	2.43	2.39	2.33	2.29	2.25	2.21	2.18	2.15	2.12	2.10	2.08	2.07
	3.56	**3.48**	**3.36**	**3.29**	**3.20**	**3.12**	**3.07**	**3.00**	**2.97**	**2.92**	**2.89**	**2.87**
16	2.37	2.33	2.28	2.24	2.20	2.16	2.13	2.09	2.07	2.04	2.02	2.01
	3.45	**3.37**	**3.25**	**3.18**	**3.10**	**3.01**	**2.96**	**2.89**	**2.86**	**2.80**	**2.77**	**2.75**
17	2.33	2.29	2.23	2.19	2.15	2.11	2.08	2.04	2.02	1.99	1.97	1.96
	3.35	**3.27**	**3.16**	**3.08**	**3.00**	**2.92**	**2.86**	**2.79**	**2.76**	**2.70**	**2.67**	**2.65**
18	2.29	2.25	2.19	2.15	2.11	2.07	2.04	2.00	1.98	1.95	1.93	1.92
	3.27	**3.19**	**3.07**	**3.00**	**2.91**	**2.83**	**2.78**	**2.71**	**2.68**	**2.62**	**2.59**	**2.57**
19	2.26	2.21	2.15	2.11	2.07	2.02	2.00	1.96	1.94	1.91	1.90	1.88
	3.19	**3.12**	**3.00**	**2.92**	**2.84**	**2.76**	**2.70**	**2.63**	**2.60**	**2.54**	**2.51**	**2.49**
20	2.23	2.18	2.12	2.08	2.04	1.99	1.96	1.92	1.90	1.87	1.85	1.84
	3.13	**3.05**	**2.94**	**2.86**	**2.77**	**2.69**	**2.63**	**2.56**	**2.53**	**2.47**	**2.44**	**2.42**
21	2.20	2.15	2.09	2.05	2.00	1.96	1.93	1.80	1.87	1.84	1.82	1.81
	3.07	**2.99**	**2.88**	**2.80**	**2.72**	**2.63**	**2.58**	**2.51**	**2.47**	**2.42**	**2.38**	**2.36**
22	2.18	2.13	2.07	2.03	1.98	1.93	1.91	1.87	1.84	1.81	1.80	1.78
	3.02	**2.94**	**2.83**	**2.75**	**2.67**	**2.58**	**2.53**	**2.46**	**2.42**	**2.37**	**2.33**	**2.31**
23	2.14	2.10	2.04	2.00	1.96	1.91	1.88	1.84	1.82	1.79	1.77	1.76
	2.97	**2.89**	**2.78**	**2.70**	**2.62**	**2.53**	**2.48**	**2.41**	**2.37**	**2.32**	**2.28**	**2.26**
24	2.13	2.09	2.02	1.98	1.94	1.89	1.86	1.82	1.80	1.76	1.74	1.73
	2.93	**2.85**	**2.74**	**2.66**	**2.58**	**2.49**	**2.44**	**2.36**	**2.33**	**2.27**	**2.23**	**2.21**
25	2.11	2.06	2.00	1.96	1.92	1.87	1.84	1.80	1.77	1.74	1.72	1.71
	2.89	**2.81**	**2.70**	**2.62**	**2.54**	**2.45**	**2.40**	**2.32**	**2.29**	**2.23**	**2.19**	**2.17**
26	2.10	2.05	1.99	1.95	1.90	1.85	1.82	1.78	1.76	1.72	1.70	1.69
	2.86	**2.77**	**2.66**	**2.58**	**2.50**	**2.41**	**2.36**	**2.28**	**2.25**	**2.19**	**2.15**	**2.13**

TABLE D *(continued)*

0.05 (lightface row) and 0.01 (boldface row) values for the distribution of F

Degrees of freedom for denominator	Degrees of freedom for numerator: 1	2	3	4	5	6	7	8	9	10	11	12	14	16	20	24	30	40	50	75	100	200	500	∞
27	4.21	3.35	2.96	2.73	2.57	2.46	2.37	2.30	2.25	2.20	2.16	2.13	2.08	2.03	1.97	1.93	1.88	1.84	1.80	1.76	1.74	1.71	1.68	1.67
	7.68	**5.49**	**4.60**	**4.11**	**3.79**	**3.56**	**3.39**	**3.26**	**3.14**	**3.06**	**2.98**	**2.93**	**2.83**	**2.74**	**2.63**	**2.55**	**2.47**	**2.38**	**2.33**	**2.25**	**2.21**	**2.16**	**2.12**	**2.10**
28	4.20	3.34	2.95	2.71	2.56	2.44	2.36	2.29	3.24	2.19	2.15	2.12	2.06	2.02	1.96	1.91	1.87	1.81	1.78	1.75	1.72	1.69	1.67	1.65
	7.64	**5.45**	**4.57**	**4.07**	**3.76**	**3.53**	**3.36**	**3.23**	**3.11**	**3.03**	**2.95**	**2.90**	**2.80**	**2.71**	**2.60**	**2.52**	**2.44**	**2.35**	**2.30**	**2.22**	**2.18**	**2.13**	**2.09**	**2.06**
29	4.18	3.33	2.93	2.70	2.54	2.43	2.35	2.28	2.22	2.18	2.14	2.10	2.05	2.00	1.94	1.90	1.85	1.80	1.77	1.73	1.71	1.68	1.65	1.64
	7.60	**5.52**	**4.54**	**4.04**	**3.73**	**3.50**	**3.32**	**3.20**	**3.08**	**3.00**	**2.92**	**2.87**	**2.77**	**2.68**	**2.57**	**2.49**	**2.41**	**2.32**	**2.27**	**2.19**	**2.15**	**2.10**	**2.06**	**2.03**
30	4.17	3.32	2.92	2.69	2.53	2.42	2.34	2.27	2.21	2.16	2.12	2.09	2.04	1.99	1.93	1.89	1.84	1.79	1.76	1.72	1.69	1.66	1.64	1.62
	7.56	**5.39**	**4.51**	**4.02**	**3.70**	**3.47**	**3.30**	**3.17**	**3.06**	**2.98**	**2.90**	**2.84**	**2.74**	**2.66**	**2.55**	**2.47**	**2.38**	**2.29**	**2.24**	**2.16**	**2.13**	**2.07**	**2.03**	**2.01**
32	4.15	3.30	2.90	2.67	2.51	2.40	2.32	2.25	2.19	2.14	2.10	2.07	2.02	1.97	1.91	1.86	1.82	1.76	1.74	1.69	1.67	1.64	1.61	1.59
	7.50	**5.34**	**4.46**	**3.97**	**3.66**	**3.42**	**3.25**	**3.12**	**3.01**	**2.94**	**2.86**	**2.80**	**2.70**	**2.62**	**2.51**	**2.42**	**2.34**	**2.25**	**2.20**	**2.12**	**2.08**	**2.02**	**1.98**	**1.96**
34	4.13	3.28	2.88	2.65	2.49	2.38	2.30	2.23	2.17	2.12	2.08	2.05	2.00	1.95	1.89	1.84	1.80	1.74	1.71	1.67	1.64	1.61	1.59	1.57
	7.44	**5.29**	**4.42**	**3.93**	**3.61**	**3.38**	**3.21**	**3.08**	**2.97**	**2.89**	**2.82**	**2.76**	**2.66**	**2.58**	**2.47**	**2.38**	**2.30**	**2.21**	**2.15**	**2.08**	**2.04**	**1.98**	**1.94**	**1.91**
36	4.11	3.26	2.86	2.63	2.48	2.36	2.28	2.21	2.15	2.10	2.06	2.03	1.89	1.93	1.87	1.82	1.78	1.72	1.69	1.65	1.62	1.59	1.56	1.55
	7.39	**5.25**	**4.38**	**3.89**	**3.58**	**3.35**	**3.18**	**3.04**	**2.94**	**2.86**	**2.78**	**2.72**	**2.62**	**2.54**	**2.43**	**2.35**	**2.26**	**2.17**	**2.12**	**2.04**	**2.00**	**1.94**	**1.90**	**1.87**
38	4.10	3.25	2.85	2.62	2.46	2.35	2.26	2.19	2.14	2.09	2.05	2.02	1.96	1.92	1.85	1.80	1.76	1.71	1.67	1.63	1.60	1.57	1.54	1.53
	7.35	**5.21**	**4.34**	**3.86**	**3.54**	**3.32**	**3.15**	**3.02**	**2.91**	**2.82**	**2.75**	**2.69**	**2.59**	**2.51**	**2.40**	**2.32**	**2.22**	**2.14**	**2.08**	**2.00**	**1.97**	**1.90**	**1.86**	**1.84**
40	4.08	3.23	2.84	2.61	2.45	2.34	2.25	2.18	2.12	2.07	2.04	2.00	1.95	1.90	1.84	1.79	1.74	1.69	1.66	1.61	1.59	1.55	1.53	1.51
	7.31	**5.18**	**4.31**	**3.83**	**3.51**	**3.29**	**3.12**	**2.99**	**2.88**	**2.80**	**2.73**	**2.66**	**2.56**	**2.49**	**2.37**	**2.29**	**2.20**	**2.11**	**2.05**	**1.97**	**1.94**	**1.88**	**1.84**	**1.81**
42	4.07	3.22	2.83	2.59	2.44	2.32	2.24	2.17	2.11	2.06	2.02	1.90	1.94	1.89	1.82	1.78	1.73	1.68	1.64	1.60	1.57	1.54	1.51	1.49
	7.27	**5.15**	**4.29**	**3.80**	**3.49**	**3.26**	**3.10**	**2.96**	**2.86**	**2.77**	**2.70**	**2.64**	**2.54**	**2.46**	**2.35**	**2.26**	**2.17**	**2.08**	**2.02**	**1.94**	**1.91**	**1.85**	**1.80**	**1.78**
44	4.06	3.21	2.82	2.58	2.43	2.31	2.23	2.16	2.10	2.05	2.01	1.98	1.92	1.88	1.81	1.76	1.72	1.66	1.63	1.58	1.56	1.52	1.50	1.48
	7.24	**5.12**	**4.26**	**3.78**	**3.46**	**3.24**	**3.07**	**2.94**	**2.84**	**2.75**	**2.68**	**2.62**	**2.52**	**2.44**	**2.32**	**2.24**	**2.15**	**2.06**	**2.09**	**1.92**	**1.88**	**1.82**	**1.78**	**1.75**
46	4.05	3.20	2.81	2.57	2.42	2.30	2.22	2.14	2.09	2.04	2.00	1.97	1.91	1.87	1.80	1.75	1.71	1.65	1.62	1.57	1.54	1.51	1.48	1.46
	7.21	**5.10**	**4.24**	**3.76**	**3.44**	**3.22**	**3.05**	**2.92**	**2.82**	**2.73**	**2.66**	**2.60**	**2.50**	**2.42**	**2.30**	**2.22**	**2.13**	**2.04**	**1.98**	**1.90**	**1.86**	**1.80**	**1.76**	**1.72**
48	4.04	3.19	2.80	2.56	2.41	2.30	2.21	2.14	2.08	2.03	1.99	1.96	1.90	1.86	1.79	1.74	1.70	1.64	1.61	1.56	1.53	1.50	1.47	1.45
	7.19	**5.08**	**4.22**	**3.74**	**3.42**	**3.20**	**3.04**	**2.90**	**2.80**	**2.71**	**2.64**	**2.58**	**2.48**	**2.40**	**2.28**	**2.20**	**2.11**	**2.02**	**1.96**	**1.88**	**1.84**	**1.78**	**1.73**	**1.70**

TABLE D *(concluded)*

Degrees of freedom for denominator	Degrees of freedom for numerator																						
	1	2	3	4	5	6	7	8	9	10	11	12	14	16	20	24	30	40	50	75	100	200	500	∞
50	4.03	3.18	2.79	2.56	2.40	2.29	2.20	2.13	2.07	2.02	1.98	1.95	1.90	1.85	1.78	1.74	1.69	1.63	1.60	1.55	1.52	1.48	1.46	1.44
	7.17	**5.06**	**4.20**	**3.72**	**3.41**	**3.18**	**3.02**	**2.88**	**2.78**	**2.70**	**2.62**	**2.56**	**2.46**	**2.39**	**2.26**	**2.18**	**2.10**	**2.00**	**1.94**	**1.86**	**1.82**	**1.76**	**1.71**	**1.68**
55	4.02	3.17	2.78	2.54	2.38	2.27	2.18	2.11	2.05	2.00	1.97	1.93	1.88	1.83	1.76	1.72	1.67	1.61	1.58	1.52	1.50	1.46	1.43	1.41
	7.12	**5.01**	**4.16**	**3.68**	**3.37**	**3.15**	**2.98**	**2.85**	**2.75**	**2.66**	**2.59**	**2.53**	**2.43**	**2.35**	**2.23**	**2.15**	**2.06**	**1.96**	**1.90**	**1.82**	**1.78**	**1.71**	**1.66**	**1.64**
60	4.00	3.15	2.76	2.52	2.37	2.25	2.17	2.10	2.04	1.99	1.95	1.92	1.86	1.81	1.75	1.70	1.65	1.59	1.56	1.50	1.48	1.44	1.41	1.39
	7.08	**4.98**	**4.13**	**3.65**	**3.34**	**3.12**	**2.95**	**2.82**	**2.72**	**2.63**	**2.56**	**2.50**	**2.40**	**2.32**	**2.20**	**2.12**	**2.03**	**1.93**	**1.87**	**1.79**	**1.74**	**1.68**	**1.63**	**1.60**
65	3.99	3.14	2.75	2.51	2.36	2.24	2.15	2.08	2.02	1.98	1.94	1.90	1.85	1.80	1.73	1.68	1.63	1.57	1.54	1.49	1.46	1.42	1.39	1.37
	7.04	**4.95**	**4.10**	**3.62**	**3.31**	**3.09**	**2.93**	**2.79**	**2.70**	**2.61**	**2.54**	**2.47**	**2.37**	**2.30**	**2.18**	**2.09**	**2.00**	**1.90**	**1.84**	**1.76**	**1.71**	**1.64**	**1.60**	**1.56**
70	3.98	3.13	2.74	2.50	2.35	2.32	2.14	2.07	2.01	1.97	1.93	1.89	1.84	1.79	1.72	1.67	1.62	1.56	1.53	1.47	1.45	1.40	1.37	1.35
	7.01	**4.92**	**4.08**	**3.60**	**3.29**	**3.07**	**2.91**	**2.77**	**2.67**	**2.59**	**2.51**	**2.45**	**2.35**	**2.28**	**2.15**	**2.07**	**1.98**	**1.88**	**1.82**	**1.74**	**1.69**	**1.62**	**1.56**	**1.53**
80	3.96	3.11	2.72	2.48	2.33	2.21	2.12	2.05	1.99	1.95	1.91	1.88	1.82	1.77	1.70	1.65	1.60	1.54	1.51	1.45	1.42	1.38	1.35	1.32
	6.96	**4.88**	**4.04**	**3.56**	**3.25**	**3.04**	**2.87**	**2.74**	**2.64**	**2.55**	**2.48**	**2.41**	**2.32**	**2.24**	**2.11**	**2.03**	**1.94**	**1.84**	**1.78**	**1.70**	**1.65**	**1.57**	**1.52**	**1.49**
100	3.94	3.09	2.70	2.46	2.30	2.19	2.10	2.03	1.97	1.92	1.88	1.85	1.79	1.75	1.68	1.63	1.57	1.51	1.48	1.42	1.39	1.34	1.30	1.28
	6.90	**4.82**	**3.98**	**3.51**	**3.20**	**2.99**	**2.82**	**2.69**	**2.59**	**2.51**	**2.43**	**2.36**	**2.26**	**2.19**	**2.06**	**1.98**	**1.89**	**1.79**	**1.73**	**1.64**	**1.59**	**1.51**	**1.46**	**1.43**
125	3.92	3.07	2.68	2.44	2.29	2.17	2.08	2.01	1.95	1.90	1.86	1.83	1.77	1.72	1.65	1.60	1.55	1.49	1.45	1.39	1.36	1.31	1.27	1.25
	6.84	**4.78**	**3.94**	**3.47**	**3.17**	**2.95**	**2.79**	**2.65**	**2.56**	**2.47**	**2.40**	**2.33**	**2.23**	**2.15**	**2.03**	**1.94**	**1.85**	**1.75**	**1.68**	**1.59**	**1.54**	**1.46**	**1.40**	**1.37**
150	3.91	3.06	2.67	2.43	2.27	2.16	2.07	2.00	1.94	1.89	1.85	1.82	1.76	1.71	1.64	1.59	1.54	1.47	1.44	1.37	1.34	1.29	1.25	1.22
	6.81	**4.75**	**3.91**	**3.44**	**3.13**	**2.92**	**2.76**	**2.62**	**2.53**	**2.44**	**2.37**	**2.30**	**2.20**	**2.12**	**2.00**	**1.91**	**1.83**	**1.72**	**1.66**	**1.56**	**1.51**	**1.43**	**1.37**	**1.33**
200	3.89	3.04	2.65	2.41	2.26	2.14	2.05	1.98	1.92	1.87	1.83	1.80	1.74	1.69	1.62	1.57	1.52	1.45	1.42	1.35	1.32	1.26	1.22	1.19
	6.76	**4.71**	**3.38**	**3.41**	**3.11**	**2.90**	**2.73**	**2.60**	**2.50**	**2.41**	**2.34**	**2.28**	**1.17**	**2.09**	**1.97**	**1.88**	**1.79**	**1.69**	**1.62**	**1.53**	**1.48**	**1.39**	**1.33**	**1.28**
400	3.86	3.02	2.62	2.39	2.23	2.12	2.03	1.96	1.90	1.85	1.81	1.78	1.72	1.67	1.60	1.54	1.49	1.42	1.38	1.32	1.28	1.22	1.16	1.13
	6.70	**4.66**	**3.83**	**3.36**	**3.06**	**2.85**	**2.69**	**2.55**	**2.46**	**2.37**	**2.29**	**2.23**	**2.12**	**2.04**	**1.92**	**1.84**	**1.74**	**1.64**	**1.57**	**1.47**	**1.42**	**1.32**	**1.24**	**1.19**
1,000	3.85	3.00	2.61	2.38	2.22	2.10	2.02	1.95	1.89	1.84	1.80	1.76	1.70	1.65	1.58	1.53	1.47	1.41	1.36	1.30	1.26	1.19	1.13	1.08
	6.66	**4.62**	**3.80**	**3.34**	**3.04**	**2.82**	**2.66**	**2.53**	**2.43**	**2.34**	**2.26**	**2.20**	**2.09**	**2.01**	**1.89**	**1.81**	**1.71**	**1.61**	**1.54**	**1.44**	**1.38**	**1.28**	**1.19**	**1.11**
∞	3.84	2.99	2.60	2.37	2.21	2.09	2.01	1.94	1.88	1.83	1.79	1.75	1.69	1.64	1.57	1.52	1.46	1.40	1.35	1.28	1.24	1.17	1.11	1.00
	6.64	**4.60**	**3.78**	**3.32**	**3.02**	**2.80**	**2.64**	**2.51**	**2.41**	**2.32**	**2.24**	**2.18**	**2.07**	**1.99**	**1.87**	**1.79**	**1.69**	**1.59**	**1.52**	**1.41**	**1.36**	**1.25**	**1.15**	**1.00**

HOW TO USE TABLE D_1

A difference in variances is significant at $\alpha = 0.05$ with df_1 and df_2 if it *equals* or *exceeds* the upper value in each cell or is *less than or equal to* the lower value in that cell; for example, if $\hat{s}_1^2 = 8.69$, df = 12 and $\hat{s}_2^2 = 2.63$, df = 9, $F = 3.30$. The critical values at df_{12} and df_9 are 0.291 and 3.87. Because obtained F is between these values, we fail to reject the hypothesis of homogeneity of variances. However, had we calculated F with $\hat{s}_1^2$ in the denominator, the critical lower and upper values at 9 and 12 df would have been 0.259 and 3.44.

TABLE D_1

Critical values of F that cut off the upper and lower 2.5% of the F-distributions

df	1	2	3	4	5	6	7	8	9	10	11	12	15	20	24	30	40	50	60	100	200	500
	.002	.026	.057	.082	.100	.113	.124	.132	.139	.144	.149	.153	.161	.170	.175	.180	.184	.187	.189	.193	.196	.198
1	648	800	864	900	922	937	978	957	963	969	973	977	985	993	997	1000	1010	1010	1010	1010	1020	1020
	.001	.026	.062	.094	.119	.138	.153	.165	.175	.183	.190	.196	.210	.224	.232	.239	.247	.251	.255	.261	.266	.269
2	38.5	39.0	39.2	39.2	39.3	39.3	39.4	39.4	39.4	39.4	39.4	39.4	39.4	39.4	39.4	39.5	39.5	39.5	39.5	39.5	39.5	39.5
	.001	.026	.065	.100	.129	.152	.170	.185	.197	.207	.216	.224	.241	.259	.269	.279	.289	.295	.299	.308	.314	.318
3	17.4	16.0	15.4	15.1	14.9	14.7	14.6	14.5	14.5	14.4	14.4	14.3	14.3	14.2	14.1	14.1	14.0	14.0	14.0	14.0	13.9	13.9
	.001	.026	.066	.104	.135	.161	.181	.198	.212	.224	.234	.243	.263	.284	.296	.308	.320	.327	.332	.342	.351	.356
4	12.2	10.6	9.98	9.60	9.36	9.20	9.07	8.98	8.90	8.84	8.79	8.75	8.66	8.56	8.51	8.46	8.41	8.38	8.36	8.32	8.29	8.27
	.001	.025	.067	.107	.140	.167	.189	.208	.223	.236	.248	.257	.280	.304	.317	.330	.344	.353	.359	.370	.380	.386
5	10.0	8.43	7.76	7.39	7.15	6.98	6.85	6.76	6.68	6.62	6.57	6.52	6.43	6.33	6.28	6.23	6.18	6.14	6.12	6.08	6.05	6.03
	.001	.025	.068	.109	.143	.172	.195	.215	.231	.246	.258	.268	.293	.320	.334	.349	.364	.375	.381	.394	.405	.415
6	8.81	7.26	6.60	6.23	5.99	5.82	5.70	5.60	5.52	5.46	5.41	5.37	5.27	5.17	5.12	5.07	5.01	4.98	4.96	4.92	4.88	4.86
	.001	.025	.068	.110	.146	.176	.200	.221	.238	.253	.266	.277	.304	.333	.348	.364	.381	.392	.399	.413	.426	.433
7	8.07	6.54	5.89	5.52	5.29	5.12	4.99	4.90	4.82	4.76	4.71	4.67	4.57	4.47	4.42	4.36	4.31	4.28	4.25	4.21	4.18	4.16
	.001	.025	.069	.111	.148	.179	.204	.226	.244	.259	.273	.285	.313	.343	.360	.377	.395	.407	.415	.431	.442	.450
8	7.57	6.06	5.42	5.05	4.82	4.65	4.53	4.43	4.36	4.30	4.24	4.20	4.10	4.00	3.95	3.89	3.84	3.81	3.78	3.74	3.70	3.68
	.001	.025	.069	.112	.150	.181	.207	.130	.248	.265	.279	.291	.320	.352	.370	.388	.408	.420	.428	.446	.459	.467
9	7.21	5.71	5.08	4.72	4.48	4.32	4.20	4.10	4.03	3.96	3.91	3.87	3.77	3.67	3.61	3.56	3.51	3.47	3.45	3.40	3.37	3.35
	.001	.025	.069	.113	.151	.183	.210	.233	.252	.269	.283	.296	.327	.360	.379	.398	.419	.431	.441	.459	.474	.483
10	6.94	5.46	4.83	4.47	4.24	4.07	3.95	3.85	3.78	3.72	3.66	3.62	3.52	3.42	3.37	3.31	3.26	3.22	3.20	3.15	3.12	3.09
	.001	.025	.069	.114	.152	.185	.212	.236	.256	.273	.288	.301	.332	.368	.386	.407	.429	.442	.450	.472	.485	.495
11	6.72	5.26	4.63	4.28	4.04	3.88	3.76	3.66	3.59	3.53	3.47	3.43	3.33	3.23	3.17	3.12	3.06	3.03	3.00	2.96	2.92	2.90
	.001	.025	.070	.114	.153	.186	.214	.238	.259	.276	.292	.305	.337	.374	.394	.416	.437	.450	.461	.481	.498	.508
12	6.55	5.10	4.47	4.12	3.89	3.73	3.61	3.51	3.44	3.37	3.32	3.28	3.18	3.07	3.02	2.96	2.91	2.87	2.85	2.80	2.76	2.74

TABLE D_1 *(concluded)*

df	1	2	3	4	5	6	7	8	9	10	11	12	15	20	24	30	40	50	60	100	200	500
	.001	.025	.070	.116	.156	.190	.219	.244	.265	.284	.300	.315	.349	.389	.410	.433	.458	.474	.485	.508	.526	.538
15	6.20	4.76	4.15	3.80	3.58	3.41	3.29	3.20	3.12	3.06	3.01	2.96	2.86	2.76	2.70	2.64	2.59	2.55	2.52	2.47	2.44	2.41
	.001	.025	.071	.117	.158	.193	.224	.250	.273	.292	.310	.325	.363	.406	.430	.456	.484	.503	.514	.541	.562	.575
20	5.87	4.46	3.86	3.51	3.29	3.13	3.01	2.91	2.84	2.77	2.72	2.68	2.57	2.46	2.41	2.35	2.29	2.25	2.22	2.17	2.13	2.10
	.001	.025	.071	.117	.159	.195	.227	.253	.277	.297	.315	.331	.370	.415	.441	.468	.498	.518	.531	.562	.585	.599
24	5.72	4.32	3.72	3.38	3.15	2.99	2.87	2.78	2.70	2.64	2.59	2.54	2.44	2.33	2.27	2.21	2.15	2.11	2.08	2.02	1.98	2.95
	.001	.025	.071	.118	.161	.197	.229	.257	.281	.302	.321	.337	.378	.426	.453	.482	.515	.535	.551	.585	.610	.625
30	5.57	4.18	3.59	3.25	3.03	2.87	2.75	2.65	2.57	2.51	2.46	2.41	2.31	2.20	2.14	2.07	2.01	1.97	1.94	1.88	1.84	1.81
	.001	.025	.071	.119	.162	.199	.232	.260	.285	.307	.327	.344	.387	.437	.466	.498	.533	.556	.573	.610	.641	.662
40	5.42	4.05	3.46	3.13	2.90	2.74	2.62	2.53	2.45	2.39	2.33	2.29	2.18	2.07	2.01	1.94	1.88	1.83	1.80	1.74	1.69	1.66
	.001	.025	.071	.120	.163	.202	.235	.264	.290	.313	.333	.351	.396	.450	.481	.515	.555	.581	.600	.641	.680	.704
60	5.29	3.93	3.34	3.01	2.79	2.63	2.51	2.41	2.33	2.27	2.22	2.17	2.06	1.94	1.88	1.82	1.74	1.70	1.67	1.60	1.54	1.51
	.001	.025	.072	.120	.165	.204	.238	.268	.295	.318	.340	.359	.406	.464	.498	.536	.580	.611	.633	.684	.729	.762
120	5.15	3.80	3.23	2.89	2.67	2.52	2.39	2.30	2.22	2.16	2.10	2.05	1.95	1.82	1.76	1.69	1.61	1.56	1.53	1.45	1.39	1.34

TABLE E
Transformation of r to z_r

r	z_r	r	z_r	r	z_r
.01	.010	.34	.354	.67	.811
.02	.020	.35	.366	.68	.829
.03	.030	.36	.377	.69	.848
.04	.040	.37	.389	.70	.867
.05	.050	.38	.400	.71	.887
.06	.060	.39	.412	.72	.908
.07	.070	.40	.424	.73	.929
.08	.080	.41	.436	.74	.950
.09	.090	.42	.448	.75	.973
.10	.100	.43	.460	.76	.996
.11	.110	.44	.472	.77	1.020
.12	.121	.45	.485	.78	1.045
.13	.131	.46	.497	.79	1.071
.14	.141	.47	.510	.80	1.099
.15	.151	.48	.523	.81	1.127
.16	.161	.49	.536	.82	1.157
.17	.172	.50	.549	.83	1.188
.18	.181	.51	.563	.84	1.221
.19	.192	.52	.577	.85	1.256
.20	.203	.53	.590	.86	1.293
.21	.214	.54	.604	.87	1.333
.22	.224	.55	.618	.88	1.376
.23	.234	.56	.633	.89	1.422
.24	.245	.57	.648	.90	1.472
.25	.256	.58	.663	.91	1.528
.26	.266	.59	.678	.92	1.589
.27	.277	.60	.693	.93	1.658
.28	.288	.61	.709	.94	1.738
.29	.299	.62	.725	.95	1.832
.30	.309	.63	.741	.96	1.946
.31	.321	.64	.758	.97	2.092
.32	.332	.65	.775	.98	2.298
.33	.343	.66	.793	.99	2.647

HOW TO USE TABLE F

A given value of r_s is statistically significant if it equals or exceeds the tabled value at the designated α-level at a given N. To interpolate, sum the critical values above and below the N of interest and divide by 2. Thus, the critical value at $\alpha = 0.05$, two-tailed test, when $N = 21$, is $(0.450 + 0.428)/2 = 0.439$.

TABLE F
Critical values of r_s

	Level of significance for one-tailed test			
	.05	**.025**	**.01**	**.005**
	Level of significance for two-tailed test			
N*	**.10**	**.05**	**.02**	**.01**
5	.900	1.000	1.000	—
6	.829	.886	.943	1.000
7	.714	.786	.893	.929
8	.643	.738	.833	.881
9	.600	.683	.783	.833
10	.564	.648	.746	.794
12	.506	.591	.712	.777
14	.456	.544	.645	.715
16	.425	.506	.601	.665
18	.399	.475	.564	.625
20	.377	.450	.534	.591
22	.359	.428	.508	.562
24	.343	.409	.485	.537
26	.329	.392	.465	.515
28	.317	.377	.448	.496
30	.306	.364	.432	.478

* N = number of pairs.

TABLE G
Functions of *r*

r	$\sqrt{r}$	r^2	$\sqrt{r - r^2}$	$\sqrt{1 - r}$	$1 - r^2$	$\sqrt{1 - r^2}$	$100(1 - k)$	r
						k	% EFF	
1.00	1.0000	1.0000	0.0000	0.0000	0.0000	0.0000	100.00	1.00
.99	.9950	.9801	.0995	.1000	.0199	.1411	85.89	.99
.98	.9899	.9604	.1400	.1414	.0396	.1990	80.10	.98
.97	.9849	.9409	.1706	.1732	.0591	.2431	75.69	.97
.96	.9798	.9216	.1960	.2000	.0784	.2800	72.00	.96
.95	.9747	.9025	.2179	.2236	.0975	.3122	68.78	.95
.94	.9695	.8836	.2375	.2449	.1164	.3412	65.88	.94
.93	.9644	.8649	.2551	.2646	.1351	.3676	63.24	.93
.92	.9592	.8464	.2713	.2828	.1536	.3919	60.81	.92
.91	.9539	.8281	.2862	.3000	.1719	.4146	58.54	.91
.90	.9487	.8100	.3000	.3162	.1900	.4359	56.41	.90
.89	.9434	.7921	.3129	.3317	.2079	.4560	54.40	.89
.88	.9381	.7744	.3250	.3464	.2256	.4750	52.50	.88
.87	.9327	.7569	.3363	.3606	.2431	.4931	50.69	.87
.86	.9274	.7396	.3470	.3742	.2604	.5103	48.97	.86
.85	.9220	.7225	.3571	.3873	.2775	.5268	47.32	.85
.84	.9165	.7056	.3666	.4000	.2944	.5426	45.74	.84
.83	.9110	.6889	.3756	.4123	.3111	.5578	44.22	.83
.82	.9055	.6724	.3842	.4243	.3276	.5724	42.76	.82
.81	.9000	.6561	.3923	.4359	.3439	.5864	41.36	.81
.80	.8944	.6400	.4000	.4472	.3600	.6000	40.00	.80
.79	.8888	.6241	.4073	.4583	.3759	.6131	38.69	.79
.78	.8832	.6084	.4142	.4690	.3916	.6258	37.42	.78
.77	.8775	.5929	.4208	.4796	.4071	.6380	36.20	.77
.76	.8718	.5776	.4271	.4899	.4224	.6499	35.01	.76
.75	.8660	.5625	.4330	.5000	.4375	.6614	33.86	.75
.74	.8602	.5476	.4386	.5099	.4524	.6726	32.74	.74
.73	.8544	.5329	.4440	.5196	.4671	.6834	31.66	.73
.72	.8485	.5184	.4490	.5292	.4816	.6940	30.60	.72
.71	.8426	.5041	.4538	.5385	.4959	.7042	29.58	.71
.70	.8367	.4900	.4583	.5477	.5100	.7141	28.59	.70
.69	.8307	.4761	.4625	.5568	.5239	.7238	27.62	.69
.68	.8246	.4624	.4665	.5657	.5376	.7332	26.68	.68
.67	.8185	.4489	.4702	.5745	.5511	.7424	25.76	.67
.66	.8124	.4356	.4737	.5831	.5644	.7513	24.87	.66
.65	.8062	.4225	.4770	.5916	.5775	.7599	24.01	.65
.64	.8000	.4096	.4800	.6000	.5904	.7684	23.16	.64
.63	.7937	.3969	.4828	.6083	.6031	.7766	22.34	.63
.62	.7874	.3844	.4854	.6164	.6156	.7846	21.54	.62
.61	.7810	.3721	.4877	.6245	.6279	.7924	20.76	.61
.60	.7746	.3600	.4899	.6325	.6400	.8000	20.00	.60
.59	.7681	.3481	.4918	.6403	.6519	.8074	19.26	.59
.58	.7616	.3364	.4936	.6481	.6636	.8146	18.54	.58
.57	.7550	.3249	.4951	.6557	.6751	.8216	17.84	.57
.56	.7483	.3136	.4964	.6633	.6864	.8285	17.15	.56

TABLE G *(continued)*

r	$\sqrt{r}$	r^2	$\sqrt{r - r^2}$	$\sqrt{1 - r}$	$1 - r^2$	$\sqrt{1 - r^2}$	$100(1 - k)$	r
						k	% EFF	
.55	.7416	.3025	.4975	.6708	.6975	.8352	16.48	.55
.54	.7348	.2916	.4984	.6782	.7084	.8417	15.83	.54
.53	.7280	.2809	.4991	.6856	.7191	.8480	15.20	.53
.52	.7211	.2704	.4996	.6928	.7296	.8542	14.58	.52
.51	.7141	.2601	.4999	.7000	.7399	.8602	13.98	.51
.50	.7071	.2500	.5000	.7071	.7500	.8660	13.40	.50
.49	.7000	.2401	.4999	.7141	.7599	.8717	12.83	.49
.48	.6928	.2304	.4996	.7211	.7696	.8773	12.27	.48
.47	.6856	.2209	.4991	.7280	.7791	.8827	11.73	.47
.46	.6782	.2116	.4984	.7348	.7884	.8879	11.21	.46
.45	.6708	.2025	.4975	.7416	.7975	.8930	10.70	.45
.44	.6633	.1936	.4964	.7483	.8064	.8980	10.20	.44
.43	.6557	.1849	.4951	.7550	.8151	.9028	9.72	.43
.42	.6481	.1764	.4936	.7616	.8236	.9075	9.25	.42
.41	.6403	.1681	.4918	.7681	.8319	.9121	8.79	.41
.40	.6325	.1600	.4899	.7746	.8400	.9165	8.35	.40
.39	.6245	.1521	.4877	.7810	.8479	.9208	7.92	.39
.38	.6164	.1444	.4854	.7847	.8556	.9250	7.50	.38
.37	.6083	.1369	.4828	.7937	.8631	.9290	7.10	.37
.36	.6000	.1296	.4800	.8000	.8704	.9330	6.70	.36
.35	.5916	.1225	.4770	.8062	.8775	.9367	6.33	.35
.34	.5831	.1156	.4737	.8124	.8844	.9404	5.96	.34
.33	.5745	.1089	.4702	.8185	.8911	.9440	5.60	.33
.32	.5657	.1024	.4665	.8246	.8976	.9474	5.25	.32
.31	.5568	.0961	.4625	.8307	.9039	.9507	4.93	.31
.30	.5477	.0900	.4583	.8367	.9100	.9539	4.61	.30
.29	.5385	.0841	.4538	.8426	.9159	.9570	4.30	.29
.28	.5292	.0784	.4490	.8485	.9216	.9600	4.00	.28
.27	.5196	.0729	.4440	.8544	.9271	.9629	3.71	.27
.26	.5099	.0676	.4386	.8602	.9324	.9656	3.44	.26
.25	.5000	.0625	.4330	.8660	.9375	.9682	3.18	.25
.24	.4899	.0576	.4271	.8718	.9424	.9708	2.92	.24
.23	.4796	.0529	.4208	.8775	.9471	.9732	2.68	.23
.22	.4690	.0484	.4142	.8832	.9516	.9755	2.45	.22
.21	.4583	.0441	.4073	.8888	.9559	.9777	2.23	.21
.20	.4472	.0400	.4000	.8944	.9600	.9798	2.02	.20
.19	.4359	.0361	.3923	.9000	.9639	.9818	1.82	.19
.18	.4243	.0324	.3842	.9055	.9676	.9837	1.63	.18
.17	.4123	.0289	.3756	.9110	.9711	.9854	1.46	.17
.16	.4000	.0256	.3666	.9165	.9744	.9871	1.29	.16
.15	.3873	.0225	.3571	.9220	.9775	.9887	1.13	.15
.14	.3742	.0196	.3470	.9274	.9804	.9902	.98	.14
.13	.3606	.0169	.3363	.9327	.9831	.9915	.85	.13
.12	.3464	.0144	.3250	.9381	.9856	.9928	.72	.12
.11	.3317	.0121	.3129	.9434	.9879	.9939	.61	.11

TABLE G *(concluded)*

r	$\sqrt{r}$	r^2	$\sqrt{r - r^2}$	$\sqrt{1 - r}$	$1 - r^2$	$\sqrt{1 - r^2}$	$100(1 - k)$	r
						k	% EFF	
.10	.3162	.0100	.3000	.9487	.9900	.9950	.50	.10
.09	.3000	.0081	.2862	.9539	.9919	.9959	.41	.09
.08	.2828	.0064	.2713	.9592	.9936	.9968	.32	.08
.07	.2646	.0049	.2551	.9644	.9951	.9975	.25	.07
.06	.2449	.0036	.2375	.9695	.9964	.9982	.18	.06
.05	.2236	.0025	.2179	.9747	.9975	.9987	.13	.05
.04	.2000	.0016	.1960	.9798	.9984	.9992	.08	.04
.03	.1732	.0009	.1706	.9849	.9991	.9995	.05	.03
.02	.1414	.0004	.1400	.9899	.9996	.9998	.02	.02
.01	.1000	.0001	.0995	.9950	.9999	.9999	.01	.01
.00	.0000	.0000	.0000	1.0000	1.0000	1.0000	.00	.00

TABLE H
Binomial coefficients

N	$\binom{N}{0}$	$\binom{N}{1}$	$\binom{N}{2}$	$\binom{N}{3}$	$\binom{N}{4}$	$\binom{N}{5}$	$\binom{N}{6}$	$\binom{N}{7}$	$\binom{N}{8}$	$\binom{N}{9}$	$\binom{N}{10}$
0	1										
1	1	1									
2	1	2	1								
3	1	3	3	1							
4	1	4	6	4	1						
5	1	5	10	10	5	1					
6	1	6	15	20	15	6	1				
7	1	7	21	35	35	21	7	1			
8	1	8	28	56	70	56	28	8	1		
9	1	9	36	84	126	126	84	36	9	1	
10	1	10	45	120	210	252	210	120	45	10	1
11	1	11	55	165	330	462	462	330	165	55	11
12	1	12	66	220	495	792	924	792	495	220	66
13	1	13	78	286	715	1287	1716	1716	1287	715	286
14	1	14	91	364	1001	2002	3003	3432	3003	2002	1001
15	1	15	105	455	1365	3003	5005	6435	6435	5005	3003
16	1	16	120	560	1820	4368	8008	11440	12870	11440	8008
17	1	17	136	680	2380	6188	12376	19448	24310	24310	19448
18	1	18	153	816	3060	8568	18564	31824	43758	48620	43758
19	1	19	171	969	3876	11628	27132	50388	75582	92378	92378
20	1	20	190	1140	4845	15504	38760	77520	125970	167960	184756

HOW TO USE TABLE I

In Table I, x is the frequency in the P category, and $N - x$ is the frequency in the Q category. The obtained x or $N - x$ must be *equal to* or *greater than* the value shown for significance at the chosen level. Dashes indicate that no decision is possible for N at the given α-level.

TABLE I
Critical values of x or $N - x$ (whichever is larger) at 0.05 and 0.01 levels when $P = Q = 1/2$

	One-tailed test		Two-tailed test	
N	0.05	0.01	0.05	0.01
5	5	—	—	—
6	6	—	6	—
7	7	7	7	—
8	7	8	8	—
9	8	9	8	9
10	9	10	9	10
11	9	10	10	11
12	10	11	10	11
13	10	12	11	12
14	11	12	12	13
15	12	13	12	13
16	12	14	13	14
17	13	14	13	15
18	13	15	14	15
19	14	15	15	16
20	15	16	15	17
21	15	17	16	17
22	16	17	17	18
23	16	18	17	19
24	17	19	18	19
25	18	19	18	20
26	18	20	19	20
27	19	20	20	21
28	19	21	20	22
29	20	22	21	22
30	20	22	21	23
31	21	23	22	24
32	22	24	23	24
33	22	24	23	25
34	23	25	24	25
35	23	25	24	26
36	24	26	25	27
37	24	27	25	27
38	25	27	26	28
39	26	28	27	28
40	26	28	27	29
41	27	29	28	30
42	27	29	28	30
43	28	30	29	31
44	28	31	29	31
45	29	31	30	32
46	30	32	31	33
47	30	32	31	33
48	31	33	32	34
49	31	34	32	35
50	32	34	33	35

HOW TO USE TABLE J

Table J was prepared to expedite decision making when dealing with binomial populations in which $P \neq Q$. *Example:* A researcher has conducted 12 independent repetitions of the same study, using $\alpha = 0.01$. Four of these studies achieved statistical significance. Is this result (4 out of 12 statistically significant outcomes) itself statistically significant, or is it within chance expectations? Looking in the column headed .01 opposite $N = 12$, we find that two or more differences significant at $\alpha = .01$ is in itself significant at $\alpha = .01$. Thus, the researcher may conclude that the overall results of his or her investigations justify rejecting H_0.

A given value of x is significant at a given α-level if it equals or exceeds the critical value shown in the table. All values shown are one-tailed. Since the binomial is not symmetrical when $P \neq Q \neq 1/2$, there is no straightforward way to obtain two-tailed values.

TABLE J

Critical values of x at $\alpha = 0.05$ (lightface) and $\alpha = 0.01$ (boldface) at varying values of P and Q for N's equal to 2 through 49

N \ P	.01	.02	.03	.04	.05	.06	.07	.08	.09	.10	.11	.12	.13	.14	.15	.16	.17	.18	.19	.20	.21	.22	.23	.24	.25
Q	.99	.98	.97	.96	.95	.94	.93	.92	.91	.90	.89	.88	.87	.86	.85	.84	.83	.82	.81	.80	.79	.78	.77	.76	.75
2	1	1	2	2	2	2	2	2	2	2	2	2	2	2	2	2	2	2	2	2	2	2	—	—	—
	1	**2**	**2**	**2**	**2**	**2**	**2**	**2**	**2**	**2**	—	—	—	—	—	—	—	—	—	—	—	—	—	—	—
3	1	2	2	2	2	2	2	2	2	2	2	2	2	3	3	3	3	3	3	3	3	3	3	3	3
	2	**2**	**2**	**2**	**2**	**3**	**3**	**3**	**3**	**3**	**3**	**3**	**3**	**3**	**3**	**3**	**3**	**3**	**3**	**3**	**3**	—	—	—	—
4	1	2	2	2	2	2	2	2	2	3	3	3	3	3	3	3	3	3	3	3	3	3	3	3	4
	2	**2**	**2**	**2**	**3**	**3**	**3**	**3**	**3**	**3**	**3**	**3**	**3**	**3**	**4**	**4**	**4**	**4**	**4**	**4**	**4**	**4**	**4**	**4**	**4**
5	1	2	2	2	2	2	2	3	3	3	3	3	3	3	3	3	3	3	4	4	4	4	4	4	4
	2	**2**	**2**	**3**	**3**	**3**	**3**	**3**	**3**	**3**	**4**	**4**	**4**	**4**	**4**	**4**	**4**	**4**	**4**	**4**	**4**	**4**	**5**	**5**	**5**
6	2	2	2	2	2	2	3	3	3	3	3	3	3	3	3	4	4	4	4	4	4	4	4	5	5
	2	**2**	**3**	**3**	**3**	**3**	**3**	**3**	**4**	**4**	**4**	**4**	**4**	**4**	**4**	**4**	**4**	**5**	**5**	**5**	**5**	**5**	**5**	**5**	**5**
7	2	2	2	2	2	3	3	3	3	3	3	3	4	4	4	4	4	4	4	4	4	4	5	5	5
	2	**2**	**3**	**3**	**3**	**3**	**3**	**4**	**4**	**4**	**4**	**4**	**4**	**4**	**5**	**5**	**5**	**5**	**5**	**5**	**6**	**6**	**6**	**6**	**6**
8	2	2	2	2	3	3	3	3	3	3	3	4	4	4	4	4	4	4	4	5	5	5	5	5	5
	2	**3**	**3**	**3**	**3**	**3**	**4**	**4**	**4**	**4**	**4**	**4**	**5**	**5**	**5**	**5**	**5**	**5**	**5**	**6**	**6**	**6**	**6**	**6**	**6**
9	2	2	2	2	3	3	3	3	3	4	4	4	4	4	4	4	5	5	5	5	5	5	5	5	5
	2	**3**	**3**	**3**	**3**	**4**	**4**	**4**	**4**	**4**	**5**	**5**	**5**	**5**	**5**	**5**	**5**	**6**	**6**	**6**	**6**	**6**	**6**	**6**	**6**
10	2	2	2	3	3	3	3	3	4	4	4	4	4	4	4	5	5	5	5	5	5	5	6	6	6
	2	**3**	**3**	**3**	**4**	**4**	**4**	**4**	**4**	**5**	**5**	**5**	**5**	**5**	**5**	**6**	**6**	**6**	**6**	**6**	**6**	**7**	**7**	**7**	**7**
11	2	2	2	3	3	3	3	4	4	4	4	4	4	5	5	5	5	5	5	6	6	6	6	6	6
	2	**3**	**3**	**3**	**4**	**4**	**4**	**4**	**5**	**5**	**5**	**5**	**5**	**6**	**6**	**6**	**6**	**6**	**6**	**7**	**7**	**7**	**7**	**7**	**7**
12	2	2	2	3	3	3	3	4	4	4	4	4	5	5	5	5	5	5	6	6	6	6	6	6	7
	2	**3**	**3**	**4**	**4**	**4**	**4**	**5**	**5**	**5**	**5**	**5**	**6**	**6**	**6**	**6**	**6**	**7**	**7**	**7**	**7**	**7**	**7**	**8**	**8**
13	2	2	3	3	3	3	4	4	4	4	4	5	5	5	5	5	6	6	6	6	6	6	7	7	7
	2	**3**	**3**	**4**	**4**	**4**	**5**	**5**	**5**	**5**	**5**	**6**	**6**	**6**	**6**	**7**	**7**	**7**	**7**	**7**	**7**	**8**	**8**	**8**	**8**

TABLE J (continued)

N \ P	.26	.27	.28	.29	.30	.31	.32	.33	.34	.35	.36	.37	.38	.39	.40	.41	.42	.43	.44	.45	.46	.47	.48	.49	.50
Q	.74	.73	.72	.71	.70	.69	.68	.67	.66	.65	.64	.63	.62	.61	.60	.59	.58	.57	.56	.55	.54	.53	.52	.51	.50
2	—	—	—	—	—	—	—	—	—	—	—	—	—	—	—	—	—	—	—	—	—	—	—	—	—
	—	**—**	**—**	**—**	**—**	**—**	**—**	**—**	**—**	**—**	**—**	**—**	**—**	**—**	**—**	**—**	**—**	**—**	**—**	**—**	**—**	**—**	**—**	**—**	**—**
3	3	3	3	3	3	3	3	3	3	3	3	—	—	—	—	—	—	—	—	—	—	—	—	—	—
	—	**—**	**—**	**—**	**—**	**—**	**—**	**—**	**—**	**—**	**—**	**—**	**—**	**—**	**—**	**—**	**—**	**—**	**—**	**—**	**—**	**—**	**—**	**—**	**—**
4	4	4	4	4	4	4	4	4	4	4	4	4	4	4	4	4	4	4	4	4	4	—	—	—	—
	4	**4**	**4**	**4**	**4**	**4**	**—**	**—**	**—**	**—**	**—**	**—**	**—**	**—**	**—**	**—**	**—**	**—**	**—**	**—**	**—**	**—**	**—**	**—**	**—**
5	4	4	4	4	4	4	4	4	4	5	5	5	5	5	5	5	5	5	5	5	5	5	5	5	5
	5	**5**	**5**	**5**	**5**	**5**	**5**	**5**	**5**	**5**	**5**	**5**	**5**	**5**	**—**	**—**	**—**	**—**	**—**	**—**	**—**	**—**	**—**	**—**	**—**
6	5	5	5	5	5	5	5	5	5	5	5	5	5	5	5	6	6	6	6	6	6	6	6	6	6
	5	**5**	**5**	**5**	**6**	**6**	**6**	**6**	**6**	**6**	**6**	**6**	**6**	**6**	**6**	**6**	**6**	**6**	**6**	**6**	**6**	**—**	**—**	**—**	**—**
7	5	5	5	5	5	5	5	5	5	6	6	6	6	6	6	6	6	6	6	6	6	6	7	7	7
	6	**6**	**6**	**6**	**6**	**6**	**6**	**6**	**6**	**6**	**7**	**7**	**7**	**7**	**7**	**7**	**7**	**7**	**7**	**7**	**7**	**7**	**7**	**7**	**7**
8	5	5	5	6	6	6	6	6	6	6	6	6	6	6	6	7	7	7	7	7	7	7	7	7	7
	6	**6**	**6**	**6**	**7**	**7**	**7**	**7**	**7**	**7**	**7**	**7**	**7**	**7**	**7**	**7**	**8**	**8**	**8**	**8**	**8**	**8**	**8**	**8**	**8**
9	6	6	6	6	6	6	6	6	6	7	7	7	7	7	7	7	7	7	7	8	8	8	8	8	8
	7	**7**	**7**	**7**	**7**	**7**	**7**	**7**	**7**	**8**	**8**	**8**	**8**	**8**	**8**	**8**	**8**	**8**	**8**	**8**	**9**	**9**	**9**	**9**	**9**
10	6	6	6	6	6	7	7	7	7	7	7	7	7	7	8	8	8	8	8	8	8	8	8	8	9
	7	**7**	**7**	**7**	**8**	**8**	**8**	**8**	**8**	**8**	**8**	**8**	**8**	**9**	**9**	**9**	**9**	**9**	**9**	**9**	**9**	**9**	**9**	**9**	**10**
11	6	6	7	7	7	7	7	7	7	8	8	8	8	8	8	8	8	8	9	9	9	9	9	9	9
	7	**8**	**8**	**8**	**8**	**8**	**8**	**8**	**9**	**9**	**9**	**9**	**9**	**9**	**9**	**9**	**9**	**10**	**10**	**10**	**10**	**10**	**10**	**10**	**10**
12	7	7	7	7	7	7	8	8	8	8	8	8	8	8	9	9	9	9	9	9	9	9	10	10	10
	8	**8**	**8**	**8**	**8**	**9**	**9**	**9**	**9**	**9**	**9**	**9**	**10**	**10**	**10**	**10**	**10**	**10**	**10**	**10**	**10**	**11**	**11**	**11**	**11**
13	7	7	7	8	8	8	8	8	8	8	9	9	9	9	9	9	9	10	10	10	10	10	10	10	10
	8	**8**	**9**	**9**	**9**	**9**	**9**	**9**	**10**	**10**	**10**	**10**	**10**	**10**	**10**	**10**	**11**	**11**	**11**	**11**	**11**	**11**	**11**	**11**	**12**

TABLE J *(continued)*

N \ *P* / *Q*	.01 / .99	.02 / .98	.03 / .97	.04 / .96	.05 / .95	.06 / .94	.07 / .93	.08 / .92	.09 / .91	.10 / .90	.11 / .89	.12 / .88	.13 / .87	.14 / .86	.15 / .85	.16 / .84	.17 / .83	.18 / .82	.19 / .81	.20 / .80	.21 / .79	.22 / .78	.23 / .77	.24 / .76	.25 / .75
14	2	2	3	3	3	3	4	4	4	4	5	5	5	5	5	6	6	6	6	6	7	7	7	7	7
	2	**3**	**3**	**4**	**4**	**4**	**5**	**5**	**5**	**5**	**6**	**6**	**6**	**6**	**7**	**7**	**7**	**7**	**7**	**8**	**8**	**8**	**8**	**8**	**9**
15	2	2	3	3	3	4	4	4	4	5	5	5	5	5	6	6	6	6	6	7	7	7	7	7	8
	2	**3**	**3**	**4**	**4**	**5**	**5**	**5**	**5**	**6**	**6**	**6**	**6**	**7**	**7**	**7**	**7**	**8**	**8**	**8**	**8**	**8**	**9**	**9**	**9**
16	2	2	3	3	3	4	4	4	4	5	5	5	5	6	6	6	6	7	7	7	7	7	8	8	8
	3	**3**	**4**	**4**	**4**	**5**	**5**	**5**	**6**	**6**	**6**	**6**	**7**	**7**	**7**	**7**	**8**	**8**	**8**	**8**	**8**	**9**	**9**	**9**	**9**
17	2	2	3	3	4	4	4	4	5	5	5	5	6	6	6	6	7	7	7	7	7	8	8	8	8
	3	**3**	**4**	**4**	**4**	**5**	**5**	**5**	**6**	**6**	**6**	**7**	**7**	**7**	**7**	**8**	**8**	**8**	**8**	**9**	**9**	**9**	**9**	**9**	**10**
18	2	2	3	3	4	4	4	5	5	5	5	6	6	6	6	7	7	7	7	8	8	8	8	8	9
	3	**3**	**4**	**4**	**5**	**5**	**5**	**6**	**6**	**6**	**7**	**7**	**7**	**7**	**8**	**8**	**8**	**8**	**9**	**9**	**9**	**9**	**10**	**10**	**10**
19	2	3	3	3	4	4	4	5	5	5	6	6	6	6	7	7	7	7	8	8	8	8	9	9	9
	3	**3**	**4**	**4**	**5**	**5**	**5**	**6**	**6**	**6**	**7**	**7**	**7**	**8**	**8**	**8**	**8**	**9**	**9**	**9**	**9**	**10**	**10**	**10**	**10**
20	2	3	3	3	4	4	4	5	5	5	6	6	6	7	7	7	7	8	8	8	8	9	9	9	9
	3	**3**	**4**	**4**	**5**	**5**	**6**	**6**	**6**	**7**	**7**	**7**	**8**	**8**	**8**	**8**	**9**	**9**	**9**	**9**	**10**	**10**	**10**	**10**	**11**
21	2	3	3	3	4	4	5	5	5	6	6	6	6	7	7	7	8	8	8	8	9	9	9	9	10
	3	**3**	**4**	**4**	**5**	**5**	**6**	**6**	**6**	**7**	**7**	**7**	**8**	**8**	**8**	**9**	**9**	**9**	**10**	**10**	**10**	**10**	**11**	**11**	**11**
22	2	3	3	4	4	4	5	5	5	6	6	6	7	7	7	8	8	8	8	9	9	9	9	10	10
	3	**3**	**4**	**5**	**5**	**5**	**6**	**6**	**7**	**7**	**7**	**8**	**8**	**8**	**9**	**9**	**9**	**10**	**10**	**10**	**10**	**11**	**11**	**11**	**11**
23	2	3	3	4	4	4	5	5	6	6	6	6	7	7	7	8	8	8	9	9	9	9	10	10	10
	3	**4**	**4**	**5**	**5**	**6**	**6**	**6**	**7**	**7**	**7**	**8**	**8**	**9**	**9**	**9**	**9**	**10**	**10**	**10**	**11**	**11**	**11**	**12**	**12**
24	2	3	3	4	4	5	5	5	6	6	6	7	7	7	8	8	8	9	9	9	9	10	10	10	11
	3	**4**	**4**	**5**	**5**	**6**	**6**	**7**	**7**	**7**	**8**	**8**	**8**	**9**	**9**	**9**	**10**	**10**	**10**	**11**	**11**	**11**	**12**	**12**	**12**
25	2	3	3	4	4	5	5	5	6	6	6	7	7	8	8	8	8	9	9	9	10	10	10	11	11
	3	**4**	**4**	**5**	**5**	**6**	**6**	**7**	**7**	**7**	**8**	**8**	**9**	**9**	**9**	**10**	**10**	**10**	**11**	**11**	**11**	**12**	**12**	**12**	**13**

TABLE J *(continued)*

N \ *P*	.26	.27	.28	.29	.30	.31	.32	.33	.34	.35	.36	.37	.38	.39	.40	.41	.42	.43	.44	.45	.46	.47	.48	.49	.50
Q	**.74**	**.73**	**.72**	**.71**	**.70**	**.69**	**.68**	**.67**	**.66**	**.65**	**.64**	**.63**	**.62**	**.61**	**.60**	**.59**	**.58**	**.57**	**.56**	**.55**	**.54**	**.53**	**.52**	**.51**	**.50**
14	7	8	8	8	8	8	8	9	9	9	9	9	9	9	10	10	10	10	10	10	11	11	11	11	11
	9	**9**	**9**	**9**	**9**	**10**	**10**	**10**	**10**	**10**	**10**	**10**	**11**	**11**	**11**	**11**	**11**	**11**	**11**	**12**	**12**	**12**	**12**	**12**	**12**
15	8	8	8	8	9	9	9	9	9	9	10	10	10	10	10	10	10	11	11	11	11	11	11	12	12
	9	**9**	**9**	**10**	**10**	**10**	**10**	**10**	**10**	**11**	**11**	**11**	**11**	**11**	**11**	**12**	**12**	**12**	**12**	**12**	**12**	**12**	**13**	**13**	**13**
16	8	8	9	9	9	9	9	9	10	10	10	10	10	10	11	11	11	11	11	11	12	12	12	12	12
	9	**10**	**10**	**10**	**10**	**10**	**11**	**11**	**11**	**11**	**11**	**11**	**12**	**12**	**12**	**12**	**12**	**12**	**13**	**13**	**13**	**14**	**14**	**14**	**14**
17	8	9	9	9	9	9	10	10	10	10	10	11	11	11	11	11	12	12	12	12	12	12	13	13	13
	10	**10**	**10**	**10**	**11**	**11**	**11**	**11**	**11**	**12**	**12**	**12**	**12**	**12**	**13**	**13**	**13**	**13**	**13**	**13**	**14**	**14**	**14**	**14**	**14**
18	9	9	9	9	10	10	10	10	10	11	11	11	11	11	12	12	12	12	12	13	13	13	13	13	13
	10	**10**	**11**	**11**	**11**	**11**	**12**	**12**	**12**	**12**	**12**	**13**	**13**	**13**	**13**	**13**	**13**	**14**	**14**	**14**	**14**	**14**	**14**	**15**	**15**
19	9	9	10	10	10	10	10	11	11	11	11	12	12	12	12	12	13	13	13	13	13	13	14	14	14
	11	**11**	**11**	**11**	**12**	**12**	**12**	**12**	**12**	**13**	**13**	**13**	**13**	**13**	**14**	**14**	**14**	**14**	**14**	**15**	**15**	**15**	**15**	**15**	**15**
20	10	10	10	10	10	11	11	11	11	12	12	12	12	12	13	13	13	13	13	14	14	14	14	14	15
	11	**11**	**11**	**12**	**12**	**12**	**12**	**13**	**13**	**13**	**13**	**14**	**14**	**14**	**14**	**14**	**15**	**15**	**15**	**15**	**15**	**16**	**16**	**16**	**16**
21	10	10	10	11	11	11	11	12	12	12	12	12	13	13	13	13	14	14	14	14	14	15	15	15	15
	11	**12**	**12**	**12**	**12**	**13**	**13**	**13**	**13**	**14**	**14**	**14**	**14**	**14**	**15**	**15**	**15**	**15**	**16**	**16**	**16**	**16**	**16**	**17**	**17**
22	10	10	11	11	11	11	12	12	12	12	13	13	13	13	14	14	14	14	15	15	15	15	15	16	16
	12	**12**	**12**	**13**	**13**	**13**	**13**	**14**	**14**	**14**	**14**	**15**	**15**	**15**	**15**	**15**	**16**	**16**	**16**	**16**	**17**	**17**	**17**	**17**	**17**
23	11	11	11	11	12	12	12	12	13	13	13	13	14	14	14	14	15	15	15	15	16	16	16	16	16
	12	**12**	**13**	**13**	**13**	**13**	**14**	**14**	**14**	**15**	**15**	**15**	**15**	**15**	**16**	**16**	**16**	**16**	**17**	**17**	**17**	**17**	**18**	**18**	**18**
24	11	11	11	12	12	12	13	13	13	13	14	14	14	14	15	15	15	15	16	16	16	16	17	17	17
	13	**13**	**13**	**13**	**14**	**14**	**14**	**14**	**15**	**15**	**15**	**15**	**16**	**16**	**16**	**16**	**17**	**17**	**17**	**17**	**18**	**18**	**18**	**18**	**19**
25	11	12	12	12	12	13	13	13	13	14	14	14	15	15	15	15	16	16	16	16	17	17	17	17	18
	13	**13**	**13**	**14**	**14**	**14**	**15**	**15**	**15**	**15**	**16**	**16**	**16**	**17**	**17**	**17**	**17**	**18**	**18**	**18**	**18**	**19**	**19**	**19**	**19**

TABLE J *(continued)*

N \ P/Q	.01/.99	.02/.98	.03/.97	.04/.96	.05/.95	.06/.94	.07/.93	.08/.92	.09/.91	.10/.90	.11/.89	.12/.88	.13/.87	.14/.86	.15/.85	.16/.84	.17/.83	.18/.82	.19/.81	.20/.80	.21/.79	.22/.78	.23/.77	.24/.76	.25/.75
26	2	3	3	4	4	5	5	6	6	6	7	7	7	8	8	8	9	9	9	10	10	10	11	11	11
	3	**4**	**4**	**5**	**5**	**6**	**6**	**7**	**7**	**8**	**8**	**8**	**9**	**9**	**10**	**10**	**10**	**11**	**11**	**11**	**12**	**12**	**12**	**13**	**13**
27	2	3	3	4	4	5	5	6	6	6	7	7	8	8	8	9	9	9	10	10	10	11	11	11	12
	3	**4**	**4**	**5**	**6**	**6**	**6**	**7**	**7**	**8**	**8**	**9**	**9**	**9**	**10**	**10**	**11**	**11**	**11**	**12**	**12**	**12**	**13**	**13**	**13**
28	2	3	4	4	4	5	5	6	6	7	7	7	8	8	8	9	9	10	10	10	11	11	11	12	12
	3	**4**	**4**	**5**	**6**	**6**	**7**	**7**	**8**	**8**	**8**	**9**	**9**	**10**	**10**	**10**	**11**	**11**	**12**	**12**	**12**	**13**	**13**	**13**	**14**
29	2	3	4	4	5	5	5	6	6	7	7	8	8	8	9	9	9	10	10	10	11	11	12	12	12
	3	**4**	**5**	**5**	**6**	**6**	**7**	**7**	**8**	**8**	**9**	**9**	**9**	**10**	**10**	**11**	**11**	**11**	**12**	**12**	**13**	**13**	**13**	**14**	**14**
30	2	3	4	4	5	5	6	6	6	7	7	8	8	8	9	9	10	10	10	11	11	11	12	12	13
	3	**4**	**5**	**5**	**6**	**6**	**7**	**7**	**8**	**8**	**9**	**9**	**10**	**10**	**10**	**11**	**11**	**12**	**12**	**12**	**13**	**13**	**14**	**14**	**14**
31	2	3	4	4	5	5	6	6	7	7	7	8	8	9	9	9	10	10	11	11	11	12	12	12	13
	3	**4**	**5**	**5**	**6**	**6**	**7**	**7**	**8**	**8**	**9**	**9**	**10**	**10**	**11**	**11**	**12**	**12**	**12**	**13**	**13**	**14**	**14**	**14**	**15**
32	2	3	4	4	5	5	6	6	7	7	8	8	8	9	9	10	10	10	11	11	12	12	12	13	13
	3	**4**	**5**	**5**	**6**	**7**	**7**	**8**	**8**	**9**	**9**	**10**	**10**	**10**	**11**	**11**	**12**	**12**	**13**	**13**	**13**	**14**	**14**	**15**	**15**
33	2	3	4	4	5	5	6	6	7	7	8	8	9	9	9	10	10	11	11	12	12	12	13	13	13
	3	**4**	**5**	**5**	**6**	**7**	**7**	**8**	**8**	**9**	**9**	**10**	**10**	**11**	**11**	**12**	**12**	**12**	**13**	**13**	**14**	**14**	**15**	**15**	**15**
34	2	3	4	4	5	6	6	7	7	7	8	8	9	9	10	10	11	11	11	12	12	13	13	13	14
	3	**4**	**5**	**6**	**6**	**7**	**7**	**8**	**8**	**9**	**9**	**10**	**10**	**11**	**11**	**12**	**12**	**13**	**13**	**14**	**14**	**14**	**15**	**15**	**16**
35	2	3	4	5	6	6	6	7	7	8	8	9	9	9	10	10	11	11	12	12	12	13	13	14	14
	3	**4**	**5**	**6**	**6**	**7**	**7**	**8**	**9**	**9**	**10**	**10**	**11**	**11**	**12**	**12**	**13**	**13**	**13**	**14**	**14**	**15**	**15**	**16**	**16**
36	3	3	4	5	5	6	6	7	7	8	8	9	9	10	10	11	11	11	12	12	13	13	14	14	14
	3	**4**	**5**	**6**	**6**	**7**	**8**	**8**	**9**	**9**	**10**	**10**	**11**	**11**	**12**	**12**	**13**	**13**	**14**	**14**	**15**	**15**	**15**	**16**	**16**
37	3	3	4	5	5	6	6	7	7	8	8	9	9	10	10	11	11	12	12	13	13	13	14	14	15
	3	**4**	**5**	**6**	**6**	**7**	**8**	**8**	**9**	**9**	**10**	**11**	**11**	**12**	**12**	**13**	**13**	**13**	**14**	**14**	**15**	**15**	**16**	**16**	**17**

TABLE J (continued)

N \ P	.26	.27	.28	.29	.30	.31	.32	.33	.34	.35	.36	.37	.38	.39	.40	.41	.42	.43	.44	.45	.46	.47	.48	.49	.50
Q	.74	.73	.72	.71	.70	.69	.68	.67	.66	.65	.64	.63	.62	.61	.60	.59	.58	.57	.56	.55	.54	.53	.52	.51	.50
26	12	12	12	12	13	13	13	14	14	14	14	15	15	15	16	16	16	16	17	17	17	17	18	18	18
	13	**14**	**14**	**14**	**14**	**15**	**15**	**15**	**16**	**16**	**16**	**16**	**17**	**17**	**17**	**18**	**18**	**18**	**18**	**19**	**19**	**19**	**19**	**20**	**20**
27	12	12	12	13	13	13	14	14	14	15	15	15	15	16	16	16	17	17	17	17	18	18	18	18	19
	14	**14**	**14**	**15**	**15**	**15**	**15**	**16**	**16**	**16**	**17**	**17**	**17**	**18**	**18**	**18**	**18**	**19**	**19**	**19**	**19**	**20**	**20**	**20**	**20**
28	12	13	13	13	13	14	14	14	15	15	15	16	16	16	16	17	17	17	18	18	18	18	19	19	19
	14	**14**	**15**	**15**	**15**	**16**	**16**	**16**	**17**	**17**	**17**	**17**	**18**	**18**	**18**	**19**	**19**	**19**	**19**	**20**	**20**	**20**	**21**	**21**	**21**
29	13	13	13	14	14	14	14	15	15	15	16	16	16	17	17	17	18	18	18	18	19	19	19	20	20
	14	**15**	**15**	**15**	**16**	**16**	**16**	**17**	**17**	**17**	**18**	**18**	**18**	**19**	**19**	**19**	**19**	**20**	**20**	**20**	**21**	**21**	**21**	**21**	**22**
30	13	13	14	14	14	15	15	15	16	16	16	17	17	17	17	18	18	18	19	19	19	20	20	20	20
	15	**15**	**15**	**16**	**16**	**16**	**17**	**17**	**17**	**18**	**18**	**18**	**19**	**19**	**19**	**20**	**20**	**20**	**21**	**21**	**21**	**21**	**22**	**22**	**22**
31	13	14	14	14	15	15	15	16	16	16	17	17	17	18	18	18	19	19	19	20	20	20	20	21	21
	15	**15**	**16**	**16**	**16**	**17**	**17**	**17**	**18**	**18**	**19**	**19**	**19**	**19**	**20**	**20**	**20**	**21**	**21**	**21**	**22**	**22**	**22**	**23**	**23**
32	14	14	14	15	15	15	16	16	16	17	17	17	18	18	18	19	19	19	20	20	20	21	21	21	22
	15	**16**	**16**	**16**	**17**	**17**	**18**	**18**	**18**	**19**	**19**	**19**	**20**	**20**	**20**	**21**	**21**	**21**	**22**	**22**	**22**	**22**	**23**	**23**	**24**
33	14	14	15	15	15	16	16	16	17	17	17	18	18	19	19	19	20	20	20	21	21	21	22	22	22
	16	**16**	**16**	**17**	**17**	**18**	**18**	**18**	**19**	**19**	**19**	**20**	**20**	**20**	**21**	**21**	**21**	**22**	**22**	**22**	**23**	**23**	**23**	**24**	**24**
34	14	15	15	15	16	16	16	17	17	18	18	18	19	19	19	20	20	20	21	21	21	22	22	22	23
	16	**16**	**17**	**17**	**17**	**18**	**18**	**19**	**19**	**20**	**20**	**20**	**21**	**21**	**21**	**22**	**22**	**22**	**23**	**23**	**23**	**24**	**24**	**24**	**25**
35	14	15	15	16	16	16	17	17	18	18	18	19	19	19	20	20	21	21	21	22	22	22	23	23	23
	16	**17**	**17**	**18**	**18**	**18**	**19**	**19**	**20**	**20**	**20**	**21**	**21**	**21**	**22**	**22**	**23**	**23**	**23**	**24**	**24**	**24**	**25**	**25**	**25**
36	15	15	16	16	16	17	17	18	18	18	19	19	20	20	20	21	21	21	22	22	22	23	23	24	24
	17	**17**	**18**	**18**	**18**	**19**	**19**	**20**	**20**	**20**	**21**	**21**	**22**	**22**	**22**	**23**	**23**	**23**	**24**	**24**	**25**	**25**	**25**	**26**	**26**
37	15	16	16	16	17	17	18	18	18	19	19	20	20	20	21	21	22	22	22	23	23	23	24	24	24
	17	**18**	**18**	**18**	**19**	**19**	**20**	**20**	**20**	**21**	**21**	**22**	**22**	**22**	**23**	**23**	**24**	**24**	**24**	**25**	**25**	**25**	**26**	**26**	**27**

TABLE J *(continued)*

N / P	.01	.02	.03	.04	.05	.06	.07	.08	.09	.10	.11	.12	.13	.14	.15	.16	.17	.18	.19	.20	.21	.22	.23	.24	.25
Q	**.99**	**.98**	**.97**	**.96**	**.95**	**.94**	**.93**	**.92**	**.91**	**.90**	**.89**	**.88**	**.87**	**.86**	**.85**	**.84**	**.83**	**.82**	**.81**	**.80**	**.79**	**.78**	**.77**	**.76**	**.75**
38	3	3	4	5	5	6	6	7	8	8	9	9	10	10	10	11	11	12	12	13	13	14	14	15	15
	3	**4**	**5**	**6**	**7**	**7**	**8**	**8**	**9**	**10**	**10**	**11**	**11**	**12**	**12**	**13**	**13**	**14**	**14**	**15**	**15**	**16**	**16**	**17**	**17**
39	3	3	4	5	5	6	6	7	8	8	9	9	10	10	11	11	12	12	13	13	14	14	14	15	15
	3	**4**	**5**	**6**	**7**	**7**	**8**	**9**	**9**	**10**	**10**	**11**	**11**	**12**	**12**	**13**	**13**	**14**	**14**	**15**	**15**	**16**	**16**	**17**	**17**
40	3	3	4	5	5	6	7	7	8	8	9	9	10	10	11	11	12	12	13	13	14	14	15	15	16
	3	**4**	**5**	**6**	**7**	**7**	**8**	**9**	**9**	**10**	**10**	**11**	**12**	**12**	**13**	**13**	**14**	**14**	**15**	**15**	**16**	**16**	**17**	**17**	**18**
41	3	3	4	5	6	6	7	7	8	8	9	10	10	11	11	12	12	13	13	14	14	15	15	15	16
	3	**4**	**5**	**6**	**7**	**8**	**8**	**9**	**9**	**10**	**11**	**11**	**12**	**12**	**13**	**13**	**14**	**14**	**15**	**16**	**16**	**17**	**17**	**18**	**18**
42	3	4	4	5	6	6	7	7	8	9	9	10	10	11	11	12	12	13	13	14	14	15	15	16	16
	3	**4**	**5**	**6**	**7**	**8**	**8**	**9**	**10**	**10**	**11**	**11**	**12**	**12**	**13**	**14**	**14**	**15**	**15**	**16**	**16**	**17**	**17**	**18**	**18**
43	3	4	4	5	6	6	7	8	8	9	9	10	10	11	11	12	13	13	14	14	15	15	16	16	17
	3	**5**	**5**	**6**	**7**	**8**	**8**	**9**	**10**	**10**	**11**	**12**	**12**	**13**	**13**	**14**	**14**	**15**	**16**	**16**	**17**	**17**	**18**	**18**	**19**
44	3	4	4	5	6	6	7	8	8	9	9	10	11	11	12	12	13	13	14	14	15	15	16	16	17
	3	**5**	**5**	**6**	**7**	**8**	**9**	**9**	**10**	**11**	**11**	**12**	**12**	**13**	**14**	**14**	**15**	**15**	**16**	**16**	**17**	**17**	**18**	**18**	**19**
45	3	4	4	5	6	7	7	8	8	9	10	10	11	11	12	12	13	13	14	15	15	16	16	17	17
	4	**5**	**6**	**6**	**7**	**8**	**9**	**9**	**10**	**11**	**11**	**12**	**13**	**13**	**14**	**14**	**15**	**15**	**16**	**17**	**17**	**18**	**18**	**19**	**19**
46	3	4	4	5	6	7	7	8	9	9	10	10	11	11	12	13	13	14	14	15	15	16	16	17	17
	4	**5**	**6**	**6**	**7**	**8**	**9**	**9**	**10**	**11**	**11**	**12**	**13**	**13**	**14**	**15**	**15**	**16**	**16**	**17**	**17**	**18**	**19**	**19**	**20**
47	3	4	5	5	6	7	7	8	9	9	10	10	11	12	12	13	13	14	15	15	16	16	17	17	18
	4	**5**	**6**	**7**	**7**	**8**	**9**	**10**	**10**	**11**	**12**	**12**	**13**	**14**	**14**	**15**	**15**	**16**	**17**	**17**	**18**	**18**	**19**	**19**	**20**
48	3	4	5	5	6	7	7	8	9	9	10	11	11	12	12	13	14	14	15	15	16	16	17	18	18
	4	**5**	**6**	**7**	**7**	**8**	**9**	**10**	**10**	**11**	**12**	**12**	**13**	**14**	**14**	**15**	**16**	**16**	**17**	**17**	**18**	**19**	**19**	**20**	**20**
49	3	4	5	5	6	7	8	8	9	10	10	11	11	12	13	13	14	14	15	16	16	17	17	18	18
	4	**5**	**6**	**7**	**8**	**8**	**9**	**10**	**11**	**11**	**12**	**13**	**13**	**14**	**15**	**15**	**16**	**16**	**17**	**18**	**18**	**19**	**19**	**20**	**21**

TABLE J *(concluded)*

N \ **P**	**.26**	**.27**	**.28**	**.29**	**.30**	**.31**	**.32**	**.33**	**.34**	**.35**	**.36**	**.37**	**.38**	**.39**	**.40**	**.41**	**.42**	**.43**	**.44**	**.45**	**.46**	**.47**	**.48**	**.49**	**.50**
Q	**.74**	**.73**	**.72**	**.71**	**.70**	**.69**	**.68**	**.67**	**.66**	**.65**	**.64**	**.63**	**.62**	**.61**	**.60**	**.59**	**.58**	**.57**	**.56**	**.55**	**.54**	**.53**	**.52**	**.51**	**.50**
38	15	16	16	17	17	18	18	18	19	19	20	20	20	21	21	22	22	22	23	23	24	24	24	25	25
	17	**18**	**18**	**19**	**19**	**20**	**20**	**20**	**21**	**21**	**22**	**22**	**23**	**23**	**23**	**24**	**24**	**24**	**25**	**25**	**26**	**26**	**26**	**27**	**27**
39	16	16	17	17	17	18	18	19	19	20	20	20	21	21	22	22	22	23	23	24	24	24	25	25	26
	18	**18**	**19**	**19**	**20**	**20**	**20**	**21**	**21**	**22**	**22**	**23**	**23**	**23**	**24**	**24**	**25**	**25**	**25**	**26**	**26**	**27**	**27**	**27**	**28**
40	16	17	17	17	18	18	19	19	20	20	20	21	21	22	22	23	23	23	24	24	25	25	25	26	26
	18	**19**	**19**	**20**	**20**	**20**	**21**	**21**	**22**	**22**	**23**	**23**	**23**	**24**	**24**	**25**	**25**	**26**	**26**	**26**	**27**	**27**	**28**	**28**	**28**
41	16	17	17	18	18	19	19	20	20	20	21	21	22	22	23	23	23	24	24	25	25	26	26	26	27
	18	**19**	**19**	**20**	**20**	**21**	**21**	**22**	**22**	**23**	**23**	**23**	**24**	**24**	**25**	**25**	**26**	**26**	**26**	**27**	**27**	**28**	**28**	**28**	**29**
42	17	17	18	18	19	19	19	20	20	21	21	22	22	23	23	23	24	24	25	25	26	26	26	27	27
	19	**19**	**20**	**20**	**21**	**21**	**22**	**22**	**23**	**23**	**23**	**24**	**24**	**25**	**25**	**26**	**26**	**27**	**27**	**27**	**28**	**28**	**29**	**29**	**29**
43	17	18	18	18	19	19	20	20	21	21	22	22	23	23	24	24	24	25	25	26	26	27	27	27	28
	19	**20**	**20**	**21**	**21**	**22**	**22**	**23**	**23**	**23**	**24**	**24**	**25**	**25**	**26**	**26**	**27**	**27**	**28**	**28**	**28**	**29**	**29**	**30**	**30**
44	17	18	18	19	19	20	20	21	21	22	22	23	23	24	24	24	25	25	26	26	27	27	28	28	28
	19	**20**	**21**	**21**	**21**	**22**	**22**	**23**	**23**	**24**	**24**	**25**	**25**	**26**	**26**	**27**	**27**	**28**	**28**	**28**	**29**	**29**	**30**	**30**	**31**
45	18	18	19	19	20	20	21	21	22	22	23	23	24	24	24	25	25	26	26	27	27	28	28	29	29
	20	**20**	**21**	**21**	**22**	**22**	**23**	**23**	**24**	**24**	**25**	**25**	**26**	**26**	**27**	**27**	**28**	**28**	**29**	**29**	**29**	**30**	**30**	**31**	**31**
46	18	18	19	20	20	21	21	22	22	22	23	23	24	24	25	25	26	26	27	27	28	28	29	29	30
	20	**21**	**21**	**22**	**22**	**23**	**23**	**24**	**24**	**25**	**25**	**26**	**26**	**27**	**27**	**28**	**28**	**29**	**29**	**30**	**30**	**30**	**31**	**31**	**32**
47	18	19	19	20	20	21	21	22	22	23	23	24	24	25	25	26	26	27	27	28	28	29	29	30	30
	21	**21**	**22**	**22**	**23**	**23**	**24**	**24**	**25**	**25**	**26**	**26**	**27**	**27**	**28**	**28**	**29**	**29**	**30**	**30**	**31**	**31**	**31**	**32**	**32**
48	19	19	20	20	21	21	22	22	23	23	24	24	25	25	26	26	27	27	28	28	29	29	30	30	31
	21	**21**	**22**	**22**	**23**	**24**	**24**	**25**	**25**	**26**	**26**	**27**	**27**	**28**	**28**	**29**	**29**	**30**	**30**	**31**	**31**	**32**	**32**	**33**	**33**
49	19	19	20	21	21	22	22	23	23	24	24	25	25	26	26	27	27	28	28	29	29	30	30	31	31
	21	**22**	**22**	**23**	**23**	**24**	**24**	**25**	**26**	**26**	**27**	**27**	**28**	**28**	**29**	**29**	**30**	**30**	**31**	**31**	**32**	**32**	**33**	**33**	**34**

TABLE K
Percentage points of the Studentized range

Error df	α	K = Number of means or number of steps between ordered means									
		2	3	4	5	6	7	8	9	10	11
5	.05	3.64	4.60	5.22	5.67	6.03	6.33	6.58	6.80	6.99	7.17
	.01	5.70	6.98	7.80	8.42	8.91	9.32	9.67	9.97	10.24	10.48
6	.05	3.46	4.34	4.90	5.30	5.63	5.90	6.12	6.32	6.49	6.65
	.01	5.24	6.33	7.03	7.56	7.97	8.32	8.61	8.87	9.10	9.30
7	.05	3.34	4.16	4.68	5.06	5.36	5.61	5.82	6.00	6.16	6.30
	.01	4.95	5.92	6.54	7.01	7.37	7.68	7.94	8.17	8.37	8.55
8	.05	3.26	4.04	4.53	4.89	5.17	5.40	5.60	5.77	5.92	6.05
	.01	4.75	5.64	6.20	6.62	6.96	7.24	7.47	7.68	7.86	8.03
9	.05	3.20	3.95	4.41	4.76	5.02	5.24	5.43	5.59	5.74	5.87
	.01	4.60	5.43	5.96	6.35	6.66	6.91	7.13	7.33	7.49	7.65
10	.05	3.15	3.88	4.33	4.65	4.91	5.12	5.30	5.46	5.60	5.72
	.01	4.48	5.27	5.77	6.14	6.43	6.67	6.87	7.05	7.21	7.36
11	.05	3.11	3.82	4.26	4.57	4.82	5.03	5.20	5.35	5.49	5.61
	.01	4.39	5.15	5.62	5.97	6.25	6.48	6.67	6.84	6.99	7.13
12	.05	3.08	3.77	4.20	4.51	4.75	4.95	5.12	5.27	5.39	5.51
	.01	4.32	5.05	5.50	5.84	6.10	6.32	6.51	6.67	6.81	6.94
13	.05	3.06	3.73	4.15	4.45	4.69	4.88	5.05	5.19	5.32	5.43
	.01	4.26	4.96	5.40	5.73	5.98	6.19	6.37	6.53	6.67	6.79
14	.05	3.03	3.70	4.11	4.41	4.64	4.83	4.99	5.13	5.25	5.36
	.01	4.21	4.89	5.32	5.63	5.88	6.08	6.26	6.41	6.54	6.66
15	.05	3.01	3.67	4.08	4.37	4.59	4.78	4.94	5.08	5.20	5.31
	.01	4.17	4.84	5.25	5.56	5.80	5.99	6.16	6.31	6.44	6.55
16	.05	3.00	3.65	4.05	4.33	4.56	4.74	4.90	5.03	5.15	5.26
	.01	4.13	4.79	5.19	5.49	5.72	5.92	6.08	6.22	6.35	6.46
17	.05	2.98	3.63	4.02	4.30	4.52	4.70	4.86	4.99	5.11	5.21
	.01	4.10	4.74	5.14	5.43	5.66	5.85	6.01	6.15	6.27	6.38
18	.05	2.97	3.61	4.00	4.28	4.49	4.67	4.82	4.96	5.07	5.17
	.01	4.07	4.70	5.09	5.38	5.60	5.79	5.94	6.08	6.20	6.31
19	.05	2.96	3.59	3.98	4.25	4.47	4.65	4.79	4.92	5.04	5.14
	.01	4.05	4.67	5.05	5.33	5.55	5.73	5.89	6.02	6.14	6.25
20	.05	2.95	3.58	3.96	4.23	4.45	4.62	4.77	4.90	5.01	5.11
	.01	4.02	4.64	5.02	5.29	5.51	5.69	5.84	5.97	6.09	6.19
24	.05	2.92	3.53	3.90	4.17	4.37	4.54	4.68	4.81	4.92	5.01
	.01	3.96	4.55	4.91	5.17	5.37	5.54	5.69	5.81	5.92	6.02
30	.05	2.89	3.49	3.85	4.10	4.30	4.46	4.60	4.72	4.82	4.92
	.01	3.89	4.45	4.80	5.05	5.24	5.40	5.54	5.65	5.76	5.85
40	.05	2.86	3.44	3.79	4.04	4.23	4.39	4.52	4.63	4.73	4.82
	.01	3.82	4.37	4.70	4.93	5.11	5.26	5.39	5.50	5.60	5.69
60	.05	2.83	3.40	3.74	3.98	4.16	4.31	4.44	4.55	4.65	4.73
	.01	3.76	4.28	4.59	4.82	4.99	5.13	5.25	5.36	5.45	5.53
120	.05	2.80	3.36	3.68	3.92	4.10	4.24	4.36	4.47	4.56	4.64
	.01	3.70	4.20	4.50	4.71	4.87	5.01	5.12	5.21	5.30	5.37
∞	.05	2.77	3.31	3.63	3.86	4.03	4.17	4.29	4.39	4.47	4.55
	.01	3.64	4.12	4.40	4.60	4.76	4.88	4.99	5.08	5.16	5.23

TABLE L

Squares, square roots, and reciprocals of numbers from 1 to 1,000

N	N^2	$\sqrt{N}$	$1/N$	N	N^2	$\sqrt{N}$	$1/N$	N	N^2	$\sqrt{N}$	$1/N$
1	1	1.0000	1.000000	51	2601	7.1414	.019608	101	10201	10.0499	.00990099
2	4	1.4142	.500000	52	2704	7.2111	.019231	102	10404	10.0995	.00980392
3	9	1.7321	.333333	53	2809	7.2801	.018868	103	10609	10.1489	.00970874
4	16	2.0000	.250000	54	2916	7.3485	.018519	104	10816	10.1980	.00961538
5	25	2.2361	.200000	55	3025	7.4162	.018182	105	11025	10.2470	.00952381
6	36	2.4495	.166667	56	3136	7.4833	.017857	106	11236	10.2956	.00943396
7	49	2.6458	.142857	57	3249	7.5498	.017544	107	11449	10.3441	.00934579
8	64	2.8284	.125000	58	3364	7.6158	.017241	108	11664	10.3923	.00925926
9	81	3.0000	.111111	59	3481	7.6811	.016949	109	11881	10.4403	.00917431
10	100	3.1623	.100000	60	3600	7.7460	.016667	110	12100	10.4881	.00909091
11	121	3.3166	.090909	61	3721	7.8102	.016393	111	12321	10.5357	.00900901
12	144	3.4641	.083333	62	3844	7.8740	.016129	112	12544	10.5830	.00892857
13	169	3.6056	.076923	63	3969	7.9373	.015873	113	12769	10.6301	.00884956
14	196	3.7417	.071429	64	4096	8.0000	.015625	114	12996	10.6771	.00877193
15	225	3.8730	.066667	65	4225	8.0623	.015385	115	13225	10.7238	.00869565
16	256	4.0000	.062500	66	4356	8.1240	.015152	116	13456	10.7703	.00862069
17	289	4.1231	.058824	67	4489	8.1854	.014925	117	13689	10.8167	.00854701
18	324	4.2426	.055556	68	4624	8.2462	.014706	118	13924	10.8628	.00847458
19	361	4.3589	.052632	69	4761	8.3066	.014493	119	14161	10.9087	.00840336
20	400	4.4721	.050000	70	4900	8.3666	.014286	120	14400	10.9545	.00833333
21	441	4.5826	.047619	71	5041	8.4261	.014085	121	14641	11.0000	.00826446
22	484	4.6904	.045455	72	5184	8.4853	.013889	122	14884	11.0454	.00819672
23	529	4.7958	.043478	73	5329	8.5440	.013699	123	15129	11.0905	.00813008
24	576	4.8990	.041667	74	5476	8.6023	.013514	124	15376	11.1355	.00800452
25	625	5.0000	.040000	75	5625	8.6603	.013333	125	15625	11.1803	.00800000
26	676	5.0990	.038462	76	5776	8.7178	.013158	126	15876	11.2250	.00793651
27	729	5.1962	.037037	77	5929	8.7750	.012987	127	16129	11.2694	.00787402
28	784	5.2915	.035714	78	6084	8.8318	.012821	128	16384	11.3137	.00781250
29	841	5.3852	.034483	79	6241	8.8882	.012658	129	16641	11.3578	.00775194
30	900	5.4772	.033333	80	6400	8.9443	.012500	130	16900	11.4018	.00769231
31	961	5.5678	.032258	81	6561	9.0000	.012346	131	17161	11.4455	.00763359
32	1024	5.6569	.031250	82	6724	9.0554	.012195	132	17424	11.4891	.00757576
33	1089	5.7446	.030303	83	6889	9.1104	.012048	133	17689	11.5326	.00751880
34	1156	5.8310	.029412	84	7056	9.1652	.011905	134	17956	11.5758	.00746269
35	1225	5.9161	.029571	85	7225	9.2195	.011765	135	18225	11.6190	.00740741
36	1296	6.0000	.027778	86	7396	9.2736	.011628	136	18496	11.6619	.00735294
37	1369	6.0828	.027027	87	7569	9.3274	.011494	137	18769	11.7047	.00729927
38	1444	6.1644	.026316	88	7744	9.3808	.011364	138	19044	11.7473	.00724638
39	1521	6.2450	.025641	89	7921	9.4340	.011236	139	19321	11.7898	.00719424
40	1600	6.3246	.025000	90	8100	9.4868	.011111	140	19600	11.8322	.00714286
41	1681	6.4031	.024390	91	8281	9.5394	.010989	141	19881	11.8743	.00709220
42	1764	6.4807	.023810	92	8464	9.5917	.010870	142	20164	11.9164	.00704225
43	1849	6.5574	.023256	93	8649	9.6437	.010753	143	20449	11.9583	.00699301
44	1936	6.6332	.022727	94	8836	9.6954	.010638	144	20736	12.0000	.00694444
45	2025	6.7082	.022222	95	9025	9.7468	.010526	145	21025	12.0416	.00689655
46	2116	6.7823	.021739	96	9216	9.7980	.010417	146	21316	12.0830	.00684932
47	2209	6.8557	.021277	97	9409	9.8489	.010309	147	21609	12.1244	.00680272
48	2304	6.9282	.020833	98	9604	9.8995	.010204	148	21904	12.1655	.00675676
49	2401	7.0000	.020408	99	9801	9.9499	.010101	149	22201	12.2066	.00671141
50	2500	7.0711	.020000	100	10000	10.0000	.010000	150	22500	12.2474	.00666667

TABLE L *(continued)*

N	N^2	$\sqrt{N}$	$1/N$	N	N^2	$\sqrt{N}$	$1/N$	N	N^2	$\sqrt{N}$	$1/N$
151	22801	12.2882	.00662252	201	40401	14.1774	.00497512	251	63001	15.8430	.00398406
152	23104	12.3288	.00657895	202	40904	14.2127	.00495050	252	63504	15.8745	.00396825
153	23409	12.3693	.00653595	203	41209	14.2478	.00492611	253	64009	15.9060	.00395257
154	23716	12.4097	.00649351	204	41616	14.2829	.00490196	254	64516	15.9374	.00393701
155	24025	12.4499	.00645161	205	42025	14.3178	.00487805	255	65025	15.9687	.00392157
156	24336	12.4900	.00641026	206	42436	14.3527	.00485437	256	65536	16.0000	.00390625
157	24649	12.5300	.00636943	207	42849	14.3875	.00483092	257	66049	16.0312	.00389105
158	24964	12.5698	.00632911	208	43264	14.4222	.00480769	258	66564	16.0624	.00387597
159	25281	12.6095	.00628931	209	43681	14.4568	.00478469	259	67081	16.0935	.00386100
160	25600	12.6491	.00625000	210	44100	14.4914	.00476190	260	67600	16.1245	.00384615
161	25921	12.6886	.00621118	211	44521	14.5258	.00473934	261	68121	16.1555	.00383142
162	26244	12.7279	.00617284	212	44944	14.5602	.00471698	262	68644	16.1864	.00381679
163	26569	12.7671	.00613497	213	45369	14.5945	.00469484	263	69169	16.2173	.00380228
164	26896	12,8062	.00609756	214	45796	14.6287	.00467290	264	69696	16.2481	.00378788
165	27225	12,8452	.00606061	215	46225	14.6629	.00465116	265	70225	16.2788	.00377358
166	27556	12.8841	.00602410	216	46656	14.6969	.00462963	266	70756	16.3095	.00375940
167	27889	12.9228	.00598802	217	47089	14.7309	.00460829	267	71289	16.3401	.00374532
168	28224	12.9615	.00595238	218	47524	14.7648	.00458716	268	71824	16.3707	.00373134
169	28561	13.0000	.00591716	219	47961	14.7986	.00456621	269	72361	16.4012	.00371747
170	28900	13.0384	.00588235	220	48400	14.8324	.00454545	270	72900	16.4317	.00370370
171	29241	13.0767	.00584795	221	48841	14.8661	.00452489	271	73441	16.4621	.00369004
172	29584	13.1149	.00581395	222	49284	14.8997	.00450450	272	73984	16.4924	.00367647
173	29929	13.1529	.00578035	223	49729	14.9332	.00448430	273	74529	16.5227	.00366300
174	30276	13.1909	.00574713	224	50176	14.9666	.00446429	274	75076	16.5529	.00364964
175	30625	13.2288	.00571429	225	50625	15.0000	.00444444	275	75625	16.5831	.00363636
176	30976	13.2665	.00568182	226	51076	15.0333	.00442478	276	76176	16.6132	.00362319
177	31329	13.3041	.00564972	227	51529	15.0665	.00440529	277	76729	16.6433	.00361011
178	31684	13.3417	.00561798	228	51984	15.0997	.00438596	278	77284	16.6733	.00359712
179	32041	13.3791	.00558659	229	52441	15.1327	.00436681	279	77841	16.7033	.00358423
180	32400	13.4164	.00555556	230	52900	15.1658	.00434783	280	78400	16.7332	.00357143
181	32761	13.4536	.00552486	231	53361	15.1987	.00432900	281	78961	16.7631	.00355872
182	33124	13.4907	.00549451	232	53824	15.2315	.00431034	282	79524	16.7929	.00354610
183	33489	13.5277	.00546448	233	54289	15.2643	.00429185	283	80089	16.8226	.00353357
184	33856	13.5647	.00543478	234	54756	15.2971	.00427350	284	80656	16.8523	.00352113
185	34225	13.6015	.00540541	235	55225	15.3297	.00425532	285	81225	16.8819	.00350877
186	34596	13.6382	.00537634	236	55696	15.3623	.00423729	286	81796	16.9115	.00349650
187	34969	13.6748	.00534759	237	56169	15.3948	.00421941	287	82369	16.9411	.00348432
188	35344	13.7113	.00531915	238	56644	15.4272	.00420168	288	82944	16.9706	.00347222
189	35721	13.7477	.00529101	239	57121	15.4596	.00418410	289	83521	17.0000	.00346021
190	36100	13.7840	.00526316	240	57600	15.4919	.00416667	290	84100	17.0294	.00344828
191	36481	13.8203	.00523560	241	58081	15.5242	.00414938	291	84681	17.0587	.00343643
192	36864	13.8564	.00520833	242	58564	15.5563	.00413223	292	85264	17.0880	.00342466
193	37249	13.8924	.00518135	243	59049	15.5885	.00411523	293	85849	17.1172	.00341297
194	37636	13.9284	.00515464	244	59536	15.6205	.00409836	294	86436	17.1464	.00340136
195	38025	13.9642	.00512821	245	60025	15.6525	.00408163	295	87025	17.1756	.00338983
196	38416	14.0000	.00510204	246	60516	15.6844	.00406504	296	87616	17.2047	.00337838
197	38809	14.0357	.00507614	247	61009	15.7162	.00404858	297	88209	17.2337	.00336700
198	39204	14.0712	.00505051	248	61504	15.7480	.00403226	298	88804	17.2627	.00335570
199	39601	14.1067	.00502513	249	62001	15.7797	.00401606	299	89401	17.2916	.00334448
200	40000	14.1421	.00500000	250	62500	15.8114	.00400000	300	90000	17.3205	.00333333

TABLE L *(continued)*

N	N^2	$\sqrt{N}$	$1/N$	N	N^2	$\sqrt{N}$	$1/N$	N	N^2	$\sqrt{N}$	$1/N$
301	90601	17.3494	.00332226	351	123201	18.7350	.00284900	401	160801	20.0250	.00249377
302	91204	17.3781	.00331126	352	123904	18.7617	.00284091	402	161604	20.0499	.00248756
303	91809	17.4069	.00330033	353	124609	18.7883	.00283286	403	162409	20.0749	.00248139
304	92416	17.4356	.00328047	354	125316	18.8149	.00282486	404	163216	20.0998	.00247525
305	93025	17.4642	.00328947	355	126025	18.8414	.00281690	405	164025	20.1246	.00246914
306	93636	17.4929	.00326797	356	126736	18.8680	.00280899	406	164836	20.1494	.00246305
307	94249	17.5214	.00325733	357	127449	18.8944	.00280112	407	165649	20.1742	.00245700
308	94864	17.5499	.00321675	358	128164	18.9209	.00279330	408	166464	20.1990	.00245098
309	95481	17.5784	.00323625	359	128881	18.9473	.00278552	409	167281	20.2237	.00244499
310	96100	17.6068	.00322581	360	129600	18.9737	.00277778	410	168100	20.2485	.00243902
311	96721	17.6352	.00321543	361	130321	19.0000	00277008	411	168921	20.2731	.00243309
312	97344	17.6635	.00320513	362	131044	19.0263	.00276243	412	169744	20.2978	.00242718
313	97969	17.6918	.00319489	363	131769	19.0526	.00275482	413	170569	20.3224	.00242131
314	98596	17.7200	.00318471	364	132496	19.0788	.00274725	414	171396	20.3470	.00241546
315	99225	17.7482	.00317460	365	133225	19.1050	.00273973	415	172225	20.3715	.00240964
316	99856	17.7764	.00316456	366	133956	19.1311	.00273224	416	173056	20.3961	.00240385
317	100489	17.8045	.00315457	367	134689	19.1572	.00272480	417	173889	20.4206	.00239808
318	101124	17.8326	.00314465	368	135424	19.1833	.00271739	418	174724	20.4450	.00239234
319	101761	17.8606	.00313480	369	136161	19.2094	.00271003	419	175561	20.4695	.00238663
320	102400	17.8885	.00312500	370	136900	19.2354	.00270270	420	176400	20.4939	.00238095
321	103041	17.9165	.00311526	371	137641	19.2614	.00269542	421	177241	20.5183	.00237530
322	103684	17.9444	.00310559	372	138384	19.2873	.00268817	422	178084	20.5426	.00236967
323	104329	17.9722	.00309598	373	139129	19.3132	.00268097	423	178929	20.5670	.00236407
324	104976	18.0000	.00308642	374	139876	19.3391	.00267380	424	179776	20.5913	.00235849
325	105625	18.0278	.00307692	375	140625	19.3649	.00266667	425	180625	20.6155	.00235294
326	106276	18.0555	.00306748	376	141376	19.3907	.00265957	426	181476	20.6398	.00234742
327	106929	18.0831	.00305810	377	142129	19.4165	.00265252	427	182329	20.6640	.00234192
328	107584	18.1108	.00304878	378	142884	19.4422	.00264550	428	183184	20.6882	.00233645
329	108241	18.1384	.00303951	379	143641	19.4679	.00263852	429	184041	20.7123	.00233100
330	108900	18.1659	.00303030	380	144400	19.4936	.00263158	430	184900	20.7364	.00232558
331	109561	18.1934	.00302115	381	145161	19.5192	.00262467	431	185761	20.7605	.00232019
332	110224	18.2209	.00301205	382	145924	19.5448	.00261780	432	186624	20.7846	.00231481
333	110889	18.2483	.00300300	383	146689	19.5704	.00261097	433	187489	20.8087	.00230947
334	111556	18.2757	.00299401	384	147456	19.5959	.00260417	434	188356	20.8327	.00230415
335	112225	18.3030	.00298507	385	148225	19.6214	.00259740	435	189225	20.8567	.00229885
336	112896	18.3303	.00297619	386	148996	19.6469	.00259067	436	190096	20.8806	.00229358
337	113569	18.3576	.00296736	387	149769	19.6723	.00258398	437	190969	20.9045	.00228833
338	114244	18.3848	.00295858	388	150544	19.6977	.00257732	438	191844	20.9284	.00228311
339	114921	18.4120	.00294985	389	151321	19.7231	.00257069	439	192721	20.9523	.00227790
340	115600	18.4391	.00294118	390	152100	19.7484	.00256410	440	193600	20.9762	.00227273
341	116281	18.4662	.00293255	391	152881	19.7737	.00255754	441	194481	21.0000	.00226757
342	116964	18.4932	.00292398	392	153664	19.7990	.00255102	442	195364	21.0238	.00226244
343	117649	18.5203	.00291545	393	154449	19.8242	.00254453	443	196249	21.0476	.00225734
344	118336	18.5472	.00290698	394	155236	19.8494	.00253807	444	197136	21.0713	.00225225
345	119025	18.5742	.00289855	395	156025	19.8746	.00253165	445	198025	21.0950	.00224719
346	119716	18.6011	.00289017	396	156816	19.8997	.00252525	446	198916	21.1187	.00224215
347	120409	18.6279	.00288184	397	157609	19.9249	.00251889	447	199809	21.1424	.00223714
348	121104	18.6548	.00287356	398	158404	19.9499	.00251256	448	200704	21.1660	.00223214
349	121801	18.6815	.00286533	399	159201	19.9750	.00250627	449	201601	21.1896	.00222717
350	122500	18.7083	.00285714	400	160000	20.0000	.00250000	450	202500	21.2132	.00222222

TABLE L *(continued)*

N	N^2	$\sqrt{N}$	$1/N$	N	N^2	$\sqrt{N}$	$1/N$	N	N^2	$\sqrt{N}$	$1/N$
451	203401	21.2368	.00221729	501	251001	22.3830	.00199601	551	303601	23.4734	.00181488
452	204304	21.2603	.00221239	502	252004	22.4054	.00199203	552	304704	23.4947	.00181159
453	205209	21.2838	.00220751	503	253009	22.4277	.00198807	553	305809	23.5160	.00180832
454	206116	21.3073	.00220264	504	254016	22.4499	.00198413	554	306916	23.5372	.00180505
455	207025	21.3307	.00219870	505	255025	22.4722	.00198020	555	308025	23.5584	.00180180
456	207936	21.3542	.00219298	506	256036	22.4944	.00197628	556	309136	23.5797	.00179856
457	208849	21.3776	.00218818	507	257049	22.5167	.00197239	557	310249	23.6008	.00179533
458	209764	21.4009	.00218341	508	258064	22.5389	.00196850	558	311364	23.6220	.00179211
459	210681	21.4243	.00217865	509	259081	22.5610	.00196464	559	312481	23.6432	.00178891
460	211600	21.4476	.00217391	510	260100	22.5832	.00196078	560	313600	23.6643	.00178571
461	212521	21.4709	.00216920	511	261121	22.6053	.00195695	561	314721	23.6854	.00178253
462	213444	21.4942	.00216450	512	262144	22.6274	.00195312	562	315844	23.7065	.00177936
463	214369	21.5174	.00215983	513	263169	22.6495	.00194932	563	316969	23.7276	.00177620
464	215296	21.5407	.00215517	514	264196	22.6716	.00194553	564	318096	23.7487	.00177305
465	216225	21.5639	.00215054	515	265225	22.6936	.00194175	565	319225	23.7697	.00176991
466	217156	21.5870	.00214592	516	266256	22.7156	.00193798	566	320356	23.7908	.00176678
467	218089	21.6102	.00214133	517	267289	22.7376	.00193424	567	321489	23.8118	.00176367
468	219024	21.6333	.00213675	518	268324	22.7596	.00193050	568	322624	23.8328	.00176056
469	219961	21.6564	.00213220	519	269361	22.7816	.00192678	569	323761	23.8537	.00175747
470	220900	21.6795	.00212766	520	270400	22.8035	.00192308	570	324900	23.8747	.00175439
471	221841	21.7025	.00212314	521	271441	22.8254	.00191939	571	326041	23.8956	.00175131
472	222784	21.7256	.00211864	522	272484	22.8473	.00191571	572	327184	23.9165	.00164825
473	223729	21.7486	.00211416	523	273529	22.8692	.00191205	573	328329	23.9374	.00174520
474	224676	21.7715	.00210970	524	274576	22.8910	.00190840	574	329476	23.9583	.00174216
475	225625	21.7945	.00210526	525	275625	22.9129	.00190476	575	330625	23.9792	.00173913
476	226576	21.8174	.00210084	526	276676	22.9347	.00190114	576	331776	24.0000	.00173611
477	227529	21.8403	.00209644	527	277729	22.9565	.00189753	577	332929	24.0208	.00173310
478	228484	21.8632	.00209205	528	278784	22.9783	.00189394	578	334084	24.0416	.00173010
479	229441	21.8861	.00208768	529	279841	23.0000	.00189036	579	335241	24.0624	.00172712
480	230400	21.9089	.00208333	530	280900	23.0217	.00188679	580	336400	24.0832	.00172414
481	231361	21.9317	.00207900	531	281961	23.0434	.00188324	581	337561	24.1039	.00172117
482	232324	21.9545	.00207469	532	283024	23.0651	.00187970	582	338724	24.1247	.00171821
483	233289	21.9773	.00207039	533	284089	23.0868	.00187617	583	339889	24.1454	.00171527
484	234256	22.0000	.00206612	534	285156	23.1084	.00187266	584	341056	24.1661	.00171233
485	235225	22.0227	.00206186	535	286225	23.1301	.00186916	585	342225	24.1868	.00170940
486	236196	22.0454	.00205761	536	287296	23.1517	.00186567	586	343396	24.2074	.00170648
487	237169	22.0681	.00205339	537	288369	23.1733	.00186220	587	344569	24.2281	.00170358
488	238144	22.0907	.00204918	538	289444	23.1948	.00185874	588	345744	24.2487	.00170068
489	239121	22.1133	.00204499	539	290521	23.2164	.00185529	589	346921	24.2693	.00169779
490	240100	22.1359	.00204082	540	291600	23.2379	.00185185	590	348100	24.2899	.00169492
491	241081	22.1585	.00203666	541	292681	23.2594	.00184843	591	349281	24.3105	.00169205
492	242064	22.1811	.00203252	542	293764	23.2809	.00184502	592	350464	24.3311	.00168919
493	243049	22.2036	.00202840	543	294849	23.3024	.00184162	593	351649	24.3516	.00168634
494	244036	22.2261	.00202429	544	295936	23.3238	.00183824	594	352836	24.3721	.00168350
495	245025	22.2486	.00202020	545	297025	23.3452	.00183486	595	354025	24.3926	.00168067
496	246016	22.2711	.00201613	546	298116	23.3666	.00183150	596	355216	24.4131	.00167785
497	247009	22.2935	.00201207	547	299209	23.3880	.00182815	597	356409	24.4336	.00167504
498	248004	22.3159	.00200803	548	300304	23.4094	.00182482	598	357604	24.4540	.00167224
499	249001	22.3383	.00200401	549	301401	23.4307	.00182149	599	358801	24.4745	.00166945
500	250000	22.3607	.00200000	550	302500	23.4521	.00181818	600	360000	24.4949	.00166667

TABLE L *(continued)*

N	N^2	$\sqrt{N}$	$1/N$	N	N^2	$\sqrt{N}$	$1/N$	N	N^2	$\sqrt{N}$	$1/N$
601	361201	24.5153	.00166389	651	423801	25.5147	.00153610	701	491401	26.4764	.00142653
602	302404	24.5357	.00166113	652	425104	25.5343	.00153374	702	492804	26.4953	.00142450
603	363609	24.5561	.00165837	653	426409	25.5539	.00153139	703	494209	26.5141	.00142248
604	364816	24.5764	.00165563	654	427716	25.5734	.00152905	704	495616	26.5330	.00142045
605	366025	24.5967	.00165289	655	429025	25.5930	.00152672	705	497025	26.5518	.00141844
606	367236	24.6171	.00165017	656	430336	25.6125	.00152439	706	498436	26.5707	.00141643
607	368449	24.6374	.00164745	657	431649	25.6320	.00152207	707	499849	26.5895	.00141443
608	369664	24.6577	.00164474	658	432964	25.6515	.00151976	708	501264	26.6083	.00141243
609	370881	24.6779	.00164204	659	434281	25.6710	.00151745	709	502681	26.6271	.00141044
610	372100	24.6982	.00163934	660	435600	25.6905	.00151515	710	504100	26.6458	.00140845
611	373321	24.7184	.00163666	661	436921	25.7099	.00151286	711	505521	26.6646	.00140647
612	374544	24.7386	.00163399	662	438244	25.7294	.00151057	712	506944	26.6833	.00140449
613	375769	24.7588	.00163132	663	439569	25.7488	.00150830	713	508369	26.7021	.00140252
614	376996	24.7790	.00162866	664	440896	25.7682	.00150602	714	509796	26.7208	.00140056
615	378225	24.7992	.00162602	665	442225	25.7876	.00150376	715	511225	26.7395	.00139860
616	379456	24.8193	.00162338	666	443556	25.8070	.00150150	716	512656	26.7582	.00139665
617	380689	24.8395	.00162075	667	444889	25.8263	.00149925	717	514089	26.7769	.00139470
618	381924	24.8596	.00161812	668	446224	25.8457	.00149701	718	515524	26.7955	.00139276
619	383161	24.8797	.00161551	669	447561	25.8650	.00149477	719	516961	26.8142	.00139082
620	384400	24.8998	.00161290	670	448900	25.8844	.00149254	720	518400	26.8328	.00138889
621	385641	24.9199	.00161031	671	450241	25.9037	.00149031	721	519841	26.8514	.00138696
622	386884	24.9399	.00160772	672	451584	25.9230	.00148810	722	521284	26.8701	.00138504
623	388129	24.9600	.00160514	673	452929	25.9422	.00148588	723	522729	26.8887	.00138313
624	389376	24.9800	.00160256	674	454276	25.9615	.00148368	724	524176	26.9072	.00138122
625	390625	25.0000	.00160000	675	455625	25.9808	.00148148	725	525625	26.9258	.00137931
626	391876	25.0200	.00159744	676	456976	26.0000	.00147929	726	527076	26.9444	.00137741
627	393129	25.0400	.00159490	677	458329	26.0192	.00147710	727	528529	26.9629	.00137552
628	394384	25.0599	.00159236	678	459684	26.0384	.00147493	728	529984	26.9815	.00137363
629	395641	25.0799	.00158983	679	461041	26.0576	.00147275	729	531441	27.0000	.00137174
630	396900	25.0998	.00158730	680	462400	26.0768	.00147059	730	532900	27.0185	.00136986
631	398161	25.1197	.00158479	681	463761	26.0960	.00146843	731	534361	27.0370	.00136799
632	399424	25.1396	.00158228	682	465124	26.1151	.00146628	732	535824	27.0555	.00136612
633	400689	25.1595	.00157978	683	466489	26.1343	.00146413	733	537289	27.0740	.00136426
634	401956	25.1794	.00157729	684	467856	26.1534	.00146199	734	538756	27.0924	.00136240
635	403225	25.1992	.00157480	685	469225	26.1725	.00145985	735	540225	27.1109	.00136054
636	404496	25.2190	.00157233	686	470596	26.1916	.00145773	736	541696	27.1293	.00135870
637	405769	25.2389	.00156986	687	471969	26.2107	.00145560	737	543169	27.1477	.00135685
638	407044	25.2587	.00156740	688	473344	26.2298	.00145349	738	544644	27.1662	.00135501
639	408321.	25.2784	.00156495	689	474721	26.2488	.00145138	739	546121	27.1846	.00135318
640	409600	25.2982	.00156250	690	476100	26.2679	.00144928	740	547600	27.2029	.00135135
641	410881	25.3180	.00156006	691	477481	26.2869	.00144718	741	549081	27.2213	.00134953
642	412164	25.3377	.00155763	692	478864	26.3059	.00144509	742	550564	27.2397	.00134771
643	413449	25.3574	.00155521	693	480249	26.3249	.00144300	743	552049	27.2580	.00134590
644	414736	25.3772	.00155280	694	481636	26.3439	.00144092	744	553536	27.2764	.00134409
645	416025	25.3969	.00155039	695	483025	26.3629	.00143885	745	555025	27.2947	.00134228
646	417316	25.4165	.00154799	696	484416	26.3818	.00143678	746	556516	27.3130	.00134048
647	418609	25.4362	.00154560	697	485809	26.4008	.00143472	747	558009	27.3313	.00133869
648	419904	25.4558	.00154321	698	487204	26.4197	.00143266	748	559504	27.3496	.00133690
649	421201	25.4755	.00154083	699	488601	26.4386	.00143062	749	561001	27.3679	.00133511
650	422500	25.4951	.00153846	700	490000	26.4575	.00142857	750	562500	27.3861	.00133333

TABLE L *(continued)*

N	N^2	$\sqrt{N}$	$1/N$	N	N^2	$\sqrt{N}$	$1/N$	N	N^2	$\sqrt{N}$	$1/N$
751	564001	27.4044	.00133156	801	641601	28.3019	.00124844	851	724201	29.1719	.00117509
752	565504	27.4226	.00132979	802	643204	28.3196	.00124688	852	725904	29.1890	.00117371
753	567009	27.4408	.00132802	803	644809	28.3373	.00124533	853	727609	29.2062	.00117233
754	568516	27.4591	.00132626	804	646416	28.3549	.00124378	854	729316	29.2233	.00117096
755	570025	27.4773	.00132450	805	648025	28.3725	.00124224	855	731025	29.2404	.00116959
756	571536	27.4955	.00132275	806	649636	28.3901	.00124069	856	732736	29.2575	.00116822
757	573049	27.5136	.00132100	807	651249	28.4077	.00123916	857	734449	29.2746	.00116686
758	574564	27.5318	.00131926	808	625864	28.4253	.00123762	858	736164	29.2916	.00116550
759	576081	27.5500	.00131752	809	654481	28.4429	.00123609	859	737881	29.3087	.00116414
760	577600	27.5681	.00131579	810	656100	28.4605	.00123457	860	739600	29.3258	.00116279
761	579121	27.5862	.00131406	811	657721	28.4781	.00123305	861	741321	29.3428	.00116144
762	580644	27.6043	.00131234	812	659344	28.4956	.00123153	862	743044	29.3598	.00116009
763	582169	27.6225	.00131062	813	660969	28.5132	.00123001	863	744769	29.3769	.00115875
764	583696	27.6405	.00130890	814	662596	28.5307	.00122850	864	746496	29.3939	.00115741
765	585225	27.6586	.00130719	815	664225	28.5482	.00122699	865	748225	29.4109	.00115607
766	586756	27.6767	.00130548	816	665856	28.5657	.00122549	866	749956	29.4279	.00115473
767	588289	27.6948	.00130378	817	667489	28.5832	.00122399	867	751689	29.4449	.00115340
768	589824	27.7128	.00130208	818	669124	28.6007	.00122249	868	753424	29.4618	.00115207
769	591361	27.7308	.00130039	819	670761	28.6182	.00122100	869	755161	29.4788	.00115075
770	592900	27.7489	.00129870	820	672400	28.6356	.00121951	870	756900	29.4958	.00114943
771	594441	27.7669	.00129702	821	674041	28.6531	.00121803	871	758641	29.5127	.00114811
772	595984	27.7849	.00129534	822	675684	28.6705	.00121655	872	760384	29.5296	.00114679
773	597529	27.8029	.00129366	823	677329	28.6880	.00121507	873	762129	29.5466	.00114548
774	599076	27.8209	.00129199	824	678976	28.7054	.00121359	874	763876	29.5635	.00114416
775	600625	27.8388	.00129032	825	680625	28.7228	.00121212	875	765625	29.5804	.00114286
776	602176	27.8568	.00128866	826	682276	28.7402	.00121065	876	767376	29.5973	.00114155
777	603729	27.8747	.00128700	827	683929	28.7576	.00120919	877	769129	29.6142	.00114025
778	605284	27.8927	.00128535	828	685584	28.7750	.00120773	878	770884	29.6311	.00113895
779	606841	27.9106	.00128370	829	687241	28.7924	.00120627	879	772641	29.6479	.00113766
780	608400	27.9285	.00128205	830	688900	28.8097	.00120482	880	774400	29.6848	.00113636
781	609961	27.9464	.00128041	831	690561	28.8271	.00120337	881	776161	29.6816	.00113507
782	611524	27.9643	.00127877	832	692224	28.8444	.00120192	882	777924	29.6985	.00113379
783	613089	27.9821	.00127714	833	693889	28.8617	.00120048	883	779689	29.7153	.00113250
784	614656	28.0000	.00127551	834	695556	28.8791	.00119904	884	781456	29.7321	.00113122
785	616225	28.0179	.00127389	835	697225	28.8964	.00119760	885	783225	29.7489	.00112994
786	617796	28.0357	.00127226	836	698896	28.9137	.00119617	886	784996	29.7658	.00112867
787	619369	28.0535	.00127065	837	700569	28.9310	.00119474	887	786769	29.7825	.00112740
788	620944	28.0713	.00126904	838	702244	28.9482	.00119332	888	788544	29.7993	.00112613
789	622521	28.0891	.00126743	839	703921	28.9655	.00119190	889	790321	29.8161	.00112486
790	624100	28.1069	.00126582	840	705600	28.9828	.00119048	890	792100	29.8329	.00112360
791	625681	28.1247	.00126422	841	707281	29.0000	.00118906	891	793881	29.8496	.00112233
792	627264	28.1425	.00126263	842	708964	29.0172	.00118765	892	795664	29.8664	.00112108
793	628849	28.1603	.00126103	843	710649	29.0345	.00118624	893	797449	29.8831	.00111982
794	630436	28.1780	.00125945	844	712336	29.0517	.00118483	894	799236	29.8998	.00111857
795	632025	28.1957	.00125786	845	714025	29.0689	.00118343	895	801025	29.9166	.00111732
796	633616	28.2135	.00125628	846	715716	29.0861	.00118203	896	802816	29.9333	.00111607
797	635209	28.2312	.00125471	847	717409	29.1033	.00118064	897	804609	29.9500	.00111483
798	636804	28.2489	.00125313	848	719104	29.1204	.00117925	898	806404	29.9666	.00111359
799	638401	28.2666	.00125156	849	720801	29.1376	.00117786	899	808201	29.9833	.00111235
800	640000	28.2843	.00125000	850	722500	29.1548	.00117647	900	810000	30.0000	.00111111

TABLE L *(concluded)*

N	N^2	$\sqrt{N}$	$1/N$	N	N^2	$\sqrt{N}$	$1/N$	N	N^2	$\sqrt{N}$	$1/N$
901	811801	30.0167	.00110988	936	876096	30.5941	.00106838	971	942841	31.1609	.00102987
902	813604	30.0333	.00110865	937	877969	30.6105	.00106724	972	944784	31.1769	.00102881
903	815409	30.0500	.00110742	938	879844	30.6268	.00106610	973	946729	31.1929	.00102775
904	817216	30.0666	.00110619	939	881721	30.6431	.00106496	974	948676	31.2090	.00102669
905	819025	30.0832	.00110497	940	883600	30.6594	.00106383	975	950625	31.2250	.00102564
906	820836	30.0998	.00110375	941	885481	30.6757	.00106270	976	952576	31.2410	.00102459
907	822649	30.1164	.00110254	942	887364	30.6920	.00106157	977	954529	31.2570	.00102354
908	824464	30.1330	.00110132	943	889249	30.7083	.00106045	978	956484	31.2730	.00102249
909	826281	30.1496	.00110011	944	891136	30.7246	.00105932	979	958441	31.2890	.00102145
910	828100	30.1662	.00109890	945	893025	30.7409	.00105820	980	960400	31.3050	.00102041
911	829921	30.1828	.00109769	946	894916	30.7571	.00105708	981	962361	31.3209	.00101937
912	831744	30.1993	.00109649	947	896809	30.7734	.00105597	982	964324	31.3369	.00101833
913	833569	30.2159	.00109529	948	898704	30.7896	.00105485	983	966289	31.3528	.00101729
914	835396	30.2324	.00109409	949	900601	30.8058	.00105374	984	968256	31.3688	.00101626
915	837225	30.2490	.00109290	950	902500	30.8221	.00105263	985	970225	31.3847	.00101523
916	839056	30.2655	.00109170	951	904401	30.8383	.00105152	986	972196	31.4006	.00101420
917	840889	30.2820	.00109051	952	906304	30.8545	.00105042	987	974169	31.4166	.00101317
918	842724	30.2985	.00108932	953	908209	30.8707	.00104932	988	976144	31.4325	.00101215
919	844561	30.3150	.00108814	954	910116	30.8869	.00104822	989	978121	31.4484	.00101112
920	846400	30.3315	.00108696	955	912025	30.9031	.00104712	990	980100	31.4643	.00101010
921	848241	30.3480	.00108578	956	913936	30.9192	.00104603	991	982081	31.4802	.00100908
922	850084	30.3645	.00108460	957	915849	30.9354	.00104493	992	984064	31.4960	.00100806
923	851929	30.3809	.00108342	958	917764	30.9516	.00104384	993	986049	31.5119	.00100705
924	853776	30.3974	.00108225	959	919681	30.9677	.00104275	994	988036	31.5278	.00100604
925	855625	30.4138	.00108108	960	921600	30.9839	.00104167	995	990025	31.5436	.00100503
926	857476	30.4302	.00107991	961	923521	31.0000	.00104058	996	992016	31.5595	.00100402
927	859329	30.4467	.00107875	962	925444	31.0161	.00103950	997	994009	31.5753	.00103842
928	861184	30.4631	.00107759	963	927369	31.0322	.00103842	998	996004	31.5911	.00100200
929	863041	30.4795	.00107643	964	929296	31.0483	.00103734	999	998001	31.6070	.00100100
930	864900	30.4959	.00107527	965	931225	31.0644	.00103627	1000	1000000	31.6228	.00100000
931	866761	30.5123	.00107411	966	933156	31.0805	.00103520				
932	868624	30.5287	.00107296	967	935089	31.0966	.00103413				
933	870489	30.5450	.00107181	968	937024	31.1127	.00103306				
934	872356	30.5614	.00107066	969	938961	31.1288	.00103199				
935	874225	30.5778	.00106952	970	940900	31.1448	.00103093				

TABLE M
Random digits

Row number										
00000	10097	32533	76520	13586	34673	54876	80959	09117	39292	74945
00001	37542	04805	64894	74296	24805	24037	20636	10402	00822	91665
00002	08422	68953	19645	09303	23209	02560	15953	34764	35080	33606
00003	99019	02529	09376	70715	38311	31165	88676	74397	04436	27659
00004	12807	99970	80157	36147	64032	36653	98951	16877	12171	76833
00005	66065	74717	34072	76850	36697	36170	65813	39885	11199	29170
00006	31060	10805	45571	82406	35303	42614	86799	07439	23403	09732
00007	85269	77602	02051	65692	68665	74818	73053	85247	18623	88579
00008	63573	32135	05325	47048	90553	57548	28468	28709	83491	25624
00009	73796	45753	03529	64778	35808	34282	60935	20344	35273	88435
00010	98520	17767	14905	68607	22109	40558	60970	93433	50500	73998
00011	11805	05431	39808	27732	50725	68248	29405	24201	52775	67851
00012	83452	99634	06288	98033	13746	70078	18475	40610	68711	77817
00013	88685	40200	86507	58401	36766	67951	90364	76493	29609	11062
00014	99594	67348	87517	64969	91826	08928	93785	61368	23478	34113
00015	65481	17674	17468	50950	58047	76974	73039	57186	40218	16544
00016	80124	35635	17727	08015	45318	22374	21115	78253	14385	53763
00017	74350	99817	77402	77214	43236	00210	45521	64237	96286	02655
00018	69916	26803	66252	29148	36936	87203	76621	13900	94400	56418
00019	09893	20505	14225	68514	46427	56788	96297	78822	54382	14598
00020	91499	14523	68479	27686	46162	83554	94750	89923	37089	20048
00021	80336	94598	26940	36858	70297	34135	53140	33340	42050	82341
00022	44104	81949	85157	47954	32979	26575	57600	40881	22222	06413
00023	12550	73742	11100	02040	12860	74697	96644	89439	28707	25815
00024	63606	49329	16505	34484	40219	52563	43651	77082	07207	31790
00025	61196	90446	26457	47774	51924	33729	65394	59593	42582	60527
00026	15474	45266	95270	79953	59367	83848	82396	10118	33211	59466
00027	94557	28573	67897	54387	54622	44431	91190	42592	92927	45973
00028	42481	16213	97344	08721	16868	48767	03071	12059	25701	46670
00029	23523	78317	73208	89837	68935	91416	26252	29663	05522	82562
00030	04493	52494	75246	33824	45862	51025	61962	79335	65337	12472
00031	00549	97654	64051	88159	96119	63896	54692	82391	23287	29529
00032	35963	15307	26898	09354	33351	35462	77974	50024	90103	39333
00033	59808	08391	45427	26842	83609	49700	13021	24892	78565	20106
00034	46058	85236	01390	92286	77281	44077	93910	83647	70617	42941
00035	32179	00597	87379	25241	05567	07007	86743	17157	85394	11838
00036	69234	61406	20117	45204	15956	60000	18743	92423	97118	96338
00037	19565	41430	01758	75379	40419	21585	66674	36806	84962	85207
00038	45155	14938	19476	07246	43667	94543	59047	90033	20826	69541
00039	94864	31994	36168	10851	34888	81553	01540	35456	05014	51176
00040	98086	24826	45240	28404	44999	08896	39094	73407	35441	31880
00041	33185	16232	41941	50949	89435	48581	88695	41994	37548	73043
00042	80951	00406	96382	70774	20151	23387	25016	25298	94624	61171
00043	79752	49140	71961	28296	69861	02591	74852	20539	00387	59579
00044	18633	32537	98145	06571	31010	24674	05455	61427	77938	91936

TABLE M *(continued)*

Row number										
00045	74029	43902	77557	32270	97790	17119	52527	58021	80814	51748
00046	54178	45611	80993	37143	05335	12969	56127	19255	36040	90324
00047	11664	49883	52079	84827	59381	71539	09973	33440	88461	23356
00048	48324	77928	31249	64710	02295	36870	32307	57546	15020	09994
00049	69074	94138	87637	91976	35584	04401	10518	21615	01848	76938
00050	09188	20097	32825	39527	04220	86304	83389	87374	64278	58044
00051	90045	85497	51981	50654	94938	81997	91870	76150	68476	64659
00052	73189	50207	47677	26269	62290	64464	27124	67018	41361	82760
00053	75768	76490	20971	87749	90429	12272	95375	05871	93823	43178
00054	54016	44056	66281	31003	00682	27398	20714	53295	07706	17813
00055	08358	69910	78542	42785	13661	58873	04618	97553	31223	08420
00056	28306	03264	81333	10591	40510	07893	32604	60475	94119	01840
00057	53840	86233	81594	13628	51215	90290	28466	68795	77762	20791
00058	91757	53741	61613	62669	50263	90212	55781	76514	83483	47055
00059	89415	92694	00397	58391	12607	17646	48949	72306	94541	37408
00060	77513	03820	86864	29901	68414	82774	51908	13980	72893	55507
00061	19502	37174	69979	20288	55210	29773	74287	75251	65344	67415
00062	21818	59313	93278	81757	05686	73156	07082	85046	31853	38452
00063	51474	66499	68107	23621	94049	91345	42836	09191	08007	45449
00064	99559	68331	62535	24170	69777	12830	74819	78142	43860	72834
00065	33713	48007	93584	72869	51926	64721	58303	29822	93174	93972
00066	85274	86893	11303	22970	28834	34137	73515	90400	71148	43643
00067	84133	89640	44035	52166	73852	70091	61222	60561	62327	18423
00068	56732	16234	17395	96131	10123	91622	85496	57560	81604	18880
00069	65138	56806	87648	85261	34313	65861	45875	21069	85644	47277
00070	38001	02176	81719	11711	71602	92937	74219	64049	65584	49698
00071	37402	96397	01304	77586	56271	10086	47324	62605	40030	37438
00072	97125	40348	87083	31417	21815	39250	75237	62047	15501	29578
00073	21826	41134	47143	34072	64638	85902	49139	06441	03856	54552
00074	73135	42742	95719	09035	85794	74296	08789	88156	64691	19202
00075	07638	77929	03061	18072	96207	44156	23821	99538	04713	66994
00076	60528	83441	07954	19814	59175	20695	05533	52139	61212	06455
00077	83596	35655	06958	92983	05128	09719	77433	53783	92301	50498
00078	10850	62746	99599	10507	13499	06319	53075	71839	06410	19362
00079	39820	98952	43622	63147	64421	80814	43800	09351	31024	73167
00080	59580	06478	75569	78800	88835	54486	23768	06156	04111	08408
00081	38508	07341	23793	48763	90822	97022	17719	04207	95954	49953
00082	30692	70668	94688	16127	56196	80091	82067	63400	05462	69200
00083	65443	95659	18238	27437	49632	24041	08337	65676	96299	90836
00084	27267	50264	13192	72294	07477	44606	17985	48911	97341	30358
00085	91307	06991	19072	24210	36699	53728	28825	35793	28976	66252
00086	68434	94688	84473	13622	62126	98408	12843	82590	09815	93146
00087	48908	15877	54745	24591	35700	04754	83824	52692	54130	55160
00088	06913	45197	42672	78601	11883	09528	63011	98901	14974	40344
00089	10455	16019	14210	33712	91342	37821	88325	80851	43667	70883

TABLE M *(continued)*

Row number										
00090	12883	97343	65027	61184	04285	01392	17974	15077	90712	26769
00091	21778	30976	38807	36961	31649	42096	63281	02023	08816	47449
00092	19523	59515	65122	59659	86283	68258	69572	13798	16435	91529
00093	67245	52670	35583	16563	79246	86686	76463	34222	26655	90802
00094	60584	47377	07500	37992	45134	26529	26760	83637	41326	44344
00095	53853	41377	36066	94850	58838	73859	49364	73331	96240	43642
00096	24637	38736	74384	89342	52623	07992	12369	18601	03742	83873
00097	83080	12451	38992	22815	07759	51777	97377	27585	51972	37867
00098	16444	24334	36151	99073	27493	70939	85130	32552	54846	54759
00099	60790	18157	57178	65762	11161	78576	45819	52979	65130	04860
00100	03991	10461	93716	16894	66083	24653	84609	58232	88618	19161
00101	38555	95554	32886	59780	08355	60860	29735	47762	71299	23853
00102	17546	73704	92052	46215	55121	29281	59076	07936	27954	58909
00103	32643	52861	95819	06831	00911	98936	76355	93779	80863	00514
00104	69572	68777	39510	35905	14060	40619	29549	69616	33564	60780
00105	24122	66591	27699	06494	14845	46672	61958	77100	90899	75754
00106	61196	30231	92962	61773	41839	55382	17267	70943	78038	70267
00107	30532	21704	10274	12202	39685	23309	10061	68829	55986	66485
00108	03788	97599	75867	20717	74416	53166	35208	33374	87539	08823
00109	48228	63379	85783	47619	53152	67433	35663	52972	16818	60311
00110	60365	94653	35075	33949	42614	29297	01918	28316	98953	73231
00111	83799	42402	56623	34442	34994	41374	70071	14736	09958	18065
00112	32960	07405	36409	83232	99385	41600	11133	07586	15917	06253
00113	19322	53845	57620	52606	66497	68646	78138	66559	19640	99413
00114	11220	94747	07399	37408	48509	23929	27482	45476	85244	35159
00115	31751	57260	68980	05339	15470	48355	88651	22596	03152	19121
00116	88492	99382	14454	04504	20094	98977	74843	93413	22109	78508
00117	30934	47744	07481	83828	73788	06533	28597	20405	94205	20380
00118	22888	48893	27499	98748	60530	45128	74022	84617	82037	10268
00119	78212	16993	35902	91386	44372	15486	65741	14014	87481	37220
00120	41849	84547	46850	52326	34677	58300	74910	64345	19325	81549
00121	46352	33049	69248	93460	45305	07521	61318	31855	14413	70951
00122	11087	96294	14013	31792	59747	67277	76503	34513	39663	77544
00123	52701	08337	56303	87315	16520	69676	11654	99893	02181	68161
00124	57275	36898	81304	48585	68652	27376	92852	55866	88448	03584
00125	20857	73156	70284	24326	79375	95220	01159	63267	10622	48391
00126	15633	84924	90415	93614	33521	26665	55823	47641	86225	31704
00127	92694	48297	39904	02115	59589	49067	66821	41575	49767	04037
00128	77613	19019	88152	00080	20554	91409	96277	48257	50816	97616
00129	38688	32486	45134	63545	59404	72059	43947	51680	43852	59693
00130	25163	01889	70014	15021	41290	67312	71857	15957	68971	11403
00131	65251	07629	37239	33295	05870	01119	92784	26340	18477	65622
00132	36815	43625	18637	37509	82444	99005	04921	73701	14707	93997
00133	64397	11692	05327	82162	20247	81759	45197	25332	83745	22567
00134	04515	25624	95096	67946	48460	85558	15191	18782	16930	33361

TABLE M *(continued)*

Row number										
00135	83761	60873	43253	84145	60833	25983	01291	41349	20368	07126
00136	14387	06345	80854	09279	43529	06318	38384	74761	41196	37480
00137	51321	92246	80088	77074	88722	56736	66164	49431	66919	31678
00138	72472	00008	80890	18002	94813	31900	54155	83436	35352	54131
00139	05466	55306	93128	18464	74457	90561	72848	11834	79982	68416
00140	39528	72484	82474	25593	48545	35247	18619	13674	18611	19241
00141	81616	18711	53342	44276	75122	11724	74627	73707	58319	15997
00142	07586	16120	82641	22820	92904	13141	32392	19763	61199	67940
00143	90767	04235	13574	17200	69902	63742	78464	22501	18627	90872
00144	40188	28193	29593	88627	94972	11598	62095	36787	00441	58997
00145	34414	82157	86887	55087	19152	00023	12302	80783	32624	68691
00146	63439	75363	44989	16822	36024	00867	76378	41605	65961	73488
00147	67049	09070	93399	45547	94458	74284	05041	49807	20288	34060
00148	79495	04146	52162	90286	54158	34243	46978	35482	59362	95938
00149	91704	30552	04737	21031	75051	93029	47665	64382	99782	93478
00150	94015	46874	32444	48277	59820	96163	64654	25843	41145	42820
00151	74108	88222	88570	74015	25704	91035	01755	14750	48968	38603
00152	62880	87873	95160	59221	22304	90314	72877	17334	39283	04149
00153	11748	12102	80580	41867	17710	59621	06554	07850	73950	79552
00154	17944	05600	60478	03343	25852	58905	57216	39618	49856	99326
00155	66067	42792	95043	52680	46780	56487	09971	59481	37006	22186
00156	54244	91030	45547	70818	59849	96169	61459	21647	87417	17198
00157	30945	57589	31732	57260	47670	07654	46376	25366	94746	49580
00158	69170	37403	86995	90307	94304	71803	26825	05511	12459	91314
00159	08345	88975	35841	85771	08105	59987	87112	21476	14713	71181
00160	27767	43584	85301	88977	29490	69714	73035	41207	74699	09310
00161	13025	14338	54066	15243	47724	66733	47431	43905	31048	56699
00162	80217	36292	98525	24335	24432	24896	43277	58874	11466	16082
00163	10875	62004	90391	61105	57411	06368	53856	30743	08670	84741
00164	54127	57326	26629	19087	24472	88779	30540	27886	61732	75454
00165	60311	42824	37301	42678	45990	43242	17374	52003	70707	70214
00166	49739	71484	92003	98086	76668	73209	59202	11973	02902	33250
00167	78626	51594	16453	94614	39014	97066	83012	09832	25571	77628
00168	66692	13986	99837	00582	81232	44987	09504	96412	90193	79568
00169	44071	28091	07362	97703	76447	42537	98524	97831	65704	09514
00170	41468	85149	49554	17994	14924	39650	95294	00556	70481	06905
00171	94559	37559	49678	53119	70312	05682	66986	34099	74474	20740
00172	41615	70360	64114	58660	90850	64618	80620	51790	11436	38072
00173	50273	93113	41794	86861	24781	89683	55411	85667	77535	99892
00174	41396	80504	90670	08289	40902	05069	95083	06783	28102	57816
00175	25807	24260	71529	78920	72682	07385	90726	57166	98884	08583
00176	06170	97965	88302	98041	21443	41808	68984	83620	89747	98882
00177	60808	54444	74412	81105	01176	28838	36421	16489	18059	51061
00178	80940	44893	10408	36222	80582	71944	92638	40333	67054	16067
00179	19516	90120	46759	71643	13177	55292	21036	82808	77501	97427

TABLE M *(concluded)*

Row number										
00180	49386	54480	23604	23554	21785	41101	91178	10174	29420	90438
00181	06312	88940	15995	69321	47458	64809	98189	81851	29651	84215
00182	60942	00307	11897	92674	40405	68032	96717	54244	10701	41393
00183	92329	98932	78284	46347	71209	92061	39448	93136	25722	08564
00184	77936	63574	31384	51924	85561	29671	58137	17820	22751	36518
00185	38101	77756	11657	13897	95889	57067	47648	13885	70669	93406
00186	39641	69457	91339	22502	92613	89719	11947	56203	19324	20504
00187	84054	40455	99396	63680	67667	60631	69181	96845	38525	11600
00188	47468	03577	57649	63266	24700	71594	14004	23153	69249	05747
00189	43321	31370	28977	23896	76479	68562	62342	07589	08899	05985
00190	64281	61826	18555	64937	13173	33365	78851	16499	87064	13075
00191	66847	70495	32350	02985	86716	38746	26313	77463	55387	72681
00192	72461	33230	21529	53424	92581	02262	78438	66276	18396	73538
00193	21032	91050	13058	16218	12470	56500	15292	76139	59526	52113
00194	95362	67011	06651	16136	01016	00857	55018	56374	35824	71708
00195	49712	97380	10404	55452	34030	60726	75211	10271	36633	68424
00196	58275	61764	97586	54716	50259	46345	87195	46092	26787	60939
00197	89514	11788	68224	23417	73959	76145	30342	40277	11049	72049
00198	15472	50669	48139	36732	46874	37088	63465	09819	58869	35220
00199	12120	86124	51247	44302	60883	52109	21437	36786	49226	77837

TABLE N_1

Critical values of U and U' for a one-tailed test at $\alpha = 0.005$ or a two-tailed test at $\alpha = 0.01$

To be significant for any given N_1 and N_2: Obtained U must be equal to or *less than* the value shown in the table. Obtained U' must be equal to or *greater than* the value shown in the table. *Example:* If $\alpha = 0.01$, two-tailed test, $N_1 = 13$, $N_2 = 15$, and obtained $U = 150$, we cannot reject H_0 since obtained U is within the upper (153) and lower (42) critical values.*

N_2 \ N_1	1	2	3	4	5	6	7	8	9	10	11	12	13	14	15	16	17	18	19	20
1	--	--	--	--	--	--	--	--	--	--	--	--	--	--	--	--	--	--	--	--
2	--	--	--	--	--	--	--	--	--	--	--	--	--	--	--	--	--	--	0	0
																			38	40
3	--	--	--	--	--	--	--	--	0	0	0	1	1	1	2	2	2	2	3	3
									27	30	33	35	38	41	43	46	49	52	54	57
4	--	--	--	--	--	0	0	1	1	2	2	3	3	4	5	5	6	6	7	8
						24	28	31	35	38	42	45	49	52	55	59	62	66	69	72
5	--	--	--	--	0	1	1	2	3	4	5	6	7	7	8	9	10	11	12	13
					25	29	34	38	42	46	50	54	58	63	67	71	75	79	83	87
6	--	--	--	0	1	2	3	4	5	6	7	9	10	11	12	13	15	16	17	18
				24	29	34	39	44	49	54	59	63	68	73	78	83	87	92	97	102
7	--	--	--	0	1	3	4	6	7	9	10	12	13	15	16	18	19	21	22	24
				28	34	39	45	50	56	61	67	72	78	83	89	94	100	105	111	116
8	--	--	--	1	2	4	6	7	9	11	13	15	17	18	20	22	24	26	28	30
				31	38	44	50	57	63	69	75	81	87	94	100	106	112	118	124	130
9	--	--	0	1	3	5	7	9	11	13	16	18	20	22	24	27	29	31	33	36
			27	35	42	49	56	63	70	77	83	90	97	104	111	117	124	131	138	144
10	--	--	0	2	4	6	9	11	13	16	18	21	24	26	29	31	34	37	39	42
			30	38	46	54	61	69	77	84	92	99	106	114	121	129	136	143	151	158
11	--	--	0	2	5	7	10	13	16	18	21	24	27	30	33	36	39	42	45	48
			33	42	50	59	67	75	83	92	100	108	116	124	132	140	148	156	164	172
12	--	--	1	3	6	9	12	15	18	21	24	27	31	34	37	41	44	47	51	54
			35	45	54	63	72	81	90	99	108	117	125	134	143	151	160	169	177	186
13	--	--	1	3	7	10	13	17	20	24	27	31	34	38	42	45	49	53	56	60
			38	49	58	68	78	87	97	106	116	125	125	144	153	163	172	181	191	200
14	--	--	1	4	7	11	15	18	22	26	30	34	38	42	46	50	54	58	63	67
			41	52	63	73	83	94	104	114	124	134	144	154	164	174	184	194	203	213
15	--	--	2	5	8	12	16	20	24	29	33	37	42	46	51	55	60	64	69	73
			43	55	67	78	89	100	111	121	132	143	153	164	174	185	195	206	216	227
16	--	--	2	5	9	13	18	22	27	31	36	41	45	50	55	60	65	70	74	79
			46	59	71	83	94	106	117	129	140	151	163	174	185	196	207	218	230	241
17	--	--	2	6	10	15	19	24	29	34	39	44	49	54	60	65	70	75	81	86
			49	62	75	87	100	112	124	148	148	160	172	184	195	207	219	231	242	254
18	--	--	2	6	11	16	21	26	31	37	42	47	53	58	64	70	75	81	87	92
			52	66	79	92	105	118	131	143	156	169	181	194	206	218	231	243	255	268
19	--	0	3	7	12	17	22	28	33	39	45	51	56	63	69	74	81	87	93	99
		38	54	69	83	97	111	124	138	151	164	177	191	203	216	230	242	255	268	281
20	--	0	3	8	13	18	24	30	36	42	48	54	60	67	73	79	86	92	99	105
		40	57	72	87	102	116	130	144	158	172	186	200	213	227	241	254	268	281	295

*Dashes in the body of the table indicate that no decision is possible at the stated level of significance.

TABLE N_2

Critical values of U and U' for a one-tailed test at $\alpha = 0.01$ or a two-tailed test at $\alpha = 0.02$

To be significant for any given N_1 and N_2: Obtained U must be equal to or *less than* the value shown in the table. Obtained U' must be equal to or *greater than* the value shown in the table.*

N_2 \ N_1	1	2	3	4	5	6	7	8	9	10	11	12	13	14	15	16	17	18	19	20
1	--	--	--	--	--	--	--	--	--	--	--	--	--	--	--	--	--	--	--	--
2	--	--	--	--	--	--	--	--	--	--	--	--	0 26	0 28	0 30	0 32	0 34	0 36	1 37	1 39
3	--	--	--	--	--	--	0 21	0 24	1 26	1 29	1 32	2 34	2 37	2 40	3 42	3 45	4 47	4 50	4 52	5 55
4	--	--	--	--	0 20	1 23	1 27	2 30	3 33	3 37	4 40	5 43	5 47	6 50	7 53	7 57	8 60	9 63	9 67	10 70
5	--	--	--	0 20	1 24	2 28	3 32	4 36	5 40	6 44	7 48	8 52	9 56	10 60	11 64	12 68	13 72	14 76	15 80	16 84
6	--	--	--	1 23	2 28	3 33	4 38	6 42	7 47	8 52	9 57	11 61	12 66	13 71	15 75	16 80	18 84	19 89	20 94	22 98
7	--	--	0 21	1 27	3 32	4 38	6 43	7 49	9 54	11 59	12 65	14 70	16 75	17 81	19 86	21 91	23 96	24 102	26 107	28 112
8	--	--	0 24	2 30	4 36	6 42	7 49	9 55	11 61	13 67	15 73	17 79	20 84	22 90	24 96	26 102	28 108	30 114	32 120	34 126
9	--	--	1 26	3 33	5 40	7 47	9 54	11 61	14 67	16 74	18 81	21 87	23 94	26 100	28 107	31 113	33 120	36 126	38 133	40 140
10	--	--	1 29	3 37	6 44	8 52	11 59	13 67	16 74	19 81	22 88	24 96	27 103	30 110	33 117	36 124	38 132	41 139	44 146	47 153
11	--	--	1 32	4 40	7 48	9 57	12 65	15 73	18 81	22 88	25 96	28 104	31 112	34 120	37 128	41 135	44 143	47 151	50 159	53 167
12	--	--	2 34	5 43	8 52	11 61	14 70	17 79	21 87	24 96	28 104	31 113	35 121	38 130	42 138	46 146	49 155	53 163	56 172	60 180
13	--	0 26	2 37	5 47	9 56	12 66	16 75	20 84	23 94	27 103	31 112	35 121	39 130	43 139	47 148	51 157	55 166	59 175	63 184	67 193
14	--	0 28	2 40	6 50	10 60	13 71	17 81	22 90	26 100	30 110	34 120	38 130	43 139	47 149	51 159	56 168	6 178	65 187	69 197	73 207
15	--	0 30	3 42	7 53	11 64	15 75	19 86	24 96	28 107	33 117	37 128	42 138	47 148	51 159	56 169	61 179	66 189	70 200	75 210	80 220
16	--	0 32	3 45	7 57	12 68	16 80	21 91	26 102	31 113	36 124	41 135	46 146	51 157	56 168	61 179	66 190	71 201	76 212	82 222	87 233
17	--	0 34	4 47	8 60	13 72	18 84	23 96	28 108	33 120	38 132	44 143	49 155	55 166	60 178	66 189	71 201	77 212	82 224	88 234	93 247
18	--	0 36	4 50	9 63	14 76	19 89	24 102	30 114	36 126	41 139	47 151	53 163	59 175	65 187	70 200	76 212	82 224	88 236	94 248	100 260
19	--	1 37	4 53	9 67	15 80	20 94	26 107	32 120	38 133	44 146	50 159	56 172	63 184	69 197	75 210	82 222	88 235	94 248	101 260	107 273
20	--	1 39	5 55	10 70	16 84	22 98	28 112	34 126	40 140	47 153	53 167	60 180	67 193	73 207	80 220	87 233	93 247	100 260	107 273	114 286

*Dashes in the body of the table indicate that no decision is possible at the stated level of significance.

TABLE N_3

Critical values of U and U' for a one-tailed test at $\alpha = 0.025$ or a two-tailed test at $\alpha = 0.05$

To be significant for any given N_1 and N_2: Obtained U must be equal to or *less than* the value shown in the table. Obtained U' must be equal to or *greater than* the value shown in the table.*

N_2 \ N_1	1	2	3	4	5	6	7	8	9	10	11	12	13	14	15	16	17	18	19	20
1	--	--	--	--	--	--	--	--	--	--	--	--	--	--	--	--	--	--	--	--
2	--	--	--	--	--	--	--	0 16	0 18	0 20	0 22	1 23	1 25	1 27	1 29	1 31	2 32	2 34	2 36	2 38
3	--	--	--	--	0 15	1 17	1 20	2 22	2 25	3 27	3 30	4 32	4 35	5 37	5 40	6 42	6 45	7 47	7 50	8 52
4	--	--	--	0 16	1 19	2 22	3 25	4 28	4 32	5 35	6 38	7 41	8 44	9 47	10 50	11 53	11 57	12 60	13 63	13 67
5	--	--	0 15	1 19	2 23	3 27	5 30	6 34	7 38	8 42	9 46	11 49	12 53	13 57	14 61	15 65	17 68	18 72	19 76	20 80
6	--	--	1 17	2 22	3 27	5 31	6 36	8 40	10 44	11 49	13 53	14 58	16 62	17 67	19 71	21 75	22 80	24 84	25 89	27 93
7	--	--	1 20	3 25	5 30	6 36	8 41	10 46	12 51	14 56	16 61	18 66	20 71	22 76	24 81	26 86	28 91	30 96	32 101	34 106
8	--	0 16	2 22	4 28	6 34	8 40	10 46	13 51	15 57	17 63	19 69	22 74	24 80	26 86	29 91	31 97	34 102	36 108	38 111	41 119
9	--	0 18	2 25	4 32	7 38	10 44	12 51	15 57	17 64	20 70	23 76	26 82	28 89	31 95	34 101	37 107	39 114	42 120	45 126	48 132
10	--	0 20	3 27	5 35	8 42	11 49	14 56	17 63	20 70	23 77	26 84	29 91	33 97	36 104	39 111	42 118	45 125	48 132	52 138	55 145
11	--	0 22	3 30	6 38	9 46	13 53	16 61	19 69	23 76	26 84	30 91	33 99	37 106	40 114	44 121	47 129	51 136	55 143	58 151	62 158
12	--	1 23	4 32	7 41	11 49	14 58	18 66	22 74	26 82	29 91	33 99	37 107	41 115	45 123	49 131	53 139	57 147	61 155	65 163	69 171
13	--	1 25	4 35	8 44	12 53	16 62	20 71	24 80	28 89	33 97	37 106	41 115	45 124	50 132	54 141	59 149	63 158	67 167	72 175	76 184
14	--	1 27	5 37	9 47	13 51	17 67	22 76	26 86	31 95	36 104	40 114	45 123	50 132	55 141	59 151	64 160	67 171	74 178	78 188	83 197
15	--	1 29	5 40	10 50	14 61	19 71	24 81	29 91	34 101	39 111	44 121	49 131	54 141	59 151	64 161	70 170	75 180	80 190	85 200	90 210
16	--	1 31	6 42	11 53	15 65	21 75	26 86	31 97	37 107	42 118	47 129	53 139	59 149	64 160	70 170	75 181	81 191	86 202	92 212	98 222
17	--	2 32	6 45	11 57	17 68	22 80	28 91	34 102	39 114	45 125	51 136	57 147	63 158	67 171	75 180	81 191	87 202	93 213	99 224	105 235
18	--	2 34	7 47	12 60	18 72	24 84	30 96	36 108	42 120	48 132	55 143	61 155	67 167	74 178	80 190	86 202	93 213	99 225	106 236	112 248
19	--	2 36	7 50	13 63	19 76	25 89	32 101	38 114	45 126	52 138	58 151	65 163	72 175	78 188	85 200	92 212	99 224	106 236	113 248	119 261
20	--	2 38	8 52	13 67	20 80	27 93	34 106	41 119	48 132	55 145	62 158	69 171	76 184	83 197	90 210	98 222	105 235	112 248	119 261	127 273

*Dashes in the body of the table indicate that no decision is possible at the stated level of significance.

TABLE N_4

Critical values of U and U' for a one-tailed test at $\alpha = 0.05$ or a two-tailed test at $\alpha = 0.10$

To be significant for any given N_1 and N_2: Obtained U must be equal to or *less than* the value shown in the table. Obtained U' must be equal to or *greater than* the value shown in the table.*

N_2 \ N_1	1	2	3	4	5	6	7	8	9	10	11	12	13	14	15	16	17	18	19	20
1	--	--	--	--	--	--	--	--	--	--	--	--	--	--	--	--	--	--	0 19	0 20
2	--	--	--	--	0 10	0 12	0 14	1 15	1 17	1 19	1 21	2 22	2 24	2 26	3 27	3 29	3 31	4 32	4 34	4 36
3	--	--	0 9	0 12	1 14	2 16	2 19	3 21	3 24	4 26	5 28	5 31	6 33	7 35	7 38	8 40	9 42	9 45	10 47	11 49
4	--	--	0 12	1 15	2 18	3 21	4 24	5 27	6 30	7 33	8 36	9 39	10 42	11 45	12 48	14 50	15 53	16 56	17 59	18 62
5	--	0 10	1 14	2 18	4 21	5 25	6 29	8 32	9 36	11 39	12 43	13 47	15 50	16 54	18 57	19 61	20 65	22 68	23 72	25 75
6	--	0 12	2 16	3 21	5 25	7 29	8 34	10 38	12 42	14 46	16 50	17 55	19 59	21 63	23 67	25 71	26 76	28 80	30 84	32 88
7	--	0 14	2 19	4 24	6 29	8 34	11 38	13 43	15 48	17 53	19 58	21 63	24 67	26 72	28 77	30 82	33 86	35 91	37 96	39 101
8	--	1 15	3 21	5 27	8 32	10 38	13 43	15 49	18 54	20 60	23 65	26 70	28 76	31 81	33 87	36 92	39 97	41 103	44 108	47 113
9	--	1 17	3 24	6 30	9 36	12 42	15 48	18 54	21 60	24 66	27 72	30 78	33 84	36 90	39 96	42 102	45 108	48 114	51 120	54 126
10	--	1 19	4 26	7 33	11 39	14 46	17 53	20 60	24 66	27 73	31 79	34 86	37 93	41 99	44 106	48 112	51 119	55 125	58 132	62 138
11	--	1 21	5 28	8 36	12 43	16 50	19 58	23 65	27 72	31 79	34 87	38 94	42 101	46 108	50 115	54 122	57 130	61 137	65 144	69 151
12	--	2 22	5 31	9 39	13 47	17 55	21 63	26 70	30 8	34 86	38 94	42 102	47 109	51 117	55 125	60 132	64 140	68 148	72 156	77 163
13	--	2 24	6 33	10 42	15 50	19 59	24 67	28 76	33 84	37 93	42 101	47 109	51 118	56 126	61 134	65 143	70 151	75 159	80 167	84 176
14	--	2 26	7 35	11 45	16 54	21 63	26 72	31 81	36 90	41 99	46 108	51 117	56 126	61 135	66 144	71 153	77 161	82 170	87 179	92 188
15	--	3 27	7 38	12 48	18 57	23 67	28 77	33 87	39 96	44 106	50 115	55 125	61 134	66 144	72 153	77 163	83 172	88 182	94 191	100 200
16	--	3 29	8 40	14 50	19 61	25 71	30 82	36 92	42 102	48 112	54 122	60 132	65 143	71 153	77 163	83 173	89 183	95 193	101 203	107 213
17	--	3 31	9 42	15 53	20 65	26 76	33 86	39 97	45 108	51 119	57 130	64 140	70 151	77 161	83 172	89 183	96 193	102 204	109 214	115 225
18	--	4 32	9 45	16 56	22 68	28 80	35 91	41 103	48 114	55 123	61 137	68 148	75 159	82 170	88 182	95 193	102 204	109 215	116 226	123 237
19	0 19	4 34	10 47	17 59	23 72	30 84	37 96	44 108	51 120	58 132	65 144	72 156	80 167	87 179	94 191	101 203	109 214	116 226	123 238	130 250
20	0 20	4 36	11 49	18 62	25 75	32 88	39 101	47 113	54 126	62 138	69 151	77 163	84 176	92 188	100 200	107 213	115 225	123 237	130 250	138 262

*Dashes in the body of the table indicate that no decision is possible at the stated level of significance.

TABLE O

Critical values of T

The symbol T denotes the smaller sum of ranks associated with differences that are all of the same sign. For any given N (number of ranked differences), the obtained T is significant at a given level if it is equal to or *less than* the value shown in the table. All entries are for the *absolute* value of T.

	Level of significance for one-tailed test					Level of significance for one-tailed test			
	.05	.025	.01	.005		.05	.025	.01	.005
	Level of significance for two-tailed test					Level of significance for two-tailed test			
N	.10	.05	.02	.01	N	.10	.05	.02	.01
5	0	--	--	--	28	130	116	101	91
6	0	0	--	--	29	140	126	110	100
7	3	2	0	--	30	151	137	120	109
8	5	3	1	0	31	163	147	130	118
9	8	5	3	1	32	175	159	140	128
10	10	8	5	3	33	187	170	151	138
11	13	10	7	5	34	200	182	162	148
12	17	13	9	7	35	213	195	173	159
13	21	17	12	9	36	227	208	185	171
14	25	21	15	12	37	241	221	198	182
15	30	25	19	15	38	256	235	211	194
16	35	29	23	19	39	271	249	224	207
17	41	34	27	23	40	286	264	238	220
18	47	40	32	27	41	302	279	252	233
19	53	46	37	32	42	319	294	266	247
20	60	52	43	37	43	336	310	281	261
21	67	58	49	42	44	353	327	296	276
22	75	65	55	48	45	371	343	312	291
23	83	73	62	54	46	389	261	328	307
24	91	81	69	61	47	407	378	345	322
25	100	89	76	68	48	426	396	362	339
26	110	98	84	75	49	446	415	379	355
27	119	107	92	83	50	466	434	397	373

Slight discrepancies will be found between the critical values appearing in the table above and in Table 2 of F. Wilcoxon and R. A. Wilcox, *Some Rapid Approximate Statistical Procedures,* rev. ed. (New York: Lederle Laboratories, 1964). The disparity reflects the latter's policy of selecting the critical value nearest a given significance level, occasionally overstepping that level. For example, for $N = 8$,

the probability of a T of 3 = 0.0390 (two-tail),

and

the probability of a T of 4 = 0.0546 (two-tail).

Wilcoxon and Wilcox select a T of 4 as the critical value at the 0.05 level of significance (two-tail), whereas Table J reflects a more conservative policy by setting a T of 3 as the critical value at this level.

ACKNOWLEDGMENTS

We are grateful to the following authors and publishers for permission to adapt from the following tables.

Table B	R. A. Fisher, *Statistical Methods for Research Workers*, 14th ed. Reprinted with permission of Macmillan Publishing Company, Inc. Copyright © 1970, University of Adelaide.
Table C	Table III of R. A. Fisher and F. Yates, *Statistical Tables for Biological, Agricultural, and Medical Research,* 6th ed. London: Longman Group, 1974, p. 46. (Previously published by Oliver and Boyd, Edinburgh.) Reprinted with permission of the authors and publisher.
Table D and Table D_1	G. W. Snedecor and William G. Cochran, *Statistical Methods,* 7th ed. Ames: Iowa State University Press, © 1980.
Table E	Q. McNemar, Table B of *Psychological Statistics.* New York: John Wiley and Sons, 1962.
Table F	E. G. Olds, "The 5 Percent Significance Levels of Sums of Squares of Rank Differences and a Correction," *Ann. Math. Statist.* 20 (1949), pp. 117–18 and E. G. Olds, "Distribution of Sums of Squares of Rank Differences for Small Numbers of Individuals," *Ann. Math. Statist.* 9 (1938), pp. 133–48.
Table G	W. V. Bingham, Table XVII of *Aptitudes and Aptitude Testing.* New York: Harper, 1937.
Table H	S. Siegel, *Nonparametric Statistics.* New York: McGraw-Hill, 1956.
Table I	R. P. Runyon, Table A of *Nonparametric Statistics.* Reading, MA.: Addison-Wesley, 1977.
Table J	R. P. Runyon, Table B of *Nonparametric Statistics.* Reading, MA: Addison-Wesley, 1977.
Table K	E. S. Pearson and H. O. Hartley, *Biometrika Tables for Statisticians,* vol. 1, 2d ed. New York: Cambridge University Press, 1958.
Table L	A. L. Edwards, *Statistical Analysis,* 3d ed. New York: Holt, Rinehart and Winston, 1969 and J. W. Dunlap and A. K. Kurtz, *Handbook of Statistical Nomographs, Tables, and Formulas.* New York: World Book, 1932.
Table M	Rand Corporation, *A Million Random Digits.* Glencoe, IL: Free Press, 1955.

Table N H. B. Mann and D. R. Whitney, "On a Test of Whether One of Two Random Variables Is Stochastically Larger Than the Other," *Ann. Math. Statist.* 18 (1947), pp. 52–54 and D. Auble, "Extended Tables for the Mann-Whitney Statistic," *Bulletin of the Institute of Educational Research at Indiana University* 1, no. 2 (1953).

Table O F. Wilcoxon, S. Katti, and R. A. Wilcox, *Critical Values and Probability Levels for the Wilcoxon Rank Sum Test and the Wilcoxon Signed Rank Test*. New York: American Cyanamid Co., 1963 and F. Wilcoxon and R. A. Wilcox, *Some Rapid Approximate Statistical Procedures*. New York: Lederle Laboratories, 1964.

APPENDIX D

Glossary of Terms

From
Abscissa (X-axis)
to
Within-group variance

abscissa (X-axis) Horizontal axis of a graph.

absolute value of a number The value of a number without regard to sign.

addition rule If A and B are mutually exclusive events, the probability of obtaining *either of them* is equal to the probability of A plus the probability of B. Symbolically

$$p(A \text{ or } B) = p(A) + p(B)$$

alpha (α) level The level of significance set by the researcher for inferring the operation of nonchance factors.

alternative hypothesis (H_1) A statement specifying that the population parameter is some value other than the one specified under the null hypothesis.

analysis of variance (ANOVA) A method, described initially by R. A. Fisher, for partitioning the sum of squares for experimental or survey data into known components of variation.

a posteriori comparisons Comparisons not planned in advance to investigate specific hypotheses concerning population parameters. *A posteriori* means "after the fact."

a priori or planned comparisons Comparisons planned in advance to investigate specific hypotheses concerning population parameters. *A priori* means "before the fact."

array An arrangement of data according to their magnitude from the smallest to the largest value.

asymmetric measure of association A measure of the one-way effect of one variable upon another.

average deviation See *mean deviation.*

bar graph A form of graph that uses bars to indicate the frequency of occurrence of observations within each nominal or ordinal category.

between-group sum of squares (SS_{bet}) The sum of the sum of squares between each group.

between-group variance An estimate of variance based on variability between groups.

bias In sampling, when selections favor certain events or certain collections of events.

biased estimate of a parameter An estimate that does not equal, on the average, the value of the parameter.

binomial distribution A model with known mathematical properties used to describe the distributions of discrete random variables.

centile A percentage rank that divides a distribution into 100 equal parts. Same as a percentile.

central limit theorem If random samples of a fixed N are drawn from *any* population (regardless of the form of the population distribution), as N becomes larger, the distribution of sample means approaches normality, with the overall mean approaching μ, the variance of the sample means $\sigma_{\bar{X}}^2$ being equal to σ^2/N, and a standard error of $\sigma_{\bar{X}}$ of $\sigma/\sqrt{N}$.

coefficient of determination (r^2) The ratio of the explained variation to the total variation.

coefficient of multiple determination (R^2) A measure of the proportion of total variation in a dependent variable that is explained jointly by two or more independent variables.

coefficient of nondetermination ($1 - r^2$) The proportion of variation not explained in terms of the correlation between the two variables.

concordant pair Two cases are ranked similarly on two variables.

conditional distribution The distribution of the categories of one variable under the differing conditions or categories of another.

conditional probability The probability of an event that is dependent on the presence of another event. Represented symbolically as $p(A \mid B)$, the probability of A given that B has occurred.

conditional table A contingency table that summarizes the relationship between two variables for categories or conditions of one or the other.

confidence interval Specifies a range of values for a parameter bounded by two endpoints called confidence limits. Common confidence intervals are 95% and 99%.

confidence limits The two endpoints of a confidence interval.

contingency coefficient A nominal measure of association based on χ^2 and used primarily for square tables, making it the most versatile of the three measures of association.

contingency table A table showing the cross-tabulation or joint distribution of two variables.

continuous variables Variables that can assume an unlimited number of intermediate values.

control variable A variable whose subgroups or categories are used in a conditional table to examine the relationship between two variables.

correlated samples design See *matched-group design.*

correlation coefficient A measure that expresses the extent to which two variables are related.

correlation matrix A summary of the statistical relationships between all possible pairs of variables.

covariation The extent to which two variables vary together.

Cramer's V A nominal measure of association based on χ^2 suitable for tables of any dimension.

critical region The portion of the area under a curve that includes those values of a statistic that lead to rejection of the null hypothesis.

critical values Those values that bound the critical rejection regions corresponding to varying levels of significance.

cross tabulation See *conditional distribution.*

cumulative frequency The number of cases (frequencies) at and below a given point.

cumulative frequency curve A curve that shows the number of cases below the upper true limit of an interval.

cumulative percentage The percentage of cases or frequencies at and below a given point.

cumulative percentage distribution A distribution that shows the cumulative percentage at and below the upper true limit of the corresponding class interval.

data Numbers or measurements that are collected as a result of observations, interviews, and so forth.
decile A percentage rank that divides a distribution into 10 equal parts.
degrees of freedom (df) The number of values that are free to vary after we have placed certain restrictions on our data.
dependence See *nonindependence*.
dependent variable The variable that is being predicted. Also referred to as the criterion variable.
descriptive statistics Procedures used to organize and present data in a convenient, usable summary form.
deviation The distance and direction of a score from a reference point.
directional hypothesis An alternative hypothesis that states the direction in which the population parameter differs from the one specified under H_0.
discordant pair Two cases are ranked on the opposite order on two variables.
discrete variables (discontinuous variables) Variables that have equality of counting units.
dispersion The spread or variability of scores about the measure of central tendency.
epsilon (ϵ) The percentage difference within a category of the dependent variable between the two extreme categories of the independent variable.
error sum of squares See *unexplained variation.*
exhaustive A grouped frequency distribution is said to be exhaustive when all possible scores can be placed within established categories.
explained variation Variation of predicted scores about the mean of the distribution.
***F*-ratio** The between-group variance estimate divided by the within-group variance estimate.
frequency curve (frequency polygon) A form of graph, representing a frequency distribution, in which a continuous line is used to indicate the frequency of the corresponding scores.
gamma (γ) A symmetric measure of association for ordinal-level data based on pair-by-pair comparison with a PRE interpretation.
grouped frequency distribution A frequency distribution in which the values of the variable have been grouped into class intervals.
histogram A form of bar graph used with interval- or ratio-scaled frequency distribution.
homogeneity of variance The condition that exists when two or more sample variances have been drawn from populations with equal variances.
independence The condition that exists when the occurrence of a given event will not affect the probability of the occurrence of another event. Symbolically:

$$p(A \mid B) = p(A) \qquad \text{and} \qquad p(B \mid A) = p(B)$$

independent variable The predictor variable. Referred to as the experimental variable in an experiment.
inferential or inductive statistics Procedures used to arrive at broader generalizations or inferences from sample data to populations.
inflated *N* An error produced whenever several observations are made on the same individual and treated as though they were independent observations.
interaction Two variables are said to have interaction when their association is not uniform across all categories of a third variable.
interquartile range A measure of variability obtained by subtracting the score at the 1st quartile from the score at the 3rd quartile.
interval estimation The determination of an interval within which the population parameter is presumed to fall.

interval scale Scale in which exact distances can be known between categories. The zero point in this scale is arbitrary, and arithmetic operations are permitted.
intervening variable A variable that causally links two other variables.
joint (or successive) occurrence The occurrence of two events simultaneously. Such events cannot be mutually exclusive.
joint probability The probability of two events occurring simultaneously. Symbolically:

$$p(A \text{ and } B)$$

Kendall's tau-*b* A symmetric measure of association for ordinal-level data.
lambda (λ) An asymmetric or symmetric measure of association for nominal-level data.
law of large numbers As the sample size increases, the standard error of the mean decreases.
least squares property of the mean Measure of central tendency that makes the sum of the squared deviations around it minimal.
leptokurtic distribution A bell-shaped distribution characterized by a piling up of scores in the center of the distribution.
line of best fit See *regression line.*
Mann-Whitney *U*-test A powerful nonparametric statistical test commonly used as an alternative to the Student *t*-ratio when the measurements fail to achieve interval scaling.
marginal probability A probability that reflects independent or unconditional events.
marginals The column and row totals of a contingency table.
matched-group design A design in which pairs of individuals are matched on a variable correlated with the dependent variable. Each member of a pair receives different experimental conditions.
mean The sum of the scores or values of a variable divided by their number.
mean deviation Sum of the deviation of each score from the mean, without regard to sign, divided by the number of scores.
mean square The sum of the squared deviations from the mean divided by degrees of freedom.
measurement The assignment of numbers to objects or events according to sets of predetermined (or arbitrary) rules.
measure of central tendency Index of central location used in the description of frequency distributions.
median The score in a distribution of scores, above and below which one-half of the frequencies fall.
mesokurtic distribution A bell-shaped distribution; "ideal" form of normal curve.
mode The score that occurs with the greatest frequency.
multiple correlation coefficient (*R*) A measure of the linear relationship between a dependent variable and the combined effects of two or more independent variables.
multiple regression coefficient A measure of the influence of an independent variable on a dependent variable when the effects of all other independent variables in the multiple regression equation have been held constant. It can be standardized or unstandardized.
multiplication rule Given two events, *A* and *B*, the probability of obtaining both *A* and *B* jointly is the product of the probability of obtaining one of these events times the conditional probability of obtaining one event, given that the other event has occurred. Symbolically:

$$p(A \text{ and } B) = p(A)p(B \mid A) = p(B)p(A \mid B)$$

multivariate statistical technique A technique used to determine the nature of the relationships between three or more variables.

mutually exclusive Categories are said to be mutually exclusive because it is impossible for a person's score to belong to more than one category.

negatively skewed distribution A distribution that has relatively fewer frequencies at the low end of the horizontal axis.

negative relationship Variables are said to be negatively related when high scores on one variable tend to be associated with low scores on the other; conversely, low scores on one variable tend to be associated with high scores on the other.

nominal numbers Numbers used to name.

nominal scale A scale in which the categories are homogeneous, mutually exclusive, exhaustive, and unordered.

nondirectional hypothesis An alternative hypothesis (H_1) that states only that the population parameter is *different* from the one specified under H_0.

nonindependence The condition that exists when the occurrence of a given event affects the probability of the occurrence of another event.

normal curve A frequency curve with a characteristic bell-shaped form.

null hypothesis (H_0) A statement that specifies hypothesized values for one or more of the population parameters. It commonly, although not necessarily, involves the hypothesis of "no difference" and can be thought of as the hypothesis to be nullified by a statistical test.

ogive See *cumulative frequency curve.*

one-tailed probability (p) values Probability values obtained by examining only one tail of the distribution.

one-variable test ("goodness-of-fit" technique) A test of whether or not a significant difference exists between the *observed* number of cases falling into each category and the *expected* number of cases, based on the null hypothesis.

one-way analysis of variance A statistical analysis of various categories, groups, or levels of one independent (experimental) variable.

order of a conditional table The order of a table is the number of control or test variables that are included.

order of a partial correlation coefficient The order of a partial correlation coefficient indicates the number of control or test variables.

ordinal numbers Numbers used to represent position or order in a series.

ordinal scale A scale in which the classes can be rank ordered, that is, expressed in terms of the algebra of inequalities (e.g., $a < b$ or $a > b$).

ordinate (Y-axis) Vertical axis of a graph.

pair-by-pair comparison An approach to prediction for ordinal-level data in contingency form.

parameter Any characteristic of a population that is measurable.

partial correlation coefficient A measure of the linear relationship between two interval-level variables controlling for one or more other interval-level variables.

partial table See *conditional table.*

Pearson's r (product-moment correlation coefficient) A correlation coefficient used with interval- or ratio-scaled variables.

percentage A proportion that has been multiplied by 100.

percentage difference Differences in percentages normally measured between the two extreme categories of the independent variable within a category of the dependent variable. Also referred to as epsilon (ϵ).

percentile rank The number that represents the percentage of cases in a distribution that had scores at or lower than the one cited.

percentiles Numbers that divide a distribution into 100 equal parts. Same as a centile.

perfect relationship A relationship in which knowledge of the independent variable allows a perfect prediction of the dependent variable, or vice versa.
phi coefficient A nominal measure of association based on χ^2 used with 2×2 tables.
platykurtic distribution A frequency distribution characterized by a flattening in the central position.
point estimation An estimate of a population parameter that involves a single sample value selected by the criterion of "best estimate."
population A complete set of individuals, objects, or measurements having some common observable characteristic.
positively skewed distribution A distribution that has relatively fewer frequencies at the high end of the horizontal axis.
positive relationship High scores on one variable tend to be associated with high scores on the other; conversely, low scores on one variable tend to be associated with low scores on the other.
post hoc fallacy Faulty causal inferences from correlational data.
probability A theory concerned with possible outcomes of studies. Symbolically:

$$p(A) = \frac{\text{number of outcomes in which } A \text{ occurs}}{\text{total number of outcomes}}$$

proportion A value calculated by dividing the quantity in one category by the total of all the components.
proportional reduction in error (PRE) A ratio of the prediction errors without information about the independent variable to the prediction errors having information about the independent variable.
quartile A percentage rank that divides a distribution into four equal parts.
random sampling A method of selecting samples so that each sample of a given size in a population has an equal chance of being selected.
range A measure of dispersion; the scale distance between the largest and the smallest score.
rate A ratio of the occurrences in a group category to the total number of elements in the group with which we are concerned.
ratio The number of cases in one category divided by the number of cases in another category.
ratio scale Same as interval scale, except that there is a true zero point.
real limits See *true limits.*
regression line A straight line that best represents the linear relationship between two variables, X and Y.
regression sum of squares (Reg SS) See *explained variation.*
regression to the mean Individuals high or low on one testing are found to be closer to (regress toward) the mean on subsequent testing.
research design The plan for collecting data.
residual The size and direction of the error in prediction or the vertical distance from the observed data coordinate to the regression line.
residual sum of squares (RSS) See *unexplained variation.*
residual variance Variance around the regression line.
restricted range A truncated range on one or both variables resulting in a deceptively low correlation between these variables.
robust test A statistical test from which statistical inferences are likely to be valid even when there are fairly large departures from normality in the population distribution.
sample A subset or part of a population.
sampling distribution A theoretical probability distribution of a statistic that would result from drawing all possible samples of a given size from some population.

scatter diagram A graphic device used to summarize visually the relationship between two variables.

significance level A probability value that is considered so rare in the sampling distribution specified under the null hypothesis that one is willing to assert the operation of nonchance factors. Common signficance levels are 0.05 and 0.01, and 0.001.

sign test A nonparametric statistical test for ordinally scaled variables, used with matched or correlated samples. The sign test simply utilizes information concerning the *direction* of the differences between pairs of scores.

simple random sampling A method of selecting samples so that each sample of a given size in a population has an equal chance of being slected.

skewed distribution A distribution that departs from symmetry and tails off at one end.

Somer's *d* An asymmetrical measure of association for ordinal-level data that incorporates tied ranks.

Spearman's rho (r_s) A measure of association for ordinal-level data that provides a measure of the extent to which two sets of ranks are in agreement or disagreement.

spurious relationship Exists when the zero-order relationship between two variables disappears or becomes significantly weaker with the introduction of a control variable.

standard deviation A measure of dispersion defined as the square root of the sum of the squared deviations from the mean, divided by *N*. Also can be defined as the square root of the variance.

standard error of estimate Standard deviation of scores around the regression line.

standard error of the mean ($s_{\bar{X}}$) A theoretical standard deviation of sample means, of a given sample size, drawn from some specified population. When based on a known population standard deviation, $\sigma_{\bar{X}} = \sigma/\sqrt{N}$; when estimated from a single sample, $s_{\bar{X}} = s/\sqrt{N-1}$.

standard error of the proportion An estimate of the standard deviation of the sampling distribution of proportions.

standard normal distribution A frequency distribution that has a mean of 0, a standard deviation of 1, and a total area equal to 1.00.

standard score (z) A score that represents the deviation of a specific score from the mean, expressed in standard deviation units.

statistic A number that describes a characteristic of a sample.

statistical elaboration The process of introducing a control variable to determine whether a bivariate relationship remains the same or varies under the different categories or conditions of the control variable.

statistics A collection of numerical facts expressed in summarizing statements; method of dealing with data: a tool for collecting, organizing, and analyzing numerical facts or observations that are collected in accordance with a systematic plan.

stratified random selection A method of random sampling in which sub-groups in the population are identified and randomly sampled.

sum of squares Deviations from the mean, squared and then summed.

sum of squares for explained variance in *Y* See *explained variation.*

sum of squares for unexplained variance in *Y* See *unexplained variation.*

symmetric measure of association A measure of the mutual association between two variables.

systematic selection A method of sampling in which individuals are selected from a list at equal intervals.

***t*-distributions or Student's *t*-distributions** Theoretical symmetrical sampling distributions with a mean of zero and a standard deviation that becomes smaller as degrees of freedom (df) increase. Used in relation to the Student *t*-ratio.

test variable See *control variable.*

***t*-ratio** A test statistic for determining the significance of a difference between means (two-sample case) or for testing the hypothesis that a given sample mean was drawn from a population with the mean specified under the null hypothesis (one-sample case). Used when population standard deviation (or standard deviations) is unknown.

tied pair Two cases are ranked similarly on one or both of two variables.

total sum of squares (TSS) Variation of scores around the sample mean. Same as the total variation.

total sum of squares for *Y* *See total sum of squares.*

total variation See *total sum of squares.*

tree diagram A method for illustrating the sequence of several events. The outcome of each event has two or more alternatives.

true limits of a number The true limits of a value of a continuous variable are equal to that number plus or minus one-half of the unit of measurement. Sometimes referred to as *real limits.*

truncated range See *restricted range.*

two-tailed probability (*p*) values Probability values that take into account both tails of the distribution.

type I error (type α error) The rejection of H_0 when it is actually true. The probability of a type I error is given by the α-level.

type II error (type β error) The probability of accepting H_0 when it is actually false. The probability of a type II error is given by β.

unbiased estimate of a parameter An estimate that equals, on the average, the value of the corresponding parameter.

unconditional probability See *marginal probability.*

unexplained variation Variation of scores around the regression line. Same as the residual sum of squares.

ungrouped frequency distribution Shows the number of times each score occurs when the values of a variable are arranged in order according to their magnitudes.

variable Any characteristic of a person, group, or environment that can vary or denotes a difference.

variance The sum of the squared deviations from the mean, divided by N.

variance estimate See *mean square.*

weighted mean The sum of the mean of each group multiplied by its respective weight (the N in each group), divided by the sum of the weights (total N).

Wilcoxon matched-pairs signed-rank test A nonparametric statistical test for ordinally scaled variables used with matched or correlated samples; more powerful than the sign test since it utilizes information concerning the *magnitude* of the differences between pairs of scores.

within-group sum of squares (SS_w) A sum of the sum of squares within each group.

within-group variance An estimate of variability based on variance within groups.

APPENDIX E

References

From American Bar Foundation to World Population Data Sheet of the Population Reference Bureau

American Bar Foundation. *The Lawyer Statistical Report: A Statistical Profile of the U.S. Legal Profession in the 1980s.* Chicago: American Bar Foundation, 1985.

Anas, N.; V. Namasthoni; and M. Ginsburg. "Criteria for Hospitalizing Children Who Have Ingested Products Containing Hydrocarbons." *Journal of the American Medical Association,* no. 246 (1981), pp. 840–43.

Auble, D. "Extended Tables for the Mann-Whitney Statistic." *Bulletin of the Institute of Educational Research at Indiana University* 1, no. 2 (1953).

Benson, P. L.; S. A. Karabenick; and R. M. Lerner. "Pretty Pleases: The Effects of Physical Attractiveness, Race, and Sex on Receiving Help." *Journal of Experimental Social Psychology* 12 (1976), pp. 409–15.

Bentler, P. M., and M. D. Newcomb. "Longitudinal Study of Marital Success and Failure," *Journal of Consulting and Clinical Psychology* 46 (1978), pp. 1053–70.

Berenson, W. M.; K. W. Elifson; and T. Tollerson, III. "Preachers in Politics: A Study of Political Activism among the Black Ministry." *Journal of Black Studies* 6 (1976), pp. 373–83.

Bingham, W. V. *Aptitudes and Aptitude Testing.* New York: Harper and Bros., 1937.

Black Elected Officials: A National Roster. Washington, D.C.: Joint Center for Population Studies, annual.

Blalock, H. M. *Social Statistics,* 2d ed. New York: McGraw-Hill, 1979.

Bohmer, P., and S. Sitton. "The Influence of Birth Order and Family Size on Notable American Women's Selection of Careers." *Psychological Record* 43 (1993), pp. 375–80.

Caballero, C. M.; P. Giles; and P. Shaver. "Sex-Role Traditionalism and Fear of Success." *Sex Roles* 1 (1975), pp. 319–26.

Cassileth, B.; et al. "Psychological Status in Chance Illness." *New England Journal of Medicine* 311 (1984), pp. 506–10.

Centers for Disease Control and Prevention. *Vital Statistics of the United States.* Vol. 11, *Mortality,* Part A, Public Health Service. Washington D.C.: U.S. Government Printing Office, 1993.

Cowens, E. L. "Help Is Where You Find It." *American Psychologist* 37 (1982), pp. 385–95.

Davis, James Allan and Smith,Tom W.: *General Social Surveys, 1972–1994.*

Digest of Educational Statistics, 1977–1978. National Center for Education Statistics, 1979.

Dunlap, J. W., and A. K. Kurtz. *Handbook of Statistical Nomographs, Tables, and Formulas.* New York: World Book Company, 1932.

Edwards, A. L. *Statistical Analysis,* 3d ed. New York: Holt, Rinehart and Winston, 1969.

Elifson, K. W.; D. M. Petersen; and C. K. Hadaway. "Religion and Delinquency: A Contextual Analysis." *Criminology* 21 (1983), pp. 505–27.

Feinstein, A. R.; D. M. Sosin; and C. K. Wells. "The Will Rogers Phenomenon: Stage Migration and New Diagnostic Techniques as a Source of Misleading Statistics for Survival in Cancer." *New England Journal of Medicine* 12, no. 25 (1985), pp. 1604–08.

Fisher, R. A. *Statistical Methods for Research Workers.* Edinburgh: Oliver and Boyd, 1950.

Fisher, R. A., and F. Yates. *Statistical Tables for Biological, Agricultural, and Medical Research,* 6th ed. London: Longman, 1974.

Freeman, S.; M. R. Walker; R. Borden; and B. Latane. "Diffusion of Responsibility and Restaurant Tipping: Cheaper by the Bunch." *Personality and Social Psychology Bulletin* 1 (1975), pp. 584–87.

Friedman, E. "Pet Ownership and Coronary Heart Disease Patient Survival." *Circulation,* no. 168 (1978), pp. 57–58.

Gerard, H. B.; R. A. Wilhelmy; and E. S. Conolley. "Conformity and Group Size." *Journal of Personality and Social Psychology* 8 (1968), pp. 79–82.

Henkel, R. E. "Part-Whole Correlations and the Treatment of Ordinal and Quasi-Interval Data as Interval Data." *Pacific Sociological Review* (1975), pp. 3–26.

Henry, G. *Practical Sampling.* Newbury Park, CA: Sage Publications, 1990.

Huff, D. *How to Lie with Statistics.* New York: W. W. Norton, 1954.

Hyde, J. S.; Fennema, E.; and Lamon, S. J. and "Gender Differences in Mathematics Performance. A Meta-Analysis." *Psychological Bulletin* 107 (1990), pp. 139–55.

Kiesler, S., and T. Finholt. "The Mystery of RSI." *American Psychologist* 43 (1988), pp. 1004–15.

Labovitz, S. "The Assignment of Numbers to Rank Order Categories." *American Sociological Review* 35:515–24.

Langan, P. A., and C. A. Innes. "The Risk of Violent Crime." *Bureau of Justice Statistics Special Report,* NCJ-97119, 1985.

Mann, H. B., and D. R. Whitney. "On a Test of Whether One of Two Random Variables Is Stochastically Larger Than the Other." *Annals of Mathematical Statistics* 18 (1947), pp. 52–54.

McNemar, Q. *Psychological Statistics.* New York: John Wiley and Sons, 1962.

Meyer, G. E., and K. Hilterbrand. "Does It Pay to Be "Bashful"? The Seven Dwarfs and Long-Term Memory." *American Journal of Psychology* 97 (1984), pp. 47–55.

Milgram, S.; L. Bickman; and L. Berkowitz. "Note on the Drawing Power of Crowds." *Journal of Personality and Social Psychology* 13 (1969), pp. 79–82.

Milligan, G. W.; D. S. Wong; and P. A. Thompson. "Robustness Properties of Nonorthogonal Analysis of Variance." *Psychological Bulletin* 101 (1987), pp. 464–70.

National Center for Education Statistics. *120 Years of American Education: A Statistical Portrait.* Washington, D.C.: National Center for Education Statistics, 1993.

Olds, E. G. "The 5 Percent Significance Levels of Sums of Squares of Rank Differences and a Correction." *Annals of Mathematical Statistics* 20 (1949), pp. 117–18.

O'Leary, K. D.; et al. "Prevalence and Stability of Physical Aggression between Spouses: A Longitudinal Analysis." *Journal of Consulting and Clinical Psychology* 57 (1989), pp. 263–68.

Pearson, E. S., and H. O. Hartley. *Biometrika Tables for Statisticians*, vol. 1, 2d ed. New York: Cambridge University Press, 1958.

Platt, R.; B. F. Polk; B. Murdock; and B. Rosner. "Mortality Associated with Nosocomial Urinary-Tract Infection." *New England Journal of Medicine* 307 (1982), pp. 637–41.
Rand Corporation. *A Million Random Digits.* Glencoe, IL: Free Press, 1955.
Ravenholt, R. T. Letter to the editor. *New England Journal of Medicine* (1982), pp. 307–12.
Ruback, R. N., and C.A. Innes. "The Relevance and Irrelevance of Psychological Research. The Examples of Prison Crowding." *American Psychologist* 43 (1988), pp. 683–702.
________. *Non-Parametric Statistics.* Reading, MA: Addison-Wesley, 1977.
Runyon, R. P. "A Statistical Sampling Experiment." Chap. 7 of *Fundamentals of Statistics in the Biological, Medical, and Health Sciences.* Boston: Duxbury Press, 1985.
________. *Winning with Statistics.* Reading, MA: Addison-Wesley, 1977.
Seiden, R. H. "Campus Tragedy: A Story of Student Suicide." *Journal of Abnormal Social Psychology* 71, pp. 389–99.
Siegel, S., and N. J. Castellan, Jr. *Nonparametric Statistics,* 2d ed. New York: McGraw-Hill, 1988.
Snedecor, G. W., and W. G. Cochran. *Statistical Methods,* 6th ed. Ames: Iowa State University Press, 1956.
Thorton, B. "Toward a Linear Prediction Model of Marital Happiness." *Personality and Social Psychology Bulletin* 3 (1977), pp. 674–76.
Tukey, J. W. *The Problem of Multiple Comparisons.* Princeton, NJ: Princeton University, 1953.
U.S. Bureau of the Census. *The Social and Economic Status of the African-American Population in the United States: An Historical View, 1790–1978,* Series P-23, no. 80, *Current Population Reports.*
U.S. Bureau of the Census. *City and County Data Book.* Washington, D.C., 1994.
U.S. Bureau of the Census. *Statistical Abstract of the United States, 1995,* 115th ed. Washington, D.C., 1995.
U.S. Bureau of the Census. U.S. Census of the Population, *Current Population Reports* and unpublished data.
U.S. Bureau of Prisons. *Statistical Report.* Washington, D.C., annual.
U.S. Center for Health Statistics. *Vital Statistics of the United States.* Washington, D.C., annual.
U.S. Congressional Directory. Washington, D.C., biannual.
U.S. Department of Commerce. *Social Indicators.* Washington, D.C., annual.
U.S. Department of Defense. *Selected Manpower Statistics.* Washington, D.C., annual.
U.S. Federal Bureau of Investigation. *Crime in the United States.* Washington, D.C., annual.
________. *Uniform Crime Reports.* Washington, D.C., 1994.
U.S. Department of Labor. *Working Women: A Chartbook.* Bulletin 2385. Washington, D.C., 1991.
U.S. Department of Labor, Bureau of Labor Statistics. *Bureau of Labor Statistics Bulletin.* Washington, D.C., monthly.
________. *Current Wage Developments.* Washington, D.C., monthly.
U.S. Immigration and Naturalization Service. Washington, D.C., annual report.
U.S. Merit System Protection Board. *Sexual Harassment in the Federal Work Place: Trends, Progress, Continuing Challenges.* Washington, D.C., 1995.
Van Bree, N. S. "Undergraduate Research." *Nursing Outlook,* January 1981, pp. 39–41.
Wilcoxon, F.; S. Katti; and R. A. Wilcox. *Critical Values and Probability Levels for the Wilcoxon Rank Sum Test and the Wilcoxon Signed Rank Test.* New York: American Cyanamid Co., 1963.
Wilcoxon, F., and R. A. Wilcox. *Some Rapid Approximate Statistical Procedures.* New York: Lederle Laboratories. 1964.
World Health Organization. *World Health Statistics,* annual.
World Population Data Sheet of the Population Reference Bureau, 1996.

PART VI

Answers to Selected Exercises

Answers to Selected Exercises

From Chapter 1 to Chapter 17

In problems involving many steps, you may occasionally find a discrepancy between the answers you obtained and those shown here. Where the discrepancies are small, they are probably due to rounding errors. These disparities are more common today because of the wide differences in methods used; that is, varying degrees of sophistication among computers, calculators, and hand calculations.

Chapter 1

1. (*a*) Constant (*b*) Variable (*c*) Constant (*d*) Variable (*e*) Constant (*f*) Variable (*g*) Constant (*h*) Variable (*i*) Constant

3. (*a*) No

(*b*) Increases could result from greater availability of illicit drugs, purer illicit drugs, and media information that downplays the dangers of illicit drug use for pregnant women. Decreases could follow a lessened availability of illicit drugs or recent legislation that allows authorities to take addicted infants from their mother or guardian.

5. These are not statistics, but data. Statistics that may be calculated from these data include proportion or percentage of passes completed by each team, proportion or percentage of yards gained on the ground or in the air, proportion or percentage of time of possession. (See Chapter 2 for a discussion of proportions and percentages.)

7. (*b*) Variable

9. (*b*) Statistic

11. (*a*) Parameter

13. For example, did you exclude men, women, or anyone else?

15. (*a*) Single women, public officials and personalities, the very rich, and those persons not in the current directory due to change of address, and so on, are among those who tend to have unlisted numbers and hence would be underrepresented.

(*b*) Random digit dialing procedures would provide a more representative sample because all persons with active telephone numbers would have a chance of being included in the sample.

17. It would be impossible because no comprehensive list of residents is available in any major U.S. city.

19. (*a*) Statistic (*b*) Inference from a statistic (*c*) Data
(*d*) Data (*e*) Inference from a statistic

Chapter 2

1. (*a*) 149 (*b*) 16 (*c*) 87 (*d*) −392

3. Given: $N = 4$
$20 + N = Y + 2$
Therefore: $20 + 4 = Y + 2$
$24 = Y + 2$
$Y = 22$

5. $N = 4$

7. $$s^2 = \frac{\Sigma(X - \overline{X})^2}{N}$$

$$s^2 = \frac{240}{12}$$

$$s^2 = 20$$

9. $$\sum_{i=1}^{N} X_i^2 = 4^2 + 5^2 + 7^2 + 9^2 + 10^2 + 11^2 + 14^2 = 588$$

$$\left(\sum_{i=1}^{N} X_i\right)^2 = (4 + 5 + 7 + 9 + 10 + 11 + 14)^2 = 60^2 = 3600$$

$588 \neq 3600$

11. (*a*) Nominal (*b*) Ordinal (*c*) Nominal (*d*) Ordinal (*e*) Ratio

13. (*a*) Continuous (*b*) Discrete (*c*) Continuous (*d*) Discrete (*e*) Discrete

15. (*a*) 100.00 (*b*) 46.41 (*c*) 2.96 (*d*) 0.01
(*e*) 16.46 (*f*) 1.05 (*g*) 86.21 (*h*) 10.00

17.

	African-American and white males	African-American and white females	Total
1982	17,350	3,922	21,272
1992	19,587	5,199	24,786

(*a*) Using these figures, which were calculated using the original data, the male : female ratio can be calculated by year.

1982 $$\frac{17{,}350}{3{,}922} = 4.42$$
Therefore, the male : female ratio is 4.42 : 1

1992 $$\frac{19{,}587}{5{,}199} = 3.77$$
Therefore, the male : female ratio is 3.77 : 1

(*b*) The calculations below are based on the original data and show the male : female ratio by race and year.

	Whites	African Americans
1982	$\frac{9{,}620}{2{,}179} = 4.41$, or 4.41 : 1	$\frac{7{,}730}{1{,}743} = 4.43$, or 4.43 : 1
1992	$\frac{9{,}456}{3{,}012} = 3.14$, or 3.14 : 1	$\frac{10{,}131}{2{,}187} = 4.63$, or 4.63 : 1

19. 20.13 million are less than 15 and 18.87 million are over 64.

$$\frac{20.13 + 18.87}{86.80} \times 100 = 44.93$$

21. (*a*) For example, to calculate women's earnings in 1960 as a percentage of men's earnings in 1960, you must divide the women's earnings in 1960 by the men's earnings in 1960 and convert the resulting proportion to a percentage by multiplying by 100. Thus:

$$\frac{3{,}293}{5{,}417} = 0.6079 \times 100 = 60.8\%$$

(*b*) To determine the percentage change of women's earnings from 1960 to 1975, you must use equation (2.3). The value for time 1 for the women will be 3,293 and the value for time 2 will be 7,504. Thus:

$$\frac{t_2 - t_1}{t_1} \times 100 = \frac{7{,}504 - 3{,}293}{3293} \times 100$$

$$= +1.2788 \times 100$$

$$= +127.88\%$$

(c) The percentage change of men's earnings from 1960 to 1975 is +135.52%.

23. time 1 = 38 + 25 = 63
time 2 = 38

Using equation (2.3) $\frac{38 - 63}{63} \times 100 = -39.68\%$

25. (*a*) −19.69%
(*b*) +80.31%

27. (*a*)

Percentage of females	
Business administration	20.00%
Education	75.00
Humanities	57.14
Science	28.57
Social science	50.00

(*b*)	(*c*)	(*d*)
38.10%	13.33%	58.33% are males
4.76	20.00	41.67% are females
14.29	26.67	
23.81	13.33	
19.05	26.67	

29.

	Population per lawyer	Lawyers per 1,000
Alaska	297	3.37
Arkansas	717	1.39
California	365	2.74
D.C.	25	39.91
Georgia	493	2.03
Illinois	352	2.84
New York	280	3.57

Chapter 3

1.

	True limits	Width	Midpoint
(*a*)	7.5–12.5	5	10
(*b*)	5.5–7.5	2	6.5
(*c*)	(−0.5)–(+2.5)	3	1
(*d*)	4.5–14.5	10	9.5
(*e*)	(−8.5)–(−1.5)	7	−5
(*f*)	2.45–3.55	1.1	3
(*g*)	1.495–1.755	0.26	1.625
(*h*)	(−3.5)–(+3.5)	7	0

3.

Class intervals	True limits	Midpoint	*f*	Cumulative *f*	Cumulative %
40–44	39.5–44.5	42	1	1	2.5
45–49	44.5–49.5	47	1	2	5.0
50–54	49.5–54.5	52	1	3	7.5
55–59	54.5–59.5	57	0	3	7.5
60–64	59.5–64.5	62	3	6	15.0
65–69	64.5–69.5	67	3	9	22.5
70–74	69.5–74.5	72	4	13	32.5
75–79	74.5–79.5	77	11	24	60.0
80–84	79.5–84.5	82	8	32	80.0
85–89	84.5–89.5	87	4	36	90.0
90–94	89.5–94.5	92	3	39	97.5
95–99	94.5–99.5	97	1	40	100.0

5. (*a*) and (*b*). The following grouped frequency distribution would be one possible solution.

Class intervals	*f*	True limits
37–41	1	36.5–41.5
42–46	3	41.5–46.5
47–51	2	46.5–51.5
52–56	2	51.5–56.5
57–61	1	56.5–61.5
62–66	1	61.5–66.5
67–71	3	66.5–71.5

(*concluded*)

Class intervals	*f*	True limits
72–76	0	71.5–76.5
77–81	10	76.5–81.5
82–86	8	81.5–86.5
87–91	3	86.5–91.5
92–96	5	91.5–96.5
97–101	1	96.5–101.5

(*c*) The number of clients per caseload ranges from 37 to 98, and the majority of the 40 caseloads are very large.

7. Constructing a grouped frequency distribution from ungrouped scores can provide a meaningful and concise summary of the raw scores. Creating categories is impractical if there are few scores or if each of the raw score values has a high frequency of occurrence.

9.

Class intervals	*f*
3–7	1
8–12	0
13–17	5
18–22	0
23–27	9
28–32	0
33–37	14
38–42	0
43–47	11
48–52	0
53–57	7
58–62	0
63–67	3

11.

Class intervals	*f*
4–5	1
6–7	0
8–9	0
10–11	0
12–13	1
14–15	2
16–17	2
18–19	0
20–21	0
22–23	2
24–25	3
26–27	4
28–29	0
30–31	0
32–33	3
34–35	4
36–37	7
38–39	0
40–41	0
42–43	2
44–45	7
46–47	2

(concluded)

Class intervals	f
48–49	0
50–51	0
52–53	2
54–55	3
56–57	2
58–59	0
60–61	0
62–63	1
64–65	1
66–67	1

13.

Class intervals	f	cum f	%	cum %
0–2	0	0	0.0	0.0
3–5	17	17	34.0	34.0
6–8	15	32	30.0	64.0
9–11	8	40	16.0	80.0
12–14	4	44	8.0	88.0
15–17	3	47	6.0	94.0
18–20	1	48	2.0	96.0
21–23	1	49	2.0	98.0
24–26	0	49	0.0	98.0
27–29	1	50	2.0	100.0

(*a*) Histogram of number of previous arrests for 50 inmates at a state prison.

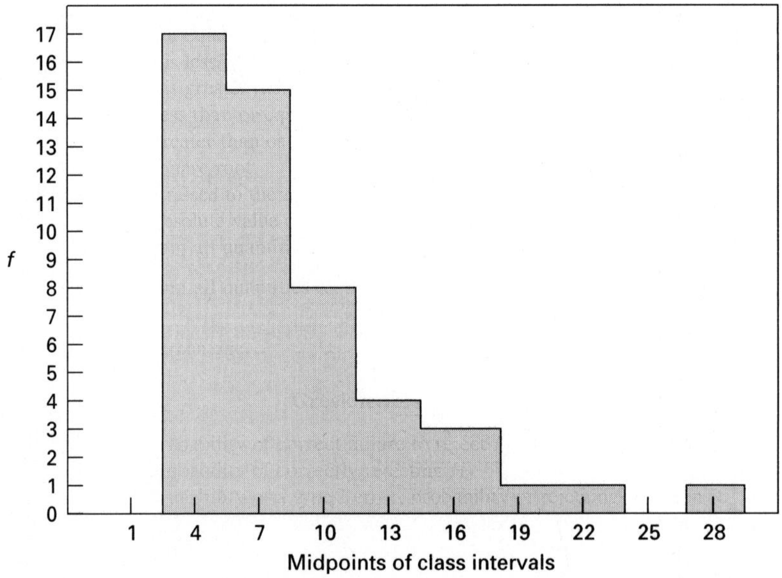

(*b*) Frequency curve of number of previous arrests for 50 inmates at a state prison

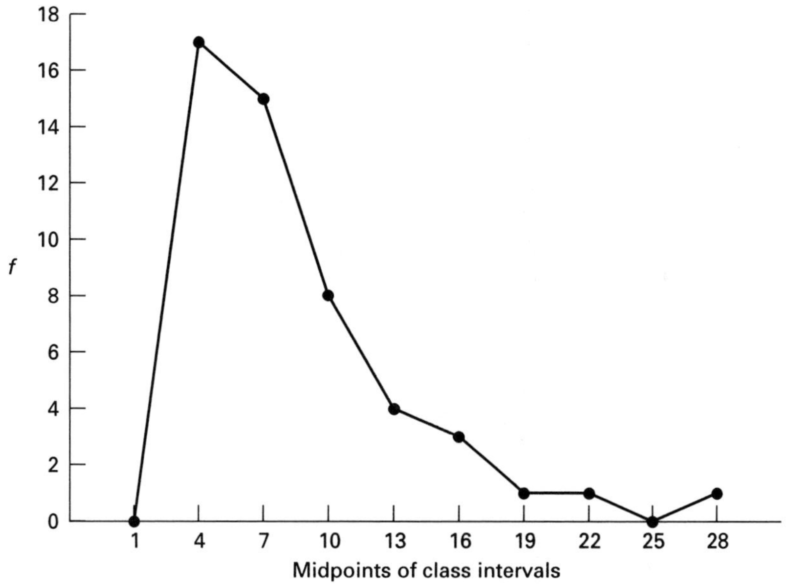

(*c*) Cumulative frequency curve of number of previous arrests for 50 inmates at a state prison

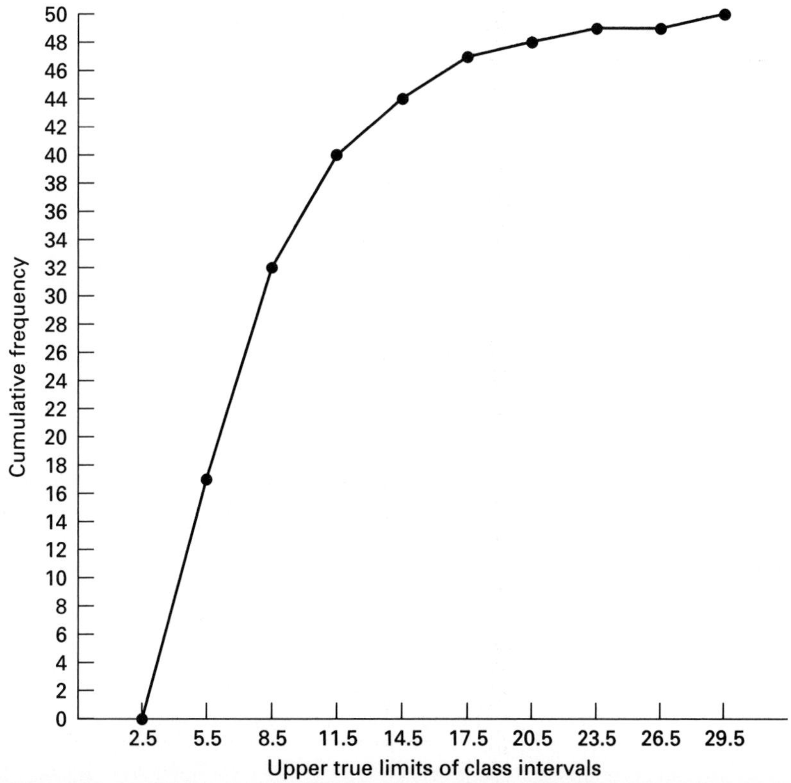

15. (*a*) positively skewed (*b*) normal (*c*) normal (*d*) bimodal

17.

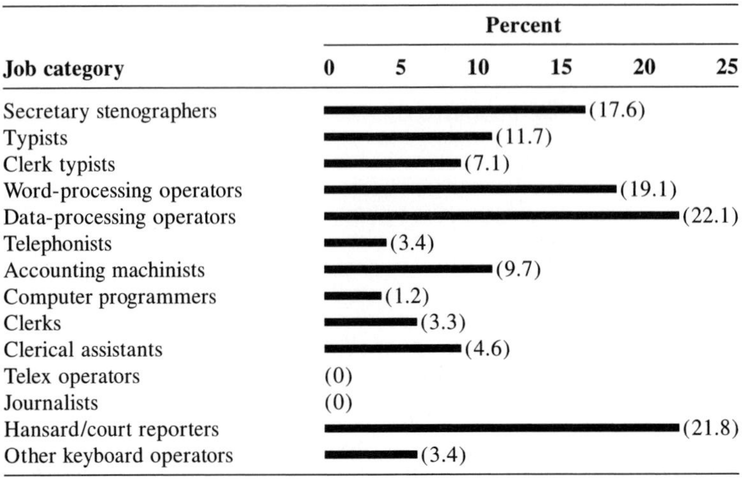

19.

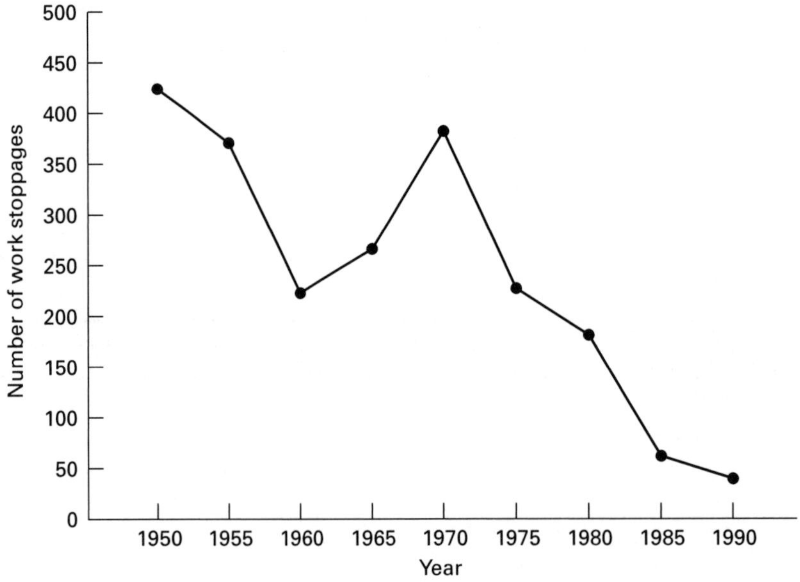

The number of work stoppages has declined markedly since 1970.

21. (*a*) and (*b*)

Age	Proportion of white suicides	Proportion of white homicides	Proportion of African-American suicides	Proportion of African-American homicides
15–24	0.2273	0.2400	0.1852	0.2089
25–34	0.4545	0.5200	0.5926	0.6329
35–44	0.2045	0.2000	0.1852	0.1266
45–54	0.0682	0.0400	0.0370	0.0253
55–64	0.0227	0.0000	0.0000	0.0063
65–74	0.0227	0.0000	0.0000	0.0000
Totals	1.0000	1.0000	1.0000	1.0000

(*c*)

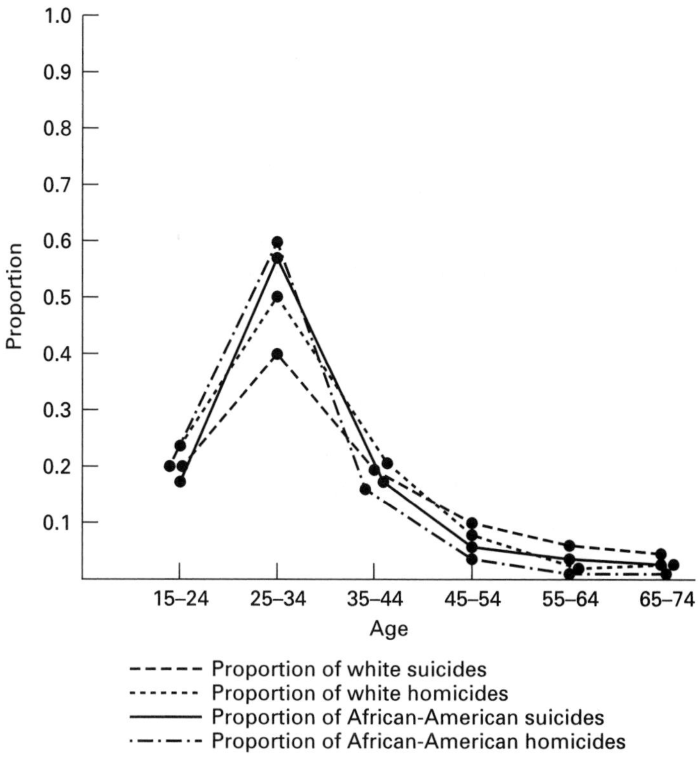

Chapter 4

1. A percentile rank is the percentage of scores that are at or below a given score. Using the percentile rank we are able to convert a test score into a score that will reflect its relative position in a distribution.
3. (*a*) Using equation (4.2), we obtain:

$$\text{percentile rank of 1} = 0 + \frac{\left(\frac{1 - (-0.5)}{5}\right)(19.7)}{259.6} \times 100$$

$$= 0 + \frac{\left(\frac{1.5}{5}\right)(19.7)}{259.6} \times 100$$

$$= 0.02277 \times 100$$

$$= 2.28$$

5. (*a*) First, calculate the cum f of the score at the 25th percentile.

$$\text{cum} f = \frac{\text{percentile rank} \times N}{100}$$

$$= \frac{25 \times 259.6}{100} = 64.9$$

Second, calculate the age at the 25th percentile.

$$\text{score at a given percentile} = X_{ll} + \frac{i(\text{cum } f - \text{cum } f_{ll})}{f_i}$$

$$= 14.5 + \frac{5(64.9 - 57.4)}{17.6} = 16.63$$

7. (*a*) Using equation (4.2), we obtain:

$$\text{percentile rank of an inmate arrested six times} = \frac{17 + \left(\frac{6 - 5.5}{3}\right)(15.0)}{50} \times 100$$

$$= 39.0$$

(*b*) $Q_1 = C_{25}$; therefore, using equation (4.3), we get:

$$\text{cum} f = \frac{25 \times 50}{100} = 12.5$$

Using equation (4.4), we have:

$$\text{score at the 25th percentile} = 2.5 + \frac{3(12.5 - 0)}{17}$$

$$= 4.7 \text{ arrests}$$

9.

Interval	f	cum f	%	cum %
0–2	12	12	33.3	33.3
3–5	10	22	27.8	61.1
6–8	9	31	25.0	86.1
9–11	5	36	13.9	100.0

(*a*) We wish to find the score corresponding to a percentile rank of 75 (Q_3).

$$\text{cum } f = \frac{75 \times 36}{100} = 27$$

Using equation (4.4), we obtain:

$$\text{score at the 75th percentile} = 5.5 + \frac{3(27 - 22)}{9}$$

$$= 7.17$$

Therefore, any score above 7.17 would be above the 3rd quartile.

11. A. 88.8, B. 77.2, C. 25.6, D. 61.6, E. 42.0, F. 42.0, G. 96.4, H. 61.6, I. 77.2, J. 13.2, K. 77.2, L. 61.6, M. 4.8, N. 25.6, O. 88.8, P. 42.0, Q. 25.6, R. 4.8, S. 0.4, T. 13.2, U. 42.0, V. 13.2, W. 61.6, X. 25.6, Y. 42.0

13. (*a*) 35th percentile
(*b*) 77th percentile
(*c*) cannot be calculated since the class is open-ended. The class "7 or more persons" is open-ended.

15. (*a*)

Sum of two scores	f
0	1
1	2
2	3
3	4
4	5
5	6
6	7
7	6
8	5
9	4
10	3
11	2
12	1
	$N = 49$

(*b*)

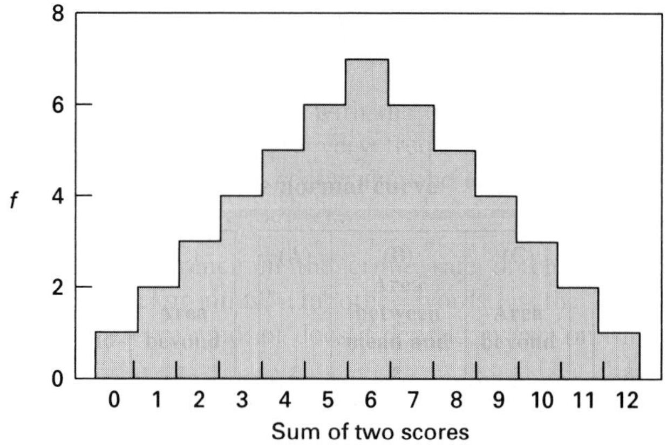

(*c*) Both distributions are symmetrical and bell-shaped.

Chapter 5

1. (*a*) Using equation (5.1)

$$\bar{X} = \frac{\Sigma X}{N} = \frac{10 + 8 + 6 + 0 + 8 + 3 + 2 + 5 + 8 + 0}{10}$$

$$\bar{X} = \frac{50}{10}$$

$$\bar{X} = 5$$

$$\text{Median location} = \frac{N + 1}{2} = \frac{10 + 1}{2} = 5.5$$

Place the scores into an array:

0, 0, 2, 3, 5, 6, 8, 8, 8, 10

$$\text{Median} = \frac{5 + 6}{2} = 5.5$$

The mode = 8 which is the most frequently occurring score.
(*b*) $\overline{X} = 5.0$ median = 5.0 mode = 5.0
(*c*) $\overline{X} = 17.5$ median = 4.0 mode = 4

3. All measures of central tendency will be multiplied by 100.

5. Using equation (5.3)

$$\overline{X} = \frac{\Sigma f X_m}{N} = \frac{4390}{110} = 39.91$$

$$M_0 = 42 \text{ (midpoint of the class interval 40–44)}$$

$$\text{median} = 42$$

Hint: Compute the cumulative frequency for Table 3.3, find the location of the middle frequency, and select the midpoint of the class in which the middle frequency occurs.

Note that when calculating measures of central tendency from the same data set in both an ungrouped and a grouped frequency distribution, the values may differ. The mean will equal 39.88 and the median and mode will equal 40.00 if they are calculated from Table 3.2.

7. (*a*) $\overline{X} <$ Median; therefore negative skew
(*b*) $\overline{X} >$ Median; therefore positive skew
(*c*) $\overline{X} =$ Median; therefore no skew
(*d*) $\overline{X} =$ Median; therefore no skew, 2 modes, therefore bimodal

9. $\overline{X} = 5.0$ (*a*) $\overline{X} = 7.0$ (*b*) $\overline{X} = 3.0$ (*c*) $\overline{X} = 26.7$
(*d*) $\overline{X} = 10$ (*e*) $\overline{X} = 2.5$

11. The distribution is symmetrical.

13. (*a*) $\overline{X}_w = \dfrac{\Sigma f \overline{X}}{N_t} = \dfrac{15{,}099}{210} = 71.9$

(*b*) There does not appear to be a relationship between class size and mean grades on the final examination.

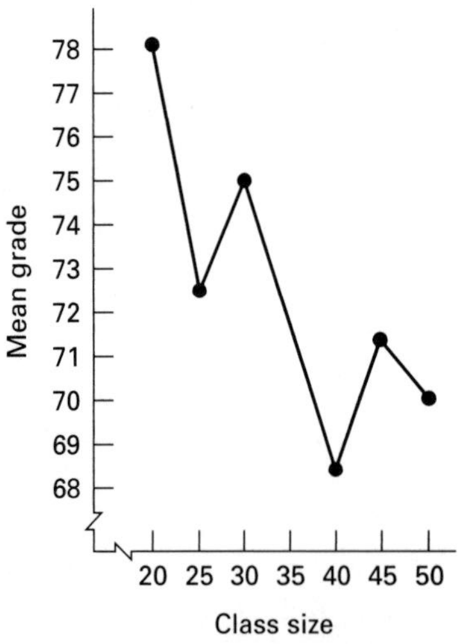

15. Raise median: (c)
Raise mean: (b)

17. 3.04

19.

Age	Sex	Attitude toward pornography
Mean = 39.1		Mean = 29.7
Median = 36		Median = 27
Mode = 21	Mode = *F*	Mode = 24

21.

1950	$\bar{X}$ = 4,004.7
1955	$\bar{X}$ = 5,661.2
1960	$\bar{X}$ = 4,036.0
1965	$\bar{X}$ = 3,727.6
1970	$\bar{X}$ = 6,477.7
1975	$\bar{X}$ = 4,106.4
1980	$\bar{X}$ = 4,251.3
1985	$\bar{X}$ = 6,000.0
1990	$\bar{X}$ = 4,204.5

There does not appear to be a consistent trend other than the mean number of workers involved in work stoppages from 1950 to 1990 has ranged between 4,000 and 6,500.

23. (*a*)

X_1	X_2	X_3	Mean	Median
6	6	2	4.7	6.0
4	1	1	2.0	1.0
6	5	5	5.3	5.0
6	4	3	4.3	4.0
4	2	1	2.3	2.0
5	4	3	4.0	4.0
4	4	3	3.7	4.0
6	6	4	5.3	6.0
5	3	2	3.3	3.0
6	3	3	4.0	3.0

X_1	X_2	X_3	Mean	Median
4	3	2	3.0	3.0
6	4	1	3.7	4.0
6	4	2	4.0	4.0
5	1	1	2.3	1.0
6	5	4	5.0	5.0
2	1	1	1.3	1.0
5	4	3	4.0	4.0
5	4	4	4.3	4.0
4	3	1	2.7	3.0
4	2	2	2.7	2.0

X_1	X_2	X_3	Mean	Median
6	5	3	4.7	5.0
5	1	1	2.3	1.0
6	5	2	4.3	5.0
6	3	3	4.0	3.0
6	6	5	5.7	6.0
6	5	4	5.0	5.0
6	2	1	3.0	2.0
5	4	3	4.0	4.0
5	4	1	3.3	4.0
6	3	1	3.3	3.0

(*b*)

	Means f	Medians f
1	1	4
2	4	3
3	7	6
4	11	9
5	6	5
6	1	3

23. (*c*)

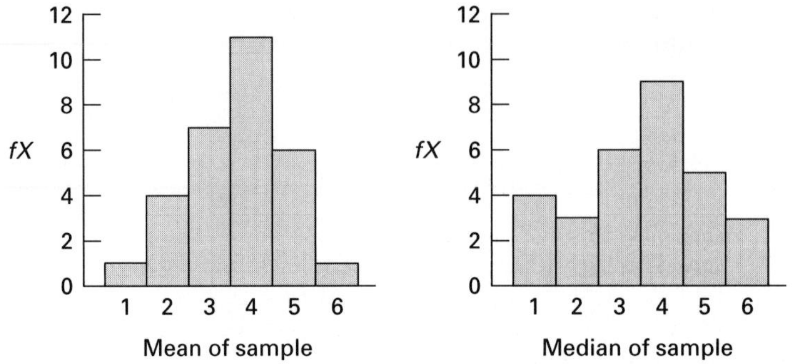

(*d*)

(i) If we put all 30 sample means and medians into separate hats, the probability of selecting a mean of 5.5 or greater is 1/30 or 3.33%. The probability of selecting a median of 5.5 or greater is 3/30 or 10%.

(ii) If we put all 30 sample means and medians into separate hats, the probability of selecting a mean of 1.5 or less is 1/30 or 3.33%. The probability of selecting a median of 1.5 or less is 4/30 or 13.33%.

(iii) If we put all 30 sample means and medians into separate hats, the probability of selecting a mean of 1.5 or less or a mean greater than 5.5 is 2/30 or 6.66%. The probability of selecting a median of 1.5 or less or a median greater than 5.5 is 7/30 or 23.33%.

Chapter 6

1. $s^2 = 1.66$; $s = 1.29$ (*a*) No change (*b*) Increase

3. (*a*) 3.5 (*b*) 2.3 (*c*) 5.9 (*d*) 0.0

5. (*a*) 10 (*b*) 8 (*c*) 20 (*d*) 0
The range is a misleading measure of variability when an extreme score is included in the data (see *c*, which includes a 20 among several smaller scores).

7. $\overline{X} = 746.67$
$s = 703.91$
$s^2 = 495{,}489.3$

9. $s = 1.64$
$s^2 = 2.69$

11. Class II had the most variability and Class I had the least.

13. The class in which the lecturer was present achieved the highest mean final examination score. It is quite possible that a few individual students in the experimental group achieved a higher score on the final examination than anyone in the control group.

15. Neighborhood *A*; $s = 4.34$; $\overline{X} = 36.3$ (most homogeneous)
Neighborhood *B*; $s = 8.36$; $\overline{X} = 83.2$ (most affluent)
Neighborhood *C*; $s = 17.74$; $\overline{X} = 37.5$ (most heterogeneous)
Neighborhood *D*; $s = 5.32$; $\overline{X} = 14.8$ (least affluent)

17. $s = 1{,}131.8$
$s^2 = 1{,}280{,}958.5$

Chapter 7

1. (*a*) 0.94 (*b*) −0.40 (*c*) 0.00 (*d*) −1.32 (*e*) 2.23 (*f*) −2.53

3. (*a*) 0.0202 (*c*) 0.4013 (*e*) 0.0495
(*b*) 0.0287 (*d*) 0.3446 (*f*) 0.0250

5. (*a*) Arithmetic: $z = 1.21$; verbal comprehension: $z = 0.77$; geography: $z = -0.29$
(*b*) Arithmetic; geography
(*c*) 0.1131, 0.2206, 0.6141
(*d*) We must assume the data are normally distributed.
(*e*) 62.53

7. a, b, c, and e

9. (*a*) $\mu = 72$, $\sigma = 8$:
(*a*) 66.64
(*b*) 77.36
(*c*) 82.24
(*d*) $z = 1.00$
15.87% of scores are above 80
(*e*) $z = -0.75$
22.66% of scores are below 66
(*f*) 66.64 − 77.36

(*b*) $\mu = 72$, $\sigma = 4$:
(*a*) 69.32
(*b*) 77.36
(*c*) 77.12
(*d*) $z = 2.00$
2.28% of scores are above 80
(*e*) $z = -1.5$
6.68% of scores are below 66
(*f*) 69.32 − 74.68

(*c*) $\mu = 72$, $\sigma = 2$:
(*a*) 70.66
(*b*) 73.34
(*c*) 74.56
(*d*) $z = 4.00$
0.003% of scores are above 80
(*e*) $z = -3.00$
0.135 of scores are below 66
(*f*) 70.66–73.34

11. No, z scores merely reflect the form of the distributions from which they were derived. Normally distributed variables will yield normally distributed z scores.

13. Assume $z = 1.27$. Her percentile rank is 89.80.

15. (*a*) 780 (*c*) 565; 780 (*e*) 98.66%
(*b*) 780 (*d*) 270; 410 (*f*) Assume $z = 1.96$; 310, 710

17. (*a*) $\overline{X} = 5.42$ (*b*) Yes (*c*) Assume $z = -0.67$, 4.29 days
$s = 1.68$
(*d*) 4 days or less
$z = -0.85$, proportion $= 0.1977$
7 days or more
$z = +0.94$, proportion $= 0.6736$

19. (*a*) Females: $z = -0.5$, 30.85%; males: $z = -2.5$, 0.62% (less than 1%)
(*b*) Females: $z = 2.0$, 97.72%; males: $z = 0$, 50%

21. (*a*) *A*, $z = 2.00$, percentile rank = 97.72
(*b*) *D*, $z = -1.50$, percentile rank = 6.68

23. The smaller the standard deviation is, the smaller the deviations of scores about the mean. When the mean is used to predict a given score, the error will be, on the average, small when the standard deviation is small. In the limiting case, when $s = 0.00$, all of the scores are identical. There is no error in prediction.

Chapter 8

1. Percentaging down

	Low	Moderate	High
High	0.0	25.0	50.0
Moderate	60.0	50.0	33.3
Low	40.0	25.0	16.7
Total	100.0	100.0	100.0

Percentaging across

	Low	Moderate	High	Total
High	0.0	25.0	75.0	100.0
Moderate	42.9	28.6	28.6	100.1*
Low	50.0	25.0	25.0	100.0

* Does not sum to 100.0 because of rounding error.

Percentaging on the total

	Low	Moderate	High	Total
High	0.0	6.7	20.0	
Moderate	20.0	13.3	13.3	
Low	13.3	6.7	6.7	
				100.0

3. $G = 0.560$
$d_{yx} = 0.378$
tau-$b = 0.384$

5. $\lambda = 0.125$

7.

Reason for not seeking work	Sex: Male	Sex: Female	
In school	51.1 (693)	24.0 (681)	(1374)
Ill or disabled	24.0 (326)	13.9 (394)	(720)
Keeping house	2.4 (32)	43.2 (1226)	(1258)
Thinks cannot get a job	22.5 (305)	19.0 (540)	(845)
Total	100.0 (1356)	100.1* (2841)	$N = 4197$

* Does not add to 100.0 because of rounding error.

$\lambda = 0.193$

9.

Racial composition of marriage partners	Year: 1970	1977	1984
Husband African American, wife white	13.2 (41)	22.6 (95)	14.6 (111)
Wife African American, husband white	7.7 (24)	7.1 (30)	8.4 (64)
Husband African American, wife other	2.6 (8)	4.8 (20)	2.2 (17)
Wife African American, husband other	1.3 (4)	0.5 (2)	0.8 (6)
Husband white, wife other	44.8 (139)	42.0 (177)	44.6 (340)
Wife white, husband other	30.3 (94)	23.0 (97)	29.4 (224)
Total	99.9* (310)	100.0 (421)	100.0 (762)

* Does not add to 100.0 because of rounding error.

11. The strengths of lambda include a range in value from 0 to 1, no assumptions concerning the distribution of variables (a normal distribution is not necessary), and a versatility that allows it to be used with tables of any dimension. Lambda does have two weaknesses. First, lambda has no sign and offers no indication of the direction of the relationship, a limitation that follows from its use with nominal level data. The second weakness results from the prediction rules for lambda. Lambda equals 0 whenever *all* the within-category modes of the independent variable occur in the row containing the modal category of the dependent variable.

Tau-*b*, gamma, and Somer's d_{yx} share several strengths including being based on pair-by-pair comparison, having signs which indicate if a relationship is positive or negative, and being appropriate for tables of any dimension. The values for gamma and Somer's d_{yx} conveniently range from -1 to $+1$, whereas a weakness of tau-b is that its maximum value is less than ± 1 when the number of rows does not equal the number of columns in a table. Gamma ignores all ties and is the most liberal (yielding inflated values) of these three measures of association for ordinal data. Somer's d_{yx} and tau-b incorporate ties in their computation, and hence are more cumbersome to calculate. Gamma and Somer's d_{yx} share the restrictive assumption that the variables are linearly related.

13. (*a*) Table A Lambda = 1

		(X) C_1	C_2	C_3	
	r_1	0	0	20	20
(Y)	r_2	0	40	0	40
	r_3	30	0	0	30
					$N = 90$

Applying equation (8.2)

$$\lambda = \frac{(30 + 40 + 20) - 40}{90 - 40}$$

$$= \frac{90 - 40}{90 - 40}$$

$$= \frac{50}{50}$$

$$= 1$$

Table B Lambda = 0

		(X) C_1	C_2	C_3	
	r_1	50	40	30	120
(Y)	r_2	40	30	20	90
	r_3	30	20	10	60
					$N = 270$

Applying equation (8.2)

$$\lambda = \frac{(50 + 40 + 30) - 120}{270 - 120}$$

$$= \frac{120 - 120}{270 - 120}$$

$$= \frac{0}{150}$$

$$= 0$$

Note: All the within-category modes of the independent variable occur in r_1 (row one), therefore, lambda = 0.

Table C Tau-b, G and $d_{yx} = 1$

		(X) C_1	C_2	C_3
	r_1	0	0	20
(Y)	r_2	0	30	0
	r_3	50	0	0

Table D Tau-b, G, and $d_{yx} = 0$

		(X) C_1	C_2	C_3
	r_1	10	10	10
(Y)	r_2	10	10	10
	r_3	10	10	10

13. (*b*) Applying equation (8.5)

$$\text{tau-}b = \frac{3100 - 0}{\sqrt{(3100 + 0 + 0)(3100 + 0 + 0)}}$$

$$= \frac{3{,}100}{3{,}100}$$

$$= 1$$

Applying equation (8.5)

$$\text{tau-}b = \frac{900 - 900}{\sqrt{(900 + 900 + 900)(900 + 900 + 900)}}$$

$$= \frac{0}{2{,}700}$$

$$= 0$$

13. (*c*) Applying equation (8.3)

$$G = \frac{3{,}100 - 0}{3{,}100 + 0} = \frac{3{,}100}{3{,}100} = 1$$

Applying equation (8.3)

$$G = \frac{900 - 900}{900 + 900} = \frac{0}{1{,}800} = 0$$

13. (*d*) Applying equation (8.4)

$$d_{yx} = \frac{3{,}100 - 0}{3{,}100 + 0 + 0} = \frac{3{,}100}{3{,}100} = 1$$

Applying equation (8.4)

$$d_{yx} = \frac{900 - 900}{900 + 900 + 900} = \frac{0}{2{,}700} = 0$$

15. (*a*)

	Use of cocaine		
Use of condoms	**Never**	**Sometimes**	**Frequently**
Always	56.8	38.5	3.3
Sometimes	34.1	38.5	30.0
Never	9.1	23.1	66.7
	100.0	100.1*	100.0

* Does not add to 100.0% due to rounding error.

(*b*) $G = -0.70$
$d_{yx} = -0.51$
tau-b $= -0.50$

(*c*) There is a strong negative relationship between cocaine use and condom use among female prostitutes. As cocaine use increases, the likelihood of using condoms decreases.

17. (*a*)

	Size of work group		
Group cohesion	**3–6**	**7–10**	**11–14**
High	59.8	34.1	35.0
Moderate	25.3	36.6	15.0
Low	14.9	29.3	50.0
	100.0	100.0	100.0

(*b*) $G = -0.344$

Chapter 9

1. (*a*) $r = +0.89$
(*b*) Reversing the scoring of fear of crime results in the following scores: 14, 9, 10, 2, 3 and $r = -0.89$

3. (*a*) Nonlinear relationship and/or restricted range (*b*) Restricted range (*c*) Restricted range

5. $r = 0.00$; $r_s = +0.50$
When there are tied ranks on either or both the *X* and the *Y* variables, the Spearman equation yields an inflated value, particularly when the number of tied ranks is high.

7. The scatter diagram indicates that the relationship between membership growth and distance from the CBD is reasonably linear; however, churches 3 and 8 can be considered deviant cases or outliers in that they depart markedly from the clustering of the remaining 18 churches.

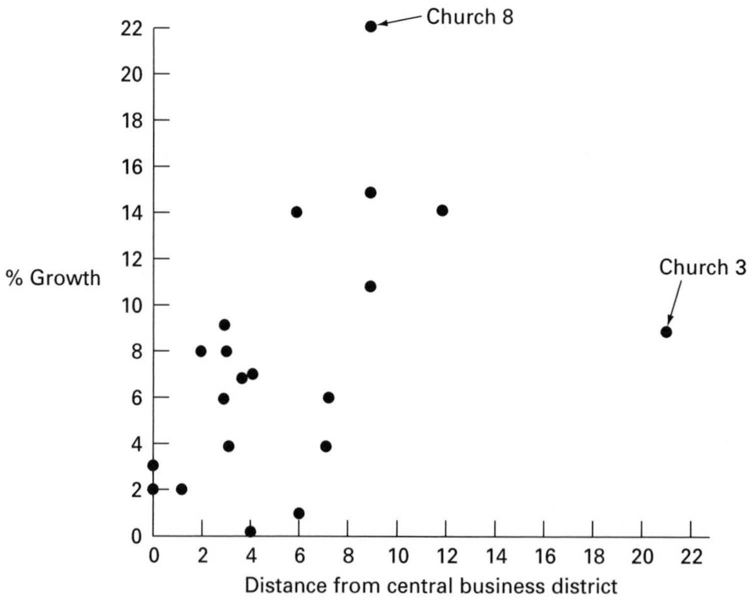

9. Strongest is -0.89; weakest is $+0.32$; negative is -0.89.

11. The correlation between age and attitude toward the police ($r = -0.14$) tells us that age has a weak, negative relationship with attitude toward the police in that older African-American ministers are slightly more likely to hold a negative attitude toward the police than younger African-American ministers. The correlation between church size and minister's education ($r = +0.41$) indicates that well-educated ministers tend to serve larger churches than less-educated ministers.

13. $r = -0.76$ indicates that two variables have a moderately strong, negative relationship, whereas $r = +0.76$ indicates that two variables have a moderately strong, positive relationship. The two coefficients indicate the relationships are equally strong.

15. (*a*) c (*b*) a (*c*) d (*d*) b

17. (*a*) $r = 0.85$

17. (*b*)

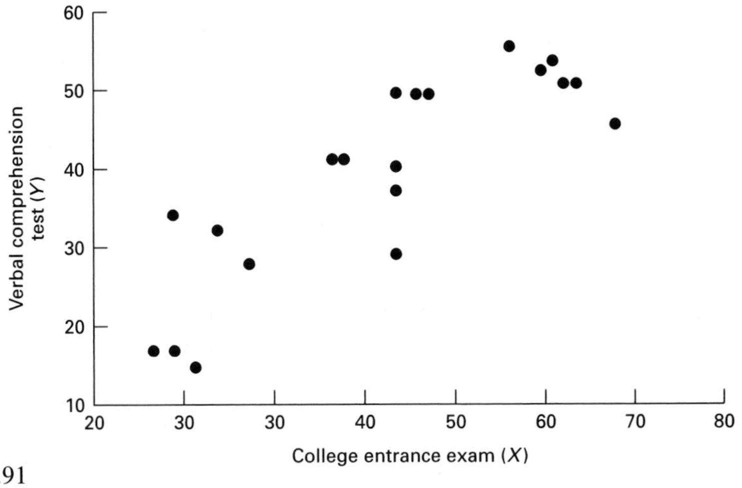

19. $r = 0.91$

21. $r = 0.80$

Students who attended many rock concerts tended to smoke marijuana more frequently than did those students who attended few or no concerts.

23. Nonlinear relationships give rise to artificially low Pearson's r correlation coefficients.

25. (*a*) Pearson's r or Spearman's r_s may be computed.

(*b*) The following matrix is based on Pearson's r.

	1	2	3
1. Order of recall	1.00		
2. Recalled %	−0.92	1.00	
3. Recognized %	−0.69	0.57	1.00

27. (*a*) For Data Set 1, $r = +0.84$; for Data Set 2, $r = +0.42$

(*b*)

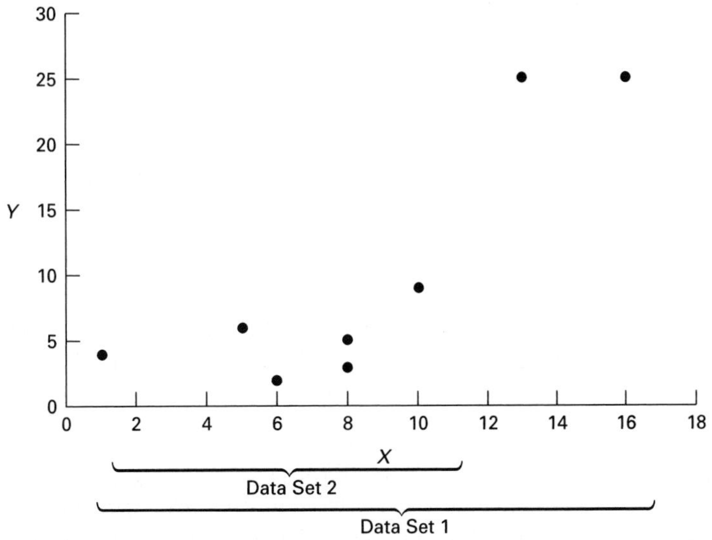

(*c*) The larger correlation coefficient for Data Set 1 reflects the influence of the extreme scores, given the small sample.

29. The correlation between age and educational attainment is −0.2593; the correlation between age and income is −0.0987; the correlation between income and educational attainment is +0.4373.

Chapter 10

1. $Y' = 5.7 - 0.9X$

3. TSS = 10; RSS = 1.9; RegSS = 8.1
$r = -0.9$; $r^2 = +0.81$; standard error of estimate = 0.80.

5. $r^2 = 0.25$; $1 - r^2 = 0.75$; 25% of the variation in Y is explained and 75% is not explained.

7. (*a*) The total sum of squares is 0.42 + 0.54 = 0.96; the standard error of estimate is 0.30; $r^2 = 0.44$.

(*b*) $Y' = 2.06 + 0.02\ X_1$

(*c*)

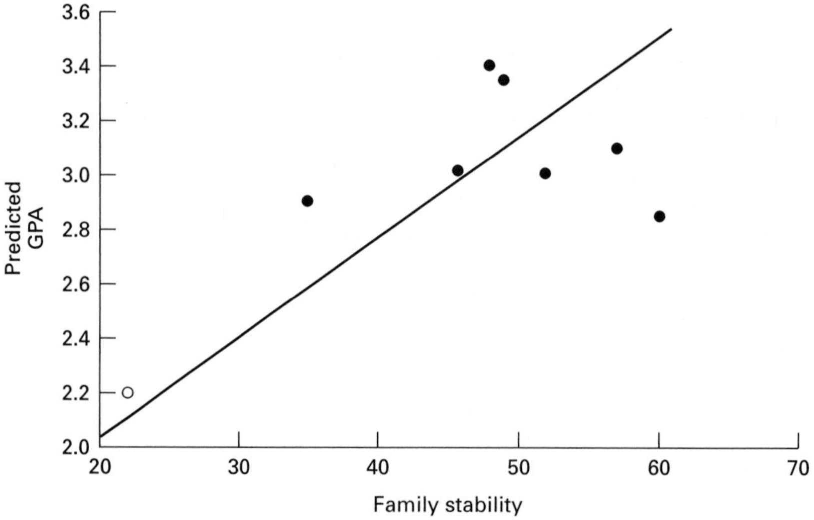

(*d*)

	Family stability	College GPA	Predicted GPA	Residuals for GPA
1	22.00	2.20	2.49	−.29
2	35.00	2.90	2.75	+.15
3	46.00	3.00	2.97	+.03
4	48.00	3.40	3.01	+.39
5	49.00	3.35	3.03	+.32
6	52.00	3.00	3.09	−.09
7	57.00	3.10	3.19	−.09
8	60.00	2.85	3.25	−.40

9. (*a*) 0.29 (*b*) −.65 (*c*) 0.75 (*d*) −0.2

(*e*) The slope of the line is the correlation multiplied by ratio of the standard deviation of the *Y* variable divided by the standard deviation of the *X* variable. When the correlation is greater than 0 the slope of the line will be positive. When the correlation is less than 0, the slope of the line will be negative. When the standard deviation of the *Y* variable is greater than the standard deviation of the *X* variable, the slope will be a large number. When the standard deviation of the *Y* variable is smaller than the *X* variable, the slope will be small. Only the correlation coefficient indicates the degree of relatedness between the two variables.

(*f*) Many researchers make the mistake of assuming that the larger the slope, the better. From an inspection of the four data sets you should be able to see that the size of the slope does not necessarily indicate the magnitude of the relationship between *X* and *Y*. It is true that when the correlation is zero, the slope will be zero. Contrast data sets *c* and *d* which are characterized by the smallest correlation ($r = .25$) and the largest correlation ($r = -.8$) yet the slope associated with the smallest correlation is 0.75 and the slope associated with the largest correlation is considerably smaller (−0.2). Of course different values of r and $\frac{S_y}{S_x}$ produce different slopes. Therefore, only the correlation coefficient can be used to describe the magnitude of the relation between two variables.

11. (*a*) If group size equals 15, the predicted group cohesiveness score is 3.61.

(*b*) 57.75%

13. This is an example of the post hoc fallacy. There may be other variables besides educational attainment that account for these data. Perhaps students who stay in school longer are more likely to live in a social and economic environment that allows them to achieve financial success without resorting to crime. In other words, it is not the education that influences or "causes" the person's chances of becoming a criminal, but the environment in which he or she lives.

15. Not necessarily. All the factors that can lead to spurious low correlation also can account for a small slope because $b = r\left(\frac{S_y}{S_x}\right)$.

17. (*a*) $r = -0.85$ (*b*) 3.78

19. (*a*) 5.56 (*b*) 4.16

Chapter 11

1. Multivariate statistical techniques allow us to determine the nature of a relationship between three or more variables. We can examine the relationship between two variables [e.g., age (*X*) and happiness (*Y*)] under different conditions with a *multivariate contingency table* by introducing a control or test variable. If our control variable had three categories (e.g., low, medium, and high income), three conditional or partial tables would result and we could contrast the relationship between age and happiness for the three income levels.

Partial correlation analysis provides us with a measure of the linear relationship between two interval level variables controlling for one or more other variables. This multivariate technique can also be used to differentiate between a spurious or an intervening relationship.

Multiple regression analysis measures the influence of an independent variable on a dependent variable when the effects of all other independent variables have been held constant. Included in a multiple regression analysis is valuable information provided by standardized regression coefficients which measure the relative importance of two or more independent variables as predictors of a common dependent variable and the coefficient of multiple determination which is a measure of the proportion of total variation in a dependent variable that is explained jointly by two or more independent variables.

3. Original Table

(*Y*) Favor HMOs?	(*X*) Age: Young	Old	Total
Yes	34.7 (51)	63.6 (82)	(133)
No	65.3 (96)	36.4 (47)	(143)
Total	100.0 (147)	100.0 (129)	$N = 276$

The two tables below show that the introduction of a two category control variable (Income) reveals that the relationship between age and favoring HMOs differs by income level. The attitudes of young and old persons of low income differ very little whereas there is a considerable difference by age among high income persons in the extent to which they favor HMOs.

Favor HMOs?	Low income: Young	Old	Total
Yes	45.5 (30)	56.5 (35)	(65)
No	54.5 (36)	43.5 (27)	(63)
	100.0 (66)	100.0 (62)	$N = 128$

Favor HMOs?	High income: Young	Old	Total
Yes	25.9 (21)	70.1 (47)	(68)
No	74.1 (60)	29.9 (20)	(80)
	100.0 (81)	100.0 (67)	$N = 148$

5. (*a*) TABLE A

Sentence length by time period

Sentence in months	Time period: Year 1	Year 2	Total
1–12	30.1	24.5	2,289
13–35	17.3	17.3	1,434
36–59	24.5	26.5	2,099
60+	28.1	31.6	2,451
Total	100.0	99.9*	$N = 8{,}273$

* Does not add to 100.0% due to rounding error.

Table B

Sentence Length by Time Period and Type of Offense

Sentence in months	Marijuana Year 1	Marijuana Year 2	Narcotics Year 1	Narcotics Year 2	Controlled substances (prescribed drugs) Year 1	Controlled substances (prescribed drugs) Year 2
1–12	38.7	30.8	25.8	20.6	34.4	28.1
13–35	23.3	20.2	14.0	16.4	22.8	16.6
36–59	22.8	31.3	25.5	25.9	22.8	23.4
60+	15.2	17.8	34.8	37.0	20.0	31.9
Total	100.0	100.1*	100.1*	99.9*	100.0	100.0
	$N = 1{,}987$		$N = 4{,}935$		$N = 1{,}351$	

* Does not add to 100.0% due to rounding error.

(*b*) The control variable is the type of substance involved (marijuana, narcotics, or controlled substances). Looking across the rows it is evident that, in the majority of cases, the percentage of short sentences has declined from year 1 to year 2. The percentage of longer sentences has tended to increase from year 1 to year 2 for all three types of substances.

7. (*a*) $r_{21.3} = -0.278$

(*b*) The correlation between church attendance and self-reported delinquent acts is -0.32 whereas the computed first-order partial correlation between church attendance and self-reported delinquent acts, controlling for drug usage is -0.278. By comparing the correlation coefficient with the partial correlation coefficient we can conclude that the relationship between church attendance and delinquent acts is, in part, spurious, due to their relationship with drug usage.

9. The partial correlation coefficient is a "weighted average" of the correlation between two variables across all categories of the control variable and would be misleading if the association were not uniform across all categories of the control variable.

11. The Y-intercept equals 1.1 and indicates that the regression line crosses the Y-axis at $+1.1$. The regression coefficients are unstandardized and may be interpreted in the following manner. The coefficient for income (X_1) equals $+0.35$ and indicates that with each unit increase in income, job satisfaction increases $+0.35$ units when controlling for the effect of seniority. The coefficient for seniority (X_2) equals $+0.12$ and indicates that with each unit increase in seniority, job satisfaction increases $+0.12$ units when controlling for the effect of income.

13.

Employee	Y'	Residual
1	4.57	1.43
2	6.39	−1.39
3	6.07	0.93
4	10.71	−1.71
5	20.26	0.74

15. (*a*) Unstandardized equation:

$$Y' = 2.11 - 2.01X_1 + 0.93X_2 - 2.46X_3 - 0.55X_4 + 1.00X_5 - 0.74X_6 - 0.11X_7$$

Standardized equation:

$$Y' = -0.20X_1 + 0.12X_2 - 0.12X_3 - 0.11X_4 + 0.10X_5 - 0.09X_6 + 0.01X_7$$

(*b*) The unstandardized coefficient of −0.55 associated with grade point average indicates that if a student's grade point average increases one unit, his or her delinquency score will decrease 0.55 units when the remaining independent variables are statistically controlled. The standardized coefficient of −0.11 associated with grade point average indicates that as one's grade point average increases one standard deviation unit, his or her delinquency score will decrease 0.11 standard deviation units when the remaining independent variables are statistically controlled.

(*c*) The *Y*-intercept tells us that the multidimensional structure (hyperstructure) characterizing the multiple regression equation crosses the *Y*-axis at +2.11. The *Y*-intercept for a standardized equation always equals 0; therefore, it is not shown here.

(*d*) The dependent variable is the weighted delinquency scale and the seven independent variables are shown in Table 11.6.

(*e*) The independent variables have jointly explained 17 percent of the variation in the weighted delinquency scale. The unexplained percentage of variance is 83 percent.

(*f*) Friends smoke marijuana is the best predictor because its standardized regression coefficient is largest, whereas importance of religion is the poorest predictor.

Chapter 12

1. Mr. Smyth is incorrect in his assumption and his conclusion represents an example of the gambler's fallacy. The probability that Mrs. Smyth will have a girl is the same as it has been for all the other pregnancies. Each pregnancy is independent of the other with respect to sex. Therefore, if we assume that having a boy or a girl is equally likely, then there is a 50% probability that Mrs. Smyth will have a girl.

3. Denise has engaged, quite literally, in the misuse of the "man-who" statistic. While it may be true that her grandfather is a long-term smoker and has lived for quite some time, a single case does not necessarily discredit the statistical generalization that people who smoke have, on average, a shorter life span than those who do not smoke.

5. (*a*) 0.1250
(*b*) 0.1250
(*c*) 0.3750
(*d*) 0.5000

7. (*a*) 0.1667
(*b*) 0.1667
(*c*) 0.2778
(*d*) 0.5000

9. (*a*) $\frac{1}{11}$ (*b*) $\frac{1}{66}$ (*c*) $\frac{14}{99}$

11. (*a*) This is not random sampling. Although Sociology 101 is a popular course, it is not taken by all students. There may be other problems with selecting this course. For example, only freshmen and sophomores may take the class. Also, systematic selection is not, technically speaking, a true form of random sampling. An alternative technique would be to generate a list of random numbers that corresponds to student ID numbers and then select those students.

(*b*) The *population* is defined as all people who watch the show, not just those in the audience. The people in the audience may not well represent the population of viewers.

An alternative technique would be to call people at random during the airing of the show and ask if they are viewing the show. Other techniques also can be created.

(*c*) In this example, we should be suspicious of how each homeroom teacher selects the student. Will the teacher pick only well-behaved students? The selection process should be random and independent of any characteristic of the student unless those characteristics are essential for the study (e.g., sex, class, class rank).

(*d*) The problem with this technique is limiting the calling to Saturday. Is there a chance that a segment of the population will be out of the house on this day? The calling should remain random and be spread out over several days.

13.

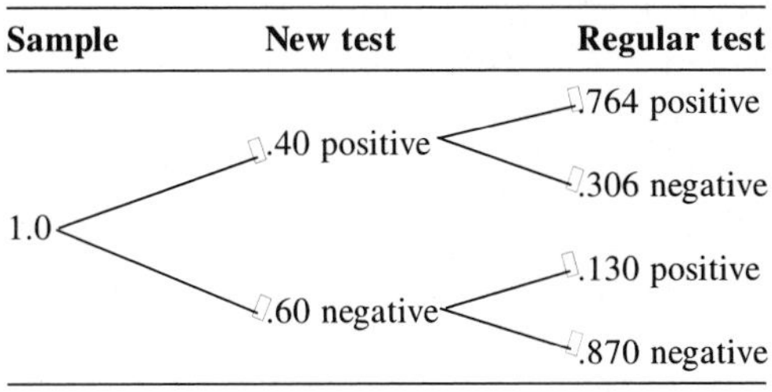

(*a*) When the test results are positive, there is a 76.4% chance that the results are correct.

(*b*) When the test results are negative, there is a 13.0% chance that the results are incorrect.

(*c*) p (true positive) $= .40 \times .764 = 0.306$
p (true negative) $= .60 \times .870 = 0.522$
p (correct) $= .306 + .522 = 0.828$
There is an 82.8% chance that the test will produce correct results.

15. (*a*) .9998 (*b*) .6916 (*c*) 488 (*d*) 94.95 (*e*) 2.56 (*f*) 432–568

17. (*a*) High income 0.39
(*b*) Socialist 0.06
(*c*) Socialist and high income 0.02
(*d*) Not Republican 0.48
(*e*) Not Democrat and low income 0.10
(*f*) Not Republican and not Socialist 0.42
(*g*) Not Republican and not moderate income . 0.31

19.

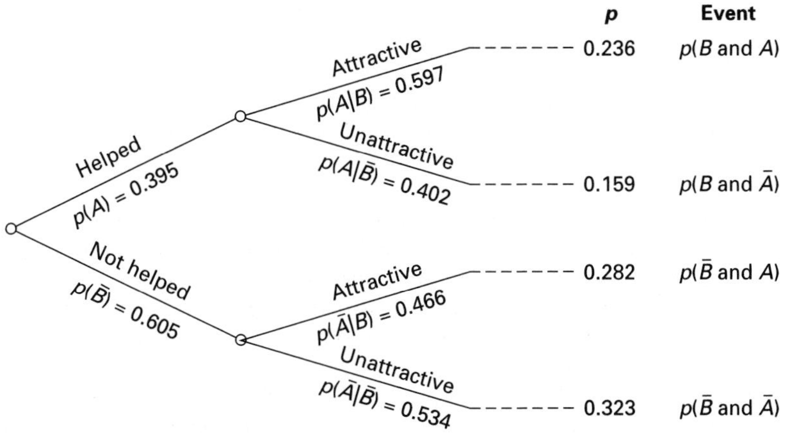

21. (*a*)

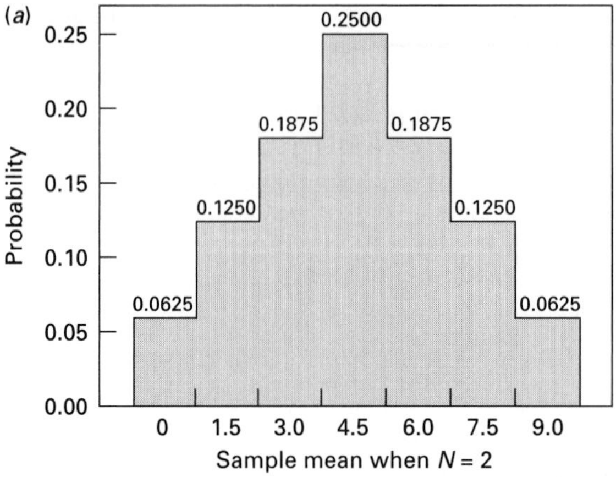

(*b*)

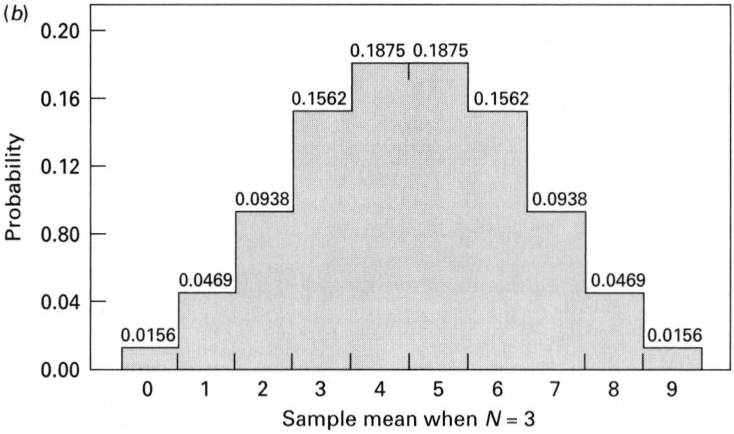

Chapter 13

1. Because populations can rarely be studied exhaustively in the social and behavioral sciences, data from samples are used to draw inferences about the population. The inferences that are made are termed conditional because the conclusions cannot be stated as absolutely correct. There is a probability that other conclusions are correct and our inference is wrong.

3. The null hypothesis cannot be proved. Evidence is found either to support or reject it. Failure to reject the null hypothesis does not constitute proof that the null hypothesis is correct.

5. (*a*) H_0 (*b*) H_1 (*c*) H_1 (*d*) H_0

7. (*a*) Type II (*b*) Type II (*c*) No error

9. By chance, one would expect five differences to be statistically significant at the 0.05 level.

11. Yes. Two tailed H_1: There is a difference in the recidivism rates for female and male parolees. One tailed H_1: The recidivism rate for female parolees is less than for male parolees.

13. (*b*)

15. (*a*) h (*b*) a

17.

		True status of H_0	
	H_0: Person has no disorder	**Person has no disorder (H_0: true)**	**Person has a disorder (H_0: false)**
Decision	Fail to reject H_0 (treat person as having no disorder)	Correct failure to reject	Incorrect decision (type II error) Do not treat person with a disorder
	Reject H_0 (treat person as having a disorder)	Incorrect decision (type I error) Person with no disorder treated as having a disorder	Correct rejection

19. On the basis of the data, we would reject H_0. However, since H_0 is true, we have made a type I or type α error.

21. We fail to reject H_0. Since H_0 is false, we have failed to reject a false H_0. Therefore, we have made a type II or type β error.

23. We reject H_0. Since H_0 is false, we have made a correct decision.

Chapter 14

1. (*a*) As sample size increases, the dispersion of sample means decreases.

(*b*) As you increase the number of samples, you are more likely to obtain extreme values of the sample mean. For example, suppose the probability of obtaining a sample mean of a given value is 0.01. If the number of samples drawn is 10, you probably will not obtain any sample means with that value. However, if you draw as many as 1,000 samples, you would expect to obtain approximately 10 sample means with values so extreme that the probability of their occurrence is 0.01.

3. (*a*) 21.71–26.29 (*b*) 20.82–27.18

5. Reject H_0; $z = 2.68$ in which $z_{0.01} = \pm 2.58$

7. In exercise 5 the value of the population standard deviation is known; thus, we may employ the z-statistic and determine probability values in terms of areas under the normal curve.

Because the t-distributions are more spread out than the normal curve, the proportion of area beyond a specific value of t is greater than the proportion of area beyond the corresponding value of z. Thus, a larger value of t is required to mark off the bounds of the critical region of rejection. In exercise 5 the absolute value of the obtained z must equal or exceed 2.58.

To generalize: The probability of making a type II error is less when we know the population standard deviation.

9. (*a*) $z = 2.73, p = 0.9968$
(*b*) $z = -0.91, p = 0.1814$
(*c*) $z = 1.82, p = 0.0344$
(*d*) $p = 0.6372$

11. $-2.08 = \dfrac{29.61 - 32.11}{\dfrac{6.0}{\sqrt{25}}}$, $t_{0.01} = -2.49$: fail to reject H_0

13. $t = 1.75$, df $= 625$

15. (*a*) $\mu = 6.0, \sigma = 3.42$

17. (*a*) $p = \frac{1}{12}$ (*b*) $p = \frac{1}{12}$ (*c*) $p = \frac{5}{9}$ (*d*) $p = \frac{1}{36}$

19. The conclusion we draw depends on the nature of the alternative hypothesis. If directional hypotheses are used and we employ $\alpha = .05$, we reject H_0 since the obtained r_s of 0.438 exceeds the value required (interpolating for $N = 17$, the critical value of r_s for $\alpha = .05$, one-tailed test is 0.412). However, if we employed a two-tailed test, we would not be able to reject H_0.

21. The statistics $\overline{X}$ and $\hat{s}$ describe the distribution of a sample and allow us to make inferences from the sample statistics to the population. These values are determined empirically from the sample data. We use $\mu_{\overline{X}}$ and $\sigma^2_{\overline{X}}$ to describe the sampling distribution of means. These values are estimated using the sample statistics and the central limit theorem.

23. The statistic $\hat{s}^2$ is an unbiased estimate of σ^2. When we use $N - 1$ in the denominator of the equation we create a better estimate of the population variance.

25. Using the example in Section 14.7 of the text, we find the 99% confidence interval:

$$\text{upper limit } \mu_0 = 108 + (2.787)(3.0) = 116.36$$

$$\text{lower limit } \mu_0 = 108 - (2.787)(3.0) = 99.64$$

Thus, the 99% confidence limits are 99.64–116.36 compared to the 95% confidence limits: 101.82–114.18.

27. (*a*) Married couples: $t = 5.219$; df $= 51$; $p < 0.05$
Divorced couples: $t = 0.329$; df $= 22$; not significant
(*b*) Married couples: $t = 1.688$; df $= 51$; not significant
Divorced couples: $t = 0.615$; df $= 22$; not significant

29. $r_{s(0.05)} = 0.450$

Chapter 15

1.

Source	SS	df	MS	F
Between groups	39.636	3	13.212	6.25
Within groups	33.824	16	2.114	
Total	73.460	19		

(*a*) There were four levels of the independent variable.
(*b*) 5
(*c*) 3, 16
(*d*) 3.24
(*e*) Yes. 6.25 > 3.24

3. When we use the 0.05 level, 1 out of every 20 comparisons will be significant *by chance.* Thus, a significant difference at the 0.05 level in 1 of 10 studies can be attributed to chance.

5. $F = 10.43$; df $= 2, 12$; HSD $= 7.16$

7. (*a*) 3 levels of the independent variable
(*b*) 22 subjects
(*c*) The F-ratio was significant ($p < .05$)

9.

Source of variation	Sum of squares	Degrees of freedom	Mean square	F
Between groups	26.80	2	13.40	9.35
Within groups	17.20	12	1.43	
Total	44.00	14		

11.

Source of variation	SS	df	MS	F
Between-groups	90.95	3	30.32	1.54
Within-groups	314.80	16	19.67	
Total	405.75	19		

Note that $F(3, 16) = 1.54$, $p > .05$; therefore, there is no reason to compare the means using Tukey's HSD test.

13.

Source of variation	Sum of squares	Degrees of freedom	Mean square	F
Between groups	919.79	3	306.60	6.43
Within groups	954.17	20	47.71	
Total	1873.96	23		

Chapter 16

1. (*a*) H_0: Last-born women will be equally likely to be a scientist, social reformer, performing artist, or writer.
(*b*) H_1: Last-born women will not be equally likely to enter these occupations.
(*c*) Significance test: The χ^2 one-variable test is appropriate.
(*d*) The significance level: $\alpha = 0.05$
(*e*) Sampling distribution: The sampling distribution is the χ^2 distribution with df $= k - 1$. In this example, $k = 4$; therefore df $= 4 - 1 = 3$.
(*f*) Critical region: Table B in Appendix C shows that for df $= 3$, $\alpha = 0.05$, the critical region consists of all values of $\chi^2 \geq 7.815$. Using equation (16.1):

$$\chi^2 = \frac{(23-21)^2}{21} + \frac{(13-21)^2}{21} + \frac{(34-21)^2}{21} + \frac{(14-21)^2}{21}$$

$$= 0.19 + 3.05 + 8.05 + 2.33$$

$$= 13.62$$

We reject H_0 because the calculated χ^2 exceeds the critical value of 7.815.

3.

20	20	40	$\chi^2 = 0$; phi = 0
20	20	40	
40	40		

5. H_0: sexual orientation is independent of one's fear of AIDS. $\chi^2 = 44.46$; $V = 0.50$

		Sexual orientation: Homosexual males	Sexual orientation: Heterosexual males
Fear of AIDS	Great	57.1	13.6
	Moderate	28.6	31.8
	Low	14.3	54.5
		100.0	99.9*

* Due to rounding error.

7. $$\chi^2 = \frac{(41 - 37)^2}{37} + \frac{(50 - 37)^2}{37} + \frac{(20 - 37)^2}{37}$$

$$= 0.43 + 4.57 + 7.81$$

$$= 12.81$$

Assume $\alpha = 0.05$, df $= 2$. The critical region consists of all values of $\chi^2 \geq 5.991$. We can reject H_0 that the CD covers are equally attractive to the consumers.

9. $\chi^2 = 20.46$, df $= 1$, reject H_0

11. $\chi^2 = 1.94$, df $= 1$, do not reject H_0

13. ϕ, C, and V are unique with respect to each other in that ϕ may only be used with tables having 2 rows and 2 columns, C should only be used with tables having an equal number of rows and columns, and V may be used with tables of any dimension. ϕ and V may have a range of values from 0 to 1; C shares the lower limit of 0 but its maximum value is determined by the table size. All three coefficients are based on χ^2 and may be used with nominal level variables in a contingency table context.

15. (*a*) MDs: 97.9% survived, 2.1% died; RNs: 93.4% survived, 6.6% died; Others: 92.5% survived, 7.5% died.
(*b*) Chi-square test of independence.
(*c*) Obtained $\chi^2 = 16.18$; critical value at $\alpha = 0.01$ level $= 9.210$; df $= 2$. Reject H_0. The mortality rate is related to the caregiver who inserts the catheter.

17. (*a*) The χ^2 test of the independence.
(*b*) $\chi^2 = 0.70$, df $= 1$. The obtained χ^2 falls short of the critical value of 3.841 at $\alpha = 0.05$, df $= 1$.

Chapter 17

1. (*a*) Sign test, $N = 10$, $x = 7$ (*b*) Wilcoxon matched-pairs test; $N = 10$, $T = 10$
(*c*) Mann-Whitney U-test; U = 23, U′ = 77

3. (*a*) The null hypothesis should state that the training program is no more effective than the control group. The alternative hypothesis should state that there are systematic differences between the two groups.

(*b*) The Mann-Whitney U-test would be the best test to use with these data. The groups are independent of each other, and the scores appear to be ordinal.

(*c*) $U = 18, U' = 103$

(*d*) Reject H_0.

5. (*a*) The null hypothesis should state that there are no differences between husbands and wives concerning political attitudes. The alternative hypothesis should state that there are systematic differences between the husbands and wives.

(*b*) The sign test would be the best test to use with these data. The data represent pairs of scores, the pairing being based on marital status.

(*c*) $T = 48$

(*d*) Fail to reject H_0.

7. Sign test, $N = 10$, $x = 6$; Wilcoxon, $T = -12$

INDEX

List of Equations *(continued)*

Number	Equation	Page
(10.10)	standard error of estimate $= s_{\text{est } y} = \sqrt{\dfrac{\Sigma(Y - Y')^2}{N - 2}}$	226
(10.11)	$\underset{\text{Total sum of squares}}{\Sigma(Y - \overline{Y})^2} = \underset{\text{Unexplained variation}}{\Sigma(Y - Y')^2} + \underset{\text{Explained variation}}{\Sigma(Y' - \overline{Y})^2}$	228
(10.12)	r square $= r^2 = \dfrac{\text{explained variation}}{\text{total variation}} = \dfrac{\Sigma(Y' - \overline{Y})^2}{\Sigma(Y - \overline{Y})^2}$	229
(10.13)	coefficient of nondetermination $= 1 - r^2 = \dfrac{\text{unexplained variation}}{\text{total variation}} = \dfrac{\Sigma(Y - Y')^2}{\Sigma(Y - \overline{Y})^2}$	229
(11.1)	partial correlation coefficient $= r_{XY.Z} = \dfrac{r_{XY} - r_{XZ}r_{YZ}}{\sqrt{(1 - r_{XZ}^2)(1 - r_{YZ}^2)}}$	245
(11.2)	predicted $Y = Y' = a_y + b_1X_1 + b_2X_2$	247
(12.4)	$p(A \text{ or } B) = p(A) + p(B)$, when the events are *mutually exclusive*	274
(12.6)	$P + Q = 1.00$, when the events are *mutually exclusive* and *exhaustive*	275
(12.9)	$p(A \text{ and } B) = p(A)p(B)$, when the events are *independent*	279
(12.10)	$p(A \text{ and } B) = p(A)p(B \mid A) = p(B)p(A \mid B)$	280
(14.3)	z-score $= z = \dfrac{\overline{X} - \mu_0}{\sigma_{\overline{X}}}$	332
(14.8)	estimated $\sigma_{\overline{X}} = s_{\overline{X}} = \dfrac{s}{\sqrt{N - 1}} = \sqrt{\dfrac{\Sigma(X - \overline{X})^2}{N(N - 1)}}$	337
(14.9)	t-ratio $= t = \dfrac{\overline{X} - \mu_0}{s_{\overline{X}}}$	338
(14.10)	upper limit $\mu_0 = \overline{X} + (t_{0.05})(s_{\overline{X}})$	345
(14.11)	lower limit $\mu_0 = \overline{X} - (t_{0.05})(s_{\overline{X}})$	345
(14.14)	standard error of the proportion $= \sigma_P = \sqrt{\dfrac{P(1 - P)}{N}}$	348